NEWCOMER'S HANDBOOK®

FOR MOVING TO AND LIVING IN THE

San Francisco Bay Area

*Including San Jose, Oakland,
Berkeley, and Palo Alto*

3rd Edition

D0668214

FIRST BOOKS®

6750 SW Franklin
Portland, OR 97223
503-968-6777
www.firstbooks.com

Author: Sabrina Crawford
Contributors: Ruth Rayle and Michael Bower
Series Editor: Linda Weinerman
Publisher: Jeremy Solomon
Cover and Interior design: Erin Johnson Design
Maps: Scott Lockheed, Jim Miller/fennana design
Transit map courtesy of Bay Area Rapid Transit

ISBN-13: 978-0-912301-63-1
ISBN-10: 0-912301-63-5
ISSN: 1557-9921

What readers are saying about Newcomer's Handbooks:

I recently got a copy of your Newcomer's Handbook for Chicago, and wanted to let you know how invaluable it was for my move. I must have consulted it a dozen times a day preparing for my move. It helped me find my way around town, find a place to live, and so many other things. Thanks.

—Mike L.
Chicago, Illinois

Excellent reading (Newcomer's Handbook for San Francisco and the Bay Area) ... balanced and trustworthy. One of the very best guides if you are considering moving/relocation. Way above the usual tourist crap.

—Gunnar E.
Stockholm, Sweden

I was very impressed with the latest edition of the Newcomer's Handbook for Los Angeles. It is well organized, concise and up-to-date. I would recommend this book to anyone considering a move to Los Angeles.

—Jannette L.
Attorney Recruiting Administrator for a large Los Angeles law firm

I recently moved to Atlanta from San Francisco, and LOVE the Newcomer's Handbook for Atlanta. It has been an invaluable resource — it's helped me find everything from a neighborhood in which to live to the local hardware store. I look something up in it everyday, and know I will continue to use it to find things long after I'm no longer a newcomer. And if I ever decide to move again, your book will be the first thing I buy for my next destination.

—Courtney R.
Atlanta, Georgia

In looking to move to the Boston area, a potential employer in that area gave me a copy of the Newcomer's Handbook for Boston. It's a great book that's very comprehensive, outlining good and bad points about each neighborhood in the Boston area. Very helpful in helping me decide where to move.

—no name given (online submit form)

TABLE OF CONTENTS

CONTENTS

CONTENTS

CONTENTS

S AN FRANCISCO IS THE LAND OF THE 49ER GOLD RUSH, THE GREAT
1906 earthquake, and the missionary expeditions of the Spanish; it is
the birthplace of Levi's jeans and home of railroad tycoon Leland
Stanford; it is host to one of greatest feats of engineering, the Golden Gate
Bridge; and as a cultural epicenter, it fueled the hippie flower-power revolution, gave rise to *Rolling Stone* magazine, and played host to beat generation poets. Although the bursting of the dot-com bubble has slowed the
influx into Silicon Valley of young college grads seeking venture capital
opportunities and entrepreneurship, the southern end of the nine-county
San Francisco Bay Area is still home to many large high-tech companies
including Hewlett Packard, Sun Microsystems, Google, Oracle, and Apple.
Today, new economic power centers are slowly emerging—most notably
in the biotech field. While newcomers to the Bay Area may come for such
employment opportunities, many come for a simpler reason—sheer love of
the city itself. With thriving art, music, and literary scenes, endless opportunities to enjoy outdoor activities, and one of the country's most stunning
urban landscapes, the city continues to attract young professionals, artists,
and recent college graduates from all across the country, and from around
the world.

Truly America's melting pot, San Francisco is home to a lively and
diverse mix of cultures, including a large Chinese population, as well as
substantial Vietnamese, Russian, Eastern European, Mexican, and Central
and South American communities. The city is also host to a vibrant gay
and lesbian community. Well known as *the* liberal mecca of the left coast,
the Bay Area pulses with political activism—from impassioned struggles
over local development issues, to heated election runoffs, to leading the
charge on a host of statewide, national, and international causes: from the
environment, to health care, to women's rights, to immigration reform, to
gay marriage.

With stately Victorians nestled all along dramatic hilltops, the beauty and expanse of the Bay and the Pacific Ocean all around, and mountain hikes or walks in the redwoods just moments away, the city is the rarest of gems—a place that offers the culture, excitement, and opportunity of urban life with the scenic and recreational joys of the great outdoors. The Bay Area is the only place in America where you can ride a moving national landmark (cable cars) while taking in some of the world's most beautiful scenery, including the Bay, Alcatraz Island, Golden Gate Bridge, Golden Gate Park, and the city skyline itself.

Then of course, there's the weather—blissfully mild with blue skies, fog near the coast, and cooling off with light winds in the evening. Many would agree that Bay Area meteorologists have one of the easiest jobs around. The weather forecast is consistently "low clouds and fog overnight, clearing by mid-morning, giving way to afternoon sunshine," with the temperature rarely dipping below 40° or above 80° Fahrenheit. The one exception to that rule comes with the much anticipated Indian summer months of September and October, when it can get into the 80s and on extremely rare occasions, over 100° Fahrenheit. The fall and winter rainy seasons begin with a few drizzles in October, becoming outright downpours in the rainy months of December and January, and continuing intermittently through March and sometimes into April. Communities located away from the ocean, particularly those in the South and East Bay, are, as a general rule, likely to have weather that is drier, warmer, and smoggier.

Thankfully gone are the infamous days of a citywide 1% vacancy rate; but rents in San Francisco still consistently remain among the most expensive in the country. Reflecting the bursting of the dot-com boom bubble, however, average rental prices have dropped between 11% and 30% in the last five years. Sharing a large Victorian or Edwardian flat with roommates is common for the younger set. Those looking for more space and better prices, but still wanting to keep that "in the city" feel, cross the bay, heading east to Berkeley or increasingly to Oakland.

Real estate throughout the Bay Area is like gold, and purchasing prices, following yet another statewide boom in 2004, are still steadily rising, sending many to look for housing elsewhere. Although housing prices remain quite high (and many anticipate an eventual burst to the real estate "bubble"), overall population figures for the area have remained essentially flat for the last 4 years. Some first-time homebuyers are heading just south of the city to San Bruno and South San Francisco to take advantage of a new crop of condos; those working in Silicon Valley often opt for townhouses further south in Sunnyvale or San Jose; and families desiring single-family homes with spacious backyards are looking east to Vallejo or even Sacramento. To the north of San Francisco, in Marin County, you'll find small but burgeoning communities with dramatic landscapes, stunning vistas, and great hiking, biking and camping. East, toward Sonoma and Napa counties, are charming vineyards tucked in among rolling hills.

This *Newcomer's Handbook*® is intended to help make your move here as seamless and enjoyable as possible. It describes San Francisco and surrounding Bay Area neighborhoods/communities in detail, and provides lists of neighborhood resources, including neighborhood web sites, police stations, post offices, libraries, hospitals, public schools, and community groups. Transportation routes are also covered. In addition to profiling area neighborhoods and communities, this guide will assist you with the biggest of Bay Area challenges: locating a new home (**Finding a Place to Live**), as well as getting your belongings here (**Moving and Storage**), setting up your bank accounts (**Money Matters**) and utilities (**Getting Settled**), where to go to buy a shower curtain, area rug, or mop and broom (**Shopping for the Home**), and places to go to kick back and relax in a welcoming patch of green (**Greenspace and Beaches**). It's all here, and much more.

LOCAL LINGO

Like many communities, San Francisco has its own slang. If you find yourself scratching your head, here are a few phrases that may help you out:

- The City (capitalized) is the way most natives and local newspapers refer to San Francisco: wherever you are in the Bay Area, "the City" with a capital "C" always means San Francisco.
- BART: Bay Area Rapid Transit, the under- and aboveground subway-style train network that connects the East Bay and peninsula with San Francisco
- MUNI: Municipal Rail Network, the city's bus and light rail system
- The Chron: The Chronicle, the city's major daily newspaper
- Pink Section: special weekend arts and entertainment supplement in The Chronicle
- The Haight: the Haight-Ashbury neighborhood, also often refers specifically to the retail shopping district along the upper section of Haight Street
- SOMA: area south of Market Street
- South Bay: Santa Clara County
- East Bay: Alameda and Contra Costa counties, but often just refers to Oakland or Berkeley
- North Bay: Marin and Sonoma counties
- The Boom: the 1990s high-tech computer and internet economic explosion

- The Bust: the end of said dot-com explosion
- Ex-dot-comers: those who were heavily involved in the high tech explosion and have since moved on to other, often non-tech-related career pursuits
- Oaktown: Oakland
- The Avenues: the numbered streets in the Sunset and Richmond neighborhoods running out toward the ocean
- General: San Francisco General Hospital
- Mavericks: the big wave, daredevil surf competition on the west coast, also the name of the actual surfing spot, just off the shore of Pillar Point Harbor in Half Moon Bay
- Mitchell's: famous locally made ice cream
- See's: famous locally made chocolates

SAN FRANCISCO'S 43 HILLS PREVENTED CITY PLANNERS FROM implementing a grand, area-wide roadway grid system, so finding the desired street address here can be a challenge. A good map or atlas is highly recommended. Avoid the small tourist maps; they often distort proportions and exclude big chunks of geography that will prove important to a resident. Transit maps are useful if you're not relying on your car to get around but they don't offer enough detailed information to serve as your primary guidance tool.

City maps are available at stores across the Bay Area, but cartography buffs will want to check out the Thomas Bros. Maps store at 550 Jackson Street in San Francisco. The company's Thomas Guide is the most detailed representation of the city you can buy. Call 800-899-6277 or check online at www.thomas.com for more information. You can also get maps free from the American Automobile Association (AAA) if you're a member.

With map in hand you may want to spend a few moments locating the major streets and highways listed below:

- First there's Market Street. It's San Francisco's main downtown street, and it starts across from the Ferry Building. As with all east-west running streets that begin at the downtown's eastern edge, address numbers begin there and increase as you head towards the ocean. Market serves as the border between the Financial District, Union Square and Tenderloin areas to the north, and the South of Market (SOMA) district to the south. For north-south running streets, address numbering begins at Market, with the lowest numbers at Market. On streets north of Market, the numbers increase as you go north. On the other side, the street numbers increase as you travel south.
- Another main street is Van Ness Avenue, which runs north-south and begins one block west of 10th Street, crossing Market. It serves as part of the Highway 101 connection to the Golden Gate Bridge, along with

Lombard Street, Marina Boulevard, and Doyle Drive. Street numbers increase as you travel north on Van Ness.

- Geary Street splits off from Market in the downtown area, runs east-west, and goes all the way out to the Pacific Ocean, although once it crosses into "the Avenues" its name changes to Geary Boulevard. Numbering begins downtown and increases as you go west.

- "The Avenues" is the locally accepted name for the area served by the numbered roadways in the Richmond District, 3rd Avenue through 46th Avenue, and it's important to know because the City also has numbered "streets," 1st Street through 30th Street. Don't confuse the streets and the avenues as they are entirely different neighborhoods. The avenues also extend down into the Sunset and Parkside districts. The numbered streets begin in the SOMA and run north-south until the Mission District where they run east-west into the Potrero Hill, Bernal Heights, Castro, Noe Valley districts after 14th Street. Thus when someone tells you that the store you want is on "24th" you'll need to clarify, "24th Street or 24th Avenue?"

- Nineteenth Avenue is a good roadway to become familiar with since it serves as another connector road, along with Park Presidio Boulevard, to the Golden Gate Bridge from Interstate 280 and Highway 1. Both run into the city from San Mateo County to the south. Nineteenth Avenue splits off from 280/1 just inside the San Francisco city limits, runs right in front of San Francisco State University, out through the Sunset District and into Golden Gate Park. Its name changes to Park Presidio Boulevard on the northern side of the park. If traffic is really bad on 19th Avenue, and it often is, Sunset Boulevard is just a few blocks to the west and is usually a good route through the Sunset.

- Highway 101 also enters San Francisco from the south, however it splits off to head for the Oakland-San Francisco Bay Bridge where I-80 begins. Interstate 80 will take you through the northern half of the East Bay, out to Sacramento, the Sierra Nevada, all the way to New York City.

BEYOND SAN FRANCISCO

Two major highways, running north and south, connect San Francisco with the Peninsula and the South Bay, Highway 101 and Interstate 280. Highway 101 is notoriously crowded and weaves through the heavily populated cities of the Peninsula and South Bay. Highway 101 goes all the way from Los Angeles to the state of Washington. A more scenic drive and often less crowded is I-280 (known as Junipero Serra Freeway), which starts near the Bay Bridge on the San Francisco side and goes south past Daly City, continues down the west side of the Bay, and culminates at the I-680 junction. Close to the San Francisco Airport, I-380 links Highway 101 with I-

280. Highway 85, also known as Stevens Creek Freeway, connects 101 with 280 from Mountain View to Cupertino. Interstate 880 is another connector for 101 and 280, slicing through the city of San Jose. Father north, Highway 92 runs through the Peninsula, around San Mateo, and traverses west all the way to the coast ending in Half Moon Bay. Another coastal connector is Highway 84, which links Redwood City with Woodside and then, like Highway 92, goes all the way to the coast, ending at Highway 1. Certainly the most scenic highway in the Bay Area, and arguably in the country, Highway 1 twists and turns itself along the western edge of the US, going south to LA and north to Washington.

Both the San Mateo Bridge and the Dumbarton Bridge connect the South Bay with the East Bay. The longest bridge in the Bay Area, the 6.8 mile San Mateo Bridge, links Foster City with Hayward via Highway 92. The Dumbarton Bridge connects Fremont and Newark in the East Bay with Palo Alto and Menlo Park. The southernmost bridge crossing the Bay, the Dumbarton Bridge is part of Highway 84, which can be accessed via the Willow Road off-ramp from Highway 101.

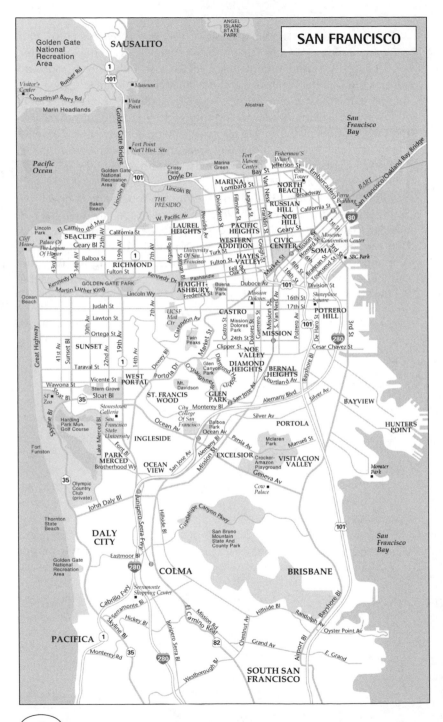

SAN FRANCISCO

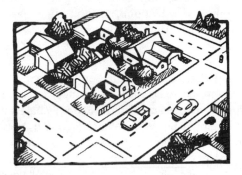

CITY OF SAN FRANCISCO

WELCOME TO SAN FRANCISCO (NEVER CALL IT "FRISCO" OR everyone will know you're not a native). More than seven million people live in the Bay Area, yet only about 800,000 people live in San Francisco proper. The city's population almost doubles during weekdays when hundreds of thousands arrive for work, clogging the local freeways. Traffic flowing out of San Francisco is sometimes worse than the commute into the city. In fact, some of the nation's worst morning and evening commutes are here, despite the existence of the sleek, clean, and usually efficient Bay Area Rapid Transit (BART) system. Where the BART trains don't go, more than two dozen other transit systems do, including buses, trolleys, cable cars, commuter trains, shuttles, and ferryboats.

Only 7 by 7 square miles in size, San Francisco is compact when compared to such cities as New York, Los Angeles, or Chicago. Every inch of the city teems with activity, from roller-blading, hiking, and biking in Golden Gate Park, to surfing or hang gliding at Ocean Beach, to dining or shopping in Chinatown or North Beach, and the list goes on.

You will quickly notice that one of the dominant features of San Francisco life is fog. London is perhaps the only city more famous for its fog. Locals here call it "Mother Nature's air conditioner," and it's especially prevalent during the Indian summer months of September and October. Neighborhoods are defined by the amount of sun, or lack thereof, that shines. Some areas of the city, such as The Mission, Potrero Hill, Noe Valley, and the Castro neighborhoods, are less fog-bound than others, but you won't be able to avoid it entirely. After you've been here for awhile, chances are you'll grow to love the fog, if you don't already. For those six to eight weeks of Indian summer, residents, especially in such neighborhoods as the Richmond, the Sunset District, Stonestown, and Diamond

Heights, awaken in homes blanketed by a fog so dense it almost looks solid. It usually burns away by noon, giving way to clear blue skies and temperatures into the 90s. Then, just when you can't take the heat anymore, the fog tumbles into the Bay Area from the Pacific Ocean to the west, cooling temperatures down to the 40s and 50s.

Certain smells also help to define San Francisco's neighborhoods. Fresh brewed, dark Italian and French roast coffee, and baking focaccia are the scents of North Beach; steamed crab and freshly baked sourdough permeate the Northpoint/Fisherman's Wharf area; and the smell of yeasty bagels and dim sum wafts through the air in the Richmond. A salty ocean bite spices the air along the western edge of the Sunset, and the sometimes-disturbing odor of cable car brakes hits you while descending some of the city's steepest slopes on Russian Hill and Nob Hill. Go to Chinatown for the smell of exotic herbs intermingled with fresh dumplings, and throughout the city's parks you'll learn to savor the unforgettable aroma of wet eucalyptus.

Aside from its stunning physical beauty, much of San Francisco's charm and vitality stems from its ethnic diversity. The earliest non-native settlers came from Russia, Italy, Ireland, Germany, China, Japan, and the Philippines, all of them establishing their own neighborhoods at first, and then branching out. That intra-city migration continues today, most notably the Chinatown population spreading out into formerly Italian-dominated North Beach.

HISTORY AND LOCAL COLOR

Called by those who live here "the City" (with a capital C), San Francisco has a rich and vivid history. Originally the area was home to the Ohlone American Indians; Europeans first laid eyes on the San Francisco Bay in 1579, when the English explorer Sir Francis Drake landed at Point Reyes, about 35 miles north of San Francisco. Drake, for whom that northern bay is today named, noted the sweeping vistas, thick fog, and dramatic cliffs, saying that the area reminded him of the famous White Cliffs of Dover of his homeland. But it wasn't until nearly two centuries later that colonization, led by Spanish soldiers and missionaries, began in San Francisco.

In 1776, Colonel Juan Bautista de Anza built a presidio near the Golden Gate, and later that year Franciscan priests opened Mission Dolores, which still stands in the heart of the Mission and is the city's oldest surviving building. A tiny village known as Yerba Buena ("good herb" in Spanish) sprang up between the mission and the presidio. In 1847, Yerba Buena officially became San Francisco, and in 1848 the territory was ceded to the United States at the end of the Mexican war. That same year, miners struck gold in the Sierra Nevada Mountains, and prospectors with dreams of riches packed their bags and headed west, spiraling the city's tiny population from 500 to 25,000 within a year. In 1850, the same year that California became the 31st state in the union, the City of San Francisco was officially incorporated.

From the famous 49er Gold Rush and the rowdy, lawless debauchery of the Barbary Coast days in the 19th century, to the massive devastation of the 1906 Earthquake and fire that ushered in the 20th century, to the 1950s poetry spark that ignited the Beat generation and electrified North Beach, to the famous 1960s "make love not war" counterculture of Haight-Ashbury, to the political and cultural birth of the gay rights revolution and sexual liberation movement in the 1970s, San Francisco has been and continues to be the liberal heartbeat of the nation.

Culturally, the city has long been a creative mecca, drawing artists, photographers, musicians, and writers from across the country and around the world. San Francisco's illustrious past includes legions of rock and roll greats like the Grateful Dead and Jefferson Airplane, as well as notable photographers Ansel Adams and Dorothea Lange. Murals painted by Diego Rivera dot the city—turning up in the most unexpected places—from the San Francisco City College campus to the stairwells of a downtown skyscraper, the City Club of San Francisco.

A vibrant spirit of creativity still flourishes here today, as witnessed by the Mission's rich, colorful murals, a plethora of small galleries, and a handful of world-class museums. San Francisco is also home to a thriving, tight-knit independent rock music community, a host of collective visual art groups and spaces, and a budding local literary scene. Throughout the year, countless festivals, parades, and celebrations pay homage to the city's rich cultural heritage—from the dizzying acrobatics of the lion dancers at Chinatown's annual Chinese New Year's Day parade, to the rhythmic beats and dancing in the streets that mark the Mission's Carnival celebration, to the outlandish drag outfits at the yearly Gay Pride weekend extravaganza hosted in the Castro (the city is, of course, well known for its large, politically active gay and lesbian population).

Liberal bent aside, San Francisco is an economic powerhouse: Along Market Street stand the towering temples of capitalism and economic power that make up the compact downtown Financial District, home to the largest concentration of banks and financial service companies west of the Mississippi, the Pacific Stock Exchange. Also in the heart of San Francisco's downtown is Union Square, resplendent in its recent $25 million makeover, with the ultra-chic designer boutiques of Dior, Armani, and Marc Jacobs, as well as numerous upscale department stores. The square itself, an elevated open green, is perfect for resting your feet, people watching, or coffee sipping. One more thing, you won't go hungry here: There are more restaurants per capita here than in any other US city, offering every cuisine and price range imaginable. Union Square also offers free wireless access—a perk that Mayor Gavin Newsom is looking into extending to the whole city.

All of these features make San Francisco a vibrant and stimulating locale to call home. The city comprises more than two dozen neighborhoods or districts, each of which can be clearly defined, despite the fact that some are only a few blocks long and many meld into one another at the edges. The neighborhood profiles that follow this introduction focus on the general characteristics and histories of each neighborhood and provide information about neighborhood housing, weather, public transit, post office locations, emergency services, hospitals, public safety agencies, and local attractions.

We start at the northeast corner of the city with the historically Italian neighborhood of North Beach, then climb up the steep slopes of upscale Nob Hill and Russian Hill, through the bustling Tenderloin, then work our way west to posh Pacific Heights, the Marina District and Cow Hollow, continuing on toward the foggy Pacific Ocean beaches of the Richmond, and the breathtaking views of Seacliff. We then head south across Golden Gate Park to the crisp air and cool coastal shores of the Sunset, continuing south to Stonestown and Park Merced. Turning east we begin to work our way back toward the center of town through the colorful Victorians of Haight-Ashbury, and the Western Addition, to Civic Center, and the lofts and nightclubs of SOMA. We then journey south to the murals of the Mission District, through the famous Castro, to Noe Valley, Glen Park, and Diamond Heights, before working our way up to the peaks of Potrero Hill and Bernal Heights. Then it's out to the Excelsior, Ingleside, Portola, and Visitacion Valley, before winding up at the city's southeastern most edge, Bayview/Hunter's Point, and stopping at the San Mateo County line.

HOUSING

Expect varied types of housing in San Francisco. The famous and oft-depicted Victorians are wood-framed buildings, which range from relatively simple cottages to extremely ornate gingerbread-style mansions. Styles include Italianate Victorians, Queen Anne Victorians, and others, which you might enjoy learning to identify once you live here. Built between the 1870s and the 1910s, Victorians have interiors as distinctive as their external features. High ceilings are the norm along with elaborate ceiling fixtures and wainscoting that can range from simple wooded slats to ornate carvings. The rooms tend to be small but generally have double doors that, when opened, create one large room out of two smaller rooms, great for creating a cozy home office. Often the rooms are entered from a railway hall, which runs from the front of the house or flat to the kitchen in the back. The grander Victorians still have fireplaces and marble fixtures, and the front rooms nearly all have bay windows. Also common here are Edwardians, built in the 1900s and 1910s. Some are wooden and similar to Victorians although less ornate. They often have bay windows, but gone are the Victorian-styled railway halls and the odd little rooms. Many have double doors between bedroom and living room; some even have closets equipped with Murphy beds. Built-in oak or fir cupboards are common in the dining room. Apartment buildings, many of which were built in the 1920s, are generally of stucco and brown brick. They often sport a web of fire escapes in front and/or back, and typically are steam-heated via radiators. Often the kitchen has some built-in glass cupboards, and maybe a table and ironing board.

Many of the homes of the Richmond and Sunset districts were built during the Depression. Places built during this time are snug and comfortable, often featuring fireplaces, hardwood floors, and built-in book cabinets. Housing from the 1950s, '60s and '70s, which is scattered throughout the city, tends to be a little boxy. Rooms are smaller, walls and ceilings are plain, and bathrooms and kitchens sometimes lack windows. Once you get to South San Francisco and Daly City, you will find entire neighborhoods composed of this architectural style.

New housing borrows features from the city's past and incorporates these into modern designs. Bay windows are the norm. New condos and apartments tend to be colorful, sometimes asymmetrical, with special attention paid to natural lighting. Generally speaking, the city's newest housing is concentrated in the South of Market Area (SOMA), particularly in the Mission Bay neighborhood, which is in the midst of wide-scale redevelopment.

Despite a sluggish local economy in recent years, living here remains expensive. In fact, according to the cost of living index compiled in 2004 by the ACCRA, a nonprofit organization that researches community and economic development, San Francisco is the third most expensive city in America to call home.

Throughout this book, unless otherwise noted, housing statistics are from the California Association of Realtors (CAR), www.car.org; Metro-Rent, www.metrorent.com; or DataQuick, www.dataquick.com. Visit their web sites for the latest information on local housing prices. While economists and housing experts do not believe the upward spiral of the housing market is sustainable, nothing so far, except for the glitch caused by the bursting of the dot-com bubble, has altered the ever upward course of Bay Area real estate. The median home price according to the California Association of Realtors (www.car.org) in San Francisco proper as of April 2005 was $755,000, still up over 20% from the previous year. For more specifics on Bay Area housing, refer to the **Finding a Place to Live** chapter.

GETTING AROUND SAN FRANCISCO

The city is notoriously tricky to navigate by car owing to an abundance of one-way streets, too many "no left turn" signs, the strangely curving main street, Market Street, which turns any semblance of grid-like order on its head, and of course, perpetual parking woes. However, San Francisco is a pedestrian and bike friendly city—at least for those able to navigate the steeper hills. Public transportation, made up primarily of a large army of gas and electric buses operated by San Francisco Municipal Railway (MUNI), is relatively easy to use, though getting out of town is another matter entirely. Beautifully restored antique streetcars traverse Market Street and the palm-lined bayfront of the Embarcadero, while old-time cable cars climb a few of the city's steepest hills. Bay Area Rapid Transit (known as BART) has a handful of stops in San Francisco, most of them downtown, though locals will tell you not nearly enough. But MUNI's growing light rail network, most notably the 3rd Street Light Rail expansion (opening in 2006) and talk of a future "Central Subway" metro link north of market to Union Square and Chinatown, promises to make public transit options more efficient and pleasant to use.

CITY RESOURCES

San Francisco is a bit of an anomaly in that is both a city and a county. Politically, the city is divided into 11 geographic districts. It is run jointly by the mayor and a Board of Supervisors—the board being elected by voters within each district. This spicy mix has led to two hotly contested mayoral elections in recent years, both ultimately decided by rousing run-offs.

Specific community resources and information are listed beneath each neighborhood profile, but here are a few basic citywide numbers you're likely to need no matter which neighborhood you choose to call home.

City Web Site: www.ci.sf.ca.us or www.sfgov.org
Board of Supervisors: 415-554-5184, TTY: 415-554-5227
Mayor's Office: 415-554-6141, TTY: 415-252-3107
City Hall: 415-554-4000
Public Transportation: MUNI, 415-673-6864, TTY: 415-923-6373, www.sfmuni.com
Parks, Open Space and Gardens: For detailed information, hours, maps, and complete park listings, contact the **San Francisco Parks and Recreation Department**, 415-831-2700, www.parks. sfgov.org or the **Neighborhood Parks Council**, 415-621-3260, www.sfneighborhoodparks.org. For information about community gardens contact the **San Francisco Urban Gardeners League (SLUG)**, 415-285-SLUG, www.grass-roots.org/usa/slug.shtml.

NEIGHBORHOODS

NORTH BEACH, TELEGRAPH HILL

CHINATOWN

Boundaries: North: Fisherman's Wharf; **East**: The Embarcadero; **South**: Broadway; **West**: Columbus Ave (Telegraph Hill is at the east corner of North Beach, with Stockton St as the border)

Don't bring your bathing suit to **North Beach**, just an appreciation for fine Italian food and a loaded wallet. North Beach is famous for its mouth-watering aromas of olive oil, garlic, and espresso, as well as its vibrant nightlife. These perks, coupled with its close proximity to downtown, make it a favorite neighborhood for young professionals, empty-nesters, and a burgeoning Chinese-American population, many of whom are moving from nearby Chinatown.

North Beach, Telegraph Hill

Famously the one-time home of the beat generation, North Beach became a gathering place for poets, writers, and critical thinkers of the 1950s and '60s, coined "beatniks" by *San Francisco Chronicle* columnist Herb Caen. Adorned in black with sandals, berets, and dark glasses, beatniks opposed mainstream beliefs and spoke out against complacency. The most famous of the bunch included San Francisco's first Poet Laureate, Lawrence Ferlinghetti, who opened the City Lights Bookstore, Jack Kerouac, Allen Ginsberg, and Gary Snyder.

Historically, the heart of the city's Red Light District, Broadway boasts neon signs that flicker and flash all night long, gleaming down on crowded sidewalks and a string of gentleman's clubs, host to a seemingly endless stream of bachelor parties. The late night vibe, minus the X-rated content, has spilled over onto Columbus and Grant Avenues, creating a bustling nightlife with music, dancing, and late night cafés. A smattering of blues bars line upper Grant Avenue, including the popular Grant & Green Blues Club and The Saloon, an intimate, old-time corner spot that has been serving up raucous, down home blues since the mid 1800s, and claims to be both San Francisco's oldest bar and the world's greatest blues bar. Meanwhile the swank, art deco Bimbos 365 Club on Columbus Avenue features bigger name rock bands and a velvet interior to make you feel like a 1950s movie star.

For a true San Franciscan experience head to the city's longest running musical, Beach Blanket Babylon, at Club Fugazi, 678 Beach Blanket Boulevard (Green Street). In addition to low-end blues and rock bars, upper Grant Avenue is home to trendy clothing shops and vintage jewelry stores. Because of spiraling rents, some merchants are being replaced by expensive boutiques, but no chain stores, thanks to neighborhood groups that have fought vehemently to keep North Beach's character intact.

Locals take a break from the food and frenzy of their neighborhood at Washington Square Park, one of the city's oldest public spaces. In the early morning, older Chinese-Americans congregate here, moving their limbs at glacial speed as they practice the ancient art of tai chi. At the same hour you can smell the focaccia baking across the street at Liguria Bakery, 1700 Stockton Street, in business since 1911. Throughout the day, neighbors, sunbathers, and artists gather at the park, which hosts numerous art and music festivals throughout the year. Above it all, the neo-gothic St. Peter and Paul's Catholic Church, 666 Filbert Street, towers majestically. The church, famous for its midnight Easter services, also hosts masses in both Italian and Chinese.

At dusk, Italian old timers play bocce ball at a small court near Aquatic Park, while nearby at the Joe DiMaggio Playground (formerly the North Beach Playground) on Lombard and Mason streets, teens gather for pick-up basketball games and tiny tots frolic in the playground. This is where baseball hall-of-famer Joe DiMaggio swung the bat around with his kid brothers.

True to its name, there used to be a long beach along the area's northern edge, between Telegraph Hill on the east and Russian Hill on the west. Shortly after the 1906 Earthquake, the city dumped debris from the earthquake and built a series of breakwaters and piers that combined to create the tourist mecca of Fisherman's Wharf and Pier 39. At the northern end of the Embarcadero, you'll find dozens of seafood restaurants and tourist shops, including Ghirardelli Square, a former chocolate factory that still serves the dark confection in various forms.

Most North Beach residents live in three-story Edwardian apartments, flats, or condos built on the ashes of the fire from the 1906 Earthquake. North Beach still is home to many Italian families (though that number has diminished significantly over the years) as well as Chinese-Americans. Young, mostly single, professionals enjoy North Beach for its food, nightlife, and easy commute downtown. Vacancies are not always easy to come by.

If you live in North Beach and work downtown, you may decide not to own a car, as parking is difficult (sometimes downright impossible), plus buses and cable cars are frequent. If you do have a car, you'll need to get a parking permit. Remember to curb your wheels when parking on a hill. If the car is facing downhill, your front wheels must turn in towards the curb. If the car faces uphill, the front wheels should turn out from the curb. (Parking control officers will ticket you for not obeying the curbing rule.) And, set that parking brake! If your apartment doesn't come with a garage (most here don't), check the newspaper's rental section and you may be able to find a garage to rent.

If you choose to make North Beach your home, undoubtedly you will find your own favorite restaurant. For breakfast, lunch, or dinner, you'll find espressos and cappuccinos available on every block. If you want to mix opera with your coffee, try Caffe Trieste at 609 Vallejo Street, one of the oldest coffeehouses in the neighborhood. If the opera's not live, it's being played on the jukebox. Neighborhood activities for hearty souls include swimming in the chilly waters at Aquatic Park, directly in front of Ghirardelli Square. The Dolphin Club and the South End Rowing Club both provide facilities and encouragement for your plunge into the cold water.

Another desirable place to live, and not as hectic as North Beach, is nearby **Telegraph Hill**. Formerly called Goat Hill, it became Telegraph Hill in 1853 because it was the site of the West Coast's first telegraph station. Here spotters scouted for ships entering San Francisco Bay through the Golden Gate. After sighting a ship, spotters used Morse code to notify port officials of the ship's impending arrival. The "Hill," as locals call the area, features breathtaking bay views, including Alcatraz Island, the former home of the notorious prison and convicts, such as Al Capone and the "Birdman of Alcatraz" (who actually never kept birds there). Here you'll find narrow streets lined with quaint cottages and picture-windowed condominiums, beautiful gardens, and even fewer rental vacancies than the rest of North Beach. Many residents must walk up tiny stairways and paths to their compact homes (compact due to the city's 40-foot height limit here).

Coit Tower, the most prominent feature of this area, rises 210 feet from the top of Telegraph Hill. A monument to the city's firefighters, Coit Tower was built in 1934, funded by the private contribution of Lillie Hitchcock Coit, an eccentric San Franciscan known for going against the grain (when she was 15 she served as a volunteer firefighter). The area around the tower is a romantic spot to bring a bottle of wine and watch the sunset or the boats on the Bay beneath you. If romance isn't in your cards, try climbing the 377 Filbert Street steps to Coit Tower for exercise. Listen carefully for the famous neighborhood parrots up in the trees. Though their origins are uncertain, most people believe the flock, now totaling over 100 birds, was started by a few birds that escaped from their cages. A documentary film was recently made about these local legends. (For daily sightings check www.pelicanmedia.org/wildparrots.html.)

Often touted as the largest Chinatown in the USA, San Francisco's **Chinatown** is a whirlwind of culture and history. Passing through the large, ornate entry gates to the south, you wind up on the main drag, Grant Avenue. Here, you'll find a host of shops selling everything from traditional Chinese clothing, to "I heart San Francisco" T-shirts, to endless bric-a-brac. Many of the retail shops here are tourist traps—but tucked in between you can find the occasional gem—fine imported fabric stores, specialty tea shops, and vegetable stands. And of course, there are restaurants, restaurants, restaurants. Wander off the main tourist drag up Washington and Sacramento streets to find the most popular local spots. One favorite with locals and tourists alike is House of Nanking on Kearny, where you'll find long lines day and night. Stockton—which connects Chinatown to North Beach at one end and to Union Square at the other—is filled with more practical, less tourist-oriented stores. On Saturdays, this street is packed with large trucks delivering durian fruits, lychees, and Asian pears to the various markets and the sidewalk is a sea of wall-to-wall people.

The city's legacy with regard to Chinese immigrants is an ugly one. Chinese men began coming to California in the 1850s to help build the railroads. At first they were welcomed as a hard-working, inexpensive source of labor, but when the Gold Rush began to die out they were villainized as unwanted competitors. Demonized as the so-called yellow peril, Chinese immigrants faced severe discrimination as a series of racist laws were enacted in the 1870s and 1880s. Interracial marriages were banned, Chinese people were not allowed to own property, to vote, or to have their families join them, Chinese children attended segregated schools, and the Chinese Exclusion Act of 1882 barred further Chinese immigration.

It was amid this chaos that Chinatown was born, as restaurants, boarding houses and opium dens sprang up around what was then the city center—Portsmouth Square—serving miners, and providing a sense of community for Chinese immigrants. Like much of the city, Chinatown was leveled in the 1906 Earthquake and fire, and rose from the ashes with the help of a wealthy businessman into the collection of tiny storefronts, Edwardian apartments, and alleyways you see today.

Today, many elderly Chinese-Americans and recently arrived young Chinese immigrants live in Chinatown, while younger families have largely moved out the Richmond and Sunset districts.

At night, wandering through the small alleyways you can often catch traditional Lion Dance troupes practicing, or stroll into a bar for a heated game of Majong. And the neighborhood especially comes alive once a year when it hosts the Chinese New Year Parade.

Web Site: www.ci.sf.ca.us
Area Code: 415
Zip Codes: 94133, 94108

Post Office: North Beach Station, 1640 Stockton St, 800-275-8777, www.usps.com

Police Station: Central Police Station, 756 Vallejo St, 415-315-2400; main non-emergency number, 415-553-0123

Emergency Hospitals: California Pacific Medical Center, 2333 Buchanan St, 415-600-6000, www.cpmc.org; Saint Francis Memorial Hospital, 900 Hyde St, 415-353-6000, www.saintfrancismemorial.org

Library: North Beach Library, 2000 Mason St, 415-355-5626, www.sfpl.org

Public Schools: San Francisco Unified School District, 555 Franklin St, 415-241-6000, http://portal.sfusd.edu

Community Resources: Telegraph Hill Dwellers, P.O. Box 330159, 94133, 415-273-1004, www.thd.org; North Beach Neighbors, P.O. Box 330115, 94113, www.northbeachneighbors.org; Telegraph Hill Neighborhood Center, 660 Lombard St, 415-421-6443, www.tel-hi.org; North Beach Citizens, 720 Columbus Ave, 415-772-0918; North Beach Chamber of Commerce, 556 Columbus Ave, 415-989-2220; The Dolphin Club, 502 Jefferson St, 415-441-9329; South End Rowing Club, 500 Jefferson St, 415-776-7372; Chinese Cultural Center, temporarily relocated to 555 Montgomery St, 16th floor, 415-986-1822, www.c-c-c.org

Public Transportation: MUNI, 415-673-6864, TTY 415-923-6373, www.sfmuni.com; *MUNI buses*: 15 Third, 30 Stockton, 10 Townsend, 41 Union, 39 Coit; *Cable Car* access to Hyde St line at Ghirardelli Square area and to Mason St line at Bay and Taylor sts. MUNI bus and cable car connections to BART and Light Rail stations along Market St

RUSSIAN HILL, NOB HILL

LOWER NOB HILL

Boundaries: *Russian Hill*: **North**: Aquatic Park; **East**: Columbus Ave; **South**: Broadway; **West**: Van Ness Ave; *Nob Hill*: **North**: Broadway; **East**: Kearny St; **South**: California St; **West**: Van Ness Ave

You won't come across *samovars*, *piroshki*, or *borscht* on **Russian Hill**, nor will you find the graves of the Russian sailors buried here before the Gold Rush. What you will find is one of San Francisco's most charming and exclusive neighborhoods, dotted with tiny gardens and parks known only to the locals. The top of Russian Hill is crowded with high-rise condominiums and apartment buildings, serviced by brass-buttoned doormen. These buildings stand interspersed with Victorian mansions, a few con-

Russian Hill, Nob Hill

verted firehouses, relatively humble Edwardian flats, and numerous dolled-up "earthquake cottages" built originally as temporary housing following the 1906 Earthquake. Tucked into the neighborhood, you'll find several small playgrounds for children, including the delightful Michelangelo Park on Greenwich Street and Ina Coolbrith Park off of Taylor Street. Sterling Park has public tennis courts with a stunning view of the Bay that might take an opponent's mind off the ball.

The streets are steep or winding, or both. And just when you're tired of asphalt, you'll find a surprising patch of green. Sometimes-rickety staircases ensure access to these public spaces. The architectural and green patchwork that makes up Russian Hill is embroidered together with cable car lines, invented by Andrew Hallidie back in 1873. It's said that Hallidie's pity for the horses strenuously pulling wagons up the hills is what inspired him to invent the cable cars. At its peak, the cable car system ran eight lines and more than 100 miles of track throughout the city. Today three lines remain, two of which serve both Russian Hill and Nob Hill (the Mason and Hyde lines); the third rumbles through Nob Hill and the Financial District along California Street.

Some of San Francisco's oldest homes keep watch from a lovely enclave between Taylor and Jones streets. Russian Hill boasts one of the crookedest (Lombard) and the steepest (Filbert between Hyde and Leavenworth) streets in the city. (Actually, the street with the most turns is in Potrero Hill, but don't tell the hordes of tourists.) The twisting Lombard Street is situated on the eastern slope of Russian Hill, between Hyde and Leavenworth streets. Local residents, who pay a pretty penny for the honor of living here, are privy to the near-constant click of camera shutters and vehicle fumes, as gleeful motorists navigate the eight near-hairpin turns in just one block.

On the north side of Russian Hill is the San Francisco Art Institute, 800 Chestnut Street, with its public exhibitions and Diego Rivera murals. Although the institute educates many budding artists, most of Russian Hill is not the bohemian enclave it was in the early 1900s when poets, painters, and photographers such as Ina Coolbrith, Maynard Dixon, and Dorothea Lange populated the area. Today, bankers, suited professionals, and the so-called San Francisco elite live here.

Russian Hill's commercial area is to the west, on upper Polk and Hyde streets. You'll find excellent and pricey restaurants in Russian Hill, but for less expensive fare try one of the many hole-in-the-wall Chinese food places where owners still charge non-elite prices. Opened in 1948, Swensen's Ice Cream store, at the corner of Union and Hyde streets, is a classic San Francisco establishment. Upper Polk Street is home to small coffee shops, boutique stores selling vintage furniture and antiques, upscale consignment shops, and used bookstores. The lower half of Polk Street, once riddled by drugs and prostitution, still remains a little rough in patches bordering the Tenderloin but has been undergoing a revival in recent years, and now hosts a lively array of restaurants, bars and cafés.

Named after the well-to-do of the post–Gold Rush era who built their enormous mansions here, **Nob Hill** is perhaps the most famous of San Francisco's hills. In 19th-century San Francisco, the newly rich were known as nobs or more derogatorily as nabobs, which was used interchangeably with the word snob. Ask around, and you'll find no one seems to mind the slightly unflattering origin of the neighborhood's name. Area residents are quite content to call Nob Hill home. Located south of Russian Hill and only minutes from downtown, Nob Hill is slightly less expensive than its northerly neighbor.

At the top of the hill are several eyesores—1960s high rises—mixed in with stately older buildings, where lucky tenants enjoy a panoramic view of the city. Some humbler apartment buildings and garden apartment bargains turn up on the market from time to time. Nob Hill's original mansions went up in smoke in the fire that followed the 1906 Earthquake, and in their stead are the city's grand hotels: the Fairmont, the Mark Hopkins, the Stanford Court, and the Clift. They all have excellent restaurants and bars, many with spectacular city and Bay views. The most famous is the Top of the Mark at the Mark Hopkins Hotel. Across the way is the Fairmont's Tonga Room, a 1960s style tiki bar replete with fabulous fruit drinks and faux rainstorms. The impressive sandstone-exterior Flood Mansion at 1000 California Street, built by James Clair Flood, who made his millions in mining stocks, is the only survivor of the grand houses of the 19th century and today houses the exclusive Pacific-Union Club.

Huntington Park, at the apex of Nob Hill, with its flowerbeds, bubbling fountains, and church bell serenades, is a lovely place to while away a Sunday afternoon (as long as you don't have to find parking). On Wednesday evenings, locals gather at the park with their dogs for a little wine and social bantering. Across the street from the park are the stunning gothic spires of the Episcopalian Grace Cathedral, home to the Cathedral

Choir of Men and Boys, and host of world-renowned musicians. For interesting lectures or big performances check out Nob Hill Masonic Center at 1111 California Street (go to www.masonicauditorium.com for information about upcoming events).

Close to the city's downtown shopping, theater, and hotel district, **Lower Nob Hill** lies between California Street on the north, Powell Street to the east, Geary Boulevard to the south, and Polk Street to the west. Called Lower Nob Hill by realtors, some refer to it as "Tenderloin Heights" or "The Tenderenob," due to its proximity to the Tenderloin, San Francisco's most downtrodden part of town. Lower Nob Hill is home to posh hotels, exclusive restaurants, and all of the leading private clubs. There are plenty of apartment buildings, some with art deco masterpieces like Egyptian-styled foyers or gilt-caged elevators, as well as inexpensive youth hostels. Views also run the gamut, ranging from brick walls to breathtaking urban panoramas. Many of the buildings have hidden gardens, complete with goldfish ponds and loquat trees. With some of the most plentiful and affordable studio and one-bedroom apartment options, Lower Nob Hill is a popular choice for those looking for a moderately priced, centrally located place to live. Some consider Lower Nob Hill to be the most urban of San Francisco's neighborhoods, "like Manhattan with hills," claim homesick New Yorkers. Yet oddly and fortunately, in a region of pigeons, taxi whistles, and "untrendified" diners, a definite neighborhood feel prevails here. The corner store may extend credit, the café remembers your usual, and the dry cleaner doesn't have to ask your name. Parking is impossible, although monthly rentals at commercial garages are available. The hill is traversed with bus and cable cars, but most people who live here walk to work, either to the Financial District, South of Market, or Union Square. Generally safe, centrally located, bustling, and well serviced, Lower Nob Hill is worth looking into for newcomers comfortable in such teeming surroundings.

Web Sites: www.ci.sf.ca.us, www.rhn.org; www.nobhillassociation.org
Area Code: 415
Zip Code: 94109
Post Office: Pine Street Station, 1400 Pine St, 800-275-8777
Police Station: Central Station, 756 Vallejo St, 415-315-2400; main non-emergency number, 415-553-0123
Emergency Hospitals: California Pacific Medical Center, 2333 Buchanan St, 415-600-6000, www.cpmc.org; Saint Francis Memorial Hospital, 900 Hyde St, 415-353-6000, www.saintfrancismemorial.org
Library: North Beach Branch, 2000 Mason St, 415-355-5626, Main Branch, 100 Larkin St, 415-557-4400; Chinatown Branch, 1135 Powell St, 415-355-2888, www.sfpl.org
Public Schools: San Francisco Unified School District, 555 Franklin St, 415-241-6000, http://portal.sfusd.edu

Community Publication: *Nob Hill Gazette*, 5 Third St, Suite 222, 415-227-0190, www.nobhillgazette.com

Community Resources: Russian Hill Neighbors, 1819 Polk St, #221, 415-267-0575, www.rhn.org; Nob Hill Association, 1177 California St, Suite A, 415-346-8720, www.nobhillassociation.org; Cable Car Museum, 1201 Mason St, 415-474-1887, www.cablecarmuseum.org

Public Transportation: MUNI, 415-673-6864, TTY 415-923-6373, www.sfmuni.com: *Russian Hill MUNI buses*: 1 California, 27 Bryant, 19 Polk, 31 Balboa, 41 Union, 45 Union-Stockton, 30 Stockton; *Cable Cars*: Hyde, Mason, and California St lines (MUNI bus and cable cars provide access to BART and MUNI Light Rail stations along Market St); *Nob Hill MUNI buses*: 1 California, 3 Jackson, 4 Sutter; *Cable Cars*: California, Mason, and Hyde lines, all Market St lines

TENDERLOIN

Boundaries: North: California St; **East**: Powell St; **South**: Market St; **West**: Van Ness Ave

Long considered San Francisco's seediest neighborhood, the Tenderloin is experiencing some improvement, with new construction and new faces. Used by many recently arrived immigrants as a kind of gateway neighborhood, you'll also find young urbanites and students living here. Located just a few blocks from Union Square, the Tenderloin is named for the days when policemen were paid more to patrol its notoriously mean streets, thereby enabling them to afford prime cuts of meat from the butcher. Others refer to it as the Theater District, with the Orpheum Theatre at 1192 Market Street; the George Coates Performance Works at

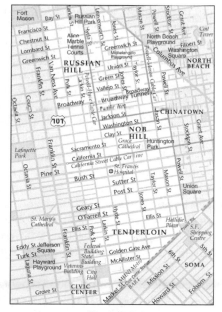

Tenderloin

110 McAllister Street; the Golden Gate Theatre at 1 Taylor Street; and the Geary Theater at 415 Geary Street, home to A.C.T. (American Conservatory

Theater), all within its boundaries. On Friday and Saturday evenings the sidewalks fill up with well-dressed theater-going crowds, and parking rates at local garages correspondingly increase.

After the devastation brought on by the 1906 Earthquake and fire, the Tenderloin had to rebuild. In preparation for the 1915 Panama-Pacific International Exposition, small hotels with ornate architecture sprang up. In addition to these smaller hotels, many of which still remain, you'll find huge hotels, like the Hilton at 333 O'Farrell Street, and the Nikko, 222 Mason Street. During World War II, when San Francisco served as a military logistics center, many shipyard and military employees lived in the single-room hotels. Interspersed throughout the neighborhood are a number of government buildings, including the Federal and State buildings, the Main Library, City Hall, the new Asian Art Museum, and the University of California Hastings Law School.

Union Square, San Francisco's answer to New York's Fifth Avenue and Times Square all rolled into one, is also nearby. This shopping magnet, packed with towering upscale department stores and pricey designer fashion boutiques, recently underwent a multimillion-dollar facelift. On weekends, the square frequently hosts a variety of outdoor events and exhibits—from free jazz shows to modern technology showcases. There is also free wireless, and a fantastic outdoor café, making Union Square an increasingly popular spot to relax in the sunshine with a cup of coffee and check your e-mail. For a fantastic view grab dessert at the Cheesecake Factory—located atop Macy's. Though it can be chilly, the outdoor balcony tables offer a bird's eye view of the hustle and bustle below.

Dozens of excellent, inexpensive Vietnamese, Chinese, and Indian restaurants dot the Tenderloin area, and on Sunday mornings and Wednesday afternoons, the Civic Center hosts a market of the old world variety, where you can buy fresh fish, fruit, and vegetables.

Tenderloin street life is busy, day and night. According to the Tenderloin Task Force, crime rates here are consistently among the city's highest. Drugs, prostitution, and burglaries are common problems and local amenities are sparse—there is no large supermarket, or even a bank in the neighborhood. Take a drive through and you will see that the streets are full of liquor stores, saloons, X-rated movie houses, and many boarded storefronts. The recently refurbished Sgt. John Macaulay Park at O'Farrell and Larkin streets, a shining diamond in the rough, is a much welcome addition, as is the neighborhood school, Tenderloin Elementary, 627 Turk Street, in this neighborhood of 3,500-plus children. The local community resource is the Glide Memorial Church at 330 Ellis Street. Run for more than four decades by the Reverend Cecil Williams and his wife, poet Janice Mirikitani, Glide is considered a Tenderloin institution, offering a multitude of programs to help the homeless, including free meals, medical services, counseling, and job training. Many volunteers offer their services to the church throughout the year, particularly during Thanksgiving and Christmas. The church's renowned Sunday gospel services regularly draw crowds from across the city and visitors from around the world.

As you might expect, rents in the Tenderloin are much lower than in the rest of the city, and landlords may not even require the first and last month's rent when signing a lease. Short-term weekly and month-to-month options are more plentiful here than anywhere else in town, making it a popular transition spot for newcomers planning to do their house hunting in person once they arrive. Affordable studios and one-bedroom apartments are also more plentiful in the Tenderloin than in any other part of town. Despite the area's rough reputation, if you search carefully, you may find a nice, clean, sunny little spot in a semi-secure art-deco building, with terrific views, an elevator, and if you are really lucky, a doorman. In addition, transportation here is top notch as many MUNI lines pass straight down Market Street, and BART stops at the Civic Center.

Web Sites: www.ci.sf.ca.us, www.tndc.org

Area Code: 415

Zip Code: 94102

Post Office: Civic Center, 101 Hyde St, Federal Building Finance Station, 450 Golden Gate Ave, 800-275-8777, www.usps.com

Police Station: Tenderloin Station, 301 Eddy St, 415-345-7300, TTY 415-474-5763; main non-emergency number, 415-553-0123

Emergency Hospitals: California Pacific Medical Center, 2333 Buchanan St, 415-600-6000, www.cpmc.org; Saint Francis Memorial Hospital, 900 Hyde St, 415-353-6000, www.saintfrancismemorial.org

Library: Main Branch, 100 Larkin St, 415-557-4400, www.sfpl.org

Public Schools: San Francisco Unified School District, 555 Franklin St, 415-241-6000, http://portal.sfusd.edu

Community Resources: Bay Area Women's and Children's Center, 318 Leavenworth St, 415-474-2400; Glide Memorial Church, 330 Ellis St, 415-674-6040, www.glide.org; North of Market Senior Services, 333 Turk St, 415-885-2274; Tenderloin Neighborhood Development Corporation, 201 Eddy St, 415-776-2151, www.tndc.org

Public Transportation: MUNI, 415-673-6864, TTY 415-923-6373, www.sfmuni.com; *MUNI buses*: 19 Polk, 27 Bryant, 31 Balboa, 38 Geary, 76 Marin Headlands, all Market St buses

date, check out Perry's, near the corner of Laguna Street. It's a longtime favorite pick-up place, and the food's pretty good too. Parking, especially along Union Street, between Fillmore and Van Ness, is a challenge at best, particularly on the weekends when visitors flock to the area.

Union Street is also home to a variety of popular annual festivities, including the holiday electric spectacular Fantasy of Lights, where the entire street comes aglow with twinkling white lights for the season, a June Art Festival, and San Francisco's only Spring Celebration and Easter Parade—featuring dozens of kids' activities including a bonnet contest.

After the 1906 Earthquake and fire, San Franciscans brushed off the ash and rubble and rebuilt their city with astonishing speed. They were so proud of what they had accomplished that they leapt at the opportunity to show off to the world and hosted the 1915 Panama-Pacific International Exposition at the west end of the Marina District. Architect Bernard Maybeck designed the Palace of Fine Arts on Lyon Street, between Bay and Jefferson streets, for the expo, which today houses one of the Bay Area's most popular attractions, the Exploratorium. Much more than just a hands-on science museum, the Exploratorium is a place where you can get your whole body involved in many of the more than 600 exhibits and demonstrations. Call ahead to reserve space at the Tactile Dome (415-561-0362), a huge darkened sphere. Groups have even been known to reserve the Dome privately and explore in the buff!

Prior to the exposition, the land around the **Marina District** was created by landfill, mostly from the debris caused by the earthquake and fire. Hundreds of mostly Mediterranean-style homes were resurrected here in the 1920s and '30s. The 1989 Loma Prieta earthquake hit the Marina District hard. Along Marina Boulevard, scores of the most desirable homes and apartment buildings were destroyed by a blaze that broke out when gas lines ruptured. The homes were rebuilt to higher seismic standards, but the ground underneath remains comparatively unstable, and seismic maps show the neighborhood as a high danger area in the event of another major earthquake.

Historically, the neighborhood was a quiet area occupied by long-time residents, many of them older and of Italian descent. But in the past decade, the Marina has been transformed into the premier playground of the city's 20- and 30-something upwardly mobile set. Catching the spillover from Union Street in Cow Hollow (just a few blocks south of the Marina), Chestnut Street bustles every day of the week with trendy shops, eateries, and bars. When not shopping or eating, locals head north to the Marina Green and the Presidio for outdoor fun. The Marina Green is optimum for kite flying as well as informal soccer and football matches. Running, biking, and roller-blading are also popular along the waterfront.

The eastern end of the Marina District is home to Fort Mason, a former military facility that now houses museums, bookstores, art galleries, public service organizations, and a renowned vegetarian restaurant, Greens (Building A in Fort Mason), with one of the city's most spectacular water-front views. Home to a number of nonprofit groups as well as a theater and an art gallery, the Fort Mason Center also frequently hosts exhibitions. It's a great place to take classes ranging from yoga to photography to driver's education. Stop by Fort Mason to grab a monthly newsletter and calendar or contact the center at 415-441-3400, www.fortmason.org.

At the western end of the Marina District sits the **Presidio**, the former military base, now an art, history, and cultural center, spectacular national park, and shorebird lagoon, among other things. Crissy Field, a popular spot with joggers, dog walkers, and bird watchers, offers 100 acres of open shoreline. An excellent place for an evening stroll, and a prime spot to sun-bathe, pack a picnic, or view windsurfing beneath the Golden Gate Bridge on a warm day, thanks to the smooth, paved Golden Gate Promenade, Crissy Field is now also easily accessible to bicycles, wheelchairs, strollers, and roller-bladers. Substantial habitat restoration work is in progress, so just steer clear of restricted areas, which are noted by posted signs. The Crissy Field Center runs a number of environmental education programs throughout the year, with a variety of hands-on programs for children.

Unique in the national parks system, the Presidio is run jointly by the National Park Service and the Presidio Trust, an independent federal agency. The US Congress mandated that the Presidio be completely self-sufficient by the year 2013, and to that end, the Presidio Trust has had to be creative about how to stay afloat. Finding big business tenants seems to be the way the Trust has decided to go, much to the dismay of area environ-mentalists. *Star Wars* maverick George Lucas, headquartered at Skywalker Ranch in the North Bay, is among the first occupants. The extended San Francisco arm of Lucas Films, a new multimedia mega-complex, the Letterman Digital Arts Center, opened in the Presidio in 2005. Other large-scale future projects may include a theater built by Robert Redford's Sundance Institute. In recent years, an increasing number of nonprofit and arts organizations have set up shop here, converting former army build-ings into offices.

The Presidio is also home to a small, upscale residential community with a handful of privately owned spectacular homes. Other housing options, set aside primarily for those who work here, include a few small cottages, dormitories, and a coast-side enclave of basic, compact, afford-able units known as the Baker Beach apartments, which offer stunning nat-ural surroundings and breathtaking views at very reasonable prices; however, there is a waiting list.

The area called **Presidio Heights** sits between the Presidio, Presidio Ave, Arguello Boulevard, and California Street, and differs little from Pacific Heights except for the view. Many of the homes here overlook cypress and eucalyptus groves, the golf course of the Presidio, or Julius Kahn Park. Sacramento Street, from Divisadero to Walnut, offers antique stores; chic clothing for men, women, and children; high-end consignment shops; gift shops; housewares stores; hair and nail salons; and a smattering of restaurants with outdoor seating (bring a sweater).

Laurel Heights, which extends to Laurel Village a little farther to the south of Pacific Heights, is served by the accessible shopping area called Laurel Village. Retailers include gourmet food and wine shops, well-stocked grocery stores, including Cal-Mart and Bryan's, which has a locally famous meat market, plus several children's stores, an independent bookshop, a stationery store, a clothing boutique, a classic five-and-dime, and an old-fashioned diner. There are many ornate single-family homes, but some apartments, flats, and even brand-new condos are also available. Prices here, though perhaps a little less than Pacific Heights, are still among the city's highest.

With easy access to the Presidio, Marin County, and downtown San Francisco, many people find the Pacific Heights, Cow Hollow, and Marina neighborhoods desirable, if not always affordable. Marina and Cow Hollow attract a significant number of single professionals. For the more settled/family-oriented, Pacific, Presidio, and Laurel Heights might be your best choice.

Web Site: www.ci.sf.ca.us

Area Code: 415

Zip Codes: Pacific Heights, 94115; Marina, 94123; Presidio, 94129; Laurel and Presidio Heights, 94118

Post Offices: Marina Station, 2055 Lombard St; Presidio Station, 950 Lincoln Blvd, Building #210; 800-275-8777, www.usps.com

Police Stations: Northern Station, 1125 Fillmore St, 415-614-3400, TTY: 415-558-2404, main non-emergency number, 415-553-0123

Emergency Hospitals: California Pacific Medical Center, 2333 Buchanan St, and 3700 California St, 415-600-6000, www.cpmc.org; Saint Francis Memorial Hospital, 900 Hyde St, 415-353-6000, www.saintfrancismemorial.org

Libraries: Presidio Branch, 3150 Sacramento St, 415-355-2880; Golden Gate Valley Branch, 1801 Green St, 415-355-5666; Marina Branch, 1890 Chestnut St, 415-355-2823, www.sfpl.org

Public Schools: San Francisco Unified School District, 555 Franklin St, 415-241-6000, http://portal.sfusd.edu

Community Publications: *New Fillmore and Marina Times*, 415-931-0515

Community Resources: Marina Neighborhood Association, 3727 Fillmore St, #201, 94123; Cow Hollow Association, 2867 Green St, 415-567-8611; Cow Hollow Neighbors in Action, 2742 Baker St, 94123; Golden Gate Valley Neighborhood Association, P.O. Box 29086, Presidio, 94129; San Francisco Recreation Harbor Tenants Association, P.O. Box 470428, 94147; Marina Merchants Association, 2269 Chestnut St, #235, 94123, 415-441-0848; Union St Association, 1686 Union St, 415-441-7055; Presidio Homeowners' Association, 650 Presidio Ave, 94129; Pacific Heights Residents Association, 2585 Pacific St, 94115; the Exploratorium, 3601 Lyon St, 415-397-5673, www.exploratorium.edu; Fort Mason Center, 415-441-3400, www.fortmason.org; Presidio National Park, 415-561-4323, TTY 415-561-4314, www.nps.gov/prsf; Crissy Field Center, 415-561-7752, www.crissyfield.org; Palace of Fine Arts, 3301 Lyon St, 415-567-6642, www.palaceoffinearts.org; Jewish Community Center, 3200 California St, 415-346-6040; Friends of the SF Pubic Library Book Bay, Bldg C South, Fort Mason, 415-771-1076

Public Transportation: MUNI, 415-673-6864, TTY 415-923-6373, www.sfmuni.com; *Pacific Heights, Presidio, and Laurel Heights MUNI buses*: 1 California, 24 Divisadero, 41 Union, 45 Union-Stockton; *Marina and Cow Hollow MUNI buses*: 22 Fillmore, 28 19th Ave, 30 Stockton, 41 Union, 43 Masonic, 45 Union-Stockton

THE RICHMOND, SEACLIFF

INNER RICHMOND
OUTER RICHMOND
WEST CLAY PARK

Boundaries: *Richmond*: **North**: Lincoln Park and the Presidio; **East**: Arguello Blvd; **South**: Fulton St and Golden Gate Park; **West**: The Great Highway/Pacific Ocean; *Seacliff*: **North**: Sea Cliff Ave/Pacific Ocean; **East**: 27th Ave; **South**: California St; **West**: Lincoln Park/Legion of Honor

Although there is no definitive agreement on how this neighborhood came by its name, one popular theory credits early settler George Turner Marsh of Richmond, Australia, who, upon seeing what was then a sea of sandy dunes stretched out before him, was reminded of his distant homeland. According to urban legend, after Mark Twain visited San Francisco's Richmond District, he declared the coldest winter he ever experienced was the summer he spent in San Francisco. Located on the edge of the Pacific Ocean, this is the part of the city that is first to greet the wind and fog blowing in from the ocean, and there are many days when the rest of the city is clear and sunny

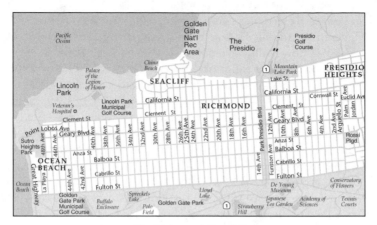

The Richmond, Seacliff

while the Richmond is blanketed in fog—something to keep in mind if you are thinking about setting up house here. It's a great zone for people who like sweater weather; because of San Francisco's microclimates, it is often possible to drive just a few blocks or miles to find the sun.

In recent years, the **Inner Richmond**, composed primarily of stucco single-family homes, a smattering of lavish Edwardians, and 1920s duplexes, has increasingly attracted young professionals drawn by some of the city's most affordable rentals and the somewhat less frantic pace. It is also is home to a large Asian-American community, and is often referred to as the "New Chinatown," boasting some of San Francisco's best Chinese, Thai, and Vietnamese restaurants and markets. Pretty much any prepared Asian food or ingredients you can imagine are available in a host of cozy family-owned eateries and shops that are clustered along Clement Street, the main drag. Clement Street is also home to an array of discount shops, hardware and video stores as well as one of the city's most beloved independent bookstores, Green Apple Books, at 506 Clement Street with an annex at 520 Clement Street. Lit lovers come from all over the city to wander along the creaky hardwood floors and browse the expansive collection of new and used books, as well as videos and DVDs.

Because it's a little further inland, the Inner Richmond sometimes manages to escape the perennial fog that blankets the outer avenues—but not always. Generally, though it's not quite as cool and misty here, though outright clear and sunny days—and the accompanying warmth—are a rarity.

Though outside the main hub, with Geary Boulevard as its main artery, the neighborhood is within minutes of nearby Japantown and the Fillmore District and is still within easy, direct reach of downtown. On the flip side, heading west on Geary will lead you straight to two of the city's great natural gems, Golden Gate Park and the Pacific Ocean.

A little west, beyond the busy pulse of the Inner Richmond, lies 25th Avenue. Cutting through the central heart of the Richmond district, this road provides easy access to the Presidio, Lincoln Park, and Land's End. Featured prominently in Alfred Hitchcock's classic noir flick, *Vertigo*, Land's End is perched majestically above 32nd Avenue and El Camino Del Mar. Overlooking the Golden Gate Bridge, this segment of the Golden Gate Recreation Area offers one of the city's most breathtaking ocean vistas.

Jefferson Starship's Paul Kantner and Grace Slick used to live in the wooden house perched on the cliff at the beginning of the Land's End trail. When walking the trail, beware of flying golf balls from the not-so-talented golfers enjoying nearby Lincoln Park Golf Course. The trail winds along the coast just below the picturesque Palace of the Legion of Honor Museum, culminating at the concrete ruins of Sutro Baths. Built in 1863 but later destroyed by a fire, Sutro Baths was once the world's largest public swimming hole.

For a slightly more bizarre and infamous local landmark, check out the Black House, an Addams Family–style black and purple Victorian at 6114 California Street, owned by the late Anton LaVey, founder of the Church of Satan. Though it is in messy disrepair and in danger of being torn down, a battle is afoot to make the site a recognized landmark.

Formerly an army base, the nearby Presidio is now a lush national park, complete with a world-class golf course, numerous hiking and biking trails, and superb beach access. The base is prime real estate, and thanks to the fact that it is now federally protected, it won't be sold off to developers. Today, a number of nonprofit organizations work in the Presidio. Private businesses are also calling the Presidio home, including George Lucas's multimedia mega-complex, the Letterman Digital Arts Center, which opened there in 2005.

When the fog lifts and the sun is shining, there is perhaps no better place to live than the **Outer Richmond**. Within walking distance of Ocean Beach and Golden Gate Park, the outer avenues are the perfect choice for lovers of the great outdoors and those looking for a little peace and quiet amid the chaos of city life. Once the city's burial ground and dismissively dubbed "the Great Sand Waste," the Outer Richmond as a neighborhood began to really take shape when waves of Russian, Irish, and European Jewish immigrants moved in following World War I. The post–World War II building boom, which went hand-in-hand with the baby boom, brought more residents, including those of Japanese and Chinese descent.

Since then the multiple generations of Asian-Americans, as well as continuing immigration waves from Russia, Eastern Europe, and Ireland, have left their indelible mark on the Outer Richmond—coming together to create one of the city's most ethnically diverse and family-oriented neighborhoods. Walking down Geary Boulevard, you can see the towering, gilded domes of Russian Orthodox Churches, grab a pint of beer at a bustling Celtic pub, or munch on dim sum at one of the many Chinese eateries, all while inhaling the scent of baking bread wafting from the numerous Russian bakeries.

The Outer Richmond continues to attract young families, drawn by the prospect of renting or even owning their own single-family homes with large backyards that are set along quiet streets and provide a distinctly residential feel. Once snubbed by young professionals as too removed and too dull, the neighborhood has been winning converts from the 20- and 30-something set, lured by moderate rents, plenty of on-street parking, and easy access to the Presidio. A leisurely walk through the remnants of the old Sutro Baths, breathtaking views at the historic, recently restored Cliff House, and kite flying at Ocean Beach are all just a short walk away. When it comes to beaches, the smaller, more scenic, and less crowded Baker Beach, on the edge of the Presidio, is one of the city's best-hidden gems. Here, you can enjoy the roar and crash of the thundering Pacific while taking in the fresh, salty ocean air and spectacular views of the nearby Golden Gate Bridge. A longstanding favorite with nude sunbathers, the beach features a small swimsuit-optional section close to the bridge. China Beach, which is farther south, is a little more protected from the wind, smaller, and family friendly.

Unfortunately, those dreaming of lazy, sunshine-filled afternoons by the seashore should be forewarned—the weather here is colder than most parts of the city. Like its neighbor across the park, the Outer Sunset, which is bordered by the Pacific Ocean to its west, the Outer Richmond is typically foggy, windy, and chilly. Long pants, sweatshirts and jackets are the norm even for summer outings. Ocean temperatures hover around 56° Fahrenheit. Those who desire to brave the cold and take a plunge—and there are a few—should heed posted signs: Swim only in designated swimming areas as the undertow and rip currents are powerful and dangerous.

While the Outer Richmond is just about as far away as you can get from the hustle and bustle and still be in San Francisco, Geary Boulevard provides a direct link to the city center. The 38 Geary bus frequently traverses the busy thoroughfare—depending on traffic, downtown is roughly a 20-minute ride away.

The Outer Richmond boasts its own little gems, including the Beach Chalet Brewery, located off the Great Highway where the edge of Golden Gate Park meets the ocean, just above the Golden Gate Park Visitor's Center. The brewery, a favorite with locals and tourists alike, has spectacular 1930s murals displaying a mini history of the area, and sells large, refillable casks of locally brewed beer to go. The Java Beach Café at 1396 La Playa Boulevard is frequented by surfers, retired businessmen, and young singles who mix freely, enjoying the sound of the pounding waves across the way.

Though it is often socked-in with fog, the beaches, backyard barbecues, and quaint neighborhood feel make the Outer Richmond one of San Francisco's coziest places to call home. Move here and you'll get to know many on a first-name basis, including your neighbors, the butcher at the local grocery store, and many of the restaurant proprietors.

Elite enclaves, such as West Clay Park and Seacliff, offer a peek at some of San Francisco's most spectacular mansions and stunning Golden Gate Bridge and ocean views. Sandwiched between Lincoln Park to the west and the Presidio to the east, **Seacliff** is a gorgeous neighborhood with, wouldn't you know it, sea cliffs, cypress trees, winding streets, and spectacular views of the Golden Gate Bridge. Home to San Francisco's social elite and a handful of celebrities, this neighborhood boasts large houses with carefully manicured lawns and multimillion-dollar price tags.

West Clay Park, tucked in between 22nd and 24th avenues, is another unique San Francisco neighborhood, full of children and lovely houses, and perhaps best known as the home of legendary photographer Ansel Adams.

Web Sites: www.ci.sf.ca.us, www.richmondsf.org

Area Code: 415

Zip Codes: Inner Richmond, 94118; Outer Richmond, 94121

Post Office: Golden Gate Station, 3245 Geary Blvd; Geary Station, 5654 Geary Blvd, 800-275-8777, www.usps.com

Police Station: Richmond Station, 461 6th Ave, 415-666-8000; TTY 415-666-8059, main non-emergency number, 415-553-0123

Public Schools: San Francisco Unified School District, 555 Franklin St, 415-241-6000, http://portal.sfusd.edu

Emergency Hospitals: California Pacific Medical Center, 2333 Buchanan and 3700 California St, 415-600-6000, www.cpmc.org; UCSF Medical Center, 505 Parnassus Ave, 415-476-1000, ucsfhealth.org; St. Mary's Medical Center, 450 Stanyan St, 415-668-1000, www.stmarysmedicalcenter.org

Library: Richmond Branch, 351 9th Ave, 415-355-5600, www.sfpl.org

Community Publication: *Richmond ReView*, 415-831-0463, www.sunsetbeacon.com

Community Resources: Palace of the Legion of Honor, 34th Ave and Clement St, 415-863-3330, www.legionofhonor.org; Lincoln Park Golf Course, 300 34th Ave, 415-750-GOLF, www.playlincoln.com; the Richmond District Neighborhood Center, 741 30th Ave, 415-751-6600, www.rdnc.org; PAR (Planning Association for the Richmond), 145 Geary Blvd., #205, 415-974-9332, www.sfpar.org

Public Transportation: MUNI, 415-673-6864, TTY 415-923-6373, www.sfmuni.com: *Inner Richmond MUNI buses*: 1 California, 2 Clement, 3 Jackson, 4 Sutter, 5 Fulton, 21 Hayes, 28L-19th Ave Limited (to Daly City BART), 29 Sunset, 31 Balboa, 33 Stanyan, 38 Geary; *Outer Richmond MUNI buses*: 1 California, 2 Clement, 3 Jackson, 4 Sutter, 5 Fulton, 18 46th Ave, 28L-19th Ave Limited (to Daly City BART), 29 Sunset, 31 Balboa, 33 Stanyan, 38 Geary; *Golden Gate Park Free Shuttle*, 415-831-2727, www.goldengateparkconcourse.org

SUNSET DISTRICT—INNER AND OUTER, PARKSIDE

GOLDEN GATE HEIGHTS
ST. FRANCIS WOOD
FOREST HILL
WEST PORTAL

Boundaries: *Sunset*: **North**: Golden Gate Park and Lincoln Way; **East**: Stanyan St; **South**: Ortega St; **West**: Great Highway/Pacific Ocean; *Parkside*: **North**: Ortega St; **East**: Dewey and Laguna Honda boulevards; **South**: Sloat Blvd; **West**: Great Highway

If you choose to make the **Sunset District** your home, be prepared with some cozy, thick sweaters, even in the summer, and know that it may be days before you actually watch a sunset here, as the neighborhood frequently is encased in fog. Rest assured, however, that the skies do clear, offering a fabulous view of the ocean and the sunset. The weather in the

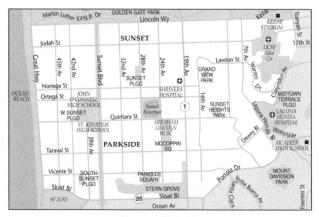

Sunset, Parkside

Sunset actually acts as a housing market deterrent, keeping values here slightly lower than in many other parts of the city. In addition, the Sunset's low crime rate, decent public schools, and manageable street parking make it an ideal family neighborhood. It is also home to students and professionals, particularly those attending classes or working at the University of California at San Francisco (UCSF) Medical Center—a premier research and teaching hospital. The neighborhood has a large Chinese-American population and many seniors as well.

Residents here are privy to one of San Francisco's greatest treasures, Golden Gate Park, right in their backyard. (See **Greenspace and Beaches** for more details.) Access to outdoor activities is easy, including endless running and bike trails, museums galore, horseback riding, rowing on Stow Lake, and soccer, polo, or lacrosse at the polo fields. You can even learn to fly fish in the park. Ocean Beach beckons from the west, where daring souls swim or surf in the cold Pacific—beware of the strong undertow. And for the more daring, Fort Funston, on the Great Highway, is a popular place to walk your dog or to hang glide. If your fear of heights dissuades you from the sport, you can still enjoy it as a spectator from the viewing area.

The Sunset comprises the **Inner Sunset** (west from UCSF Medical Center to 19th Avenue) and the **Outer Sunset** (west of 19th Avenue to the Great Highway). And, while many locals consider the entire area the Sunset, technically the homes to the south of Ortega Street and all the way to Sloat Boulevard are actually in **Parkside**; and the hilly area around Lomita and 16th avenues, known as **Golden Gate Heights**, is also considered by many as the Sunset. When the fog lifts, the views from Golden Gate Heights, perched atop a 725-foot bluff, are stunning.

Architecturally, the Inner Sunset is comprised of a number of Victorians and Edwardians, while the Outer Sunset is predominantly Mediterranean- and Spanish-style stuccos. Some of the homes along the hilly, tree-lined streets have spectacular views of the ocean and the park. Others, especially those west of 19th Avenue, are just plain unoriginal. Designed by Henry Doelger in the 1930s, they were built quickly and sold for about $5,000. While uninspiring, these "white cliffs of Doelger" usually have small gardens, and street parking is not a problem.

Two upscale neighborhoods, **St. Francis Wood** and **Forest Hill**, border the Sunset on the east; here you'll find some of the loveliest, best-tended homes in the city with prices to match. Many of the homes in St. Francis Wood, which with its large engraved entry pillars feels slightly like a gated community, were designed by renowned local architect Julia Morgan. The lots are large, giving these exquisite homes substantial space. The streets are gently winding and tree-lined.

A little further down the hill and to the west is another of San Francisco's great hidden treasures, **West Portal**. With its 1950s charm, friendly mom-and-pop establishments, and an old-time movie house, West Portal feels like a small town you'd stumble upon somewhere in middle America. Seemingly plunked in the middle of a densely packed urban city, it is a refreshing and often overlooked family-oriented enclave, complete with quiet side streets and neatly tended single-family homes. City dwellers sometimes stumble into the heart of this quiet neighborhood quite by accident, some while riding the MUNI Metro, which runs through a tunnel here, linking it with downtown. On West Portal Avenue, an old-fashioned looking main street, independent shops and restaurants thrive and chain stores are refreshingly absent, save for a Starbucks Coffee. West Portal is just minutes from San Francisco State University via MUNI.

The main north-south artery in the Sunset is 19th Avenue, which slices through the neighborhood. (It's easy to keep track of direction here, as the streets along 19th Avenue are alphabetical from Judah Street south to Wawona Street.) Frequently crammed with vehicles, 19th Avenue links Interstate 280, coming up from San Mateo County, with Highway 1, heading north toward the Golden Gate Bridge and Marin County. (Be aware that 19th Avenue changes to Park Presidio Boulevard when it crosses Fulton Street, just north of Golden Gate Park.)

Residents of the Sunset happily boast that they can find just about everything they need within their neighborhood—from daily staples to exotic food, coin-operated laundries, electronics stores, and clothing outlets. In the Inner Sunset, the commercial areas run along Irving and Judah streets. More upscale shopping, including clothing boutiques, coffeehouses, and ethnic eateries, is centered along 9th Avenue and Irving. Go west on Irving to about 20th Avenue for the neighborhood Chinatown, which is chock full of produce markets and Asian delicacies. One block south of Irving is Judah Street, which offers easy access to the Light Rail Vehicles (LRV). Called the MUNI Metro or Metrolines, they will take you quickly to the Financial District's Embarcadero station. A number of regular bus lines also go that way, but the LRV is the most popular choice for those headed downtown.

At the southern end of 19th Avenue, near the Stonestown neighborhood, is San Francisco State University (SFSU). With almost 29,000 students, it is one of the largest schools in the California State University System, and thus many students call the Sunset, particularly the Outer Sunset/Parkside environs, home. The best time to find a place here is early summer, when many of the students take a year's worth of laundry home to mom and dad's house, vacating their San Francisco digs.

The Sigmund Stern Grove, located on Sloat Avenue, is a natural amphitheater surrounded by giant eucalyptus groves, redwoods, and firs.

Since 1938, Stern Grove has hosted Sunday afternoon concerts for all types of music lovers. The Midsummer Music Festival features opera, operetta, symphonic, choral, jazz, rock and roll, and Broadway music...and it's all free! For the best seats, arrive early; otherwise you'll have to settle for lounging on the hillside lawn on your blanket. If you plan far enough in advance, you can call ahead and reserve a picnic table.

With its proximity to the airport and Interstate 280, many newcomers are choosing to live in the Sunset and commute to Silicon Valley. In addition, transportation to downtown San Francisco is quick, making it an optimum choice for professionals who work in the city. And, unlike most of the rest of the city, parking here is not too difficult.

Web Site: www.ci.sf.ca.us

Area Code: 415

Zip Codes: Sunset, 94122; Parkside, 94116

Post Offices: Sunset Station, 1314 22nd Ave; Parkside Station, 1800 Taraval St, 800-275-8777, www.usps.com

Police Station: Taraval Station, 2345 24th Ave, 415-759-3100, TTY 415-351-2924, main non-emergency number, 415-553-0123

Emergency Hospital: UCSF Medical Center, 505 Parnassus Ave, 415-476-1000, ucsfhealth.org

Libraries: Sunset Branch, 1305 18th Ave, 415-355-2808, Merced Branch, 155 Winston Dr, 415-355-2825, Parkside Branch, 1200 Taraval St, 415-355-5770, www.sfpl.org

Public Schools: San Francisco Unified School District, 555 Franklin St, 415-241-6000, http://portal.sfusd.edu

Community Publication: *Sunset Beacon*, 415-831-0463, www.sunset beacon.com

Community Resources: Sunset Neighborhood Beacon Center, 3925 Noriega St, 415-759-3690, www.snbc.org; Inner Sunset Merchants Association, 917 Irving St, 415-731-2884; Golden Gate Park Visitors Center, 415-751-2766, www.parks.sfgov.org; Stern Grove Festival, 415-252-6252, www.sterngrove.org; Golden Gate Heights Neighborhood Association, P.O. Box 27608, 94127, www.gghna.org

Public Transportation: MUNI, 415-673-6864, TTY 415-923-6373, www.sfmuni.com; *Sunset MUNI buses*: 6 Parnassus, 17 Parkmerced, 18 46th Ave, 26 Valencia, 29 Sunset, 66 Quintara, 71 Haight-Noriega; *LRV*: N-Judah; *Parkside MUNI buses*: 17 Parkmerced, 18 46th Ave, 23 Monterey, 28 19th Ave, 29 Sunset, 35 Eureka, 48 Quintara-24th St, 52 Excelsior, 66 Quintara, 89 Laguna Honda; *LRV*: L-Taraval, K-Ingleside, M-Oceanview; *Golden Gate Park Free Shuttle*, 415-831-2727, www.goldengateparkconcourse.org

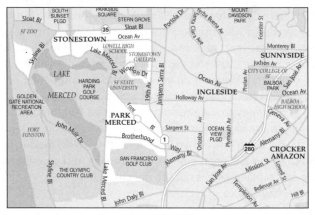

Stonestown, Park Merced

STONESTOWN, PARK MERCED

LAKESHORE

Boundaries: *Stonestown*: **North**: Sloat Blvd; **East**: 19th Ave; **South**: Brotherhood Way; **West**: Lake Merced Blvd; *Lakeshore*: **North**: Sloat Blvd; **West**: Great Highway/Pacific Ocean; **East**: Lake Merced Blvd; **South**: San Francisco/San Mateo County Line; *Park Merced*: **North**: Holloway Ave; **East**: 19th Ave; **South**: Brotherhood Way; **West**: Merced Blvd

The neighborhoods of Stonestown, Park Merced, and Lakeshore meld together and surround the compact campus of San Francisco State University (SFSU), which serves 29,000 students. Today the school is known for its education, business, and creative arts departments. In the 1960s, however, it was one of the flash points of the student protests. Well-known alumni include actress Annette Bening, pianist Vince Guaraldi (he did the music for the "You're a Good Man, Charlie Brown" cartoons), singer Johnny Mathis (rumor has it Mathis quit at SFSU after being told he'd never sing), and author Anne Rice.

The often fog-bound **Stonestown** area, simply a southern extension of the Parkside district, comes with its own mall, the Stonestown Galleria. This is a shopping destination for people from near and far that boasts major department stores, upscale boutiques, restaurants and coffee shops, a supermarket, movie theaters, medical offices, and, perhaps most important in this city, oodles of free parking. Stonestown is also the name of a pleasant collection of apartments adjacent to the Galleria. Here, you'll find scores of units, many of which are occupied by middle-aged and older residents who've lived here for years, and by students of nearby SFSU.

Just south of the campus is an even larger residential complex known as the Villas Park Merced. Metropolitan Life Insurance Company developed the 200-acre project in 1948 to house San Francisco's elderly. Today, it is a haven for SFSU students, especially if mom and dad are paying the rent for their garden or tower apartment that's just a five-minute walk to campus. **Park Merced**, with an array of one-, two-, and three-bedroom townhouses, is also home to many families and older residents. The multi-acre development has become a mini neighborhood in its own right, with a local grocery store, Montessori school, MUNI bus lines, lovely shaded trails, and ample green space. A state-of-the-art fitness center, movie theater, and conference space were recently added as part of an overall renovation effort. The shores of Lake Merced are just minutes away, as is access to I-280 and 101 south, making this a popular spot with commuters who work on the Peninsula or in the South Bay.

Across Lake Merced Boulevard, to the west of Park Merced, is Lake Merced, one of San Francisco's main reservoirs, which is surrounded by a wooded park and the 18-hole Harding Park golf course. Paddle boats and rowboats are available for rent. The western edge of Lake Merced is known as **Lakeshore**, where few San Franciscans ever visit, unless they're hang-gliders destined for the cliffs of Fort Funston or they're lucky and well off enough to have scored one of the luxury apartments or condominiums lining John Muir Drive. Rents here are steep, amenities exceptional, and the atmosphere serene, but vacancies are rare. If you can afford it and if living this far from the hustle and bustle is for you, keep checking—someone's bound to move out eventually.

Web Site: www.ci.sf.ca.us

Area Code: 415

Zip Codes: 94132

Post Offices: Stonestown Station, 180 Napoleon St, 800-275-8777, www.usps.com

Police Stations: Taraval Station, 2345 24th Ave, 415-759-3100, TTY 415-351-2924; Ingleside Station, 1 Sergeant John V. Young Lane, 415-404-4000, TTY 415-404-4009; main non-emergency number, 415-553-0123

Emergency Hospital: UCSF Medical Center, 505 Parnassus Ave, 415-476-1000, www.ucsfhealth.org

Library: Merced Branch, 155 Winston Dr, 415-355-2825, www.sfpl.org

Public Schools: San Francisco Unified School District, 555 Franklin St, 415-241-6000, http://portal.sfusd.edu

Community Resources: San Francisco Zoo, Sloat Blvd at 47th Ave, 415-753-7080, www.sfzoo.org; San Francisco State University, 1600 Holloway Ave, 415-338-1111, www.sfsu.edu; San Francisco Golf Club, Junipero Serra Blvd and Brotherhood Way, 415-469-4100; Harding Park Golf Course, Harding Dr off of Skyline Dr, 415-664-4690; Lake

Merced, Lake Merced Blvd, 415-831-2700, www.lakemerced.org; Fort Funston, Fort Funston Rd and Skyline Blvd, 415-239-2366.

Public Transportation: MUNI, 415-673-6864, TTY 415-923-6373, www.sfmuni.com; *Stonestown MUNI buses*: 17 Park Merced, 18 46th Ave, 23 Monterey, 26 Valencia, 28 19th Ave, 29 Sunset; *MUNI Metro*: M Oceanview; *MUNI LRV*: K-Ingleside, M-Oceanview; *Lake Merced MUNI buses*: 18 46th Ave, 88 BART shuttle (to nearby Daly City BART station)

HAIGHT–ASHBURY

COLE VALLEY
BUENA VISTA PARK
PARNASSUS/ASHBURY HEIGHTS

Boundaries: *Haight-Ashbury*: **North**: Oak St; **East**: Divisadero St; **South**: Parnassus St; **West**: Stanyan St; *Buena Vista Park*: **North**: Haight St; **East**: Divisadero; **South**: Roosevelt Way; **West**: Masonic Ave; *Parnassus/Ashbury Heights*: **North**: Parnassus Ave; **East**: Buena Vista Ave and Roosevelt Way; **South**: Clarendon Ave and Tank Hill Park; **West**: UCSF Medical Center

Haight-Ashbury

Once dubbed "Hashbury" by legendary San Francisco columnist Herb Caen, Haight-Ashbury (or the Haight) is best known for its glory days in the sixties as the epicenter of the "make love not war" generation. Back then the Haight was *the* place for free love, psychedelic drugs, and lazy days in the park listening to the rock bands of the time, including the Grateful Dead. But times have changed; today, the Haight has moved far beyond its counterculture and anti–Vietnam war roots to become an established and desirable neighborhood. At its core, Haight-Ashbury consists of a busy commercial zone filled with retail shops and restaurants, surrounded by restored Victorian houses, flats, and apartments. Set on tree-lined hills, the unique mansions that rock-and-roll bands once bought for a song and painted purple and orange are now tastefully restored and worth a fortune. Had you lived here in the Haight's heyday, your neighbors could have been such musical icons as Janis Joplin and members of the Grateful Dead and Jefferson Airplane, or more disturbingly, members of Charles Manson's cult.

Today, young professionals, as well as many students and employees of nearby UCSF Medical Center and the University of San Francisco, call the Haight home. Life is a tad more like it was in the 1960s the closer you get to Haight Street itself, where young people, struggling to make ends meet, often get together to share flats in large old Victorian or Edwardian houses. If you like the hubbub of a busy street, and don't mind sharing a place, such apartments are sometimes reasonably priced; some buildings feature hardwood floors, large fireplaces, views of Golden Gate Park, and cupolas.

Haight Street itself is lined with trendy boutiques selling vintage clothing, fetish shoes, used furniture, and toys for grown-ups. Not surprisingly, there are still plenty of stores that sell used records, clothes, books, comics, vintage rock-and-roll posters (even some of the "black light" variety), and new age and hippie paraphernalia, including incense, body oils, and tarot cards. Throughout the Haight vestiges of hippiedom remain, including folks with flowers in their hair wearing tie-dyes and sandals and strumming acoustic guitars. It's also commonplace to be approached on the street by folks selling all manner of illegal drugs, and there are plenty of panhandlers, some neo-hippie, some neo-punk, and some just plain annoying.

Those considering making their home here may want to "try the neighborhood out" first with a stay at the Red Victorian bed and breakfast, 1665 Haight Street, 415-864-1978, www.redvic.com. The Red Victorian Movie House, known as the Red Vic, just down the street at 1727 Haight, screens a mix of alternative, independent, and cult films. The theater is small but friendly and features bowls of yeast-flavored popcorn and old loveseats in the front rows.

Having a popular retail corridor close at hand can be both a blessing and a curse. Though Haightsters often roll their eyes at the hordes of suburban weekend warrior shoppers and tourists that crowd the sidewalks on Saturday and Sunday afternoons, living here is convenient and mostly pleasant. All the basics are here: a good local video store, a friendly hardware shop, a mid-sized grocery store, a well-stocked bookstore, and Amoeba Music, 1855 Haight, with its mind-boggling aisles filled with new and used country, rock, blues, and everything in between—voted year after year in the *San Francisco Bay Guardian's* reader polls as the city's best music store.

Eating out is a popular pastime here, where a mix of inexpensive restaurants reflecting the city's diversity—Asian, Latin American, Italian—

NEWCOMER'S HANDBOOK FOR THE SAN FRANCISCO BAY AREA

line the block. Spanish tapas can be had at the favorite Cha! Cha! Cha! at 1801 Haight Street. Weekends find the Haight's handful of popular brunch spots serving up huge plates of eggs and waffles, with plenty of coffee and mimosas, to blurry-eyed, jam-packed crowds well into the late afternoon; arrive early if you don't want to wait in line.

Outdoor recreation, including dog walking and Frisbee playing, is an option in Golden Gate Park's "panhandle," conveniently located between Oak and Fell streets from Stanyan to Baker. The panhandle is a finger-like extension of the 1,000-plus-acre park that stretches all the way out to Ocean Beach. The park, which was once nothing but sand dunes, is laced with walking trails and has sports fields, playground equipment, an antique carousel, a science museum, an art museum, a riding stable, polo fields, an angling pond, Dutch windmills, and more.

Cole Valley, a small, friendly neighborhood located on the southern edge of Haight-Ashbury, is bounded by Carl and Cole streets. It's quieter than the Haight and home to doctors and medical students from the nearby UCSF Medical Center as well as families and young professionals. The local shopping area on Cole Street is packed with cafés, bakeries, bars, and restaurants, ranging from low-cost creperies to elegant dining. Hardware stores, flower shops, health-food stores, and dry cleaners are also available. The neighborhood pub, the Kezar Bar and Restaurant, 900 Cole, is a good place to check for any unadvertised apartment rentals. The UCSF has a housing board (www.sfsu.edu/~housing/board.html) that posts a variety of shared rentals and one-bedroom apartment options. Homes here are typically a little more expensive than in the Haight. The commute to downtown is convenient; just hop on the MUNI LRV N-Judah and you'll get there in less than ten minutes.

The **Buena Vista Park** neighborhood, which surrounds the 36-acre Buena Vista Park, has curvy, hilly streets, magnificent homes, and plenty of wealthy occupants. In fact, this neighborhood has a history of well-to-do residents, including the members of the Spreckels family, who made a sweet living in the sugar refining industry. One of two Spreckels homes in the city is at the west end of the Haight, overlooking Buena Vista Park. Built in 1887 and located at 737 Buena Vista Avenue West, this mansion is exquisite, and typical of some of the other homes lining the avenue. (If you think this place is grand, take a trip over to the second Spreckels palace at 2080 Washington Street in Pacific Heights. Kind of makes one wonder if there are any openings in the sugar refinery biz.)

Visit the lookout at the top of the Buena Vista Park and you'll find a vast panorama that includes San Bruno Mountain to the south, Mount Diablo to the east, Mount Tamalpais and the Golden Gate Bridge to the north, and the Farallon islands to the west. Though right in the midst of the city, this park, with its eucalyptus groves and stately pines, makes you feel like you've left the city behind entirely. In the early morning and early evening, the park is a popular spot for local dog walkers.

For more charming neighborhoods with old, refurbished homes, check nearby **Parnassus** and **Ashbury Heights**, located south of Haight Street. These neighborhoods have plenty of ornate Victorians and Edwardians, as well as a few apartment buildings and large homes converted into apartments. Residents here claim that the wild parrots of Telegraph Hill come to visit, often in flocks of twenty or more. (To learn about these notorious birds and daily sightings, check their web page at www.pelicanmedia.org/wildparrots.html.) Rents and house prices in this area and in Buena Vista Park are higher than in the rest of the upper Haight.

Web Sites: www.ci.sf.ca.us, www.haightashbury.org

Area Code: 415

Zip Code: 94117

Post Office: Clayton St Station, 554 Clayton St, 800-275-8777, www.usps.com

Police Station: Park Station, 1899 Waller St, 415-242-3000, TTY 415-681-6487, main non-emergency number, 415-553-0123

Emergency Hospitals: St. Mary's Medical Center, 450 Stanyan St, 415-668-1000, www.stmarysmedicalcenter.org; UCSF Medical Center, 505 Parnassus Ave, 415-476-1000, www.ucsfhealth.org

Library: Park Branch, 1833 Page St, 415-355-5656, www.sfpl.org

Public Schools: San Francisco Unified School District, 555 Franklin St, 415-241-6000, http://portal.sfusd.edu

Community Resources: The Haight-Ashbury Free Medical Clinic, 558 Clayton St, 415-487-5632, www.hafci.org; Haight Ashbury Neighborhood Council, P.O. Box 170518, 94117, 415-753-0932, www.hanc-sf.org; Haight Ashbury Neighborhood Council Recycling Center, 780 Frederick St, 415-753-0932; Cole Valley Improvement Association, P.O. Box 170611, 94117; Haight Ashbury Merchants, www.haightashburymerchants.com

Public Transportation: MUNI, 415-673-6864, TTY 415-923-6373, www.sfmuni.com; MUNI buses: 5 Fulton, 6 Parnassus, 7 Haight, 33 Stanyan, 37 Corbett, 43 Masonic, 21 Hayes, 24 Divisadero, 66 Quintara, 71 Haight-Noriega: MUNI LRV: N-Judah

WESTERN ADDITION, CIVIC CENTER

THE FILLMORE
JAPANTOWN
LOWER HAIGHT
ALAMO SQUARE
HAYES VALLEY
LOWER PACIFIC HEIGHTS

Boundaries: *Western Addition*: **North**: Pine St and Pacific Heights; **East**: Polk St and the Tenderloin; **South**: Haight St and The Lower Haight; **West**: Masonic and Richmond; *Civic Center*: **North**: Turk St; **East**: Larkin St; **South**: Market St; **West**: Gough St

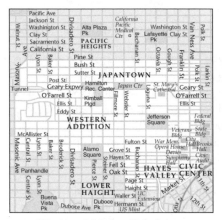

Western Addition, Civic Center

Nestled between the upscale neighborhood of Pacific Heights and the colorful Haight-Ashbury, the Western Addition is one of the most ethnically and economically diverse neighborhoods in the city. Boasting rows of restored Victorians, the area features ritzy bed and breakfasts and cozy, chic restaurants as well as auto repair shops and thrift stores. Housing choices are varied, including apartments, railway flats, colorful mansions, single-family Victorians, brand new condos, and public housing, and housing costs are inching ever upward. Despite this, affordable housing can still be found in the Western Addition, bringing young professionals and accompanying commercial development to the neighborhood. Hayes Valley in particular, with its trendy boutiques and upscale eateries, and the nearby construction of the much-awaited Octavia Grand Boulevard, is becoming popular.

Until its development in the 1850s, this large land area, covering what is now the center of San Francisco, was a wasteland of sand dunes. Situated west of the already settled section of the city, the expansion was aptly named the **Western Addition**. The neighborhood survived the 1906 Earthquake and fire without much damage; the buildings, many of which were built on top of bedrock, did not topple, and it was beyond the downtown fire zone. After the great fire, many Japanese-Americans sought refuge here. Then, during World War II, African-Americans flooded into the vacancies left by the interned Japanese population. It was during this era that the jazz scene flourished on Fillmore Street. However, in the decades following World War II, this neighborhood was hit with the combination of suburban flight and the introduction of public housing, which spiraled the area into urban decay. A city-sponsored urban renewal plan was largely unsuccessful, and eventually many of the long-standing Victorians were either demolished or moved to other areas of town. For years, vacant lots scarred the once vibrant Fillmore Street. It wasn't until the real estate crunch of the 1980s and '90s that developers and real estate agents began to uncover the area's potential.

Fillmore Street, with its mix of high-end boutiques and locally owned shops, is shared by both Pacific Heights and the Western Addition. Upper Fillmore, part of neighboring Pacific Heights, is lined with exclusive clothing and home design stores, trendy restaurants, an art film house, and upscale chain stores. Lower Fillmore is home to a multiplex theater, eateries, cafés, and an eclectic mix of independent neighborhood stores. Remnants of the Fillmore District's 1940s jazz heyday continue today with the famous Fillmore Auditorium, John Lee Hooker's Boom Boom Room, and Rasselas Jazz Club. Every summer, the neighborhood comes together to relive its glory days as the heart and soul of the city's jazz scene with the Fillmore Jazz Festival.

Part of the Lower Fillmore area, **Japantown** sports sushi bars, specialty stores, and cultural events. Of particular note is the Japan Center, with the Kabuki Theater Cinema Complex and the relaxing Kabuki Springs and Spa. Japanese necessities, from stationery and books to kimonos and cosmetics to fresh seafood and wasabi, are all available in Japantown. As you would expect, there are a number of sushi palaces, noodle shops, and yes, karaoke bars. The Cherry Blossom Festival takes place here in April. Old Victorians, newly built public housing, and even a high-rise apartment building make up the housing options in this part of the Western Addition.

More urban and slightly gritty, Divisadero Street is the less gentrified artery of the Western Addition. Divisadero Street separates the **Lower Haight** from the Upper Haight or Haight-Ashbury. The Lower Haight has a distinctly different feel from its more famous sister. For the last couple of decades, students, artists, musicians, herbalists, and the like have lived in the Lower Haight's cheap and cavernous railway flats. Garages and gas stations hinder the cohesiveness of the street's commercial center, but independent and imaginative business owners maintain a stronghold in the neighborhood. A barbecue restaurant, karate studio, video store, and a popular record store are testament to the street's diversity. Divisadero Street is also home to several popular cafés, one of which has an adjoining international magazine and newspaper stand. And one of the few places

groceries and laundry, and Civic Center's section of Market Street is still host to a number of adult entertainment spots. But, if you look hard, you may be lucky enough to find an affordable, spacious apartment with a secured entrance on a quiet street.

Web Site: www.ci.sf.ca.us

Area Code: 415

Zip Codes: 94115, 94117, 94102

Post Offices: Steiner St Station, 1849 Geary St; Clayton St Station, 554 Clayton St, 800-275-8777, www.usps.com

Police Stations: east of Steiner St: Northern Station, 1125 Fillmore St, 415-614-3400, TTY 415-558-2404; west of Steiner St: Park Station, 1899 Waller St, 415-242-3000, TTY 415-681-6487

Emergency Hospitals: California Pacific Medical Center, Pacific Campus, 2333 Buchanan St, 415-600-6000, www.cpmc.org; California Pacific Medical Center, Davies Campus, Castro and Duboce sts, 415-600-6000, www.cpmc.org; St. Francis Memorial Hospital, 900 Hyde St, 415-353-6300

Library: Main Library, 100 Larkin St, 415-557-4400; Western Addition Branch, 1550 Scott St, 415-355-5727, www.sfpl.org

Public Schools: San Francisco Unified School District, 555 Franklin St, 415-241-6000, http://portal.sfusd.edu

Community Resources: Alliance Française de San Francisco, 1345 Bush St, 415-775-7755, www.afsf.com; Audium (a theater for audiophiles), 1616 Bush St, 415-771-1616, www.audium.org; The Fillmore, 1805 Geary Blvd, 415-346-6000, www.thefillmore.com; San Francisco Performing Arts Library and Museum, 399 Grove St, 415-255-4800; Ella Hill Hutch Community Center, 1050 McAllister St, 415-921-6276; War Memorial Opera House, 199 Grove St, 415-864-3330, www.sfopera.com; San Francisco Ballet, 415-865-2000, www.sfballet.org; Louise M. Davies Symphony Hall, 201 Van Ness Ave, 415-864-6000, www.sfsymphony.org; Bill Graham Civic Auditorium, 99 Grove St, 415-974-4060, www.billgrahamcivic.com; Alamo Square Neighbors Association, P.O. Box 15372, 94115, 415-567-5197; North of Panhandle Neighborhood Association, NOPNA, P.O. Box 591504, 94159-6113, www.nopa.org; Hayes Valley Neighborhood Association, P.O. Box 423978, 94142-3978, www.hayesvalleysf.org; Hamilton Recreation Center and Pool, Geary Blvd and Steiner St, 415-292-2001

Public Transportation: MUNI, 415-673-6864, TTY 415-923-6373, www.sfmuni.com: *MUNI buses*: east-west: 38 Geary, 2 Clement, 3 Jackson, 4 Sutter, 5 Fulton; north-south: 22 Fillmore, 24 Divisadero, 43 Masonic, 42 Downtown Loop, 49 Van Ness-Mission, 47 Van Ness; inter-city: 76 Marin/Headlands; *Golden Gate Transit buses* (to and from Marin County): 10, 20, 60, 70, 80, 90

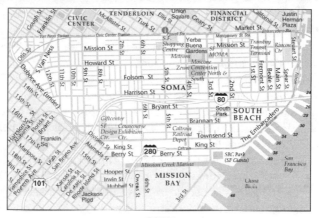

SOMA

SOUTH OF MARKET AREA (SOMA)

SOUTH PARK
SOUTH BEACH
MISSION BAY/CHINA BASIN/MISSION CREEK

Boundaries: **North** and **West**: Market St; **South**: 16th St; **East**: San Francisco Bay

In the 1990s, amid the dot-com boom, San Francisco's **South of Market Area** (SOMA) transformed almost overnight from a somewhat rundown commercial area to the "it" place to live and work. Old industrial warehouses were rapidly converted into internet businesses and bustling high-end live/work lofts. But when the economic tide turned, SOMA was hit hard, as legions of small start-ups, one after another, closed up shop for good.

In the dot-com aftermath, SOMA has been forging a new identity, returning to its earlier roots as an artists' enclave, with an array of newly established art studios, galleries, and small theaters. The neighborhood also offers a smattering of fine restaurants and cafés, many of them tucked semi-secretly away.

Locals who live in SOMA, long the seat of the city's nightclub scene, enjoy an easy walk to live music spots, busy bars, and dance clubs—something to keep in mind for those looking for a quiet neighborhood to call home. In particular, 11th, Folsom, Harrison, and Howard streets are often bustling, packed with cars, and noisy late into the night.

Housing options range from newly built condos and lofts to small Edwardian apartments in wood-framed buildings on tiny alleyways, to residential high-rise units in the bayfront areas. Residents can walk to work in the nearby Financial District or downtown. Numerous top-name clothing and furniture outlet stores in SOMA attract shoppers citywide, including the Burlington Coat Factory, 899 Howard Street, and the ever-popular Flower Mart, 640 Brannan Street, where morning shoppers can choose from an array of fresh cut flowers and potted plants.

You can grab a bite to eat, see a live performance, and do your laundry all in one sitting at Brainwash, 1122 Folsom Street. And Trader Joe's, Costco, Rainbow Grocery Co-op, and a new Whole Foods are all nearby to meet basic shopping needs.

The Moscone Convention Center (named for Mayor George Moscone, who was assassinated along with Supervisor Harvey Milk in 1978) attracts thousands of people for conventions and conferences. The Yerba Buena Center for the Performing Arts and the $87 million Museum of Modern Art solidify SOMA's flourishing art scene. A new permanent home for the 30-year-old Mexican Museum (temporarily relocated to Fort Mason) is underway, and plans were recently unveiled for a new 60,000-square-foot building for the Contemporary Jewish Museum (currently located at 121 Steuart Street). The Sony Metreon, a gigantic urban techno-mall, with shops, restaurants, an IMAX theater, and a 15-screen movie theater, is situated at 101 4th Street. And just across from the Metreon is the Zeum Children's Museum, nestled in a large indoor complex that features a playground, old-fashioned merry-go-round, production studios, a bowling alley, and an ice skating rink. SOMA's heart, the sprawling expanse of lawn of the Yerba Buena Gardens, hosts a number of free outdoor events—from mini theater shows to music concerts to political fests and rallies.

Eagerly anticipated is Yerba Buena Lane, whose dozen shops and restaurants, scheduled to open in 2006, will connect Market Street to Yerba Buena Gardens, and a $380 million Bloomingdale's shopping center, slated to transform the ghost-like shell of the once grand Emporium. Nearby 6th Street boasts a mix of hipster bars, makeshift art galleries, mini nightclubs, and inexpensive eateries. But with its smattering of boarded-up buildings and ramshackle residential hotels, this is still one of the rougher spots in town.

The **South Park** section of SOMA originated in the mid-1850s as an upscale residential area with elegant English-style townhouses. It surrounds an oval, European-style park between 2nd and 3rd and Bryant and Brannan streets, and was the first posh neighborhood in San Francisco. Today, the park remains, but the mansions do not. Wealthy San Franciscans moved to newer neighborhoods after the 1906 Earthquake and fire ruined their homes, and in the years that followed, this area became decidedly more industrial than residential. By the late 1970s photographers, graphic designers, and artists, attracted by cheap rents, moved into the neighborhood. In the 1980s a couple of restaurants tested the waters, and in the 1990s some multi-media startups rented space in ware-houses that had been converted into live-work spaces, creating what was known as "Multimedia Gulch." Today, a few hearty businesses remain, but the area is now slower paced with a decidedly residential feel. Bordering the park, you'll find excellent cafés and elegant restaurants including the South Park Café, 108 South Park; Ecco, 101 South Park; and the Infusion Bar and Restaurant, 555 2nd Street; as well as housewares and clothing shops, and architecture and design firms.

In the last decade, a massive urban renewal project has brought a number of waterfront condominium and apartment complexes to SOMA's **South Beach** area, near the west end of the Bay Bridge and along the Embarcadero, from Market Street to 3rd Street. South Beach is dominated by the SBC Park, the massive outdoor stadium that is home to San Francisco's beloved Giants baseball team. On a warm day, you can sometimes see boats floating along the marina here, hovering in hopes of catching a fly-away ball. A number of upscale bars and restaurants surround the ballpark.

Once a weedy wasteland, with crumbling, abandoned commercial buildings and pothole-filled streets, after decades of planning, **Mission Bay**—or **China Basin** as it is referred to by old timers—is now the city's urban renewal heartland, with construction of condominiums, apartment, and office buildings, and the MUNI 3rd Street Light Rail project, connecting the city's southeast neighborhoods (Visitation Valley, the Bayview, and Mission Bay) to downtown San Francisco, all underway. Long one of the city's last underdeveloped outposts, Mission Bay is undergoing a multimillion-dollar facelift—transforming more than 300 acres of abandoned rail yard to an ultramodern high-density urban hub—that will continue into the next decade.

Today, in the southwest corner of Mission Bay, the transformation is largely complete. A handful of tall condo complexes, luxury apartments, and glassy offices with ground floor retail have sprung up in the once vacant area between 3rd and 4th streets, along King Street. The swanky restaurants, winding bayfront walkways and bike paths, and the well-manicured pockets of green space with gently swaying waterfront palms, come together to create a natural extension of the revitalized Embarcadero. Folks visit to watch the boats bob in the breeze at nearby South Beach Harbor, walk along the fishing pier, and take in stunning views of the Bay Bridge or a Giants game at the SBC Park. A spacious new Safeway grocery store recently opened here as well as a Borders bookstore, both on King Street. A Mission Bay branch library as well as a senior community is scheduled to open in 2006.

As the 3rd Street Light Rail project nears completion in 2006, this area, already a short ride on the N-Judah from downtown, will likely attract more young professionals and accompanying retail services.

Originally part of a larger waterway—a bay, marsh, and mudflat system that connected Mission Creek to San Francisco Bay—Mission Bay was crossed by Long Bridge, a wooden causeway (where 3rd Street is now) constructed in the mid 19th century to improve links to the waterfront shipyards at Potrero Point and Hunter's Point, cutting off most of Mission Creek's mouth. After the 1906 Earthquake, rubble was dumped here, filling in and further compromising Mission Bay. Then Southern Pacific Railroad settled in, using this area for its rail yards.

Long-term plans for Mission Bay include 6,000 units of housing; 49 acres of new park space, which will include preserved wetlands; an entertainment complex; and a 43-acre UCSF Mission Bay research campus, which is already partially up and running.

With its distinctly modern high-density flavor, the redevelopment of Mission Bay is a good example of "new urbanism." The mixed-use matrix, being organized by one large developer, has been criticized by many for being ultramodern, too chain store friendly, and out of step with San Francisco's character, but none would disagree that this languishing area has desperately needed an overhaul. Touted by its developers as "San Francisco's newest neighborhood," Mission Bay will take a good two decades to truly come into its own, but those who enjoy an urban atmosphere and desire easy access to downtown, happening nightclubs, excellent restaurants, and the Bay should feel quite at home. Newcomers looking for a neighborhood with a more residential feel will want to head elsewhere.

Buried amid the noise of all the new construction and tucked under Interstate 280 is an old San Francisco gem, the **Mission Creek** Marina, host to a small houseboat community. Less well-to-do than Sausalito's floating home communities, the tiny, tight-knit enclave floating on Mission Creek is one of the city's hidden treasures. Established in the 1960s, this mini oasis was once legendary for its hodgepodge of gypsies and artists—not far from a one-time traveling hobo camp near the railroad tracks—and its wild parties on the water. Today, most residents are in their 50s and 60s, have been here many years, and life is quieter, though a communal spirit is still very much alive here. Rents are very low, with only a handful of berth spaces, and turnover is almost nonexistent. Mission Creek Park, a bit raggedy and overrun with weeds, has been getting a little more attention lately, with planned construction of a new Mission Creek bikeway and greenbelt along its banks. A variety of birds call this area home, giving it the feel of a tiny island of nature amid new four- and five-story towering structures.

Web Site: www.ci.sf.ca.us
Area Code: 415
Zip Codes: 94103, 94105, 94107
Post Offices: Bryant Station, 1600 Bryant St; Rincon Finance Station, 180 Steuart St; Brannan St Station, 460 Brannan St, 800-275-8777, www.usps.com
Police Station: Southern Station, 850 Bryant St, 415-553-1373; main non-emergency number, 415-553-0123
Emergency Hospital: San Francisco General Hospital, 1001 Potrero Ave, 415-206-8000, www.dph.sf.ca.us/chn/SFGH/default.asp
Library: Main Branch, 100 Larkin St, 415-557-4400, www.sfpl.org
Public Schools: San Francisco Unified School District, 555 Franklin St, 415-241-6000, http://portal.sfusd.edu
Community Resources: San Francisco Museum of Modern Art, 151 3rd St, 415-357-4000, TTY 415-357-4154, www.sfmoma.org; Yerba Buena Center for the Arts, 701 Mission St, 415-978-2787, www.ybca.org; Cartoon Art Museum, 415-227-8666, www.cartoon art.org; Counter PULSE, 1310 Mission St, 415-626-2060, www.counter pulse.org; Gene Friend Recreational Center, 6th and Folsom streets, 415-554-9532; SomArts Cultural Center, 934 Brannan St, 415-552-2131, www.somarts.org; California Historical Society, 678 Mission St, 415-357-1848; SBC Ballpark, 24 Willie Mays Plaza, 415-972-2000, http://sanfrancisco.giants.mlb.com; UCSF Mission Bay Campus, 16th and Owens streets, http://pub.ucsf.edu/missionbay/, 415-476-9000; South Beach Harbor, The Embarcadero at Pier 40, 415-495-4911, www.southbeachharbor.com; South of Market Community Action Network, 965 Mission St, 415-348-1945; Mission Bay Golf Center, 1200 6th St, 415-431-7888; Natoma/SOMA Neighborhood Association, 544 Natoma St, 94103, 415-864-7440, www.sfdistricts.org
Public Transportation: MUNI, 415-673-6864, TTY 415-923-6373, www.sfmuni.com: *MUNI buses*: 9 San Bruno, 12 Folsom, 14 Mission, 15 3rd St, 26 Valencia, 27 Bryant, 30 Stockton, 45; *MUNI LRV*: all routes along Market St; *BART*: all trains along Market St; Transbay Bus Terminal for AC Transit, Sam Trans, Golden Gate Transit and Greyhound buses, on Mission St, between 1st and Fremont sts; *CalTrain Station* on 4th and King sts

MISSION DISTRICT

MISSION DOLORES

Boundaries: North and East: Highway 101; **South:** Cesar Chavez (formerly Army) St; **West:** Valencia St

Mission District

Taking its name from Mission Dolores, the whitewashed, gilded-topped monument to California's early days as the stomping ground of Spanish religious conquesting zeal, the **Mission District** is one of San Francisco's oldest neighborhoods. The traditional heart of San Francisco's Latin American community, over the years, the growing intersection of emerging artists, new trendy restaurants, and young urban hipsters has turned the Mission District into one of the city's most diverse, vibrant, and distinctive neighborhoods. Here, amid the roving mariachi bands, you can step outside your door and grab an enormous, tasty burrito on almost every corner, enjoy a lazy, sunny afternoon in one of the city's most luscious stretches of urban greenery, Dolores Park, or get your drink on at an endless string of dive and high end bars. Just past the city's fog line, the Mission also boasts some of San Francisco's most consistent sunny, warm, and therefore most welcoming weather.

Opened in 1776, the mission, officially named Mission of St. Francis de Asis but known to all as Mission Dolores, bears the distinctive title of San Francisco's oldest building. The sixth California mission founded by Spanish missionary Father Junipero Serra, its spectacular ceiling is covered by a mural with Indian basket designs. Today, Roman Catholics from all over the city congregate for mass at Mission Dolores. The noon mass is conducted in Spanish.

From its inception as a mission, various ethnic groups have settled this area. By the 1850s, the neighborhood was filled with German and Scandinavian immigrants, with the Italians and Irish moving here en masse after the 1906 Earthquake and fire displaced them from their North Beach and South of Market homes. In fact, the three-day fire following the 8.3 Richter earthquake leveled much of San Francisco, but stopped short at the adobe tower of Mission Dolores. So fond were locals of the Mission that, faced with the spreading flames that destroyed much of what the great earthquake missed, firefighters, hoping to preserve it, dynamited the Convent and School of Notre Dame across the way, a move later determined probably unnecessary. The anecdote remains poignant today as a testament to the neighborhood's history as well as to its inhabitants' determination and grit.

Perhaps more than any other, this neighborhood, a mix of old-timers, Mexican and Central American families, and young artists, activists, and hipsters, has a fierce sense of community unity and pride.

In the 1990s dot-com boom, tensions ran high as the Mission became a key economic and cultural battleground between preservationists and well-financed commercial opportunists. Despite the chaos and friction, when the bubble burst, an artistic and cultural vortex was left in its stead. Today, high-end restaurants sit next to independent stalwarts, such as the Roxie Theater, 3117 16th Street, an old movie house that features alternative films and documentaries; Theater Artaud, 450 Florida Street; and Theater Rhinoceros, 2926 16th Street. And new creative paragons, local writer Dave Eggers' 826 Valencia, a writing center with free programs for teens, and art collaborative Cell Space, 2050 Bryant Street, have opened.

At the heart of it all is Valencia Street, the bustling epicenter for nightlife with a continuously opening string of swank "must try" eateries. Coffeehouses, restaurants, and of course bars are open late here and along 16th Street, and the proprietors won't rush you as you nurse your latte or espresso. During the day, the street is abuzz with a mix of trendy clothing stores, furniture shops, several top-notch independent bookstores, the progressive New College, whose motto is "Education and Social Change." In recent years, the Valencia vibe has spilled over onto nearby Guerrero Street, which has seen a number of new eateries, bars, and independent boutiques open recently.

Heading south to 24th Street brings you to the heart of the Mission, where Spanish is the dominant language and Mexican taquerias and Salvadoran bakeries dot the street. The street scene is sprinkled with galleries, small shops, and amazingly colorful mural-filled alleys, especially Balmy Alley, between 24th and 25th streets, and Folsom and Harrison, where every garage door and backyard fence sports a mural. The Precita Eyes Mural Arts and Visitor Center, 2981 24th Street, sponsors an art walk that features 75 murals in six blocks. And no area comes more brilliantly alive for Carnival and the Day of the Dead.

Filled primarily with massive, old wooden Victorians divided into two, three or more flats, the Mission is teaming with spacious three- and four-bedroom apartments—and living with multiple roommates is definitely the norm. The ability to split the rent many ways translates into many of the city's best opportunities for cheap, relatively speaking, rent. The lowest-cost rental options are shared homes where at least one person has been on the lease for a long time, and where the apartment is rent-controlled (a general rule of thumb that applies to all neighborhoods). The great rental speculation explosion of the nineties shot the prices of empty apartments way up, but in general, prices here are still lower than much of the city. In addition to the city's first-time home buyers program, prospective home-owners may want to check out the more neighborhood-specific Mission Economic Development Association (MEDA) at 415-282-3334.

Inching west toward the Castro is **Mission Dolores**, where the vibe and the prices become increasingly more upscale. The Mission Dolores area (a rectangular neighborhood with Market Street to the north, 20th Street to the south, Church Street to the west, and Valencia Street on the east) is a quiet enclave in this often-boisterous neighborhood. It consists of classic, single-family Victorian and Edwardian houses and some contem-porary apartment buildings. Rents here are higher than in the rest of the Mission, but still lower than most of the city.

Though most of San Francisco is fairly dog friendly, the proximity of Dolores Park makes the more upscale western end of the neighborhood particularly prime for those with four-legged friends. Lined by friendly cof-fee shops, this stretch of rolling green, home to tennis courts, picnics, run-ners, and bicyclists, is the perfect place to spend Sunday in the park with George—or whomever.

On the east side of Dolores Park is Dolores Street, one of San Francisco's most attractive boulevards, which runs south from Market Street until it merges with San Jose Avenue. Unlike many of the other streets in the neighborhood, Dolores Street is a wide, divided residential boulevard with an oasis of leafy palms. Housing along Dolores Street is a mixture of traditional Mediterranean stucco houses and apartments; some of the homes are quite ornate, while others are more box-like and modern.

Transportation in the Mission is top notch, with both MUNI buses and BART easily available.

Web Site: www.ci.sf.ca.us, www.sfmission.com
Area Code: 415
Zip Code: 94110
Post Office: Mission Station, 1198 South Van Ness Ave; Potrero Center, 16th and Bryant streets, 800-275-8777, www.usps.com
Police: Mission Station, 630 Valencia St, 415-558-5400
Emergency Hospital: San Francisco General Hospital, 1001 Potrero Ave, 415-206-8000
Library: 300 Bartlett St, 415-355-2800, www.sfpl.org
Public Schools: San Francisco Unified School District, 555 Franklin St, 415-241-6000, http://portal.sfusd.edu

Community Resources: Mission Neighborhood Centers, 362 Capp St, 415-206-7747, Mission Cultural Center, 2868 Mission St, 415-821-1155 (offers classes in dance, art, and more); Women's Building, 3543 18th St, 415-431-1180, www.womensbuilding.org; Inner Mission Neighbors, 2922 Mission St, Suite 106, 94110; Precita Eyes Mural Arts and Visitor Center, 2981 24th St, 415-285-2287; New College, 777 Valencia St, 415-437-3400, www.newcollege.edu; Mission Merchants Association, P.O. Box 40280, 94110, 415-979-4171, www.mission merchants.com; Mission Economic Development Association (MEDA), 3505 20th St, 415-282-3334, www.medasf.org; Cell Space, 2050 Bryant, 415-648-7562, www.cellspace.org; 826 Valencia writing center, 826 Valencia St, 415-642-5905, www.826valencia.org; Dolores Park, Dolores and 19th streets, 415-831-2700

Public Transportation: MUNI, 415-673-6864, TTY 415-923-6373, www.sfmuni.com: *MUNI buses*: 9 San Bruno, 12 Folsom, 14 Mission, 22 Fillmore, 26 Valencia, 27 Bryant, 33 Stanyan, 48 Quintara, 49 Mission, 53 Southern Heights, 67 Bernal Heights; *BART*: 16th St Station and 24th St Station

THE CASTRO

CORONA HEIGHTS
DUBOCE TRIANGLE

Boundaries: *Castro*: **North** and **West**: Market St; **East**: Dolores St; **South**: 22nd St

The Castro

Technically known as Eureka Valley, the Castro occupies a small but vibrant area of the city that spills across Market Street into the Upper Market area. Since the 1970s, the Castro has been the center of San Francisco's dynamic and politically powerful gay community. For a number of years the Castro has hosted one of the nation's largest and most ribald Halloween celebrations. Tens of thousands of people dressed to the nines, if dressed at all, cram into the blocked-off street to stand cheek to cheek, to cheek to cheek, as a near-solid block of humanity. In recent years, the rowdy, uncontrolled vibe has been checked by better security, an army of volunteers, and more formal planning centered around large stages with live music, dancing, and cabaret-style shows. Still, every year, the highlight undoubtedly remains the dazzling array of costumed revelers informally parading up and down the street, many offering their own impromptu performances.

AIDS hit this tight-knit community hard in the 1980s, transforming the freewheeling, sexual liberation spirit of the 1970s into a new kind of activism based on promoting HIV/AIDS awareness, safe sex education, scientific research, and treatment. These days, residential life in the neighborhood is quieter and increasingly family-oriented. But at night, the heart of the neighborhood, Castro Street, with its bustling nightclubs, bars, and drag shows, still hosts a pulsing nightlife.

The Castro boasts some of the city's most beautifully maintained homes, including dozens of Victorian and Edwardian cottages, rows of two- and three-story Edwardian apartments, and a smattering of 1920s stucco flats. Streets here are often tree-lined and many of the houses have been recently renovated. Finding that perfect place in the Castro can be a challenge, as most who move into the neighborhood tend to stay for the long haul, leaving few vacancies for newcomers. Those spaces that do open tend to be in the upper middle to high end of the rental price spectrum. If you don't mind sharing, consider pooling together with two or three roommates to rent one of the neighborhood's large Victorians or, easier yet, try to find a space in an already established household. If prices seem high at first glance, don't be discouraged. A little patience and persistence can pay off.

For area shopping, Castro Street offers a variety of boutiques selling everything from jewelry, clothing, leather goods, and sexual aids to health foods, hamburgers, coffees, teas, and pastries. Castro Street also is where you'll find more mundane needs, with drug, hardware, and grocery stores scattered throughout. Locals consider Cliff's Variety Store at 479 Castro Street a neighborhood fixture, offering more than just hardware. Taking in a show is easy at the beautiful 1930s Spanish Colonial style Castro Theatre, 429 Castro Street, with its huge Wurlitzer; arrive early to hear the resident organist pipe out live tunes. It's one of the city's cultural landmarks. If you like old movies, including musicals and art flicks, this is the place to go. It is also one of the venues for many local film festivals.

Walk across Market Street, the northern boundary of the Castro, and you'll find yourself in the so-called **Corona Heights** area. Almost like a bedroom community for the Castro, Corona Heights has well-tended Victorian homes along steep and narrow streets. A good selection of contemporary apartments can be found in this area, many of which offer sweeping views of the southeastern section of the city and the Bay. Rentals are rare in this upscale section. Turnover is slower here than in some areas of the city, as people who put down roots here tend to stay—sometimes making rental pickings slim.

Twin Peaks shelters both Upper Market and the Castro, keeping much of the fog away, and many of these homes have sun decks in the back or on the roofs. Some even have small swimming pools. There's plenty of tight, tanned skin here, and few residents are shy about showing it off.

Children come from all over the city to visit the Randall Museum, on Museum Way in Corona Heights, which features an earthquake exhibit, live animals, art and science programs, films, lectures, concerts, and plays.

Also to the north, the three-way intersection of Market, Duboce, and Castro streets forms **Duboce Triangle**. This small, quaint, and increasingly popular neighborhood straddles the North of Market Area and the ever extended arm of the Western Addition—both of which claim it. Yet, like so many of San Francisco's micro neighborhoods, Duboce Triangle really belongs to neither but, with its unique and individual character truly stands on its own. Clustered around tree-lined Noe Street, this picturesque neighborhood is home to a smattering of small restaurants, cafés, and upscale shops. Bordered by Duboce Park, a small but ever-popular spot of green (especially with dog owners), Duboce Triangle boasts some of the city's most beautifully restored Victorian flats. Sandwiched between the Castro and the Lower Haight, the neighborhood is centrally located, with a large Safeway, excellent restaurants, and your choice of a popular beer joint or semi-swank martini bar, all within easy walking distance. Housing prices are on the higher end, but young professionals who can afford it are increasingly finding Duboce Triangle a good option.

Web Site: www.ci.sf.ca.us

Area Code: 415

Zip Code: 94114

Post Office: 18th St Station, 4304 18th St, 800-275-8777, www.usps.com

Police Station: Mission Station, 630 Valencia St, 415-558-5400, TTY 415-431-6241, main non-emergency number, 415-553-0123

Emergency Hospitals: San Francisco General Hospital, 1001 Potrero Ave, 415-206-8000, www.dph.sf.ca.us/chn/SFGH/default.asp; California Pacific Medical Center, Davies Campus, Castro and Duboce streets, 415-600-6000, www.cpmc.org.

Library: Noe Valley Branch, 451 Jersey St, 415-355-5707, www.sfpl.org

Public Schools: San Francisco Unified School District, 555 Franklin St, 415-241-6000, http://portal.sfusd.edu

Community Resources: Metropolitan Community Church, 150 Eureka St, 415-863-4434, www.mccsf.org; Randall Museum, 199 Museum

Way, 415-554-9600, www.randallmuseum.org; Eureka Valley
Promotion Association, P.O. Box 14137, 94114, www.evpa.org; Castro
Theatre, 429 Castro St, 415-621-6120, www.thecastrotheatre.com;
Eureka Valley Recreation Center, 19th and Collingwood sts, 415-
554-9528

Community Newspaper: *Castro Star*, 415-863-6397, www.sf
observer.com

Public Transportation: MUNI, 415-673-6864, TTY 415-923-6373,
www.sfmuni.com: *MUNI buses*: 24 Divisadero, 33 Stanyan, 35
Eureka, 48 Quintara-24th; *MUNI LRV*: F-Market, J-Church, K-Ingleside,
M-Oceanview; Shuttle: S-Castro to downtown; *BART*: 24th St Station

NOE VALLEY

Boundaries: **North**: 22nd St; **East**: Dolores St; **South**: 30th St; **West**:
Diamond Heights Blvd

Noe Valley

Surrounded by hills, Noe Valley
is geographically separate from
the rest of the city, yet still easily
accessible to downtown and the
South Bay. In a city where you
can regularly go for days or
weeks without ever seeing a
child under age five, Noe Valley
is a bit of an anomaly as a family-
friendly oasis. A mix of well-to-
do young families and singles of
all persuasions and from virtually every corner of the globe
inhabit Noe Valley. Local comic
Marga Gomez characterizes the
area as ambitious and spiritual, sort of a "yuppie Tibet." Indeed, Noe has a
progressive ambiance similar to Berkeley, but completely unlike its boister-
ous neighbor, the Castro. Residents of Noe Valley, named after Jose Noe,
San Francisco's last Mexican *alcalde* (town administrator), are proud of
their quiet neighborhood, their homes, and their colorful gardens.

Architecturally, you'll find rows of two-story Victorian homes accom-
panied by a smattering of Edwardians and Tudors. And, with many
homeowners busily renovating their houses, it seems there's always at
least one construction project happening on every block. Some even opt
to tear out an existing house and build from scratch. The array of large,

single-family homes with gardens is impressive; add to this the many strollers bobbing up and down the steep hills, and you'll quickly realize you've come to a family-focused neighborhood. Children and infants are everywhere, especially at the playgrounds. Local residents designed the popular Douglass Playground, nestled underneath Twin Peaks and shaded by looming pine trees.

From Castro to Church, 24th Street is the local shopping area, and is jam-packed with coffee shops, restaurants, Irish pubs, mom-and-pop markets, one-of-a-kind clothing stores, bookshops, and vintage clothing stores as well. A quick drive east on 24th Street, and you'll end up in the heart of the Mission, where taquerias and Mexican bakeries replace the coffee shops and boutique clothing stores of Noe. Church Street, from about 24th to 30th streets, is another commercial area dotted with neighborhood stores, such as Drewes Brothers Meats at 1706 Church Street, a local favorite that has been in the neighborhood since 1889.

While it costs a bundle to live here, it hasn't a trace of chic about it. In the mornings tie-dyed t-shirt–wearing kids who attend local public schools abound, mixing in with the uniformed kids being carpooled around the city to attend private schools. There's a small town feel to this community, and overall it's a place where you'd have little to complain about. The Noe Valley Ministry, 1021 Sanchez Street, is a Presbyterian church that also hosts community groups, classes, and concerts. Concerts vary from religious (it is a church, after all) to jazz, folk, and classical. Classes range from belly dancing to ecology. Another neighborhood center for those who are expecting or are new parents is Natural Resources, 816 Diamond Street, 415-550-2611, located one block up from 24th Street. Here, you can enroll in pregnancy, childbirth, CPR, and early parenting classes, or just peruse their library.

Noe Valley offers easy access to public transit, including buses and BART. For those making the commute to the South Bay, Interstate 280 is accessible from Dolores Street/San Jose Avenue, only a few minutes away. You can access CalTrain at the 22nd and Pennsylvania Street station.

Web Sites: www.ci.sf.ca.us, www.noevalley.com
Area Code: 415
Zip Codes: 94114, 94131
Post Office: Noe Valley Station, 4083 24th St, 800-275-8777, www.usps.com
Police Station: Mission Station, 630 Valencia St, 415-558-5400, TTY 415-431-6241, main non-emergency number, 415-553-0123
Emergency Hospitals: San Francisco General Hospital, 1001 Potrero Ave, 415-206-8000, www.dph.sf.ca.us/chn/SFGH/default.asp; California Pacific Medical Center, Davies Campus, Castro and Duboce sts, 415-600-6000, www.cpmc.org

Library: Noe Valley Branch, 451 Jersey St, 415-355-5707, www.sfpl.org

Public Schools: San Francisco Unified School District, 555 Franklin St, 415-241-6000, http://portal.sfusd.edu

Community Resources: Noe Valley Ministry, 1021 Sanchez St, 415-282-2317, www.noevalleyministry.org; Friends of Noe Valley, 415-282-9918, www.friendsofnoevalley.com; Upper Noe Neighbors, 169 Valley St, 94131, 415-285-0473; Natural Resources, 816 Diamond St, 415-550-2611, www.naturalresourcesonline.com

Community Newspapers: Noe Valley Voice, 1021 Sanchez St, 415-821-3324, www.noevalleyvoice.com

Public Transportation: MUNI, 415-673-6864, TTY 415-923-6373, www.sfmuni.com: *MUNI buses*: 24 Divisadero, 33 Stanyan, 35 Eureka, 48 Quintara 24th; *MUNI LRV*: J-Church, K-Ingleside, M-Oceanview; *BART*: 24th St Station

GLEN PARK, DIAMOND HEIGHTS

Boundaries: **North**: Clipper St; **East**: Dolores St/San Jose Ave; **South**: Bosworth St; **West**: O'Shaughnessy Blvd

Glen Park, Diamond Heights

Affordable property (by San Francisco standards) and a cozy neighborhood feel make **Glen Park** worth exploring. A rural community at the turn of the century, Glen Park replaced Cow Hollow, which suffered from a cholera outbreak, as the dairy capital of the area. Shortly thereafter, San Francisco bought Glen Canyon Park in 1922 and sold residential lots. Today, this hilly area located south of Noe Valley is made up of a quaint collection of single-family homes, Victorian flats, and apartments that run along narrow, curvy streets. In fact, for a moment you may wonder if you've detoured into a small, twisting mountain village. The main shopping area around Chenery and Diamond streets is nestled in the hillside surrounding the Glen Park BART Station. Close to the station you'll find a handful of cozy cafés and restaurants. For newcomers particularly concerned about temblors, this neighborhood survived last century's two great earthquakes relatively unscathed. Though slowly growing, Glen Park is still largely undiscovered, relatively quiet, and, in general, considerably less expensive than its trendy neighbor, Noe Valley. With a busy BART station at its center, transit to and from downtown San Francisco is quick and easy, as are daily commutes to the East Bay and peninsula along the BART corridor.

The neighborhood is named for the lovely Glen Canyon Park, San Francisco's second largest park. Because this 70-acre park is off the beaten path, few people who live in San Francisco even know this eucalyptus-rich area exists. Many locals walk their dogs in the canyon. In addition to hiking trails there are tennis courts, a children's playground, baseball field, and an 80-foot band of sandstone for beginner climbers. (Beware of poison oak!) The recreation center in the park has a basketball court and offers dance and art classes. (See listings below.) Another natural gem close at hand is Mount Davidson, the city's highest peak, which rises 938 feet above sea level. Here, springtime hikers can catch a glimpse of an incredible array of wildflowers.

The hilltop residential area of **Diamond Heights** was one of the last areas settled in San Francisco. Overlooking Glen Park to the north, it contains row upon row of sizable apartment complexes, a shopping center, and some superb views of the city and the San Francisco Bay below. Parking is not a problem and affordable rental housing can be found here, despite the general rule of thumb that the higher the elevation the higher the price. One drawback to living here is the fog and the wind, both of which will send you scurrying for cover. Across Market Street, to the north of Diamond Heights, sit the famous Twin Peaks. Climb up here on clear days to view the snow-capped Sierra Nevada mountain range 200 miles to the east. Nearby Sutro Tower is a strange looking structure, and many would call it an eyesore, but it's an accepted part of the San Francisco skyline. Used by television and radio stations to beam their signals to the masses below, at 981 feet, it is actually the tallest structure in the city.

Web Site: www.ci.sf.ca.us

Area Code: 415

Zip Code: 94131

Post Office: Diamond Heights Station, 5262 Diamond Heights Blvd, 800-275-8777, www.usps.com

Police Station: Ingleside Station, 1 Sergeant John V. Young Lane, 415-404-4000, TTY 415-404-4009; main non-emergency number, 415-553-0123

Emergency Hospitals: San Francisco General Hospital, 1001 Potrero Ave, 415-206-8000, www.dph.sf.ca.us; St. Luke's Hospital, 3555 Cesar Chavez St, 415-647-8600, www.stlukes-sf.sutterhealth.org

Library: Glen Park Branch, 653 Chenery St, 415-337-4740, www.sfpl.org

Public Schools: San Francisco Unified School District, 555 Franklin St, 415-241-6000, http://portal.sfusd.edu

Community Resources: Glen Park Association, P.O. Box 31292, 94131, 415-908-6728; Glen Park Recreation Center, 70 Elk St, 415-337-4705; Diamond Heights Community Association, P.O. Box 31529, 94131; Friends of Glen Canyon Park, 140 Turquoise Way, 94131, 415-648-0862; Glen Canyon Park, O'Shaughnessy Blvd and Bosworth St, 415-831-2700

Public Transportation: MUNI, 415-673-6864, TTY 415-923-6373, www.sfmuni.com; *MUNI buses*: 23 Monterey, 26 Valencia, 35 Eureka, 44 O'Shaughnessy, 52 Excelsior; *MUNI LRV*: J-Church line; *BART*: Glen Park Station

POTRERO HILL

DOGPATCH

Boundaries: North: 15th St; **East**: San Francisco Bay; **South**: Cesar Chavez St; **West**: Highway 101

Potrero Hill

Much like the Mission, its neighbor to the west, Potrero Hill is one of the sunniest areas of the city as the fog seldom makes its way this far south and east. Atop Potrero Hill you'll also experience some of the best views of the Bay. Because of its proximity to Highway 101 on the west and 280 on the east, the Potrero district is easily accessible for those facing a daily freeway commute and is therefore considered a choice place to live by young professionals.

If you want to live in Potrero Hill, make sure you're ready to climb. Potrero, which means "pasture" in Spanish, was nicknamed "Billy Goat Hill" around the turn of the century when goats spent their days scrambling up the hillside. These hills also gave rise to the most crooked street in San Francisco, which is located on the slope of 20th and Vermont streets. Unlike Lombard Street, Vermont Street, with its six hairpin turns and 14.3% grade, does not play host to tourists lined up in cars waiting to experience the ride, nor is it as photogenic. Nearby you'll find a small, windswept playground at McKinley Square Park. In fact, you'll find many ultra-steep hills here that offer fantastic views of the city skyline below.

Housing in Potrero Hill is varied and includes many renovated Victorians, dark-shingled Edwardians, 1920s art-deco stucco apartment buildings, and not-so-attractive apartments from the 1960s and '70s, as well as more recently constructed live/work loft spaces. To the south lie the housing projects where O.J. Simpson grew up.

Once a predominantly working class neighborhood and home to many recently arrived immigrants and artists, the neighborhood suffered the pains of rapid gentrification in the late nineties, but now has settled into a vibrant and comfortable cultural mix. Local cafés, restaurants, and grocers, primarily clustered along a few short blocks on 18th Street near Connecticut Street, are friendly neighborhood gathering spots and quiet compared to many of San Francisco's more frenetic neighborhoods. Comfortable coffeehouses, like Farley's at 1315 18th Street, dot the neighborhood, making it easy for you to grab a cup of coffee on your way out in the morning or to sit down and visit. There are also friendly corner bars, including Bloom's Saloon, 1318 18th Street, and excellent restaurants offering everything from fine French food to gourmet pizza to Thai food and tiki bar drinks. To hear rock music in an intimate setting, try the Bottom of the Hill Club on 17th Street and Missouri. Gardeners will be interested to know about the community gardens located at San Bruno and 20th Street, and Connecticut and 22nd streets. Newcomers looking to learn how to dance the tango, swing, or lindy hop should check out the Metronome Ballroom, 1830 17th Street, regularly voted by the *San Francisco Bay Guardian* readers' poll as the best place to learn to dance.

Outside of those searching for a good view or a taste of fine beer, not many venture into Potrero Hill. Consider this a bonus, particularly on those gloriously clear mornings when you can relax on your hilltop perch and pat yourself on the back for moving to the city that's spread out before you.

Heading further east to the outskirts of Potrero Hill, between Mariposa Street and Islais Creek, is a small "in between" spot, with a personality all its own, known as **Dogpatch**. A diverse neighborhood in the flats on the eastern edge of Potrero Hill, Dogpatch was recognized as a Historic District by the city of San Francisco in 2003. The area, one of the few to survive the 1906 Earthquake and fire, includes a number of old Victorians and the city's largest collection of 19th and early 20th century workers' cottages. Today, like the rest of Potrero Hill, the area also contains a number of ultra-modern live/work lofts constructed during the 1990s dot-com explosion.

Along Potrero's watery edge is a smattering of warehouses and old industrial buildings, some historically significant, some simply ghost-like shells, which speak to this area's industrial past. Known as the Central

Waterfront, this spot was once home to such heavy industry giants as Tubbs Cordage Company, the Spreckels Sugar refinery, and the gasworks company that would become PG&E. At its heart is Pier 70, a long-time shipbuilding and repair hub. During World War II, under the direction of Union Iron Works/Bethlehem Steel, a flurry of ships was constructed, and in 1967, the transit tubes—57 sections, each 325 feet long and weighing 800 tons—that carry BART beneath the Bay were built here. By the 1970s manufacturing declined, and in 1982, the land was transferred to the City of San Francisco for $1. Today, the San Francisco Drydock continues with the business of ship repair, and a number of artists, drawn by low rents, have set up workspaces in this cluster of old brick buildings. Amid vacant warehouses, you'll find Agua Vista Park, with a few picnic tables and up-close views of the giant tankers and a public fishing pier (be sure to read signs about acceptable levels of fish consumption, as the Bay has high levels of mercury). Though much of Pier 70 still sits largely abandoned, with many structures in need of rehabilitation or razing, as well as environmental clean-up issues, the expansion of the nearby UCSF Mission Bay Campus and the completion of the 3rd Street Light Rail clearly demonstrate the impending redevelopment of Potrero's waterfront. Planning sessions are afoot at the Port of San Francisco to determine the future of this massive public trust land.

Web Site: www.ci.sf.ca.us

Area Code: 415

Zip Code: 94107

Post Office: Brannan St Station, 460 Brannan St, 800-275-8777, www.usps.com

Police Station: Bayview Station, 201 Williams St, 415-671-2300, TTY 415-671-2346, main non-emergency number, 415-553-0123

Emergency Hospital: San Francisco General Hospital, 1001 Potrero Ave, 415-206-8000

Library: Potrero Branch, 1616 20th St, 415-355-2822, www.sfpl.org

Public Schools: San Francisco Unified School District, 555 Franklin St, 415-241-6000, http://portal.sfusd.edu

Community Publication: *The Potrero View Newspaper*, 953 DeHaro St, 415-824-7516

Community Resources: Potrero Hill Neighborhood House, 953 DeHaro St, 415-826-8080; Potrero Hill Family Resource Center, 415-206-2121; Potrero Hill Health Center, 1050 Wisconsin St, 415-648-3022, www.dph.sf.ca.us/chn/HlthCtrs/PotreroHill.htm

Public Transportation: MUNI, 415-673-6864, TTY 415-923-6373, www.sfmuni.com: *MUNI buses*: 10 Townsend, 15 3rd St, 19 Polk, 22 Fillmore, 48 Quintara-24th St, 53 Southern Heights; *CalTrain*: 22nd St Station

BERNAL HEIGHTS

Boundaries: North: Cesar Chavez St; **East**: Highway 101; **South**: Interstate 280/Alemany Blvd; **West**: San Jose Ave

Formerly a rough, working class neighborhood, Bernal Heights, located in the southeast section of San Francisco, is now considerably safer and generally more affordable than much of the rest of the city. Indeed, because of its off-the-beaten-path location and affordable prices, many artists, musicians, writers, and young families have made Bernal Heights their home. Considered an alternative to the predominantly gay male culture of the Castro, Bernal Heights has

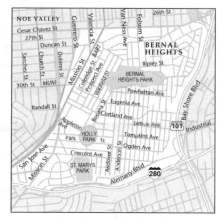

Bernal Heights

also become a welcoming home to a growing lesbian community. And the view from atop the brown bald hill (brown in the summer and green in the winter) offers a spectacular panorama of the city below.

Named for Don Jose Cornelio de Bernal, to whom the land was granted in 1839 by the Mexican government as part of larger parcel, Bernal Heights was originally a grazing area for cows, goats, and other livestock. By the 1860s, small plots had been sold to Irish and Italian immigrants, and farming continued, giving the area the nickname "nanny goat hill." As it was essentially unscathed after the 1906 Earthquake, Bernal Heights is where many displaced Italians from North Beach came to start anew.

Today, Bernal Heights is an intimate, progressive, and child-friendly community where neighbors know each other and come together to fight for area causes, including safer streets and improved playgrounds. Each August, residents host a hill-wide garage sale. Visit the playground behind the public library on 500 Cortland Avenue and you'll quickly realize you've arrived in a melting pot. Residents hail from Japan, China, Italy, and Mexico, among other countries. Take a tour of this neat and tidy neighborhood and it is apparent that quite a few residents spend their free time tending their yards or planting at one of the community gardens. Many of the streets are lined with small, Victorian cottages and some contemporary (1960s and '70s) box-like homes. Today, some of the smaller homes are being torn down and replaced by larger structures. Though the streets are narrow, parking is usually not a challenge.

Cortland Avenue offers a number of shopping options, from a classic barbershop, coffee shops, and a bookstore to produce stands and pet shops. Chain stores are almost nonexistent here and the neighborhood prides itself on supporting local, independent businesses. The recently remodeled and expanded health food store, the Good Life Grocery at 448 Cortland Avenue, is always bustling, as is Bernal Books, 401 Cortland Avenue. The Liberty Café, 410 Cortland, is a local favorite for home-style cooking featuring a rotating array of fresh seasonal items. Attached, you'll find the Liberty Wine Cottage and Bakery; the smell of fresh, tasty baked goods and the cozy outdoor patio attract morning crowds, while wine buffs flock to evening tastings.

For bigger shopping needs, head to the Saturday morning Alemany Farmers' Market at 100 Alemany Boulevard (near the 101-280 interchange). Many consider this, the oldest farmers' market in the city, to be the most affordable. Selections and other goods come from all over the state. Bargain hunters should return on Sunday mornings when the site hosts a flea market.

Bus service in Bernal Heights is not as frequent or swift as in the neighboring Mission District. However, the neighborhood is connected to the downtown area via MUNI, and offers fast access to both I-101 and 280 for commuters.

To learn more about the neighborhood, stop by the Bernal Heights Neighborhood Center at 515 Cortland Avenue.

Web Sites: www.ci.sf.ca.us, www.bernalheightsonline.com

Area Code: 415

Zip Code: 94110

Post Office: Bernal Heights Finance Station, 189 Tiffany Ave, 800-275-8777, www.usps.com

Police Station: Ingleside Station, 1 Sergeant John V. Young Lane, 415-404-4000, TTY 415-404-4009; main non-emergency number, 415-553-0123

Emergency Hospitals: St. Luke's Hospital, 3555 Cesar Chavez St, 415-647-8600, www.stlukes-sf.sutterhealth.org; San Francisco General Hospital, 1001 Potrero Ave, 415-206-8000

Library: Bernal Heights Branch, 500 Cortland Ave, 415-355-2810, www.sfpl.org

Public Schools: San Francisco Unified School District, 555 Franklin St, 415-241-6000, http://portal.sfusd.edu

Community Resources: Bernal Heights Neighborhood Center, 515 Cortland Ave, 415-206-2140, www.bhnc.org; Alemany Farmers'

Market, 100 Alemany Blvd, 415-647-9423; The Writing Salon, for creative writing instruction, 415-642-9793, www.writingsalons.com
Public Transportation: MUNI, 415-673-6864, TTY 415-923-6373, www.sfmuni.com: *MUNI buses*: 9 San Bruno, 12 Folsom, 14 Mission, 23 Monterey, 24 Divisadero, 27 Bryant, 49 Van Ness-Mission, 67 Bernal Heights

EXCELSIOR, MISSION TERRACE/OUTER MISSION, CROCKER AMAZON, INGLESIDE, VISITACION VALLEY, PORTOLA

Boundaries: *Excelsior*: **North**: Alemany Blvd; **East**: McLaren Park; **South**: Geneva Ave; **West**: Mission St; *Mission Terrace/Outer Mission*: **North and West**: Interstate 280; **East**: Mission St; **South**: San Mateo County Line; *Crocker Amazon*: **North and West**, Mission St; **North** and **East**: Geneva Ave; **South**: San Mateo County Line; *Ingleside*: **North**: Monterey Blvd; **East**: Interstate 280; **South**: San Mateo County Line; **West**: 19th Ave; *Visitacion Valley*: **North**: Mansell St; **East**: Bayshore Blvd; **South**: San Mateo County Line; **West**: McLaren Park; *Portola*: **North**: Interstate 280; **East**: Highway 101; **South**: Mansell St; **West**: Cambridge to Silver to Madison

Located in the foggy, windswept southern section of San Francisco, near the San Mateo County border, these neighborhoods are all primarily residential and are considered inexpensive, at least by San Francisco standards. Because of the neighborhoods' relative affordability, this is one of

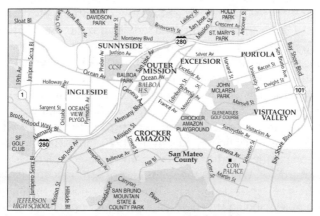

Excelsior, Mission Terrace/Outer Mission,
Crocker Amazon, Ingleside, Visitacion Valley, Portola

the rare areas in San Francisco where the dream of home ownership still remains within reach for those other than the wealthy. A true melting pot, the area is home to a variety of ethnic groups especially Asian, Latino, and African-American, as well as a host of student residents, many of whom attend San Francisco City College (north of Ingleside in Sunnyside).

Visiting the **Excelsior** and **Outer Mission** neighborhoods, you'll find row upon row of single-family stucco homes, flats, apartment complexes, duplexes, and townhouses, varying from immaculate to those in need of serious renovation. Look for housing here and you may find a hidden treasure in the form of an affordable, mother-in-law rental unit tucked away in a sun-baked backyard garden. Residents here have an easy commute into downtown San Francisco to the north or into the shopping mall–rich suburbia of San Mateo County to the south. Buses run frequently along Mission Street, and the two nearby BART Stations are Glen Park and Balboa Park. Geneva Avenue and Mission Street are home to inexpensive yet tasty Asian and Latin restaurants. In recent years, the Outer Mission has seen a handful of fancier, pricier eateries spring up, along with popular nightclubs and bars, which are transforming the strip of Mission Street (from Cesar Chavez south to 30th Street) into a nighttime destination spot, especially on weekends. In the summer, folks head in droves to Mitchell's Ice Cream, 688 San Jose Avenue, to sample its famous frozen confections. Family run for more than 50 years, Mitchell's has been voted "best ice cream" six years in a row by the *San Francisco Bay Guardian* readers' poll.

The triangular-shaped **Crocker Amazon** lies directly south of Excelsior. These homes and the ones in Daly City supposedly served as the inspiration for the Malvina Reynolds song (made famous by folk singer Pete Seeger) that refers to "the little boxes, on a hilltop and they're all made out of ticky tacky." The Crocker Amazon Playground, the biggest playground in the city, is a popular family weekend outing. It's also home to San Francisco's first and so far only skateboard park. In Crocker Amazon, neighborhood lines blur with Daly City's own Crocker neighborhood boundaries. The only way to tell which town you're officially in is by the street signs—San Francisco's are white and Daly City's are blue.

Situated west of Outer Mission, the **Ingleside** district is a hodgepodge of single-family homes built in the 1920s and '30s. Ingleside was home to one of the city's first racetracks, and today's Urbano Drive traces the old racecourse. While not the safest area of San Francisco, Ingleside is far from being the most dangerous. There are a number of charming pockets along quiet winding streets where families take pride in their homes, lawns are green, traffic is sparse, and neighbors are...neighborly.

Visitacion Valley, named in 1777 by Franciscan priests, is perhaps a bit more lively than Crocker Amazon, but it's by no means exciting. What may be exciting to home seekers is that some of the least expensive homes in the city are here, both for purchase and rent. Housing includes single stuccos, wood-framed apartments, Victorian flats, townhouses, and duplexes. In an effort to improve the neighborhood, one of the city's largest and most troubled public housing projects, Geneva Towers, was demolished in 1998. The other, the 700-plus Sunnydale complex, remains and continues to struggle with difficulties arising from gang activity. Such problems still plague the neighborhood, despite residents' efforts to make the streets safer.

McLaren Park, which comes with its own golf course, makes up Visitacion Valley's western border with **Excelsior**. The world-famous Cow Palace sits a bit to the south of McLaren Park, along Geneva Avenue. The Beatles played at the Cow Palace, as have hundreds of other big-name acts over the years. The arena also hosts sports and boat shows, dog and cat exhibitions, consumer electronics auctions, car auctions, motorcycle races, tractor-pulls, and, true to its cowboy roots, a popular annual rodeo.

Jutting out into the Bay, just across Highway 101, sits the large open-air stadium Monster Park (previously 3COM Park but called Candlestick Park by most), the current home of the National Football League's 49ers. The park is a cold and windy place, except for a few days in the summer, which was one of the reasons the Giants built their own facility in the city's South Park/China Basin/Mission Bay area. The 49ers are working on building a new stadium as well, but they want to stay at Candlestick Point.

Just north of Visitacion Valley, south of Bernal Heights, is **Portola**, an area similar to Bernal Heights when it comes to housing options, climate, and residential makeup. It also has a rich Italian and Jewish heritage, much of which survives to this day, especially in the thriving commercial zone along San Bruno Avenue, the district's southern border with Visitacion Valley. Local shopping options are practical, including an Italian butcher shop, mom-and-pop grocers, and flower shops. With McLaren Park nearby, there's plenty of open space for recreational activities.

Web Site: www.ci.sf.ca.us

Area Code: 415

Zip Codes: Excelsior, Outer Mission, Crocker Amazon, Ingleside, 94112; Portola, Visitacion Valley, 94134

Post Offices: Excelsior Station, 15 Onondaga Ave; Vista Grande Station, 6025 Mission St; Visitacion Valley, 68 Leland Ave; McLaren Station, 2755 San Bruno Ave, 800-275-8777, www.usps.com

Police Stations: Ingleside Station, 1 Sergeant John V. Young Lane, 415-404-4000, TTY 415-404-4009; 201 Williams St, 415-671-2300, TTY 415-671-2346; main non-emergency number, 415-553-0123

Emergency Hospital: San Francisco General Hospital, 1001 Potrero Ave, 415-206-8000

Libraries: Excelsior Branch, 4400 Mission St, 415-337-4735; Visitacion
  Valley, 45 Leland Ave, 415-355-2848; Portola, 2450 San Bruno Ave,
  415-355-5660; Ingleside Branch, 1649 Ocean Ave, 415-355-2898
Public Schools: San Francisco Unified School District, 555 Franklin St,
  415-241-6000, http://portal.sfusd.edu/template/index.cfm
Community Publication: *Visitacion Valley Grapevine*, 415-467-9300
Community Resources: Excelsior District Improvement Association,
  P.O. Box 12005, 94112-0005 www.excelsiordistrict.org; Visitacion
  Valley Children's Center, 325 Leland Ave, 415-585-9320; Visitacion
  Valley Child and Family Development Center, 103 Tucker Ave, 415-
  467-5565; Visitacion Valley Community Center, 50 Raymond Ave,
  415-467-6400; McLaren Park, Geneva and La Grande aves, Gleneagles
  International Golf Course, 2100 Sunnydale Ave, 415-587-2425
Public Transportation: MUNI, 415-673-6864, TTY 415-923-6373,
  www.sfmuni.com: *Excelsior, MUNI buses*: 14 Mission, 29 Sunset, 43
  Masonic, 49 Van Ness-Mission, 52 Excelsior, 54 Felton, *MUNI LRV*:
  J-Church, K-Ingleside, M-Ocean View; *Crocker Amazon, MUNI buses*:
  14 Mission, 43 Masonic, 49 Van Ness-Mission, 88 BART shuttle; *Visitacion
  Valley, MUNI buses*: 9 San Bruno, 15 3rd St, 29 Sunset, 56 Rutland

BAYVIEW/HUNTERS POINT

Boundaries: **North**: Highway 280; **East** and **South**: the Bay; **West**:
Bayshore Blvd

Bayview, Hunters Point

Offering some of the city's
warmest weather, easy access to
the Peninsula and South Bay,
and majestic hilltop views of the
Bay, the long neglected, troubled Bayview/Hunters Point
stands today at the crossroads
of change.

Walking though the neigh-
borhood, located on the sunny
southeastern tip of San Francisco,
you'll find evidence of this everywhere. Bright, boxy, pink, green,
and yellow two-story stuccos
line the rolling hillsides, while a
handful of exquisite Victorians hide away amid public housing projects in
various states of upkeep.

Plagued for years by economic depression, some of the city's highest violent crime rates, as well as health and environmental concerns resulting from its proximity to a large power plant, sewage treatment facility, and a former US navy shipyard, all eyes have turned to Bayview/Hunters Point as massive redevelopment here gets underway.

MUNI's 3rd Street light rail extension, scheduled to open in 2006, will connect the once isolated neighborhood quickly and easily with downtown.

Plans are in the works to close the polluting power plant, and the long-awaited redevelopment of the Hunters Point Naval Shipyard is finally underway.

Bulldozers roll up and down 3rd Street, the main thoroughfare, which is home to host to a handful of shops, corner stores, and restaurants. Local merchants have long struggled to make ends meet here, and the only major grocery store in the area, Safeway, closed in the mid-1990s citing lack of business and high crime rates. But, with the ongoing MUNI Metro extension and the rehab of the shipyard, more business owners are considering setting up shop in the area.

Recently a new Saturday morning farmers market opened at Galvez Avenue and Third Street, a blessing for residents who often complained about the lack of fresh produce and other healthy food options nearby. The historic Bayview Opera House, 4705 3rd Street, which offers music, theater and dance programs, and community classes, received a large refurbishment grant aimed to restore the theater to its original grandeur and greatly expand its art and culture offerings.

For more than a decade, the biggest issue in Hunters Point, located in the area's southeast corner, has been the future of the 500-acre former US Naval shipyard, now a Superfund site. In 1867, Hunters Point was the first permanent dry dock on the Pacific Coast, and in 1939 the US Navy purchased the land for use as a dry dock and shipbuilding operation. During World War II, Hunters Point base, a ship repair yard, provided a large number of high-paying blue-collar jobs, and the Hunters Point/Bayview community boasted the highest percentage of home ownership in the city. But things began to slow down in the 1960s and '70s, and in 1974 the shipyards were closed. Since then the neighborhood has been plagued by high unemployment and high crime rates. Though the facility closed over three decades ago, the city and the Navy have been at odds over the environmental cleanup and transfer of land to the city. To date, the Navy has spent over $100 million to help rid the area of toxins, but residents and city officials remain concerned about higher rates of cancer and asthma among children. In 2004, a major hurdle was cleared when both sides agreed to a plan to turn the land over to city for redevelopment.

And now the first phase, a $600 million project that will include 1,600 new apartments and townhouses, with close to a third set aside for affordable housing; 300,000 square feet of commercial space; and more than 30 acres of open space is underway. Residents and city officials are hoping new jobs created by the massive redevelopment of the shipyard will go to local residents, driving economic revitalization and social improvements in the Hunters Point and Bayview communities. Still, cleanup of the most polluted areas of the site needs to be completed, and it will likely be several decades before the face of the old shipyard is fully transformed.

With lots of undeveloped space, Hunters Point has a surprising amount of wildlife. The stunning Candlestick Point Recreation Area—home to blue herons, possums, barn owls, seals, jackrabbits, foxes, raccoons, falcons and red-tailed hawks—is popular with joggers, windsurfers and fishermen. Though still considered rough in many spots, this neighborhood has attracted waves of artists over the years, and continues to do so today.

Near the San Mateo County line you'll also find the home of the 49ers, Monster Park (otherwise known as Candlestick Park), jutting out over the Bay. There has been talk for years about rebuilding the windy outdoor stadium or finding a new spot for it altogether, but no concrete plans are underway.

Locals fear displacement as Bayview—the city's largest African-American neighborhood, home to more than 4,000 families with children, and a large population of seniors—goes through growing pangs. While residents are eager to improve their neighborhood, they fear being priced out of their homes by gentrification. And in fact, property prices have increased dramatically over the last few years and are expected to continue to climb.

Web Site: www.ci.sf.ca.us

Area Code: 415

Zip Code: 94124, 94134, 94107

Emergency Hospital: San Francisco General Hospital, 1001 Potrero Ave, 415-206-8000

Post Office: Bayview Station, 2111 Lane St; Hunters Point: San Francisco Manual Processing Facility; 180 Napoleon St, 800-275-8777, www.usps.com, www.usps.com

Police: Bayview Station, 201 Williams, 415-671-2300, TTY 415-671-2346

Library: Bayview Branch, 5075 3rd St, 415-355-5757, www.sfpl.org

Public Schools: San Francisco Unified School District, 555 Franklin St, 415-241-6000, http://portal.sfusd.edu

Community Publications: *San Francisco Bay View*, 4917 3rd St, 415-671-0789, www.sfbayview.com

Community Resources: Bayview Opera House, 4705 3rd St, 415-824-0386, www.bayviewoperahouse.org (theater, dance, African-American center, aftercare and arts programs); Burnett Child Development Center, 1520 Oakdale Ave, 415-695-5660; Shipyard

Trust for the Arts, Hunters Point Shipyard, Bldg 101-1317, 415-822-0922; The Point, Hunters Point Shipyard, Building 101, 415-822-9675, www.thepointart.com; Hunters Point Naval Shipyard Redevelopment, www.hunterspointshipyard.com; Southeast Community Facility, 1800 Oakdale Ave, 415-821-1534; Joseph Lee Recreation Center, 1395 Mendell St, 415-822-9040; Candlestick Point State Recreation Area, Hunters Point Expressway, 415-671-0145

Public Transportation: MUNI, 415-673-6864, TTY 415-923-6373, www.sfmuni.com: *MUNI buses*: 9 San Bruno, 15 3rd, 19 Polk, 23 Monterey, 24 Divisadero, 29 Sunset, 44 O'Shaughnessey, 54 Felton

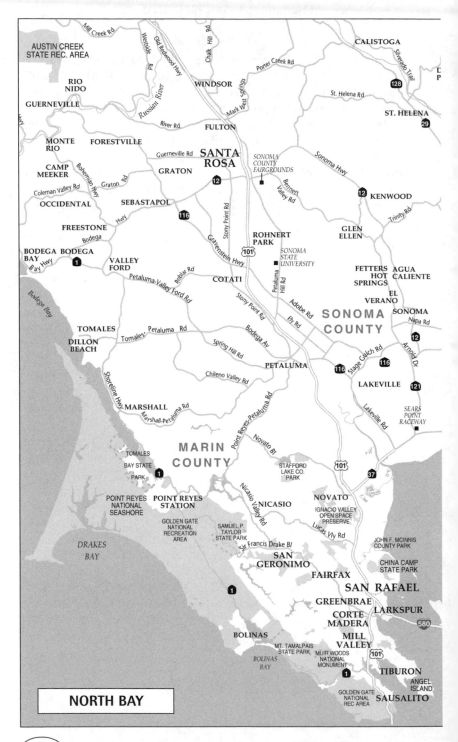

NORTH BAY

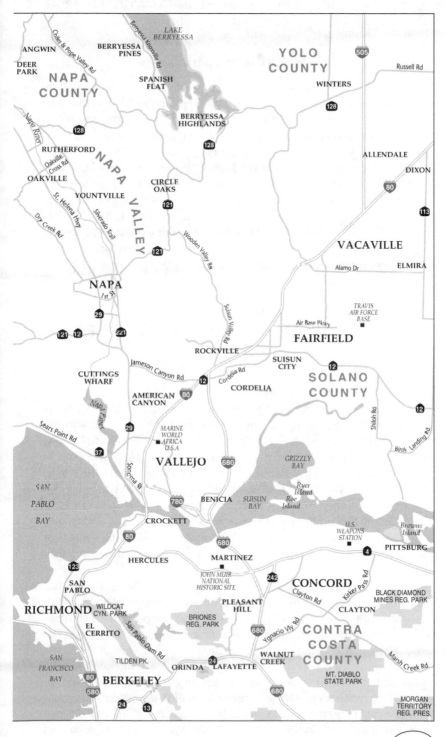

SURROUNDING AREAS

Many coming to the Bay Area choose to live outside of San Francisco proper. The reasons are varied—perhaps the city is too expensive, too congested, too foggy, some want to live in the country or suburbs, and many are looking to set up house near their office, which very often is outside of San Francisco. More than seven million people live in the nine Bay Area counties of Alameda, Contra Costa, Marin, Sonoma, San Mateo, Napa, Solano, Santa Clara, and San Francisco, and the numbers continue to increase. What follows is an overview of these counties, divided into four regions, the **North Bay, East Bay, Peninsula,** and **South Bay**. The following profiles are by no means comprehensive, but intended as a launch to your exploration of the greater Bay Area. Unless otherwise noted, housing statistics were supplied by the California Association of Realtors (CAR). See www.car.org for the latest information on Bay Area homes.

NORTH BAY
(MARIN, SONOMA, NAPA, SOLANO COUNTIES)

MARIN COUNTY

Just north of San Francisco, across the Golden Gate Bridge, the weather is warmer and life more relaxed. Encased by the Bay on the east and the Pacific Ocean on the west, Marin County's terrain is hilly and full of oak trees, eucalyptus groves, redwoods, and other evergreens. The Coastal Miwok Indians inhabited Marin first, followed by the Spaniards, the seafarers, and eventually San Franciscans, who settled in droves after the Golden Gate Bridge opened in 1937; with easy access to San Francisco, Marin County was no longer a hidden, hard-to-reach enclave. Today with a total population just over 250,000, 84% of Marin County still consists of natural preserves, public lands, parks, open space, watershed, and agricultural lands.

Home to CEOs, CFOs, old money, and new money, Marin County has the highest average per capita income in the state, though a few less affluent artists, writers, and musicians remain. The wooded northern community once elicited hedonistic images of hot tubs and peacock feathers. The 1980 movie made from the book, *The Serial: A Year in the Life of Marin County*, parodied this milieu, and although the book was intended to poke fun at the hot-tubbing, affair-having, therapizing, divorcing stereotypes of the locals, some believe it did not stray far from the truth. These days you'll find life in Marin pretty mainstream, although vestiges of the past still can be found, particularly in the sixties-era Volkswagen mini-buses decorated with peace signs and batiked curtains, and the occasional hitchhiker waving her thumb along the roadside.

Most of the western part of Marin is dramatic, with wooded mountains and hills bordering the Pacific Ocean. California's stunning North Coast offers a visual feast, from Sausalito all the way up to the Oregon border. In the summer, sun worshippers flock to Muir Beach and Stinson Beach on the frequently glorious weekends, clogging Highway 1 and turning it into the proverbial "parking lot," one of the Bay Area's most frustrating traffic problems. Residents of Marin have one of the grandest views of the entire Bay Area, made especially photogenic when the fog hovers on the Bay or around the bridge. From Mount Tamalpais' wooded vantage point, you can often see for over 100 miles in any direction.

The southwestern end of Marin County encompasses the 1,000-acre Golden Gate National Recreation Area, which includes the Marin Headlands, Muir Woods, and the remains of wartime batteries and bunkers of Fort Cronkite. During World War II, 12-foot guns sat aimed toward the sea in the expectation of enemies invading the USA from the Pacific, invaders who, thankfully, never materialized. If you enjoy hiking or camping, you may want to make the 90-minute drive from San Francisco to the 66,000-acre Point Reyes National Seashore, north of Stinson Beach. The seashore curls gracefully around Drake's Bay, so named for the explorer Sir Francis Drake, who is credited with "discovering" San Francisco Bay in 1579.

Marin County consistently ranks among the least affordable places to live in the nation. According to the California Association of Realtors, the median price for a home in April 2005 was $801,000, up 21% from the previous year. Sausalito, Mill Valley, Tiburon, and Belvedere are the most expensive cities in the county. The towns located farther north of San Francisco, such as San Rafael, Corte Madera, and Novato, are more affordable, and the most affordable towns here are the West Marin towns of San Geronimo Valley, Inverness, Tomales, and Marshall.

MARIN COUNTY
Web Sites: www.co.marin.ca.us, www.marin.org
Zip Codes: 94965, 94941, 94920, 94901, 94925, 94945, 94930
Area Code: 415
Sheriff: Marin County Sheriff Department, 3501 Civic Center Dr, #167, San Rafael, 415-499-7250
Emergency Hospital: Marin General Hospital, 250 Bon Air Road, Greenbrae, 415-925-7000
Library: Main Branch, 3501 Civic Center Dr, San Rafael, 415-499-6056, www.co.marin.ca.us/depts/lb/main/
Public Schools: Marin County Office of Education, 415-472-4110, http://marin.k12.ca.us

Community Publications: *Marin Independent Journal*, 150 Alameda del Prado, Novato, 415-883-8600, www.marinij.com; *The Ark Newspaper*, 1550 Tiburon Blvd, Tiburon, 415-435-2652; *The Coastal Post*, P.O. Box 31, Bolinas, 415-868-1600, www.coastalpost.com; Marin Scope Community Newspapers (*Mill Valley Herald, Ross Valley Reporter, Twin Cities Times, San Rafael News Pointer,* and *Marin Scope*), P.O. Box 1689, Sausalito, 94966, 415-339-8510, www.marinscope.com; *Novato Advance*, P.O. Box 8, Novato, 415-898-7084; *Pacific Sun*, P.O. Box 5553, Mill Valley, 415-383-4500; *Point Reyes Light*, P.O. Box 210, Point Reyes Station, 415-663-8404, www.ptreyeslight.com

County/Community Resources: Marin Services for Women, 415-924-5995; Bay Area Discovery Museum, Fort Baker, 557 McReynolds Rd, Sausalito, 415-339-3900; Marin Civic Center, Ave of the Flags, San Rafael, 415-499-7331; City of San Rafael Community Center, 618 B St, San Rafael, 415-485-3333; Golden Gate National Recreation Area, Fort Mason, Building 201, 415-561-4700, www.nps.gov/goga; Point Reyes National Seashore, Point Reyes, 415-464-5100, www.nps.gov/pore; Muir Woods National Monument, 415-388-2595, www.visitmuirwoods.com; Mount Tamalpais State Park, 801 Panoramic Highway, Mill Valley, 415-388-2070; Marin County Parks, 3501 Civic Center Drive Room #415, San Rafael, 415-499-6387, www.co.marin.ca.us; Corte Madera Creek Watershed, 415-457-6045, www.friendsofcortemaderacreek.org

Public Transportation: *Golden Gate Transit*, 415-455-2000; *Blue & Gold Fleet*, 415-705-5555 (advance tickets), 415-773-1188 (recorded schedule); *Angel Island Ferry*, 415-435-2131; *RIDES for Bay Area Commuters*, 511

SAUSALITO, MILL VALLEY, TIBURON

Just across the Golden Gate Bridge, where the weather is always warmer, you'll find the upscale and highly desirable communities of Sausalito, Mill Valley, and Tiburon. **Sausalito** (population 7,374), which means "little willow" in Spanish, hosts splendid mansions with views of San Francisco and the Bay. Down on the water, the Sausalito Harbor shelters thousands of boats and houseboats, including the Taj Mahal, a replica of the Indian monument, only this one is smaller and floats. Tourists flock to Sausalito via the ferry from San Francisco and on weekends they virtually take over Bridgeway, the main street. To avoid the crowds and the overabundance of t-shirt shops and art galleries on Bridgeway, locals prefer to gather on Caledonia Street, one block east from the Bay. Away from the clicking cameras, residents of Sausalito have an active community, from the Sausalito Women's Club, which works to improve the city, to the yachties putzing on their boats, to resident artists inspired by their surroundings. The Sausalito Arts Festival, held every Labor Day, brings people from all over the Bay Area in search of good art and live music. Residents celebrate the arts year round with the Sausalito Art Walk held the second Wednesday evening of every month on Caledonia Street.

Once a bohemian, hippie-type enclave, Sausalito is now joining the rank and file of the rest of the Bay Area with a wealthy population, soaring housing costs, and a number of high-tech businesses. The hills above downtown Sausalito are peppered with a broad range of abodes, from artist cabin/studios, craftsman homes, ranch-style houses, condos, and apartments to Victorians and contemporary mansions. Many of the homes have exquisite bay views and gardens, and garage space is at a premium, especially on the hillside. Median home prices are high, $651,000 as of April 2005 according to the CAR, but actually considerably lower than the previous year. Rental vacancies are rare and generally costly.

Those commuting to San Francisco generally rely on the Sausalito Ferry or Golden Gate Transit.

Formerly a lumber town, **Mill Valley** (population 13,686) has more rentals and available property than Sausalito, and it is not as touristy. Located northwest of Sausalito at the foot of Mount Tamalpais, Mill Valley has a popular downtown with charming restaurants, a coffee shop, and other stores. The famous Depot Bookstore & Café is here, located smack center in the town square where people play chess, hackysack, or chat with their neighbors. The square gives the city a real community feel, somewhat reminiscent of town squares in Mexico. The Mill Valley Market is another landmark, featuring a gourmet deli that's ideal for hungry bikers or hikers. Just off of Highway 101 is the recently renovated Strawberry Village Shopping Center, where you'll find a large Safeway, cafés, restaurants, bookstores, and boutiques. With Mount Tamalpais as a backdrop, many Mill Valley residents spend their free time hiking, biking, or just walking trails. Since 1905, runners have gathered to race the seven-mile rigorous Dipsea Race (www.dipsea.org), which starts in Mill Valley and ends at Stinson Beach. The Mill Valley Film Festival (www.mvff.com), held each fall, is gaining worldwide respect.

Many of the homes here were constructed during Mill Valley's lumber days and are Craftsman types, built with exquisite redwood. You'll also find many traditional homes, some Victorians, and a number of apartments, townhouses, and condominiums. Average selling prices for a home in Mill Valley hover close to the million-dollar mark.

Located 18 miles north of San Francisco, nearby **Tiburon** (population 8,772), which means "shark" in Spanish, is even more upscale than Mill

Valley and Sausalito, with homes typically priced well above Mill Valley's average. Many houses are either on the water or up in the hills. The Belvedere Peninsula sports some of the most upscale homes in Marin County. Many of these stately mansions were built more than a hundred years ago, and some have their own docks.

In downtown Tiburon you can catch the ferry to San Francisco, or better yet, to Angel Island—a delightful 750-acre state park in San Francisco Bay that is part wilderness and part former army base. In the early 1900s, many Asian immigrants came to the island first for government processing; later in the century nuclear Titan missiles were based here. Parts of the immigration station remain; you can still find graffiti, names, and even a poem etched into the walls of the buildings where the immigrants were held.

Restaurants on Tiburon's Main Street, notably Sam's Anchor Café, 27 Main Street, are popular, though pricey. The Sweden House Bakery, 35 Main Street, bakes some of the best éclairs and cookies, not to mention delicious Swedish pancakes. Views of Angel Island from the shops and restaurants on Main Street, many of which have large outdoor back patios that open out onto the Bay, are lovely. The Tiburon Playhouse movie theater, 40 Main Street, 415-435-3585, has a soundproof private viewing booth, ideal for those with infants. And a few years ago, Tiburon began hosting its own film festival, which while still in its infancy, is increasingly attracting crowds from San Francisco (go to www.tiburonfilmfestival.com for more information). Boat owners can take their pick from one of three yacht clubs: San Francisco Yacht Club (in nearby Belvedere), and Corinthian and Tiburon Yacht Clubs. Bikers enjoy the scenic ride on Paradise Loop or the path by Blackie's Pasture along Tiburon Boulevard.

SAUSALITO
Web Site: www.ci.sausalito.ca.us
Area Code: 415
Zip Codes: 94965, 94966
Post Office: 150 Harbor Dr, 800-275-8777, www.usps.com
Police Station: 29 Caledonia, 415-289-4170
Library: 420 Litho St, 415-289-4100, www.ci.sausalito.ca.us/library
Public Schools: Sausalito Marin City School District, 630 Nevada St, Sausalito, 415-332-3190, www.sausalitomarincityschooldistrict.org
Parks, Gardens, and Open Space: Parks and Recreation Department, 420 Litho St, 415-289-4152, www.ci.sausalito.ca.us

MILL VALLEY
Web Sites: www.cityofmillvalley.org, www.gomillvalley.com
Area Code: 415
Zip Codes: 94941, 94942

Post Office: 751 East Blithedale Ave, 800-275-8777, www.usps.com

Police Station: One Hamilton Dr, 415-389-4100

Library: Mill Valley Public Library, 375 Throckmorton Ave, 415-389-4292, www.millvalleylibrary.org

Public Schools: Mill Valley School District, 411 Sycamore Ave, Mill Valley, 415-389-7700, www.mvschools.org

Parks, Gardens, and Open Space: Mill Valley Parks and Recreation Commission, 26 Corte Madera Ave, 415-383-1370, www.cityof millvalley.org

TIBURON

Web Site: www.tiburon.org

Area Code: 415

Zip Code: 94920

Post Office: 6 Beach Road, Tiburon, 800-275-8777, www.usps.com

Police Station: 1155 Tiburon Blvd, 415-789-2801

Library: 1501 Tiburon Blvd, Tiburon, 415-789-2665, www.bel-tib-lib.org

Public Schools: Reed Union School District, 277A Karen Way, Tiburon, 415-381-1112, http://rusd.marin.k12.ca.us

Parks, Gardens, and Open Space: Belvedere/Tiburon Recreation Department, 1505 Tiburon Blvd, Suite A, 415-435-4355, www.tiburon.org

SAN RAFAEL

Situated north of Tiburon, **San Rafael** is the largest city in Marin County and the oldest. Founded in 1817 as a mission, San Rafael (population 57,224) is home to both blue- and white-collar populations. Compared to Sausalito and Mill Valley, rental housing here is plentiful and more affordable. According to the CAR, the median April 2005 price for a home in San Rafael was $782,000, up more than 29% from the previous year. Architecturally, homes range from apartments to ranch style homes, cottages, and Mediterranean-style villas.

Nestled beneath wooded mountains, San Rafael's claim to fame is the Marin County Civic Center, a national historic landmark, designed in the early 1960s by Frank Lloyd Wright. With its salmon-colored arches and a blue-domed roof, the building's colors are intended to merge with the colors of nature. It was featured in George Lucas' first feature film, *THX-1138* (look for the golden escalator). Fourth Street, San Rafael's main drag, also found its way onto the cinematic map, as the place to cruise in your big Buick or Chevrolet in Lucas's *American Graffiti*. Throckmorton is another shopping street, home to chic clothing stores and quaint one-of-a-kind boutiques. In addition to the unique Civic Center, the Falkirk Cultural Center, 1408 Mission Ave, 415-485-3328, www.falkirkcurlturalcenter.org, is a historic Queen Anne Victorian built in 1888. The Falkirk hosts contemporary art exhibits, art classes, and poetry readings. You'll also find the gorgeously restored Art Deco Christopher B. Smith Rafael Film Center here. Known to most simply as the "Rafael," the movie theater screens a selection of independent and art house films and annually plays host to the Mill Valley Film Festival (www.mvff.com).

The San Rafael to San Francisco commute via Highway 101 can be frustrating. Many locals prefer to take the ferry or Golden Gate Transit. The ferry service is fast and scenic—board at the Larkspur Ferry Terminal. On the way out of Larkspur, the ferry passes San Quentin State Prison, still in operation, as well as Alcatraz Island, which has been closed since the mid-1960s. Drinks and snacks are served on the ride.

SAN RAFAEL
Web Site: www.cityofsanrafael.org
Area Code: 415
Zip Codes: 94901, 94902, 94903
Post Office: 40 Bellam Blvd, San Rafael, 800-275-8777, www.usps.com
Police Station: 1400 5th Ave, 415-485-3000
Library: 1100 East St, San Rafael, 415-485-3323, www.srpubliclibrary.org
Public Schools: San Rafael City Schools, San Rafael City Schools, 310 Nova Albion Way, San Rafael, 415-492-3200, www.srcs.org/~district/
Parks, Gardens, and Open Space: San Rafael Parks and Recreation Commission, 618 B St, 415-485-3333, www.cityofsanrafael.org/parkandrecreation

CORTE MADERA, NOVATO, HAMILTON, FAIRFAX

Tucked between Mount Tamalpais to the west and Highway 101 to the east, the town of **Corte Madera** (population 9,378), which means "cut wood" in Spanish, is small and quaint. With slightly more affordable home prices—by Marin County standards—the town boasts a large park, historical village square and two shopping centers. Corte Madera is also home to popular independent bookstore Book Passage, 51 Tamal Vista Boulevard, whose literary events draw crowds from throughout the county. The best way to commute to the city is via the Larkspur Ferry.

A little farther north, homes in **Novato** (population 50,586) are also considered affordable for this area, averaging $700,000. Novato quickly outgrew its dairy and fruit orchard days when developers built condominiums and inexpensive tract homes, but you will also find large estates hidden in the hills. Novato has the ingredients of classic suburbia, with sprawling malls, theaters, fast food eateries, and family restaurants, as well as the $100 million Buck Center for Research in Aging. Perhaps the biggest challenge about taking up residence in sunny Novato is the commute to San Francisco. It's even longer and more arduous than the San Francisco commute from San Rafael, although the Larkspur Ferry is an excellent option.

Near the edge of San Pablo Bay is old Hamilton Air Field. Opened in 1935, Hamilton Air Field was named in honor of the first American pilot to fly with the Royal Flying Corps during World War I, Lt. Lloyd Hamilton. Used at points by both the Army and the Navy, the base reached its peak of activity during World War II, when it was home to 20,000 servicemen. Decommissioned in 1975, Hamilton Air Field sat untouched for two decades while city officials, the community, and developers struggled to agree upon a plan for the site. Finally, in the 1990s, developers purchased the land from the US government for a reported $13 million and set to work on a massive redevelopment plan that included environmental cleanup, infrastructure rehabilitation, and new housing construction.

The airfield has now been transformed into a thriving planned community, sort of a small town within Novato, simply called **Hamilton.** Here, the very new—quiet culs-de-sac, new homes, outdoor trails, parks, and a large open community green—blends with the very old—restored Spanish-style buildings now converted for community uses. Clusters of modern tract homes, from spacious luxury houses to townhomes, form the heart of Hamilton. Senior apartments, as well as some affordable housing units, are also underway, though both of these are expected to have waiting lists before completion.

Other pluses include an historic outdoor amphitheater, a large park, a community swimming pool, a history museum, bat sanctuary, restored wetlands, and a city arts center home to Indian Valley Artists and a number of individual artist studios. Old hangars are in the process of being converted into office space; there are two large hotels here, and a free shuttle bus runs through the area. A few vestiges of the site's early military days linger on in the form of the US Coast Guard's Pacific Strike Team, which still maintains an installation including Coast Guard housing here.

With hundreds of new homes being built, and a new community center on the way, Hamilton has definitely moved beyond its airfield days. Today, the community is a living testament to what cities can do, working together, to rehabilitate shuttered military bases to meet their housing and community needs. Once finished, Hamilton will have roughly 1,000 new housing units. All together, the ambitious project is expected to take at least two decades to finish. For more information visit www.hamiltown.com.

Away from busy Highway 101, **Fairfax** is a charming small town (population 7,309) with a quaint downtown and plenty of open space for hiking, biking, horseback riding, and pondering life. Proudly defining itself as one of the most progressive and eco-conscious communities in Marin County, Fairfax has placed strict limitations on development and banned chain stores. Once a year, the community comes together for the annual Fairfax Festival, which has recently been expanded to include an EcoFest as well.

The Fairfax-Bolinas Road is not only scenic, but provides access to the coast. Fairfax's claim to fame is being home of the mountain bike, which was "invented" here in 1974. Other than the long commute to the city, the only other negative Fairfax residents must contend with is the risk of flooding from the creeks each winter.

CORTE MADERA

Web Site: www.ci.corte-madera.ca.us
Area Code: 415
Zip Codes: 94925
Post Office: Main, 7 Pixely Ave, Corte Madera, 800-275-8777, www.usps.com
Police Station: 950 Doherty Dr, Larkspur, 415-927-5150
Library: 707 Meadowsweet Dr, Corte Madera, 415-924-4844, www.co.marin.ca.us/depts/lb/main/corte/index.cfm
Public Schools: Larkspur School District, 230 Doherty Dr, Larkspur, 415-927-6960, www.larkspurschools.org
Parks, Gardens, and Open Space: Corte Madera Recreation Department, 300 Tamalpais Dr, 415-927-5072, www.ci.corte-madera.ca.us

NOVATO/HAMILTON

Web Site: www.ci.novato.ca.us
Area Code: 415
Zip Codes: 94945, 94948, 94949
Post Office: 1537 South Novato Blvd, 800-275-8777, www.usps.com
Police Station: 908 Sherman Ave, 415-897-4378
Library: 1720 Novato Blvd, 415-898-4623, www.co.marin.ca.us/depts/lb/main/novato/index.cfm
Public Schools: Novato Unified School District, 1015 7th St, Novato, 415-897-4201, http://nusd.marin.k12.ca.us
Parks, Gardens, and Open Space: Novato Community Services, 75 Rowland Way, #200, 415-899-8200, www.ci.novato.ca.us

FAIRFAX

Web Site: www.town-of-fairfax.org
Area Code: 415
Zip Codes: 94930
Post Office: 773 Center Blvd, 800-275-8777, www.usps.com

Police Station: 144 Bolinas Road, 415-453-5330
Library: 2097 Sir Francis Drake Blvd, 415-453-8092, www.co.marin.
ca.us/library/fairfax/index.cfm
Public Schools: Ross Valley District, 110 Shaw Dr, San Anselmo, 415-454-2162, http://rvsd.marin.k12.ca.us/
Parks, Gardens, and Open Space: Fairfax Parks Department, 142 Bolinas Road, 415-453-1584, www.town-of-fairfax.org

WEST MARIN COUNTY

Though much of Marin County is super expensive, many of the homes in West Marin, which includes the coastal and sometimes tucked-away communities of **Muir Beach** (www.muirbeach.com), **Stinson Beach**, (www.stinsonbeachonline.com), **Bolinas, Nicasio, Olema, Inverness, Point Reyes Station, Tomales** (http://tomales.com), **Marshall, San Geronimo, Woodacre** and **Dillon Beach**, are slightly more affordable—though still pricey even by Bay Area standards. More information on these communities can be found at www.pointreyes.org. (To discourage the hordes of tourists that descend upon these beach communities, residents of Bolinas have been known to tear down the town's street sign indicating the turn-off.)

Point Reyes National Seashore is the area's crown jewel, as well as Tomales Bay, which is famous for its oysters. Filmmaker George Lucas (*Star Wars*) has his famous 4,000-acre Skywalker Ranch headquarters in Nicasio, along Lucas Valley Road. Up in Marshall, the Strauss family has been making organic milk, butter, and yogurt for years. Check your local health food store for the "skinny." In many of these towns you'll find homes, complete with redwoods and acreage, that can still be purchased for prices on the lower end of the countywide median. For lovers of the great outdoors and the quiet life, these semi-secluded small towns offer plentiful hiking, biking, and horseback riding opportunities, not to mention easy access to miles of spectacular coastline via Highway 1. In San Geronimo you'll also find a popular 18-hole golf course, and Woodacre is home to the Spirit Rock Meditation Center, 5000 Sir Francis Drake Boulevard, offering a variety of programs (www.spiritrock.org).

WEST MARIN COUNTY
Web Sites: www.co.marin.ca.us, www.marin.org, www.pointreyes.org
Zip Codes: see Marin County above
Area Code: 415
Sheriff: Marin County Sheriff Department, 3501 Civic Center Dr, #167, San Rafael, 415-499-7250

Emergency Hospital: Marin General Hospital, 250 Bon Air Road, Greenbrae, 415-925-7000

Library: Main Branch, 3501 Civic Center Dr, San Rafael, 415-499-6056, www.co.marin.ca.us/depts/lb/main/

Public Schools: Marin County Office of Education, 415-472-4110, http://marin.k12.ca.us

Community Publications: *Marin Independent Journal*, 150 Alameda del Prado, Novato, 415-883-8600, www.marinij.com; *Point Reyes Light*, P.O. Box 210, Point Reyes Station, 415-663-8404, www.pt reyeslight.com; *The Coastal Post*, P.O. Box 31, Bolinas, 415-868-1600, www.coastalpost.com

County/Community Resources: West Marin Chamber of Commerce, 415-663-9232, www.pointreyes.org; San Geronimo Valley Community Center, 415-488-8888, www.sgvcc.org; Point Reyes National Seashore, Point Reyes, 415-464-5100, www.nps.gov/pore; Marin County Parks, 3501 Civic Center Dr Room #415, San Rafael, 415-499-6387, www.co.marin.ca.us; Golden Gate National Recreation Area, Fort Mason, Building 201, 415-561-4700, www.nps. gov/goga

Public Transportation: *Golden Gate Transit*, 415-455-2000

SONOMA COUNTY

North and northeast of Marin County, Sonoma County consists of rolling, green, tree- or vineyard-covered hills, dramatic coastline, seamless skies, glorious weather (most of the time), and some of the world's top chefs. Sonoma County, along with neighboring Napa County, is internationally known for the wines produced in this region. Hundreds of wineries dot the countryside, hosting visitors from around the world who come to sample and learn about the fine art of making wine. Housing options are varied, ranging from apartments and condominiums to single-family homes and stately Victorians. You'll also find farms and ranches, mobile home parks, and summer cottages.

SONOMA COUNTY

Web Site: www.sonoma-county.org

Area Code: 707

Zip Codes: 95403, 95404, 95405, 95406, 95476

Sheriff: 2796 Ventura Ave, Santa Rosa, 707-565-2650

Emergency Hospitals: Sutter Hospital, 3325 Chanate Rd, Santa Rosa, 707-576-4000; Palm Dr Hospital, 501 Petaluma Ave, Sebastopol, 707-823-8511; Santa Rosa Memorial, 1165 Montgomery Dr, Santa Rosa,

707-546-3210; Sonoma Valley Hospital, 347 Andrieux St, Sonoma, 707-935-5000

Libraries: Sonoma County Library, Petaluma Branch, 100 Fairgrounds Dr, 707-763-9801, www.sonoma.lib.ca.us

Public Schools: Sonoma County Office of Education, 5340 Skylane Blvd, Santa Rosa, 707-524-2600, www.sonoma.k12.ca.us

Community Publications: *Santa Rosa Press Democrat*, 427 Mendocino Ave, Santa Rosa, 707-546-2020, www.pressdemocrat.com; *Marin Independent Journal*, 150 Alameda Del Prado, Novato, 415-883-8600, www.marinij.com; *Sonoma Index-Tribune*, P.O. Box C, Sonoma, 95476, 707-938-2111, www.sonomanews.com

Community Resources: Sonoma Valley Chamber of Commerce, 651-A Broadway, Sonoma, 707-996-1033, www.sonomachamber.com; Sonoma Community Center, 276 East Napa St, Sonoma, 707-938-4626; Sonoma Valley Chorale, P.O. Box 816, Sonoma, 95476, 707-935-1576, www.sonomavalleychorale.org; Sonoma State University, 1801 East Cotati Ave, Rohnert Park, 94928, 707-664-2880, www.sonoma.edu

Public Transportation: Sonoma County Transit, 800-345-7433, www.transitinfo.org

Parks, Gardens, and Open Space: Sonoma County Regional Parks, 2300 County Center Dr, 120A, Santa Rosa, 707-565-2041, www.sonoma-county.org/parks; Sonoma County Farm Trails, 800-207-9464, www.farmtrails.org

SANTA ROSA

Recently named one of the nation's "Most Livable Communities" by the Partners for Livable Communities, Santa Rosa prides itself on maintaining a small town feel despite a booming population. Home to the county seat and located 50 miles north of San Francisco in central Sonoma County, the city is popular with young families, first-time homeowners, and retired seniors. Long considered one of the more affordable spots to buy a home, prices here have soared in recent years. According to the CAR, the April 2005 median price for a home in this picturesque town was $499,000—up over 17% from the previous year. City officials here are picky about the look of new buildings and businesses, so you'll find Santa Rosa easy on the eyes. Despite the close tabs kept on development, Santa Rosa is growing (population 156,268), as is traffic congestion, especially going "crosstown" from east to west or vice versa. In addition, Highway 101, which splits the city in two going north and south, is now too narrow for the number of vehicles it must handle on a daily basis.

Surrounded by a handful of picturesque, lovingly restored historic neighborhoods, the downtown area comes alive every Wednesday evening from mid-May through August with the Santa Rosa Downtown Market—renowned as Sonoma County's largest farmers market. Also downtown is the Prince Memorial Greenway, a new curving terraced pedestrian and bike pathway that snakes along the banks of the Santa Rosa Creek, providing a scenic link to the city's Historic Railroad Square. In addition to scores of popular suburban ranch-style homes, Santa Rosa is also home to 14 mobile home parks, as well as two unique spots —Valley Vista I and II—where mobile home owners own the land. To encourage upkeep and maintain affordability, the city maintains a rent control program for the private parks and offers rehabilitation loans. For a taste of local history you can visit the home, greenhouse, and gardens of horticulturist Luther Burbank or take a tour of the Charles M. Schulz Museum and Research Center, named in honor of the beloved "Peanuts" creator and long-time Santa Rosa resident (www.charlesmschulzmuseum.org).

SANTA ROSA
Web Site: www.ci.santa-rosa.ca.us
Zip Codes: 95403, 95404, 95405, 95406
Area Code: 707
Post Office: 730 2nd St, 800-275-8777, www.usps.com
Police: 965 Sonoma Ave, 707-543-3600
Library: Santa Rosa Branch of the Sonoma County Library, 3rd and E sts, 707-545-0831, www.sonoma.lib.ca.us/branches/Central.html
Community Resources: Downtown Market, www.srdowntown market.com; Sonoma County Museum, www.sonomacountymuseum. com; Luther Burbank Center for the Arts, www.lbc.net
Parks, Gardens, and Open Space: Santa Rosa Parks and Recreation Commission, 618 B St, 415-485-3333, www.cityofsanrafael. org/parkandrecreation; Hood Mountain Regional Park, 3000 Los Alamos Rd; Maddux Ranch Park, 4655 Lavelle Rd; Shiloh Regional Park, 5750 Faught Rd; Spring Lake Park, 5390 Montgomery Dr

SONOMA

Sonoma, sometimes called by locals "Slo-noma" for its tranquil, small town feel, is the commercial heart of Sonoma Valley, the so-called Valley of the Moon. Surrounded by vineyards, the entire valley is a mecca for wine lovers. On weekends, particularly in the summer, the city's population explodes as scores of tourists clog Route 12 to sample world-renowned local cabernets, pinots, and merlots. A picture-postcard small community (population 9,834), rich in history, culinary treasures, and health resorts, Sonoma is also home to Sonoma State University. If you have to commute to San Francisco though, plan on at least one hour each way in the car, longer by bus.

Architecturally, single-family homes, many of them ranch style, were built between 1950 and 1970. On the outskirts, you'll find older family farms, as well as stately vineyard estates. The median price for a home here in April 2005 was $611,000, up almost 26% from the previous year. History buffs should visit the Mission San Francisco de Solano, or Sonoma Mission, the last and northernmost of the Franciscan missions along the California Coast. Literature and nature lovers will enjoy the serene surroundings of author Jack London's former ranch and final resting place, now an 800-plus acre state park located in nearby Glen Ellen. Heading out of the city, throughout the valley you'll find clusters of small towns and villages, many of them home to popular natural hot springs, spas, dairy farms, and of course, wineries.

SONOMA
Web Site: www.sonomacity.org
Area Code: 707
Zip Codes: 95476
Post Office: 617 Broadway, 800-275-8777, www.usps.com
Police: 175 1st St West, 707-996-3602
Library: Sonoma Branch of the Sonoma County Library, 755 Napa St, 707-996-5217, www.sonoma.lib.ca.us/branches/Sonoma.html
Parks, Gardens, and Open Space: Sonoma Parks and Public Works Department, #1 the Plaza, 707-938-3332, www.sonomacity.org; Maxwell Farms Regional Park, 100 Verano Ave

NAPA COUNTY

ST. HELENA, RUTHERFORD, YOUNTVILLE, NAPA, CALISTOGA

East of Sonoma County lies Napa Valley, a place where you can indulge your taste buds with fine wine and gourmet meals. With a mild, Mediterranean-like climate, Napa Valley produces hundreds of thousands of gallons of wine including zinfandels, merlots, cabernets, pinot noirs, and chardonnays. Premier grapes are grown on the vine, then aged in the casks, and finally bottled and corked with an end result rivaling the best in France. On weekends, thousands of wine lovers take to Highway 29, the road that runs north-south through Napa County, stopping along the way at the vineyards, wineries, and picturesque small towns, such as

St. Helena, Rutherford, and **Yountville**. A typical day visit might begin with one or two tastings in the cool basement of a winery, followed by a picnic lunch break in a park, then a few more wineries before dinner. If you enjoy wine and bucolic hills, it's a delightful way to spend a day. Better yet, it might be an ideal place to call home. One interesting geological note about Yountville is its recent earthquake history. In September 2000, a magnitude 5.2 earthquake struck Napa County, the epicenter of which was in Yountville, which sits about six miles northwest of Napa. It caused millions of dollars' worth of damage to buildings throughout the county, though thankfully no fatalities. Today, Yountville is known for its world-class restaurants, chief among them the French Laundry, which recently ranked number 3 on the 50 Best restaurants in the World List, put together annually by World Press.

The **City of Napa** is the center of county government. If the hot air from the politicians is too much, try hot air ballooning, an ideal way to soar in Napa's often-sunny skies fanned by gentle breezes. Set up house here, and you can sample the wine year round. The average home price in April 2005 was $544,000, an 18% increase over the previous year. In addition to ranch-style homes, popular with families, a handful of mobile home parks—many of them designed especially for seniors—offer tranquil life for retirees.

Calistoga, at the northern end of the Napa Valley, attracts people ready to be pampered with a mud bath, herbal wrap, mineral bath, and/or a massage. (For more see the **Quick Getaways** chapter.) There's also a natural geyser, called the Old Faithful (not to be confused with Yellowstone's Old Faithful) that shoots 350° water 60 feet into the air. The owner claims Old Faithful acts erratically about 2 to 14 days before the area experiences a significant earthquake.

NAPA COUNTY
Web Site: www.co.napa.ca.us
Area Code: 707
Zip Codes: 94558, 94559, 94574, 94508
Sheriff: 1125 Third St, Napa, 707-253-4440
Libraries: Napa City-County Library, 580 Coombs St, 707-253-4241, www.co.napa.ca.us/library/
Public Schools: Napa Valley Unified School District, 2425 Jefferson St, Napa, 707-253-3715, www.nvusd.k12.ca.us
Community Publications: *The Napa Valley Register*, 1615 Second St, Napa, 707-226-3711, www.napanews.com; *St. Helena Star*, 1200 Main St, C, St. Helena, 707-963-2731, www.sthelenastar.com
Community Resources: Community Resources for Children, 5

Financial Plaza #224, Napa, 707-253-0366; Wildlife Rescue, P.O. Box 2571, 707-224-4295; Napa County Historical Society, 1545 Second St, 707-224-1739, www.napahistory.org; Napa Valley Museum, 55 Presidents Circle, Yountville, 707-944-0500, www.napavalley museum.org; Napa Community Resources Department, 1100 West St, 707-257-9529

Public Transportation: CalTrain, 800-660-4287; Napa Valley Transit, 800-696-6443, www.transitinfo.org; Napa Valley Wine Train, 800-427-4124, www.winetrain.com

Parks, Gardens, and Open Space: Napa Valley Parks, 1195 Third St, Room 310, Napa, 707-253-4580, www.co.napa.ca.us; The Petrified Forest, 707-942-6667; Old Faithful Geyser, 707-942-6463; Bothe-Napa Valley State Park, 800-444-7275; Bothe Napa Valley State Park, 5 miles north of St. Helena and 4 miles south of Calistoga on Highway 29/128; Bale Grist Mill State Historic Park, 3369 North Saint Helena Highway (Highway 29)

SOLANO COUNTY

East of Napa County, Solano County is one of the fastest growing counties in the Bay Area, with housing developments and new businesses springing up from Vallejo in the southwestern corner of the county to Vacaville and Fairfield farther inland. So-called refugees from the big city seem to be arriving en masse and are snatching up many of the new homes. From April 2004 to April 2005, home prices in Solano County increased almost 22% (from $330,000 to $402,000), which offers a good indication of where things are headed. Crime rates are relatively low here, and schools, in general, are better than their counterparts in San Francisco and Oakland.

SOLANO COUNTY
Web Site: www.co.solano.ca.us
Area Code: 707
Zip Codes: 94533, 94587, 95687, 95688, 94589, 94590
Sheriff: 530 Union Ave, Suite 100, Fairfield, 707-421-7040
Libraries: Solano County Library, 1150 Kentucky St, Fairfield, 707-421-6500, http://solanolibrary.com/
Public Schools: Solano County Office of Education, Superintendent's Office, 5100 Business Center Dr, Fairfield, 94534, 707-399-4400, www.solanocoe.k12.ca.us
Community Publications: *Vallejo Times Herald*, 440 Curtola Pkwy, Vallejo, 707-644-1141; *Daily Republic*, 1250 Texas St, 707-425-4646; *Vacaville Reporter*, 318 Main St, Vacaville, 707-448-6401; *Benicia*

Herald, P.O. Box 65, Benicia, 707-745-0733; *Dixon Tribune*, 145 East A
St, Dixon, 916-678-5594; *River News Herald and Journal*, P.O. Box 786,
Rio Vista, 707-374-6431

Community Resources: Six Flags Marine World, 2001 Marine World
Pkwy, 707-643-6722, www.sixflags.com; Solano County Fair, 707-
644-4401; Solano County Family and Children Services, 100 Cement
Hill Rd, Suite 500, Fairfield, 707-427-6600

Public Transportation: Vallejo Baylink Ferry, 800-640-2877; Vallejo
Transit Buses, 800-640-2877; Vacaville City Coach, 707-449-6000;
Fairfield-Suisun Transit, 707-422-2877; RIDES, 511, www.511.org

Parks, Gardens, and Open Space: Solano County Parks, 707-784-
7514, www.co.solano.ca.us

FAIRFIELD, VACAVILLE

Fairfield and **Vacaville** are typical American towns, with tract homes,
apartment complexes, duplexes, townhouses, strip malls, and shopping
centers. Located northeast of San Francisco along Interstate 80, they offer
easy access to University of California at Davis and the state capital in
Sacramento. Except for a strange blanket of fog that rolls in nightly over I-
80, the weather here is dry and hot, hot, hot. On the upside, homes here
are more affordable and many have swimming pools. Fairfield hosts Travis
Air Force Base, one of the few military installations left open in California.
Vacaville's claim to fame is the local state prison that cares for mentally ill
inmates. Nearby Rio Vista recently rose from the empty desert-like landscape as an oasis with the opening of Trilogy, a planned retirement community—complete with spacious homes, state-of-the-art recreation
complex, and a massive golf course.

FAIRFIELD
Web Site: www.ci.fairfield.ca.us
Area Code: 707
Zip Codes: 94533, 94587
Post Office: 600 Kentucky St, 800-275-8777, www.usps.com
Police: 1000 Webster, 707-428-7307
Library: Fairfield Branch, 1150 Kentucky St, 707-421-6510,
http://solanolibrary.com/fairfield.cfm
Parks, Gardens, and Open Space: Fairfield Park Division, 1000
Webster St, 707-428-7407, www.ci.fairfield.ca.us; Grizzly Island State
Wildlife Area, Highway 12; Rockville Hills Regional Park, Rockville Rd,
www.rockvillepark.org

VACAVILLE

Web Site: www.ci.vacaville.ca.us
Area Code: 707
Zip Codes: 95688, 95687
Post Office: 98 Cernon St, 800-275-8777, www.usps.com
Police: 630 Merchant St, 707-449-5200
Libraries: Cultural Center Branch, 1020 Ulatis Dr, 707-449-6290, http://solanolibrary.com/vacaville.cfm; Town Square Branch, 1 Town Square Place, 707-469-4590, http://solanolibrary.com/vacts.cfm
Parks, Gardens, and Open Space: Vacaville Community Services Department, 40 Eldridge Ave, 707-449-5629, www.ci.vacaville.ca.us; City of Vacaville Park Facilities, 707-449-5100, www.cityofvacaville.com/content/city_information/parks.php

VALLEJO

With home prices consistently among the lowest in the Bay Area, the City of Vallejo has become an attractive option for legions of families looking to fulfill what can seem the impossible dream here—homeownership. Although Vallejo's median home price increased over 20% between April 2004 and April 2005, according to the California Association of Realtors, at $399,500, it is still a bargain by regional standards.

San Francisco is just 32 miles away, and the high-speed Vallejo Bay Link Ferry catamaran offers one of the most pleasant commute options around. Daily, the ferry glides across the Bay, carrying 2,000 people to work in San Francisco (the stop is the Ferry Building), with the trip taking just under an hour each way. Commuting by car would take almost double the time.

Founded by General Mariano G. Vallejo in 1844, Vallejo originated as an important shipping and naval center. Around that time, a temporary capital building was built in Vallejo in 1852, but because of the area's lack of housing the legislature moved up to Sacramento. In 1853 a devastating flood then brought the legislature back to Vallejo, but they were still dissatisfied, and moved on to Benicia, and then later returned to Sacramento.

Today, Vallejo (population 121,221) is the largest city in Solano County. Best known for being home to Six Flags Marine World, a large outdoor theme and animal park, Vallejo also features an outside farmers' market, a golf course, a yacht club, and the California Maritime Academy, a California State University School. Existing housing is an eclectic mix of homes, from beautifully restored Victorians to 1950s tract housing to lavish, newly built residences in the Northgate and Hiddenbrooke Golf Course neighborhoods.

In 1996, the Mare Island Shipyards closed, and the city is now in the process of converting the 5,252 acres to civilian use. Part of the conversion includes an estimated $81 million environmental cleanup of lead-based paint, petroleum waste, and other toxic remnants left in the shipyard. A large commercial area is already up and running here, home to more than 70 businesses including the US Forest Service, Western Regional Headquarters. The final plans call for 1,400 new housing units ranging from apartments to single-family homes, a total of 7 million square feet of office space, new parks, and a large area of restored open space. The first 126 new single family homes are scheduled to open in 2005, model homes have been available for view since April 2005, and the community celebrated its grand opening in Summer 2005. Watch for reported median home prices in Vallejo to rise as these homes, whose prices start in the $600,000's, begin to sell.

With the Mare Island rehabilitation underway, including plans to revitalize the downtown area and revamp the waterfront, the City of Vallejo is at a crossroads. In the next two decades, the waterfront project will convert 110 acres into a thriving connected core of 1,090 new housing units, 562,000 square feet of commercial space, and 28 acres of parks. A new $52 million transit center to improve bus and ferry links, complete with a massive new commuter parking garage, is also in the works, as are a new performing arts center and waterfront promenade. Meanwhile, the planned $120 million downtown project will overhaul a smattering of empty lots to create 800 new housing units and 68,000 square feet of retail and office space. With so many projects in the works and a 63% rate of homeownership, it's perhaps no surprise that *Money Magazine* recently ranked Vallejo third among all medium-sized metropolitan areas in California in its report on "The Best Places to Live in America."

Web Site: www.ci.vallejo.ca.us

Area Code: 707

Zip Codes: 94589, 94590, 94591

Post Office: 485 Santa Clara St, 800-275-8777, www.usps.com

Police: 111 Amador St, 707-648-4553

Libraries: John F. Kennedy Library, 505 Santa Clara St, 707-553-5568, http://solanolibrary.com/jfk.cfm; Springstowne Library, 1003 Oakwood Ave, 707-553-5546, http://solanolibrary.com/springstowne.cfm

Parks, Gardens, and Open Space: Greater Vallejo Recreation District, 395 Amador St, 707-648-4600, www.gvrd.org

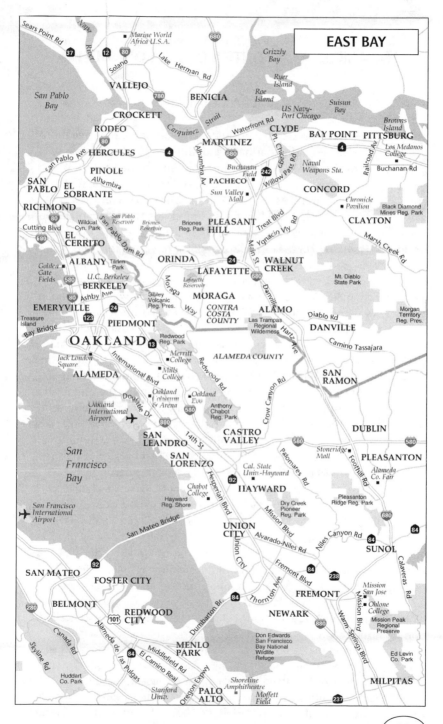

EAST BAY

EAST BAY
(ALAMEDA AND CONTRA COSTA COUNTIES)

ALAMEDA COUNTY

The East Bay is the most densely populated region of the Bay Area, from Crockett and Hercules at the northern end, through Pinole, Richmond, El Cerrito, Albany, Berkeley, Oakland, and Alameda in the center; to San Leandro, Castro Valley, Hayward, Union City, and Fremont on the southern end, and Livermore, Pleasanton, Dublin, Concord, Walnut Creek, Martinez, Pittsburg, and Antioch out east. In fact, the East Bay contains so many enclaves it's difficult to generalize about life here, except to say that it's not San Francisco. For the most part, you'll find parking the car is not as arduous a task compared to the city, rents are somewhat lower and rental property is more available, and the weather is generally clearer and warmer than in San Francisco. However, the biggest drawback to living in the East Bay is commuting to San Francisco by car. Fortunately, the entire area is served, and served well, by an extensive criss-crossing network of public transit systems, including buses, trains, and Bay Area Rapid Transit (BART). Another asset is the Oakland International Airport, one of the friendliest airports you're likely to find anywhere in the United States. Here, when you dial information, real human beings still answer the phone and are happy to assist you with everything from driving directions to parking suggestions, to tips for quick and easy passenger drop-off. While officials at both San Francisco International Airport and San Jose International Airport often warn passengers about overflowing parking lots, their Oakland counterpart generally can proclaim hassle-free parking.

Many fleeing San Francisco's exorbitant prices, or simply looking for more family-oriented single-family housing options, look to cities in the East Bay to call home. And the East Bay has a lot to offer. The lush parks have an array of outdoor activity options including hiking, biking, boating, picnicking, and swimming. Berkeley's Tilden Park, the crown jewel of East Bay's park system, has hiking and biking trails, a swimming hole, a carousel, a petting zoo, a steam train and much more. Another escape to the outdoors is Mount Diablo State Park, located in eastern Contra Costa County. As the highest peak in the Bay Area, Mount Diablo is a popular weekend destination for hikers, campers, and families. Oakland's 140-acre saltwater Lake Merritt, spread out beneath the downtown Oakland skyline, hosts joggers, walkers, and bikers at all times of the day. You can even hire an authentic Venetian gondola to chauffeur you on a romantic glide across the lake.

The East Bay contains several colleges and universities, most prominently the University of California, Berkeley, or "Cal" (the only school in the

University of California system so called). Cal State East Bay has campuses in the Hayward hills and the Concord foothills of Mount Diablo, as well as a professional development center in Oakland. Private colleges and universities in the East Bay include Saint Mary's in the densely wooded community of Moraga, John F. Kennedy University in Orinda, and Mills College in Oakland. The northern environs of the East Bay are a stone's-throw away, if you've got a strong arm, from the University of California at Davis, Sacramento State University in Sacramento, and the University of the Pacific in Stockton.

ALAMEDA COUNTY

Web Site: www.co.alameda.ca.us
Area Code: 510
Sheriff: 1401 Lakeside Dr, 12th Floor, 510-272-6900, http://alameda-countysheriff.org
Emergency Hospitals: Alameda Hospital, 2070 Clinton Ave, 510-522-3700, www.alamedahospital.org; Fairmont Hospital, 15400 Foothill Blvd, San Leandro, 510-667-7800, www.acmedctr.org; Highland Hospital, 1411 East 31st St, Oakland, 510-437-4800, www.acmedctr.org; St. Rose Hospital, 27200 Calaroga Ave, Hayward, 510-264-4000, www.strosehospital.org; Kaiser Medical Center, 27400 Hesperian Blvd, Hayward, 510-784-4000, www.kaiserpermanente.org; Alta Bates Medical Center, 2450 Ashby Ave, Berkeley, 510-204-4444, www.altabates.com; Children's Hospital Oakland, 747 52nd St, Oakland, 510-428-3000, www.childrenshospitaloakland.org
Library: Alameda County Library Foundation, 2450 Stevenson Blvd, Fremont, 510-745-1500, www.aclibrary.org
Public Schools: Alameda County Office of Education, 313 West Winton Ave, Hayward, 510-887-0152, www.alameda-coe.k12.ca.us.
Community Publications: *Oakland Tribune*, 510-208-6300, www.insidebayarea.com/oaklandtribune, (the Alameda Newspaper Group also owns the *Alameda Times-Star* and the *Fremont Argus*); *East Bay Express*, 510-879-3700, www.eastbayexpress.com; *Contra Costa Times* (covers Contra Costa and east Alameda County), 800-598-4637, www.ContraCostaTimes.com (also owns a handful of smaller local publications including the *Berkeley Voice*, *Alameda Journal*, the *Montclarion*, and the *Piedmonter*); *The Berkeley Daily Planet*, 510-841-5600, www.berkeleydailyplanet.com; U.C. Berkeley Publications: *The Daily Californian*, www.dailycal.org; *North Gate News On-line*, http://journalism.berkeley.edu/ngno/
County/Community Resources: Alameda One-Stop Career Center, 510-981-7564; Bananas (childcare referrals), 510-658-7353, direct referral line: 510-658-0381, www.bananasinc.org; Alameda County Social Services Agency, 510-596-0110, alamedasocialservices.org;

Eden Information and Referral for Social Services, 510-537-2710, www.edenir.org; Ohlone Community College, 510-659-6000, www.ohlone.edu; Childcare Links, 510-791-9256 www.childcare links.org; Alameda County Art Commission, (510) 208-9646 www.co.alameda.ca.us/arts/

Public Transportation: AC *(Alameda-Contra Costa) Transit*, 510-891-4700, TTY 800-448-9790, www.actransit.org; *BART*, 510-465-2278, TTY 510-839-2278, www.bart.gov; *Alameda-Oakland Ferry*, 510-522-3300, www.eastbayferry.com; *Emery-Go-Round*, 510-451-3862, next bus hotline, 510-451-3862, www.emergygoround.com; *RIDES*, 511, www.rideshare.511.org; *Amtrak*, 800-USA-RAIL, TTY 800-523-6590, www.amtrak.com; *Greyhound*, 800-229-9424, TTY: 800-345-3109, www.greyhound.com

Parks, Gardens, and Open Space: East Bay Regional Park District, 2950 Peralta Oaks Court, P.O. Box 5381, Oakland, 94605, 510-562-PARK, www.ebparks.org; maintains 62 parks throughout the region, many of them with large open areas, nature trails, and shorelines

HAYWARD, FREMONT, NEWARK, UNION CITY

A sprawling, often hot, expanse of suburbia, **Hayward** (population 146,027) comes complete with a standard fare of strip malls, shopping centers, gigantic car dealerships, and fast food restaurants. This family-oriented city includes large Hispanic and Asian populations. In the eastern part of the city, California State University East Bay perches high atop a hill, offering dynamic views of the Bay Area below. Formerly called and still known locally as Cal State Hayward, the campus is in the process of expanding—adding a new Business Technology Center, revamped student union, and new housing. As is true with all of California's public colleges, though it keeps creeping up, tuition is—relatively speaking—inexpensive, and a variety of programs are geared to part-time students in the workforce looking to change careers, get new training, or simply enrich their lives.

Because of its relatively more affordable home prices, both for single-family homes and condos, Hayward continues to grow at a steady rate. Housing prices have also grown at a more than steady rate, with median home prices in April 2005 according to the CAR reaching $510,500, over a 27% increase above the previous year. Many new Bay Area residents opt to set down roots here and commute the 25 miles northeast to San Francisco or the 26 miles south to Silicon Valley, all for the sake of home ownership. Thanks to the Hayward–San Mateo Bridge, crossing the bay to the Peninsula is relatively easy—though commute hour traffic can be brutal despite a recent widening.

The cities of **Fremont**, **Newark**, and **Union City** lie to the south of Hayward, and are similar in appearance, socioeconomic components, housing options, and the like. All of these suburban communities began to absorb a mass exodus about two decades ago, as families fled San Francisco, the peninsula and the South Bay—heading east across the bay in search of suburban family living and affordable home ownership opportunities. As a result, these towns are very family-friendly with quiet neighborhood streets, good local parks, more affordable homes, and significantly higher rates, generally speaking, of home ownership. Like Hayward, all three cities lie off of the seemingly-always-clogged I-880—which frequently resembles a parking lot during the morning and evening rush hours.

Popular with young families, Fremont's largest population segment—more than 20%—is children under age 14, according to the most recent US Census. Residents here frequent Lake Elizabeth for boating, walking, and picnics. The city offers easy, direct—though not always swift—access to Silicon Valley via the Dumbarton Bridge. Two active and popular community centers—Centerville and Irvington—offer an array of community programs, classes, recreation activities and even mini branch libraries. The main route through town, Fremont Boulevard, is filled with large outdoor strip malls, and connects to the smaller neighboring town of Newark. For local shopping, the New Park Mall in Newark is one of the busiest malls in the Bay Area. A little further north, Union City has a collection of large shopping centers right off of the freeway. The largest of these is Union Landing, on Alvarado-Niles Street. Its biggest draw on weekends is a gigantic movie theater with more than two-dozen screens. During the Krispy Kreme craze, Union City drew hundreds of doughnut tourists—literally forming lines around the block—as it had the distinction of being among the first cities in northern California to open the popular doughnut shop. For prospective homeowners, the city's biggest enticement is its comparatively lower home prices. With relatively affordable rates, Union City boasts an owner occupancy rate of more than 70%, according to the city.

HAYWARD
Web Site: www.ci.hayward.ca.us
Area Code: 510
Zip Codes: 94540, 94541, 94542, 94543, 94544, 94545, 94546, 94552, 94557
Post Offices: 822 C St; 24438 Santa Clara St; 2163 Aldengate Way, 800-275-8777, www.usps.com
Police: Hayward Police Department, 300 West Winton Ave, 510-293-7000
Library: Hayward Main Library, 835 C St, 510-293-8685; Weekes Branch, 27300 Patrick Ave, 510-782-2155

Public Schools: Hayward Unified School District, 24411 Amador St, 510-784-2600, www.husd.k12.ca.us

Parks, Gardens, and Open Space: Hayward Area Recreation and Park District, 1099 E St, 510-881-6700, www.hard.dst.ca.usp

FREMONT

Web Site: www.ci.fremont.ca.us

Area Code: 510

Zip Codes: 94536, 94537, 94538, 94539, 94555

Post Offices: Fremont: 37010 Dusterberry Way; 160 J St; 41041 Trimboli Way; 43456 Ellsworth St; 240 Francisco Lane, 800-275-8777, www.usps.com

Police: Fremont Police Department, 2000 Stevenson Blvd, 510-790-6800

Library: Fremont Main Library, 2400 Stevenson Blvd, 510-745-1400, TTY 510-796-9749, www.aclibrary.org

Public Schools: Fremont Unified School District, 4210 Technology Dr, 510-657-2350, www.fremont.k12.ca.us

Parks, Gardens, and Open Space: Fremont Recreation Services, 3300 Capitol Ave, Building B, 510-494-4600

NEWARK

Web Site: www.ci.newark.ca.us

Area Code: 510

Zip Code: 94560

Post Office: Newark Post Office, 6655 Clark Ave, 800-275-8777, www.usps.com

Library: Newark Library, 6300 Civic Terrace Ave, 510-795-2627

Public Schools: Newark Unified School District, 5715 Musick Ave, 510-794-2141

Parks, Gardens, and Open Space: Newark Recreation Services, Community Center, 35501 Cedar Blvd, 510-742-4437, www.ci.newark.ca.us/rc/rcrecgd.html

UNION CITY

Web Site: www.ci.union-city.ca.us

Area Code: 510

Zip Code: 94587

Post Office: Main Post Office, 33170 Alvarado-Niles Rd; 3861 Smith St, 800-275-8777, www.usps.com

Library: Union City Library, 34007 Alvarado-Niles Rd, 510-745-1464, TTY: 510-489-1655

Parks, Gardens, and Open Space: Leisure Services Administration, 34009 Alvarado-Niles Rd, 510-675-5353, www.ci.union-city.ca.us/ leisure/ucls.htm

ALAMEDA

Located just south of Oakland, the City of Alameda (population 74,581) is mostly an island, tucked alongside the East Bay. Flat as a pancake and with one long beach, Alameda connects to the mainland via a number of bridges and tunnels. In the late 1800s Alameda was a popular resort for San Franciscans and Oaklanders who sought its mild climate and comfortable sand. Seawater pools were even lighted and heated to accommodate nighttime swimmers. During World War II, the Navy built the Alameda Naval Air Station, creating a bustling naval base here until its decommissioning in 1997. Today the 800-plus acre site, now called Alameda Point, is slowly undergoing a $2 billion plus facelift, converting it into a mix of new residential neighborhoods, shopping areas, recreational facilities, and business parks. The terminal for the Alameda to San Francisco Ferry is also here. The city hasn't fully recovered from its button-down Navy days, as is evidenced by the downtown area, which still feels small and unpolished, as though from another era. Compared to the frenzy of much of the rest of the Bay Area, it seems local residents appreciate the calm, unsophisticated environment. Alameda has all your basic shopping needs, though not generally in the form of chain stores.

Robert Crown Memorial Beach, equipped with picnic tables and showers, is a mile-and-a-half beach, good for beginning windsurfers and kiteboarders. Washington Park, just before the beach, has a number of tennis courts, a baseball field, and a dog park. Taking your dogs to the beach, however, could cost you a large fine. And for golfers, butting up right next to the Oakland International Airport is the Chuck Corica Golf Complex on Harbor Bay Island, One Clubhouse Memorial Road, 510-747-7800, www.ci.alameda.ca.us/golf/corica.html.

Architecturally, Alameda has some of the most beautifully restored Victorians in the Bay Area. You'll also find a few that haven't yet been renovated, and you may be lucky enough to find one at a decent price. But real estate here, once available at comparatively bargain prices, is now keeping pace with much of the Bay Area. According to the California Association of Realtors, in April 2005, the median home price, while still lower than San Francisco's, was up 21% from the previous year to $649,000. Certainly, as Alameda continues to dust off its old Navy image, it will become a more sought after locale with ever-higher prices to match.

ALAMEDA
Web Site: www.ci.alameda.ca.us
Area Code: 510
Zip Codes: 94501, 94502
Post Offices: 2201 Shoreline Dr; 2 Eagle Rd; 1415 Webster St, 800-275-8777, www.usps.com
Police: Alameda Police Department, 1555 Oak St, 510-337-8340
Library: Alameda Main Library, 2200 A Central Ave, 510-747-7777, TTY 510-522-2072
Public Schools: Alameda Unified School District, 2200 Central Ave, 510-337-7000, www.alameda.k12.ca.us
Community Resources: Alameda Chamber of Commerce, 1416 Park Ave, 510-522-0414, www.alamedachamber.com; Altarena Playhouse, 1409 High St, 510-523-1553, www.altarena.org; Bill Osborne Model Airplane Field on Doolittle St, 510-747-7529; Alameda Museum and Alameda Historical Society, 2324 Alameda Ave, 510-521-1233, www.alamedamuseum.org; USS Hornet Museum, Alameda Point, Pier 3, 510-521-8448, www.uss-hornet.org; Alameda Civic Light Opera, 2200 Central Ave, 510-864-2256, www.aclo.com; Mastick Senior Center, 1155 Santa Clara Ave, 510-747-7500
Parks, Gardens, and Open Space: Recreation and Parks, 1327 Oak St, 510-747-7529, TTY 510-522-7538, www.ci.alameda.ca.us/arpd

EMERYVILLE

Sandwiched between Oakland and Berkeley and virtually at the foot of the Bay Bridge, Emeryville was originally an industrial area, with not much else happening. By the late 1980s and early 1990s, the 1.2-square-mile city set out on a path of transformation. Old industrial sites metamorphosed into huge shopping centers, warehouses became loft-style apartments and offices, and new apartments and condominiums sprang up. Today over 8,000 people call Emeryville home, while about 20,000 commute here to work at businesses such as Chiron (biotech) and Pixar (the computer animation company that created *Finding Nemo* and *The Incredibles*).

To help the 20,000 employees get to work, Emeryville has a free shuttle, the Emery-Go-Round, which transports people to and from BART (MacArthur Station) and Amtrak. In addition, bike paths wind throughout the city. Another progressive attribute of Emeryville is a city-run daycare facility, known as the Child Development Center, 1220 53rd Street, 510-596-4343. The Center operates year-round and provides childcare services for 90 infants and toddlers whose parents are working, in training, or in school. In 1999, Ex'pression College for Digital Art, 877-833-8800, www.expression.edu, which is devoted exclusively to digital visual media and sound arts technology, opened its doors.

The city is also a regional shopping magnet, drawing people from all across the East Bay to its dense core of retail plazas. Numerous chain stores, such as Borders, Good Guys, Trader Joe's, and Ross Dress for Less occupy space in Emeryville. Meanwhile, IKEA's 274,000-square-foot (equivalent to five football fields), semi do-it-yourself furniture funhouse attracts people from all over the Bay Area. For food, the Emeryville Public Market, 5800 Shellmound Street, is a favorite with its inexpensive ethnic dishes, from Korean BBQ to French crepes to Japanese noodles, served cafeteria style.

A good example of "new urbanism," most of the city's new housing takes the form of condos and townhouses situated within mixed-use plazas, such as the Bay Street development project, now nearing completion. Most Emeryville residents live in some kind of rental situation, with apartment complexes, condominiums, or loft warehouses the most common housing options. You'll find some single-family detached homes in "the triangle" area, on San Pablo Avenue, mostly Craftsman-style houses built in the 1920s and '30s. Waterfront living is available at the 1970s era Watergate Condominiums, which have a spectacular view of the Bay. Other Emeryville residents live in the 30-story Pacific Park Plaza, with its 650 condominium units. Although many of Emeryville's original loft residents were artists, today professionals are moving into the unique spaces created in these old industrial buildings. Emeryville's population is mostly young, single professionals and students, though a number of families are arriving. Compared with most other communities in the Bay Area, median home prices here ($385,000 in April 2005, according to the CAR) remain reasonable, reflecting the preponderance of condos rather than single-family homes.

EMERYVILLE
Web Site: www.ci.emeryville.ca.us
Area Code: 510
Zip Code: 94608, 94662
Post Office: Emeryville Branch, 1585 62nd St, 800-275-8777, www.usps.com
Police: Emeryville Police Department, 2449 Powell St, 510-596-3700
Library: Golden Gate Library, 5606 San Pablo Ave, 510-597-5023
Public Schools: Emery Unified School District, 4727 San Pablo Ave, 510-601-4000, www.emeryusd.k12.ca.us
Community Resources: Emeryville Chamber of Commerce, 5858 Horton St, Suite 130, 510-652-5223, www.emeryvillechamber.com; Emeryville Senior Center, 4321 Salem St, 510-596-3730; Emeryville Child Development Center, 1220 53rd St, 510-596-4343; Emery-Go-Round

Free Shuttle, 510-451-3862 or 511, next bus hotline: 510-451-3862, www.emerygoround.com; Amtrak, 5885 Horton Street, 800-USA-RAIL, www.amtrak.com; First Time Homebuyers Program, 510-596-4316.

Parks, Gardens, and Open Space: Emery Recreation Department, 4300 San Pablo Ave, 510-596-3782, www.ci.emeryville.ca.us

ALBANY

Just north of Berkeley, Albany is one of the Bay Area's best-kept secrets. Like Emeryville, it's small—just a little over one square mile, with about 17,000 residents. But here, in a city that prides itself on its small town feel, and is in no way a commuter magnet, life is decidedly family-oriented. Local public schools are considered better than average, and parents who live in other cities have been known to stretch the truth a tad in order to have their children attend Albany schools. The crime rate is among the lowest in the region, and Albany is located only 30 to 50 minutes from downtown San Francisco. Housing includes a number of single-family homes as well as apartments from the 1940s and '50s. But people are catching on to Albany's charm, a fact that was reflected in rapidly increasing housing prices in the earlier years of the decade. Increases have since leveled off somewhat, and median home prices are still relatively reasonable compared with San Francisco, at $580,000 in April of 2005, according to the CAR.

The commercial strip of Solano Avenue is shared with Berkeley. Once a railroad thoroughfare, Solano Avenue offers day-to-day services and shopping options, all within walking distance from most parts of Albany. Among the selections are bookstores, boutique clothing stores, restaurants, cafés, a supermarket, and a movie theater. Locals rave about Rivoli Restaurant, 1539 Solano Avenue. Each fall the mile-long stretch of Solano Avenue is closed for the "Solano Avenue Stroll," a weekend festival of food, music and entertainment. The west side of town, where I-80 and I-580 meet, is bounded by the Bay and home to the mudflats, which are popular with bird watchers, walkers, and joggers. An extension of the Bay Trail is underway here, as is work on Eastshore State Park. If you like to play the ponies, or just watch them run, Golden Gate Fields Racetrack, one of the largest thoroughbred tracks in the country, is also here (510-559-7300, www.goldengatefields.com).

ALBANY
Web Site: www.albanyca.org
Area Code: 510

Zip Code: 94706, 94710
Post Office: 1191 Solano Ave, 800-275-8777, www.usps.com
Police: Albany Police Department, 1000 San Pablo Ave, 510-525-7300
Library: Albany Library, 1247 Marin Ave, 510-526-3720
Public Schools: Albany Unified School District, 904 Talbot Ave, 510-558-3750, www.albany.k12.ca.us
Community Resources: Albany Chamber of Commerce, 1108 Solano Ave, 510-525-1771, www.albanychamber.org; Solano Avenue Association, 1563 Solano Ave, #101, 510-527-5358, www.solano avenueassn.org
Parks, Gardens, and Open Space: Albany Recreation and Community Services Department, 1249 Marin Ave, 510-524-9283, www. albanyca.org

PIEDMONT

Surrounded by Oakland, but a city in itself, Piedmont is one of the wealthiest communities in the East Bay—and indeed the Bay Area. Incorporated in 1907, only 1.8 square miles in size, and with a population hovering around 11,000, Piedmont is a tiny enclave of large estates, mansions, tennis courts, immaculate wooded parks, and civility. This city is also known for its excellent school district. Don't go looking for an apartment here; you won't find one. As a matter of fact, rental property of any type is virtually nonexistent here. If the name Piedmont rings a bell, it may be because the local high school has for years been the host of a national bird-calling contest, the winners of which are invited to appear on "The Tonight Show."

PIEDMONT
Web Site: www.ci.piedmont.ca.us
Area Code: 510
Zip Codes: 94611, 94610, 94618, 94602, 94620
Post Office: (nearest one) 195 41st St, Oakland, 800-275-8777, www.usps.com
Police: Piedmont Police Department, 401 Highland Ave, 510-420-3000
Public Schools: Piedmont Unified School District, 760 Magnolia Ave, 510-594-2600, www.piedmont.k12.ca.us
Community Resources: City Hall, 120 Vista Ave, 510-420-3040; Piedmont Adult School 510-594-2655, piedmontadultschool.org
Parks, Gardens, and Open Space: Piedmont Recreation Department, 358 Hillside Ave, 510-420-3070, www.ci.piedmont.ca.us

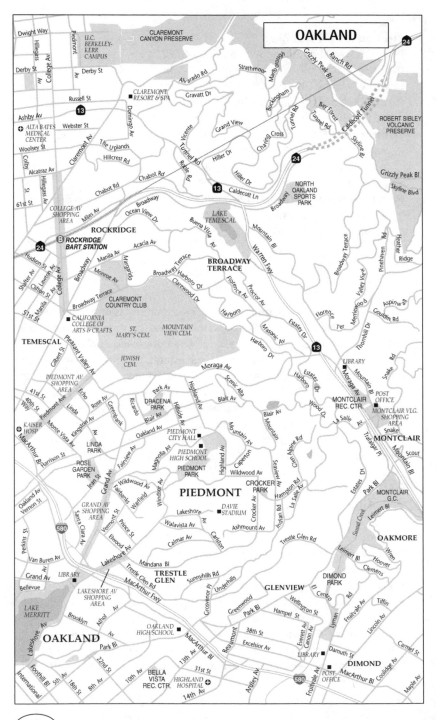

OAKLAND

OAKLAND

DOWNTOWN OAKLAND
LAKE MERRITT
MONTCLAIR
CLAREMONT HILLS
ROCKRIDGE

Across the Bay in Oakland is another Mayor Brown, but he's not related to San Francisco's famous former mayor, Willie Brown. Mayor Jerry Brown, former Governor of California (1975–1983) and three-time presidential candidate, is making waves in Oakland. With people and companies being priced out of San Francisco, many have sought "shelter" in Oakland, and Mayor Brown has welcomed them with open arms and business tax incentives. Housing costs are moderate here too, at least when compared with much of the rest of the Bay Area. As of April 2005, the median home price in Oakland was still averaging about 40% less than that in San Francisco.

For sports fans, living in Oakland means you'll have a number of professional teams to root for. Oakland is home to the NFL's Raiders, Major League Baseball's Oakland Athletics (A's), and the NBA's Golden State Warriors. The A's and the Raiders play at McAfee Coliseum (Oakland–Alameda County Coliseum complex) known locally as simply the Oakland Coliseum, and the Warriors play at the Oakland Arena, off I-880 in southern Oakland.

As Brooklyn is to Manhattan, so Oakland has become to San Francisco. Though many commute to San Francisco for work and nightlife, Oakland, packed with locally owned businesses, championship sports teams, and local color and culture, including old-time movie houses, inspires civic pride and loyalty among its residents. Oakland is a happening place with all the amenities that a city of over 400,000 can offer. Home to a large and established African-American community, Oakland also boasts a growing Asian-American population, and in recent years it has drawn an increasing number of young artists, writers, and musicians. An excellent place to be if you play an instrument, Oakland is known locally as a kind of hipster haven. Its bustling independent music scene includes a network of nightclubs, hometown record labels, radio stations, and above all, rock bands.

In the 1930s, Oakland was a cluster of ranches, farms, and lavish summer estates. A lot has changed since then. Although much of Oakland is green and middle-class, some problems with crime and the presence of impoverished areas have had a tarnishing effect over the years. Under Mayor Brown, Oakland is now moving away from its diminished reputation and is developing nicely. In his inaugural year, Brown launched a program known as the 10K Downtown Housing Initiative—its intended goal to attract 10,000 new residents to downtown Oakland. As part of that plan, 5,000 new housing units have been completed or are in the final stages of construction, and the city has plans to build another 1,000 or so in the near future. Despite these efforts, be aware that core gentrification efforts are not complete, and the downtown area is still peppered with a number of empty storefronts. Until the local and national economy turns completely around, the city may continue to struggle to fill commercial vacancies.

The neighborhoods that make up Oakland are as different as water and oil. Generally speaking, the more upscale neighborhoods are found higher up on the hills, complete with bay views; down the hills and further west are what many would consider the rougher neighborhoods. **Downtown's** Old Oakland, adjacent to the City Center, has a collection of vintage Victorian buildings that were spared from the bulldozer. Known as Preservation Park, this area is a commercial zone, with a lovely fountain in the center. Paramount Theatre, an art deco landmark at 2025 Broadway, is another downtown highlight.

A world-class port, Oakland's waterfront teems with activity, bringing in an estimated $25 billion worth of goods each year, mostly from Asia. Situated next to the boats, Jack London Square is a destination place to dine, shop, and stroll along the waterfront, much like San Francisco's Pier 39, only not as crowded. Here, you can eat sushi and listen to jazz at the popular Yoshi's Jazz and Sushi Club, 510 Embarcadero West. Also located at the pier is Franklin Delano Roosevelt's 165-foot USS Potomac, which was frequented by the late president, close advisors, and congressional leaders for informal strategy sessions. Every Sunday year round, locals gather at the Pier for the farmers' market, which also opens midday on Wednesdays for an extended summer season. From here you can also take the ferry into San Francisco, or just cross the street to the Amtrak station at 245 2nd Street. On Fridays, check out the Old Oakland Farmers' Market, an old-fashioned open-air market filled with fruit, veggies, and seafood, held at the revitalized Swan's Marketplace, on Ninth Street between Broadway and Clay streets, near Chinatown.

If you want the best of both worlds—city life and natural beauty— **Lake Merritt** may be your best option. Just moments from downtown, the three-mile lagoon is a scenic sanctuary amid the sometimes gritty hustle and bustle of urban life. Home to 90 species of birds, including a huge flock of Canada geese, the lake proudly bills itself as the nation's oldest wildlife refuge. During the morning, the shores are packed with joggers and dog walkers, while at night, the picturesque waters are lit up by a string of white lights, making Lake Merritt undoubtedly one of Oakland's most scenic neighborhoods.

Though not the least expensive option in town, Lake Merritt is reasonably priced. Around Lake Merritt are abundant apartments in older brick buildings from the 1920s, two- and three-bedroom homes from the 1940s and '50s, and condos from the 1960s and '70s. In the early 19th century, elite estates were built around the lake. Only one home remains today, the Camron Stanford House, 1418 Lakeside Drive. Lake Merritt residents who work in downtown Oakland enjoy a quick commute, as well as the natural beauty and outdoor recreation amenities of lakeside living. In the summer the lake comes alive with canoes, kayaks, and windsurfing, while fall ushers in breezy moonlight walks and the popular Moon Viewing Festival.

In October 1991, a massive fire struck the Oakland Hills destroying more than 2,500 homes and killing 25 people. Fire investigators believe an arsonist set the fire that raged for days in the hills above the city. Responding fire trucks had a difficult time trying to navigate the narrow, winding, and tree-lined roads. Though it's been well over a decade since the fires, the horrific specter of that disaster still haunts Oakland. Since the tragedy, the city implemented new fire codes and constructed roads wide enough to allow emergency vehicle accessibility to outlying areas. A mural at the Rockridge BART Station commemorates the fire victims. One of the areas hardest hit by the fires was the upscale **Montclair** district, which has been largely rebuilt. The homes immediately surrounding the main shopping area along Mountain Boulevard are wood-framed stuccos with a Mediterranean look. Others are Craftsman-style bungalows, some nearly hidden by trees and having back yards that open up to rambling redwood groves. Other homes perched on the hills are privy to views of the Bay and San Francisco. Montclair also hosts several apartment complexes for would-be renters. Many Montclair residents commute into San Francisco, which, without traffic, is only 15 to 20 minutes; with traffic it's sometimes triple that. Although Montclair is a pricey district for Oakland, purchasing a house here is considerably less costly than buying a hilltop home in San Francisco.

The **Claremont Hills** area, just north of Montclair, also suffered from the fire of 1991. These wooded environs have large dwellings mixed in with a smattering of smaller, sometimes student-occupied homes as well as a few apartments. Access to Interstate 24 makes commuting to San Francisco or the South Bay easier. Nearby Redwood Regional Park provides for miles of secluded serenity amidst the redwoods.

Of all the areas that make up Oakland, many would argue that **Rockridge**, located south of Berkeley, offers the quintessential "neighborhood" feel. Created after the 1906 earthquake destroyed San Francisco, this former hayfield originally was developed as a racially exclusive housing tract. Today, the area known as Lower Rockridge (between Claremont and Broadway) is an ethnically diverse and upscale area. In fact, many consider this to be one of Oakland's hippest neighborhoods. Some students and employees of UC live here, and many young professionals commuting into San Francisco or the South Bay call Rockridge home. BART's central location at College and Shafter makes the commute a breeze. Homes here are typically stucco and wood-shingled Craftsman-style bungalows with small cottage gardens. Residents can stroll along tree-lined streets to the gourmet restaurants and trendy shops clustered around the strip of College Avenue between Alcatraz and Broadway.

Upper Rockridge (above Broadway), built during the post-war housing booms of the 1920s and 1940s, extends into the hills northeast toward Lake Temescal. Many of the homes destroyed in the 1991 fire were replaced by a unique "tract" of million-dollar custom homes. As a result, housing is on the expensive end of Oakland's price scale. Apartments are scarce as the area has zoning restrictions on buildings with more than four units. Finding a rental here is easiest in the early summer when many UC students go home for the break.

Shopping and dining are the main attractions in Rockridge. Its heart is College Avenue, which boasts excellent eateries, fine antique shops, art galleries, and clothing boutiques. Rockridge Market Hall, 5655 College Avenue, touts a European-style shopping experience with specialty grocery shops located under one open-air roof. Restaurants here reflect the ethnic diversity of Oakland and include several Mexican eateries as well as Ethiopian, Italian, Japanese, Chinese, and Irish cuisine. Specialty pizza at Zachary's, 5801 College Avenue, is always standing room only. Meanwhile a mix of coffee shops and comfortable pubs with well-lit pool tables cater to locals as well as UC students that filter down from Berkeley. For those looking for a good book, the Sierra Club bookstore, 6014 College Avenue, Pendragon's new and used books, 5560 College Avenue, and a branch library, 5366 College Avenue, should satisfy most literary tastes.

The public schools for this district are Hillcrest Elementary and Middle School (K–8, enrollment about 275) and Chabot Elementary (K–5, enrollment about 440). Both schools traditionally rank among the top in the Oakland Unified School District.

OAKLAND

Web Sites: www.ci.oakland.ca.us or www.oaklandnet.com, www.rockridge.org

Area Code: 510

Zip Codes: 94601–94627, 94643, 94649, 94659, 94660, 94661, 94662, 94666

Post Office: Oakland Main, 1675 Seventh St, 800-275-8777, www.usps.com

Police: Oakland Police Department, 455 7th St, 510-777-3333
Libraries: Oakland Public Library, Main Branch, 125 14th St, 510-238-3134, www.oaklandlibrary.org; Asian Branch 388 9th St, Suite 190, 510-238-3400; Brookfield Branch, 9255 Edes Ave, 510-615-5725; César E. Chávez Branch, 3301 East 12th St (services in Spanish), 510-535-5620; Dimond Branch, 3565 Fruitvale Ave, 510-482-7844; Eastmont Branch, 7200 Bancroft, Suite 211 (Eastmont Town Center), 510-615-5726; Elmhurst Branch, 1427 88th Ave, 510-615-5727; Golden Gate Branch, 5606 San Pablo Ave, 510-597-5023; Lakeview Branch, 550 El Embarcadero, 510-238-7344; Martin Luther King Branch, 6833 International Blvd, 510-615-5728; Melrose Branch, 4805 Foothill Blvd, 510-535-5623; Montclair Branch, 1687 Mountain Blvd, 510-482-7810; Piedmont Avenue Branch, 160 41st St, 510-597-5011; Rockridge Branch, 5366 College Ave, 510-597-5017; Temescal Branch, 5205 Telegraph Ave, 510-597-5049; West Oakland Branch, 1801 Adeline St, 510-238-7352
Public Schools: Oakland Unified School District, 1025 Second Ave, 510-879-8200, http://webportal.ousd.k12.ca.us
Community Publications: *Oakland Tribune*, 510-208-6300, www.insidebayarea.com/oaklandtribune (also owns the *Alameda Times Star*, the *Fremont Argus* and a handful of smaller local papers); *East Bay Express*, 510-879-3700, www.eastbayexpress.com; *Contra Costa Times* (covers Contra Costa and east Alameda County), 800-598-4637, www.ContraCostaTimes.com (also owns Hills News, which puts out *Berkeley Voice*, *Alameda Journal*, the *Montclarion* and the *Piedmonter*)
Community Resources: Oakland Zoo, 9777 Golf Links Rd, 510-632-9525, www.oaklandzoo.org; McAfee Coliseum (Oakland–Alameda County Coliseum), 7000 Coliseum Way, 510-569-2121; Chabot Observatory and Science Center, 10000 Skyline Blvd, 510-336-7300, www.chabotspace.org; Oakland A's Baseball, 510-638-4900, www.oaklandathletics.com; Golden State Warriors Basketball, 510-986-2222, www.nba.com/warriors; Oakland Raiders Football, 510-864-5000, www.raiders.com; Oakland DMV, 5300 Claremont Avenue, 800-777-0133; Claremont Country Club, 5295 Broadway Terrace, 510-653-6789
Cultural Resources: Alameda County Arts Commission, P.O. Box 29004, Oakland, 94604, 510-208-9646, www.acgov.org/arts; Oakland Museum of California, 1000 Oak St, 510-238-2200, www.museumca.org; Oakland East Bay Symphony, 510-444-0801, www.oebs.org; Oakland Ballet, 510-452-9288, www.oaklandballet.org; Museum of Children's Art, 538 9th St, 510-465-8770, www.mocha.org; Pro Arts, Inc., 461 Ninth St, 510-763-4361,

www.proartsgallery.org; California College of Arts & Crafts, 5212 Broadway, 510-594-3600, www.cca.edu

Parks, Gardens, and Open Space: Oakland Parks and Recreation, 250 Frank Ogawa Plaza, Suite 3330, 510-238-PARK, TTY 510-615-5883, www.ci.oakland.ca.us (Oakland's Community Gardening Coordinator can be reached at 510-238-2197); Lake Temescal Regional Recreation Area, 6500 Broadway, 510-652-1155, www.ebparks.org/parks/temescal.htm

BERKELEY

NORTH BERKELEY
BERKELEY HILLS
SOUTH BERKELEY
CLAREMONT, ELMWOOD
DOWNTOWN/CENTRAL BERKELEY
WEST BERKELEY

Nicknamed the "The People's Republic of Berkeley" and many other more or less affectionate monikers, Berkeley conjures images of student protests, hippies, Birkenstocks, counterculture, and, above all, independent thinking. This was the first city in the nation to replace Columbus Day observances with Indigenous Peoples Day, honoring the Native Americans who lived here before Columbus arrived. The uproar caused when the Reverend Jerry Falwell claimed that the purple Teletubby, Tinky Winky, was homosexual resulted in the Berkeley City Council passing a resolution in support of this diminutive television character. With its colorful residents and liberal leanings, Berkeley beckons the young, the politically active, and those who seek an intellectual existence. Many find it a stimulating and relaxed place to call home. According to the California Association of Realtors, the median home price in Berkeley, well above that in Oakland, is only slightly less than San Francisco's ($720,000 in April 2005).

Berkeley is home to about 104,500 people from all walks of life. The city proudly proclaims that 83% of those who live here call Berkeley an "excellent" or "good" place to live. A bike-friendly, eco-conscious, and art-loving town, Berkeley boasts fantastic parks and open space for outdoor adventurers as well as excellent food from all over the world and myriad cultural offerings. Every year locals celebrate their unique brand of civic pride with the outlandish How Berkeley Can You Be Parade and Festival.

The University of California at Berkeley ("Cal") and Lawrence Livermore laboratory are the city's largest employers. Founded in 1868, Cal spreads out between the downtown area and the Berkeley hills, and has more than 33,000 undergraduate and graduate students in attendance. The reputation of today's students is not as liberal as it was in the 1960s when Mario Savio rallied against the university's policies, sparking the free speech movement, or when Berkeley students protested the Vietnam War. Today, protests revolve around changes in admission requirements, tuition increases, and the negative impacts of state budget cuts. In addition to the many local coffeehouses, Berkeley's milieu of evening entertainment includes more than 30 movie theaters, 50 bookstores, and 400 restaurants—certainly a lot of food for thought.

North Berkeley, considered to be the calmer side of town, is home to many graduate students, professors, and young families. Strollers glide past the American Craftsman-style bungalows, rolling over to the many small parks spread throughout the area.

North on Shattuck Avenue, from Rose until Hearst, you'll find the "Gourmet Ghetto," which is equipped with restaurants and specialty shops. It was 1971 when Alice Waters pioneered serving organic food at her restaurant, Chez Panisse, 1517 Shattuck Avenue. She has since instigated serving organic foods in Berkeley's public schools. Other gourmet delights in this area abound; just take a stroll down Shattuck Avenue for anything from pasta and pizza to *pad thai* and matzo-ball soup. Intimate Walnut Square, between Walnut and Shattuck, is home to the original Peet's Coffee & Tea at 2124 Vine Street. Black Oak Books at 1491 Shattuck Avenue is an established independent that features guest authors several times a week. Additional shopping is available on Hopkins Street (known as "Gourmet Ghetto West").

Following Shattuck south across University Avenue, you hit the heart of downtown. Here, you'll find a mix of shops and restaurants, and a centrally located BART station for easy access to San Francisco. There is also a cluster of movie theaters—both commercial and art house—within a short radius. Homes around the downtown area have the blessing of being both centrally located—within blocks of the action—and reasonably serene. As you move away from the main drag, streets become heavily tree-lined, shrouding stately Victorians and bungalows, roads narrow, speed limits drop, and bike lanes abound.

Up in the **Berkeley Hills**, which run from the North Campus area east to Berkeley's magnificent Tilden Park and then north to Kensington, you'll discover magnificent views and be surrounded by the lovely smell of eucalyptus. To get to the Berkeley Hills take either Euclid Avenue north all the way to Grizzly Peak, coming through Tilden Park at its northernmost entrance, or start at the football stadium and take Centennial Drive up to Grizzly Peak. Along your drive you'll see exquisite Craftsman-style homes, some with striking bay views and fabulous gardens. If you are willing to navigate the hill every day, you may be able to rent a room in one of these homes.

Along Euclid Street, the higher the ascent, the more spectacular the homes. The Berkeley Rose Garden on Euclid Street (between Eunice and Bayview Place) offers great bay views and lovely aromas. For a romantic sunset, the benches at the top of the garden are front row seats. Traveling up the hills via the Centennial route will bring you to the Botanical Gardens in Strawberry Canyon. Considered one of the world's leading gardens in terms of plant variety and quality, the gardens are home to Chinese medicinal herbs and soaring redwoods. Also on the hill is the Lawrence Hall of Science, which sports one of the best views of the city as well as a first-rate public science center with a multitude of hands-on educational programs for children and exhibits that are fun for people of all ages.

Visitors come from all over to enjoy the 2,065 acres of open meadows and forests of Tilden Park, which include 30 miles of hiking and horse trails, an 18-hole public golf course, swimming at Anza Lake, pony rides, a petting farm, carousel, and a steam train. There are no shopping options atop the hill, so you'll need to take care of all your errands before heading up.

Located directly south of the campus and west of the Berkeley Hills, **South Berkeley's** population is composed predominantly of students, many of whom live in dormitories, cooperatives, and fraternity or sorority houses. This is the rowdy area of Berkeley, with activity at all times of the day and night. Some of the most architecturally interesting homes are the large mansions that house the college fraternities and sororities. The Sigma Phi house on Durant and Piedmont is a classic Arts and Crafts style home, designed by the Greene brothers in 1909. Julia Morgan designed the outdoor Greek Theatre, and Bernard Maybeck, architect of San Francisco's Palace of Fine Arts, also made his mark on many Berkeley homes.

Much of the 1960s free speech movement and the anti-Vietnam War protests centered around Telegraph Avenue and Sproul Plaza. The plaza still hosts student protests, and when there is little to yell about, musicians, politicians, prophets, and students take center stage. Telegraph Avenue, which begins in downtown Oakland, runs into the southern side of the Cal campus. The Berkeley section of Telegraph is a bustling shopping zone catering to students with clothing, book, and music stores; coffee shops; cheap eats; and cafés. Street vendors set up daily, selling handmade jewelry and tie-dyed clothes. Locals have a choice of four well-known independent bookstores on the 2400 block: Cody's, Moe's, Shakespeare & Co., and Shambhala. Every Christmas season the Telegraph Avenue Street Fair hosts an arts and crafts show. UC Berkeley has two concert sites: the outdoor Greek Theater and the indoor Zellerbach Hall, which features national and international performers. Another popular annual event is the ArtCar Fest, a motorcade showcasing some of the most creative, unique, and bizarre vehicles you'll ever see. The fest kicks off in Berkeley with a drive across the Bay Bridge to San Francisco.

The hustle and bustle of university life quiets down once you head south, away from the campus. Close to College Avenue, the **Claremont** neighborhood, bordering Oakland (east of the Elmwood District and west of the Claremont Resort), is one of Berkeley's grandest and most expensive neighborhoods. The area is named for the huge, 22-acre resort called the Claremont Resort and Spa, which is so large it can be seen from across the bay. Designed by Charles Dickey, the Claremont has tennis courts and a large outdoor swimming pool. Some of the elegant homes that make up Claremont have bay views. Two small shopping areas serve the neighborhood: the Uplands Street area and Domingo Avenue, where you'll find Berkeley's famous Peet's Coffee, across from the Claremont Resort.

The **Elmwood District**, just down the street and west from the Claremont, is a pleasant area of two- and three-story, brown-shingle homes surrounded by tall trees. Housing here is pricey, and to supplement income, many families find tenants for their backyard cottages, basements, or attic rooms.

Downtown Berkeley's civic heart is the Martin Luther King Jr. Civic Center Park, 2151 Martin Luther King Jr. Way, a stretch of green at the foot of city hall. Berkeley's main post office and library are in the 2000 block of Allston way. Though not as chic as Fourth Street or College Avenue (see below), Shattuck Avenue offers a variety of shopping, from furniture, to clothing, to tiny boutiques, to toy stores and movie theaters. For fresh fruits and vegetables, the farmers' market is a local favorite. Held twice a week on Martin Luther King Jr. Way, the market attracts people from all over seeking produce straight from the farmers. On Saturdays, the market is at Center Street and Martin Luther King (10 a.m. to 3 p.m.; on Tuesdays head for Derby Street and Martin Luther King Jr. Way, from 2 p.m. to 6 p.m.; on Thursdays, there is an all organic market at Shattuck Avenue and Rose Street, open 3 p.m. to 7 p.m. (see www.ecologycenter.org/bfm for more information).

Downtown is home to Berkeley's theater scene, with the Berkeley Repertory Theatre, 2025 Addison Street, being most familiar. Though not in downtown proper, Zellerbach Auditorium on the UC campus also sponsors live performances, from the Kirov Ballet to John Cleese. Also in downtown, and noteworthy because it is a Bay Area rarity, you'll find Iceland, 2727 Milvia Street, a true ice rink.

Downtown's central hub for mass transit includes BART (Shattuck and Center) and AC Transit. Just down the street from the BART Station, people line up early in the morning to carpool into the city; three persons in a car constitute a carpool, plus you do not have to pay the $3 bridge toll.

Also known as the "Flatlands," **West Berkeley** is considered a transitional area with affordable fixer-upper bungalows, new lofts, and relatively inexpensive rents. This area is neither as safe nor as aesthetically pleasing as other parts of Berkeley; however, proximity to the waterfront and to the Fourth Street shopping district is an asset. South of University Avenue, along the numbered streets, you'll find a cluster of commercial warehouses and unique arts and crafts studio-shops. Nearby San Pablo Avenue not only is a major route through town, but has become a popular neighborhood gathering spot with a small stretch that's home to a smattering of restaurants, cafés, and independent boutiques. Berkeley initiatives to enhance this area are well underway including the addition of new bike routes, a revamping of the West Berkeley train station and transit plaza, and improvements to the waterfront area. The Berkeley Marina is a mecca for water sports, including sailing, kayaking, and windsurfing. On the Berkeley pier, fishing is the main pastime. Both California Adventures and the California Sailing Club offer sailing and windsurfing lessons. Also on the waterfront is Adventure Playground, a popular outdoor area for children.

Vibrant Fourth Street, which includes an inviting outdoor shopping mall, is perhaps Berkeley's most upscale shopping district, chock-full of popular restaurants, home and garden shops, boutiques, and outlet stores. Locals rave about brunch at Bette's Ocean View Diner, 1807A Fourth Street (expect a two-hour wait on Sundays). Newcomers often head to the Crate & Barrel outlet at 1785 Fourth Street to stock up on home necessities; Restoration Hardware and Cody's bookstore also grace this block.

BERKELEY

Web Sites: www.ci.berkeley.ca.us

Area Codes: 510, 341

Zip Codes: 94701, 94702, 94703, 94704, 94705, 94707, 94708, 94709

Main Post Office: 2000 Allston Way, Berkeley, 800-275-8777, www.usps.com

Police: Berkeley Police Department, 2100 Martin Luther King Jr. Way, 510-981-5900, TTY: 510-981-5799

Libraries: Berkeley Public Library, Central Branch, 2090 Kittredge Street, Berkeley, 510-981-6100; Claremont Branch, 2940 Benvenue Avenue, 510-981-6280; South Branch, 1901 Russell Street, 510-981-6260; North Branch, 1170 The Alameda, 510-981-6250; West Branch, 1125 University Avenue, 510-981-6270, www.berkeleypubliclibrary.org

Public Schools: Berkeley Unified School District, 2134 Martin Luther King Jr. Way, Berkeley, 510-644-6348, www.berkeley.k12.ca.us; college: www.berkeley.edu

Community Publications: East Bay Express, 510-879-3700, www.east-bayexpress.com; *Contra Costa Times* (covers Contra Costa and east Alameda County) 800-598-4637, www.ContraCostaTimes.com (also owns Hills News, which puts out *Berkeley Voice, Alameda Journal,* the *Montclarion,* and the *Piedmonter*); *Berkeley Daily Planet,* 510-841-5600, www.berkeleydailyplanet.com; UC.Berkeley Publications: *Daily Californian,* www.dailycal.org; *North Gate News On-line* http://journalism.berkeley.edu/ngno/

Community Resources: Berkeley Chamber of Commerce, 1834 University Ave, 510-549-7000, www.berkeleychamber.com; Tool Lending Library, 1901 Russell St, 510-981-6101; Iceland, 2727 Milvia St, 510-647-1620, www.berkeleyiceland.com; Berkeley First Source employment program, 510-981-7550; Berkeley Art Center, 1275 Walnut St, 510-644-6893, www.berkeleyartcenter.org

Cultural Resources: University of California, Berkeley Art Museum, 2626 Bancroft Way, 510-642-0808, www.bampfa.berkeley.edu; Pacific Film Archive Theater, 2575 Bancroft Way, 510-642-1124, www.bampfa.berkeley.edu; Lawrence Hall of Science, Centennial Drive below Grizzly Peak, 510-642-5132, www.lhs.berkeley.edu; Judah L. Magnes Memorial Museum, 2911 Russell St, 510-549-6950, www.magnes.org; La Pena Cultural Center, 3105 Shattuck Ave, 510-849-2568, www.lapena.org; Ames Gallery of American Folk Art, 2661 Cedar St, 510-845-4949, www.amesgallery.com; Black Repertory Group, 3201 Adeline St, 510-652-2120; Julia Morgan Center for the Arts, 2640 College Ave, 510-845-8542; Berkeley Repertory Theatre, 510-647-2949, www.berkeleyrep.org

Parks and Open Space: Berkeley Parks Recreation and Waterfront Department, 2180 Milvia St, Third Floor, 510-981-6700, TTY 510-981-6903, www.ci.berkeley.ca.us (Berkeley Community Gardening Collaborative can be reached at 510-883-9096, www.ecology center.org/bcgc); Marina Experience Program/Shorebird Park and Nature Center and Adventure Playground, 160 University Ave, 510-981-6720; call the parks and recreation department for information about local climbing parks

CONTRA COSTA COUNTY

Contra Costa County, with just over one million people, is on the eastern side of the East Bay Hills, out where the weather is warm, warmer, and warmest. The population is diverse, with all economic levels represented. Housing options are also varied, ranging from old farmhouses and massive, gated apartment complexes to duplexes, condominiums, and sprawling, newly landscaped housing developments. Many apartment complexes offer swimming pools and recreation centers. Housing costs are slightly lower than most Bay Area counties, but are increasing at a similar rate (according to the California Association of Realtors, median home prices in April 2005 were $517,000, an over 21% increase from the previous year).

CONTRA COSTA COUNTY

Web Site: www.co.contra-costa.ca.us

Area Codes: 510, 925

Sheriff: 651 Pine St, 7th Floor, Martinez, 925-646-2441

Libraries: Contra Costa County Library, Pleasant Hill/Central Branch, 1750 Oak Park Blvd, 925-646-6434, http://cclib.org, branches throughout the county

Emergency Hospitals: Contra Costa Health Services: Contra Costa Regional Medical Center, 20 Allen St, Martinez (operates community health centers in Antioch, Bay Point, Brentwood, Pittsburg, Richmond and Concord), 800-495-8885 or 877-905-4545, www.cchealth.org; John Muir Medical Center, 1601 Ygnacio Valley Rd, Walnut Creek, 925-939-3000, www.jmmdhs.com; Mt. Diablo Medical Center, 2540 East St, Concord, 925-682-8200, www.jmmdhs.com; San Ramon Regional Medical Center, 6001 Norris Canyon Rd, 925-275-9200

Public Schools: West Contra Costa Unified School District, 1108 Bissell Ave, Richmond, 94801, 510-234-3825, www.wccusd.k12.ca.us; Contra Costa Office of Education, 77 Santa Barbara Rd, Pleasant Hill, 925-942-3388, www.cccoe.k12.ca.us

Community Publications: *Oakland Tribune*, 510-208-6300, www.insidebayarea.com/oaklandtribune (also owns the *Alameda Times-Star* and the *Fremont Argus*); *East Bay Express*, 510-879-3700, www.eastbayexpress.com; *Contra Costa Times* (covers Contra Costa and east Alameda County) 800-598-4637, www.ContraCosta Times.com

Community/County Resources: Richmond Art Center, Civic Center Plaza, 2540 Barrett Ave, 510-620-6772, www.therichmondart center.org; Richmond Museum of History, 400 Nevin Ave, 510-235-7387; Alvarado Adobe House and Blume House (the San Pablo Historical Society), 510-215-3046; John Muir National Historic Site, 4202 Alhambra Ave, Martinez, 925-228-8860, www.nps.gov/jomu; Blake Garden, 70 Rincon Rd, Kensington, 510-524-2449; Martinez Marina, 925-313-0942; Contra Costa HIV/AIDS Program Resource Line, 925-313-6770; Recreation Services, City Hall, 525 Henrietta St, Martinez, 925-372-3510; Concord Police Community Action and Awareness Line, 925-671-3237

Public Transportation: AC (*Alameda-Contra Costa*) *Transit*, 510-891-4700, TTY 800-448-9790, www.actransit.org; *BART*, 510-465-2278, TTY 510-839-2278, www.bart.gov; *Benicia Transit*, 707-745-0815,

County Connection, 925-676-7500; *RIDES*, 511, www.rides.511.org; *Tri-Delta Transit*, 925-754-4040, *WestCat*, 510-724-7993; *Amtrak*, 800-872-7245

Parks, Gardens, and Open Space: East Bay Regional Park District, 2950 Peralta Oaks Court, P.O. Box 5381, Oakland, 94605, 510-562-PARK, www.ebparks.org, maintains 62 parks throughout the region, many with large open areas, nature trails and shorelines

MARTINEZ, WALNUT CREEK, CONCORD

The City of **Martinez**, www.cityofmartinez.org, is the site of naturalist John Muir's historic home, a well-maintained hillside Victorian mansion that is open to the public. With a population of nearly 37,000, Martinez boasts average home prices a little under the county median.

Walnut Creek, www.ci.walnut-creek.ca.us, is home to more than 66,000 people. With its fine arts programs, including the Dean Lesher Regional Center for the Arts and Bedford Gallery, 1601 Civic Dr, 925-295-1400, its open space projects, public gardens, equestrian center, and the Boundary Oak Golf Course, 3800 Valley Vista Rd, 925-934-4775, it is considered by many to be one of the most desirable cities in Contra Costa County. Commensurate with its desirability, housing prices run higher, averaging $656,000 in April 2005, up almost 28% from the previous year, according to the CAR.

Concord, www.ci.concord.ca.us, has the most people, with a population of about 125,000. Houses along the corridor of Highway 680 are going up rapidly because it is possible to live here and drive to Silicon Valley in under an hour. Although housing prices are increasing more rapidly than in most other areas, median home prices, according to the CAR, were still on the low end for the Bay Area, averaging $495,000 in April 2005. Concord is also home to an upper-division and graduate campus of Cal State East Bay.

June through September finds the homes on the east side of Highway 24's Caldecott Tunnel basking in heat. Opened in 1937, the Tunnel connects Oakland to Orinda. During the summer it's not unusual to find temperatures 60° in San Francisco and over 100° in Concord, Martinez, or Walnut Creek.

MARTINEZ
Web Site: www.cityofmartinez.org
Area Code: 925
Zip Code: 94553
Post Office: 4100 Alhambra Ave

Library: Martinez Library, 740 Court St, 925-646-2898
Public Schools: Martinez Unified School District, 921 Susana St, 925-313-0480, www.martinez.k12.ca.us, and Mt. Diablo Unified School District, 1936 Carlotta Dr, 925-682-8000, www.mdusd.k12.ca.us
Parks, Gardens, and Open Space: Parks, Recreation and Community Services, 525 Henrietta St, 925-372-3510

WALNUT CREEK
Web Site: www.ci.walnut-creek.ca.us
Area Code: 925
Zip Code: 94596
Post Office: 2070 N Broadway
Library: Walnut Creek, 1644 N. Broadway, 925-646-6773, www.wc library.org
Public Schools: Walnut Creek School District, 960 Ygnacio Valley Rd, 925-944-6850, www.wcsd.k12.ca.us, and Mt. Diablo Unified School District, 1936 Carlotta Dr, 925-682-8000, www.mdusd.k12.ca.us
Parks, Gardens, and Open Space: Arts, Recreation and Community Services Division, 1666 North Main St, 925-943-5858

CONCORD
Web Site: www.ci.concord.ca.us
Area Code: 925
Zip Code: 94519, 94520
Post Office: 2121 Meridian Park Blvd
Library: Concord Library, 2900 Salvio St, 925-646-5455
Public Schools: Mt. Diablo Unified School District, 1936 Carlotta Dr, 925-682-8000, www.mdusd.k12.ca.us
Parks, Gardens, and Open Space: Parks Department, 1950 Parkside Dr, 925-671-3329

RICHMOND

POINT RICHMOND

Richmond, the northernmost city in Contra Costa County, was established as a shipyard town with the onset of World War II. Many ships destined for the Pacific front left port from Richmond. Today, many Richmond residents are descended from individuals who arrived here for work in the mid-1930s and '40s. Richmond has since fallen upon hard times, suffering from lack of employment. Richmond has gotten a bit of a bad reputation over the years, as the city has been plagued by economic depression and high crime rates. However, Richmond is slowly improving, though enhancing safety remains a preeminent concern in the community. BART quickly connects the area with nearby Oakland and Berkeley, as well as San Francisco. The city is largely African-American with a growing Latino population. Compared with the rest of the East Bay, rents and property here are much cheaper. Indeed, the April 2005 median home price of $405,000 is the county's lowest, but still represents over a 30% increase from the previous year, according to the CAR.

One lovely enclave in Richmond is **Point Richmond**, which is invitingly situated close to the bay. Here, you'll find a bayside artist/sailing community with a quaint, old-fashioned downtown with cafés and restaurants, as well as a flower shop and grocery store. The community atmosphere is cozy, with neighbors looking out for one another, and shopkeepers remembering customers' names. The Richmond Yacht Club, 351 Brickyard Cove, is a popular socializing spot. Many of the homes near the yacht club have their own private docks. Public swimming is normally available in the Richmond Plunge, the Bay Area's largest heated indoor pool at 1 East Richmond Avenue. The Plunge was closed for extensive seismic upgrades, with completion slated for 2007 or 2008; meanwhile its programs have relocated to the Swim Center (see details below).

RICHMOND
Web Site: www.ci.richmond.ca.us
Area Code: 510
Zip Codes: 94801–8, 94820, 94850, 94875, 94530
Post Offices: 104 Washington Ave; 1025 Nevin Ave; 2100 Chanslor Ave; 200 Broadway, 800-275-8777, www.usps.com
Police: Richmond Police Department, 401 27th St, 510-620-6648
Library: Richmond Main Library, 325 Civic Center Plaza, 510-620-6561
Public Schools: West Contra Costa Unified School District, 1108 Bissell Ave, 510-234-3825, www.wccusd.k12.ca.us
Community Resources: Point Richmond Online, www.point richmond.com; Richmond Yacht Club, 351 Brickyard Cove, 510-237-2821; Richmond Plunge, 1 East Richmond Ave, 510-620-6820, Swim Center, Richmond Swim Center at 45th St and Cutting Blvd, 510-620-6654; Masquers Playhouse, 105 Park Place, 510-232-4031
Parks, Gardens, and Open Space: Richmond Recreation and Parks, 3230 Macdonald Ave, 510-620-6788; East Bay Regional Park District, 2950 Peralta Oaks Court, P.O. Box 5381, Oakland, 94605, 510-562-PARK

SAN RAMON

Located about 25 miles east of Oakland, in the heart of the San Ramon Valley, is the City of **San Ramon**. Here, what started out as a small, sleepy, well-to-do bedroom community is now a burgeoning city in its own right, with a bustling commercial center at its core and exploding job growth. Though historically known as San Ramon for more than 100 years, the city did not officially incorporate until 1983, making it a relatively new municipality. Since then, economic growth has driven a rapid population expansion along with accompanying construction, a trend that city officials expect to continue. In 2002, voters approved plans to build a dense core of new homes in the northwest part of town, with the caveat that the new area must include open space and parks.

Despite the hustle and bustle, San Ramon (population just over 51,000) retains its small town suburban charm. With its semi-secluded location, safe streets, and friendly neighborhood parks, this affluent community is the quintessential family town. More than 60% of households here are home to married couples, many with children. Spacious two-, three-, and four-bedroom single-family homes, built in the 1980s or later, dot the quiet residential roads. Many boast the well-manicured front lawns, sunny backyards, and modern amenities characteristic of newer suburban houses.

People who come to San Ramon tend to stay. Along with having one of the county's highest median incomes, San Ramon also boasts relatively high home prices, averaging $766,000 in April 2005, an increase of about 21% over the previous year, according to the CAR. Nonetheless, the city's housing office reports that San Ramon's rate of home ownership is almost 70%. Nestled in an area of natural beauty, San Ramon is only moments away from the hiking trails of Mount Diablo, the area's highest peak at 3,849 feet. Peppered with unique rock formations and wildflowers, Mount Diablo draws crowds from all over the Bay Area most weekends for hiking, camping, and horseback riding. From the peak on a clear day, you can see 35 of California's 58 counties.

A network of creeks dots San Ramon's landscape, which, while giving a bucolic feel, can create flooding problems during heavy rains, especially for those who live close to San Ramon, San Catanio, or South San Ramon creek. Those looking to buy a home in these areas should consult FEMA's flood maps, www.fema.gov, and consider purchasing flood insurance.

As part of the Tri-Valley area, known for wealthy enclaves, lush golf courses, and local wineries, San Ramon shares services and amenities with a larger family of cities including Pleasanton, Livermore, and Danville. Every March, the nearby City of Dublin hosts the Bay Area's largest St. Patrick's Day celebration.

San Ramon's central commercial area, a 580-acre office park known as Bishop Ranch, is host to roughly 200 regional and corporate headquarters, including Pacific Bell, Chevron-Texaco, AT&T, Toyota, Bank of America, and United Parcel Service. Roughly 70,000 people work in San Ramon, and city officials predict another 16,000 jobs will be added to the area over the next 15 years.

Like its Tri-Valley neighbors, San Ramon connects to the urban cores of Oakland, San Francisco, and San Jose via two major highways, I-680 and I-580—which become severely congested during commute hours. San Ramon actively promotes the use of alternative transit and has in place several innovative programs, many of which run in partnership with local employers, the county, or neighboring cities. Incentives include $60 gas vouchers for starting a new carpool or adding a new rider, free parking and lockers at the local transit center, and the Carpool to School program, www.pooltoschool.org. In fact, San Ramon was awarded the EPA's 2004 Bay Area's Best Workplaces for Commuters Award for its commitment to reducing traffic and air pollution.

For this former village, which once boasted "San Ramon Population 100," the challenge in coming years will be to balance its historically suburban character with continuing growth.

SAN RAMON
Web Site: www.ci.san-ramon.ca.us
Area Code: 925
Zip Code: 94582, 94583,
Post Office: 12935 Alcosta Blvd, 800-275-8777, www.usps.com
Police: 2220 Camino Ramon, 925-973-2700
Library: San Ramon Library, 100 Montgomery St, 925-973-2850
Public Schools: San Ramon Valley Unified, 699 Old Orchard Dr, Danville, CA 94526, 925-552-5500, www.srvusd.k12.ca.us
Community Resources: San Ramon Olympic Pool and Aquatic Park, 9900 Broadmoor Dr, 925-973-3240; Senior Center, 9300 Alcosta Blvd, 925-973-3250; San Ramon Royal Vista Golf Course and San Ramon Golf Club, 9430 Fircrest Lane, 925-828-6100, www.sanramongolfclub.com; The Bridges Golf Club, 9000 South Gale Ridge Rd, 925-735-4253, www.thebridgesgolf.com; Child Day Schools and Hidden Canyon School, 18868 Bollinger Canyon Rd, 925-820-2515; San Ramon Historical Foundation, http://sanramonhistoricfoundation.org/
Community Publications: *Tri-Valley Herald*, 510-208-6300, www.insidebayarea.com/trivalleyherald; *San Ramon Observer*, www.sanramonobserver.org

Public Transportation: *County Connection*, 925-676-7500, www.cccta.org; *AC (Alameda-Contra Costa) Transit*, 510-891-4700, TTY 800-448-9790, www.actransit.org; *BART*, 510-465-2278, TTY 510-839-2278, www.bart.gov; *Amtrak*, 800-USA-RAIL, TTY 800-523-6590, www.amtrak.com, *ACE (Altamont Commuter Express)*, 800-411-RAIL, www.acerail.com

Parks, Gardens, and Open Space: San Ramon Parks and Recreation and Community Center, 925-973-3200, www.ci.san-ramon.ca.us; San Ramon Community Center and Central Park, 12501 Alcosta Blvd, 925-973-3200

ADDITIONAL CITY WEB SITES—CONTRA COSTA COUNTY

Antioch: www.ci.antioch.ca.us
Danville: www.ci.danville.ca.us
El Cerrito: www.el-cerrito.ca.us
Lafayette: www.ci.lafayette.ca.us
Livermore: www.ci.livermore.ca.us
Orinda: www.ci.orinda.ca.us
Pinole: www.ci.pinole.ca.us
Pittsburg: www.ci.pittsburg.ca.us
Pleasanton: www.ci.pleasanton.ca.us
San Leandro: www.ci.san-leandro.ca.us

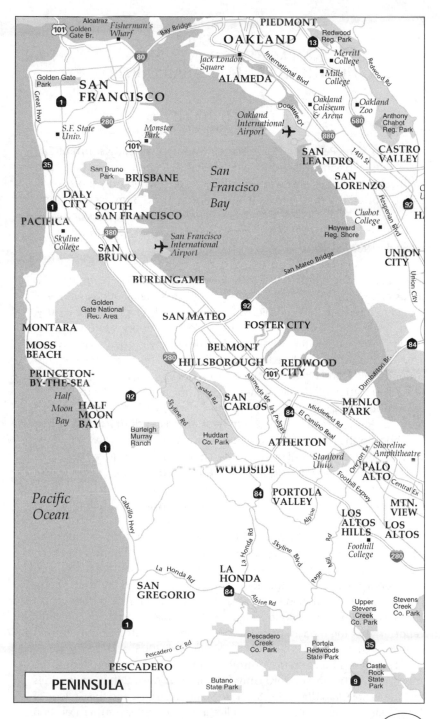

PENINSULA

THE PENINSULA
(SAN MATEO COUNTY AND
NORTHERN SANTA CLARA COUNTY)

SAN MATEO COUNTY

Known as "The Peninsula," San Mateo County is directly south of San Francisco, with Santa Clara County a little farther south and east. It's hard to imagine what this area was like 100 years ago when only a few small towns dotted the road between San Francisco and San Jose. Belmont, Hillsborough, Woodside, Atherton, and Palo Alto were not cities or towns, but rather garden spots with estates where wealthy San Franciscans relaxed in tranquil surroundings and glorious weather.

Today San Mateo County, which became independent of San Francisco in 1856, consists of 21 cities, many of which are booming with industry and commerce. The eastern half of San Mateo County, with easy access to Interstate 280 and Highway 101, is heavily populated and busy. Fortunately, the folks who live here have plenty of options to escape civilization since roughly the western half of the county is open space, where wooded mountains are laced with superb hiking and biking trails, campgrounds, lakes, and beaches.

Filled with single-family homes, green front lawns, and the usual array of outdoor shopping malls, San Mateo County, with its cozy suburban feel, has long attracted a more family-oriented set than its busy urban neighbor to the north. The most populous city of the county, Daly City, borders San Francisco and marks the beginning of the suburbs. Here at the northernmost edge, longtime San Francisco bedroom communities including San Bruno and South San Francisco are beginning to attract more young professionals and younger families with the development of new, more moderately priced condos and townhouses.

A little further to the south, in the mid-county, which includes San Mateo (the city), Burlingame, and Belmont, the price of homes has been edging up, nudging past the middle-class price mark. Neatly tucked between San Francisco to the north and Silicon Valley to the south, commuter traffic here flows in both directions and can be rough during rush hours, sometimes grinding to a halt. The California Association of Realtors reported that the median price for a home in San Mateo County moved from $620,000 in April 2004 to $750,000 in April 2005, a 21% increase.

The Peninsula contains a number of universities and colleges, the most famous being Stanford University in Palo Alto. Other universities include Santa Clara University, San Jose State University, and the College of Notre Dame in Belmont. And, if you live in the center or northern portion of the Peninsula, you will not be far from San Francisco State University.

San Francisco International Airport (SFO) is located on the bayside of the Peninsula, in the South San Francisco/Millbrae/San Bruno area. The airport is a madhouse practically everyday, but especially on holidays, and is notorious for living under a perpetual cloud of fog, causing frequent flight delays. The Peninsula is also served by the CalTrain commuter service and a number of bus lines including SamTrans (the San Mateo County bus service), which runs into San Francisco. But by far the most exciting development in recent years here has been the expansion of BART service. Rather than terminating in Daly City, the trains have added stops further south—Colma, San Bruno, South San Francisco, Millbrae, and most exciting, SFO. The new stops offer an excellent park-and-ride option for commuters headed to San Francisco or the East Bay, though so far ridership in these areas has been a little slow to take off. BART is also working with local buses and CalTrain, which has remodeled several peninsula stations and begun "baby bullet" express service between San Francisco and San Jose, to create better transit links.

People living in the East Bay commute to San Mateo County and Silicon Valley via the San Mateo–Hayward Bridge or the Dumbarton Bridge (to Fremont). During the past decade, as more and more people have moved east in search of more affordable homes, traffic has increased considerably. The San Mateo–Hayward Bridge was recently widened in hopes of alleviating some of the strain, but traffic along Highway 92 (the route that crosses the bridge) still frequently moves at a slow crawl during peak times. From the late afternoon into the evening, cars are frequently backed up from the ocean to the Bay (and sometimes vice versa, with coastsiders heading home from work), past jammed intersections with both of the area's major freeways—101 and 280—all along the bridge itself, and continuing well into the bottlenecks of the East Bay.

To the west, you'll find the ocean-side edge of San Mateo County. This area is trimmed with Highway 1, one of the most beautiful roadways in the world, tracing the Pacific coastline from the beach city of Pacifica to the pumpkins of Half Moon Bay to the boardwalk of Santa Cruz. Be on the lookout for gray whales. The coastline is often blanketed with fog, giving the beaches a chilly, romantic feeling.

SAN MATEO COUNTY
Web Site: www.co.sanmateo.ca.us
Area Code: 650
Sheriff: San Mateo County Sheriff's Office, 400 County Center, Redwood City, 650-599-1664
Emergency Hospitals: San Mateo Medical Center, 222 West 39th Ave, San Mateo, 650-573-2222; Sequoia Hospital, 170 Alameda de las

Pulgas, Redwood City, 650-369-5811, www.sequoiahospital.org; Seton Medical Center, 1900 Sullivan Ave, Daly City, 650-992-4000, www.setonmedicalcenter.org; Stanford Medical Center, 300 Pasteur Dr, Stanford, 650-723-4000, www.stanfordhospital.com

Library: Peninsula Library System, 25 Tower Rd, San Mateo, 650-780-7018, www.plsinfo.org

Public Schools: San Mateo County Office of Education, 101 Twin Dolphin Dr, Redwood City, 650-802-5300, www.smcoe.k12.ca.us

Community Publication: *San Mateo County Times,* 650-348-4321, www.insidebayarea.com/sanmateocountytimes

Community Resources: San Mateo County Convention and Visitors Bureau, 111 Anza Blvd, Suite 410, Burlingame, 650-348-7600; ARTshare, 1219 Ralston Ave, Twin Pines Art Center, Belmont, 650-591-2101, www.artshare.org; TIES (information, advice and resources for seniors and disabled), 800-675-8437 or 650-573-3900, TTY: 800-994-6166

Public Transportation: *RIDES,* 511, www.511.org; *CalTrain,* 800-660-4287, TTY: 415-508-6448, www.caltrain.com; *SamTrans,* 800-660-4287, TTY: 650-508-6448, www.samtrans.com.

Parks, Gardens, and Open Space: San Mateo County Park and Recreation Department, 455 County Center, 4th Floor, Redwood City, 650-363-4020, www.eparks.net

DALY CITY

Calling itself the "The Gateway to the Peninsula," Daly City is directly south of San Francisco, just off of Interstate 280. Immediately after the 1906 Earthquake and fire, many San Franciscans sought refuge in the open countryside of Daly City. Today, this 7.5-square-mile city is the most populous community in the county, with over 104,000 residents.

In the Bay Area, Daly City is even more notorious for its fog than its big city neighbor to the north. It's frequently cool and gray here even when the sun is shining down on all of San Francisco. But for those who don't mind sweater weather, Daly City, which offers family-oriented living just minutes from San Francisco, may be the perfect place to call home.

Part of what gives Daly City its unique character is the fact that it is home to a large, established, and vibrant Filipino-American community. According to the most recent US Census, Filipino-Americans make up more than 30% of the city's total population. In fact, Filipino families who live here have nicknamed Daly City "Little Manila." Asian specialty markets are scattered throughout the city, and there is no place better in the Bay Area to grab pancit noodles and a tasty lumpia roll.

Daly City has its own BART station, located at 500 John Daly Boulevard, providing easy access to downtown San Francisco. For those driving to the station, BART provides 1,400 parking spaces; even so, these spaces fill up quickly, so arrive early or look for parking on a nearby street. San Francisco Airport is less than ten minutes away, which is a plus if you need to fly, though many locals complain about the noise. If you are commuting to Silicon Valley, it could take you anywhere from 40 minutes to 2 hours, depending on traffic.

Henry Doelger, designer of much of the bland housing that is found in parts of San Francisco's Sunset District, continued in his blah though practical style in Daly City—a one-car garage at the base that supports the common rooms, which overlook the street and are finished off with two bedrooms, one bath, and a (now) huge tree in the front yard. These "cliffs of Doelger" inspired Malvina Reynolds to write a song about Daly City homes, calling them "...the little boxes made of ticky tacky..." Indeed, though many of the homes here are painted different colors, they are very similar.

Daly City is considered one of the most affordable cities of San Mateo County. Apartments, duplexes, townhouses, condominiums, and single-family homes can be found throughout, and many of the homes on the hill have bay and ocean views. Though still relatively affordable when compared with San Francisco, property prices in Daly City increased 15% between April 2004 and April 2005, with the median price up to $650,000, according to the California Association of Realtors.

For those who can afford it, the posh, tree-lined neighborhood of **Westlake**, bordering San Francisco, has its own shopping plaza undergoing massive renovations, and is within minutes of Lake Merced. To get a feel for the neighborhood and learn all about local lore, stop in at Joe's of Westlake on the corner of John Daly Boulevard and Lake Merced Boulevard. To the west, you'll find single-family and newer luxury homes perched atop steep cliffs overlooking the pounding waves of the Pacific below. In recent years, some hillside spots have had trouble with erosion, and even landslides, so you may want to ask for a geological assessment before settling here.

In addition to the ticky tacky homes, Daly City also has one of the area's major shopping malls, the Serramonte Shopping Center. Home Depot, Nordstrom Rack and a second Target (in case the first at Serramonte is missing that sweater you want in your size) are south on I-280 at the Metro Shopping Center in the neighboring city of Colma. Also just off the freeway, you'll find a large multiplex cinema packed every Friday and Saturday night, as well as two popular fast food pit stops—In-N-Out Burger and Krispy Kreme Doughnuts. New plans in the works include efforts to revitalize Mission Street, which connects to San Francisco, with a new community center, and a new, but controversial, medium-density mixed-use commercial/housing development.

Locals enjoy easy access to three golf courses, including Lake Merced Country Club, which also features tennis courts. Although there is much coastline, there is little coastal access here, and so determined dog walkers have been known to frequent the path down to the city's only beach, Thornton, even though the path remains officially closed from severe storm damage due to safety concerns. The renovated Thornton Beach Vista recently reopened (west end of John Daly Boulevard, off of Skyline Boulevard [Highway 35]), so you can at least enjoy looking down at the beach once again from above.

DALY CITY
Web Site: www.ci.daly-city.ca.us
Area Codes: 415, 650
Zip Codes: 94014, 94015
Post Office: 1100 Sullivan Ave, 800-275-8777, www.usps.com
Police Station: Daly City Police Department, 333 90th St, 650-991-8119
Emergency Hospital: Seton Hospital, 1900 Sullivan Ave, 650-992-4000, www.setonmedicalcenter.org
Library: Serramonte Main Library, 40 Wembley Dr, 650-991-8023, www.dalycitylibrary.org
Public Schools: Jefferson Elementary School District, 101 Lincoln Ave, 650-746-2400, www.jsd.k12.ca.us; Jefferson Union High School District, 699 Serramonte Blvd, #100, 650-550-7900, www.juhsd.k12.ca.us
Community Resources: Daly City-Colma Chamber of Commerce, 355 Gellert Blvd, Suite 138, 650-755-3900, www.dalycity-colmachamber.org; Doelger Senior Center, 101 Lake Merced Blvd, 650-991-8012, www.doelgercenter.com
Parks, Gardens, and Open Space: Parks and Recreation Department, 111 Lake Merced Blvd, 650-991-8001, www.ci.daly-city.ca.us/city_services/depts/park_rec/parks.htm

PACIFICA

Pacifica (population 38,678), is no longer a small beach town without sidewalks. The word is out and people are moving in. Populated by middle- to upper-income families and singles who love living in fog, Pacifica (which means "peace" in Spanish) is just 15 miles south of San Francisco, and only 5 miles from the San Francisco Airport. Don't look for the town center, because it doesn't exist. What you will find instead, is a string of shopping enclaves. Near the water's edge, Rockaway Beach Plaza, the Pacific Manor area, and Pedro Point, with their mix of cozy waterside cafés, seafood restaurants, pubs, antique stores, and of course surfboard shops, are alive with a quaint, quintessential beach town spirit. Others, like the Linda Mar Shopping Center east of Highway 1, have a more outdoor strip mall feel, while offering such basic necessities as a large grocery store.

People move to Pacifica for one main reason, to be close to the ocean. And you can find lovely apartments and homes, many of them overlooking the Pacific. Architecturally, the homes are mostly California ranch style, but you'll also see Queen Anne Victorians and Cape Cods, a few beach shacks, and a handful of new two-story luxury homes. Boxy 1970s style two-story apartment buildings, scattered throughout the town, attract crowds of young professionals who commute via Highway 1 and Interstate 280 to San Francisco every morning. While not much to look at on the outside, many of these apartments have small balconies perfect for kicking back with a good book (and a very warm sweater) and taking in the breathtaking foggy ocean vistas. For roughly the rent of a studio in San Francisco's Tenderloin, you can get a spacious one-bedroom with excellent views, parking, and quick and easy freeway access. Pacifica is quiet, cool, foggy, and friendly. Its traditional working class roots have kept prices relatively affordable, but people are catching on to its charm. From April 2004 to April 2005, property prices in Pacifica increased nearly 24%, reaching a median of $711,500, according to the California Association of Realtors.

Pacifica offers an abundance of outdoor activities, including surfing, scuba diving, fishing, paragliding, hiking, birding, golf, tennis, and horseback riding. Surfers from all over ride the waves at Pedro Point and Rockaway Beach, and on warm days crowds cast their fishing lines off of Pacifica Pier. Most of the sandy shores here are not nearly as crowded as those in nearby Half Moon Bay; the same goes for the local parks and golf courses, except at the end of September when the city hosts thousands of visitors at the annual Pacific Coast Fog Fest. Activities include music, food, and artists' booths.

PACIFICA

Web Site: www.ci.pacifica.ca.us
Area Code: 650
Zip Code: 94044
Post Office: 50 West Manor Dr, 800-275-8777, www.usps.com
Police Station: 2075 Coast Highway, 650-738-7314
Libraries: Pacifica Library, 104 Hilton Way, Pacifica, 650-355-5196; Sanchez Library, 1111 Terra Nova, 650-359-3397, www.pacifica library.org

Public Schools: Pacifica School District, 375 Reina Del Mar, 650-738-6600, www.pacificasd.org; Jefferson Union High School District, 699 Serramonte Blvd, #100, Daly City, 650-550-7900, www.juhsd.k12.ca.us

Community Resources: Pacifica Resource Center, 1809 Palmetto Ave, 650-738-7470; Pacifica Performances, 1220A Linda Mar Blvd, 650-355 1882, www.pacificaperformances.org; Pedro Point Surf Club, http://pedropoint.typepad.com

Community Publications: *Pacifica Tribune,* 650-359-6666, www.pacificatribune.com

Beaches, Parks, Gardens, and Open Space: Parks, Beaches and Recreation Department, 650-738-7381, www.ci.pacifica.ca.us/CITYHALL/dept.html

HALF MOON BAY

A beachfront community about 25 miles south of San Francisco, Half Moon Bay (12,688) spans some of the most beautiful coastline in California. The smell of salt air permeates this coastal town. A little over a decade ago, the farming of flowers and specialty vegetables was one of the main occupations here. And even today you can still find excellent fresh fruits and veggies for sale at a handful of regular roadside stands. More recently the area has become a bedroom community for San Francisco and Silicon Valley, with housing prices to match. Higher even than San Francisco's average, Half Moon Bay's median home prices reached $840,000 in April 2005, according to the CAR. The good news, though, is that figure represents a tiny 1.8% increase over the 2004 figures.

During October, locals enjoy the annual Great Pumpkin Contest, where gourd growers from around the country bring their pumpkins and weigh-off against global competitors, hoping to enter the record books (a recent winner tipped the scales at 1229 pounds). The historic downtown area is a hodgepodge of antique shops, clothing boutiques, arts and crafts shops, tiny restaurants and cafés, and cozy bed-and-breakfasts. During the summer, the monthly flower mart is colorful and fragrant. Recreation opportunities include two golf courses, along with plenty of access to beaches for surfing, horseback riding, hiking, and biking. Tres Amigos, 200 North Cabrillo Highway, is a local favorite for inexpensive yet delicious Mexican food. Fundraising is currently underway to build a new, much larger main library to replace the current facility.

Nearby, you'll find a handful of smaller, semirural coastside towns including El Granada, Montara, Moss Beach, and a tiny fishing village known affectionately as Princeton-by-the-Sea. Home to Pillar Point Harbor, this little hot spot attracts surfers, sailors, and fishermen year round. Residents and visitors alike routinely venture down to the docks here to buy fresh fish and crab straight from the boats. Just off Pillar Point you'll find the world-famous Mavericks surf spot, which hosts an annual big wave contest that attracts pros from around the world. A little farther south on Highway 1 is Año Nuevo State Reserve, home to thousands of elephant seals.

Half Moon Bay is a delightful and tranquil community, which feels worlds away from the hectic pace of San Francisco or Silicon Valley. Commuting to San Francisco via Highway 1 may be delayed, especially during winter, because of mudslides around the so-called "Devil's Slide." Those commuting west on Route 92 marvel at the change of weather, especially in the summer, when it can be downright hot and sticky inland, but once they reach the ridge near Half Moon Bay, the fog brings instant cooling relief.

HALF MOON BAY
Web Site: www.half-moon-bay.ca.us
Area Code: 650
Zip Codes: 94018, 94019, 94038
Post Office: 500 Stone Pine Rd, 800-275-8777, www.usps.com
Police Station: 537 Kelly Ave, 650-726-8288
Library: Half Moon Bay Library, 620 Correas St, 650-726-2316, www.half moonbaylibrary.org
Public Schools: Cabrillo Unified School District, 498 Kelly Ave, 650-712-7100, www.cabrillo.k12.ca.us
Community Resources: The Coastsider, http://coastsider.com; Coastside Children's Programs, 494 Miramontes Ave, 650-726-7413, www.coastsidechildren.org; Coastside Opportunity Center, 99 Ave Alhambra, El Granada, 650-726-9071
Community Publications: Half Moon Bay Review, 650-726-4424, www.hmbreview.com
Beaches, Parks, Gardens, and Open Space: Parks and Recreation Department, 535 Kelly Ave, 650-726-8297

SAN BRUNO, SOUTH SAN FRANCISCO, BRISBANE

Nestled amid the rolling hills to the south of San Bruno Mountain, both San Bruno and its onetime heavy industry neighbor **South San Francisco** (www.ci.ssf.ca.us) used to be filled with dark plumes of smoke, the sound of crunching metal, and the roar of airplanes from nearby SFO flying low overhead. In fact, both areas were considered sort of ugly stepchildren of San Mateo County. But today, much of that—except for the airplane noise, which remains anathema for those on the east side of town—seems to be changing. These days, South San Francisco, home of research giant Genentech, while still displaying its large white mountainside "South San Francisco, the industrial city," sign, is also becoming the biotech city. With a population of almost 62,000, South San Francisco does indeed sit on the northern edge of the airport; however, its median home prices have still increased almost 25% in the last year, reaching $710,250 in April 2005, according to the CAR.

Meanwhile next door, the city of **San Bruno** (population 42,215) is in the midst of a home-building frenzy—adding hundreds of new condos, apartments, townhouses, and luxury homes each year. Twelve miles south of San Francisco, San Bruno, with a sleek new BART station, efforts afoot to renovate the sleepy downtown, a major mall makeover in progress, and plans to add more than 1,000 new housing units in the near future, is attracting crowds of young professionals. Lured by the potential to own their own condos—often a near impossibility for all but the incredibly wealthy in San Francisco—20- and 30-something singles and young families are arriving here in droves. Median home prices here, according to the CAR, were $620,000 in April 2005, just over a 10% increase from the previous year.

San Bruno the city originally took its name from San Bruno the mountain. While exploring the area in 1775, Captain Bruno Heceta spotted a large mountain, which he named in honor of his patron saint, the founder of the Carthusian order of monks, San Bruno. In the 1820s, the land was part of a large grant given by the Mexican government to Jose Antonio Sanchez for his military service. After the USA won the war with Mexico in 1848, Sanchez's heirs lost their claim to the land. But their legacy lived on when in 1899 the Tanforan racetrack, named for Sanchez's grandson-in-law, a cowboy called Toribio Tanforan, opened. Though it burned down in 1964, the site of the old Tanforan Racetrack still holds many fond memories—the first west coast flight took off from here. But the site holds many disturbing memories as well. During World War II, the track was converted into an internment center for Japanese Americans, many of whom lost their homes, jobs, and businesses when they were forcibly relocated.

Today Tanforan is the site of a large indoor shopping center undergoing a multimillion-dollar makeover, in the heart of the city's rapidly transforming commercial/retail core. Nearby along El Camino Real, you'll find the 24-acre outdoor shopping plaza, San Bruno Towne Center; the new BART station; and Bayhill Drive, home to a bustling 80-acre office park that includes the Gap's corporate headquarters.

Here too, you'll find the Crossing, a 20-acre former US Navy Administration site on its way to becoming a lively high-density, transit-oriented village. Three hundred new apartments were recently completed here, with another 185 on the way. The site will also include 200-plus condos as well as new senior housing, and at least 20% percent of all units will be designated as affordable housing.

The building boom here is contagious, and new apartments and condos are springing up all across town. San Bruno is looking at adding as many as 1,400 new housing units in the coming decade. Forging ahead, the city also recently approved a $10 million master plan to revitalize a 700-plus acre redevelopment zone, including the former navy land, Tanforan, downtown, and the eastside residential areas by 2009.

East San Bruno is made up of two- and three-bedroom single-family homes from the 1950s and '60s clustered on narrow side streets off of San Bruno Avenue, one of the city's older commercial thoroughfares, and gateway to a twisting ribbon of freeway overpasses—Highways 101 and 380 (which heading west connects to I-280). The area east of 101 is dominated by the airport and businesses—long-term parking lots, rental car agencies, and hotels—that cater to it. If you don't mind the sound of jets roaring above while you sip your morning coffee, you can find some of the peninsula's most affordable single-family homes here.

To the west, you'll find woody, winding roads and more expensive homes, some with sweeping views of the Bay below. Skyline Boulevard (Highway 35) offers access to trails at Milagra and Sweeney Ridges, and links up with Highway 1 to carry you to nearby Pacifica's beaches in minutes. A good resource for continuing education, Skyline Community College is also here, and nearby 115 new upscale, two-story homes are nearing completion.

Downtown San Bruno, with its 1950s time warp feel, is clustered along a short stretch of San Mateo Avenue. Filled with small local eateries and retailers, and the peninsula's only casino-style card room, Artichoke Joe's, "the Avenue" has struggled to keep pace with newer shopping centers on nearby El Camino Real. But the city hasn't given up hope, and has been looking at ways to revive the languishing strip. City Park in the center of town is a local highlight, as are the light displays on the Fourth of July, when the city celebrates its designation as one of only two places on the peninsula where fireworks remain legal (the other is Pacifica).

A true natural gem, San Bruno Mountain (outside San Bruno's official city limits), is one of the largest urban open spaces in the USA, with 3,300 undeveloped acres. Home to the rare Mission Blue butterfly, the mountain is covered with hundreds of wildflowers in the spring. Curve around Guadalupe Canyon Road to the north side of the mountain and you'll find the small, tight-knit community of **Brisbane** (www.ci.brisbane.ca.us). With its old-fashioned downtown area, small-town vibe, and hillside homes, Brisbane is a well-kept secret—and residents want it to stay that way. But as plans inch ahead to redevelop the Baylands, an expansive former dump site alongside Highway 101, the future of the entire northern edge of San Mateo County seems destined to continue growing and changing.

SAN BRUNO
Web Site: www.sanbruno.ca.gov
Police: 1177 Huntington Ave, 650-616-7100
Area Code: 650
Zip Code: 94066
Post Office: 1300 Huntington Ave, 800-275-8777, www.usps.com
Library: 701 Angus Ave West, 650-616-7078, www.ci.sanbruno.ca.us/ Library
Public Schools: San Bruno Park School District, 500 Acacia Ave, 650-624-3100; San Mateo Union High School District, 650 North Delaware St, 650-558-2299, www.smuhsd.k12.ca.us
Community Resources: Recreation Services Department, 567 El Camino Real, 650-616-7180, San Bruno Mountain Watch, 44 Visitacion Ave, Brisbane, 415-467-6631, www.mountainwatch. org; San Bruno Senior Center, 1555 Crystal Springs Rd, 650-616-7150; Skyline Community College, 3300 College Dr, 650-738-4100, http://skylinecollege.net
Parks, Gardens, and Open Space: Parks Department, 567 El Camino Real, 650-616-7195; San Bruno Mountain Park, 555 Guadalupe Canyon Pkwy

SAN MATEO, BELMONT, BURLINGAME

San Mateo, the city (94,212), has a varied population living in a variety of homes from traditional ranch styles to English Mediterranean styles, with some condominiums, modest starter homes, and huge mansions mixed in. Once the banking capital of the Peninsula, San Mateo is now a bedroom community for Silicon Valley. According to the CAR, housing costs here are rising steadily, with the median price of a home at $748,750, up almost 18% from April 2004 to April 2005. A mini renaissance is afoot here in the once-languishing downtown, where a wave of new excellent restaurants along with a new centrally located movie theater and revamped transit center has brought new life to the area. You can browse the shops and get to know the neighbors here while sipping glasses of vino at the annual wine walk. In the heart of downtown, Central Park, with its rolling grass, busy playground, rose garden, popular Japanese tea garden, and free outdoor summer concerts, draws visitors from throughout the Peninsula.

Right now, you can play the ponies at the 83-acre Bay Meadows Racetrack, but probably not for long. The city is in talks with developers to build a massive new high-density community with 1.25 million square feet of office space, 1,250 multi-family residential units, 150,000 square feet of retail space, and 15 acres of public parks and open space that would transform the town east of the railroad tracks. A recent development on the site of the old racing practice track, at the intersection of Hillsdale Boulevard and Highway 101, brought new condos, a large corporate campus for mutual fund magnate Franklin-Templeton, a new Whole Foods Market, and a temporary home for the main library, which is being rebuilt at its old 3rd Avenue site. The city is feeling some growing pains as it looks to plan for the future, meet growing housing needs, and improve public transportation—yet maintain the single-family homes, greenery and suburban charm that have been its hallmarks through the years.

In **Belmont** (population 24,470), median home prices increased over 22% in the last year, reaching $907,500 in April 2005, according to the CAR, placing it among the first in line behind the county's wealthiest enclaves: Hillsborough, Woodside, Atherton, and Burlingame. On the west side of town, most of the homes are nestled in the lush rolling hillside and it's not at all unusual to find deer trolling through your backyard in the evening. The entrance to Crystal Springs Reservoir and the San Francisco Watershed area, with winding waterside trails popular with bicyclists and joggers throughout the peninsula, is just a few moments away off Highway 92 Just west of I-280.

Belmont is primarily a residential community, with shopping largely concentrated in a few short blocks along El Camino Real, the peninsula's main commercial thoroughfare. Residents frequently head a bit south to the cluster of upscale eateries and boutiques on Laurel Street in neighboring San Carlos. Belmont's name comes from nineteenth century banker William Ralston, who built an 80-room mansion, which he called Belmont. Today, Ralston Avenue, named in his honor, remains the main local thoroughfare here.

Homes in **Burlingame** are a bit more upscale, with higher prices to match. According to the CAR, median home prices in April 2005 were $1,250,000. For those who can afford it, this city, known for its small-town feel, elm-lined avenues, and top-notch schools, is extremely popular among young professionals planning to start families. The streets here are cozy and quiet, neighborhood parks are filled with dog walkers, and the downtown sidewalks are bustling throughout the day with moms (and a few dads) pushing strollers. Filled with dozens of restaurants and upscale shops, Burlingame Avenue, the heart of this community, has a vibe similar in some ways to University Avenue in Palo Alto. Following Burlingame east across the train tracks, past the historic train station, you'll find Washington Park—a patch of green popular with stroller mommies, dog walkers, and joggers. Also in Burlingame is the Pez Museum, 214 California Drive, 650-

347-2301, featuring hundreds of Pez dispensers. For those in the know, Edward Huss from Austria invented the Pez to help people quit smoking. To the north is Broadway, which, while it lives in the shadow of the more glamorous Burlingame Avenue, offers friendly, low-key local shopping and dining. In all three cities, you'll find young and old families, good schools, and tree-lined streets, a symbol of the Peninsula.

SAN MATEO
Web Site: www.cityofsanmateo.org
Area Code: 650
Zip Codes: 94401, 94402
Post Office: 1630 South Delaware St, 800-275-8777, www.usps.com
Police Station: 2000 South Delaware St, 650-522-7710 or 650-522-7700
Library: San Mateo Public Library, 55 West Third Ave, 650-522-7800 (At the time of this writing, the main library had temporarily relocated to 1100 Park Place, 4th Floor, during reconstruction. The new library is slated to open in the summer of 2006); Hillsdale Branch, 205 West Hillsdale Blvd, 650-522-7880; Marina Branch, 1530 Susan Court, 650-522-7890, www.smplibrary.org
Public Schools: San Mateo-Foster City School District, 51 West 41st Ave, 650-312-7777,www.smfc.k12.ca.us; San Mateo Union High School District, 650 North Delaware St, 650-558-2299, www.smuhsd.k12.ca.us
Community Resources: San Mateo United Homeowners' Association, 223 South Humboldt St; Poplar Creek Golf Course, 1700 Coyote Point Dr, 650-522-4653, www.poplarcreekgolf.com; Coyote Point Recreation Area, Coyote Point Dr, 650-573-2592; Coyote Point Museum, 1651 Coyote Point Dr, 650-342-7755, www.coyotept museum.org
Parks, Gardens, and Open Space: Parks and Recreation Department, 330 West 20th Ave, 650-522-7400, www.cityofsanmateo.org/dept/parks/

BURLINGAME
Web Site: www.burlingame.org
Area Code: 650
Zip Code: 94010
Post Office: 220 Park Rd, 800-275-8777, www.usps.com
Police Station: 1111 Trousdale Dr, 650-777-4100
Library: Burlingame Library, 480 Primrose Rd, 650-558-7444
Public Schools: San Mateo Union High School District, 650 North Delaware St, 650-558-2299, www.smuhsd.k12.ca.us; Burlingame

School District, 1825 Trousdale Dr, 650-259-3800, www.burlingame schools.com

Community Resources: Burlingame Chamber of Commerce, 650-344-1735, http://burlingamechamber.org; Burlingame Historical Society, 650-340-9960 www.burlingamehistorical.org

Parks, Gardens, and Open Space: Parks and Recreation Department, 850 Burlingame Ave, 650-558-7300, www.burlingame.org/p_r

BELMONT
Web Site: www.ci.belmont.ca.us
Area Code: 650
Zip Code: 94002
Post Office: 640 Masonic Way, 800-275-8777, www.usps.com
Police Station: Belmont Police Department, 1215 Ralston Ave, 650-595-7400
Library: Belmont Library, 1110 Alameda de las Pulgas, 650-591-8286 (temporarily closed for remodeling, slated to reopen in spring 2006)
Public Schools: Belmont-Redwood Shores School District, 2960 Hallmark Dr, 650-637-4800, www.belmont.k12.ca.us; San Mateo Union High School District, 650 North Delaware St, 650-558-2299, www.smuhsd.k12.ca.us
Community Resources: 1870 Art Center, 1870 Ralston Ave, 650-595-9679, www.1870artcenter.org; Belmont Community Players, 650-599-2720, www.belmontcommunityplayers.org; Belmont Historical Society, 650-593-4213; Notre Dame de Namur University, 1500 Ralston Ave, 650-508-3500, www.ndnu.edu
Parks, Gardens, and Open Space: Parks and Recreation Department, 30 Twin Pines Lane, 650-595-7441

HILLSBOROUGH, ATHERTON, WOODSIDE

The Peninsula also has a handful of more upscale, exclusive, and secluded towns: Hillsborough, Atherton, Woodside, and parts of Menlo Park. If you're looking for rental property, the latter is certainly your best bet. The other three communities are heavily mansioned, with homes priced in the millions. Except for a police department and a town hall, **Hillsborough** does not have much in terms of an infrastructure and is considered to be a bedroom community. Most who live here do their shopping in Burlingame, at the upscale boutiques and chains on Burlingame Avenue.

If you dream of calling **Atherton** home, you'll need especially deep pockets. Currently home to the likes of investment mogul Charles Schwab, eBay CEO Meg Whitman, and Google pioneer Eric Schmidt, Atherton was ranked the second most expensive city in the country by a recent US Census report. In May 2005, Lawrence J. Ellison of Oracle Systems, voted by *Forbes Magazine* as one of the 10 richest people in America, put his 7-bedroom, 8,000-square-foot Japanese-inspired home here on the market for $25 million.

Full of lovely old estates that were once used by wealthy San Franciscans as summer residences, Atherton is a little like the West Coast's version of the Hamptons—minus the beach. Most of Atherton's homes are hard to see from the town's handful of quiet, dark residential streets, having been set back on their large lots behind thickets of foliage and large off-putting entrance gates. The wealthy enclave is almost strictly residential, with no retail or commercial businesses here of any kind. Residents typically stroll over to nearby Menlo Park or head a little further south to Palo Alto to meet their shopping needs. In Atherton you will also find the elite Menlo School, a prep school for grades 6–12.

Woodside, named for its wooded hillsides, has a true country feel with its steep, narrow roads, natural streams, fields of wildflowers, and towering redwoods. At its heart is a small town center that still looks a little like a trading post from California's Wild West days, complete with an old-fashioned general store. You'll frequently even see horses tied up out in front of Roberts Market, whose selection of fine delicacies belies its rugged exterior. The bulletin board out front is a kind of community clearinghouse, where you'll find everything from landscaping services, to thoroughbreds for sale, to ads looking for experienced live-in nannies. Many of Woodside's estates have substantial acreage and stables are common here, although given these homes' multimillion-dollar price tags, more CEOs than cowboys live here today. Woodside was ranked the sixth most expensive city in the country in a recent report by the US Census. Rich in natural beauty, the town's crowning glory is the 973-acre Huddart Park on King's Mountain Road, with its wandering wooded trails and wide open grassy meadows. A little off the beaten track, Woodside is served by sharply curving Highway 84, which connects the town with busier suburban life in Redwood City to the northeast, and with Highway 101 and I-280. Heading southwest, Highway 84 will carry you through the redwoods to the Pacific Ocean.

HILLSBOROUGH
Web Site: www.hillsborough.net
Area Code: 650
Zip Code: 94010
Post Office: 220 Park Rd, Burlingame, 800-275-8777, www.usps.com
Police Station: Police Department, 1600 Floribunda Ave, 650-375-7470

Libraries: Burlingame Library, 480 Primrose Rd, 650-558-7444; San Mateo Library, 55 West 3rd Ave, 650-522-7800 (At the time of this writing, the main library had temporarily relocated to 1100 Park Place, 4th Floor, during reconstruction. The new library is slated to open in the summer of 2006.)

Public Schools: Hillsborough City School District, 300 El Cerrito Ave, 650-342-5193, www.hcsd.k12.ca.us; San Mateo Union High School District, 650 North Delaware St, 650-558-2299, www.smuhsd.k12.ca.us

Community Resources: *Town Newsletter*, www.hillsborough.net/depts/boards/citizens/town_newsletter.asp; also see **Burlingame** above

Parks, Gardens, and Open Space: Public Works and Parks Department, Municipal Service Center, 1320 La Honda Rd, 650-375-7444, http://www.hillsborough.net/depts/pw/parks.asp

ATHERTON
Web Site: www.ci.atherton.ca.us
Area Code: 650
Zip Code: 94027
Post Office: 3875 Bohannon Dr, Menlo Park, 800-275-8777, www.usps.com
Police Station: Atherton Police Department, 83 Ashfield Rd, 650-688-6500
Library: Atherton Public Library, 2 Dinkelspiel Station Lane, 650-328-2422
Public Schools: Menlo Park City School District, 181 Encinal Ave, Atherton, 650-321-7140, www.mpcsd.k12.ca.us; Sequoia Union High School District, 480 James Ave, Redwood City, 650-369-1411, www.seq.org
Community Resources: *The Almanac*, 650-854-2626, www.AlmanacNews.com; Holbrook-Palmer Park and Carriage House, 150 Watkins Ave, 650-752-0534
Parks, Gardens, and Open Space: Public Works, 93 Station Lane, 650-752-0535; Holbrook-Palmer Park, 150 Watkins Ave, 650-752-0534

WOODSIDE
Web Site: www.woodsidetown.org
Area Code: 650
Zip Code: 94062
Post Office: 1100 Broadway St, Redwood City, 800-275-8777, www.usps.com

Sheriff: San Mateo County Sheriff's Office, 400 County Center, Redwood City, 650-599-1664

Library: Woodside Library, 3140 Woodside Rd, Woodside, 650-851-0147, www.woodsidelibrary.org

Public Schools: Woodside Elementary School District, 3195 Woodside Rd, 650-851-1571; Sequoia Union High School District, 480 James Ave, Redwood City, 650-369-1411,www.seq.org

Community Resources: *The Almanac,* 650-854-2626, www.AlmanacNews.com; Kings Mountain Art Fair (held annually on Labor Day weekend), 650-851-2710, www.kingsmountainartfair.org; Filoli Center and Gardens, 650-364-8300, www.filoli.org; Horse Park, 650-851-2140, www.horsepark.org; The Woodside Store and history museum, 650-851-7615

Parks, Gardens, and Open Space: Huddart Park, 1100 King's Mountain Rd, 650-851-1210; Wunderlich Park, Woodside Rd, 650-851-1210

MENLO PARK

SHARON HEIGHTS

Halfway between San Francisco and San Jose, **Menlo Park**, boasting a population just over 30,000, is like old town USA where you think Kevin Arnold from "The Wonder Years" just may be cruising the street on his bicycle. A quaint, all-American city, Menlo Park's downtown Santa Cruz Avenue is lined with restaurants, coffee shops, retail stores, and ice cream shops. The quiet, tree-lined streets, public swimming pools, and tennis courts mark the 19 square miles of Menlo Park as the quintessential suburb. That's not to say nothing is going on here. Menlo Park is known for having a high number of venture capitalist companies, many of which are located along Sand Hill Road. Other noteworthy ventures include Stanford's Linear Accelerator (SLAC), which literally smashes atoms in its Menlo Park laboratory; Sun Microsystems, the largest high-tech company in the area; and the headquarters of *Sunset Magazine*.

Menlo Park received its official name in 1854 when two Irishmen, Dennis J. Oliver and D.C. McGlynn, purchased about 640 acres and built an estate, including two houses with a common entrance. On a gate, they printed the name "Menlo Park," with the date, August 1854, under it. In 1863, when the railroad came through, a railroad official looked at the gate and decided to name the station Menlo Park. The rest is history. During World War I, Menlo Park changed almost overnight from an unpopulated agricultural community into a bustling military camp housing 43,000 soldiers who trained at nearby Camp Fremont. During World War II, Menlo Park's Dibble General Hospital was built to treat thousands of soldiers injured in the South Pacific. For more about the history of Menlo Park contact the Menlo Park Historical Association and Archives, located on the lower level of the library, at 650-330-2522.

Architecturally, you'll find a range of housing options, from 1950s-style apartments to Eichler homes to ranch style homes. You can also find a number of newer apartments. The neighborhoods west of Highway 101 are more desirable. **Sharon Heights**, near the golf course, is Menlo Park's upscale neighborhood and features mountain views. With Stanford University right next door, Menlo Park is home to a number of Stanford faculty, employees, and some students. Residents also include blue- and white-collar workers, some here for generations, others recently arrived. Across San Francisquito Creek and past the stately 1,000-year-old redwood called "El Palo Alto" is the northernmost reach of Santa Clara County, and the beginning of the much-fabled Silicon Valley. Housing prices in Menlo Park are somewhat higher than you'll find in San Francisco, but here you do tend to get more house for your money. According to the California Association of Realtors, median home prices here were $900,000 in April 2005, a 25% increase over the previous year.

The city blocks off Santa Cruz Avenue during its annual Fine Arts Festival and its Fourth of July Parade. Both events are downright fun, attracting people from all over the area. Locals rave about Draeger's Bistro, 1010 University Drive, for its brunch and delicatessen. Draeger's Supermarket, at the same location, is also legendary, offering only the best, from saffron to fresh brie to vine-ripe tomatoes.

Parking is easy in Menlo Park, especially since most of the homes have garages. With Interstate 280 on the west side of the city and Highway 101 near the waterfront, access to San Francisco and Silicon Valley is quick. The East Bay is accessible via the Dumbarton Bridge; CalTrain and SamTrans buses represent mass transit options.

MENLO PARK
Web Site: www.ci.menlo-park.ca.us
Area Code: 650
Zip Code: 94025
Post Office: 3875 Bohannon Dr, 800-275-8777, www.usps.com
Police Station: 701 Laurel St, 650-330-6300
Library: 800 Alma St, 650-330-2500, www.menloparklibrary.org
Public Schools: Menlo Park City School District, 181 Encinal Ave, Atherton, 650-321-7140, www.mpcsd.k12.ca.us; Sequoia Union High School District, 480 James Ave, Redwood City, 650-369-1411, www.seq.org

Community Resources: Menlo Park Chamber of Commerce, 650-325-2818 www.menloparkchamber.com; *The Almanac*, 650-854-2626, www.AlmanacNews.com; Horse Park, 650-851-2140, www.horse park.org

Parks, Gardens, and Open Space: Community Services Department, 701 Laurel St, 650-330-2200

REDWOOD CITY

Once a woody, rural, hillside community full of country cottages, open pasture, and of course redwoods, **Redwood City** today is a modern day suburbia popular with young families. The curving, tree-lined streets are filled with post–World War II Baby Boom era cozy two- and three-bedroom single-family homes with green lawns and reasonably good-sized back-yards. You'll frequently find kids on bikes or skateboards cruising down the quiet residential streets here, or playing ball at one of a handful of eclectic mini parks that zigzag through the town.

Heading west into the area known as Emerald Hills, you'll find sprawling homes with spectacular views surpassing the million-dollar mark, and a few older charming country houses with stables and sizable acreage. A semi-secret swimming spot popular with kids, Emerald Lake is open in the summertime to neighborhood residents. Up in the western hills, you'll also find hiking trails and spectacular wildflowers at Edgewood Park, and Cañada College, located just off of I-280, an excellent community resource.

Downtown Redwood City is undergoing major revitalization—and the once languishing Broadway is now packed with restaurants and busy side-walk cafes. The old Fox Theatre keeps the historic vibe alive with a variety of theater and music programs. And a large new cinema complex is under construction. The seat of San Mateo County government is here—in a central compound that includes the courthouse, law library and county jail—and you can frequently catch D.A.'s, defense attorneys, and judges alike lunching at Bob's Courthouse Coffee Shop during the noontime hour. On the edge of the downtown area, you'll find the public library, located in a renovated historic firehouse, and Sequoia High School. Originally built as a feeder for Stanford University, this large campus with its pristine lawns, shady trees, and tiled rooftops, is among the most impressive public high school campuses you'll ever see.

On the east side of town, there is a large, vibrant Latino community—and a busy commercial strip—along Middlefield Road. Homes here are a little bit cheaper, but not by much. Heading out further toward the Bay, east of Highway 101, you'll find Redwood Shores, a planned community full of newer tract homes that has a distinct feel all its own. Similar to nearby

Foster City in look and character, Redwood Shores—built on landfill—offers fantastic Bay views, lagoons, and plentiful trails. Software development powerhouse Oracle is also located here.

Redwood City's gateway proudly boasts the old-timey welcome "Climate Best By Government Test," and test or no, it's true that the weather here, as on much of the peninsula, is warm and sunny practically year-round.

REDWOOD CITY
Web Site: www.ci.redwood-city.ca.us
Area Code: 650
Zip Code: 94061–5
Post Office: 855 Jefferson Ave; 1100 Broadway St; 800-275-8777, www.usps.com
Police Station: 1301 Maple, 650-780-7100
Library: 1044 Middlefield Rd, 650-780-7026, www.redwoodcity.org/library
Public Schools: Redwood City School District, 750 Bradford St, 650-423-2200, www.rcsd.k12.ca.us; Sequoia Union High School District, 480 James Ave, Redwood City, 650-369-1411, www.seq.org
Community Resources: Redwood City San Mateo County Chamber of Commerce, 650-364-1722; www.redwoodcitychamber.com; Cañada College, 650-306-3100, www.canadacollege.net
Parks, Gardens, and Open Space: Parks, Recreation, and Community Services Department, 1400 Roosevelt Ave, 650-780-7250

ADDITIONAL CITY WEB SITES—SAN MATEO COUNTY

Foster City, www.fostercity.org
Millbrae, www.ci.millbrae.ca.us
San Carlos, www.cityofsancarlos.org

NORTHERN SANTA CLARA COUNTY

A decade ago, Santa Clara County was one of the fastest growing counties in the Bay Area. Now, it's one of the fastest shrinking areas in the country. Here the feast and famine are all about one thing—jobs, job, jobs. Silicon Valley exploded with rapid growth during the 1990s high-tech boom, when it seemed just about anyone a little computer savvy could land a high-paying job, often with bonus perks and promising stock options, fresh out of college. Today, that's no longer the case. Pressures from a sagging economy, the aftermath of the dot-com crash, combined with out-sourcing high-tech jobs, have made the competition for top-notch positions decidedly more fierce. Couple that with one of the most expensive housing markets in the country, and new arrivals can be in for a real challenge. Nevertheless, living here has its own rewards, and for those highly skilled programmers and engineers who can land one of the remaining premium jobs, Silicon Valley can still feel like a techie paradise.

Both Palo Alto and Mountain View are a part of Santa Clara County. They are also included as part of the amorphous Silicon Valley, a term coined by Don Hoefler, a writer for the weekly *Electronic News*. He used the name in 1971 to describe the electronic firms that were mushrooming out of Santa Clara County. However, the northern end of the county has its own distinct feel in many ways, and has been able to weather the recent economic storms better than some of its southern neighbors. Palo Alto is dominated by Stanford University, while Mountain View has grown into a kind of hybrid—taking on a bit of its northern neighbor's cultural sheen, while joining the industry ranks with Sunnyvale and Santa Clara. Both cities have lovely vibrant downtown areas and the distinct advantage of being not-so-terribly-far from San Francisco as their southern counterparts.

For Santa Clara County resources, see the **South Bay** section.

PALO ALTO

OLD PALO ALTO
CRESCENT PARK
PROFESSORVILLE DISTRICT
COLLEGE TERRACE
FOREST AVENUE
BARRON PARK

While Menlo Park has street fairs, **Palo Alto** has evening balls. Indeed, Palo Alto, named after the 1,000-year-old redwood growing at the border with Menlo Park, sports a refined, cosmopolitan attitude. Located 35 miles south of San Francisco, Palo Alto is a town of cafés, bookstores, theaters, and Stanford Shopping Center, the oldest outdoor mall in the country. The city's star is the elite Stanford University, founded in 1891 by US Senator and railroad magnate Leland Stanford, when the local population was only 400. Living near the university offers distinct advantages, including access to an array of art exhibits, performances, cultural events, and lectures open to the public, not to mention the opportunity to enjoy walks, bike rides and picnics on the lovely, palm-lined grounds of the 8,200-acre campus.

Despite its small size relative to San Francisco and San Jose, Palo Alto boasts more than 30 parks, two community centers, seven libraries, including a children's library, an upscale shopping center, and a first-rate hospital. Along University Avenue, just a short walk from the Stanford campus, the downtown is quaint and busy, filled with cafés, bookstores, boutiques, and a wide variety of restaurants. For more of a hometown atmosphere, locals shop and dine on California Avenue. Three of the parks in Palo Alto are particularly magnificent due the natural settings and preserves within them: Arastradero Preserve, Foothills Park, and Palo Alto Baylands Nature Preserve. Today, over 61,000 folks from every corner of the globe call Palo Alto home. Thousands more commute into Palo Alto, often bringing the morning rush hour to a standstill.

In 1939, Hewlett-Packard began in a one-car garage located at 367 Addison Avenue. This garage is now a historical landmark with a plaque describing it as "the birthplace of Silicon Valley." With its headquarters still in Palo Alto, today Hewlett-Packard has more than 120,000 employees in 178 countries. The 650-acre Stanford Research Park has 150 high-tech and biotech companies, including XeroxParc where GUI (Graphical User Interface), the computer mouse, and *Pong* were developed. Though the high-tech industry has struggled to get back on its feet in recent years, Palo Alto, driven by the economic engine of Stanford University, a growing crop of medical and biotech research companies, and high-tech stalwarts like HP that survived the crash, seems to have fared far better and bounced back faster than the all-tech, all-the-time cities a bit further south in Santa Clara County.

Palo Alto has more than 15 different neighborhoods, each with its own charm. Oregon Expressway divides the city, and generally speaking, the neighborhoods north of the Oregon Expressway are more established, while those south of the Expressway exemplify the expansion that took place in the late 1990s to accommodate Silicon Valley. On the north side, you'll find **Old Palo Alto** and **Crescent Park**, with their magnificent mansions, including one owned by Steve Jobs, co-founder of Apple Computer. Also on the north side is **Professorville District**, so named because it is home to many Stanford faculty members, with its wood-shingled homes (some designed by Julia Morgan and Bernard Maybeck). Another established neighborhood is **College Terrace**, nestled between Stanford University and Stanford Research Park, which is home to a mix of students, engineers, musicians, and retired people.

Slightly north of Professorville is the **Forest Avenue** neighborhood, which has newer apartments and many condominiums. This neighborhood attracts a younger crowd, many of whom frequent the nearby Whole Foods and St. Michael's Alley, a club where Joan Baez used to sing. South of

Oregon Expressway, where the apricot orchards used to grow, is the largest community of Eichler homes, built from 1949 to 1970. Joseph Eichler crafted these homes, which are known for their open design (minimal interior walls in their living space), shallow pitched roofs, and glass walls. Another interesting neighborhood is **Barron Park**, just west of El Camino and south of Stanford. This area has a rural feel as there are no sidewalks, plenty of grand trees, and mailboxes detached from the homes.

Finding housing in the late summer months is difficult because you will be competing with Stanford students. Property prices are higher than those in San Francisco, with median home prices reaching $901,000 in April 2005, an 8% increase over the previous year, according to the CAR. Prospective homebuyers are looking cautiously at East Palo Alto, an area that has suffered higher crime rates and poverty since the early 1960s, but that seems to be turning around. A recently developed large shopping plaza near Highway 101, just off of University Avenue, includes IKEA and Home Depot. New homes are going in, and with prices significantly more moderate than those in Palo Alto, they've been selling fast.

PALO ALTO
Web Site: www.city.palo-alto.ca.us, www.paloaltoonline.com
Area Code: 650
Zip Codes: 94301, 94302, 94303, 94304, 94306, Stanford University 94309
Post Office: 380 Hamilton Ave, 800-275-8777, www.usps.com
Police Station: 275 Forrest Ave, 650-329-2413, www.papd.org
Public Schools: Palo Alto Unified School District, 25 Churchill Ave, 650-329-3700, www.pausd.palo-alto.ca.us
Libraries: Palo Alto Children's Library, 1276 Harriet St, 650-329-2134; Main Library, 1213 Newell Rd, 650-329-2436
Community Resources: Junior Museum and Zoo, 1451 Middlefield Rd, 650-329-2111; Lucie Stern Community Center, 1305 Middlefield Rd, 650-463-4900; Cubberley Community Center, 4000 Middlefield Rd, 650-329-2418; Stanford University, 650-723-2300, www.stanford.edu
Parks, Gardens, and Open Space: Parks Division, 3201 East Bayshore Rd, 650-463-4900, http://www.city.palo-alto.ca.us/parks/

MOUNTAIN VIEW

Located 40 miles south of San Francisco and only 8 miles north of San Jose, Mountain View (72,000) is considered the heart of Silicon Valley. For a town that originated as a stagecoach stop in 1850, a lot has happened to this 7-square-mile city. Today it is the fourth most populated city in Silicon Valley (following San Jose, Sunnyvale, and Santa Clara, respectively), and it is home to a number of high-tech companies, including AOL-Netscape Communications, Silicon Graphics, Sun Microsystems, Synopsys, and Intuit. Intel started in Mountain View before it moved to Santa Clara, and NASA's Ames Research Center is also based in Mountain View.

The population and job market exploded here during the dot-com heyday, then quickly shrank when the economy turned sour. Following the dramatic shakeup, Mountain View, like all of Silicon Valley, has been struggling to get back on even footing. Recent local economic boons include the expansion of AOL-Netscape, a new office for PayPal, and the startling success of search engine powerhouse Google, which employs more than 4,000 people, and is headquartered here.

Mountain View is predominantly home to young professionals. According to the city, more than half of the population is between 20 and 44. Locals boast that their town is well organized and clean, and the city sponsors a number of festivals, including the September Art and Wine Festival. In addition, locals also enjoy a weekly farmers' market, held every Sunday on Hope Street, between Villa and Evelyn, and easy access to the popular Shoreline Park. This 660-acre park includes a golf course, bicycling and jogging trails, and a man-made lake, which is often jumping with sailors, windsurfers, paddle-boaters and shore-side picnickers. The outdoor Shoreline Amphitheatre hosts popular musicians and festivals, including Coldplay, John Mellencamp, and Ozzfest; past headliners have included Santana, Madonna, and Pearl Jam. Downtown, Castro Street, with its restaurants, bars, and shops, is the pulsing center of activity during both the day and night.

Many single, high-tech professionals, young families, and students call Mountain View home. Apartments predominate the housing mix; in fact, Mountain View has more apartments than single-family homes. Homes that are here include Craftsman-style bungalows and some Eichler homes. During the high-tech boom, a number of small, single-family unit condominiums and townhouses were added to the housing pool. And the building continues today, especially in the downtown area. Median home prices here run fairly close to the county median; the CAR reports prices up almost 15% in the last year, to a median of $640,000 in April 2005.

Neighborhoods are changing all over the city, especially around Castro Street, with the development of both residential and commercial sites. Special incentives have been given—in the form of additional floor space and higher densities—to projects located near the transit center. Recent additions to the downtown area include Park Place South Apartments, at 851 Church Street, a four-story high-density, mixed-use retail, office, and housing complex; the 44-condo Bryant Place on Bryant; and 211 apartments at Avalon Bay.

Nearby, the Mountain View Center for the Performing Arts, 500 Castro Street, 650-903-6000, is located in a newly rebuilt downtown area centered around Castro and Church streets. The former center for anti-submarine warfare on the Pacific coast, Moffett Field Naval Air Station, now decommissioned, is in Mountain View, with a large hangar for dirigibles still in existence. Some of the complex continues to be used by NASA and federal agencies. When the President flies in, he usually lands at Moffett Airfield. The city is exploring various alternatives for Moffett's future, including looking at one plan to convert 500 acres of the old airfield into a large mixed-use development for research and development companies and residential housing. Lockheed was once the major employer in the area, but after its troubles in the 1970s, high-tech firms, support industries, and more recently biotech in Mountain View, Sunnyvale, San Jose, Palo Alto, and environs are now the major employers.

MOUNTAIN VIEW

Web Site: www.ci.mtnview.ca.us
Area Code: 650
Zip Codes: 94040, 94041, 94043, 94035, 95002
Post Office: 1768 Miramonte Ave, 800-275-8777, www.usps.com
Police Station: 1000 Villa St, 650-903-6707
Library: 585 Franklin St, 650-903-6337, http://library.ci.mtnview.ca.us
Public Schools: Mountain View-Whisman School District, 750-A San Pierre Way, 650-526-3500, www.mvwsd.k12.ca.us; Mountain View-Los Altos Union High School District, 1299 Bryant Ave, 650-940-4669, www.mvla.k12.ca.us
Community Resources: Mountain View Center for the Performing Arts, 500 Castro St, 650-903-6000, Mountain View Community Center, 201 South Rengstorff Ave, 650-903-6331, www.mvcpa.com; Shoreline Amphitheatre, One Amphitheatre Pkwy, 650-967-3000, www.shorelineamp.com
Parks, Gardens, and Open Space: Community Services Department, Recreation Division, 201 South Rengstorff Ave, 650-903-6331, www.ci.mtnview.ca.us/citydepts/cs/commsvcs.htm

LOS ALTOS

LOS ALTOS HILLS

Set in the gentle green hills just west of Mountain View, you'll find the tranquil, upscale enclave of **Los Altos**. A well-to-do bedroom community of Silicon Valley, Los Altos is home to a number of programmers, software developers and CEOs—many of whom cashed in their chips during the height of the dot-com frenzy. With its quiet streets and family-friendly attitude, Los Altos is a community that prides itself on its cozy village feel. Boutiques and locally owned shops line the well-manicured Main Street— which looks like a picture postcard of small town America. Here, you're likely to get to know your corner grocer, bookstore owner, and neighborhood police officer by name.

To the west, the pristine hills offer a stunning backdrop, plentiful open space, and fantastic views. And homes here have the high price tags to match. Nowhere is this more true than in the adjoining community of **Los Altos Hills**, the city's wealthier, secluded and decidedly more elite twin. Here, you'll find multimillion-dollar homes and estates hidden amid large trees, sharply twisting and ascending roads, and long, private drives. Incorporated in the 1950s to preserve the charms of rural life, homes in Los Altos Hills have a mandated minimum lot size of one acre—and several surpass that margin many times over. Mixed in with the mansions, you'll find a few stables and even a handful of family farms. A bicyclist's, walker's, and horseback rider's heaven, Los Altos Hills has 63 miles of roadside and off-road trails known as the pathway system. Open space is vast and outdoor gems abound, including the 75-plus acre Byrne Preserve, and the expansive 165-acre Rancho San Antonio Preserve. The town also owns a public horseback riding arena, the Town Riding Ring, operated jointly with the Los Altos Hills Horsemen's Association, that is free and open to all.

For activities, Hillview Community Center, near the heart of downtown Los Altos, has a variety of recreation and cultural programs, while Foothill College, spread out across a large, picturesque hillside campus in Los Altos Hills, offers not only a variety of classes, but first-rate theater performances, and a renowned radio broadcasting program, KFJC 89.7 FM. Because these neighboring communities are all about small town atmosphere and rural, upscale living, respectively, Los Altos and Los Altos Hills are short on large-scale shopping centers, big-chain grocery stores, megaplex theaters, and the like. Residents frequently head downhill to Mountain View for bulk shopping sprees and evening entertainment.

LOS ALTOS

Web Site: www.ci.los-altos.ca.us, www.losaltoshills.ca.gov, www.los altosonline.com

Area Code: 650

Zip Codes: 94022–4

Post Office: 100 1st St, 800-275-8777, www.usps.com

Police Station: 1 N. San Antonio Rd, 650-947-2770

Library: 13 S. San Antonio Rd, 650-948-7683, www.santaclara countylib.org/losaltos

Public Schools: Los Altos School District, 650-947-1150, www.los altos.k12.ca.us

Community Resources: Los Altos Chamber of Commerce, 321 University Ave, 650-948-1455, www.losaltoschamber.org; Los Altos Village Association, www.losaltos-downtown.org; Town Riding Ring, lahha.org; Foothill College, www.foothill.fhda.edu; *The Los Altos Town Crier*, http://latc.com

Parks, Gardens, and Open Space: Los Altos Recreation Department, 97 Hillview Ave, 650-947-2790, http://ci.los-altos.ca.us/recreation; Los Altos Hills Recreation Department, 26379 Fremont Rd, 650-941-7222, www.losaltoshills.ca.gov/recreation

SOUTH BAY (SOUTHERN SANTA CLARA COUNTY)

The heart of Silicon Valley, Santa Clara County is located on the southern tip of San Francisco Bay and extends south all the way to Gilroy (and sometimes beyond, depending on who you ask). With over 1.5 million people, the county is the center of the high-tech world, from the internet to computers, software, communications devices, and other technological wizardry. It is home to more than 6,000 high-tech companies including Cisco Systems, Hewlett-Packard, Apple Computer, Intel, Sun Microsystems, and many more.

The heartland of the 1990s dot-com boom, Silicon Valley suffered the most severe impact when that economic bubble burst. The first blows came fast and heavy, as the region watched helplessly as a full 10% of its jobs dried up, venture capitalists cut off the once seemingly endless investment cash flow, and thousands of once eager new arrivals packed up and moved away. Formerly one of the fastest growing regions in the country, in the past five years Silicon Valley has become one of the fastest shrinking. Overall, between 2001 and 2004, the area lost more than 200,000 jobs—with computer and technology industries suffering the greatest impacts, according to the 2005 Index for Silicon Valley.

Today, the economy is still struggling to recover from those heavy blows. Depending on monthly job statistic reports, economists waver between pessimistically dubbing the area still stuck in a slump, and optimistically forecasting signs of its slow recovery. The reality seems to be somewhere in the middle, and perspectives on how things are doing here vary greatly depending on your vantage point. For those who cashed in their stock options before the market tanked, purchased lovely homes, and have held onto top-paying positions, life in Silicon Valley is good. On the other hand, for those who lost jobs, watched the value of their stock market investments plummet, and are still struggling to buy homes in a housing market that continues to climb, defying all sense of reason, things aren't quite as rosy.

The local workforce shrank by 21,000 people during 2004, according to a recent article in the *San Jose Mercury News*. But computer and electronics—product manufacturing has added more jobs for the first time since 2001. Recent economic reports also show venture capital—traditionally the province of hardware and software and jobs—coming back into to town, but shifting more toward biotech.

Also on the upside, traffic congestion, once among the worst in the nation, is down, and apartment rents are down 27% from their 2000 peak, according to a study by RealFacts in 2004. Buying a home, however,

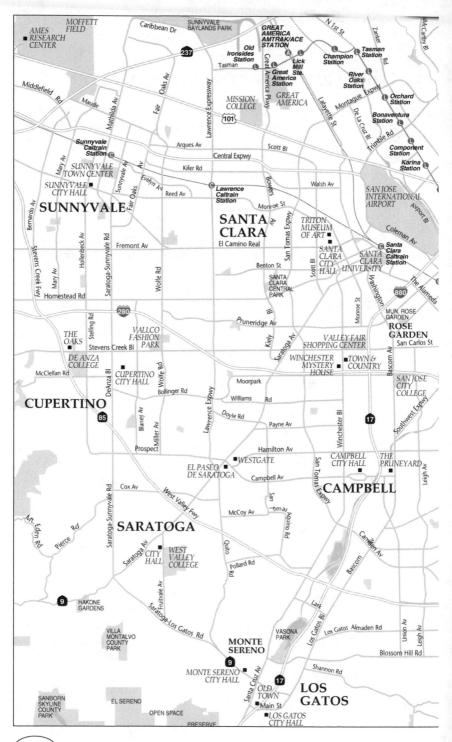

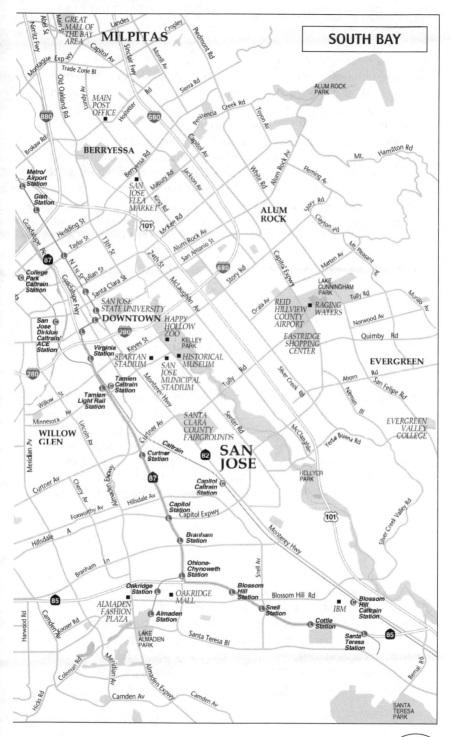

SOUTH BAY

remains pricey. Though the buyer's housing market followed suit behind the job market, peaking then spiraling down in 2000 with the high-tech economic crash, real estate quickly rebounded. The median home price in Santa Clara County in April 2005 was $632,000, up 21.5% from the previous year, according to the California Association of Realtors. Housing availability and affordability rank third—behind transportation and the economy—when it comes to residents' top concerns, according to an annual poll by the Bay Area Council. To help first-time homebuyers get a foothold in this expensive market, Santa Clara County offers a Mortgage Credit Certificate Program, providing a tax credit to first-time homebuyers for the purchase of single-family homes, townhomes, and condominiums. For more information contact the Santa Clara County Mortgage Credit Certificate Program at 408-441-4260, or check out the program's web site at www.mccprogram.com.

Weather-wise, you'll find Santa Clara County to be more Los Angeles than San Francisco, especially in the summertime. Away from the cooling effects of Pacific fog, the sky here is blue and the air warm at least 300 days a year. Tank tops, shorts, and flip-flops are the normal everyday wear here for about half of the year, and the area is famous locally for its hot summer nights. The Mediterranean-like climate is ideal for agriculture, which was capitalized upon by early settlers here, beginning with the Ohlone Indians. The Spanish settlers came to Santa Clara County in 1777 and established El Pueblo de San Jose de Guadalupe, now known as San Jose. This community raised crops and cattle for the Spanish presidios (army bases) located in San Francisco and Monterey. In 1821, after Mexico declared its independence from Spain, San Jose became a Mexican town. Twenty-seven years later, with the signing of the Treaty of Guadalupe Hidalgo, all of California joined the United States. In 1849, during the height of the Gold Rush, San Jose was declared the first state capital. In 1851 the state capital was moved to Vallejo and then eventually to Sacramento. Through the late 1800s and into much of the 1900s, agriculture was the primary industry in the area.

It was not until the latter half of the 20th century that folks started moving to the area in earnest. With high-tech inventors like David Packard, William Hewlett, and the Varian brothers (inventors of an electron tube that helped facilitate radar and microwave technology), electronic and biotech industries began to move into areas previously occupied by farmland and orchards. According to state estimates, the city of San Jose grew from 95,000 in 1950 to over 909,000 by 1999—almost a ten-fold increase—with a population today of 944,857.

SANTA CLARA COUNTY
Web Site: www.co.santa-clara.ca.us
Area Code: 408
Zip Codes: 95109–13, 95116, 95119, 95125, 95126, 95128, 95129, 95133, 95134, 95136, 95141, 95148, 95150, 95151, 95192, and more
Sheriff: Office of the Sheriff, 55 West Younger Ave, San Jose, 800-211-2220
Emergency Hospitals: Santa Clara Valley Medical Center, 751 South Bascom, San Jose, 408-885-5000; San Jose Regional Medical Center, 225 North Jackson Ave, San Jose, 408-259-5000; Good Samaritan Hospital, 2425 Samaritan Dr, San Jose, 408-559-2011; Kaiser Santa Teresa Community Medical Hospital, 250 Hospital Pkwy, San Jose, 408-972-7000
Library: Santa Clara County Library System, 14600 Winchester Blvd, Los Gatos, 408-293-2326 or 800-286-1991, www.santaclaracounty lib.org (Important Note: all libraries that are part of the Santa Clara County Library System are closed on Mondays. The library system includes libraries in the following cities: Campbell, Cupertino, Milpitas, Saratoga, Gilroy, Los Altos, and Morgan Hill.)
Public Schools: Santa Clara County Office of Education, 1290 Ridder Park Dr, San Jose, 408-453-6500, www.sccoe.k12.ca.us
Community Publications: *San Jose Mercury News*, 408-920-5000, www.mercurynews.com; *San Jose Post Record*, 408-287-4866; Metro, 408-298-8000, www.metroactive.com; *Silicon Valley-San Jose Business Journal*, 408-295-3800, http://sanjose.bizjournals.com/sanjose/
Community Resources: Symphony Silicon Valley, 408-286-2600, www.symphonysiliconvalley.org; Opera San Jose, 345 South First St, 408-437-4450, www.operasj.org; Ballet San Jose-Silicon Valley, 40 North First, 408-288-2800; Lick Observatory, 19 miles east of San Jose on Highway 130 near Mount Hamilton, 408-274-5061, www.ucolick.org; Minolta Planetarium, 21250 Stevens Creek Blvd, DeAnza Community College Campus, Cupertino, 408-864-8814, www.planetarium.deanza.edu; Tech Museum of Innovation, 201 South Market St, 408-795-6100, www.thetech.org; American Musical Theater of San Jose, Center for the Performing Arts, 408-453-7108
Public Transportation: *Santa Clara Valley Transportation Authority (SCVTA)*, 408-321-2300, www.vta.org; *RIDES*, 511, www.511.org; *CalTrain*, 800-660-4287, www.caltrain.com

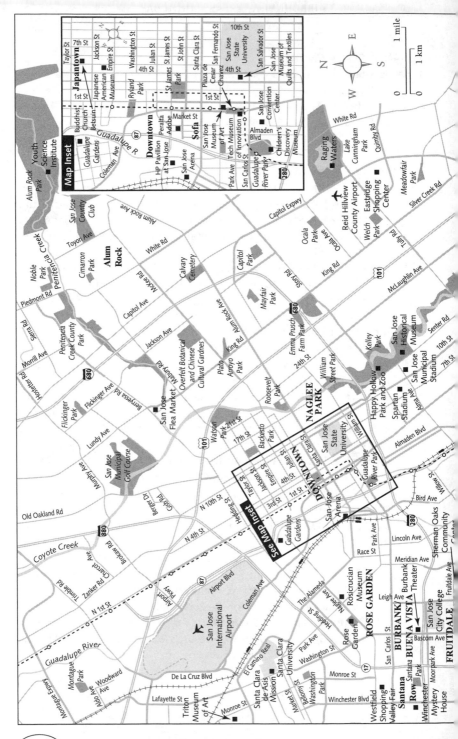

Map Inset

Japantown

Taylor St
7th St
Jackson St
Empire St
Washington St
4th St
Julian St
1st St

Buddhist Church Betsuin
Guadalupe Gardens
Coleman Ave
Guadalupe R

Jackson St
Japanese American Museum
Ryland Park

Downtown

Peralta Adobe
HP Pavillion at San Jose
San Jose Arena

Market St
Julian St
St James St
St John St
Santa Clara St

1st James Park
1st St

San Fernando St
Cesar Chavez
Plaza de

San Jose State University

10th St
San Jose State

San Salvador St
4th St

San Jose Museum of Quilts and Textiles

SoFA

San Jose Museum of Art
Tech Museum of Innovation
Almaden Blvd
Park Ave
San Carlos St
Guadalupe River Park

San Jose Convention Center
Children's Discovery Museum

White Rd

Raging Waters

0   1 mile
0   1 km

N   S   W   E

Alum Rock Park
Youth Science Institute
Alum Rock Ave

San Jose Country Club
Toyon Ave
White Rd

Cimarron Park
Alum Rock

Piedmont Rd
Noble Ave
Penitencia Creek

McKee Rd
Capitol Ave

Calvary Cemetery

Capitol Park

Capitol Expwy

Reid Hillview County Airport
Welch Park
Eastridge Shopping Center

Ocala Park
Ocala Ave

Meadowfair Park

Silver Creek Rd

Morrill Ave
Sierra Rd
Hostetter Rd

Penitencia Creek County Park
680

Jackson Ave
Capitol Ave

Overfelt Botanical and Chinese Cultural Gardens

Mabury Rd

King Rd

Mayfair Park

680

McLaughlin Ave
101

Flickinger Park
Flickinger Ave
Berryessa Rd
Lundy Ave

San Jose Flea Market

Plato Arroyo Park

King Rd
Alum Rock Ave
Story Rd

Emma Prusch Farm Park
24th St

Roosevelt Park

William Street Park

NAGLEE PARK

Kelley Park
Happy Hollow Park and Zoo
Spartan Stadium
Alma Ave

San Jose Historical Museum
Senter Rd
10th St
7th St

San Jose Municipal Stadium

Tully Rd

San Jose Municipal Golf Course
Murphy Ave

Watson Park
21st St
17th St

Backesto Park

Santa Clara St
Julian St
Empire St
4th St

DOWNTOWN

William St
San Jose State University

Guadalupe River Park

Almaden Blvd

Bird Ave

280

Old Oakland Rd
Berryessa Rd
Gish Rd

N 10th St
N 4th St

Taylor St
Jackson St
Empire St
3rd St
1st St

Guadalupe Gardens

San Jose Arena

Lincoln Ave

Sherman Oaks Community Center

See Map Inset

980
Coyote Creek
Trimble Rd
Zanker Rd
Charcot Ave
Brokaw Rd

Hedding St

Park Ave

Race St

Meridian Ave

Willow St

Montague Expwy
Airport Pkwy
Airport Blvd
87
Coleman Ave

San Jose International Airport

The Alameda
Naglee Ave
Hedding St

Rosicrucian Museum
Rose Garden

Leigh Ave
Park Ave
Washington St

ROSE GARDEN

Burbank
Lincoln Ave

Burbank Theater

San Jose City College
Fruitdale Ave

BURBANK/
BUENA VISTA

Bascom Ave

FRUITDALE

Guadalupe River
Montague Park
Aldo Ave
Woodward Ave

De La Cruz Blvd
El Camino Real

Santa Clara University
Santa Clara de Asis Mission

San Carlos St
Park Ave
Washington St
Monroe St

17

Santana Row

Moorpark Ave
Winchester Blvd

Lafayette St
Monroe St
Triton Museum of Art

Market St
Bellamy St
Washington Park

Winchester Blvd

Westfield Shopping Valley Fair
Winchester
Santana Park

Mystery House

162

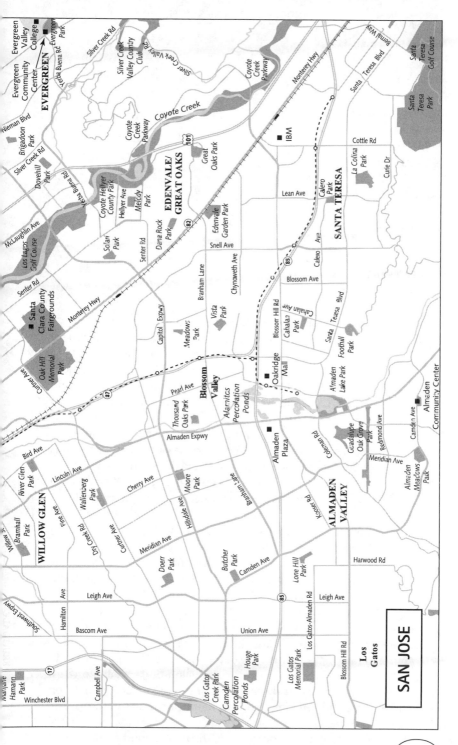

EVERGREEN

Evergreen Valley College
Evergreen Park
Evergreen Community Center

Veba Buena Rd
Silver Creek Rd
Silver Creek Valley Country Club
Silver Creek Valley Rd

Coyote Creek Parkway

Coyote Creek

Monterey Hwy
Bernal Way

Santa Teresa Blvd
Santa Teresa Golf Course

Nieman Blvd

Brigadoon Park

Silver Creek Rd
Dovehill Park

Yerba Buena Rd

Coyote Creek Parkway

IBM

Cottle Rd

101

Great Oaks Park

La Colina Park
Curie Dr

McLaughlin Ave

Los Lagos Golf Course

Coyote Hellyer County Park

Hellyer Ave

Melody Park

EDENVALE/ GREAT OAKS

82

Dana Rock Park

Edenvale Garden Park

Lean Ave

Calero Ave

Calero Park

SANTA TERESA

Caleno

Senter Rd
Solari Park
Senter Rd

Snell Ave

Branham Lane

Chynoweth Ave

85

Blossom Ave

Santa Clara County Fairgrounds

Monterey Hwy

Capitol Expwy

Meadows Park

Vista Park

Blossom Hill Rd

Cahalan Ave

Sarta Teesa Blvd

Santa Foothill Park

Oak Hill Memorial Park

Curtner Ave

87

Pearl Ave

Thousand Oaks Park

Blossom Valley

Alamitos Percolation Ponds

Oakridge Mall

Almaden Lake Park

Almaden Community Center

Camden Ave

Almaden

Bird Ave

River Glen Park

Lincoln Ave

Almaden Expwy

Almaden Plaza

Coleman Rd

Guadalupe Oak Grove Park

Redmond Ave

Meridian Ave

Almaden Meadows Park

WILLOW GLEN

Wallenberg Park

Fine Ave

Cherry Ave

Moore Park

Hillsdale Ave

Branham Lane

Bramhall Park

Willow St

Dry Creek Rd

Curtner Ave

Meridian Ave

Doerr Park

Butcher Park

Camden Ave

Koesch Rd

ALMADEN VALLEY

Lone Hill Park

Harwood Rd

Southwest Expwy

Bird Ave

Ave

Leigh Ave

Bascom Ave

Union Ave

85

Leigh Ave

Marijane Hamann Park

17

Hamilton

Campbell Ave

Winchester Blvd

Houge Park

Los Gatos Creek Park Camden Percolation Ponds

Los Gatos Memorial Park

Los Gatos-Almaden Rd

Blossom Hill Rd

Los Gatos

SAN JOSE

163

SAN JOSE

DOWNTOWN SAN JOSE
ALUM ROCK
JAPANTOWN
NAGLEE PARK
ROSE GARDEN
BURBANK/BUENA VISTA
FRUITDALE
WILLOW GLEN
EVERGREEN
EDENVALE/GREAT OAKS
SANTA TERESA
ALMADEN VALLEY

Though San Francisco gets all the attention, San Jose is actually larger—both in population (944,857 residents) and physical size (177 square miles). In fact, San Jose is the third largest city in California, behind Los Angeles and San Diego, and the eleventh largest city in the USA. San Jose International Airport is only three miles from downtown and, like Oakland International Airport, is easier and friendlier to use than San Francisco International (SFO).

In the past two decades, the self-proclaimed capital of Silicon Valley has undergone a major makeover—especially in the city center. Here streets and storefronts once sat neglected and empty, and local nightlife was virtually nonexistent. On weekends, residents regularly hopped in their cars and headed north to San Francisco in search of entertainment and culture. Today, light rail cars glide gracefully along the streets, and the tree-lined thoroughfares of Market and First Street are packed with trendy restaurants, bars, and cafés. A new state-of-the-art cultural arts complex, home to a performing arts center, civic auditorium, and convention center, has recently opened, and a handful of theaters have sprung up around its edges, earning the southern edge of downtown the nickname "SoFA" (South of First Area). With the vibrant Downtown at its heart, a thriving arts district, and an ever-growing population, San Jose is defying its reputation as a sprawling suburb and becoming a world-class city in its own right.

Architecturally, housing runs the gamut, from studio apartments, to small 1950s and '60s bungalows, to multimillion-dollar, gated estates. Most of the housing stock is fairly new, built since 1960 to meet population demands; however, you can also find neighborhoods with historic Victorians or old ranch homes built at the turn of the century. As a general rule, the further you get from downtown, the more suburban the neighborhoods' character becomes—with larger yards, quieter streets, and mammoth outdoor strip malls.

Due to its vast size, there are dozens of neighborhoods in San Jose, some officially recognized as such by city leaders, others existing only in the hearts and minds of those residing there. Among the best known neighborhoods are the Downtown Museum district, Rose Garden neighborhood, Naglee Park, Willow Glen, Evergreen, Santa Teresa, Almaden Valley, Japantown, Burbank, Buena Vista, Edenvale, and Great Oaks.

Today, life in San Jose, especially for the young professional set, is all about one thing—**Downtown**. Just 15 years ago many would say the city was suffering from an identity crisis. But today, the city's place as a leader in technology is clear. Since 1984, more than $2 billion has been pumped into the downtown area, creating museums, convention centers, theaters, a light rail system, fountains, offices, restaurants, and shopping areas. For many South Bay residents, downtown San Jose is the place to be. In the past 5 years, Downtown housing has also exploded. While you'll still find older homes ranging from bungalows to mansions clustered in a handful of neighborhoods at its edges, the recent emphasis here has been on building new ultramodern high-rise condos, apartments, and townhomes. Especially attractive to young professionals looking to be in the thick of it, Downtown housing is expected to be in continued demand—and thus plans are on the table for the building boom to continue right along with it. Since 1999, 3,000 units have been built Downtown and another 2,600 are in the works. To further encourage high-density housing here, in 2004 the city created a new program, offering developers incentives to build new multi-story housing complexes here.

The Plaza de Cesar Chavez, named for the legendary migrant labor leader and beloved local hero who led a series of massive, successful strikes against the grape growing industry, is smack in the center of the museums and just across from the renovated Fairmont Hotel. The plaza has an incredible fountain with nozzles spraying water right out of the sidewalk that make it a perfect place to cool off on a hot summer day. The $140 million, 20,000-seat HP Pavilion (also known as the San Jose Arena), mockingly called the "the tin can" by locals, is also here. Not only is the Arena home to the San Jose Sharks Hockey team, but it also hosts big name entertainers from around the world. The Sharks, a source of San Jose pride, had their 2004-2005 season cancelled along with the rest of the National Hockey League (NHL) during contract disputes—much to the dismay of local fans. But things seem to be back on track for 2005–2006. Life is running a bit more smoothly for AFL football team the San Jose SaberCats, who also play at the Pavilion, and for Major League Soccer's San Jose Earthquakes, who play at San Jose State's Spartan Stadium on 7th Street, just south of downtown San Jose.

One of the highlights of the Downtown revitalization project is the Tech Museum of Innovation, one of the Bay Area's premier science museums. Opened in the early 1990s, the Tech quickly outgrew its original quarters, and in 1998 its new 132,000-square-foot, mango-colored facility opened at the corner of Market Street and Park Avenue. The museum boasts nearly 300 hands-on exhibits that allow visitors to do such things as design their own bicycle and ride a roller coaster. You can also get a 3-D map of your head made by a rotating laser scanner, and catch a film at the state-of-the-art IMAX Dome Theater.

On the third Thursday of every month the Downtown art galleries stay open late, fostering a cultural nightlife. Also on Thursday evenings in the summer, you can enjoy live concerts in the Plaza de Cesar Chavez. And on Friday afternoons, locals frequent the farmers' market on San Pedro Street between Santa Clara and St. John streets. In the heart of Downtown, from Highway 880 at the north to Highway 280 at the south, you'll find Guadalupe River Park, a three-mile ribbon of park land currently being developed along the banks of the Guadalupe River. Guadalupe Gardens, which already features a renowned Heritage Rose Garden with over 3,700 varieties of roses, is being created adjacent to the River Park on land just south of the San Jose International Airport. A little further west you'll find Overfelt Botanical and Chinese Cultural Gardens, 2145 McKee Rd, 408-251-3323, a perfect place to take an afternoon stroll through the gardens.

A popular local landmark on the west side of San Jose is the Winchester Mystery House, 525 South Winchester Boulevard, 408-247-2000, www.winchestermysteryhouse.com, where you can wander through a dizzying maze of seemingly endless hallways, trapdoors, and staircases that lead to nowhere. Designed by the eccentric heiress to the Winchester rifle fortune to ward off the spirits of those killed with rifles, the house was continually added on to until the day Sarah Winchester died. In addition to regular tours of the house and gardens, flashlight tours are given in the evenings every Friday the 13th and annually on Halloween.

Near the Winchester Mystery House, you'll find Santana Row, which has created some competition for Downtown in recent years. An upscale shopping, living, and dining district, Santana Row boasts some of the Bay Area's finest restaurants and designer boutiques as well as a mix of luxurious rental townhomes and flats. The Portfolio at Santana Row features one- to three-bedroom loft condominiums as well three-bedroom villa condominiums for sale. Hobnobbing, window shopping, and lunching here have become so popular that the area now draws people from across the Bay Area, especially on weekends.

The building boom has radiated out beyond the immediate Downtown area to nearby neighborhood business districts. Since 1999, 4,000 apartments and condos have gone up in the areas along Alum Rock Avenue, The

Alameda, West San Carlos Street, and Japantown. Nestled within Alum Rock Canyon, in the foothills of the Diablo Mountain range, is Alum Rock Park, 16240 Alum Rock Avenue. San Jose's oldest and largest park, at 720 acres, Alum Rock Park is home to the Youth Science Institute, which houses a variety of live animals. The main drag, Alum Rock Avenue, has been undergoing redevelopment—with several new large mixed use projects—combining commercial space and new apartments. A new Mexican Heritage Plaza and Cultural Center are located in **Alum Rock**, as is Little Portugal.

Over 100 years old, **Japantown** bills itself as one of the last remaining authentic Japantowns in the USA. Located close to Downtown, between 1st and 7th streets and Jackson and Taylor streets, Japantown is home to single-story single-family homes as well as a handful of new condo projects. Clustered along Jackson Street between 4th and 6th streets you can find family-owned Japanese restaurants as well as handmade sweet shops. You can even try some homemade tofu, at the San Jose Tofu Company, 175 Jackson Street. The San Jose Buddhist Church Betsuin, 640 North 5th Street, a historic temple, is frequently crowded. To learn more about the rich Japanese history in San Jose, stop by the Japanese American Museum of San Jose, on 535 North 5th Street near Jackson. Every Sunday morning locals stop by the Japantown Farmers' Market on Jackson Street between 6th and 7th streets to pick up fresh vegetables, sweet treats, and fresh flowers.

The oldest neighborhood in San Jose, **Naglee Park**, is in the center core of the city, just east of San Jose State University, and bordered by Highway 280 on the south, Coyote Creek on the east, 10th Street to the west, and Santa Clara Street to the north. The neighborhood is named after General Henry Naglee, who owned a 140-acre estate and lived on 14th and East San Fernando streets. In addition to General Naglee's still-standing house, there are classic Victorian and Craftsman-style homes, and stately mansions dating from the early 1900s, some of which have been divided into apartments and duplexes. You'll also find a number of newer apartment complexes dating from the 1970s and '80s. Naglee Park locals enjoy the playground at William Street Park as well as the annual Bark in the Park Festival for dogs, hosted here each July. Then there's the Fourth of July parade, BBQs, and a playgroup for moms and tots each morning. Santa Clara Street, which runs east-west through the center of Naglee Park, has had a drastic facelift with a new City Hall, elementary school, and symphony. Newcomers looking at housing along Coyote Creek should be aware that the creek sometimes overflows in the winter months.

The **Rose Garden** neighborhood is centrally located in San Jose, west of Downtown, and bordered by the Alameda Roadway on the east, Interstate 880 on the northwest, and Naglee Avenue on the north. The area is named for the city's magnificent public rose garden located at Dana and Naglee avenues—a lovely place for an early morning stroll. Also in the neighborhood is the Rosicrucian Egyptian Museum and Planetarium, 1342 Naglee Avenue. With the pyramids and sphinxes, you feel like you just might be in Egypt. Housing choices in the Rose Garden neighborhood include exquisite Queen Anne Victorians, some Tudor-style homes, contemporary apartments, and many new condominiums. With San Jose State University located nearby, you'll find a lot of students here, as well as plenty of professionals and their families. Those interested in architectural preservation may want to get involved in the Rose Garden Neighborhood Preservation Association, www.rgnpa.org. The only drawback is this neighborhood's proximity to the airport and CalTrain tracks, which may present a noise problem for some.

Coming off of the freeway, you can easily miss **Burbank**, even though its main drag, West San Carlos Street, is the gateway to Downtown. The neighborhood, bounded roughly by 2nd Street, I-280, McLaughlin Avenue, and Phelan Avenue, is made up of single-family homes, apartments, and new condo developments. Within walking distance of downtown, this neighborhood has the advantage of being a bit quieter in the evenings. West San Carlos Street, a kind of mini antique alley, is a popular shopping spot to hunt for eclectic home furnishings and other vintage gems. San Jose City College is located here, as well as the old Burbank Theater. Once a year, the community comes together for the Burbank Neighborhood Jamboree, which dates back to 1948 and hosts a variety of events including an antiques show and more bizarrely, a bed race, where beds on wheels cruise down the streets. Nearby the **Buena Vista** neighborhood has a unique collection of historic bungalows with handcrafted features built between 1906 and 1930.

The **Fruitdale** area, just south of Buena Vista, is named for the fruit orchards, especially prunes, that used to grow here. Today, middle-class homes, shopping malls, and apartments have replaced the orchards. San Jose City College, 2100 Moorpark Avenue, is also located here.

Another family-preferred area is the **Willow Glen** neighborhood, just 3 miles southwest of downtown San Jose, and easily accessible to the light rail system. Named after the willow trees that grow along the creeks and Guadalupe River, the neighborhood is composed of what used to be the town of Willow Glen. Founded in 1927, it was annexed by San Jose just 9 years later (this is an oft-repeated story of San Jose's growth). Newcomers to Willow Glen who want to get involved in the community should consider joining the active Willow Glen Neighborhood Association, www.wgna.net, "a grassroots community organization dedicated to improving life in Willow Glen." Among other neighborhood improvement projects, this organization looks for ways to preserve the history of this area. Architecturally you'll see the usual Victorians mixed in with Eichlers, Tudors, some ranch-style homes, and Mediterranean-style stuccos. In recent years, a number of older houses have been torn down and replaced with larger abodes, but residents have worked hard to ensure that the neighborhood maintains its old-fashioned character and charm. Strolling along the quiet sidewalks here you'll find lovely lawns and well-tended gardens filled with fragrant, colorful flowers.

Young families find this neighborhood attractive because it is safe, comfortable, and more affordable than nearby Los Gatos and Saratoga. Many residents have lived here for a long time, and it seems few have plans to leave any time soon. During the winter holidays many of the houses here are adorned with twinkling lights, reindeer, and elaborate manger scenes, drawing people from all over the Bay Area for a neighborhood tour. Willow Glen's commercial area, along Lincoln Avenue, is quaint, with restaurants, coffee shops, boutiques, and antique shops. No chain stores here, as locals fight hard to keep this area a one-of-a-kind place. The neighborhood hosts a popular farmer's market every Saturday at the corner of Willow and Lincoln. At the time of this writing, there was discussion about relocating the market to a large area just behind Lincoln Avenue.

Southeast of downtown San Jose, on the eastern side of Highway 101, is **Evergreen**, a recently developed area of the South Bay. Housing here is relatively new, much of it built starting about 25 years ago. It is made up largely of modern apartments and large homes with three, four, and even five bedrooms. Set against the arid hills, the Evergreen Community College, 3095 Yerba Buena Road, is a wonderful local resource, offering a variety of classes and a home for the local Police Academy. Students and neighbors alike enjoy the shady, tranquil green and picturesque pond on the edge of campus—a perfect spot to relax, eat lunch, and feed the ducks. Just south of the campus is the golf course, Silver Creek Valley Country Club, 5460 Country Club Parkway, and a gated community with about 1,500 Mediterranean-style homes. Evergreen feels a world away from the bustle of downtown San Jose, and residents here seem to like it that way. Newer corner malls take care of all the basics in terms of shopping, coffee, and banking needs, and the main thoroughfare, Yerba Buena Road, links the neighborhood with nearby Highway 101.

The Edenvale, Great Oaks and Santa Teresa neighborhoods are located near the end of the light rail system. In the southeast corner of the city, just north of the Blossom Hill overpass, you'll find the adjoining neighborhoods of **Edenvale** and **Great Oaks**. Built on the site of an old racetrack, many of the streets in Edenvale and Great Oaks are named after famous racehorses. Great Oaks Park forms the boundary between the two communities. Homes here tend to be ranch-style, single-family abodes and are among the more affordable in the city. Resources here are a little lacking, but there is a local shopping center. Both neighborhoods are part of an ongoing revitalization effort—dubbed Strong Neighborhoods Initiative by the city—to improve resources, make neighborhoods cleaner and safer, and better connect them to one another. The Edenvale Roundtable Community Association can be reached at www.enative.com/ca/scl/erca. To enjoy the great outdoors, head just north of Edenvale to Coyote Hellyer County Park, located along Coyote Creek and Coyote Road.

Bordered by Blossom Hill Road on the north, Santa Teresa Boulevard on the west, and Monterey Road on the east, is **Santa Teresa**. Most homes here were built in the 1960s, though new developments have been added. A lovely expanse of greenspace is located nearby at the 1,688-acre Santa Teresa County Park, along Santa Teresa's southern border. For a view of the sprawling city and the mountains, climb Coyote Peak. The practical single-family tracts in these southeastern neighborhoods provide much of the housing for employees of the Almaden Research Center—a large IBM facility that sits on a nearly 700-acre campus in the in the nearby valley.

Home to one of the most gorgeous landscapes in America, according to the Greenbelt Alliance, **Almaden Valley** feels like an upscale, rural sub-urb of San Jose. Named for the quicksilver mines and also known as Silver Creek Valley, this large area at the southernmost edge of San Jose is roughly bordered by Almaden Expressway to the north, the Santa Teresa foothills to the east, Guadalupe Road to the west, and the city limits to the south. There is a mixture of housing here—some old, some built in the 1960s. In recent years, the area has exploded with new, multimillion-dollar mansions. Many San Jose old timers are in shock that this neighborhood has become so high priced. Almaden Lake Park, located at the intersection of Almaden Expressway and Coleman Avenue, has a sandy beach and swim area, which comes in handy during hot summer days. Also on the lake are kayaks, paddle boats, and windsurfers. Sitting atop Los Capitancillos Ridge, the 4,000-plus acre Quicksilver County Park is home to vast open meadows, gorgeous wildflowers, and 33 miles of hiking trails. The Almaden Expressway connects residents to state routes 85 and 87. To reduce congestion, plans are underway to widen this roadway. For more information on the neighborhood, check out the Almaden Valley Community Association, www.avca-sj.org. For a bit of history, head beyond the city limits and about 11 miles south you'll find the remnants of an historic mining town. Known as New Almaden, this little village, home to the Almaden Quicksilver Mining Museum, is like a living time capsule.

SAN JOSE
Web Site: www.ci.san-jose.ca.us
Area Codes: 408, 699
Zip Codes: 95109–13, 95116, 95119, 95125, 95126, 95128, 95129, 95133, 95134, 95136, 95141, 95148, 95150, 95151, 95192
Post Office: 1750 Lundy Ave, San Jose, 800-275-8777, www.usps.com

Police: 201 West Mission, 408-277-8900
Library: Dr. Martin Luther King, Jr. Library, 150 East San Fernando St, 408-808-2000, www.sjlibrary.org
Public Schools: San Jose Unified School District, 855 Lenzen Ave, 408-535-6000, www.sjusd.org
Community Publications: *San Jose Mercury News*, 408-920-5000, www.mercurynews.com; *San Jose Post Record*, 408-287-4866; Metro, 408-298-8000, www.metroactive.com; *Silicon Valley-San Jose Business Journal*, 408-295-3800, http://sanjose.bizjournals.com/sanjose
Cultural Resources: Peralta Adobe, 154 West Saint John St, 408-993-8182; History Park at Kelley Park, 1650 Senter Rd, 408-287-2290, www.history sanjose.org; Santa Clara de Asis Mission, 500 El Camino Real; Santa Clara University, 408-554-4023, www.scu.edu; San Jose Museum of Quilts and Textiles, 110 Pasco de San Antonio, 408-971-0323, www.sjquilt museum.org; San Jose Museum of Art, 110 South Market St, 408-294-2787, www.sjmusart.org; San Jose Institute of Contemporary Art, 451 South First St, 408-283-8155, www.sjica.org; Lick Observatory, 19 miles east of San Jose on Highway 130 near Mount Hamilton, 408-274-5061, www.ucolick.org; Tech Museum of Innovation, 201 South Market St, 408-795-6100, www.thetech.org; American Musical Theater of San Jose, Center for the Performing Arts, 408-453-7108; Opera San Jose, 345 South First St, 408-437-4450, www.operasj.org; Ballet San Jose Silicon Valley, 40 North First, 408-288-2800, www.balletsanjose.org; San Jose Convention and Cultural Facilities (Center for the Performing Arts, Parkside Hall, Civic Auditorium, Montgomery Theater, McEnery Convention Center), West San Carlos St and Almaden Blvd, 408-277-3900, www.sjcc.com; Children's Discovery Museum of San Jose, 180 Woz Way, 408-298-5437, www.cdm.org
Community Resources: San Jose Silicon Valley Chamber of Commerce, 310 S. First St, 408-291-5250, www.sjchamber.com; Almaden Community Center, 6445 Camden Ave, 408-268-1133; Evergreen Community Center, 4860 San Felipe Rd, 408-270-2220; Sherman Oaks Community Center, 1800A Fruitdale Ave, 408-292-2935; Rose Garden Neighborhood Preservation Association, P.O. Box 28761; Willow Glen Neighborhood Association, www.wgna.net; Japantown Neighborhood Association, www.jtownneighbors.org/
Parks, Gardens, and Open Space: Park, Recreation and Neighborhood Services, 4 North Second St, Suite 600, 408-277-4661, www.san joseca.gov/prns/regionalparks; Emma Prusch Farm Park, 647 South King Rd; Alum Rock Park, 16240 Alum Rock Ave; Overfelt Gardens (and Chinese Cultural Gardens), Educational Park Dr off of McKee Rd; Almaden Lake Park, 6099 Winfield Blvd, 408-277-5130; Kelley Park (Japanese Friendship Gardens and Happy Hollow Park and Zoo, 1300

Senter Rd, 408-277-3000, www.happyhollowparkandzoo.org, are also located here), Story and Senter rds; Rose Garden, Dana and Naglee aves, 408-277-2757; Lake Cunningham Park, 2305 South White Rd, 408-277-4319

SUNNYVALE

In the heart of Silicon Valley, **Sunnyvale** (133,086) remains home to many high-tech employees. Amenities include large numbers of parks and tennis courts, as well as theater groups, golf courses, a sports complex, a dance company, and much more. Home to 36,000 trees, Sunnyvale proudly calls itself a "Tree City USA." Residents here enjoy the Baylands Nature Preserve, 408-730-7709, located at the end of Lawrence Expressway off Highway 237, at Caribbean Drive. This 70-acre park is a bird watcher's paradise. Heritage Park, 550 East Remington Avenue, includes a pond-side plaza that is home to a community center, creative arts center, performing arts center, indoor sports complex, recreation center, and senior center.

Houses vary from multi-story condominium townhouses with the requisite pool, to red-tiled Mediterranean-style homes, to multimillion-dollar mansions. The average price for a home in April 2005 was $680,000, up 26% from 2004, according to the California Association of Realtors. Downtown Sunnyvale is undergoing serious construction with a new City Plaza, new office buildings, and a 20-screen movie theater. The historic Murphy Avenue has a number of new restaurants and shops, as well as a Saturday morning farmers' market on South Murphy Avenue, between Evelyn and Washington avenues. Recently completed projects include a new Transit Station and Plaza del Sol, 500 West Evelyn Avenue, which pays homage to the city's agricultural past with giant, colorful fruit sculptures. As part of the large-scale effort to revitalize this 184-acre central city core to create a more traditional downtown, Sunnyvale is currently looking at a $150 million plan to scrap the old downtown mall, the Sunnyvale Town Center, and replace it with a large outdoor town square that would include 1 million square feet of retail space, some small office spaces, and roughly 300 new condos or townhouses.

The 23.8 square miles of Sunnyvale are said to be home to more high-tech companies than any other city in the world. Advanced Micro Devices, Network Appliance, Yahoo!, and Lockheed Martin are only a few of the hundreds of high-tech businesses that operate here. Lockheed alone employs more than 8,500 people. Back at the turn of the century, Walter Crossman, the city's first developer, was on to something when he dubbed the scarcely populated agricultural town "the City of Destiny." If only he could see how prophetic his words were.

SUNNYVALE
Web Site: www.ci.sunnyvale.ca.us
Area Codes: 408, 669
Zip Codes: 94086, 94087, 94088, 94089
Post Office: 580 North Mary Ave, Sunnyvale, 800-275-8777, www.usps.com
Police: 700 All America, 408-730-7100
Library: Main Library, 665 West Olive Ave, Sunnyvale, 408-730-7300, http://sunnyvale.ca.gov/Departments/Library
Public Schools: Sunnyvale School District, 819 West Iowa Ave, Sunnyvale, 408-522-8200, www.sesd.org
Community Publication: *Sunnyvale Sun*, 408-200-1000, www.sunny valesun.com
Community Resources: Sunnyvale Chamber of Commerce, 101 West Olive Ave, 408-736-4971, www.svcoc.org; Sunnyvale Community Center Theater, 550 East Remington Dr, 408-733-6611; Sunnyvale Volunteer Resources, 408-730-7533
Parks, Gardens and Open Space: Parks and Recreation Department (and Sunnyvale Community Center), 550 East Remington Dr, 408-730-7350, http://sunnyvale.ca.gov/Departments/Parks+and+Recreation

LOS GATOS, MONTE SERENO

Considered by many to be one of the loveliest towns in the South Bay, **Los Gatos** is tucked away in the hills just east of the Santa Cruz Mountains, off of Highway 17. This community of about 29,000 is upscale, picture-perfect, woodsy, politically progressive, and prides itself on its strong sense of community. The hills are peppered with newly built mansions, especially in the Blossom Hill Manor area. More modest, early 1900s Victorians are still extant as well. In April 2005, the median price for a home was $965,000, up 11% from the previous year. For an even more upscale area, visit the city of **Monte Sereno** (population 3,500), right next to Los Gatos. An old, established community, it's known for its multimillion-dollar homes sitting on expansive lots. See www.montesereno.org for more information about this quaint town.

With 15 parks and 8 playgrounds, people in Los Gatos have every opportunity to enjoy the outdoors. Year round, the Los Gatos Creek Trail, just outside the downtown on Main Street, abounds with thrill-seeking cyclists, runners, and walkers. The 5-mile path winds up into the hills and around the Lexington Reservoir, providing spectacular views guaranteed to please. For an outdoor experience more suited to the family, try Vasona Park, where you can picnic, roller blade, jog, bike, or just go for a stroll. For a leisurely afternoon in the lake, rent a paddleboat. Next to Vasona Park is Oak Meadow Park, where you can ride a carousel or a miniature train, or just settle down for a picnic.

If shopping is more your thing, you'll want visit North Santa Cruz Avenue. This upscale shopping district is full of trendy boutiques, art galleries, restaurants, and cafés that lure people from all over the county. Warm evenings bring locals in to browse the sales, window shop, and stop for cappuccinos or a bite to eat. Singles frequent the Los Gatos Brewing Company, a brewpub at 130-G North Santa Cruz Avenue, and Steamers, 50 University Avenue. On Sunday evenings in the summer, head to the Civic Center lawn at 110 East Main Street for a popular free concert series. In the fall, Los Gatos High School, 20 High School Court, located just a short walk from downtown, brings in local fans to watch the Friday night football games. During the Christmas season horse-drawn carriages prance around the town. All in all life, here is pretty good, and that's without even mentioning the weather. On average, you'll find 330 sunny days per year here. Nor is it too cold or too hot; average temperatures in January are 46° Fahrenheit, in July, 71°.

Centrally located for anyone commuting to Silicon Valley, Los Gatos also offers, for those seeking more work than play, a 40-minute trip south via Highway 17 to the beach and boardwalk in Santa Cruz.

LOS GATOS
Web Site: www.los-gatos.ca.us
Area Code: 408
Zip Codes: 95030, 95031, 95032
Post Office: 101 South Santa Cruz Ave, 408-354-5801, www.usps.com
Police: 110 East Main St, in the Los Gatos Town Hall Complex, 408-354-5257
Library: 110 East Main St, in the Los Gatos Town Hall Complex, 408-354-6891, http://library.town.los-gatos.ca/us
Public Schools: Los Gatos Union School District, 1710 Roberts Rd, 408-335-2000, www.lgusd.k12.ca.us
Parks, Gardens, and Open Space: Department of Parks and Public Works, 110 East Main St, in the Los Gatos Town Hall Complex, 408-399-5781, www.losgatosca.gov/services/6a.html

CAMPBELL, CUPERTINO

Other cities to consider if you are looking in the South Bay are Campbell (38,415), and Cupertino (53,452). Located in the foothills of the Santa Cruz Mountains, both communities are very suburban, with shopping malls, parks with tennis courts and play lots, and many families. In addition, major high-tech companies, including Apple, call these cities home.

Campbell borders Willow Glen and Los Gatos. The portion of Campbell between Bascom and Meridian avenues features wide, tree-lined streets with ranch-style and Eichler homes. Named after the prune yard drying days, the Pruneyard Shopping Center on Bascom and Campbell avenues offers such stores as Starbucks, Barnes & Noble, and Trader Joe's, as well as restaurants, including the Rock Bottom Brewery, a nice place to have a burger and catch a televised sports game, and Buca di Beppo for family-style Italian food.

The old commercial heart of Campbell is along Campbell Avenue. Here you'll find internet cafés, antique shops, dry cleaners, and a hodge-podge of ethnic restaurants and mom-and-pop stores. The choice for Italian here is Mio Vicino at 384 East Campbell Avenue. Nearby at 1690 South Bascom Avenue is the popular Whole Foods, a gourmet grocery store featuring health food, organic fruits and vegetables, and freshly pre-pared meals. Many come here during their lunch hour or to pick up dinner on their way home from work. On Campbell Avenue, between First Street and Central Avenue, a year-round farmers' market held every Sunday morning, rain or shine, features farm-fresh produce.

Property prices in Campbell have increased considerably over the past decade but seem to be holding somewhat steadier. According to the California Association of Realtors, the median home price here was $615,000 in April 2005, up almost 12% from 2004. Campbell has a variety of affordable housing programs, including one to assist eligible first-time homebuyers (contact the city's housing coordinator, 408-866-2137).

The 13-square-mile city of **Cupertino** grew prodigiously after World War II, first as a weekend destination for wealthy San Franciscans, and today as a thriving residential and business community. In 1950, there were only 500 homes in Cupertino; today there are more than 18,000, according to the city's consolidated housing plan, with a population of more than 52,000. Cupertino, which borders Saratoga and Sunnyvale, does not have a true downtown center, so strip malls are common. High-tech business offices include Apple Computer, which is headquartered here, and Compaq. Primarily a bedroom community, with most residents heading to San Jose for nightlife, many families move to Cupertino for its suburban feel and top-notch schools, which have received state and national recognition for their excellence. Travel north on Highway 9 from Saratoga, which becomes Saratoga-Sunnyvale Road, and you'll know you've arrived in Cupertino when you begin to see the many Asian restaurants and grocery stores. To the west of Saratoga-Sunnyvale Road sit the Cupertino foothills, home to million-dollar mansions with acres of open space behind them. Outdoor enthusiasts come here for mountain biking and hiking. Cupertino has a brand new library on Torre Avenue that even has its own café, the popular Coffee Society, and plans are underway to revitalize the city's largest mall, Vallco Fashion Park on Wolfe Road. Right now, in addition to its handful of shops—including a large Macy's—you can find the local farmers' market at Vallco in the parking lot every Friday morning. There is a Whole Foods in Cupertino at 20830 Stevens Creek Boulevard, and next door, Fontana's, 20840 Stevens Creek Boulevard, is a romantic Italian restaurant. Locals frequent the Oaks Shopping Center at 21275 Stevens Creek Boulevard for its café, fitness center (for women only), and the popular, A Clean, Well-Lighted Place For Books. Across the street are De Anza College and the Flint Center, which features regular concerts by the San Francisco Symphony, Broadway plays, and other performances. Bargain hunters should check out the De Anza Flea Market, held on the first Saturday of every month on the De Anza College Campus in parking lots A and B. The 33-acre Blackberry Farm, www.blackberryfarm.org, with swimming picnic facilities and a 9-hole golf course, is also popular with locals.

Plans to revitalize the retail core along Stevens Creek and De Anza boulevards with new restaurants, high-density housing, and better public transit connections are underway. If you are looking for a home in Cupertino, you'll find dozens of new condominiums mixed in with single-family homes and a few older homes, located along wide boulevards. The median home price in Cupertino was $888,000 in April 2005, up almost 22% from the previous year, according to the CAR.

In 2003, the City of Cupertino developed a down payment assistance program to assist qualifying Cupertino teachers in their quest for home-ownership (for more information, contact Neighborhood Housing Services Silicon Valley, 408-279-2600, www.nhssv.org).

CAMPBELL

Web Site: www.ci.campbell.ca.us
Area Codes: 408, 669
Zip Code: 95008
Post Office: 500 West Hamilton Ave, 800-275-8777, www.usps.com
Police: 70 North First St, 408-866-2121
Library: Campbell Library, 77 Harrison Ave, 408-866-1991, www.santa claracountylib.org/campbell
Public Schools: Campbell Union School District, 155 North Third St, Campbell, 408-364-4200, www.campbellusd.k12.ca.us
Community Publications: *Campbell Express*, 408-374-9700; *Campbell Times*, 408-494-7000
Community Resources: Campbell Community Center, 1 West Campbell Ave, 408-866-2138; Campbell Chamber of Commerce, 408-378-1666, www.campbellchamber.com

Parks, Gardens, and Open Space: Recreation and Community Services Department, 1 West Campbell Ave #C-31, 408-866-2105, www.ci. campbell.ca.us/communityandarts/recreation.htm

CUPERTINO

Web Site: www.cupertino.org

Zip Codes: 95014, 95015

Area Codes: 408, 669

Post Office: 21701 Stevens Creek Blvd, Cupertino, 800-275-8777, www.usps.com

Police: Santa Clara County Sheriff's Office, 55 West Younger Ave, San Jose, 800-211-2220

Library: Cupertino Library, 10800 Torre Ave, 408-446-1677, www.santa claracountylib.org/cupertino

Public Schools: Cupertino Union School District, 10301 Vista Dr, Cupertino, 408-252-3000, http://cupertino.ca.campusgrid. net/home

Community Publication: *Cupertino Courier*, 408-200-1000, www. cupertinocourier.com

Community Resources: Cupertino Chamber of Commerce, 20455 Silverado Ave, 408-252-7054, www.cupertino-chamber.org; Quinlan Community Center, 10185 North Stelling Rd, 408-777-3120; De Anza College Flint Center for the Performing Arts, 21250 Stevens Creek Blvd, 408-864-8816; Cupertino Historical Museum, 10185 North Stelling Rd, in the Quinlan Community Center, 408-973-1495; Asian-Americans for Community Involvement, 408-975-2730; Sports Center, 21111 Stevens Creek Blvd, 408-777-3160; Minolta Planetarium, 21250 Stevens Creek Blvd, Cupertino, 408-864-8814, www.planetarium.deanza.edu

Parks, Gardens, and Open Space: Parks and Recreation Department (and Quinlan Community Center), 10185 North Stelling Rd, 408-777-3110, www.cupertino.org/city_government/departments_and_ offices/parks_recreation/index.asp

SARATOGA

Saratoga (31,000) is located 10 miles west of San Jose in the golden foothills of the Santa Cruz Mountains. Numerous creeks, wooded trails, and streets lined with mature oak trees fill the city's 12 square miles. The city is decidedly upscale: The median home price in April 2005 was over $1.5 million dollars, up more than 23% from 2004, according to the CAR.

Like Los Gatos, the community has easy access to the outdoors. The downtown area, on Big Basin Avenue, is where you'll find chic restaurants and boutique shopping.

Proximity to the Santa Cruz redwood trees put Saratoga on the map; by the mid-1800s, Saratoga had become a thriving lumber town. After lumber, agriculture in the form of fruit orchards, especially prunes, became the economy's mainstay. Around the turn of the 20th century, wealthy San Franciscans started building summer cottages here for weekend and summer getaways, which added tourism to the economy. Today the orchards are gone and the area is considered a bedroom community for Silicon Valley. Architecturally, you'll find many grand ranch style estates and two-story Victorians. Famous architect Julia Morgan (best known for the Hearst Castle) designed the Saratoga Foothill Club in 1915. Of note, Steven Spielberg graduated from Saratoga High School, and actresses Olivia de Havilland and her sister Joan Fontaine began their careers in Saratoga.

One of the highlights of Saratoga is Hakone Gardens, 21000 Big Basin Way, 408-741-4994, www.hakone.com. Created in 1918 by a former Japanese imperial gardener, it is considered to be the only authentic Japanese garden in Northern California, the Japanese Tea Garden in San Francisco notwithstanding. For summer concerts, locals frequent the Mountain Winery located at 14831 Pierce Road. Another getaway is The Villa Montalvo Cultural Center, 15400 Montalvo Road, a 175-acre estate with beautiful gardens, a bird sanctuary, and nature trails. The center hosts concerts and plays at its outdoor amphitheater. It received its initial funding from US Senator James Phelan, who, upon his death in 1930, left the estate with a mission to support the arts. Today artists live and work at the center. Rock climbers come from all over the Bay Area to Castle Rock State Park at the intersection of Route 35 and Highway 9, which offers challenging belays. Hikers, horseback riders, and mountain bikers also enjoy the 32 miles of trails at the park.

SARATOGA

Web Site: www.saratoga.ca.us
Area Code: 408
Zip Code: 95070
Post Office: 13650 Saratoga Ave, 408-867-6126, www.usps.com
Sheriff: Office of the Sheriff, West Side Substation 408-867-9715
Library: Saratoga Library, 13650 Saratoga Ave, 408-867-6126, www.santaclaracountylib.org/saratoga
Community Publication: *Saratoga News*, 408-200-1000, www.saratoga news.com
Community Resources: Mountain Winery, 14831 Pierce Rd, 408-741-2822, www.mountainwinery.com; The Villa Montalvo Cultural

Center, 15400 Montalvo Rd, 408-961-5800, www.villamontalvo.org

Public Schools: Saratoga Union School District, 20460 Forrest Hills Dr, 408-867-3424, www.susd.k12.ca.us

Parks, Gardens and Open Space: Saratoga Parks and Recreation (also the Saratoga Community Center), 19655 Allendale Ave, 408-868-1248

SANTA CLARA

The City of Santa Clara (109,100) started out in 1777 as a Spanish mission, and later evolved into a prime agricultural region with expansive orchards as well as a lumber community. Like many of the other surrounding towns, Santa Clara reaped the immediate benefits of the old-growth redwood trees. In 1874, the Pacific Manufacturing Company set up shop, cutting down thousands of redwood trees and becoming one of the largest suppliers of wood. By 1906 Santa Clara's population had increased to a whopping 5,000. By 1950, when the semiconductor chip was developed and most of the redwoods had been cut down, many of the orchards were plowed under, making way for the industrial expansion for which Santa Clara is known today. Heavyweight companies in Santa Clara include Intel, 3COM, Applied Materials, and Yahoo!

Santa Clara is more than just high-tech industry. Founded in 1851 on mission grounds, Santa Clara University is one of the West Coast's oldest universities. Fanning out alongside Saratoga Creek is the gorgeous 52-acre Central Park, 909 Kiely Boulevard. The park is home to the famous George F. Haines International Swim Center, 2625 Patricia Drive. Since its 1951 opening, more than 50 Olympians have trained here, bringing home 33 gold, 12 silver, and 10 bronze medals. You'll also find a lake, lighted tennis courts, a bowling green, softball fields, basketball courts, an amphitheater, a children's play area, a 30,000-square-foot Community Recreation Center, and the Central Park Library. For a more serene sojourn in the outdoors, visit the Ulistac Natural Area, 4901 Lick Mill Boulevard, a 40-acre open space preserve featuring wooded areas, grasslands and wetlands. Restored in large by community volunteers, Ulistac opened to the public in 2001. For more information or to get a free copy of the self-guided trail map, call 408-615-2260. Another popular family attraction is Paramount's Great America Amusement Park on Highway 101.

Because Santa Clara developed earlier than many surrounding areas, you'll find its residential neighborhoods are older. Housing is slightly more affordable than Sunnyvale or Mountain View, and therefore more appealing to young families and those just getting started. According to the California Association of Realtors, the median home price in April 2005 was

$625,000, an increase of almost 17% from the previous year. Home to a substantial Italian, Asian, and Indian immigrant population, Santa Clara offers a wide selection of restaurants reflecting this delectable diversity.

SANTA CLARA

Web Sites: www.santaclara.org, www.ci.santa-clara-ca.us
Area Codes: 408, 669
Zip Codes: 95050, 95051
Post Office: 1200 Franklin Mall on Jackson St, 800-275-8777, www.usps.com
Police: 601 El Camino Real, 408-615-4700
Library: Central Park Library, 2635 Homestead Rd, 408-615-2900
Public Schools: Santa Clara Unified School District, 1889 Lawrence Rd, 408-983-2000, www.scu.k12.ca.us
Community Publications: Santa Clara Silicon Valley Visitors' Guide, 408-244-8244
Community Resources: Santa Clara Chamber of Commerce and Convention and Visitor's Bureau, 1850 Warburton Ave, 408-244-8244; Triton Museum of Art, 1505 Warburton Ave, 408-247-3754; Intel Museum, 2200 Mission College Blvd, 408-765-0503; Santa Clara Players, Santa Clara Community Center, 408-248-7993; Louis B. Mayer Theatre, Santa Clara University, Cultural Events Line for Santa Clara Arts and Historical Consortium, 1509 Warburton Ave, 408-248-ARTS; Paramount's Great America Amusement Park, Great America Parkway off of Highway 101, 408-988-1776, www.sixflags.com/parks/greatamerica/index.asp; Santa Clara University, 500 El Camino Real, 408-554-4000, www.scu.edu; Mission Community College, 3000 Mission College Blvd, 408-988-2200, www.missioncollege.org

MILPITAS

Set amid the hilly, arid backdrop of the Mount Diablo foothills, the city of **Milpitas** boasts one of Santa Clara County's highest homeownership rates. Here, in this growing community of 65,000, close to 70% of households are owner-occupied. That's thanks largely to a rampant building boom, focused on what regional planners say is the key to the Bay Area's future—affordable, higher density, public transit–accessible housing. Recent developments include the 300-unit Monte Vista family apartments, with 50% moderately priced units, and 58 new moderately priced condos at Parc Place near the Great Mall, an area where many of the new developments are concentrated. A new 700-unit complex has also recently been approved. Working with nonprofits, developers, and federal grant agencies, Milpitas is leading the way, taking every opportunity imaginable to create new housing—including recently purchasing a large parcel of county land.

Not surprisingly, with all the recent large-scale development, you'll find mostly modern architecture here—from older 1960s tracts of single-family ranch-style homes to a seemingly endless wave of new three- and four-story affordable apartment buildings, spacious condos, and town-homes. The good news is that if you can snag one of these, you might just get a brand new place for as little as half of the county's median home price. According to the CAR, median home prices in April 2005 were up to $595,000, over a 21% increase from the previous year, but still low for Santa Clara County.

Milpitas is home to a large Asian-American community. In fact, more than 50% of the city is of Asian descent, according to the most recent US Census. Here, you'll find Northern California's largest Asian market center, Milpitas Square, a 1.5-million-square-foot mall, aptly named the Great Mall of the Bay Area. You'll also find a construction underway for a new civic center, a recently renovated sports center, and 28 parks. Chief among the parks is Ed Levin County Park, with 1,539 acres of hiking trails. Here, from Monument Peak you can take in the spectacular views of the valley floor and the Bay. Murphy Park is popular with children, while Hidden Lake Park, as its name suggests, is a serene place to relax and watch the ducks. For a workout try the Milpitas Sports Center, 1325 East Calaveras Boulevard, where locals enjoy aerobics, yoga, swimming, volleyball, and basketball in a new state-of-the-art facility.

All of this makes Milpitas an attractive option for families seeking a more suburban atmosphere in which to raise their children, as well as for Silicon Valley professionals looking to own their own condo. Milpitas, whose name means "little cornfields" in Spanish, is relatively young as cities go—just barely over 50 years old—and thus has a very modern suburban feel. A stopping point on the road between San Jose and Oakland, the area first attracted settlers in the 1850s, most of them farmers. Filled with vast orchards, sprawling sugar beet, pea, and corn fields, Milpitas remained a small agricultural community for roughly a century. During the post–World War II baby and building boom, the first of many tracts emerged in Milpitas, and in 1954, Milpitas officially became a city in its own right.

In the early 1960s Milpitas voters proved they could go it alone when they soundly defeated a ballot measure that would have made their city into an annexed arm of nearby San Jose. Milpitas leaders likened their battle for independence to the US Revolutionary War, dubbing themselves "the Milpitas Minutemen." Today, a minuteman symbol engraved on the official city seal pays tribute to that legacy, and to this day, a kind of friendly local rivalry still exists with San Jose.

With easy access to three major highways: I-680, I-880, and Highway 237, Milpitas is within easy commuting distance of both the East Bay and Silicon Valley, though the commute on these Bay Area roads can be among the region's most brutal during peak hours. To help alleviate the strain, the city is urging commuters to consider carpooling at least once a week, with "Rideshare Thursdays," organized by Rideshare (call 511 or visit www.511.org for more information).

Fortunately, the Valley Transportation Agency recently extended Santa Clara County's sleek, efficient light rail to Milpitas, greatly improving in-county commute options. Better still, plans to extend BART, linking Milpitas, San Jose, and Santa Clara with Alameda County by 2020, are also in the works. Though beset by funding woes, the BART extension project, for which Santa Clara County voters increased their local sales tax, consistently tops residents' priority list when it comes to transportation initiatives.

MILPITAS
Web site: www.ci.milpitas.ca.gov
Area Code: 408
Zip Code: 95035
Post Office: 450 S Abel St, 800-275-8777, www.usps.com
Police: 1275 North Milpitas Blvd, 408-586-2400
Library: Milpitas Library, 40 North Milpitas Blvd, 408-262-1171, www.santaclaracountylib.org/milpitas/
Public Schools: Milpitas Unified School District, 1331 East Calaveras Blvd, 408-945-5547
Community Resources: Milpitas Community Center, 457 East Calaveras Blvd, 408-586-3210; Milpitas Sports Center, 1325 East Calaveras Blvd, 408-586-3225; Milpitas Alliance for the Arts, 142 North Milpitas Blvd, Suite 330, www.milpitasarts.com; Rainbow Children's Theatre (performances at the Milpitas Community Center), 457 East Calaveras Blvd, 408-686-3210; Milpitas Chamber of Commerce, 138 North Milpitas Blvd, 408-262-2613, www.milpitaschamber.com
Parks, Gardens and Open Space: Recreation Service Department, 457 East Calaveras Blvd (and Milpitas Community Center), 408-586-3210

GORGEOUS COASTS, SPECTACULAR MOUNTAINS, HILLSIDES AND parks, excellent weather, top-tier universities, and the diverse, vibrant, and culturally rich mecca of San Francisco combine to make the Bay Area one of the country's most desirable places to live. Unfortunately, the region has the prices to match. Despite a sluggish economy, the San Francisco Bay Area still ranks among the nation's most expensive places to live. Thus for many, moving here—especially to San Francisco—means gearing up for high rents, and often pulling aside (at least for a while) the dream of homeownership. The stark reality is that only 10% of people living in the Bay Area can afford to buy a home here, according to a recent article in the *San Francisco Examiner*. The Association of Bay Area Governments (ABAG) expects the region to expand by more than a million people, topping 8.2 million by 2025.

In an effort to meet the growing need, especially for affordable housing, the state, local counties, and cities have banded together to create a variety of housing initiatives all designed with one goal in mind. To help meet the housing challenge, reduce congestion, and revitalize downtown areas, the regional emphasis here has been on "smart growth," with planners repeating the mantra "TOD" (Transit Oriented Development). The current trend is to focus on building mixed-use, higher density developments—creating communities that frequently have retail and office space, market rate or even luxury units, blended with below–market rate apartments, senior housing, condos, and townhouses near transportation hubs and in downtown areas. A number of municipalities and school districts are also starting their own programs to help attract and retain high-quality police, firefighters, nurses, and teachers by putting homeownership within reach through First Time Homebuyer assistance programs.

In San Francisco, two thirds of the city are renters, and many live with roommates to bring costs down. The good news is that rents have fallen significantly since the peak of the dot-com boom. Hopeful homebuyers are increasingly turning an eye to condos, townhouses, and, in San Francisco, tenants in common (TIC) ownership. If you dream of owning a home here, you may need to be a bit creative. A number of communities throughout the Bay Area, however, are beefing up their condo stock, with prices significantly lower than traditional single-family homes. Many families looking for that perfect suburban dream are choosing to move further east to Hayward, Fremont, and Vallejo, and even sometimes as far as Sacramento.

Housing options in the Bay Area are varied. San Francisco's most distinctive dwellings are its wood-framed Victorian homes, many of which have been remodeled and turned into flats with two to four units per building. You will also find a large number of Edwardian apartment buildings, each containing dozens of units. Here in quake country, wood-framed buildings, especially if they are built on rock, are safest because they give a little when the earth moves beneath them. Un-reinforced brick buildings are not safe in an earthquake, so if you find a nice apartment in one of these, you should be aware of the added risk. Also, if you're especially worried about earthquakes, steer clear of homes built on landfill (like in the Marina District), which tends to act like gelatin during a shaker. See the **Emergency Preparedness** chapter for more on this topic.

APARTMENT HUNTING

DIRECT ACTION

Many arriving in the Bay Area from other large US metropolitan areas are comfortable with the idea of finding their own apartment. Methods include reading the classifieds, either in printed form or online, and looking for posted rental notices on coffee shop, grocery store, and Laundromat bulletin boards, as well as on vacant apartments. Energetic souls will call a building's manager, ask everyone they know for word-of-mouth referrals, and, when all else fails, pound the pavement and talk to people on streets or in neighborhoods where they want to live. If this seems like too much work for you or if you haven't the time, check below under **Rental Agents, Relocation Services, Roommate Services**.

NEWSPAPER CLASSIFIED ADS

Perusing the newspaper classifieds is traditionally the most popular place to begin searching for an apartment. The listings will also give you a good sense of what you can expect to pay for rent each month. You'll see that rates vary significantly by location. Most rental ads are placed in the

Sunday newspapers, which are available on Saturday at convenience stores and newsstands. The perennial favorite here is the on-line community *Craig's List*, www.craigslist.org, especially for San Francisco, Oakland, Berkeley, and San Jose listings. The service is free, easy to use, and has the distinct advantage of being accessible from anyplace, which means you can peruse ahead of time, before you arrive, to get an idea of what's available. Through the Open Door Program, the San Francisco SPCA maintains a list of pet-friendly rental listings and provides support and advice for pet owners seeking new homes. For more info visit their website: www.sfspca.org/opendoor.

- **Contra Costa Times**, published daily, focuses on the East Bay, particularly Concord, Walnut Creek, Pleasant Hill, Martinez, Richmond, Hercules, Benicia, Antioch, Pittsburg, and Bay Point areas, 800-598-4637, www.ContraCostaTimes.com (also owns Hills Newspapers, a handful of smaller local publications including the *Berkeley Voice*, *Alameda Journal*, the *Montclarion*, and the *Piedmonter*).
- **The Daily Californian**, daily, UC Berkeley's student newspaper, good for rental and roommate listings, 510-548-8300, www.dailycal.org.
- **East Bay Express**, a weekly, free alternative newspaper that focuses on the East Bay. Good for rental and roommate listings. Found in newsstands and at cafés on Thursdays, 510-879-3700, www.eastbayexpress.com.
- **Marin Independent Journal**, published daily with listings for Marin, Sonoma, and Napa counties, 415-883-8600, www.marinij.com.
- **Oakland Tribune**, published daily, focuses on East Bay listings, especially Oakland, Berkeley, and Alameda areas, 510-208-6300, www.insidebayarea.com/oaklandtribune.
- **Pacific Sun**, weekly free, alternative newspaper with listings for Marin County. Good for rentals and roommate listings; found on Wednesdays at newsstands and cafés, 415-383-4500, www.pacificsun.com.
- **San Francisco Bay Guardian**, a free, weekly, alternative newspaper with extensive listings for San Francisco and the East Bay. Good for rental and roommate listings. Published Wednesdays, found at every café and newsstands all over city, 415-255-3100, www.sfbg.com.
- **San Francisco Chronicle**, the most widely read newspaper in the area; includes listings for San Francisco, North Bay, East Bay, and Peninsula counties, and some outlying areas. The Sunday paper has the most extensive listings, 415-777-1111, www.sfgate.com.
- **San Francisco Weekly**, a free, weekly, alternative newspaper with San Francisco listings; comes out Wednesdays. Good for rental and roommate listings. Found all over city at newsstands and cafés, 415-541-0700, www.sfweekly.com.

- ***San Jose Mercury News***, published daily with the most extensive listings for the South Bay, much of the Peninsula, and areas southeast of the Bay, 408-920-5000, www.mercurycenter.com.
- ***San Mateo County Times***, published daily except Sunday, with listings for much of the Peninsula, 650-348-4321, www.sanmateotimes.com.
- ***Santa Rosa Press Democrat***, published daily with listings for Sonoma, Marin, and Napa counties, 707-546-2020, www.pressdemo.com.

OTHER RENTAL PUBLICATIONS

Many property owners pay to list their units in glossy guides that are free to prospective renters. These guides, available in racks at supermarkets, bus and BART stations, and on many street corners, are designed to make the property look like the Taj Mahal. Keep in mind that while many of them are as nice as they look in the ads...others may not be.

Here are just a couple of these publications:

- ***Apartment Guide***, covers San Francisco and the greater Silicon Valley, 650-364-4900, www.apartmentguide.com
- ***Rental Guide***, covers San Francisco and the greater Bay Area, 415-929-7777, www.rentalguide.com

RENTAL AGENTS, RELOCATION SERVICES, ROOMMATE SERVICES

Now that the vacancy rate in San Francisco hovers around 6%—as opposed to its all-time high in the high-tech boom days of 1%—you should have no problem searching for a place to call home on your own. But for newcomers arriving in the Bay Area who want some expert help finding a place, a rental agency may be a worthwhile investment, if for no other reason than to save time. When it comes to professional services, the most popular option is to sign up with a listing service, which typically charges a flat fee for access to an extensive bank of available rentals. Listings are typically accessible on-line and updated daily. Some agencies will also run a credit report for you and help you put together a renter's resume when you sign up. Rental agencies that offer a more tailor-made approach, do the necessary footwork to find a place for you, and/or create customized lists frequently charge a percentage of the first month's rent. Sometimes a property owner will pay the fee, though this would certainly be an exception. If you have friends or coworkers in the area, ask if they can recommend a good agency. Always ask for a clear description of fees and services before entering into any binding agreements.

SF Renter, www.sfrenter.com, is an excellent online information source for San Francisco renters, with links to top local rental agencies and tenants' rights organizations. If you're looking at a large Bay Area apartment complex, you can find a quick free review by tenants at www.apartmentratings.com or check out what dwellers have to say and connect with your future neighbors at an online renter's forum, www.thinwalls talk.com.

For pet owners, the San Francisco SPCA, www.sfspca.org/ opendoor/index.shtml#housing, and the Humane Society Silicon Valley, www.hssv.org/RESOURCES/pet_friendly.htm, maintain free pet-friendly housing listings as well as helpful information on making the big move with your pet.

Below is a partial list of Bay Area rental agencies; check the Yellow Pages under "Apartment Finding and Rental Services" for more listings:

SAN FRANCISCO

- **American Marketing Systems Inc.**, 2800 Van Ness Ave, 800-747-7784, 415-447-2000, www.amsires.com.
- **Craig's List**, www.craigslist.com; housing is just one of the many listings found here. Check for fee and no-fee apartment listings, sublets, and parking spaces. Listings placed by property owners or current occupants looking to sublet their units.
- **Lofts Unlimited**, 17 Bluxome St, 415-901-2769, www.lofts unlimited; specializes in lofts for sale and for rent in San Francisco and the East Bay.
- **Metro-Rent**, 2021 Fillmore St, 415-563-7368, www.metro rent.com; listing service and roommate matching, $45 for 45 days' worth of rental search and $45 for 45 days' worth of Roommate Search, or a package of both ($50 for 45 days); also has listings in San Jose and the East Bay.
- **RentNet**, www.rentnet.com; national web site includes listings for apartment rentals all around the Bay Area.
- **Roommates.com**, national roommate-finder with San Francisco and San Jose listings, $20 for 30 days.
- **San Francisco for Rent**, 2261 Market St #900, 415-440-RENT, www.sf4rent.com; listing service, includes pet-friendly housing, fee is $20 for 90 days.
- **SF Real Estate Services**, 150 Lombard St, 415-788-4488, www.SFRealEstateServices.com; has a rental department.
- **SF Gate**, the *Chronicle's* web site, www.sfgate.com, lists rentals and homes for sale.
- **Saxe Real Estate**, 1188 Franklin St, 415-474-2435; 1551 Noriega St, 415-661-8110; www.saxerealestate.com.
- **The Rental Source**, 2013 16th St, 415-771-7685, www.therental source.com, free listings.

- **Trinity Properties**, 333 Bay St, 415-433-3333, specializes in short-term furnished rentals for corporate clients; does have some unfurnished units for long-term lease.
- **UCSF Campus Housing Office**, Milberry Union, 500 Parnassus, 415-476-2231, www.campuslifeservices.ucsf.edu/housing.

EAST BAY/NORTH BAY

- **Bay For Rent**, 2261 Market St #900, 415-440-RENT, www.bay 4rent.com; Bay Area listing service, includes pet-friendly housing, fee is $20 for 90 days (also operates SF4rent; see above for description).
- **Craig's List**, www.craigslist.com; see above for description.
- **E-Housing**, 2161 Shattuck Ave, Berkeley, 510-549-2000, www.ehousing.com; continuously updated databases; web, e-mail, and walk-in service provided.
- **Metro-Rent**, 2840 College Ave, Berkeley, 510-845-7821, www.metrorent.com; listing service and roommate matching, East Bay rental search, $30 for 45 days roommate search, package of both $30 for 45 days; North Bay rental search $45 for 45 days, roommate search $45 for 45 days, $50 for both.
- **Metro Roommates**, 201-845-RENT, www.metroroommates.com, online roommate matching service.
- **Share Rentals Unlimited**, 400 West 3rd St, Santa Rosa, 707-576-0904.
- **Tenant Finders**, 2110 Oak St, Concord, 925-939-2200, www.tenantfinders.com; free registration and rental lists; custom lists for 30 days cost $39.

PENINSULA

- **Bay For Rent**, 2261 Market St #900, 415-440-RENT, www.bay4 rent.com; Bay Area listing service, includes pet-friendly housing, fee is $20 for 90 days (also operates SF4rent; see above for description).
- **Craig's List**, www.craigslist.com; see above for description.
- **M&M Relocation Center**, 4906 El Camino Real, Los Altos, 650-988-0100, www.rentnet.com, click on "corporate housing." Long-term and short-term lease units available.
- **Roommate Express**, 2706 Harbor Blvd, Suite 212, Costa Mesa, 800-487-8050, www.e-roommate.com, www.roommateexpress.com; national roommate matching service with Bay Area listings.
- **HIP-Homesharing**, 364 South Railroad Ave, San Mateo, 650-348-6660, www.hiphousing.org; specializes in shared housing in San Mateo County. Call to set up an interview.

SOUTH BAY

- **Bay Area Rentals**, 3396 Stevens Creek Blvd, #3, San Jose, 408-244-4901, www.bayarearentals.com; a fee service that boasts a 95% placement rate. Service contracts are for 90 days and include detailed listings and daily updates. Also provides listings for San Mateo, San Francisco, Contra Costa, Marin, Solano, and Alameda counties. Special services available for corporate relocation.
- **Bay For Rent**, 2261 Market St #900, 415-440-RENT, www.bay4rent.com; Bay Area listing service, includes pet-friendly housing, fee is $20 for 90 days (also operates SF4rent; see above for description).
- **Craig's List**, www.craigslist.com; see above for description.
- **M&M Corporate Housing/Relocation**, 4906 El Camino, Los Altos, 650-988-0100; see above for description.
- **Metro-Rent**, 2050 South Bascom Ave, Campbell, 408-369-9700, www.metrorent.com; listing service and roommate matching.
- **Rental Experts,** 249 South Mathilda Ave, Sunnyvale, 408-732-8777, www.rentalexperts.net; a fee-listing service, offers 90 days worth of unlimited listings; will e-mail or fax apartment listings that match your criteria.
- **Roommate Express**, 1556 Halford Ave, Santa Clara, 408-727-2077 www.roommateexpress.com
- **Roommates.com**, national roommate-finder with San Francisco and San Jose listings, $20 for 30 days.
- **Santa Clara University Student Resource Center**, 500 El Camino Real, Benson Center, Room 203, Santa Clara, 408-554-4109 (available to students and non-students).

SUBLETS

If you're unsure how long you are going to stay in the Bay Area, or if you are having trouble finding a long-term place to lease, consider subletting an apartment or a house. A sublet allows you to rent a unit on a short-term basis while the original tenant is temporarily away. In San Francisco, while subletting is common, most leases prohibit a tenant from subletting to another tenant without the landlord's approval. Be sure to speak to the landlord before signing with a tenant. If you find a room, apartment, or a house to sublet for a limited time, you must vacate when the original tenant returns. If the original tenant decides not to return, you are not considered to be the legal tenant until you enter into a separate agreement with the landlord. For those wishing to stay, the landlord can require you to sign a lease at a higher rent than what you had been paying.

Subletting from a "master tenant" who is the sole lease signer, and who already lives on the premises and will continue to do so while you also live there, is common, but again must usually be approved by the landlord. While it is illegal for master tenants to charge you more than the rent they pay to the landlord, they can charge you up to the full amount in rent that they are paying, an amount they must disclose in writing. The master tenant always has the right to evict you with 30 days' written notice, for any reason.

SHARING

Considering the dozens of schools and universities, the high cost of rent, and the preponderance of rambling Victorian flats—with odd-shaped little rooms and formal dining rooms that do new duty as bedrooms—house sharing is ubiquitous in the Bay Area. For a thousand dollars a month, a studio with an efficiency kitchen may seem paltry and cramped when compared with renting a room in a house with a big kitchen, pantry, a shared dining and living room, and a backyard, all for the same amount of rent or less. Of course roommate situations are not for everybody. There are households, a better term might be co-ops, comprised solely of non-smoking, cat-loving, vegetarian political activists who go to the farmers' market together and share cooking duties each evening. And that's just one scenario. The options are endless.

There are two ways to enter into lease agreements with roommates. Some or all leasees can be "co-tenants," which means that whoever signs the lease with the landlord has equal rights and equal responsibilities. The worst case scenario here occurs if living together does not go as well as anticipated. Because everyone has signed the lease, everyone has the right to remain in the house and no one can force anyone else to go. The other lease option is to have a master tenant who signs the lease, pays the rent in one check, and deals with the landlord. The other roommate or roommates are then considered sub-tenants. Should you, as a sub-tenant, be unable to pay your rent, the landlord cannot go after you, but your roommate can. In fact, the master tenant can evict you with 30 days' written notice, regardless of cause.

Roommate situations can bring lifelong friends or a few months of living hell. While not legally binding, it's wise to get together with your prospective roomies to compose and sign a so-called "pre-nup," which may help to ensure promises made today won't go ignored tomorrow. For tips on what to include in your roommate agreement, check out www.ehow.com/how_4331_draft-roommate-agreement.html. You can print out a free template at: www.roommateconnection.com/2000TRC/headers/agreement.html.

If you don't mind paying a fee to find a roommate, hire a roommate service (see above under **Rental Agents, Relocation Services,**

Roommate Services). The cost to match you with a roommate generally is reasonable, ranging from $35 to $110. If you'd rather not pay the roommate referral service fee, there are free alternatives, chief among them bulletin boards at universities, colleges, local grocery stores (generally not the chains), and coffeehouses. The Rainbow Grocery in the Mission District at Folsom and 12th Street has a large roommate board, as does the Women's Building, 3543 18th Street. In the East Bay, the bulletin board at the Whole Foods Market at Ashby and Telegraph avenues in Oakland is a popular posting place. Housing offices at universities and colleges also may be helpful.

CHECKING IT OUT

For many people, the neighborhood is just as important as the place itself, so once you've checked out a potential apartment or house, get out and walk around. Feel free to ask neighbors if they enjoy living there as well. Maintain a sense of what you want/need and what you are willing to do without before you view a unit. Here are some things to consider during your search:

- Are the kitchen appliances clean and in working order? Do the stove's burners work? How about the oven? How's the kitchen sink? Is there sufficient counter and shelf space?
- Check the windows—do they open, close, and lock? Do the bedroom windows open onto a noisy or potentially dangerous area?
- How are the closets? Are they big enough to accommodate your belongings? Is there any private storage space?
- How's the water pressure? Try turning on the shower and the sink. Does the toilet flush adequately?
- Are there enough electrical outlets for your needs? Do the outlets work?
- Are there any signs of insects or other pests?
- What about laundry facilities? Are they in the building or is there a Laundromat nearby?
- Outside, do you feel comfortable? Will you feel safe here at night? Is there secured parking? How many spaces? If two, are they tandem (so that one car blocks the other) or side by side? Is there an extra fee for parking? What about public transportation and shopping?
- Are you responsible for paying gas, water, and/or electricity? This policy varies from place to place, and paying any combination or none at all is possible.
- Watch for discrimination. In San Francisco, it's illegal to deny housing based on race, religion, age, or any other personal basis.

Ed Sacks' *Savvy Renter's Kit* contains a thorough renter's checklist for those interested in augmenting their own lists. The California Department of Consumer Affairs also maintains various useful documents and check-lists at www.dca.ca.gov/legal/landlordbook.

STAKING A CLAIM

When you view a unit, come *prepared*. Bring your checkbook so that if the place looks good, you can hold it with a deposit. Also bring a copy of your credit report for the building manager (see **Money Matters**). Landlords will often want references from your previous residences, as well as your basic employment information. Keep in mind that when you're applying for a place, landlords can require that the amount of money you earn monthly be equivalent to three times the amount of rent you are expected to pay. Also, they can request only nonsmokers, they can prohibit pets other than a working dog, and they can bar you from having overnight guests for more than a certain number of nights per year. (If you think you'll have lots of visitors, watch out for a lease containing such a clause, as this may not bode well for your tenant/landlord relationship.)

LEASES/RENTAL AGREEMENTS AND SECURITY DEPOSITS

If you want a preview of what a typical Bay Area lease or rental agreement looks like, take a trip to any well-stocked office supply store. Standard lease/rental agreements are sold in tear-off pads. Of course, the numbers will not have been entered, but you'll at least get a glimpse at how most landlords handle deposits, rent due dates and grace periods, appliances, pets, and the like.

The law requires that a lease of one year or more be in writing. Every lease must also specify a termination date. If the termination date is not included, the tenant and landlord are considered to have entered into a month-to-month rental agreement. An oral agreement to rent for more than one year is considered a month-to-month rental agreement, not a lease. Also, unless it is a fixed-term lease, it will convert to a month-to-month rental agreement at the conclusion of the first tenancy period. Rarely, a landlord might ask you to sign another yearlong lease.

It is customary and acceptable for California landlords to demand var-ious combinations of up-front charges before entering into a lease or rental agreement with you. Those charges will likely include a fee for running a credit check (not refundable), the first month's rent, possibly last month's rent (which differs from a security deposit), a key deposit, sometimes a security/cleaning deposit, and, perhaps, a pet deposit. If the property manager asks for last month's rent, keep in mind it must be used for just that. That way, when you give your customary 30 days' notice of intent to vacate, you're paid up. No lease or rental agreement may include nonrefundable deposits. In California all deposits are returnable if all agreed-to conditions are met. Landlords are also required to pay 5% interest on security deposits at the termination of the lease, if the unit was held for longer than a year. If your security deposit is not returned within three weeks of your vacancy date, you can talk to a tenants' rights organization or seek recourse in small claims court. If you are a co-tenant or a sub-tenant, the landlord does not have to return your portion of the security deposit directly to you. The deposit on the unit is returned only when the entire unit is vacated, which means you will have to get your part of the deposit money from the co-tenants or master tenant.

Should you find yourself in the uncomfortable position of having to break a lease, you have a number of ways to mitigate the situation, making it less contentious, less costly to yourself, and more palatable to your landlord. If you need to move out before the lease is up, the landlord must make an effort to rent your unit and he/she may not double-dip; that is he/she may not accept rent from you (who have moved out) and a new tenant at the same time. When breaking a lease, try to do it with care and savvy. Give the landlord written notice of intent as far in advance as possible, and if you can, try to find a new tenant for your unit, making sure he or she is financially capable of taking on the responsibility. If you know that your old unit has been rented and you are still being held responsible for the lease, take action. Speak to the new tenant, photograph a new name on your old mailbox, and seek help from a tenants' organization (see below).

RENT AND EVICTION CONTROL

Before you've secured a place of your own, be aware that San Francisco has a Rent Stabilization and Arbitration Ordinance that offers protection against some rent increases. The ordinance does not apply to post-1979 apartment units, government regulated housing, and short-term residential hotels. For those units covered by the ordinance, landlords are allowed to raise the rent once a year, beginning on the anniversary of your move-in date, as long as a 30-day written notice is given. The amount by which the rent may be raised is determined by the San Francisco Rent Board and is announced each March. By law it will always be between 0 and 7%.

East Palo Alto also has rent control (see listing below). In San Jose only mobile homes and apartments built before September 1979 are protected by rent control. An 8% rent increase is allowable yearly for these kinds of units. Berkeley is the only other rent-controlled city in the region. The rent increase allowance is variable; check with the Berkeley Rent Stabilization Program for more information (see below).

In the remaining parts of the Bay Area, you can expect a rent increase at the end of your lease (with 30 days' notice). Also, you can be evicted without "just cause" when your lease expires, again with 30 days' notice.

Berkeley and San Francisco have stringent eviction protection for tenants. In San Francisco there are 14 "just cause" reasons for eviction, and in Berkeley there are 12. These include failure to pay rent; failure to sign a new lease that is the same as the old lease; illegal activity on the premises; breaking the terms of the lease; willful damage to property or allowing others to damage the property (Berkeley); disturbing other tenants; refusing the landlord legal access to the premises when the landlord needs entry in order to bring the unit up to code or to make substantial repairs; an owner-move-in eviction; the landlord has received a permit to demolish the unit; a subletting tenant refuses to vacate the temporary housing offered by the landlord after the landlord has repaired the tenant's prior unit (Berkeley). In addition, a newer quirk in San Francisco is landlords' use of the Ellis Act, a state law permitting owners to evict tenants on the grounds that they are permanently removing the rental units from the market.

The sale of property, the expiration of a rental agreement, or a change in the Federal Section 8 status of a unit does *not* constitute "good cause" for eviction.

The laws of every other locality are generally state tenancy laws. A comprehensive source of information on the legal aspects of tenancy, *California Tenants' Rights*, is published by Berkeley-based Nolo Press, 800-728-3555, www.nolo.com. Nolo also publishes the *California Landlord's Law Book*, for those on the other side of the rental property wall. Knowing the rights and responsibilities of both sides may prove valuable when it comes time to sign on the dotted line, and again when you're ready to move out, as security deposits, apartment cleaning, and repairs become potential issues of concern. Also, you can view the California Civil Code on the web, www.leginfo.ca.gov

If you're in need of help, you can also get information on tenants' rights from a number of offices:

- **Berkeley Rent Stabilization Program**, 2125 Milvia St, 510-644-6128, www.ci.berkeley.ca.us/rent
- **California State Fair Employment and Housing Department**, www.dfeh.ca.gov, 455 Golden Gate Ave, Suite 7600, San Francisco, 800-884-1684; 1515 Clay St, Suite 701, Oakland, 510-622-2941; 111 North Market St, Suite 810, San Jose, 408-277-1277
- **East Palo Alto Rent Stabilization Program**, 650-853-3109
- **Eviction Defense Center**, 1611 Telegraph Ave, #726, Oakland, 510-452-4541
- **Housing Rights, Inc.**, 2718 Telegraph #100, Berkeley, 510-548-8776, 800-261-2298, www.housingrights.org

- **Project Sentinel**, specializes in landlord/tenant disputes in Sunnyvale, 408-720-9888
- **St. Peter's Housing Committee**, 474 Valencia St, San Francisco, 415-487-9203
- **San Francisco Rent Board**, 25 Van Ness Ave, #320, San Francisco, 415-252-4600
- **San Francisco Tenants Union**, 558 Capp St, San Francisco, 415-282-6622, www.sftu.org
- **Bay Area Legal Aid**, 2 West Santa Clara St, 8th floor, San Jose, 408-283-3700; call for a pre-screening.
- **Legal Aid Society Housing Counseling Program**, 408-283-1540
- **San Jose Rental Rights and Referrals**, 4 North 2nd St, #600, San Jose, 408-277-5431

LANDLORD/TENANT RIGHTS AND RESPONSIBILITIES

In the state of California, landlords must rent premises (grounds, buildings, and units) that are free of rubbish and vermin. There must be adequate containers for garbage and recycling. The floors, hallways, and railings must be in good repair. Electrical wiring must be in good working order and up to the safety standards at the time of installation. There must be adequate and safe heating facilities. There must be hot and cold running water and a sewage disposal system. There must be plumbing, electricity, and gas, all in good working order. There must be effective waterproofing on the walls and roofs. Windows and doors must be unbroken, and locks must be in working order.

Landlords are not allowed to enter your premises without giving 24 hours' notice and receiving your permission, unless an emergency threatens damage to the unit. You must permit the landlord to enter to make repairs, and to show the apartment to prospective buyers, tenants, contractors, appraisers, and the like. The landlord is not allowed to harass you verbally or physically or make threats. A landlord can neither lock you out of the premises until you have been legally evicted nor turn off your utilities in an attempt to get you to vacate without due process. Tenants are responsible for maintaining the premises in working and sanitary condition, for paying the rent on time, and for following the rules written in the lease.

Renting situations in the Bay Area vary widely, from renting a typical apartment in a complex to renting an attic room in someone's home. To learn more about local ordinances order the book *California Tenants: A Guide to Residential Tenants' and Landlords' Rights and Responsibilities*, available free from the Department of Consumer Affairs. Send your request to California Tenants c/o Department of Consumer Affairs, P.O. Box 989004, West Sacramento, CA 95798-0004, or visit www.dca.ca.gov.

RENTER'S INSURANCE

Renter's insurance provides relatively inexpensive coverage against theft, water damage, fire, and in many cases personal liability. In this earthquake-prone area, try to find a policy that covers earthquake damage to personal possessions. Be sure to shop around as insurance rates vary considerably. Those with several housemates may not be eligible for coverage.

Web sites can be helpful as you search for renter's insurance. A couple that may be worth investigating include www.insure.com; Quicken, www.insuremarket.com; and www.getrentersinsurance.com. These sites offer details about what a policy should cover and tips on making a claim. Most large insurance companies (AAA, 21st Century, etc.) also offer renter's insurance. If you own a car, a good option is to check and see if your car insurance carrier also offers renter's insurance, as you may be able to get a discount for adding a new service.

BUYING

Many people come to the Bay Area with the intention of buying a house, but the sticker price often scares them into renting and longing for life back in Kansas. Despite tough economic times, the prices of Bay Area real estate continue to soar. The median price for a Bay Area home in April 2005 was $622,000, up more than 19% from the previous year, according to DataQuick.

On the bright side, interest rates for mortgages are still running relatively low, and in fact, low mortgage rates have been the major factor driving the homebuyers' market. Because of this, it is not unusual, particularly in San Francisco, for buyers to bid against each other—often in increments of thousands of dollars. As a buyer, you need patience, persistence, and stamina. Be prepared to bid on a number of houses before your bid is accepted. In the bidding process, it's not uncommon for bids to go as high as 20% above the list price.

While it's good to have a clear idea of what you want, you may need to be willing to make concessions—in terms of both price and neighborhood. To figure out what you can afford to pay for a house, the general rule of thumb is to multiply your annual salary by three or four. For example, if you make $100,000 a year, you should plan on spending no more than $400,000 on your new home. The bad news is that you will be hard pressed to find a home for $400,000 in much of the Bay Area. Another important point to remember is that you will be required to place about 20% of the purchase price as a down payment, and don't forget about closing costs, which are generally 1% to 3% of the purchase price, depending on your loan.

Before even beginning your search, most realtors suggest taking a moment to make a list of your top priorities. Think about the neighborhood, the commute, parking, schools, the number of bedrooms and bathrooms, etc. Consider your lifestyle. If you are a gourmet cook, is the kitchen spacious enough? Do you want to live in a gated community? How about a historic property? If you are looking for a fixer-upper, you'll need to consider how much time, money, and effort you will be willing to put into a place. Drafting such a list will let a real estate agent focus on what's truly important to you and your family. In addition, before meeting with a real estate agent, it's a good idea to do a little footwork on your own. Investigate the cost of properties in the neighborhood where you would like to live, and compare that to your financial situation. A good resource to check out is Fisbo's Homebuyer's Toolkit, available online at www.fisbos.com/P_Genpub/FHB.html. Another good source with lots of Bay Area–specific information including home-buying tips and articles on local real estate trends is www.nestegghomebuying.com.

GET YOUR FINANCIAL HOUSE IN ORDER

The first thing to consider when preparing to buy a home is your pocketbook. How much do you have in savings for a down payment, and what can you afford to spend on monthly mortgage payments? Typically, as mentioned above, you will be required to put down 20% of the total cost as a down payment. Don't forget that there will also be closing costs, which include insurance, appraisal, attorney's fees, taxes, and loan fees.

As a rule, your monthly housing costs should not exceed 28% of your income, and your debt load shouldn't exceed 36% of it. That said, these days lenders might tailor the 28/36 ratio depending on your situation (assets, liability, job, credit history). As a homeowner you will also be responsible for homeowner's insurance, property taxes, repairs, utilities, and condo fees, so make sure to leave space in your budget for these.

Many buyers consult with a mortgage broker or direct lender and get **pre-qualified** or even **pre-approved** for a loan prior to finding a house. **Pre-qualifying** is an educated estimate, based on your finances (income, debt, general expenses), of what you can afford. **Pre-approval** verifies your financial claims, and your ability to pay is guaranteed by the lender. For you to be pre-approved, your loan officer will need to review and verify your finances (by running a credit check, getting proof of employment and savings); then you will be given a letter stating that the bank is willing to lend you a specified amount based on your proven financial situation. Although pre-approval is a bit labor intensive, it may give you a competitive edge. This is a good idea, particularly in the Bay Area where speed is of the essence. But perhaps the best aspect of pre-approval is that you'll know before even starting your search what you can realistically afford.

Before setting up an appointment with a lender to get pre-qualified or pre-approved, you should prepare your financial documents. You will need to provide your loan officer with your name, address, previous address, social security number, documentation of financial history, and credit report, available from the three major credit bureaus (listed below). You can also visit **www.annualcreditreport.com** for online access to all three. (See also **Credit Reports** in the **Money Matters** chapter.) If your credit report isn't stellar you may still be able to qualify, but your interest rates may be higher. A substantial down payment can counteract credit flaws as well.

The major **credit bureaus** are:

- **Experian,** P.O. Box 2104, Allen, TX 75002-2104, 888-397-3742
- **TransUnion**, P.O. Box 390, Springfield, PA 19064-0390, 800-916-8800
- **Equifax**, P.O. Box 105873, Atlanta, GA 30348, 800-685-1111

If you're planning to buy a home, it's a good idea to take a thorough look at your credit report ahead of time. This will give you the opportunity to challenge any errors and get them removed. Also, if your credit score is on the lower end, you can set to work trying to bring it back up. If you have a less than perfect track record, paying your bills on time and in full for a full year will help restore your credit score and make you more appealing to lenders.

When filling out your final loan paperwork, keep in mind that it is a federal offense to intentionally put down incorrect information. Within three business days of receiving your loan application, your lender must give you a "good faith estimate" of how much your closing costs will be. Once you are approved, you can make an offer (you can make an offer when you are pre-qualified, contingent on funding). Your offer should be in writing. You may want to consider adding contingency clauses to the offer—the most critical being a requirement that the home must pass inspection. Having your prospective new place evaluated by an expert can save you from being unhappily surprised by unforeseen problems down the road. An expert will review the structure inside and out (walls, roof, floors, ceilings, windows); the electrical, plumbing, and heating systems; and the foundation, and will also provide structural and foundation assessments for seismic safety, which are crucial when considering buying a home in earthquake country.

Modern criteria for seismic design and construction have been included in the Uniform Building Code since 1973. The 1988 edition has the most up-to-date requirements. Construction of nearly all new buildings in California complies with this or a similar code. The code requires greater strength for essential facilities and for sites on soft soil, where shaking intensity is increased. It also sets minimum requirements that assure life safety but allow earthquake damage and loss of function. For more information on seismic safety, visit www.usgs.gov.

Once your offer has been accepted, you'll need to have the house appraised and inspected, and the title will need to be sent to the lender for a title search. If all goes well, you'll move into escrow, where the seller is paid, keys are exchanged, the title is transferred, and the deal is sealed.

Buying a home is a complicated process with multiple steps, only briefly touched on here. Below are some resources to help you begin your search and find a good realtor.

ONLINE RESOURCES—HOUSE HUNTING

These days you can start your search for a home on the Internet before you even arrive in the Bay Area. While searching the web probably won't get you a house, since many are sold as quickly as they are listed, it will give you a good idea about what's on the market, where you should look once you get here, and about how much you can expect to pay. Not every site lists every home in the Bay Area but every home in the Bay Area for sale is probably now listed on at least one site.

Some useful sites to help your search include:

- **www.ziprealty.com**; claims to be the first online real estate brokerage to host online transactions
- **www.cyberhomes.com**; lists homes for sale across the nation and lists other pertinent real estate information
- **http://houseandhome.msn.com**; home-buying site with information on homes for sale, moving and relocating, home improvement and more
- **www.homefair.com**; realty listings, moving tips, and more
- **www.homestore.com**; lists homes for sale, apartments, and roommates, includes moving tips, and a section on home improvement
- **www.realtylocator.com**; contains thousands of home listings nationwide; neighborhood data; discussions about real estate
- **www.homeseekers.com**; a database system of the Multiple Listing Service
- **http://realestate.yahoo.com**; this site list homes for sale, mortgage loans, community profiles, listing for home inspectors, real estate agents, title companies, and more

ONLINE RESOURCES—MORTGAGES

Everyone likes to complicate mortgages, but think of them simply as an agreement between the buyer and the lender about the amount of money being borrowed. There are a few other elements of mortgages like points, interest rates, and terms, but don't get overwhelmed by the language. Remember everything is negotiable, so shop around for the best mortgage. You may want to find a mortgage broker to assist you with the process. The web and the bookstore are good places to begin figuring out mortgages. **www.mtgprofessor.com**, a web site written by Professor Jack Guttentag of the Wharton School of the University of Pennsylvania, contains helpful information about mortgages.

Today, hundreds of web sites offer mortgage loans. If this avenue appeals to you, be aware that some online companies cannot process mortgage applications fast enough for the Bay Area's short escrow period, typically 30 days or less. Also, be sure to investigate a company's track record thoroughly, as fraud has increasingly been a problem in recent years. Check out the Better Business Bureau, www.bbb.com, to find out if a company is licensed, how long it has been in business, and if it has any history of consumer complaints. You may also want to call online companies and speak with them directly, and find out if they have a local office you can visit in person.

Below is a list of web sites to help you get started with the process:

- **www.mycountrywide.com**; offers moving services, branch locators, locked rates, mortgage rates, credit evaluations, mortgage tools, and relocation services, and more
- **http://houseandhome.msn.com**; can help you find loans, homes, and neighborhood profiles, and can help you with credit cards, auto financing, and refinancing your home
- **www.freddiemac.com**; provides information on lower cost loans and homes for renter and buyers
- **www.lendingtree.com**; helps you find any type of loan, from a mortgage to a student loan
- **www.owners.com**; offers loan status, mortgage rates, credit evaluations, mortgage tools, and virtual tours of homes for sale
- **www.realtor.com**; offers property listings, virtual tours, and lender and realtor listings

Because of the high cost of housing in the Bay Area, the state, a number of local counties, cities, and some school districts have partnered with lenders to offer a variety of mortgage and down payment assistance programs to qualified first-time homebuyers. The Clearinghouse for Affordable Housing and Community Finance Resources, 916-445-4782, www.hcd.ca.gov/clearinghouse, offers information on over 200 housing programs throughout California, including government, private lenders, and foundation grants, and the California Housing Finance Agency, 916-322-3991, www.calhfa.ca.gov, offers a variety of below–market interest rate first mortgage programs and down payment assistance programs to eligible first-time homebuyers.

CONDOMINIUMS, CO-OPS, TENANCIES-IN-COMMON

In the Bay Area, detached single-family homes are plentiful, but usually expensive. Alternative housing options include condominiums, co-ops, and tenancies-in-common.

Condominiums or "condos" are communal associations or cooperative developments where the co-owners share interest and responsibility for the common areas (elevator, garden, laundry room, and hallways), but hold sole ownership of their unit. Condos are common in the Bay Area, and new ones are rapidly being built.

A **co-op** is a corporation; owners hold shares in the property and have voting rights. An owner has the right to sell those shares, but the board members or fellow co-op members reserve the right to refuse to sell to someone whom they consider undesirable. Co-op residences are generally in larger, older buildings.

With **tenancies-in-common**, known as TICs, co-owners usually buy an existing building of two to six units. By law the co-owners all must live on the premises as their primary residences. The co-owners own a percentage of the entire building, but while they enjoy exclusive use of their unit, they do not own that unit outright. The finances of TIC co-owners, with regard to the building, are entwined, perhaps making it riskier to buy into than a condo. In San Francisco, TICs have become a popular option for those who want out of the San Francisco rental market but cannot afford to purchase a traditional, single-family home.

San Franciscans concerned about the dwindling supply of affordable rental units in the Bay Area have opposed the recent rise in condo and TIC conversions, and now San Francisco severely restricts residential condominium conversions. All two- to six-unit buildings that are not 100% owner-occupied by separate individuals living in separate units must compete in an annual lottery for the right to convert. A maximum of 200 residential units can win the right to convert each year through the lottery. Properties with more than six residential units cannot convert at all. A two- to six-unit building can qualify to convert to a TIC only when it meets occupancy requirements, wins or bypasses the annual conversion lottery, and satisfies "Tenant Intent to Purchase" requirements. But this may be on the verge of changing. At the time of this writing, the San Francisco Board of Supervisors was considering doing away with the lottery and the maximum yearly conversion cap and allowing TIC eligible groups that were 100% owner-occupied as of January 20, 2005, to move ahead.

REHABBING

High housing costs in the Bay Area tempt many would-be homeowners into considering the purchase of a fixer-upper. Be aware, fixer-uppers here usually need a lot of work. No one in this real estate market is going to sell a home for under market value when all that is needed is a fresh coat of paint, some new counter tops, and a couple of light fixtures. For those seriously in the market for a fixer-upper, and if this is where your talent lies, or what you consider a fun hobby, hunt long enough and hard enough and you can get a good price on a home that needs work. Keep in mind that materials and labor are more expensive in California. If you give up and need help, you can contact the Handyman Connection (800-466-5530, www.handymanconnection.com) for contractor referrals in your neck of the woods.

FINDING A REALTOR

Certainly, buying a home is not something you do every day, and while it is possible to find a house or condo on your own, you'll probably be better off with the help of an expert. According to the *San Francisco Chronicle*, less than 5% of homes here are bought and sold without an agent. Even if you find a home that appeals to you, say in cyberspace, you will most likely need an agent to show you the place and complete the transaction. What's more, homes in the Bay Area are often sold before they make it to the MLS (Multiple Listing Service).

One of the best ways to find a real estate agent is through word of mouth. Ask your friends, colleagues, or your employer's relocation administrator. Visiting open houses held in the neighborhood of your choice is another good way to meet agents. It's important to meet with and talk to a few agents before choosing one. Be sure to look for someone who will represent you as a buyer—a buyer's broker. A buyer's broker works exclusively for the prospective homebuyer, while a traditional broker works for the home seller, even though they show buyers around. A broker who works for you will bargain on your behalf, and try to get you the lowest possible price for the house, while a traditional broker's job is just the opposite—to get the seller the most money possible for the house. Make sure that whomever you choose, he/she is someone who seems trustworthy and has a good reputation. Check a realtor's credentials, and call his/her references to find out if his/her previous clients were satisfied.

Once you find a home you want, your realtor will help make sure that your offer is accepted, which can include pitching your "story" to the seller. When making an offer, it is also important to structure it with minimal contingencies. In today's market some buyers are willing to accept a house on an "as is" basis; some offer to pay a portion of the seller's closing costs. A real estate agent who is familiar with these and other tactics, as well as the going prices for properties, can be a great help in this market.

REAL ESTATE AGENTS

Below is a list of real estate agents to help you get started. This list is far from comprehensive.

SAN FRANCISCO

- **Century 21**, 5812 Geary Blvd, 415-863-7500, for free consultation call 877-798-7777; www.hartfordproperties.com
- **Coldwell Banker**, 1699 Van Ness Ave, 415-474-1750; 2633 Ocean Ave, 415-334-1880; multiple other Bay Area locations, 800-464-4292; www.coldwellbanker.com
- **Hill & Company**, 2107 Union St, 415-921-6000, www.hill-co.com
- **Herth Real Estate**, 555 Castro St, 415-861-5200, www.herth.com
- **Lofts Unlimited**, 461 Second St, 415-546-3100, www.lofts unlimited.com
- **McGuire Real Estate**, 2001 Lombard St; 560 Davis St; 800-4-RESULTS, www.mcguire.com
- **Pacific Union**, 6001 Van Ness Ave, 415-474-6600; 1700 California St, 415-447-6200; www.pacunion.com
- **Prudential California Realty**, 2241 Market St, 677 Portola Dr, 415-664-9400; 2200 Union St, 415-921-0113; www.prurealty.com
- **Zephyr Real Estate**, 4040 24th St, 415-695-7707; 318 Brannon St, 415-905-0250, www.zephyr-re.com

NORTH BAY

- **Coldwell Banker**, 901 Reichert Ave, Novato, 415-899-8400, www.cbnorcal.com
- **Frank Howard Allen Realtors**, 915 Diablo Ave, Novato, 415-897-3000; 215 Second St, Sausalito, 415-331-9000; 905 East Washington Blvd, Petaluma, 707-762-7766; 2245 Montgomery Dr, Santa Rosa, 707-537-3000; www.fhallen.com
- **McGuire Real Estate**, 1040 Redwood Hwy, Mill Valley, 415-383-8500, www.mcguire.com
- **Prudential California Realty**, 1604 Sir Francis Drake Blvd, San Anselmo, 415-457-7340, www.prucalmarin.com
- **RE/MAX Realty of Central Marin**, 1099 D St, Suite 201, San Rafael, 415-258-1500

EAST BAY

- **Berkeley Hills Realty**, 1714 Solano Ave, Berkeley, 510-524-9888, 800-523-2460
- **Better Homes Realty**, 5942 MacArthur Blvd, Oakland, 510-562-8600; 5353 College Ave, Oakland, 510-339-8400; www.bhr.com
- **Marvin Gardens**, 1577 Solano Ave, Berkeley, 510-527-2700, www.marvingardens.com
- **Miller & Co.**, 702 Gilman St, Berkeley 510-558-3464
- **Prudential California Realty**, 660A Central Ave, Alameda, 510-337-8670; 1539 Shattuck Ave, Berkeley, 510-849-3711; 2077 Mountain Blvd, Oakland, 510-339-9290
- **Red Oak Realty**, 1891 Solano Ave, Berkeley, 510-527-3387; 2983 College Ave, Berkeley, 510-849-9990, www.redoakrealty.com
- **RE/MAX Realtors**, 1758 Solano Ave, Berkeley, 510-526-1200; 2070 Mountain Blvd, Oakland, 510-339-4100, www.home-buy-sell.com

PENINSULA

- **Alain Pinel Realtors**, 620 Santa Cruz Ave, Menlo Park, 650-462-1111; 578 University Ave, Palo Alto, 650-323-1111, www.apr.com
- **Alhouse King Realty**, 2600 El Camino Real, Palo Alto, 650-354-1100, www.akrealty.com
- **Century 21**, 871 Hamilton Ave, Menlo Park, 650-328-6100; 385 Foster City Blvd, Foster City, 650-341-2121; 1503 Grant Rd, Mountain View, 650-966-1100; 450 Dondee Way, Pacifica, 650-355-2121; 123 South San Mateo Dr, San Mateo, 650-347-3888, www.century21 alliance.com
- **Coldwell Banker**, 496 First Ave, Los Altos, 650-947-2200; 930 Santa Cruz Ave, Menlo Park, 650-323-7751; 1745 El Camino Real, Redwood City, 650-369-8050; 2969 Woodside Rd, Woodside, 650-851-1940
- **McGuire Real Estate**, 360 Primrose Rd, Burlingame, 650-348-0222, www.mcguire.com
- **Peninsula Homes Realty**, 605 Cambridge Ave, Menlo Park, 650-324-2200, www.penhomes.com
- **Prudential California**, 1116 South El Camino Real, San Mateo, 650-578-0200, www.1prudential.com; 100 El Camino Real, Burlingame, 650-696-7020, www.pruweb1.com
- **RE/MAX Realtors**, 670 Woodside Rd, Redwood City, 650-364-2660

SOUTH BAY

- **Better Homes Realty**, 1725 South Bascom Ave, Suite 216, Campbell, 408-559-5000; 1185 Branham Lane, San Jose 408-448-5600; www.bhr.com

- **Coldwell Banker**, 1550 South Bascom Ave, Campbell, 408-559-0303; 761 First St, Gilroy 408-847-3000; 480 South Mathilda Ave, Sunnyvale, 408-616-2600; www.cbnorcal.com
- **Prudential California Realty**, 408-281-7800; 841 Blossom Hill Rd, Suite 112, San Jose, 408-281-7800; 17500 Monterey Rd, Suite A, San Jose, 408-779-7066, www.prurealty.com
- **Silicon Valley Association of Realtors**, 19400 Stevens Creek Blvd, Cupertino, 408-200-0100, www.silvar.org
- **True Vision Network Real Estate**, 2021 The Alameda, San Jose, 408-236-6650, www.true-vision.com

FOR SALE BY OWNER

Intrepid souls who want to buy or sell a house without an agent can check online sites specializing in home listings by owners:
- **www.fisbos.com**
- **http://hometoursonline.net**
- **www.HomesByOwner.com**
- **www.owners.com**
- **www.econobroker.com**, 888-989-4MLS; this service will list your home (for a fee) on the Multiple Listing Service, which is a list used by real estate agents nationwide.

HOMEOWNER'S INSURANCE

For most everyone, dealing with a bank or mortgage lender is necessary when buying a new home, and getting homeowner's insurance is a required part of the process. Coverage is typically offered at 120% to 125% of the face value of your house and belongings. Factors that insurance companies consider when determining the rate of your policy include the fire resistance of your house—wood frames cost more to insure than masonry structures—and your location. Being in a high theft neighborhood or far from a fire hydrant or fire station will add to the cost of your policy.

There are ways to get lower homeowner's insurance rates: Requesting a higher deductible can lower your premium by as much as 25%; coupling homeowner's insurance with an automobile policy may result in a discount on both; and most insurance companies offer lower premiums for homes with safety devices such as deadbolt locks, security alarm systems, and fire extinguishers.

Earthquake insurance in the Bay Area is a good idea, although it's expensive and for a while was difficult to obtain. In 1994, as a result of the costs associated with the Northridge Earthquake, many insurance companies stopped writing new homeowner's and renter's insurance policies and some pulled out of California altogether. In response, the State of California established the **California Earthquake Authority (CEA)** in 1996, which provides basic earthquake-damage coverage. Insurance companies operating in California are required to either supply their own earthquake coverage to their policyholders or to offer the CEA's policy. For more information about the CEA call 916-325-3800 or 877-797-4300, or check out www.earthquakeauthority.com. For answers to any other insurance-related questions, contact the **California Department of Insurance** at 800-927-4357 or visit www.insurance.ca.gov.

The most common type of earthquake insurance is normally added as an endorsement on a standard homeowner's insurance policy. Typically, there is a deductible of 5% to 10%, and sometimes 15%, of the value of the home. This means that for a home currently insured at $200,000, you would have to pay $10,000 to $30,000 on damages before the insurance company would pay anything. Separate deductibles may apply to contents and structure. An important coverage is temporary living expense, which pays for motel and meals if you have to move out of your home. There is usually no deductible on this coverage. The yearly cost of residential earthquake insurance is normally about $1.50 to $3 per $1,000 of coverage on the structure.

In the San Francisco Bay Area, 30% to 40% of homeowners have earthquake insurance. The percentage drops to about 25% for all of California. To find out more about earthquake insurance, ask your insurance agent or call the California State Department of Insurance at 800-927-4357 or visit www.insurance.ca.gov.

If you are looking at an older home, find out if it has been retrofitted. Though not required, this is something you want to consider. Retrofitting won't guarantee your home will escape a quake damage-free but generally speaking, reinforced structures withstand shocks better, making them safer and reducing damage in quakes. Cost varies but can be 1% to 3% of a home's total value. For shaking maps and information on making your home safer, check out http://quake.abag.ca.gov. The **US Geological Survey**, www.usgs.gov, also has a wealth of information on earthquakes and earthquake safety.

ADDITIONAL RESOURCES—HOUSE HUNTING

Following are resources that may be of interest for those in the market for a new home:

- **100 Questions Every First Time Homebuyer Should Ask: With Answers from Top Brokers from Around the Country**, 2nd edition (Times Books), by Ilyce R. Glink

- **Opening the Door to a Home of Your Own,** a pamphlet published by the Fannie Mae Foundation for first-time homebuyers; call 800-834-3377 for a copy
- **How to Buy a House in California,** 10th edition (Nolo Press), by Ralph E. Warner, Ira Serkes, and George Devine
- **Your New House: the Alert Consumer's Guide to Buying and Building a Quality New Home,** 4th edition (Windsor Peak Press), by Alan and Denise Fields; chosen by the *San Francisco Chronicle* as one of its top ten "Best Real Estate Books"
- **www.scorecard.org,** check this site if you are nervous about toxic waste issues in or near your prospective neighborhood; sponsored by the Environmental Defense Fund.

AVING FOUND AND SECURED A PLACE TO LIVE, YOU HAVE NOW the task of getting your stuff here and perhaps finding storage. The how-tos follow, as well as a section detailing which agency to contact regarding consumer complaints against moving companies, information about moving with children, and specifics regarding tax-deductible moving expenses.

TRUCK RENTALS

First determine if you are going to move it yourself or hire someone else to do it for you. If you prefer doing it all yourself, you can rent a vehicle, load it up, and hit the road. Look in the Yellow Pages under "Truck Rental" and call around and compare; also ask about any specials. Below is a list of four national truck rental companies and their toll-free numbers and web sites. For the best information, you should call a local office. Note: Most truck rental companies now offer "one-way" rentals as well as packing accessories and storage facilities. Of course, these extras are not free. If you're cost conscious you may want to scavenge boxes in advance of your move or buy some directly from a box company. (Those moving locally should check Smart and Final stores, which frequently offer empty boxes in a bin by the entrance of the store. Liquor stores are also a perennial favorite for free small and mid-size boxes.)

If you're planning to move during the peak moving months (May through September), call well in advance, at least a month ahead of when you think you'll need the vehicle. Remember that Saturday is a popular moving day; you may be able to get cheaper rates if you book a different day.

Once you're on the road, keep in mind that your rental truck may be a tempting target for thieves. If you must park it overnight or for an extended period (more than a couple of hours), try to find a safe place, preferably somewhere well-lit and easily observable by you, and do your best not to leave anything of particular value in the cab. Make sure you lock the back door and, if possible, use a steering wheel lock or other easy-to-purchase safety device.

Four national self-moving companies to consider:

- **Budget**, 800-428-7825, www.budget.com
- **Penske**, 800-222-0277, www.penske.com
- **Ryder**, 800-297-9337, www.ryder.com (now a Budget company, still operating under the Ryder name)
- **U-Haul**, 800-468-4285, www.uhaul.com

A little wary of driving the truck yourself? Commercial freight carriers, such as **ABF U-Pack**, 800-355-1696, www.upack.com, offer an in-between service; they deliver a 28-foot trailer to your home, you pack and load as much of it as you need, and they drive the vehicle to your destination (often with some other freight filling the remaining space). However, if you have to share truck space with another customer, you may arrive far ahead of your boxes—and bed. Try to estimate your needs beforehand and ask for your load's expected arrival date. You can get an online estimate from some shippers, so you can compare rates.

If you aren't moving an entire house and can't estimate how much truck space you will need, keep in mind this general guideline: Two to three furnished rooms equal a 15-foot truck; four to five rooms, a 20-foot truck.

MOVERS

INTERSTATE

First, the good news: Moving can be affordable and problem-free. The bad news: If you're hiring a mover, the chances of it being so are much less.

Probably the best way to find a mover is by **personal recommendation**. Absent a friend or relative who can recommend a trusted moving company, you can turn to what surveys show is the most popular method of finding a mover: the **Yellow Pages**. Then there's the **internet**: just type in "movers" on a search engine and you'll be directed to hundreds of more or less helpful moving-related sites.

In the past, *Consumer Reports*, www.consumerreports.org, has published useful information on moving. You might ask a local realtor, who may be able to steer you towards a good mover, or at least tell you which ones to avoid. Members of the American Automobile Association have a valuable resource at hand in **AAA's Consumer Relocation Services**, which will assign the member a personal consultant to handle every detail of the move free of charge and which offers savings from discounts arranged with premier moving companies. Call 800-839-MOVE, www.aaa.com.

Another good resource to help you avoid problems is California-based **MoveRescue**, www.moverescue.com, which offers pre-move education and consumer assistance, all aimed at helping you avoid being scammed.

But beware! Since 1995, when the federal government eliminated the Interstate Commerce Commission, the interstate moving business has degenerated into a wild and mostly unregulated industry with thousands of unhappy, ripped-off customers annually. (There are so many reports of unscrupulous carriers that we no longer list movers in this book.) Since states do not have the authority to regulate interstate movers and the federal government has been slow to respond, you are pretty much on your own when it comes to finding an honest, hassle-free mover. That's why we can't emphasize enough the importance of carefully researching and choosing who will move you.

To aid your search for an **interstate mover**, we offer a few general recommendations.

First get the names of a half-dozen movers and check to make sure they are licensed by the **US Department of Transportation's Federal Motor Carrier Safety Administration** (**FMCSA**). With the movers' Motor Carrier (MC) numbers in hand, call 888-368-7238 or 202-358-7000 (offers the option of speaking to an agent) or go online to www.fmcsa.dot.gov, to see if the carriers are licensed and insured. If the companies you're considering are federally licensed, your next step should be to check with the **Better Business Bureau**, www.bbb.org, in the state where the moving companies are licensed as well as with the states' consumer protection boards, or attorney generals (in California call the Department of Consumer Affairs, 800-952-5210, or go to www.dca.ca.gov). Also check FMCSA's **Household Goods Consumer Complaint** web site, www.1-888.dot.saft.com, where they maintain complaints that have been filed on interstate movers. Assuming there is no negative information, you can move on to the next step: asking for references. Particularly important are references from customers who did moves similar to yours. If a moving company is unable or unwilling to provide references, eliminate it from your list. Unscrupulous movers have even been known to give phony references who will falsely sing the mover's praises—so talk to more than one reference and ask questions. If something feels fishy, it probably is. One way to learn more about a prospective mover: Ask them if they have a local office (they should) and then walk in and check it out.

Once you have at least three movers you feel reasonably comfortable with, it's time to ask for price quotes (always free). Best is a binding "not-to-exceed" quote, of course in writing. This will require an on-site visual inspection of what you are shipping. If you have *any* doubts about a prospective mover, drop it from your list before you invite a stranger into your home to catalog your belongings.

Recent regulations by FMCSA require movers to supply several documents to consumers before executing a contract. These include two booklets: *Important Information for Persons Moving Household Goods (within California)*, which must be provided at the first-person contact between the consumer and the mover; and *Your Rights and Responsibilities When You Move*; a concise and accurate written estimate of charges; a summary of the mover's arbitration program; the mover's customer complaint and inquiry handling procedure; and the mover's tariff containing rates, rules, regulations, classifications, etc. For more about FMCSA's role in handling household goods, you can go to its consumer page at www.fmcsa.dot.gov/factsfigs/moving.htm.

ADDITIONAL MOVING RECOMMENDATIONS

*   If someone recommends a mover to you, get names (the salesperson or estimator, the drivers, the loaders). To paraphrase the NRA, moving companies don't move people, people do. Likewise, if someone tells you he had a bad moving experience, note the name of the company and try to avoid it.
*   Remember that price, while important, isn't everything, especially when you're entrusting all of your worldly possessions to strangers.
*   Legitimate movers charge by the hour (local moves, under 100 miles), and by weight/mileage (for long-distance moves). Be wary if the mover wants to charge by the cubic foot.
*   Ask about the other end—subcontracting increases the chances that something could go wrong.
*   In general, ask questions, and if you're concerned about something, ask for an explanation in writing. If you change your mind about a mover after you've signed on the dotted line, write a letter explaining that you've changed your mind and that you won't be using its services. Better safe than sorry.
*   Ask about insurance; the "basic" 60 cents per pound industry standard coverage is not enough. If you have homeowner's or renter's insurance, check to see if it will cover your belongings during transit. If not, ask your insurer if you can add that coverage for your move. Otherwise, consider purchasing "full replacement" or "full value" coverage from the carrier for the estimated value of your shipment. Though it's the most expensive type of coverage offered, it's probably worth it. Trucks get into accidents, they catch fire, they get stolen—if such insurance seems pricey to you, ask about a $250 or $500 deductible. This can reduce your cost substantially while still giving you much better protection in case of a catastrophic loss.

- Whatever you do, *do not* mislead a salesperson/estimator about how much and what you are moving. And make sure you tell prospective movers about how far they'll have to transport your stuff to and from the truck as well as any stairs, driveways, obstacles or difficult vegetation, long paths or sidewalks, etc. The clearer you are with your mover, the better he or she will be able to serve you.

- Think about packing. If you plan to pack yourself, you can save some money, but if something is damaged because of your packing, you may not be able to file a claim for it. On the other hand, if you hire the mover to do the packing, they may not treat your belongings as well as you will. They will certainly do it faster, that's for sure. Depending on the size of your move and whether or not you are packing yourself, you may need a lot of boxes, tape, and packing material. Mover boxes, while not cheap, are usually sturdy and the right size. Sometimes a mover will give a customer free used boxes. It doesn't hurt to ask. Also, don't wait to pack until the last minute. If you're doing the packing, give yourself at least a week to do the job; two or more is better. Be sure to ask the mover about any weight or size restrictions on boxes.

- You should transport all irreplaceable items such as jewelry, photographs, or key work documents personally. Do not put them in the moving van! Consider sending less precious items that you do not want to put in the moving truck via the US Postal Service or by UPS.

- Ask your mover what is not permitted in the truck: usually anything flammable or combustible, as well as certain types of valuables.

- Although movers will put numbered labels on your possessions, you should make a numbered list of every box and item that is going in the truck. Detail box contents and photograph anything of particular value. Once the truck arrives on the other end, you can check off every piece and know for sure what did (or did not) make it. In case of claims, this list can be invaluable. Even after the move, keep the list; it can be surprisingly useful.

- Movers are required to issue you a "bill of lading"; do not hire a mover who does not use them.

- Consider keeping a log of every expense you incur for your move, i.e., phone calls, trips to San Francisco, etc. In many instances, the IRS allows you to claim these types of expenses on your income taxes. (See **Taxes** below.)

- Be aware that during the busy season (May through September), demand can exceed supply and moving may be more difficult and more expensive than during the rest of the year. If you must relocate during the peak moving months, call and book service well in advance—a month at least—of when you plan on moving. If you can reserve service way in advance, say four to six months early, you may be able to lock in a lower winter rate for your summer move.

- Listen to what the movers say; they are professionals and can give you expert advice about packing and preparing. Also, be ready for the truck on both ends—don't make them wait. Not only will it irritate your movers, but it may cost you. Understand, too, that things can happen on the road that are beyond a carrier's control (weather, accidents, etc.) and your belongings may not get to you at the time or on the day promised.
- Treat your movers well, especially the ones loading your stuff on and off the truck. Offer to buy them lunch, and tip them if they do a good job.
- Before moving pets, attach a tag to your pet's collar with your new address and phone number in case your furry friend accidentally wanders off in the confusion of moving. Your pet should travel with you, and you should never plan on moving a pet inside a moving van. For more on moving with pets, you might want to look into *The Pet-Moving Handbook: Maximize Your Pet's Well-Being and Maintain Your Sanity*, by Carrie Straub, published by First Books (www.firstbooks.com).
- Be prepared to pay the full moving bill upon delivery. Cash or bank/cashier's check may be required. Some carriers will take VISA and MasterCard but it is a good idea to get it in writing that you will be permitted to pay with a credit card since the delivering driver may not be aware of this and may demand cash. Unless you routinely keep thousands in greenbacks on you, you could have a problem getting your stuff off the truck.

INTRASTATE AND LOCAL MOVERS

The **California Public Utilities Commission (CPUC)**, www.cpuc. ca.gov, regulates the licensing, rates, and rules of the Household Goods moving industry in California. All companies involved in the moving business must be insured and hold a license that permits them to provide moving services within or from/to California. To verify certification of your chosen mover, call the CPUC at 800-877-8867 or the **California Moving and Storage Association** (CMSA) at 800-672-1415 and have the mover's CAL T number (listed on the mover's literature) ready. The CMSA, www.thecmsa.org, is a nonprofit trade organization that offers references to legitimate movers and provides information to help consumers avoid "bandit movers" (movers that engage in unlawful practices and/or bully the customer into paying outrageous prices once the move has started). According to the CMSA, 80% of the calls to them involve complaints about bandit movers. They recommend against booking online or over the phone without investigating the company's physical address first and confirming it's licensed (with a CAL T number) with the CPUC. For moves within California, the CPUC regulations require all movers to provide each client with a written "not to exceed price" before the move commences. This price should be clearly disclosed on your Agreement for Service form. The mover will have you sign this form before the move begins.

CONSUMER COMPLAINTS—MOVERS

If a **move goes badly** and you blame the moving company, you should first file a written claim with the mover for loss or damage. If this doesn't work and it's an intrastate move, call 800-894-9444 to file a complaint with the CPUC. If the mover is a CMSA member, the CMSA will intervene on the consumer's behalf if there is a problem.

If your grievance is with an **interstate carrier**, your choices are limited. Interstate moves are regulated by the Federal Motor Carrier Safety Administration (FMCSA), 888-368-7238, www.dot.fmcsa.gov, an agency under the Department of Transportation, with whom you can file a complaint against a carrier. While its role in the regulation of interstate carriers historically has been concerned with safety issues rather than consumer issues, in response to the upsurge in unscrupulous movers and unhappy consumers, it has issued a recent set of rules "specifying how interstate household goods (HHG) carriers (movers) and brokers must assist their individual customers shipping household goods." According to its consumer page, carriers in violation of said rules can be fined, and repeat offenders may be barred from doing business. In terms of loss, however, "FMCSA does not have statutory authority to resolve loss and damage of consumer complaints, settle disputes against a mover, or obtain reimbursement for consumers seeking payment for specific charges. Consumers are responsible for resolving disputes involving these household goods matters." It is not able to represent you in an arbitration dispute to recover damages for lost or destroyed property, or to enforce a court judgment. If you have a grievance, your best bet is to file a complaint against a mover with FMCSA and with the Better Business Bureau, www.bbb.org, in the state where the moving company is licensed, as well as with that state's attorney general or consumer protection office. To seek redress, hire an attorney.

STORAGE WAREHOUSES

Storage facilities may be required when you have to ship your furniture without an apartment to receive it or if your apartment is too small for all your belongings. The CPUC regulates short-term storage (under 90 days), but not long-term or self-storage. If your mover maintains storage warehouse facilities in the city, as many do, you'll probably want to store with them. Some even offer one month's free storage. Look in the Yellow Pages under "Storage," and shop around for the best and most convenient deal. Below are a couple of major moving/storage companies. Listing here does *not* imply endorsement by First Books.

- **Door to Door Storage**, 888-366-7222, www.dtdstorage.com, has warehousing for cargo containers, which it delivers to you for packing, and then its trucks transport the container back to its facilities (several throughout the Bay Area); the company also operates a City to City moving service, which offers a full range of moving services, 888-505-3667.
- **Public Storage**, 800-447-8673, www.publicstorage.com, offers locations throughout San Francisco and the Bay Area for self-service storage, pick-up service and storage, full-service moving, and/or truck rentals.

SELF-STORAGE

The ability to rent anything from 5' x 5' rooms to storage rooms large enough to accommodate a car is a great boon to urban dwellers. This is especially true in San Francisco, where landlords frequently rent garage space separately (for those homes that have it) to monthly parkers. Collectors, people with old clothes they can't bear to give away, and those with possessions that won't fit in a sublet or shared apartment all find mini-warehouses a solution to too-small living spaces.

Rates for space in Bay Area self-storage facilities are competitive: Expect to pay at least $50 a month for a 5' x 5' (25 sq ft), $100 a month for a 5' x 10' space (50 sq ft), and so on. Some offer free pick-up; otherwise you or your mover delivers the goods. If you're looking for lower rates, inquire with the storage facility for move-in specials, upper floor discounts, or other locations.

As you shop around, you may want to check the facility for cleanliness and security. Does the building have sprinklers in case of fire? Does it have carts and hand trucks for moving in and out? Does it bill monthly, or will it automatically charge the bill to your credit card? Access should be 24-hour or nearly so, and some are air conditioned, an asset if you plan to visit your locker in the summer. Is the area well lit at night and is there a security guard on-site at all times? Is the rental month to month or is there a minimum lease? Is it easily accessible from your home?

Finally, a word of warning: Unless you no longer want your stored belongings, pay your storage bill and pay it on time. Storage companies may auction the contents of delinquent customers' lockers.

Here are a few area self-storage companies. For more options, check the Yellow Pages under "Storage."

- **AAAAA Rent-A-Space**, 800-527-7223, www.5Aspace.com, offers student and senior discounts, has locations in Alameda, Vallejo, Berkeley, San Leandro, Hayward, Castro Valley, El Sobrante, Moraga, Foster City, and Colma.
- **Central Self-Storage**, 415-861-3138, www.centralselfstorage.com, has facilities in San Francisco and Daly City.
- **Mobile Mini, Inc.**, 800-531-7253, www.mobileminiinc.com, delivers storage containers from 5' x 8' to 40' x 10' that you fill and it will transport to a location you specify or to its own secured facilities.
- **Public Storage**, 800-447-8673, www.publicstorage.com, has a variety of locations throughout the Bay Area, also offers pick-up and delivery services at certain locations, 877-777-4258, www.pspickup.com.
- **Shurgard**, 800-748-7427, www.shurgard.com, has facilities in San Francisco, South San Francisco and Daly City, also offers truck rentals and packing supplies.
- **U-Haul Self-Storage**, 800-GO-U-HAUL, www.uhaul.com, has multiple locations through the Bay Area, prices for rooms vary by their location and availability.

CHILDREN AND MOVING

Studies show that moving, especially frequent moving, can be hard on children. According to an American Medical Association study, children who move often are more likely to suffer from such problems as depression, low self-esteem, and aggression. Often their academic performance suffers as well. Aside from not moving more than is necessary, there are a few things you can do to help your children through this stressful time:
- Talk about the move with your kids. Be honest but positive. Listen to their concerns. To the extent possible, involve them in the process.
- Make sure children have their favorite possessions with them on the trip; don't pack "blankey" in the moving van.
- Make sure you have some social life planned on the other end. Your children may feel lonely in your new home, and such activities can ease the transition. If you move during the summer, you might find a local camp (check with the YWCA or YMCA) at which they can sign up for a couple of weeks in August to make new friends.
- Keep in touch with family and loved ones as much as possible. Photos and phone calls are important ways of maintaining links to the important people you have left behind.
- If your children are school age, take the time to involve yourself in their new school and in their academic life. Don't let them fall through the cracks.

- Try to schedule a move during the summer so they can start their new school at the beginning of the term.
- If possible, spend some time in the area prior to the move doing fun things in the area to which you are moving, such visiting a local playground or playing ball in a local park or checking out the neighborhood stores with teenagers. With any luck they will meet some other kids their own age.

First Books (www.firstbooks.com) offers two helpful resources for children. For those aged 6-11, *The Moving Book: A Kids' Survival Guide* by Gabriel Davis is a wonderful gift, and younger children will appreciate *Max's Moving Adventure: A Coloring Book for Kids on the Move* by Danelle Till. For general guidance, read *Smart Moves: Your Guide Through the Emotional Maze of Relocation* by Nadia Jensen, Audrey McCollum, and Stuart Copans.

TAXES AND MOVING

If your move is work-related, some or all of your moving expenses may be tax-deductible—so you may want to keep those receipts. Though eligibility varies, depending, for example, on whether you have a job or are self-employed, generally, the cost of moving yourself, your family, and your belongings is tax deductible, even if you don't itemize. The criteria: In order to take the deduction your move must be employment-related, your new job must be more than 50 miles away from your current residence, and you must be here for at least 39 weeks during the first 12 months after your arrival. If you take the deduction and then fail to meet the requirements, you will have to pay the IRS back, unless you were laid off through no fault of your own or transferred again by your employer. It's probably a good idea to consult a tax expert regarding IRS rules related to moving. However, if you're a confident soul, get a copy of IRS Form 3903 (www.irs.gov) and do it yourself!

ADDITIONAL RELOCATION
AND MOVING INFORMATION

- **www.firstbooks.com**, relocation resources and information on moving to Atlanta, Boston, Chicago, Minneapolis–St. Paul, New York, San Francisco, Seattle, Washington, D.C., as well as London, England. Also publisher of the *Newcomer's Handbook® for Moving to and Living in the USA*.
- *How to Survive A Move*, edited by Jamie Allen and Kazz Regelman, is a **Hundreds of Heads** guide (www.hundredsofheads.com). Divided into sections ranging from planning a move to packing tips, moving

with kids, and worst moves ever, this easy-to-digest book provides the wisdom, dispensed mostly in single-paragraph bites, of hundreds of people who've lived through the experience.

- **BestPlaces**, www.bestplaces.net; compares quality-of-life and cost-of-living data of US cities.
- **DataMasters**, www.datamasters.com; for basic community statistics by zip code
- *How to Move Handbook* by Clyde and Shari Steiner, an excellent general guidebook
- **http://houseandhome.msn.com**; online quotes
- **The Riley Guide**, www.rileyguide.com/relocate.html; online moving and relocation clearinghouse. Lists moving and relocation guides and web sites, offers links to sites that cover cost of living/demographics as well as real estate links and school and health care directories.
- **www.allamericanmovers.com**, 800-989-6683; online quotes
- **www.american-car-transport.com**; if you need help moving your car
- **www.erc.org**, the Employee Relocation Council, a professional organization, offers members specialized reports on the relocation and moving industries
- **www.homestore.com**; relocation resources, including a handy salary calculator that will compare the cost of living in US cities
- **www.usps.com**; relocation information from the United States Postal Service

ONE OF THE FIRST THINGS YOU'LL WANT TO DO WHEN YOU ARRIVE in the Bay Area is set up a checking and perhaps a savings account. Opening one is usually painless. Since San Francisco is a regional financial center, there is no shortage of banks, savings and loans, and credit unions.

Most financial institutions offer a variety of account options, from no-fee checking and savings with a sizable minimum balance to inexpensive service if you do all your banking by ATM. If you have time, shop around for the best deal or if you are in a rush during the move, sign up with one of the big boys, then research other banks and change later if/when you find a better deal. Keep in mind that smaller banks may be less expensive, in terms of fees, than their colossal nationwide counterparts, while offering you a more navigable bureaucracy to deal with when you need help from your bank.

CHECKING ACCOUNTS

Setting up a checking account should be relatively quick and easy, as long as you have a photo identification with your signature, an address, and some money. Some banks prefer to see that you've had an account at another financial institution, but most will not require this. Many financial institutions offer free checking account options, though most will require you to maintain a specified minimum balance in order to avoid monthly service fees. When you open your account, be sure to ask the teller for a full description of your new account, including minimum balances, available services, and fees. You may also want to ask for a map of the bank's local ATM locations, in order to avoid raking up penalty charges for using another's institution's ATMs. You will typically be issued temporary checks on the spot for use until your printed ones arrive, usually within a week to 10 days. However, many merchants don't like to accept non-printed checks. To be on the safe side, keep enough cash on hand to meet your basic needs for two weeks. Once your printed checks arrive, you should have no trouble writing checks at most places, as long as you have a driver's license or similar photo identification. Chances are you'll also get a debit/ATM card when you open your account. The card usually arrives in the mail within 7 to 10 days, ready to use. Most of your accounts can be linked to each other and to the card, making it easy to do your basic banking without ever going into a branch. Many financial institutions also offer online banking at no additional charge, which allows you to monitor your account from your personal computer.

SAVINGS ACCOUNTS

Just as easy to set up as a checking account, individual characteristics of savings accounts differ from bank to bank in fees, interest, and required minimum balances. Often your savings account can be linked to your checking account to provide overdraft protection, usually for a fee. Again, your savings account can easily be accessed with your debit/ATM card, although you may have to ask that it be set up that way.

AREA BANKS

Here's a list of some of the biggest banks in the area and their main offices. Call them for the address and phone number of neighborhood branches if you'd rather bank closer to home or work.

SAN FRANCISCO
- **Bank of America**, 345 Montgomery St, 650-615-4700, 800-227-5458, www.bankofamerica.com
- **Bank of the West**, 295 Bush St, 415-765-4886, 800-488-2265, www.bankofthewest.com
- **California Bank and Trust**, 465 California St, 415-875-1500, 800-400-6080, www.calbanktrust.com
- **Citibank**, 260 California St, 415-981-3180, 800-274-6660, www.citibank.com
- **First Republic Bank**, 101 Pine St, 415-392-1400, www.firstrepublic.com
- **Union Bank of California**, 1675 Post St, 415-202-0350, www.uboc.com
- **US Bank**, 525 Market St, 415-278-5050, 800-872-2657, www.usbank.com
- **Washington Mutual**, 401 California St, 415-788-1037, 800-788-7000, www.wamu.com

- **Wells Fargo Bank**, 464 California St, 800-869-3557, www.wells fargo.com

NORTH BAY
- **Bank of America**, 1000 4th St, San Rafael, 415-499-5151, 800-227-5458, www.bankofamerica.com
- **Bank of Marin**, 50 Madera Blvd, Corte Madera, 415-927-2265
- **Bank of the West**, 1313 Grant Ave, Novato, 415-897-1131, 800-488-2265, www.bankofthewest.com
- **Glendale Federal**, 101 Tiburon Blvd, Mill Valley, 415-381-6545
- **US Bank**, 3200 Northgate Dr, San Rafael, 415-479-4804, 800-872-2657, www.usbank.com
- **Wells Fargo**, 715 Bridgeway, Sausalito, 415-332-3355, 800-869-3557, www.wellsfargo.com

EAST BAY
- **Bank of America**: 1500 Park St, Alameda, 510-649-6600; 2129 Shattuck Ave, Berkeley, 510-649-6600; 300 Lakeside Dr, Oakland, 510-649-6600; 1400 East 14th St, San Leandro, 510-649-6600; 800-227-5458, www.bankofamerica.com
- **Bank of the West**: 1969 Diamond Blvd, Concord, 925-689-4410; 11100 San Pablo Ave, El Cerrito, 510-235-2980; 3305 Broadway, Oakland, 510-834-1780; 800-488-2265, www.bankofthewest.com
- **Mechanics Bank**: 1 Kaiser Plaza #750 Oakland, 510-452-5114; 1350 North Main, Walnut Creek, 925-210-8170
- **Union Bank**: 2333 Shattuck Ave, Berkeley, 510-843-6353; 3223 Crow Canyon Rd #100, San Ramon, 925-866-0422; 1970 Franklin St, Oakland, 510-891-9505
- **US Bank**, 2424 Santa Clara Ave, Alameda, 510-747-1657, 800-872-2657, www.usbank.com
- **Wells Fargo**, 1221 Broadway, Oakland, 510-891-2011, 800-869-3557, www.wellsfargo.com

PENINSULA
- **Bank of America**, 530 Lytton Ave, Palo Alto, 650-615-4700, 800-227-5458, www.bankofamerica.com
- **First National Bank of Northern California**, 6600 Mission St, Daly City, 800-380-9515, www.fnbnorcal.com
- **Union Bank**, 400 University, Palo Alto, 650-859-1200
- **US Bank**, 1105 El Camino Real, Menlo Park, 650-617-8330, 800-872-2657, www.usbank.com
- **Washington Mutual**, 300 Hamilton Ave, Palo Alto, 650-853-2602, 800-788-7000, www.wamu.com

- **Wells Fargo**, 400 Hamilton Ave, Palo Alto, 650-855-7677, 800-869-3557, www.wellsfargo.com

SOUTH BAY
- **Bank of America**: 777 North 1st St, San Jose, 408-983-0588; 2905 Stevens Creek Blvd, Santa Clara, 408-983-0588; 921 East Arques Ave, Sunnyvale, 408-983-0588, 800-227-5458, www.bankofamerica.com
- **Bank of the West**: 2395 Winchester Blvd, Campbell, 408-998-6769; 890 North First St, San Jose, 408-998-6800; 1705 El Camino Real, Santa Clara, 408-998-6964; 800-488-2265, www.bankofthewest.com
- **Union Bank**, 990 North 1st St, San Jose, 408-279-7400, www.uboc.com
- **US Bank**, 1099 Lincoln Ave, San Jose, 408-287-2710, 800-872-2657, www.usbank.com
- **Washington Mutual**, 55 West Santa Clara St, San Jose, 408-291-3331, 800-788-7000, www.wamu.com
- **Wells Fargo**, 7076 Santa Teresa Blvd, San Jose, 800-869-3557, www.wellsfargo.com

CREDIT UNIONS

Some of the best financial service deals are offered by credit unions. The goal of a credit union is to offer affordable, bank-like services, including checking and savings accounts, and low interest loans, and to do it in a way that makes fiscal sense for the organization. On the downside, usually credit unions offer fewer locations than banks and often do not have easily accessible teller machines. You'll have to pay a fee when using a non–credit union ATM. Generally, membership to a credit union is available through some kind of group affiliation, often your place of work or residence. To find out if your company sponsors one, check online at www.ccul.org for a list of dozens of Bay Area credit unions, or try:

- **Marin County Federal**, 30 North San Pedro Rd, #115, San Rafael 94903, 415-499-9780; Marin County employees and family members
- **Pacific Service Credit Union**, P.O. Box 8191, Walnut Creek, 94596, 925-296-6200; open to employees, and families of employees of PG&E
- **San Jose Credit Union**, 140 Asbury St, San Jose, 95110, 408-294-8800

ONLINE BANKING

Today, it is rare when a bank does not offer online banking. Generally this includes balance and other account information inquiries, making transfers, paying bills, and even applying for loans. Security should be a chief concern when accessing your private financial information over the internet. While banks should encrypt your personal information and password, the user should also take standard precautions as well. Don't share your password with anyone, and change it often; don't send confidential information through e-mail or over unsecured web space; and restrict your banking interactions to private computers—not a work computer with a shared network or at an internet cafe.

Online access services and fees vary from bank to bank, so check with individual institutions for information. Sometimes access is directly through the bank's web site; sometimes you'll first need to download a program or use specialized banking software.

CREDIT CARDS

If you're not bringing a wallet full of credit cards with you, and you'd like to apply for one or more, you'll be happy to know issuers of those cards have simplified the process in recent years. Application forms have become shorter, and many card companies will take your application over the telephone.

Here are the major ones:

- **American Express**: They offer a number of different cards, each of which requires a minimum annual income and an annual fee. In most cases your Amex balance must be paid in full each month. Call 800-528-4800, http://home.americanexpress.com
- **Diner's Club**: This card costs $95 per year just for the privilege of having it in your wallet. Call 800-234-6377, www.dinersclubus.com
- **Discover Card**: Dean Witter issues this card, which pays cash back at the end of the each anniversary year, depending on how much you use the card over the period. Call 800-347-2683, www.discovercard.com
- **VISA/MasterCard**: banks, S&Ls, and various financial institutions, as well as nearly every other organization imaginable, now offer VISA and/or MasterCard, at widely varying interest rates. Some cards are free, some offer lower interest rates, some offer frequent flyer miles...shop around for the best deal for you (see below).
- **Others**: Oil companies, department stores, home improvement outlets, electronics stores, clothing retailers, and many others offer their own credit cards, usually with high interest rates. San Francisco has Macy's, Nordstrom, JC Penney, Mervyn's, Brooks Brothers, and Eddie Bauer, to name just a few that offer credit accounts, many of them instantly with proper identification. One benefit of these types of accounts: The issuer notifies cardholders in advance of upcoming sales and specials.

A list of low-rate card issuers can be found on the internet at **CardWeb**, www.cardweb.com; the **Consumer Action** site, www.consumer-action.org; **BankRate.com**, www.bankrate.com; and **iMoneynet.com**, www.imoneynet.com.

CREDIT REPORTS

If you're interested in seeing a personal credit report, you can go to www.annualcreditreport.com, where you can obtain a free copy of your credit report once a year from each of the three main credit bureaus (Equifax, Experian, and TransUnion). It's best to get a copy from each service because each company's report may be different. If you discover any inaccuracies, you should contact the service immediately and request that it be corrected. By law they must respond to your request within 30 days. Note: checking your credit report too frequently can adversely affect your credit rating.

You can also visit or call each bureau individually:

- **Equifax**, P.O. Box 105873, Atlanta, GA 30348, 800-685-1111, www.equifax.com
- **Experian**, P.O. Box 2104, Allen, TX 75002-2104, 888-397-3742
- **TransUnion**, P.O. Box 390, Springfield, PA 19064-0390, 800-916-8800

TAXES

FEDERAL INCOME TAX

The Internal Revenue Service has offices in the Bay Area where you can pick up the forms you need to file your income tax return and get the answers to your tax questions. However, be advised that recent studies have found that the answer you get from an IRS representative often depends upon the person giving it rather than any clearly defined rule or regulation. The IRS says it is working on standardizing responses.

Many Bay Area post offices stay open until midnight on April 15th to give procrastinators extra time to fill out their return and get it in the mail with the proper postmark. To request tax forms call 800-829-3676. Tax forms are also available at most post offices and libraries during filing season (January–April), and at the Federal Building in San Francisco, 450 Golden Gate Avenue, or check online, www.irs.ustreas.gov.

IRS Taxpayer Assistance Centers can help clarify tax laws and answer specific questions about your return, your tax account, and any letters you've received from the IRS. The centers are open for walk-in assistance and no appointment is necessary. You can also get help over the phone, 800-829-1040 or 800-829-4477 (individuals), or 800-829-4933 (businesses).

If you qualify for the Earned Income Tax Credit (sometimes called the "Child Tax Credit") or your income is $36,000 or less, you may qualify for free help preparing your individual return. Stop into one of the IRS Assistance Centers listed below (all open Monday–Friday, 8:30 a.m. to 4:30 p.m.) to ask for more information and to set up an appointment:

* **Oakland**: 1301 Clay St, 510-637-2487
* **San Francisco**: 450 Golden Gate Ave, 415-522-4061
* **San Jose:** 55 South Market St, 408-817-6747
* **Santa Rosa:** 777 Sonoma Ave, 707-523-0924
* **Walnut Creek**: 185 Lennon Lane, 925-279-4000

If you have ongoing unresolved issues with the IRS, contact the Taxpayer Advocate Service, 510-637-2703 or 408-817-6850.

ELECTRONIC INCOME TAX FILING

These days, many people are choosing to file their taxes electronically, by purchasing or downloading tax software, using an online tax service, or going through an accredited agency. According to the IRS, electronic filers receive their refunds in about half the time of people who file through the mail, and e-filing costs less and is more accurate than doing it the old-fashioned way.

To research the many tax filing software options, go to your search engine and type in "tax software." **Quicken Turbo Tax**, www.turbo tax.com, is just one of many that are available.

For more information on electronic filing, check out **IRS E-file**, www.irs.gov/efile. This site includes features such as convenient payment options or direct deposit for those expecting a return, and offers a list of software brands and internet sites that are capable of handling both federal and state returns.

STATE INCOME TAX

California residents file state tax form 540, 540A, 540 2EZ, 540NR, or 540X. Generally much of the information for your California taxes will come directly from your completed federal return. State income tax forms and answers to your state income tax questions can be found at the State Franchise Tax Board offices:

* **San Francisco**: 121 Spear St, Suite 400, Monday–Friday, 8 a.m. to 5 p.m.
* **Oakland**: 1515 Clay St, Suite 305, Monday–Friday, 8 a.m. to 5 p.m.

For information and assistance with state taxes call 800-338-0505 or 800-852-5711, TDD, 800-822-6268, www.ftb.ca.gov. State tax filing deadline is the same as for federal taxes, April 15. Tax forms are available at most post offices and libraries during tax season (January–April). You can also file online with Calfile at the Franchise Tax Board's web site, www.ftb.ca.gov

SALES TAX

The local sales tax throughout the Bay Area ranges from 7.375% to 8.75%. It has risen over the years to its current level to help fund the BART transit system and to pay for earthquake damage repairs.

STARTING OR MOVING A BUSINESS

With a well-educated pool of workers, the Bay Area is a great place to start a business or move your existing business.

If your business involves sales of tangible personal property, you'll have to apply for a seller's permit from the **State of California Board of Equalization**, 800-400-7115, www.boe.ca.gov. This web site provides information about doing business in California, including employer tax forms and the *California Employer's Guide*. The Board of Equalization's information center can also answer your tax questions.

To protect your efforts and investment you should probably hire a local attorney to help you through the maze of state rules and regulations, especially if you are moving your business from another state. Resources include:

- **California State Franchise Tax Board** at 415-929-5700, 800-338-0505, www.ftb.ca.gov, the agency to check with regarding payroll, unemployment insurance, and disability insurance taxes
- **Chambers of Commerce**: Berkeley, 1834 University Ave, 510-549-7000, www.berkeleychamber.com; Oakland, 475 14th St, 510-874-4800, www.oaklandchamber.com; San Francisco, 235 Montgomery St, 12th floor, 415-392-4520, www.sfchamber.com; San Jose, 310 South First St, 408-291-5250, www.sjchamber.com
- **Internal Revenue Service**, 800-829-1040, www.irs.gov, call them for information about an employer tax ID number
- **Sfbizinfo**, connects San Francisco business with services, resources and information, 888-800-8000, www.sfbizinfo.org
- **SF Prospector**, Mayor's Office of Economic and Workforce Development web site with information for businesses looking to expand or relocate in San Francisco, www.sfprospector.org
- **Referral Service of the San Mateo County Bar Association**, which also serves Santa Clara County, 650-369-4149.

- **San Francisco Bar Association Lawyer Referral Service**, 415-989-1616, www.sfbar.org
- **Service Corps of Retired Executives (SCORE)**, 415-744-6827, 800-634-0245, www.score.org; call them for one-on-one counseling when starting a new business, free of charge
- **State Bar of California**, 415-538-2000, www.calbar.org
- **State of California's Department of Finance**, www.dof.ca.gov
- **US Small Business Administration (SBA)**, www.sbaonline. sba.gov; go online for information about starting up and financing a business, as well as learning about the SBA's services and local offices
- **Women's Initiative for Self Employment (WISE),** 415-641-3460, www.womensinitiative.org, a local nonprofit dedicated to helping low income women start and run their own businesses

Congratulations! You've found a place to live, which is never easy here. Now it's time to set up your utilities and basic services and settle in. You may want to subscribe to the local paper, find a doctor, get a library card, and register to vote while you're at it. Details follow.

UTILITIES

GAS AND ELECTRICITY

To have existing service transferred to your name or to initiate gas and electric service, call **Pacific Gas & Electric Company (PG&E)**, www.pge.com. The 24-hour number is 800-743-5000, and PG&E covers San Francisco, the North Bay, East Bay, and parts of the South Bay and the Peninsula. If you're speech or hearing impaired, the TTY number is 800-652-4712, also 24 hours. The City of Santa Clara has its own electric service, **Silicon Valley Power**, while PG&E provides gas. To find out about setting up service you can contact Silicon Valley Power between 8 a.m. and 5 p.m. at 408-615-2300, www.siliconvalleypower.com. The municipally owned and operated company recently added an eco-friendly option, **Santa Clara Green Power**. The program offers residents the option of choosing 100% renewable energy from wind and solar power sources. Silicon Valley Power estimates the additional monthly cost for going green at about $7.05 for the average Santa Clara household. For more information check out the web site listed above and click on the "Green Power" icon, or call 408-244-SAVE. The **City of Palo Alto Utilities (CPAU)**, 650-329-2161, is the only municipal utility in California that operates city-owned utility services that include electric, gas, water, and wastewater collection.

If you have questions about utilities, contact the **Public Advisor's Office** in San Francisco toll free at 866-849-8390 or visit the **California**

Public Utilities Commission's web site, www.cpuc.ca.gov. When you are settling into a new place, turn on the hot water tap to make sure the water heater is on. If you don't have hot water, you need to find out why. If the water heater is in your unit, check to see if the pilot light is on. If it's not, follow directions on the heater for lighting the flame, or, if you're nervous about doing it yourself, call your landlord or PG&E and have them do it. While you're looking at the water heater, check to see if it is strapped to the wall. Many post-quake fires are started by ruptured gas lines to water heaters, and attaching the heater to the wall is an important safety precaution here in earthquake country. (See **Emergency Preparedness** for more details.)

Most people pay their PG&E bills by mail or online. There are also numerous drug stores and other neighborhood businesses set up to collect money for PG&E. Customer service representatives should be able to tell you where one is in your area. You may also drop off your payments at any PG&E office. There are two customer service offices in San Francisco: 863 Clay Street in the Chinatown area, and at 2435 Mission Street in the Mission district. For other locations, call 800-743-5000.

TELEPHONE

At one time, you had only one choice when it came to local telephone service throughout the Bay Area, and that was Pacific Bell—now **SBC**. With ongoing industry deregulation, dozens of companies are now offering services. To search for a provider other than SBC, check the Yellow Pages under "Telecommunications." SBC is still the major operator in the Bay Area, and at the time of this writing, the company was beginning a merger with distance service giant AT&T. Phone hook-up is easy; just call 800-310-2355 Monday–Friday, 8 a.m. to 6 p.m., or Saturday, 8:30 a.m. to 5 p.m. The TTY number is 800-772-3140, available Monday–Friday, 8 a.m. to 5:30 p.m., or visit www.sbc.com.

A deposit is not required, but SBC does charge about $33 to turn on the line to your unit. That fee will be added to your bill, and may be paid in three monthly payments. Basic phone service runs about $11 a month. SBC offers other telephone services, at additional cost, including the message center, which acts as your personal answering machine, call waiting, and caller ID, as well as a variety of internet service options. Currently cable TV giant **Comcast** is making inroads in the market with special promotions offering bundled cable, internet, and, increasingly, telephone services. Prices range greatly depending on options selected. For more information visit www.comcast.com or call 800-COMCAST.

LONG-DISTANCE SERVICE

When it comes to long-distance service, there are a dizzying number of companies in this business, and they are not bashful about going after you. Below are just a few of the long-distance service providers available in the Bay Area. Several of these companies also offer local phone service, cellular phone service, and internet options. For help comparing long-distance and wireless calling plans, visit the **Telecommunications Research and Action Center** (TRAC, not affiliated with the communications industry), www.trac.org or call them at 202-263-2950. The TRAC site also provides directory assistance via the internet.

- **AT&T**, 800-222-0300, www.att.com
- **GTC Telecom**, 800-486-4030, www.gtctelecom.com
- **MCI**, 800-444-3333, www.mci.com
- **Qwest**, 800-860-2255, www.qwest.com
- **SBC**, 800-310-2355, TTY: 800-772-3140, www.sbc.com
- **Sprint**, 800-877-4646, www.sprint.com
- **Utility.com**, www.utility.com
- **Verizon**, 800-483-4000, www.verizon.com
- **Working Assets**, 800-788-0898, www.workingforchange.com, this company donates a portion of monthly fees to nonprofits.

CELLULAR PHONE SERVICES

These days it seems everyone in California carries a cell phone and there are as many cellular pricing plans as there are makes and models of phones. The market is changing rapidly, so your best bet is to call around and determine for yourself which service and pricing structures best meet your needs. The web can make it easier; www.point.com, named the best web site for cell phone information by *Forbes* magazine, allows you to compare service plans in your area, and the **Telecommunications Research and Action Center (TRAC)**, out of Washington DC, is a consumer organization that publishes charts, comparing plans and prices: www.trac.org, 202-263-2950. **TURN (The Utility Reform Network)** also operates a web site with useful consumer information on things to consider when choosing a plan, switching plans, keeping your old phone number, and deciphering cell phone charges, www.turn.org. Following are the Bay Area's largest cellular personal communication service (PCS) providers:

- **Cingular,** 800-331-0500, www.cingular.com
- **MetroPCS**, 888-8-Metro-8, www.metropcs.com
- **SBC**, 800-310-2355, TTY: 800-772-3140, www.sbc.com

- **Sprint**, 888-253-1315, www.sprintpcs.com (now includes Nextel Communications)
- **T-Mobile**, 1-800-T-MOBILE. www.t-mobile.com
- **Verizon Wireless**, 800-922-0204, www.verizonwireless.com

Most businesses that sell cellular phones can also activate them for you on the spot, saving you the trouble of having to call the service provider yourself. Some even give you the phone for free, if you sign up and pay for a service contract with the company they represent.

AREA CODES

Here in the Bay Area, area codes are pretty straightforward and relatively easy. If you get confused, consult the Customer Guide at the front section of the White Pages. Here you'll find everything from the area code for Concord to directions on how to call Scotland. Below are the basic Bay Area codes; when calling from one to another, you'll need to dial a "1" plus the area code, then the number you are calling. Check your calling plans to see what if any long-distance charges may apply.

- **415:** The master number for all of San Francisco; Marin County in the North Bay, including Marin, San Rafael, Sausalito, Novato, Mill Valley, Corte Madera, and Fairfax; and some parts of Daly City to the south
- **510:** The East Bay, Alameda County, including Berkeley, Oakland, Alameda, Emeryville, Albany, Piedmont, Hayward, Fremont, Newark, Union City; and some parts of western Contra Costa County including Richmond
- **707:** Further North Bay: Sonoma County, including Santa Rosa and Sonoma; Napa County including Napa, St. Helena, Yountville, and Calistoga; and Solano County, including Vacaville, Vallejo, and Fairfield
- **925:** Outer East Bay, Contra Costa County, including Walnut Creek, Martinez, San Ramon, Dublin, and Pleasant Hill
- **650:** The Peninsula, San Mateo County, including parts of Daly City, South San Francisco, San Bruno, Millbrae, Burlingame, San Mateo, Pacifica, Half Moon Bay, Belmont, San Carlos, Redwood City, Woodside, Atherton, Menlo Park; and some parts of northern Santa Clara County including Palo Alto and Mountain View
- **408:** The South Bay, Santa Clara County, including San Jose, Santa Clara, Sunnyvale, Campbell, Milpitas, Cupertino, Saratoga, and Los Gatos
- **916:** Sacramento, the state capital, and environs

ONLINE SERVICE PROVIDERS

Hundreds of internet service companies offer basic internet access via existing phone lines. For a complete list of internet service providers located near you, go to www.cnet.com. You can also find a list of providers in the Yellow Pages under "Internet Access."

For high-speed internet access, consider signing up for service on a digital subscriber line (known as DSL), or via cable modem access. Unlike a dial-up option, a DSL connection does not interrupt phone lines. Cable internet access is available from cable TV providers, and like DSL, the cable modem is always on. One possible disadvantage to cable modem is your access speed may decrease if your neighbors also use cable. Before you sign up for cable modem, ask the provider what speed they guarantee.

Here are a few of the companies that offer dial-up, DSL, and/or cable modem:

- **AT&T World Net**, http://download.att.net, 800-967-5363
- **America Online**, www.aol.com, 888-265-8003
- **Comcast**, www.comcast.com, 800-COMCAST
- **Earthlink**, www.earthlink.com, 800-Earthlink
- **Juno**, 800-390-5866, www.juno.com
- **Net Zero**, 888-349-0029, www.netzero.net
- **SBC/Yahoo**, 800-310-2355, or 866-Sbc-Yahoo, TTY: 800-772-3140, www.sbc.com
- **Sonic Net**, 415-354-9616, www.sonic.net
- **RCN**, 800-746-4726, www.rcn.com
- **ZR Net**, 415-920-2226, www.zrnetservice.com

ONLINE DIRECTORY ASSISTANCE

In today's web-oriented world, directory assistance does not have to cost a lot of money. An online Yellow Pages is available from SBC, www.smartpages.com, and numerous sites are dedicated to providing telephone listings and web sites, including the following:

- **www.google.com**
- **www.411.com**
- **www.altavista.com**
- **www.anywho.com**
- **www.bigbook.com**
- **http://yp.yahoo.com**
- **www.superpages.com**
- **www.whitepages.com**
- **www.worldpages.com**
- **www.infospace.com**

CONSUMER PROTECTION—UTILITY COMPLAINTS

In the state of California, utility rates and practices relating to telephone, electric, and gas are governed by the state **Public Utilities Commission (PUC)**. The San Francisco Public Utilities Commission handles water issues. Officials at both organizations strongly suggest you take your complaints first to the utility involved. If you don't get satisfaction there, then the PUCs will listen to you.

- **California PUC**, 505 Van Ness Ave, San Francisco, Public Advisor's Office in San Francisco, 866-849-8390, www.cpuc.ca.gov
- **San Francisco PUC**, 1155 Market St, 11th Floor, San Francisco, 415-554-3155, http://sfwater.org

Interestingly, if you have problems with the PUC, there is a public watchdog organization that keeps tabs on the effectiveness of each of the PUCs. It's called **TURN (The Utility Reform Network)**. If you don't get what you need from either PUC you may want to turn to TURN, 711 Van Ness Ave, San Francisco, 415-929-8876, 800-355-8876, www.turn.org.

With the break-up of Ma Bell and the proliferation of long-distance telephone service providers have come the inevitable scamsters. If you look at your phone bill and think you've been "slammed" (your long-distance provider or established services were changed without your approval) or "crammed" (calls you didn't make were added to your bill), and your local service provider and state attorney general's office cannot assist you, contact the **Federal Communications Commission's Consumer Center**, 888-CALL-FCC, www.fcc.gov, or the **Federal Trade Commission**, 877-FTC-HELP, www.ftc.gov, to file a complaint.

See the **Helpful Services** chapter for more on consumer protection.

WATER

Water in the Bay Area is provided by several water districts (see list below). Accounts and billing are handled either directly through the water district or by your city's municipal services. Bay Area renters generally are responsible for paying for water except in San Francisco apartment buildings and multi-unit flats, where usually the landlord pays.

In 1974, the United States Congress enacted a program to ensure safe drinking water for US residents. Amended in 1986, the Safe Drinking Water Act set up a comprehensive program for monitoring drinking water. Among many things, the Act banned all future use of lead pipe and lead solder in public drinking water systems, set up a monitoring system, mandated greater protection of groundwater sources of drinking water, and streamlined enforcement procedures to ensure that suppliers comply with the Safe Drinking Water provisions. About 85% of San Francisco's water supply comes from Hetch Hetchy, a remote area of Yosemite National Park in the Sierra Nevada Mountains. Because of its pristine source, the quality of San Francisco's water is higher than most cities; however, it's not entirely sterile or free of all organisms. The other 15% of San Francisco's water comes from watersheds in San Mateo, Santa Clara, and Alameda counties. To preserve water quality and improve local service, the San Francisco Public Utilities Commission has embarked on a $4.3 billion program to repair and upgrade its regional water system.

Outside of San Francisco, about two thirds of the state, or 22 million people, obtain water from the San Francisco Bay and the Sacramento Delta (located northeast of Contra Costa County) through a series of pumps and canals. In the South Bay, concern remains over water contamination caused by the gasoline additive methyl tertiary butyl ether (MTBE), mixed with gasoline to make it burn cleaner. When scientists discovered that MTBE can contaminate groundwater, and is not as readily removable as other contaminates, then-Governor Gray Davis ordered a statewide phase-out of the additive. MTBE is now officially banned, and massive clean-up efforts have taken place across the state to ensure the safety of drinking water. Nevertheless, areas that were impacted, like the Santa Clara Valley Water District, are still keeping a watchful eye on water supplies to determine whether further action is necessary. The likelihood of having MTBE in the groundwater may depend on how close you live to a gas station. If you are within 1,000 feet, check with the station to find out if they have ever had any leaks or spills. If you are moving to the South Bay, contact the Santa Clara Valley Water District, 408-265-2600, www.scvwd.dst.ca.us, for more information about the MTBE issue. Another good source of information is the State Water Resources Control Board, 916-657-1256.

If you are living in the city and are concerned about the quality of your tap water, contact the **San Francisco Water Quality Division** at 650-872-5950. Those outside of San Francisco can contact the **Water Quality Control Board, San Francisco Bay Region**, 1515 Clay Street, Oakland, 510-622-2300, www.waterboards.ca.gov/sanfranciscobay, and ask them to send you a copy of their annual report on water quality. If you feel the need to take extra precaution, contact a private laboratory to perform water quality tests. Check the Yellow Pages under "Laboratories-Analytical" or get a referral from your county health department.

For further questions on tap water quality, contact the **California Department of Health Services**, 916-445-4171, www.dhs.ca.gov; the **US Environmental Protection Agency Safe Drinking Water Hotline**, 800-426-4791; or the **Water Quality Association**, www.wqa.org. Information regarding home water filtration systems is covered in an Environmental Protection Agency pamphlet, "Home Water Treatment Units: Filtering Fact from Fiction," www.epa.gov/ogwdw.

To **set up water service** you will need to contact one of the following water districts or municipal services. Most of the web sites included here provide detailed information about setting up your account, as well as the county's annual water quality report:

- **Alameda County Water District**, 43885 South Grimmer Blvd, Fremont, 510-668-4200, www.acwd.org
- **Contra Costa Water District**, 1331 Concord Ave, Concord, 925-688-8000, www.ccwater.com
- **East Bay Municipal Utility District**, 375 11th St, 866-403-2683, www.ebmud.com
- **Marin Municipal Water District**, 220 Nellon Ave, Corte Madera, 415-945-1400, www.marinwater.org
- **North Marin Water District**, 999 Rush Creek Pl, Novato, 415-897-4133, www.nmwd.com, serves Novato and parts of West Marin
- **City of Palo Alto Utilities (CPAU)**, 250 Hamilton Ave, Palo Alto, 650-329-2161, www.cpau.com
- **San Francisco Water Department**, 1155 Market St, San Francisco, 415-554-3155, http://sfwater.org
- **Santa Clara Valley Water District**, 5750 Almaden Expy, San Jose, 408-265-2600, www.scvwd.dst.ca.us; to set up service contact one of the following:
- **California Water Service**, 650-917-0152, www.calwater.com, serves Los Altos and some areas of Cupertino, Mountain View, and Sunnyvale
- **San Jose Municipal**, 3025 Tuers Rd, San Jose, 408-277-4036, www.sjmuniwater.com, and **Great Oaks Water**, 15 Great Oaks Blvd, Suite 100, 408-227-9540, www.greatoakswater.com, serve San Jose
- **San Jose Water Co.**, 374 West Santa Clara St, San Jose, 408-279-7900, www.sjwater.com, serves Campbell, Los Gatos, and Saratoga, and parts of the cities of San Jose and Cupertino
- **Sonoma County Water Agency**, 404 Aviation Blvd, Santa Rosa, 707-526-5370, www.scwa.ca.gov to set up service in Sonoma County contact one of the following:
- **Santa Rosa Water District**, 707-543-3150, serves Santa Rosa
- **City of Sonoma City Hall**, #1 the Plaza, Sonoma, 707-938-3681, serves Sonoma

GARBAGE/RECYCLING

In San Francisco landlords pay for garbage collection for apartments, and for some duplexes and single-family homes. Homeowners must order and pay for disposal service; the collection fee is based on how many trashcans you fill up each week. Two major companies, **Norcal** and **BFI**, provide the vast majority of garbage service in the Bay Area. Contracts change, and at the time of this writing companies were locked in a fierce bidding war over much of Santa Clara County. The best way to determine your local garbage service provider is to contact your city's public works department or contact one of the following companies:

- **Norcal Waste Systems: Sunset Scavenger**, 415-330-1300, and **Golden Gate Disposal & Recycling Company**, 415-626-4000, provide service to San Francisco
- **Norcal Waste Systems of San Jose**, 408-576-0057, provides service in San Jose
- **BFI Daly City**, serving Daly City, Colma, Broadmoor, 650-756-1130, www.bfidalycity.com
- **BFI San Mateo County**, serving Atherton, Belmont, Burlingame, East Palo Alto, Foster City, Half Moon Bay, Hillsborough, Ladera, Menlo Park, North Fair Oaks, Redwood City, San Carlos, and San Mateo, 650-592-2411; http://bfisanmateocounty.com
- **Marin Sanitary Services**, Marin County, 415-456-2601, www.marinsanitary.com
- **Pleasanthill Bayshore Disposal**, serves most of Contra Costa County, 925-685-4711, www.pleasanthillbayshoredisposal.com/
- **StopWaste.org (Waste Management, Alameda County [north])**, 510-430-8509, www.stopwaste.org
- **Tri-Cities Waste Management**, East Bay, 510-624-5900
- **South San Francisco Scavenger**, northern San Mateo County (South San Francisco, Brisbane, Millbrae), 650-589-4020, www.ssf scavenger.com

Curbside recycling collection is available throughout the Bay Area and generally is included in the cost of your other garbage pickup. In San Francisco residents of apartment buildings with fewer than five units are responsible for picking up the approved plastic containers themselves. Landlords are responsible for setting up recycling programs if the building has five or more units. Landfill space is scarce in the Bay Area, making recycling all the more important. To find out more about recycling in the Bay Area contact:

- **Acterra**, 650-962-9876, www.Acterra.org
- **Marin Recycling Center**, 415-453-1404
- **Recycle Central (Norcal)**, 415-330-1400
- **Recycle Palo Alto Program,** 650-496-5910
- **RecycleWorks,** San Mateo County, 888-442-2666, www.recycle works.org
- **Santa Clara County Recycling Hotline**, 408-924-5453 or 800-533-8414, www.recyclestuff.org

- **SF Environment,** 415-355-3700, recycling hotline 415-554-7329, www.sfenvironment.com
- **StopWaste.org (Waste Management, Alameda County [north]),** recycling hotline 877-786-7927, www.stopwaste.org

Earth 911 offers a wealth of information on recycling including what items can and cannot be recycled, how to find local recycling centers, and instructions for dealing with hazardous waste, 800-CLEAN-UP, www.earth911.org. For information specifically dealing with beverage container collection centers, call the **California Department of Conservation** at 800-732-9253.

If you've got a green thumb and you'd like to compost, the ultimate recycle, contact the **San Francisco League of Urban Gardeners (SLUG)** at 415-285-SLUG. They call it the ROT-line, as opposed to a HOT-line. In the East Bay the ROT-line is run by **StopWaste.org (Alameda County Waste Management Authority),** 510-444-SOIL.

AUTOMOBILES

DRIVER'S LICENSES

If you've moved here from out-of-state and you want to drive in California, you have 10 days from your arrival to apply for a new driver's license from the Department of Motor Vehicles (DMV). While there is no penalty for filing late, if you are pulled over for a traffic violation after the 10-day grace period, the officer can give you a citation. You will need to bring your current driver's license and a birth certificate or passport for proof of age to your appointment. If the name that you use is different than the one on this document, you will also need to provide a marriage certificate or dissolution of marriage, adoption, or name change document that shows your current name.

Once there, you will be asked to fill out a formal application, provide your social security number, and pass a vision test. You will also be required to pass a written test on traffic laws and road signs. You have three chances to pass this test. The test has 36 questions. To give yourself a quick refresher course, you can take a sample test on the DMV's web site: www.dmv.ca.gov/pubs/interactive/tdrive/exam.htm. Once you pass, you'll have your thumbprint done and your picture taken. You new license will be mailed to you. In the meantime, the DMV will issue you an interim license good for 60 days. When driving with an interim license, always keep a valid photo ID handy (out-of-state driver's license or passport).

A note to international newcomers: If your license is from another country, you will also be required to take a driving test.

A driver's license costs $25 and it is good for up to four years, expiring on your birth date. If you are moving to the Bay Area from within California, you have 10 days to notify the DMV of your address change; call or go to www.dmv.ca.gov.

The DMV also handles the issuance of **state identification cards**. In order to get one you'll need to bring a birth certificate or passport and provide your Social Security number. The fee is $21 and the card is valid for six years. Seniors can get ID cards free that are good for 10 years.

AUTOMOBILE REGISTRATION & INSURANCE

If you bring a car into the state of California you are supposed to register it within 20 days of your arrival. The DMV requires that emission control devices on your car operate correctly; any non-diesel vehicle that is four years old or older must pass an emissions test. Most service stations will do the test for less than $50. When you've received emission certification, bring it, along with your current automobile registration and your checkbook, to the nearest DMV. Registration is good for one year and costs $31.

All California drivers are required by law to carry liability insurance on their vehicles and to show proof of coverage when registering an automobile at the DMV. Insurers estimate that 30% to 40% of the drivers on California roads do not carry proper coverage. All the more reason to cover yourself.

DMV OFFICES

The DMV in San Francisco is notorious for its long lines. If you can, spare this frustration and instead go to the DMV in Marin County or San Mateo County. Wherever you go, you should make an appointment, which could be the difference between a half-hour wait and a two-hour wait. The DMV now has a 24-hour hotline that handles all appointments. The automated 24-hour number is 800-921-1117; to speak with an agent, call 800-777-0133 between 8 a.m. and 5 p.m.; TTY: 800-368-4327. Appointments can also be made online at www.dmv.ca.gov. When heading to your appointment, make sure to show up early—not late—they won't wait for you! A note about hours: In general DMV offices are open 8 a.m. to 5 p.m. on Mondays, Tuesdays, Thursdays and Fridays. Due to budget cuts, offices now open one hour later on Wednesdays—at 9 a.m. The offices are also open on the third Saturday of each month. To make matters more confusing, in order to provide monthly Saturday service, DMV offices are closed on the preceding Monday. More information about operating hours, driver's license requirements, and vehicle registration can be found online at www.dmv.ca.gov.

SAN FRANCISCO/NORTH BAY
- Corte Madera, 75 Tamal Vista Blvd
- San Francisco, 1377 Fell St

EAST BAY
- Concord, 2070 Diamond Blvd
- El Cerrito, 6400 Manila Ave
- Fremont, 4287 Central Ave
- Hayward, 150 Jackson St
- Oakland, 501 85th Ave; 5300 Claremont Ave
- Walnut Creek, 1910 North Broadway

PENINSULA/SOUTH BAY
- Daly City, 1500 Sullivan Ave
- Redwood City, 300 Brewster Ave
- San Jose, 111 West Alma Ave
- San Mateo, 425 North Amphlett Blvd
- Santa Clara, 3665 Flora Vista Ave

PARKING

SAN FRANCISCO

In the City of San Francisco vacant parking spaces are some of the most sought-after real estate. Many residential areas require parking permits, which allow neighborhood residents or temporary guests to park without time limits in the neighborhood. Those without a permit are required to move their cars frequently, usually after two hours. If you're not sure if your neighborhood or the neighborhood you are visiting requires a residential parking permit, check for signs posted along the street. Also check to see when the street sweeper is coming—illegally parked vehicles on street-sweeping days will be towed.

Residential Parking Permits are available at the Residential Permit Parking office, 1380 Howard Street, 415-503-2020. In order to get your permit you'll need to bring valid car registration that shows your new address, which means you'll first need to visit the nearby DMV. Also bring proof of address: your lease, a utility bill with your address on it, a bank statement, or a personalized check. Your driver's license is not an acceptable proof of residency. The full-fledged parking permit is good for a year and will set you back $27. For more information on the program, call 415-554-5000.

When it comes to parking in San Francisco's downtown core, your choices are limited to streetside meters or parking garages. There are more than 10,000 garage spaces in the downtown area, and they are certainly the most costly option. Fees vary somewhat; in general, depositing your car in one of these spots will cost $20 to $30 a day. Some outdoor lots in the South of Market area will sell you a monthly spot for as little as $100, but more often than not those lots are sold out. For general information on parking in San Francisco, call the **Department of Parking and Traffic** at 415-554-7275 or check online at www.ci.sf.ca.us/dpt. Here are just a few of San Francisco's downtown parking garages:

- **Ellis-O'Farrell Garage**: 123 O'Farrell St, 415-986-4800, 1200+ spaces
- **Fifth and Mission Yerba Buena Garage**: 5th and Mission St, 415-982-8522, www.fifthandmission.com, 2600+ spaces
- **Portsmouth Square Garage**: 733 Kearny St, 415-982-6353, 500+ spaces
- **St. Mary's Square Garage**, 433 Kearny St, 415-956-8106, 800+ spaces
- **Sutter-Stockton Garage**: 330 Sutter St, 415-982-7275, 1800+ spaces
- **Union Square Garage**: 333 Post St, 415-397-0631, 1100+ spaces

There are many more lots in the city, so if the one you want to patronize is full or closed you'll only need to drive a couple of blocks and you'll probably find one with space. While driving around watch for the much less expensive metered parking spaces, but make certain you read and understand all the postings. The only people faster at their jobs than the meter readers are the tow truck operators they call out. **To pay a parking citation** by phone, have your VISA or MasterCard ready and dial 415-255-3999 or you can pay online at http://services.sfgov.org/PTP-Multiple Citations/intro.asp.

COLORED CURBS

You'll need to know the meaning of painted curbs:

Red   Fire Zone—don't even think of parking here
Yellow Commercial loading zone only, for times posted
White Passenger pick-up or drop-off only
Green Temporary (usually 20–30 minutes) parking only—as posted
Blue   Handicapped parking only, special placard required

PARKING FINES

The city of San Francisco Department of Parking and Traffic issues 7,000 tickets every month. Meter readers troll the streets throughout the day, and enforcement of parking rules here is aggressive. If you get a ticket, pay it right away. Delaying payment can significantly increase your fine—doubling and in some cases even tripling what you owe. Following is a list of current fees for common violations.

Failure to curb your wheels on a hill $35
Meter violation $40
Meter violation downtown $50
Parking in a red zone $75
Parking in a white zone $75
Parking in a yellow zone. $60
Parking in a green zone $50
Parking on a sidewalk. $100
Failure to move car for street sweeper . . . $40
Residential permit zone violation. $50
Blocking a bike lane $100
Blocking a driveway . . . . $75 (If a resident calls to complain, you can also be towed)
Double parking. $65
Abandoned vehicle. $200
Parking in a bus zone $250
Blocking wheelchair access ramp $250
Parking in a blue (handicapped) zone. . . $275

SURROUNDING AREAS

Fortunately parking is easier in outlying areas and there is plenty of street parking in most cities; in fact there have been cases of people moving out of San Francisco just for the parking. Some cities require a residential permit allowing you to park in your neighborhood for an extended period of time. To obtain a residential parking sticker in Sausalito, call the **Sausalito Parking Services**, 415-289-4100, ext. 144. Most of the other cities in Marin do not require parking stickers. For information on parking tickets, towing, and other unpleasantness in the North Bay, contact the **Marin County Traffic Authority**, 800-281-7275.

In the East Bay, Oakland residents should call the **Oakland Parking Bureau**, 510-238-3099 or the **Traffic Division of the Superior Court**, 510-268-7673, located in Oakland. In Berkeley, contact the Berkeley **Residential Preferential Parking (RPP) Program**, Finance Customer Service Center, 510-981-7200. For UC Berkeley call the **UC Berkeley Parking and Transportation Office**, 510-642-4283.

In the South Bay/Peninsula, call **Palo Alto Parking Permits**, 650-329-2317; **San Mateo Parking Permits, Residential & City Parking Facilities**, 650-522-7326; and in San Jose, contact the **Residential Parking Permits** at 408-277-4304.

GETTING YOUR TOWED CAR BACK

If your car is towed is San Francisco, your first step should be to call the **DPT Tow Line** 415-553-1235 to find out why it was towed and what you need to do (read: how much you'll need to pay) to get it back. Once you've figured out how much you owe, you'll need to settle your fees with **AutoReturn**, 850 Bryant Street, Room 145, 415-558-7411. To obtain your vehicle's release you must appear in person with picture identification and be prepared to pay not only the towing cost and ticket but also any outstanding parking tickets written against the vehicle, and storage costs. Ouch!

In surrounding Bay Area counties, if your car is missing, call the local police station first and they will provide you with the name of the towing company contracted out by that city. Police department numbers are listed at the end of the neighborhood profiles.

OFFICIAL DOCUMENTS
VOTER REGISTRATION

Registering to vote in the Bay Area is easy. Frequent voter registration drives literally bring the process to you, along downtown sidewalks, in malls, and in public transit facilities. You can also register by visiting the **Registrar of Voters** or **Elections Department** in the county where you live. The deadline to register is 29 days before an election.

You can register with any political party in California, sign up as an independent, or decline to state a party affiliation. Voters may cast their ballots in person or vote via absentee ballot. If you want to vote absentee, you must call your local registrar's office and request the forms. Be sure to allow ample time, usually about a month, for them to receive your forms in the mail. Your registrar's office will be able to tell you what the cut-off date is for sending in an absentee ballot.

Here are the locations and phone numbers for voter registration officials in each of the nine Bay Area counties:
* **San Francisco**, City Hall, Room 48, San Francisco, 415-554-4375
* **Alameda**, 1225 Fallon St, Oakland, 510-272-6973
* **Contra Costa**, 524 Main St, Martinez, 925-646-4166
* **Marin**, 3501 Civic Center Dr, San Rafael, 415-499-6456
* **Napa**, 900 Coombs St, Room 256, Napa, 707-253-4321
* **San Mateo**, 40 Tower Rd, San Mateo, 650-312-5222
* **Santa Clara**, 1555 Berger Dr, Building 2, San Jose, 408-299-8302
* **Solano**, 510 Clay St, Fairfield, 707-421-6675
* **Sonoma**, 435 Fiscal Dr, Santa Rosa, 707-565-1800

LIBRARY CARDS

San Francisco is home to one of the finest city libraries in the world. Opened in early 1996, **New Main**, 415-557-4400, www.sfpl.org, across the Civic Center plaza from City Hall, holds more than one million books, magazines, and research tomes. It also provides internet access and multi-media presentations via dozens of computers. The entire library system's card catalog is on computer and accessible at terminals on every floor. Library cards are free, and you don't have to be a San Francisco resident to get one. Just bring proper ID, such as a driver's license, and something else with your current address on it, such as a utility bill. The card is valid at all San Francisco library branches; addresses and phone numbers are listed in the Neighborhoods section of this book. New Main, at 100 Larkin Street, is easy to get to; it's just a short walk through the United Nations Plaza from the Civic Center BART/MUNI station. For more information on local branch libraries, see neighborhood listings, and for more on specialty libraries, see the **Cultural Life** chapter.

PASSPORTS

You need to apply in person for new passports. A number of post offices and local city halls are set up to provide this service; check http://iafdb.travel.state.gov for the office closest to you. You'll need to bring two identical 2" x 2" photographs, proof of US citizenship (birth certificate, social security card, old passport), and a valid photo identification (driver's license, state ID card, military ID), and you'll have to fill out the application available at the passport office. The fee for a new passport is $97. For general information contact the **National Passport Information Center,** 877-4USA-PPT (877-487-2778), TTY: 888-874-7793, or visit www.travel.state.gov.

If you just need to renew your passport, you can do it by mail. Simply fill out the renewal application (DS-82)—available on-line at www.travel.state.gov—and send it, along with your old passport, two identical 2" x 2" photos, and a check for $67 made out to the US Department of State, to National Passport Center, P.O. Box 371971, Pittsburgh, PA, 15250-7971.

Passports generally take about six weeks to arrive by mail, but can take longer, so it's a good idea to take care of your passport well in advance. If you need it sooner, you can pay $60 to expedite the process—plus overnight charges there and back. Expedited passports should arrive within 2 weeks. If you've been called out of town on an emergency, it is possible to get a passport sooner—in some cases even on the same day, but it will cost extra for speedy service. If this is the case, your first step should be to call the **National Passport Information Center** (see number above). You can also contact the **San Francisco Passport Agency** directly at 415-538-2700 for assistance. The services at this office are reserved for those in need of expedited service. The San Francisco Passport Agency, located at 95 Hawthorne Street, 5th Floor, is open Monday–Friday from 9 a.m. to 4 p.m. If you're crunched for time, get there when the office opens, as waits of one to two hours are not uncommon. If you are outside San Francisco, check with your local city hall. In San Jose, the **Santa Clara County Recorders Office** at the County Government Center, East Wing, 70 West Hedding Street, 408-299-2481, can process your passport application within 10 to 14 days. Passports are good for 10 years (for adults).

BROADCAST AND PRINT MEDIA

TELEVISION STATIONS

Broadcast television reception in the Bay Area is fairly good, unless you live in a particularly hilly area, in which case hooking up to the cable is the way to go. If you're not interested in cable, a standard roof antenna will probably suffice to pull in most of the stations listed below. Apartment dwellers may want to consider getting a pair of "rabbit ears," a small indoor antenna that sits on top of the television set.

CHANNEL	CALL LETTERS	NETWORK	LOCATION
2	KTVU	Fox	Oakland
4	KRON	Independent	San Francisco
5	KPIX	CBS	San Francisco
7	KGO	ABC	San Francisco
9	KQED	PBS	San Francisco
11	KNTV	NBC	San Jose
14	KDTV	Univision (Spanish)	San Francisco
20	KBWB	WBN	San Francisco
26	KTSF	Independent	San Francisco
32	KMTP	Minority Television Project	San Francisco
36	KICU	Independent	San Jose
44	KBHK	UPN	San Francisco
50	KFTY	Independent	Santa Rosa
54	KTEH	PBS	San Jose
60	KCSM	San Mateo Community College District, PBS	San Mateo
66	KFSF	Univision	Vallejo

CABLE AND SATELLITE TELEVISION

If broadcast television (those listed above) doesn't provide you with adequate entertainment options, you'll probably need to get cable or a satellite dish. Cable and satellite television are available throughout the nine Bay Area counties, with service levels governed by agreements reached with municipalities. Each provider offers various packages based on how many channels you wish to receive. Naturally, the more channels you receive, the more you pay.

Here are some of the largest local providers:

- **Direct TV**, 888-777-2454, www.directv.com
- **Comcast**, 800-Comcast, www.comcast.com
- **RCN**, 800-RING-RCN, www.rcn.com

RADIO STATIONS

There are 80 radio stations located within the nine-county Bay Area, 30 AM and 50 FM. AM reception is fairly consistent throughout the area, with no special equipment needed. FM reception can be spotty, especially if you live in a hilly area of San Francisco (which is most of the city), the East Bay, or North Bay. You may need an FM antenna in those areas. Here are some of the most listened-to stations in the Bay Area and their formats.

AM

SAN FRANCISCO

KABL 960	Oldies
KCBS 740	News
KBZS 1220	Business Network
KFRC 610	Oldies
KGO 810	News, Talk
KIQI 1010	Hispanic
KNBR 680	Sports, Talk
KYCY 1550	Country
KSFO 560	Conservative Talk
KSRO 1350	News, Talk
KOIT 1260	Adult Contemporary

NORTH BAY

KXBT 1190	Asian
KRRS 1460	Hispanic
KMZT 1510	Classical

KDIA 1640	Talk, Catholic
KSRO 1350	News, Talk, Sports

SOUTH BAY/PENINSULA

KTCT 1050	Sports
KAZA 1300	Hispanic
KSJX 1500	Vietnamese
CNN 1590	News
KAZA 1290	Hispanic
KKSJ 1370	Spanish.
KNTS 1220	News, Talk, Sports
KTCT 1050	Sports, Talk
KLIV 1590	CNN
KLOK 1170	Spanish
KSJX 1500	Vietnamese

EAST BAY

KDYA 1190	Gospel
KMKY 1310	Children, Disney
KNEW 910	Talk
KQKE 960	Liberal Talk
KVTO 1400	Asian

FM

SAN FRANCISCO

KALW 91.7	News and Information (NPR)
KBRG 100.3	Romantic, Hispanic
KISQ 98.1	Classic Soul
KBLX 102.9	Adult Contemporary
KCSM 91.1	Jazz, News (NPR)
KDFC 102.1	Classical
KFOG 104.5	Rock
KFRC 99.7	Oldies
K101 101.3	Adult Contemporary
KJOY 100.7	Oldies, Nostalgia
KITS 105.3	Live 105, Modern Rock
KKSF 103.7	Jazz, New Age
KMEL 106.1	Hip Hop
KOIT 96.5	Light Rock
KUFX 98.5	Modern Rock
KPFA 94.1	News, Information, Variety

KPOO 89.5	Music, Talk, Variety, Listener Sponsor
KQED 88.5	Public Radio News, Information (NPR)
ALICE 97.3	Modern Adult Contemporary
KUIC 95.3	Adult Contemporary
KWLD 94.9	Urban Top 40
KSJO 92.3	Rock
KUSF 90.3	College, Alternative Rock, Multicultural
KYCY 93.3	Country
KEAR 106.9	Religious
KFOG 104.5	Adult Alternative
KZQZ 95.7	Top 40
KSAN 107.7	Classic Rock

EAST BAY

KALX 90.7	College, Alternative Rock
KFJO 92.1	Rock
KPFA 94.1	Public Radio Liberal News, Culture

NORTH BAY

KJZY 93.7	Jazz
KMGG 97.7	Oldies
KRSH 98.7	Rock

SOUTH BAY/PENINSULA

KBAY 94.5	Soft Rock
KFFG 97.7	Adult Alternative
KEZR 106.5	Adult Contemporary
KFJC 89.7	Alternative Rock
KZSU 90.1	Eclectic Music

NEWSPAPERS AND MAGAZINES

- *Asian Week*, 809 Sacramento St, San Francisco, 415-397-0220, www.asianweek.com
- *Bay Area Business Woman*, classified listings of local businesses, seminars, classes, events, 510-654-7557, 5245 College Ave, Suite 501, Oakland, www.babwnews.com
- *Bay Area Consumers' Checkbook*, evaluates quality and prices of local service firms and stores; 510-763-7979, www.checkbook.org
- *Bay Area Naturally*, 7282 Sir Francis Drake Blvd, San Rafael, 800-486-4794; a free directory of community resources for natural living, published by City Spirit Publications and distributed in businesses. Includes holistic health professionals, green products and services, schools and

educational centers, a natural food restaurant guide, and a calendar of events

- **Contra Costa Times**, published daily with East Bay listings, focusing on Concord, Walnut Creek, Pleasant Hill, Martinez, Richmond, Hercules, Benicia, Antioch, Pittsburg, and Bay Point areas, 800-598-4637, www.contraCostaTimes.com (also owns Hills Newspapers, a handful of smaller local publications including the *Berkeley Voice*, *Alameda Journal*, the *Montclarion*, and the *Piedmonter*)
- **East Bay Express**, 510-879-3700, www.eastbayexpress.com, a free weekly alternative paper; focuses on the East Bay. Good for rental and roommate listings; found in newsstands and at cafés.
- **East Bay Monthly**, distributed free throughout the East Bay, 1301 59th St, Emeryville, 510-658-9811, www.themonthly.com
- **Marin Independent Journal**, published daily with listings for Marin, Sonoma, and Napa counties, 415-883-8600, www.marinij.com
- **Metro**, 408-298-8000, www.metroactive.com, the South Bay's alternative weekly
- **Oakland Tribune**, published daily with a focus on the East Bay, especially Oakland, Berkeley, and Alameda, 510-208-6300, www.inside bayarea.com/oaklandtribune (the Alameda Newspaper Group also owns the *Alameda Times-Star*, the *Fremont Argus*, and a handful of smaller local papers)
- **Pacific Sun**, a free, weekly alternative; listings for Marin County. Found in newsstands and cafés. Good for rentals and roommate listings, 415-383-4500, www.pacificsun.com.
- **San Francisco Bay Guardian**, weekly free alternative paper with extensive listings for San Francisco and the East Bay. Published Wednesdays. Found at every café, corner store, and newsstands all over city. Good for rental and roommate listings, 415-255-3100, www.sfbg.com.
- **San Francisco Business Times**, 275 Battery, San Francisco, 415-989-2522
- **San Francisco Chronicle**, the most-read newspaper in the area; includes listings for San Francisco, North Bay, East Bay, Peninsula counties, and some outlying areas, 415-777-1111, www.sfgate.com
- **San Francisco Examiner**, daily free tabloid that publishes local news, 866-733-7323, www.sfexaminer.com.
- **San Francisco Magazine**, 243 Vallejo St, San Francisco, 415-398-2800, www.sanfran.com, glossy, upscale San Francisco lifestyle magazine
- **San Francisco Weekly**, a free weekly alternative paper with San Francisco listings. Good for rental and roommate listings; published Wednesdays; found all over city at newsstands and cafés, 415-536-8100, www.sfweekly.com.

- **San Jose Mercury News**, published daily; most extensive listings for the South Bay as well as much of the Peninsula and southern East Bay, 408-920-5000, www.mercurynews.com
- **San Mateo County Times**, published daily except Sunday with listings for much of the Peninsula, 650-348-4321, www.insidebayarea.com/sanmateocountytimes
- **Santa Rosa Press Democrat**, published daily; listings for Sonoma, Marin and Napa counties, 707-546-2020, www.pressdemocrat.com
- **7 x 7 Magazine**, San Francisco lifestyle, fashion, food, design, celebrity magazine, 415-362-7797, www.7x7mag.com

FINDING A PHYSICIAN

Much like finding a place to live in the Bay Area, finding a physician is never easy. You must first consider your needs—are you looking for a pediatrician, family physician, OB/Gyn, or all of the above? Do you want someone who staffs the hospital nearest you? Are you interested in an MD or an osteopath? And perhaps most importantly, does your health plan limit whom you can see? Here in the Bay Area you will find cutting-edge, top-notch care at the **University of California San Francisco Medical Center** located at 505 Parnassus, 415-476-1000, famous for its pioneering work in areas such as pediatrics, high-risk obstetrics, organ transplantation, cancer care, cardiac care, neurosurgery, and orthopedics. However, because it is an educational facility, you may have students observing you. Probably the most popular way to find a good doctor is through word of mouth, talking to friends, neighbors, colleagues, or other doctors. To assist in your research, consider ordering the book *Top Doctors* from the *Bay Area Consumers' Checkbook*, which lists the Bay Area's outstanding physician specialists. Go to www.checkbook.org, or call 510-763-7979 and ask for the latest version of *Top Doctors*; there is a charge for the service. See the **Helpful Services** chapter for more information about *Consumers' Checkbook*. To determine if a physician you are considering is board certified, check with the American Board of Medical Specialties Board Certification Verification at 866-ASK-ABMS, or go online to www.abms.org.

If you are strapped for cash while in transition, the **Haight Ashbury Free Medical Clinic**, 558 Clayton Street, 415-487-5632, www.hafci.org, offers free primary health care and specialty care, including podiatry, chiropractic care, pediatrics, HIV testing, comprehensive HIV treatment services, and community information and referral services. The Medical Clinic welcomes everyone who walks through the door. However, the clinic is unable to treat emergency medical problems, such as broken bones, severe bleeding, trauma, abdominal pains, etc. For emergency medical problems, go immediately to the nearest hospital emergency room.

If you've only recently arrived to the Bay Area and find yourself in sudden need of a physician, the **Traveler's Medical Group**, 490 Post Street, Suite #225, 415-981-1102, can send a doctor who speaks your language, 24 hours a day, 7 days a week.

Hopefully you'll never need the following: The **Medical Board of California**, 1426 Howe Avenue, Suite 54, Sacramento, CA 95825, 800-633-2322, 916-263-2382, www.medbd.ca.gov, and the **Osteopathic Medical Board of California**, 2720 Gateway Oaks Dr, Suite 350, Sacramento, CA 95833, 916-263-3100, www.docboard.org, are the two state organizations that handle complaints against medical professionals in California. Write or call for more information.

PETS

PET LAWS & SERVICES

If you're bringing Fido, Fluffy, or Spot with you to the Bay Area, you're no doubt wondering what local ordinances may apply to your dog or cat. Area agencies can answer your specific questions about leash laws, immunizations, and the like, or at least refer you to the right organization. **SF DOG** (San Francisco Dog Owners Group), www.sfdog.org, has a comprehensive web site that lists dog-friendly areas, events, and important contact numbers. Your courthouse should be able to provide details about licensing your pets and local leash laws. Additional pet services found in the Bay Area include pet sitters and boarding and grooming establishments. Look in the Yellow Pages under "Pet Services."

You and Fido can take MUNI together, but your dog must pay her own way and wear a muzzle. Guide dogs can ride all public transit and do not need to be muzzled. Call 415-673-MUNI for more information. Also noteworthy is **PAWS**, which stands for "Pets are Wonderful Support," an organization dedicated to preserving the relationship of people with AIDS and their pets; call 415-241-1460 to volunteer or visit www.pawssf.org for more information. The *Dog Lover's Companion to the Bay Area* by Maria Goodavage provides valuable information for the best places to explore, sleep, and eat with your dog in the nine Bay Area counties. There is even a glossy quarterly magazine devoted to dogs called *The Bark*, www.thebark.com, 2810 Eighth Street, Berkeley, 877-227-5639.

What follows is a list of animal shelters, adoption services, and rescue and resource groups:

SAN FRANCISCO

- **Animal Care & Control**, 1200 15th St, 415-554-6364, TTY: 415-554-9704, www.sfgov.org/acc

- **PAWS (Pets Are Wonderful Support)**, 415-241-1460, www.paws sf.org
- **Pets Unlimited Adoption Center**, 2343 Fillmore St, 563-6700, www.petsunlimited.org
- **SF Society for the Prevention of Cruelty to Animals (SPCA)**, 2500 16th St, 415-554-3000, www.sfspca.org
- **SF DOG (Dog Owners Group)**, 415-339-7461, www.sfdog.org
- **Rocket Dog Rescue**, 415-642-4786, www.rocketdogrescue.org

EAST BAY
- **Berkeley-East Bay Humane Society**, 2700 9th St, Berkeley, 510-845-7735, www.berkeleyhumane.org
- **East Bay SPCA**, 8323 Baldwin St, Oakland, 510-569-0702, www.east bayspca.org
- **Home at Last Animal Rescue**, 510-237-1625, www.homeatlast rescue.org
- **Tri-Valley SPCA Maddie's Adoption Center**, 4651 Gleason Dr, Dublin, 925-479-9670 www.eastbayspca.org
- **Milo Foundation**, 1575 Solano Ave, Berkeley, 510-548-9301, www.milofoundation.org

SOUTH BAY/PENINSULA
- **Peninsula Humane Society**, 12 Airport Blvd, San Mateo, 650-340-8200, www.peninsulahumanesociety.org
- **Peninsula Cat Works**, 650-329-9570, www.peninsulacatworks.org/index.php
- **Humane Society Silicon Valley**, 2530 Lafayette St, Santa Clara, 408-727-3383, www.hssv.org
- **Homeless Cat Network**, 650-286-9013, www.homelesscat network.org
- **A Safe Haven For Cats**, 650-802-9686, www.safehavenforcats.com

NORTH BAY
- **Benicia-Vallejo Humane Society**, 1121 Sonoma Blvd, Vallejo, 707-645-7905, www.bvhumane.org
- **Marin County Humane Society**, 171 Bel Marin Keys Rd, Novato, 415-883-4621, www.marin-humane.org
- **Napa County Humane Society**, 942 Westimola Ave, 707-255-8118, www.napahumanesociety.org
- **Humane Society of Sonoma County**, 5345 Highway 12 West, Santa Rosa, 707-542-0882 www.sonomahumane.org
- **Second Chance Rescue**, 415-721-1721, www.secondchance rescue.com

FINDING A VETERINARIAN/EMERGENCY HOSPITALS

To alleviate the high cost of veterinarian bills, you may want to consider obtaining health coverage for your pet. Contact the national organization **Veterinary Pet Insurance**, 800-872-7387, or the pet HMO **Pet Assure**, 888-789-7387, www.petassure.com for more details.

Most neighborhoods have at least one vet. To limit your travel time, try a vet in your area first. Perhaps the best way to get the inside scoop on vets is to frequent the dog park and talk to neighborhood owners. There's **Nob Hill Cat Clinic**, 415-776-6122, and **Pets Unlimited**, 415-563-6700, in Pacific Heights, which serves many areas of the city and is also an adoption center. In addition to adoption services, the **San Francisco SPCA**, 2500 16th Street, 415-554-3030, also runs a full-service animal hospital and operates a spay-neuter clinic.

Or try the **California Veterinary Medical Association's** site at www.cvma.org. You choose the city in which you are interested, and they will give you in-depth details about selected vets there. The CVMA's parent organization at www.avma.org will also give you information on your critter questions.

If your pet has ingested anything poisonous, contact **ASPCA National Animal Poison Control Center**, 24-hour emergency informational service, 888-426-4435; there is a $50 charge. You can also go straight to an emergency pet hospital at the following locations:

SAN FRANCISCO
- **Pets Unlimited Veterinary Hospital**, 2343 Fillmore St, 415-563-6700, open 7 days a week, 24 hours for emergencies
- **All Animals Emergency Hospital**, 1333 9th Ave, 415-566-0531 or 415-837-1011, open weekday evenings from 6 p.m. to 8 a.m., weekends from noon on Saturday to 8 a.m. on Monday
- **Balboa Pet Hospital**, 3329 Balboa St, 415-752-3300
- **San Francisco Veterinary Specialists**, 600 Alabama St, 415-401-9200, www.sfvs.net, 24-hour emergency services

NORTH BAY
- **Pet Emergency Center**, 901 East Francisco Blvd, #C, San Rafael, 415-456-7372, www.petemergencycenter.com, 24-hour emergency services
- **San Francisco Veterinary Specialists**, 901 East Francisco Blvd, 415-455-8317, www.sfvs.net, 24-hour emergency services
- **Novato Veterinary Hospital**, 7454 Redwood Blvd, Novato, 415-897-2173; evening calls will be directed to call emergency number

- **Calistoga Pet Clinic**, 1124 Lincoln Ave, Calistoga, 707-942-0404, one vet on call for emergencies
- **Madera Pet Hospital**, 5796 Paradise Dr, Corte Madera, 415-927-0525

EAST BAY
- **Berkeley Dog and Cat Hospital**, 2126 Haste St, Berkeley, 510-848-5150, www.berkeleydogandcat.com
- **All Bay Animal Hospital**, 1739 Willow Pass Rd, Concord, 925-687-7346
- **Pet Emergency Treatment Service of Berkeley**, 1048 University Ave, after hours emergency services, 510-548-6684

SOUTH BAY/PENINSULA
- **Adobe Animal Hospital**, 396 First St, Los Altos, 650-948-9661, www.adobe-animal.com, 24 hour emergency care
- **Skyline Pet Hospital**, 170 Skyline Plaza, Daly City, 650-756-4877
- **Stanford Pet Clinic**, 4111 El Camino Real, Palo Alto, 650-493-4233
- **Mayfair Veterinary Hospital**, 2810 Alum Rock Ave, San Jose, 408-258-2735

OFF-LEASH AREAS

San Francisco is a dog lover's paradise. Berkeley is the birthplace of *Bark* magazine, and the greater Bay Area—which, slowly but surely, is adding new dog parks every year—isn't so bad either.

In San Francisco, one in four families includes a dog, according to local dog owners' group **SF Dog**. Four-legged furry friends are more than welcome at a multitude of neighborhood parks, beaches, and even some cafés. While most of these spots have posted signs requiring pups to stay on their leashes, there are an increasing number of designated off-leash runs and play areas where your pet can frolic freely—and legally. See the list below for dog park locations.

That said, by far and away the most popular off-leash spots in San Francisco, all located within the Golden Gate National Recreation Area (GGNRA), became strictly on-leash four years ago. But the story doesn't end there.

Every morning, evening, and weekend, these hot spots—the sandy shores of Fort Funston, Ocean Beach, and Crissy Field—are packed with wall-to-wall Golden Retrievers, Labs, and German Shepherds jogging alongside their owners. Some dogs are on leash, as the new rules require, while many others, in open defiance of the rules, are not.

Created in 1979, GGNRA's original pet policy allowed dogs to run off-leash in these areas, as well as North Baker Beach, Fort Miley, and Lands End. But in 2001, amid loud protests, the National Park Service—citing concerns about sensitive habitats, bird life, and eco-restoration areas, abruptly revoked this privilege. In response, many dog owners have refused to comply. To make matters murkier, a recent court ruling declared off-leash tickets issued at Crissy Field void, saying the pet policy was changed without adequate public input and notice. However, the park service has publicly stated it considers the off-leash ban still in effect, and plans to continue ticketing violators.

At the time of this writing, the park service was in negotiations with dog owner groups in hopes of coming up with a new policy that would be amenable to both sides. In the meantime, dogs continue to run off-leash at Crissy Field, Fort Funston, and Ocean Beach, though it remains against official rules. If you let your puppy go here, be prepared—you may get a ticket. Tickets for off-leash violations in the GGNRA are $50!

For the latest update on negotiations with the park service, and detailed information on the status of off-leash policies in the GGNRA, visit the following web sites: Crissy Field Dog Group, http://crissyfielddog.org; Fort Funston Dog Walkers' Association, www.fortfunstondog.org; and SF Dog, www.sfdog.org.

Luckily, there are a host of neighborhood parks, open greenspaces, and fenced runs that are far less embattled. Below is a list of designated spots where your doggy can run free, hassle free.

A note about off-leash etiquette: Off-leash does not mean out of control. Dogs must always be under your direct supervision, and under strict voice control. This is especially important in unfenced off-leash areas. You should always carry a leash, ask fellow dog owners if your pup can play with their pets before releasing him into the pack, and always, always, always carry waste baggies and pick up after your pet!

SAN FRANCISCO DESIGNATED OFF-LEASH AREAS

- **Alamo Square Park**, western half of the park, along Scott St between Hayes and Fulton sts
- **Alta Plaza Park**, second park terrace, Clay St between Scott and Steiner sts
- **Bernal Heights**, dogs roam free beside their owners all along the trails that wind along the top of the hill, Bernal Heights Blvd
- **Buena Vista Park**, this green spot with great city views has trails and open hilly green grass popular with pooches and their owners, Buena Vista West at Central Ave

- **Corona Heights**, upper field with fenced area near the base of the hill, adjacent to Randall Museum, Roosevelt Way, and Museum Way
- **Dolores Park**, south of tennis courts, north of soccer field, 16th St between Church and Dolores sts
- **Douglass Park**, 26th and Douglass sts
- **Eureka Valley Park**, fenced area, 19th St and Collingwood, east of baseball diamond (on a trial basis)
- **Golden Gate Park**, four off-leash areas: southeast section bounded by Lincoln Way, King Dr, 2nd and 7th aves; northeast section at Stanyan and Grove sts; south central area bounded by King Dr, Middle Dr, 34th and 38th aves; fenced training area in the north central area near 38th Ave and Fulton
- **Lafayette Park**, near Sacramento St between Octavia and Gough sts
- **Lake Merced**, north side of lake area provides lots of space for free roaming with your dog, Lake Merced Blvd and Middlefield Dr
- **McKinley Square**, western slope, San Bruno Ave and 20th St
- **McLaren Park**, two off-leash areas: top of hill at Shelly Dr and Mansell St; south section via 1600 block of Geneva or 1600 block of Sunnydale— dogs must remain outside of sensitive habitat area
- **Mountain Lake Park**, east end of park, north of Lake St at 8th Ave
- **Potrero Hill Mini-Park**, 22nd St between Arkansas and Connecticut sts
- **St. Mary's Park**, lower park terrace, fenced area, Murray Ave and Justin Dr
- **Stern Grove**, north side, Wawona Street between 21st and 23rd aves
- **Upper Noe Park**, fenced area adjacent to ball field, Day and Sanchez sts (on a trial basis)

UNOFFICIAL OFF-LEASH AREAS

As mentioned above there is quite a bit of controversy over some of San Francisco's most popular puppy sites, Fort Funston, Crissy Field, and Ocean Beach. Duboce Park, Duboce and Steiner streets, has been an "unofficial" dog park for years. However, it has never been legally designated for off-leash use. In 2005, an initiative was put forward by local pet owners urging the city to create an official fenced-in off-leash area here. At the time of this writing, the subject was still under discussion.

For additional details on city off-leash sites listed here, or for more information on citywide dog run areas, contact the Parks and Recreation Department at 415-831-2700 or the San Francisco Dog Owner's Group, 415-339-7461, www.sfdog.org. Outside of San Francisco check out Palo Alto People for Unleashed Pet Space (PUPS), 650-562-1777, www.canineworld.com/pups, and South Bay Dog Parks, http://southbay

dogparks.org; www.dogpark.com and www.thedogpark.com are also good resources.

EAST BAY

- **Cesar Chavez Park**, 11 Spinnaker Way, Berkeley
- **Crown Memorial Beach**, Alameda
- **Del Mar Dog Park**, Del Mar Dr at Pine Valley Rd, San Ramon
- **Dracena Park**, 130 Dracena, Piedmont
- **Drigon Dog Park**, fake fire hydrants, dog bone–shaped walkway, jumps, tunnels, separate small dog and large dog areas, Mission Blvd and 7th St, Union City
- **East Bay Regional Parks**: The majority of parks in the district allow dogs to be off-leash in most open space and trail areas (with a list of exceptions) as long as they are under control at all times, and the owner is carrying a leash. The park system includes a number of gems for pet lovers including a dog-swimmable shoreline at Lake Del Valle, and the puppy paradise Point Isabel—which has its own set of guidelines (see below). For detailed dog rules, off-leash areas, park listings, and trail maps visit www.ebparks.org.
- **Hardy Dog Park**, fenced, off-leash, 2.16 acres, 491 Hardy St, Oakland
- **Lake Elizabeth Dog Park**, at Central Park and Lake Elizabeth, fenced area near softball camp side of the lake, off of Stevenson Blvd, 40000 Paseo Padre Pkwy, Fremont
- **Leona Heights Park**, Campus and Canyon Oaks Dr
- **Livermore Canine Park**, Murdell Lane, Livermore
- **Lower Washington Park**, recently expanded to a half acre, 8th and Westline, Alameda
- **Marina Park**, Marina and Fairway, San Leandro
- **Memorial Park—Dog Run**, 1.3-acre fenced dog run within Memorial Park, Bollinger Canyon Rd at San Ramon Valley Blvd, San Ramon
- **Newhall Dog Park**, areas for big and small dogs, Ayers and Turtle Creek, Concord
- **Ohlone Dog Park** (Martha Scott Benedict Memorial Park), dogs allowed off-leash in entire park, membership group publishes monthly newsletter, SCOOPs, and hosts potluck meetings, Grant St and Hearst Ave, Berkeley, www.ohlonedogpark.org
- **Paso Nogal Park**, Paso Nogal Rd and Morello Ave, Pleasant Hill
- **Piedmont Park**, 711 Highland Ave, Piedmont
- **Point Isabel Regional Shoreline**, 21 acres of run-free shoreline; official off-leash area is along the south side of the canal; Central Ave, exit off I-80 East or I-580 West, Richmond, www.pido.org. Point Isabel Dog Owners and Friends, a dog owner membership group, provides

biodegradable doggy waste bags, publishes a newsletter, and sponsors monthly clean-ups. At the end of the day, you can stop by the popular Mudpuppy's Tub & Scrub and Sit & Stay café, www.mudpuppys.com, in the park to sign your pup up for a doggie bath, pick up treats and toys, and grab some coffee and snacks for yourself.

- **San Lorenzo Community Park**, half-acre site on the west side of the 30-acre park, 1970 Via Buena Vista, San Lorenzo

NORTH BAY

- **Bayfront Park**, popular 2-acre dog park, Camino Alto and Sycamore Ave, Mill Valley
- **Camino Alto Open Space Preserve**, end of Escalon Dr, West of Camino Alto, Mill Valley
- **DeTurk Roundbarn Park**, 819 Donahue St, Santa Rosa
- **Doyle Park Dog Park**, fenced dog park is behind the stadium, 700 Hoen Ave, Santa Rosa
- **Field of Dogs**, San Rafael, 3540 Civic Center Dr, fenced two thirds of the area behind Marin Civic Center, www.fieldofdogs.org
- **Galvin Dog Park**, in Don Galvin Park, next to Golf Course, 3330 Yulupa Ave, Santa Rosa
- **Marin Headlands Trails**, there are several entrances, one is at the Coastal Trail off Bunker Rd, near Rodeo Beach, Marin
- **Mc Dog**, within John F. McInnis County Park, Highway 101 to Smith Ranch Rd, San Rafael
- **Northwest Community Dog Park**, Marlow off of Gurneville Rd, Santa Rosa
- **Remington Dog Park** (also known as the Sausalito Dog Park), fenced area within the Martin Luther King Park, on Bridgeway and Ebbtide Ave, Sausalito, http://dogpark-sausalito.com
- **Rincon Valley Dog Park**, in Rincon Valley Community Park, fenced pond area for dogs, separate fenced large and small dog areas, 5108 Badger Rd, Santa Rosa
- **Rodeo Beach and Lagoon**, from the Marin Headlands Visitor Center, follow the sign west, Sausalito
- **San Pedro Mountain Open Space Preserve**, North Point San Pedro Rd, to Woodoaks Dr to the end, San Rafael
- **Terra Linda–Sleepy Hollow Divide Open Space Preserve**, end of Ridgewood Dr, San Rafael

PENINSULA

- **Boothbay Park**, Boothbay Ave and Edgewater Lane, Half Moon Bay
- **Burlingame Dog Park**, fenced area in Washington Park, Burlingame Ave east of train tracks, Burlingame

- **Cipriani Park Dog Exercise Area**, 2525 Buena Vista Ave, Belmont
- **Coastside Dog Park**, Wavecrest Rd near the Smith Field ball fields, off of Highway 1, Half Moon Bay, http://coastdogs.org
- **Foster City Dog Exercise Area**, 600 Foster City Blvd, Foster City
- **Foster City Dog Run**, fenced run, Foster City Blvd and Bounty, Foster City
- **Greer Park**, West Bayshore Rd and Amarillo St, Palo Alto
- **Heather Park**, Portofino and Melendy drs, San Carlos
- **Hoover Park**, Cowper St between Loma Verde and Colorado aves, Palo Alto
- **Mitchell Park**, 3800 Middlefield Rd, Palo Alto
- **San Bruno Dog Park**, fenced area, Maywood and Evergreen, San Bruno
- **Shoreline Dog Park**, Shoreline Recreation Area, east end of Shoreline Blvd, Mountain View

SOUTH BAY
The City of San Jose is planning to build a dog park in each of its 10 districts, starting with a one-year trial dog park in the Willow Glen neighborhood. The park will be located in Frank Bramhall Park on Willow Street.
- **Hellyer Park**, 1-acre enclosed area near Shadowbluff picnic area, 101 to Hellyer Ave, San Jose
- **Las Palmas Park**, Russet and Danforth drs, Sunnyvale
- **Lincoln Park**, fenced area, Wabash and West San Carlos, San Jose
- **Miyuki Dog Park**, small dirt enclosed area, Miyuki Dr and Autotech Lane, off of Santa Theresa Blvd, San Jose
- **Percolation Ponds**, off-leash running and swimming, Noble Ave north of Piedmont, San Jose
- **Santa Clara Dog Park**, 3450 Brookdale Dr, Santa Clara
- **Watson Dog Park**, the city's first official dog park, has a separate fenced small dog area, benches, picnic tables and grass, East Jackson and 22nd, San Jose

A WORD ABOUT SAFETY

San Francisco, and indeed the Bay Area, suffers from the same problems with crime as does most every other large metropolitan area. What's unusual here is that San Francisco suffers from an inordinate number of pedestrian fatalities. More pedestrians than occupants of motor vehicles have been killed in car accidents in San Francisco during the past 10 years, according to a study by the San Francisco Injury Center of UCSF. Pedestrian injuries were heavily concentrated in the downtown area of San Francisco and along heavily trafficked corridors. Be careful when you walk, bike, or drive. Because police can't be everywhere all the time, you need to be aware of your own safety. Fortunately, common sense can reduce your chances of being victimized. Below are a few simple urban safety tips:

- Walk with determination, and remain aware of your surroundings at all times.
- If you're carrying a handbag or backpack, do so with the strap across your chest. However, if someone demands what you are carrying, give it up! Your life is much more valuable than anything you're carrying.
- On the street, you do not owe a response to anyone who asks for one. This may seem callous but it is better to err on the side of bad manners than bad judgment.
- At all costs, avoid getting into a car with a stranger.
- On the bus, ride in the front next to the driver.
- Keep clear of abandoned/deserted areas; if you must go into an area that you feel may be unsafe, do it in the daytime and, if possible, with someone else.
- Lock your house, both when you leave and when you are at home.
- If you like to jog, try to find a running partner, particularly if you run at night.
- Know where the local police and fire stations are located.
- If something does happen to you or if you witness a crime, notify the police immediately.

Neighborhood Watch programs are on the increase throughout the Bay Area, but they're not in every community yet. These programs encourage neighbors to get to know each other and watch out for each other, and to notify authorities of anything suspicious. Check with the police department in your neighborhood to find out if a watch program is up and running, and if not, you may want to take the lead and set one up yourself. You can also visit the neighborhood watch web site at www.ncpc.org, which gives you general safety information and instructs you on how to set up a neighborhood watch in your neighborhood. In addition, the District Attorney's office set up a community DA program where district attorneys in San Francisco volunteer in their own neighborhood and share their expertise.

The San Francisco Police Department is looking for volunteers to assist in crime prevention, neighborhood policing, and other areas. For more information, contact the Volunteer Coordinator, 850 Bryant Street, Room 570, San Francisco, 415-553-9152, or fill out a request for information online at the police department's web site, www.ci.sf.ca.us/police.

In San Francisco, neighborhood crime statistics are available online with weekly breakdowns and maps at www.ci.sf.ca.us/police.

Finally, if you are a victim of a crime, contact the police immediately, by dialing 911. For family violence, the crisis hotline is 415-553-9225 during the day and 415-553-0123 after hours (non-emergency) or 911 for emergencies. For more listings, see **Crisis Lines** in the **Useful Phone Numbers & Web Sites** chapter.

If you have a complaint against a police officer in San Francisco, contact the Office of Citizen Complaints, 415-597-7711. In Oakland, contact the Citizens' Police Review Board, 510-238-3159. In San Jose, contact the Office of the Independent Police Auditor, 408-794-6226. You can also contact the police department in question directly.

N OW THAT YOU'VE FOUND A PLACE TO HANG YOUR HAT, AND
you've taken care of some of the basics like turning on electricity
and making sure your stove works, it's time to make your place feel
like home. This chapter covers appliance rentals, domestic services, finding
an automobile repair shop, receiving and sending packages, as well as
services for people with disabilities, information for international newcomers, a resource section for gays and lesbians, and more.

RENTAL SERVICES

Most Bay Area rental apartments come fully equipped with all of the basic
essentials you'll need—refrigerator, stove, etc.—with one exception. Your
odds of getting a washer and dryer in San Francisco are only about 50/50,
especially if you opt, as many locals do, for an older Victorian or Edwardian
flat. In which case, your odds are even worse. If you'd rather not shlep to
the local Laundromat with all your neighbors, you might consider renting
a washer and dryer. However, always be sure to check with your landlord
first, about logistics—where to hook it up and who will pay the increased
water (the owner if you're lucky) and electricity (almost always you) bills.
Who knows, in the process you may even be able to convince them to purchase one instead. It's worth a try.

If you're buying a house or condo and wind up missing a key appliance, or want to replace an old one with a newer one, or find yourself in
the rare but odd studio rental with a "partial kitchen" you may want to
check into appliance rental options. Generally speaking, you'll probably
save money by opting to buy instead of renting—even buying on credit is
financially better. But you just may need to rent something temporarily to
get you started.

MAJOR APPLIANCE RENTAL

SAN FRANCISCO/NORTH BAY
- **Rent-A-Center**, 2853 Mission St, 415-282-2522, or 800-665-5510, www.rentacenter.com
- **Rent-A-Center**, 1375 Fillmore St, 415-567-3313, or 800-665-5510, www.rentacenter.com
- **Rent-A-Center**, 2635 Springs Rd, Vallejo, 707-643-7368, or 800-665-5510, www.rentacenter.com
- **Rent-A-Center**, 711 Stony Point Rd #6, Santa Rosa, 707-542-6522, or 800-665-5510, www.rentacenter.com
- **Webrents**, 888-321-6170, www.webrents.com

EAST BAY
- **Rent-A-Center**, 3400 International Blvd, Oakland, 510-532-0210, or 800-665-5510, www.rentacenter.com
- **Webrents**, 888-321-6170, www.webrents.com

PENINSULA/SOUTH BAY
- **Rent-A-Center**, 1789 East Capitol Expy, San Jose, 408-532-0274
- **Mike's Appliance Rental**, 1224 Lynhurst Way, San Jose, 408-266-5640
- **Rent-A-Center**, 1605 West San Carlos St, San Jose, 408-287-2183, or 800-665-5510, www.rentacenter.com

DOMESTIC SERVICES

HOUSEKEEPING

As many of us work more than we care to, you may find there just isn't enough time to keep up with domestic details, particularly house cleaning. Rest assured, the Bay Area has a whole bunch of people who'd be more than happy to clean your abode, for a fee. Many housekeepers advertise on coffeehouse, grocery store, and university/college bulletin boards, as well as in newspaper classifieds. In San Francisco, **Parent's Place**, 1710 Scott St, 415-359-2454, has a bulletin board full of ads posted by people looking for housecleaning and childcare jobs. **Professional housecleaning services** are listed in the Yellow Pages under "House Cleaning." Here are a few numbers to get you started.

SAN FRANCISCO

- **Cinderella's Housekeeping**, 415-864-8900, www.cinderellas agency.com
- **City Maids**, 650-755-4155, www.sfcitymaids.com
- **Golden Gate Housecleaning**, 415-379-3607, www.golden gatehc.com
- **Green Maids**, 415-673-3266, www.greenmaids.com; this service uses non-toxic supplies, and specializes in working with families and children
- **Marvel Maids**, 415-546-8000
- **Merry Maids**, 415-221-6243 or 800-Merry-Maids, www.merrymaids. com
- **New Dimensions**, 415-731-4900, www.ndclean.com/agency.html
- **Self-Help for the Elderly**, 415-677-7600, www.selfhelpelderly.org; free temporary at-home assistance for qualified seniors and the disabled

NORTH BAY

- **Golden Gate Housecleaning**, 415-379-3607, www.goldengate hc.com
- **Merry Maids**, 707-545-2192 or 800-Merry-Maids, www.merrymaids. com
- **A Maid to Shine**, 415-379-9400, www.amaidtoshine.com

EAST BAY

- **Dana's Housekeeping**, 800-876-5837, www.danashousekeeping.com
- **Merry Maids**, 510-521-5878, 510-482-7770, 925-685-3750, or 800-Merry-Maids, www.merrymaids.com

PENINSULA

- **Bay Area Maintenance**, 650-368-3906
- **City Maids**, 650-755-4155, www.sfcitymaids.com
- **Merry Maids**, 650-369-6243 or 800-Merry-Maids, www.merrymaids. com

SOUTH BAY

- **Complete Cleaning**, 408-248-4162
- **European Touch**, 408-269-5210
- **Merry Maids**, 408-978-6243 or 800-Merry-Maids, www.merrymaids. com

PEST CONTROL

As with the rest of the USA, the Bay Area has some cockroaches, ants, and termites, but in general there are far fewer pests here than in many parts of the country. Some older buildings, especially those with restaurants on the premises, are prone to cockroaches. In winter months ants can be a problem. Fleas may bug you in the late fall, particularly if you live near the beach, at ground level, or have pets. Pigeons can become bothersome if they decide to roost on the ledges of your building, especially near the entryway – protect your head! In warmer, damper regions, mosquitoes can be a nuisance. Alameda, San Mateo, Santa Clara, Marin, Sonoma, Napa, Solano, and Contra Costa counties have mosquito abatement programs. The telephone numbers of the abatement programs are listed below and may be helpful regarding other pest issues. Some homes also suffer from termites; if you are in the market to buy a house, consider having it inspected for termites. In more rural areas ticks, raccoons, opossums, and skunks can be a problem.

If you are renting your place, it is the landlord's responsibility to keep your premises free from vermin, although keeping your home or apartment clean always helps. Nontoxic and humane means of controlling pests are available. Check the Yellow Pages under "Pest Control Services" for listings.

MAIL SERVICES

If you're in between addresses but still need a place to get your mail, there are dozens of businesses that will rent you a mailbox. You can also rent a mailbox at your local post office, though many have a waiting list. The following mail service companies are in San Francisco. Check your Yellow Pages under "Mailing Receiving and Forwarding Services" for a location near you.

- **Aim Mail Center**, 221 King St, 415-495-6776, www.aimmailcenters. com
- **Eagle Mailbox**, 1850 Union St, 415-921-1850
- **Jet Mail**, 2130 Fillmore St, 415-922-9402
- **Mail Access**, 2261 Market St, 415-626-2575, www.mail-access.com
- **Mail Boxes Etc. (MBE)** and **UPS Stores**: 268 Bush St, 415-765-1515; 3701 Sacramento St, 415-221-9882; 4104 24th St, 415-824-1070; 601 Van Ness Ave, 415-775-6644; 2370 Market St, 415-431-0121, 2443 Fillmore St, 415-922-6245; 1032 Irving St, 415-566-2660; multiple other San Francisco and Bay Area locations; to find the store nearest you, visit www.theupsstore.com or www.mbe.com

- **Postal Annex**, 100 First St, 415-882-1515; 350 Bay St, 415-772-9022
- **Potrero Mail n' More**, 1459 18th St, 415-826-8757
- **UPS Store** (mail boxes plus additional services; see **Mail Boxes Etc.** above)
  For mailing services, packaging help, faxing, and copying try
- **FedEx Kinko's**, 1967 Market St, 415-252-0864; 1150 Harrison St, 415-552-4628; 1800 Van Ness Ave, 415-292-2500; 555 California St, 415-986-6160; 369 Pine St, 415-834-1053, http://fedex.kinkos.com

MAIN POST OFFICES

Neighborhood post offices are listed at the end of each neighborhood profile. Check there for the one nearest you. For postal rates, post office locations, zip codes, and more, you can also contact the post office at 800-ASK-USPS, www.usps.com, or try any of the post offices listed below.

SAN FRANCISCO/NORTH BAY
- **Napa**, 1625 Trancas St (Monday-Friday, 9 a.m. to 5 p.m.; closed Saturday)
- **San Francisco**, 1300 Evans Ave (Monday-Friday, 7 a.m. to 8:30 p.m.; Saturday, 8 a.m. to 2 p.m.)
- **San Rafael**, 40 Bellam Blvd (Monday-Friday 8:30 a.m. to 5 p.m.; Saturday, 10 a.m. to 1 p.m.)
- **Santa Rosa**, 730 2nd St (Monday-Friday, 8 a.m. to 6 p.m.; Saturday, 10 a.m. to 2 p.m.)

EAST BAY
- **Berkeley**, 2000 Allston Way (Monday-Friday, 9 a.m. to 5 p.m.; Saturday, 9 a.m. to 3 p.m.)
- **Concord**, 2121 Meridian Park Blvd (Monday-Friday, 9 a.m. to 6 p.m.; Saturday, 9 a.m. to 2 p.m.)
- **Oakland**, 201 13th St, (Monday-Friday, 8:30 to 5 p.m.; Saturday, 8 a.m. to 2 p.m.)
- **Walnut Creek**, 2070 North Broadway (Monday-Friday, 8:30 a.m. to 5 p.m.; closed Saturday)

PENINSULA/SOUTH BAY
- **Palo Alto**, 2085 East Bayshore Rd (Monday-Friday, 8:30 a.m. to 5 p.m.; closed Saturday)
- **San Mateo**, 1630 South Delaware St (Monday-Friday, 8:30 a.m. to 5 p.m.; Saturday, 9 a.m. to 12:30 p.m.)
- **San Jose**, 1750 Lundy Ave (Monday-Friday, 8:30 a.m. to 8 p.m.; closed Saturday)

JUNK MAIL

Everyone gets it, and most hate it—junk mail. There are a number of strategies for curtailing the onslaught. Try writing a note, including your name and address, asking to be purged from the **Direct Marketing Association's list** (Direct Marketing Association's Mail Preference Service, P.O. Box 9008, Farmingdale, NY 11735). This may work, although some catalogue companies need to be contacted directly with a purge request. Another option is to call the **"Opt-out" line** at 888-567-8688 and request that the main credit bureaus not release your name and address to interested marketing companies pushing "pre-approved" credit and insurance offers. To keep telemarketers at bay, you can also register your home and cell phone numbers with the **National Do Not Call Registry**, 888-382-1222, TTY: 866-290-4236, www.donotcall.gov.

SHIPPING SERVICES

- **DHL Worldwide Express**, 800-225-5345, www.dhl.com
- **FedEx**, 800-238-5355, www.fedex.com
- **United Parcel Service (UPS)**, 800-742-5877, www.ups.com
- **US Postal Service Express Mail**, 800-222-1811, www.usps.com

AUTOMOBILE REPAIR

Everything in your world is going great: you have a place to live, a good job, the sun is shining...and then your car breaks down. If this happens on the freeway, hopefully you already have some kind of service plan that will get your car towed to a service station. American Automobile Association, known as AAA, is a popular plan (see below). Insurance companies that offer auto insurance, as well as some fuel companies, offer auto emergency plans similar to AAA. Your next dilemma—how do you find a reputable auto repair place? This is not an easy process, no matter where you live. Probably the most popular way to find a repair place is to ask around—friends, co-workers, neighbors, etc. Going to your auto dealer, while generally a reliable option, can be expensive. **Value Star**, a leading rating organization of local service businesses and professionals, is headquartered in Oakland. To use their rating service, go to www.valuestar.com or call 888-298-8100. At **Bay Area Consumers' Checkbook** (see below, under **Consumer Protection**) you can order the latest article on auto repair shops in the Bay Area. Remember, it's always a good idea to check with the **Better Business Bureau** (see below under **Consumer Protection**) to find out if any complaints have been filed against a service station you are considering using. And finally, on the lighter side, try calling *Car Talk* on National Public Radio, 888-CAR-TALK, or just tune in to KQED 88.5 FM, at 10 a.m. on Saturday or Sunday as Click and Clack, the Tappet brothers, discuss, in a most humorous fashion, cars and the problems of their owners. You can also pick up handy auto tips on their web site: www.cartalk.com.

AAA (AMERICAN AUTOMOBILE ASSOCIATION)

Founded at the turn of the century by Jim Wilkins, proprietor of the Cliff House, the American Automobile Association (AAA) began as an automobile club when there were only a dozen self-propelled vehicles navigating the hills of San Francisco. Today, more than 3.8 million people belong to AAA. Membership costs $49 a year plus a one-time $17 enrollment fee. As a member, you receive 24-hour emergency road service, free maps, travel services, discounts at numerous hotels, DMV services, and more. If you are caught out of gas, have a flat tire, or worse yet, a blown transmission, AAA can come rescue you. Just call their **Emergency Road Service Number** at 800-AAA-HELP (800-222-4357). You can also call 800-922-8228 to find an office near you or visit the web site for California AAA, www.csaa.com.

CONSUMER PROTECTION

The ***Bay Area Consumers' Checkbook*** is a pro-consumer guide published by the Center for the Study of Services. It is a nonprofit magazine, free of advertising, created "to provide consumers information to help them get high quality services and products at the best possible prices." The quality of information is excellent. Articles can be ordered online at www.checkbook.org or through the mail, call 510-763-7979, Monday-Friday, 8:30 a.m. to 2:30 p.m. There is a fee for ordering articles. A subscription to the magazine is $30 for two years; call the same number used for ordering articles.

For consumer protection information regarding utilities see **Consumer Protection—Utility Complaints** in the **Getting Settled** chapter.

Got a beef with a merchant or a company? Several agencies monitor consumer-related businesses and will take action when necessary. It goes without saying that the best defense against fraud and consumer victimization is to avoid it—read contracts before you sign them, save all receipts and canceled checks, get the name of telephone sales and service people, and check a contractor's license number with the Department of Consumer Affairs for complaints. But sometimes you still get stung. A dry cleaner returns your blue suit, but now it's purple and he shrugs. A shop refuses to refund as promised on the expensive gift, which didn't suit your mother. Your landlord fails to return your security deposit when you move. After $898 in repairs to your automobile's engine, the car now vibrates wildly, and the mechanic claims innocence. Negotiations, documents in hand, fail. You're angry, and embarrassed because you've been had. There is something you can do.

- **Better Business Bureau**: San Francisco, Alameda, Contra Costa, San Mateo, and Marin counties: 415-243-9999, 650-552-9222, or 510-238-1000 (all connect to main service number); Santa Clara and Santa Cruz counties, 408-278-7400; maintains consumer complaint files about businesses. You can also research businesses on their web site at www.bbb.goldengate.org.
- **Better Business Bureau Automotive Line**, 800-955-5100
- **California Attorney General**, 800-952-5225, http://caag.state.ca.us, maintains a public inquiry unit that reviews consumer complaints.
- **California State Directory Information Service**, 916-657-9900
- **California Department of Consumer Affairs**, 510-785-7554, 800-952-5210, www.dca.ca.gov, is a state agency that investigates consumer complaints.
- **Contractors State License Board**, 800-321-2752
- **SF District Attorney**, 415-552-6400, maintains a consumer protection unit that investigates and mediates consumer/business disputes.

MEDIA–SPONSORED CALL FOR ACTION PROGRAMS

The following are consumer advocacy programs operated by Bay Area television/radio stations:
- **KGO Seven On Your Side**, 900 Front St, San Francisco, CA 94111, 415-954-8151
- **KRON-TV Contact 4**, 1001 Van Ness Ave, San Francisco, 415-441-4444
- *San Jose Mercury News* **Action Line**, 750 Riddler Park Dr, San Jose, CA 95190, 888-688-6400

LEGAL MEDIATION/REFERRAL PROGRAMS

- **The Bar Association of San Francisco**, 465 California St, Suite 1100, San Francisco, 415-982-1600, www.sfbar.org, runs early mediation program jointly with San Francisco Superior Court
- **California Community Dispute Service**, 502 7th St, San Francisco, 415-865-2520
- **East Bay Community Mediation**, 1968 San Pablo Ave, Berkeley, 510-548-2377, www.ebcm.org

LEGAL ASSISTANCE FOR THE ELDERLY

- **Legal Assistance for Seniors**, 614 Grand Ave, Suite 400, Oakland, 510-832-3040
- **Legal Assistance to the Elderly**, 1453 Mission St, Suite 500, San Francisco, 415-861-4444

SMALL CLAIMS COURTS

The maximum amount of money you may sue for in small claims court is $5,000, and in accordance with state law, one individual may file up to two cases per year.

The **California Department of Consumer Affairs** maintains a helpful web site, www.dca.ca.gov/smallclaims, with information on small claims court in general, including a useful booklet, "How to Use Small Claims Court," that you can download. The site also has information and individual contacts for each county. Here are a few local county web sites to get you started.

- **Alameda County**, www.alameda.courts.ca.gov/courts/divs/small/index.shtml
- **Contra Costa County**, www.cc-courts.org/smallcl.htm
- **Marin County**, www.co.marin.ca.us/depts/MC/main/small claims.cfm
- **San Mateo County**, www.sanmateocourt.org/director.php?filename=./smallclaims/index.html
- **Santa Clara County**, www.scselfservice.org/small/default.htm
- **Solano County**, www.solanocourts.com/general/court/small.htm
- **Sonoma County**, www.sonomasuperiorcourt.com/index.php?v=civil_smcl_div

SERVICES FOR PEOPLE WITH DISABILITIES

Long before there was an Americans with Disabilities Act, the Bay Area's sensitivity to the needs of the disabled was raised by a group of handicapped college applicants who fought for admission to the Berkeley campus of the University of California. Their efforts, in the early 1970s, not only achieved the group's goal but also spawned the **Independent Living Center**, which now boasts offices across the country. Its representatives work hard to protect the rights of the disabled, and the centers offer training and rehabilitation services to those with disabilities, as well as referrals to support groups and organizations.

Rose Resnick's Lighthouse for the Blind and Visually Disabled provides assistance, equipment, support, and referrals to the visually impaired. Fully trained guide dogs are available through **Guide Dogs for the Blind**, which is based in Marin County. **The Hearing Society for the Bay Area** provides testing, education, support and referrals to the hearing impaired.

Another great resource for information on disability access in the city is *San Francisco Access*, a guide with information on hotels, dining, shopping, and local attractions. To order a copy, contact the Convention and Visitors Bureau, 900 Market St, 415-391-2000, TTY: 415-392-0328, www.AccessNCA.com.

Here's how to get in touch with several helpful organizations:

- **The ARC of San Francisco (Association of Retarded Citizens)**, 1500 Howard St, 415-255-7200
- **Center for Independent Living**, 2539 Telegraph Ave, Berkeley, 510-841-4776, TTY 510-841-3101
- **Deaf and Disabled Telecommunications Program**, 510-302-1100, TTY 510-302-1101
- **Deaf Services of Palo Alto**, P.O. Box 60651, Palo Alto, 650-856-2558
- **Guide Dogs for the Blind**, 350 Los Ranchitos Rd, San Rafael, 415-499-4000
- **Hearing Impaired Line**, San Jose, 408-998-5299
- **Hearing Society**, 870 Market St, 3rd Floor, 415-693-5870, TTY 415-834-1005
- **Independent Living Resource Center**, 649 Mission, 3rd Floor, San Francisco, 415-543-6222, TTY 415-543-6698
- **The Janet Pomeroy Center (Recreation Center for the Handicapped)**, 207 Skyline Blvd, 415-665-4100; TTY 415-665-4107, www.janetpomeroy.org
- **Rose Resnick Lighthouse for the Blind**, 214 Van Ness Ave, 415-431-1481; TTY 415-431-4572
- **Support for Families of Children with Disabilities**, 2601 Mission St, 415-282-7494

GETTING AROUND

All BART stations are wheelchair accessible with elevators at every station and available discount tickets. Most public transit buses throughout the Bay Area are also equipped to handle wheelchairs by use of ramps and lifts. Fares are significantly lower for the disabled. For more information on public transit options for the disabled call the appropriate transit agency (BART, MUNI, AC Transit, SamTrans, and CalTrain are listed in the

Transportation chapter). Wheelchair rentals are available at a number of medical equipment and supply businesses. You can also purchase new and used wheelchairs at various stores. Check under "wheelchairs" in the Yellow Pages.

Applications for handicapped parking permits are available at any local **Department of Motor Vehicles** and online at www.dmv.ca.gov, or you can request to have an application mailed to you by calling 800-777-0133, TTY: 800-368-4327. Once you complete the application, it must be signed by your doctor and brought to any local DMV office, or returned by mail to the address listed on the application. There is no fee for disabled placards.

COMMUNICATION

The **California Telephone Access Program** offers free assistance devices for the deaf, as well as the hearing-, speech-, mobility-, and visually impaired—from amplified phones, to voice enhancers, to large-button phones, to TTYs (teletypewriters). **TTY** is a small telecommunications device with a keyboard for typing and a screen for reading conversations. TTY is sometimes also referred to as **TDD (Telecommunications Device for the Deaf)**. Experts will come to your home to install the equipment and help train you to use it. To get started contact TTY: 800-806-4474 or Voice: 800-806-1191; or for services in Spanish TTY: 800-896-7670, or Voice: 800-949-5650. You can also drop by the walk-in center, CTAP Oakland Service Center, 1970 Broadway, Suite 650, Oakland, open Monday through Friday, 9 a.m. to 6 p.m.

California also has a telephone relay service, which provides a communication system for the hearing- and speech-impaired. This system allows people who are deaf or hard of hearing to phone people who do not have a TTY. The operator will contact your party and relay your conversation. **Speech to Speech Relay Service (STS)** assists those who can hear but have a speech disability, and use a voice synthesizer or voice enhancer. A specially trained operator re-voices what is being said by the STS user. The STS user hears the other party's voice directly. No special telephone equipment is required. This service is free except for any toll charges.
- TTY: 800-735-2929 or 711
- STS: 800-854-7784 or 711
- Voice: 800-735-2922 or 711

If you need help with sign language, contact the following organizations. They usually require one week's notice. **Bay Area Communication Access**, 415-356-0405, TTY: 415-356-0376; **Hands On**, 800-900-9478, TDD: 800-900-9479.

HOUSING

Some of the organizations listed above can help you with finding accessible housing, including the **Independent Living Center** in San Francisco at 415-543-6222 and the **Center for Independent Living** in Berkeley, 510-841-7776.

INTERNATIONAL NEWCOMERS

Immigration rules and regulations have become increasingly strict and bureaucratic in the USA since 9/11. If you are planning to relocate from abroad, your first step should be to visit the US consulate in your home country and find out what you need to do to prepare; that way you can have all of your paperwork in order ahead of time, and hopefully avoid any problems or delays when you arrive. The consulate should be able to provide you with information specific to your situation—applications for permanent residency, guest worker programs, and student visas, etc., as well as information on green cards, naturalization, seeking asylum, and becoming a US citizen.

A variety of helpful information can be found online at the **US Citizen and Immigration Services** web site: http://uscis.gov. If you have specific questions, you can also contact the USCIS national customer service center: 800-375-5283 or TTY: 800-767-1833. Once you know what you need to do, you'll undoubtedly need to fill out paperwork. To get the proper forms call 800-870-3676 or look on the USCIS web site (listed above).

For further assistance, you can schedule an appointment with **US Citizen and Immigration Services** by calling 800-375-5283. Below are the addresses of local USCIS district and satellite offices:

- **San Francisco District Office**: 444 Washington St, San Francisco; Note: most appointments will be directed to 630 Sansome St.
- **Asylum Office**: 75 Hawthorne St, #303S, San Francisco
- **Oakland Citizenship Office**: Oakland Federal Building, 1301 Clay St, Room 380 North, Oakland
- **South Bay Office**: 1887 Monterey Rd, San Jose

Once you've settled in, you may want to get in touch with the consulate from your home country. The consulate can often be a useful starting point when you're getting settled—providing information on local community groups and organizations that may be of interest, as well as assisting with questions you may have about your move to the USA. For US citizens planning to travel abroad—especially for work, school, or an extended stay—the consulate is also the place to go to find out about rules and regulations, visas, etc. Below is a list of the major offices in San Francisco:

INTERNATIONAL CONSULATES IN SAN FRANCISCO

- **The Consulate General of Australia**, 625 Market St, Suite 200, 415-536-1970
- **The Consulate General of Austria**, 41 Sutter, 415-951-8911
- **The Consulate General of the Arab Republic of Egypt**, 3001 Pacific Ave, 415-346-9700, www.egy2000.com/indexl.htm
- **The Consulate General of Brazil**, 300 Montgomery St, Suite 900, 415-981-8170, www.brazilsf.org
- **The British Consulate General**, 1 Sansome St, Suite 850, 415-617-1300, www.britainusa.com/consular/sf/
- **The Consulate General of Canada**, 555 Montgomery St, Suite 1288, 415-834-3180
- **The Consulate General of Chile**, 870 Market St Room 1062, 415-982-7662
- **The Consulate General of China**, 1450 Laguna St, 415-674-2900
- **The Consulate General of Ecuador**, 235 Montgomery St, Suite 944, 415-982-1819
- **The Consulate General of El Salvador**, 870 Market St, Suite 508, 415-781-7924
- **The Consulate General of France**, 540 Bush St, 415-616-4900, www.consulfrance-sanfrancisco.org
- **The Consulate General of Germany**, 1960 Jackson St, 415-775-1061
- **The Consulate General of Greece**, 2441 Gough St, 415-775-2102
- **The Consulate General of Guatemala**, 870 Market St, Suite 660, 415-788-5651
- **The Consulate General of Honduras**, 870 Market St, Suite 449, 415-392-0076
- **The Consulate General of India**, 540 Arguello Blvd, 415-668-0662, www.cgisf.org
- **The Consulate General of Indonesia**, 1111 Columbus Ave, 415-474-9571
- **The Consulate General of Ireland**, 100 Pine St, 33rd Floor, 415-392-4214
- **The Consulate General of Israel**, 456 Montgomery St, Suite 2100, 415-844-7500
- **The Consulate General of Italy**, 2590 Webster St, 415-931-4924, www.italcons-sf.org
- **The Consulate General of Japan**, 50 Fremont St, Suite 2300, 415-777-3533

- **The Consulate General of the Republic of Korea**, 3500 Clay St, 415-921-2251
- **The Consulate General of Luxembourg**, One Sansome St, Suite 830, 415-788-0816
- **The Consulate General of Mexico**, 532 Folsom St, 415-354-1700, www.sre.gob.mx/sanfrancisco/
- **The Royal Norwegian Consulate General**, 20 California St, 6th floor, 415-986-0766
- **The Consulate General of Peru**, 870 Market St, Suite 10, 415-362-5185
- **The Consulate General of The Philippines**, 447 Sutter St, 6th Floor, Philippine Center Building, 415-433-6666
- **The Consulate General of Portugal**, 3298 Washington St, 415-346-3400
- **The Consulate General of the Russian Federation**, 2790 Green St, 415-928-6878
- **The Consulate General of The Republic of Singapore**, 595 Market St, Suite 2450, 415-543-4775, www.mfa.gov.sg/sanfrancisco
- **The Consulate General of Spain**, 1405 Sutter St, 415-922-2995
- **The Consulate General of Sweden**, 120 Montgomery St, Suite 2175, 415-788-2631
- **The Consulate General of Switzerland**, 456 Montgomery St, 415-788-2272
- **The Consulate General of the Republic of Turkey**, 41 Sutter St, Suite 1581, 415-362-0912
- **The Consulate General of Ukraine**, 530 Bush St, Suite 402, 415-398-0240, www.ukrainesf.com
- **The Consulate General of Vietnam**, 1700 California St, Suite 430, 415-922-1707

IMMIGRATION RESOURCES

- **Bureau of Immigration and Customs Enforcement**, www.bice.immigration.gov
- **Customs & Border Protection**, www.cbp.gov
- **Department of Homeland Security**, www.dhs.gov, www.whitehouse.gov/deptofhomeland
- **General Government Questions**, 800-688-9889, www.firstgov.gov
- **Social Security Administration**, 800-772-1213, www.ssa.gov
- **US Bureau of Consular Affairs**, www.travel.state.gov
- **US Department of State, Visa Services**, http://travel.state.gov/visa_services

- **US Immigration Online**—Green Cards, Visas, Government Forms— USA Immigration Services, www.usaimmigrationservice.org

IMMIGRATION PUBLICATIONS

You can download a useful guide, **"Welcome to the United States: A Guide for New Immigrants"** free at http://uscis.gov/graphics/citizen-ship/imm_guide.htm. The booklet includes information on your rights and responsibilities as well as the steps to take to become a US citizen. Other publications you may find helpful include:
- *Newcomer's Handbook for Moving to and Living in the USA*, by Mike Livingston (First Books)
- *The Immigration Handbook*, 3rd edition, by Henry Liebman (First Books)

MOVING PETS TO THE USA

- *The Pet-Moving Handbook* (First Books) covers domestic and international moves, via car, airplane, ferry, etc. Primary focus is on cats and dogs.
- **Cosmopolitan Canine Carriers** out of Connecticut, 800-243-9105, has been shipping dogs and cats all over the world for over 25 years. Contact them with questions or concerns regarding air transportation arrangements, vaccinations, and quarantine times.

GAY AND LESBIAN LIFE

After years of grassroots fundraising, the **Lesbian, Gay, Bisexual and Transgender Center of San Francisco**, known simply as "The Center," opened its doors in 2002 at the corner of Market Street and Laguna. Today, the bright, primary-colored, multimillion-dollar, spacious, 40,000-square-foot facility proudly flying the rainbow flag provides a variety of programs for the LGBT community, their families and friends, including parenting classes, HIV support groups, 12-step programs, and a wide range of arts activities and presentations. The Center also has a drop-in youth center, a large auditorium for special events, a senior space, a reading room, an art gallery, a bulletin board with dozens of resources, child care, offices for a handful of nonprofit groups, a computer room, a café, and a fantastic roof terrace. To find out more, drop by 1800 Market Street, call 415-865-5555, or check out www.sfcenter.org.

For gay and lesbian nightlife, dance clubs, comedy, and theater, the Castro and the Mission districts are the places to go. Check *Gay USA: Where the Babes Go*, by Lori Hobkirk, for information about lesbian life in

San Francisco. For the leather loving set, a handful of clubs in SOMA is hopping every night. SOMA is also home to the Stud, one of the oldest gay club/bars around, which frequently draws a mixed crowd to its popular dance nights.

The biggest gay celebration in town is the annual **Gay Pride Parade** in June. Festivities are held all over the city, especially in SOMA and The Castro. See **A Bay Area Year** for more detail. Also in June, check out **The International Lesbian & Gay Film Festival**, put on annually by Frameline, 415-703-8650, www.frameline.org. For a mini tour through the evolution of queer politics, culture, and identity in San Francisco check out www.shapingsf.org/ezine/gay, part of the excellent history project **Shaping San Francisco**.

PUBLICATIONS

- *Bay Area Reporter*, 395 9th St, San Francisco, 415-861-5019, www.ebar.com, has been around for almost 30 years and offers entertainment listings, hard news, sports, classifieds, personals, and more. It is distributed citywide every Tuesday; free.
- *San Francisco Bay Times: The Gay, Lesbian, Bi, Trans Newspaper*, 3410 19th St, San Francisco, 415-626-0260, offers news, reviews, employment listings, therapy and support groups, etc. Distributed citywide every other Thursday; free.
- *Girlfriends*, a glossy, lesbian magazine with light features on queer celebrities, monthly, www.girlfriendsmag.com; the same company also publishes the racier *On Our Backs*.

BOOKSTORES

- **A Different Light Bookstore**, 489 Castro St, 415-431-0891, www.adlbooks.com, is arguably the premier gay and lesbian bookstore.
- **Modern Times**, 888 Valencia, 415-282-9246, is a progressive bookstore with a good selection of lesbian, bi, and gay literature.

WHEN MOVING TO A NEW AREA, ONE OF THE MOST CHALLENGING and overwhelming prospects parents face is finding good childcare and/or schools. While the process is not an easy one, with time and effort it is possible to find what you are looking for, be it in-home or on-site daycare, an after-school program, or a good public or private school. The keys, of course, are research and persistence. Often the best advice comes from those with the most first-hand experience, namely, other parents.

PARENTING PUBLICATIONS

If you have childcare concerns upon arriving here, it's a good idea to pick up a copy of *Bay Area Parent*, a free monthly magazine that includes a calendar of events and articles on parenting resources in San Francisco and the Bay Area. The same company also publishes several related publications including *B.a.b.y. (The Best Advice for Baby & You)* and *Parenting Bay Area Teens*. To subscribe, call their office at 408-399-4842, or visit them online at (www.bayareaparent.com). *Parents' Press*, 1454 Sixth Street, Berkeley, CA 94710, 510-524-1602, offers online magazines for parents: www.parentspress.com and www.parent-teen.com (for families with teens).

DAYCARE

Probably the best way to find a good daycare provider is by referral from someone you know and trust. That said, being new to the Bay Area might limit such an option for you. The **California Childcare Resource & Referral Network**, 111 New Montgomery Street, 7th floor, San Francisco, CA 94105, 415-882-0234, www.rrnetwork.org, an information service that provides referrals to childcare agencies throughout California, should be able to assist you with your search. **The National Association for the Education of Young Children (NAEYC)** may be helpful as well. Call or write for a list of daycare centers in your area, accredited by them: 202-232-8777, NAEYC, 1509 16th Street NW, Washington, DC 20036, or search their childcare provider database at www.naeyc.org. You can also use this service to find accredited nursery schools.

Those affiliated with a major university in the Bay Area may have access to a university-operated referral agency and/or a university-run childcare center. Inquire at the student services desk of your university. Sometimes university graduate student divisions provide such referrals and services.

For a childcare referral agency in your area check with the following:

SAN FRANCISCO/NORTH BAY

- In San Francisco, contact **Children's Council of San Francisco**, 575 Sutter St, 445 Church St, San Francisco, CA 94114, 415-276-2900, Child Care Resource and Referral Line: 415-343-3300, www.childrens council.org.
- **Wu-Yee**, 888 Clay St, Lower Level, Joy Lok Family Resource Center, San Francisco, CA 94108, 415-391-4890, www.wuyee.org/programs, an agency devoted to servicing the needs of San Francisco's large Cantonese-speaking community, operates six childcare centers in the Tenderloin, Chinatown, and Visitacion Valley. Both agencies provide a variety of services in English, Spanish, and Cantonese, including training for childcare providers, health and safety training, needs assessment and food programs, resource library, parent support information about employing in-home workers, referral service for licensed childcare, and listings of nanny services.
- In Marin County, contact **Marin Child Care Council**, 555 Northgate Dr, San Rafael, Suite 105, CA 94903, 415-472-1092, Childcare Referral Line: 415-479-CARE, www.marinchildcarecouncil.org.

EAST BAY

- For childcare referrals in Alameda County contact **Bananas**, 5232 Claremont Ave, Oakland, CA 94618, 510-658-7353, direct referral line: 510-658-0381, www.bananasinc.org; or **Child Care Links**, 1020 Serpentine Lane, Suite 102, Pleasanton, CA 94566, 925-417-8733, www.childcarelinks.org.
- For referrals in Hayward, San Leandro, and the Tri-Cities Area, call **4Cs of Alameda County**, 22351 City Center Dr, Suite 200, Hayward, CA 94541, 510-582-2182, www.4c-alameda.org, childcare referral lines: 510-582-2182 (Hayward, San Leandro, San Lorenzo, and Castro Valley) and 510-790-0655 (Fremont, Newark, and Union City).

- In Contra Costa County, call **Contra Costa Child Care Council**, 2280 Diamond Blvd, Suite 500, Concord, CA 94520, 925-676-KIDS, www.cocokids.org.

PENINSULA/SOUTH BAY

- For the San Mateo area, consult with **Child Care Coordinating Council of San Mateo County (4Cs)**, 2121 El Camino Real, Suite A-100, San Mateo, CA 94403, 650-655-6770, www.thecouncil.net.
- The **Community Child Care Council of Santa Clara County**, 111 East Gish Rd, San Jose, CA 95112, 408-487-0749, www.4c.org, provides information and referrals in Santa Clara County.

WHAT TO LOOK FOR IN DAYCARE

When searching for the best place for your child, be sure to visit prospective daycare providers—preferably unannounced. In general, look for safety, cleanliness, and caring attitudes on the part of the daycare workers. Check that the kitchen, toys, and furniture are clean and safe. Observe the other kids at the center. Do they seem happy? Are they well behaved? Ask for the telephone numbers of other parents who use the service and talk to them before committing. It's a good idea to request a daily schedule—look for both active and quiet time, and age-appropriate activities. Since the weather in California allows for year-round outdoor activities, such as sports, games, and field trips, make sure the childcare curriculum includes such things.

Keep in mind that being licensed does not necessarily guarantee service of the quality you may be seeking. If you think a provider might be acceptable, check to see if they're licensed and not in trouble for anything. To find out if a daycare is licensed, check the online registry of the **California Community Care Licensing Division**, www.ccld.ca.gov or contact the **California Child Care Resource & Referral Network**, 111 New Montgomery Street, 7th floor, San Francisco, CA 94105, 415-882-0234, www.rrnetwork.org, or any of the county referral agencies listed above.

For drop-in childcare while you go shopping or to a movie, try **Kids' Park Centers**. They have two locations close to the major shopping malls in Silicon Valley (Oakridge and Valley Fair) and accept children age 2–12 years. Call 408-260-7929 or visit www.kidspark.com for more information.

In 2005 rates were $7 per hour for one child with discounted rates for siblings. They limit the number of hours that you can use their service (5 hours per day and up to 15 hours per week) to ensure that the center provides drop-in rather than regular childcare. There is also a one-time $25 registration fee per family. While reservations are not necessary, it's a good idea to call first to be sure they have room on a particular day.

NANNIES

If you are looking for a nanny, in San Francisco or Silicon Valley you can expect to pay $1,400 to $2,000 per month for a live-in nanny, and $13 to $25 per hour for a part-time nanny, depending on the nanny's experience, education, the number of kids in your family, and whether housekeeping and driving are expected. Many agencies can assist you in finding a qualified nanny. Online, try **The Nanny Network** at www.nannynet.net or call them at 925-256-8575. This organization provides reliable nanny referral services within Alameda and Contra Costa counties. In San Francisco, **In-House Staffing @ Aunt Ann's,** 415-749-3650, www.in-house staffing.com, matches families with baby nurses, nannies, and babysitters. **A Special Nanny**, 408-379-8987, www.specialnanny.com, provides nanny care and aides for children with special needs throughout the greater Bay Area. **I Love My Nanny**, www.ilovemynanny.com, is a national service that offers help with screening and recruiting nannies and babysitters. Other useful resources for employing a nanny include **Mom's Away**, 510-559-9195, **Nannies Limited**, 925-803-1040, and the popular **Town and Country Resources**, www.tandcr.com, 415-567-0956 (San Francisco), 650-326-8570 (Palo Alto). The latter places childcare and household professionals in homes, including nannies, baby nurses, personal assistants, housekeepers, and cooks. You can also log onto **GoodConnection.com**, www.goodconnection.com, a free message board that connects parents looking for childcare with babysitters and nannies.

Be sure to check all references prior to hiring someone. Many parents choose to run background checks on prospective nannies. **Trustline**, 800-822-8490, www.trustline.org, a nonprofit state-affiliated background checking agency and registry, conducts fingerprint searches through both FBI and California Department of Justice records, and name searches for child abuse reports. This service is available to all prospective childcare employers, but keep in mind that searches usually take three to four weeks to complete.

If you decide to hire a nanny without using an agency, you will need to take care of taxes, disability, unemployment insurance, and social security. For information, call 800-NANITAX or check www.4nannytaxes.com.

AU PAIRS

The US Information Agency oversees and approves the organizations that offer this service where young adults between the ages of 18 and 26 provide a year of in-home childcare and light housekeeping in exchange for airfare, room and board, and a small stipend per week. The program offers a valuable cultural exchange between the host family and the (usually European) au pair, as well as a flexible childcare schedule for parents. Unfortunately, the program only lasts one year and the au pairs don't have the life or work experience of a career nanny. Nevertheless, in California au pairs are a popular way to satisfy families' childcare needs. In the Bay Area, most au pairs come from Poland, Germany, France, and Scandinavia. The agencies that bring over the au pairs run background checks before making placements, and orientation and training sessions once the placements have been made. Here are some of the agencies you can contact if you'd like to find an au pair:

- **Cultural Care Au Pair**, 800-333-6056, www.efaupair.org
- **Interexchange, Au Pair USA**, 800-479-0907 or 800-287-2477, www.interexchange.org/aupair
- **Au Pair In America**, 800-928-7247, www.aupairinamerica.com
- **Au Pair Care**, 800-4AU-PAIR, www.aupaircare.com

SCHOOLS

Choosing the right school for your child was probably a difficult task in your old community; factor in moving to a new city, and, for many, it becomes a stressful proposition. Add to that the reputation of California's public schools—overcrowded, staffed by underpaid and inexperienced teachers, etc.—and the search for the right school can be downright intimidating. Many parents who are new to the area rush to the conclusion that the only way to offer their child a good education here is to shell out a lot of money for an expensive private school. In fact, the Bay Area offers a great multitude of schooling possibilities, including an excellent public charter program, public and private year-round schooling programs, and myriad private options.

CHOOSING A SCHOOL

Quantitative measures such as graduation rates and test scores are important, but just as important are the subjective impressions and feelings you and your child will gain from visiting a prospective school. That's why the crucial ingredients for finding the right school are visit, visit, visit, and talk, talk, talk.

When visiting a school, your gut reactions will tell you a lot. Ask yourself these questions:
- Am I comfortable here? Will my child be comfortable here?
- Does the school feel safe? Are the bathrooms clean and free of graffiti?

- Does this school meet her/his learning style? Are elementary-age students moving around naturally, but staying on task?
- What are the halls like in junior high and high schools when classes change—how are students interacting with one another and with their teachers as their class changes?
- Are students actively engaged in discussions or projects? Is student work displayed?
- Ask elementary teachers about reading and math groups and if children move up as they build skills.
- Find out if there are any special programs offered to assist new students with their transition to their new school.
- Check for after-school or enrichment activities that your child will enjoy.
- Ask if parents are encouraged to volunteer in the classroom.
- Look at the faculty and curriculum as well as facilities and equipment. Are adults a presence in all parts of the building and grounds? Are the computer labs up-to-date with enough computers? Are instructional materials plentiful and new? Do textbooks cover areas you think are important? Does the school have a clearly articulated mission statement? Do the teachers that you observe seem to teach with that mission in mind? Can teachers speak articulately about the mission of the school and the educational philosophy? Do you see opportunities for your child to do things he/she likes to do—art, music, science, etc.?
- Finally, if the school that you are visiting is located near one of the Bay Area's many colleges and universities, ask whether there are programs that bring college students to schools for presentations and talks. Inquire about field trips to the Bay Area's museums and other attractions.

Although satisfying answers to all these questions might be a somewhat unrealistic and time-consuming dream, with research and visits, you will be able to find a good match for your child's needs and interests. The time put in at the front end of the decision-making process is definitely worth the effort.

To find out about California Public Schools' statewide accountability programs, funding, and reform efforts, as well as district and school-by-school breakdowns of recent test scores and campus rankings, visit the **California Department of Education's** web site, www.cde.ca.gov.

Another excellent site for gathering specific information about Bay Area schools is called **Great Schools**, www.greatschools.net. This non-profit organization is dedicated to providing clear and objective information about local schools. Visit their web site to learn about schools' test scores, programs, facilities, student body size, and teacher qualifications.

To orient yourself to the public schools in the Bay Area, you might want to consult several helpful publications in your local bookstore and/or online. **School Wise Press** has a number of useful resources and links on their web site, www.schoolwisepress.com. You can also order detailed individual school profiles for $6 each. They also publish a handful of resource books, and have two on-line "ask an expert" columns that offer parents advice on everything from understanding test scores to applying for school transfers. For more information or to order profiles, call 800-247-8443. Or try Mark Mastracci's **San Francisco Bay Area School Ratings**, which rates 1,100 Bay Area public schools on the basis of test scores, safety, diversity, graduation rates, and teacher/student turnover. For straightforward explanations of California's complex education policies and reform efforts, check out the nonprofit **EdSource**, www.edsource.org. If your head isn't already swimming, you can find additional facts and figures at **Ed-Data**, www.ed-data.k12.ca.us, a joint effort between the state and EdSource to provide accessible data to parents.

To become better acquainted with schools in your district, consider contacting the for-profit organization **SchoolMatch Inc.**, 800-992-5323, www.schoolmatch.com, which maintains a database including information on student-teacher ratios, test scores, and per-pupil spending for public and private schools. The cost for a basic "snapshot" of a school district is $10; you can get you a more comprehensive district "report card" for $34. Prices are higher if not ordered online. SchoolMatch's "full search service" will give you a statistical analysis of up to ten school systems in your requested area.

PRESCHOOLS

Preschools, typically for children ages 3 to 5, offer youngsters a chance to start off on the right foot, at a critical period in their early development. Multiple studies have shown that good early childhood education lays a foundation that leads to higher levels of achievement and academic aptitude throughout the school years, and even beyond. Currently, there are far fewer top-notch programs than there are families with young children. Thus, the most popular preschools all have waiting lists. As a newcomer, it's a good idea to thoroughly research schools and once you find one you like, sign up as far in advance as possible. There are a wide range of programs available, from co-ops that offer parent participation and education, to Montessori. To find accredited programs, contact the **National Association for the Education of Young Children (NAEYC)**, 202-232-8777, 1509 16th Street NW, Washington, DC, 20036, www.naeyc.org. The national **Head Start** program, www.nhsa.org, 866-763-6481, helps low-income families and children ages 0–5.

Proposition 10, the California Children and Families Act of 1998, also helps fund early childhood development services to children prenatal to 5 years of age. For more information about programs contact **California**

Children & Families Commission, First 5, 501 J Street, Suite 530, Sacramento, CA 95814, 916-323-0056, www.ccfc.ca.gov.

BAY AREA PUBLIC SCHOOLS

California's schools are in turmoil. Thirty years ago California spent more money on public schools than most other US states. However, due to property tax cuts implemented in 1978 by Proposition 13, California's spending on schools dropped dramatically—from one of the highest per pupil spending levels to near the bottom of that list today. And its overall performance went with it. California student achievement on national standardized tests ranks only above that of Louisiana and Mississippi. Despite efforts that began in 1996 to reduce class size, focusing first on the early grades of K–3, and for high school freshmen, California still has the second highest ratio of students per teacher in the nation—with an average of 20.9 students per teacher, compared with a national average of 16.1— according to a 2005 report released by nonprofit research group RAND.

In the late eighties, concerned California voters passed Proposition 98 to guarantee that minimum levels of school funding must be met. However, the "guarantee" has proven to be less than solid as the state con- tinues to struggle in the throes of a fiscal crisis. In 2004, Governor Arnold Schwarzenegger diverted $2 billion from the education fund—cited as a loan to cover the state's bottom line—but much to the dismay of many teachers and parents, the "loan" has yet to be repaid. On top of that, dis- tricts are contending with spiraling healthcare and retirement benefit costs. With public schools receiving fewer and fewer state dollars, a num- ber of districts routinely issue pink slips to teachers, unsure of whether the funds to pay their salaries will return from the state in the coming year. To save funds, districts have cut back on support staff—school librarians, sec- retaries, and janitors—cut extracurricular and enrichment programs, and a number of districts with declining enrollments have closed down cam- puses entirely. In 2005, the San Francisco School Board, citing financial troubles and an ongoing annual decrease in its student rolls of about 800 children, voted to close four local schools. Across the Bay, after struggling unsuccessfully with budget woes for several years, and with a number of its schools receiving poor performance assessments, the Oakland Unified School District was taken over by the State Department of Education. There have been feisty board meetings, mass protests, and demonstrations, including a 70-mile march to Sacramento by parents and teachers plead- ing for more money for the West Contra Costa school district, which was forced to make severe cutbacks in 2004.

Meanwhile the national education reform effort, **No Child Left Behind (NCLB)**, has become a prickly bone of contention among educators. Bogged down by federal requirements to cut class sizes and meet performance testing standards, without the funds attached to implement the changes, NCLB has left many schools reeling. To further complicate matters, not all school districts here are funded in the same way.

On the brighter side, a number of counties and cities have come together and taken it upon themselves to pass bond initiatives to help upgrade and retrofit ailing buildings, provide new equipment, science centers, and recreation facilities for their local schools. Parent groups and concerned residents have also chipped in to keep art and music programs—which have often landed on the chopping block—alive. In San Francisco initiatives were approved to restore public school arts, physical education, and other extras cut by state funding, and to add funds for after-school activities, childcare subsidies, and additional programs. Innovative efforts are underway to help educate the state's large ESL (English as a Second Language) population. Meanwhile in an effort to attract and retain good teachers, several districts have started offering to assist educators with the high costs of housing through **First Time Homebuyer Programs**.

California has a dizzying array of assessment tests and performance evaluations that even confuse many education experts. How a school measures up, according to these, in general can been seen in the annual **Academic Performance Index (API)** report—which measures various tests results on an overall scorecard. Looking at the API, you can find district and school-by-school test scores, as well as overall rankings on a scale of 1 through 10, 10 being the highest. To see how your neighborhood schools stack up, visit http://api.cde.ca.gov/reports.asp.

In 1994 Bay Area public schools adopted an **open enrollment** policy, which offers a student the option to enroll in any public school in his/her district, space permitting, if parents believe that the school within a student's immediate vicinity is not right for their child. Often with top schools, particularly high schools, there are waiting lists, and open spots are granted by lottery. If your transfer request is declined, you can appeal to the governing district school board.

Throughout the Bay Area, the length of the academic year is becoming more flexible. Now you can decide whether a **traditional ten-month** or the newly adopted and increasingly popular **yearlong academic program** is the best for your child. For instance, educators at Allendale Elementary in Oakland, one of the largest year-round elementary schools in the Bay Area, believe that year-round education offers advantages to children who, during long summer breaks, would otherwise not be exposed to educational activities. San Francisco is trying a new approach on a few campuses dubbed "Dream Schools." By keeping kids in school longer, offering more rigorous academics, enhanced extracurricular activities—and requiring uniforms—the program seeks to provide challenges and opportunities for local kids, particularly in poorer neighborhoods.

In the past decade, California public education has seen the growth of the **charter school** movement. Unlike most public schools, charter schools, which are bound by their own charter agreements, are free from some of the traditional school regulations. A charter school is a public program created by a group of individuals, usually teachers, parents, and community leaders, that must have approval of the local school district governing board. First and foremost, the purpose of a charter school is to improve student learning. To do this, many charter schools promote the use of innovative teaching methods, expand the learning base outside the classroom, and encourage parent/community involvement in the school. Charter school enrollment is voluntary and not determined by geographic location, which means parents can select any school, as long as space allows. While most charter schools do not focus on specific subjects (as do magnet schools, which often specialize in language arts or the sciences), their charters propose certain programmatic guidelines for the general educational process. For example, Aurora High School in Redwood City guarantees its students personalized learning plans, which are created to help students realize their full potential. Several charter schools in San Francisco, including Gateway and Leadership high schools, have been quite successful.

Because charter schools are designed with more academic freedom and flexibility, they are not bound by most of the regulations in the state Education Code. In some cases, charter schools have been a wonderful success. In other cases, concerns have arisen that standards aren't high enough. In California, students in charter schools are required to take part in the Standardized Testing and Reporting Program. If students in a given charter school do not perform at a certain level or meet certain goals listed in their charter agreement with the local school district governing board, the school may be closed.

In the current fiscal climate, charter schools have become more controversial, as districts worry about adding new campuses, and spreading scant resources too thin. As a result, getting charter schools approved has become increasingly difficult. For more information about charter programs and charter school policies in the Bay Area, visit www.uscharter schools.org.

Although individual class years in many public schools tend to be fairly large, there is always an opportunity for your child to get individualized attention. Inquire about programs for children with special needs, including those with learning disabilities or programs for gifted and talented children (GATE). Again, the importance of visiting schools and asking lots of questions before enrolling your child cannot be underestimated.

BAY AREA SCHOOL DISTRICTS

The following school organizations will provide you with information concerning schools in your area, as well as details about referrals, enrollment testing, and any available special programs.

- For official information on public schools in **San Francisco**, contact the **San Francisco Unified School District**, 555 Franklin St, 415-241-6000, http://portal.sfusd.edu/template/index.cfm. This district oversees 59,000 students in over 100 schools as well as many specialized educational programs in the city.
- If you plan to reside in the **North Bay**, consult the **Marin County Office of Education**, 1111 Las Gallinas Ave, San Rafael, CA 94903, 415-472-4110, http://marin.k12.ca.us
- For information on the **East Bay**, go to the **Alameda County Office of Education**, 313 West Winton Ave, Hayward, 510-887-0152, www.alameda-coe.k12.ca.us.
  - Fremont Unified School District, with a total enrollment of around 31,000. Contact them at 4210 Technology Dr, Fremont, CA 94538, 510-657-2350, www.fremont.k12.ca.us.
  - Hayward Unified School District enrolls 24,000 students, 24411 Amador St, Hayward, CA 94540, 510-784-2600, www.husd.k12.ca.us.
  - Oakland Unified School District, with enrollments of around 50,000 students in its more than 100 schools, can be contacted at 1025 Second Ave, Oakland, CA 94606, 510-879-8200, http://webportal.ousd.k12.ca.us
- For information on **Contra Costa County**, visit the **Contra Costa County Office of Education**, 77 Santa Barbara Rd, Pleasant Hill, CA 94523, 925-942-3388, www.cccoe.k12.ca.us.
- Those on the **Peninsula** should contact the **San Mateo County Office of Education**, 101 Twin Dolphin Dr, Redwood City, CA 94065, 650-802-5300, www.smcoe.k12.ca.
- For information on **Silicon Valley** and **South Bay** schools, visit the **Santa Clara County Office of Education**, 1290 Ridder Park Dr, San Jose, CA 95131, 408-453-6500, www.sccoe.k12.ca.us, which incorporates 33 elementary, high, and unified school districts. This office's publications department can also mail you a hard copy of demographic profiles of school districts in the county if you call 408-453-6879. If you would like to purchase the *Santa Clara County Public Schools Directory* ($15.16 plus tax and shipping), call 408-453-6959.

PRIVATE AND PAROCHIAL SCHOOLS

In San Francisco, an estimated 25% to 30% of children attend private and parochial schools. If you are ready to finance your child's studies, there are many different private programs in the Bay Area. You'll find private schools, which offer educational programs based on particular learning philosophies, including Montessori and Waldorf programs, as well as parochial schools, which often provide more traditional settings and curriculum. The diverse educational offerings of private schools and their smaller classroom sizes often better accommodate children's individual talents and interests. To find a private school that suits your needs, visit **www.baprivateschools.com,** which offers a guide to private schools in the Bay Area and includes information, locations, and links to private and parochial schools. In addition, the **California Department of Education**, P.O. Box 271, Sacramento, CA 95812, 800-995-4099, www.cde.ca.gov, publishes the *California Private School Directory* (they also publish a public school directory), which you can order for about $25. Other helpful publications on finding a good private school include *Peterson's Private Secondary Schools*, www.petersons.com; *The Handbook of Private Schools,* www.privateschoolsearch.com; *Private High Schools of the San Francisco Bay Area* by Betsy Little and Paula Molligan; and *Private Schools of San Francisco & Marin Counties (K-8): A Parents' Resource Guide* by Susan Vogel.

PRIVATE SCHOOLS
*   For information on area Montessori schools, contact **Montessori Schools of California**, 16492 Foothill Blvd, San Leandro, CA 94578, 510-278-1115, www.montessorica.com.
*   For **Waldorf schools** check the following:
    *   San Francisco Waldorf School, K–8, 2938 Washington St, San Francisco, CA 94115, 415-931-2750; high school, 245 Valencia St, San Francisco, 415-431-2736 www.sfwaldorf.org
    *   Marin County, 755 Idylberry Rd, San Rafael, CA 94903, 415-479-8190, www.marinwaldorf.org
    *   East Bay, 3800 Clark Rd, El Sobrante, CA 94803, 510-223-3570, www.eastbaywaldorf.org
    *   Silicon Valley, Waldorf School of the Peninsula K-8, 11311 Mora Dr, Los Altos, CA 94024, 650-948-8433, www.waldorfpeninsula.org
*   **Challenger Schools** are famous for their engaging approach to elementary and middle school education. Their mission: "to prepare children to become self-reliant, productive individuals; to teach them to think, speak, and write with clarity, precision, and independence; and

to inspire them to embrace, challenge, and find joy and self-worth through achievement." Call 888-748-1135, 408-377-2300, or 408-245-7170, or visit www.challengerschool.com for more information.

PAROCHIAL SCHOOLS

- Information regarding Catholic schools in San Francisco, San Mateo, and Marin counties is provided by the **Archdiocese of San Francisco Department of Catholic Schools**, One Peter Yorke Way, San Francisco, CA 94109, 415-614-5660, www.sfcatholicschools.org.
- The **Archdiocese of Oakland, Department of Catholic Schools**, 3014 Lakeshore Ave, Oakland, CA 94610, 510-628-2154, www.csdo.org, can give you information for Alameda and Contra Costa counties.
- In the South Bay, contact the **Archdiocese of San Jose, Office of Education**, 900 Lafayette St, Suite 301, Santa Clara, CA 95050, 408-983-0185, www.dsj.org.
- For information on **Jewish education** in the Bay Area, go to www.sfjcf.org/resource, where you'll find *The Resource: A Guide to Jewish Life in the Bay Area*, which provides listings and brief information on all the Jewish schools in the Bay Area.

Since admission to private schools can be competitive, the sooner you call a school to find out about admission deadlines and open houses the better. The registration process begins as early as October of the year prior to the desired academic start date. Be sure to visit schools to learn about their unique philosophies and teaching methodologies. As private schools are not required to follow state standards (though most do), a visit can be an extremely important aspect of the admissions process. Many parents and children have a visceral reaction when walking into a school, and can often sense whether a school is "right" for them. Since private schooling is expensive and signing up for a private program is an often-arduous task, finding a good match between child and school is important.

HOMESCHOOLING

Homeschooling is becoming increasingly popular in the state of California at large, and in the Bay Area specifically. Many parents believe that they, with their in-depth knowledge of their child's psychological and intellectual needs, are better suited to design an educational program that will engage and challenge their youngsters to the utmost. If you have the time and energy to plan and execute a comprehensive study program for your children, you'll find many organizations to assist you. For information and support for your homeschooling project, visit the **HomeSchool Association of California** at www.hsc.org. The mission of this organization is to provide information, monitor legislation, and cultivate connections among homeschoolers and the society at large. Another organization that might be helpful is **California Homeschool Network**, http://californiahomeschool.net; it too provides information on homeschooling and works to protect the rights of the family to educate children at home.

ADDITIONAL PARENTING RESOURCES

- **Parents Place**, www.parentsplaceonline.org: In **San Francisco** offers a drop-in playgroup for children 5 and under every Tuesday, where kids can play and parents can meet, 1710 Scott St, Koret Family Resource Center, San Francisco, 415-359-2454. A variety of programs are also available in **Palo Alto**, 650-688-3040, **San Rafael**, 415-491-7958, and **Sonoma**, 707-571-8131.
- **Support for Families of Children with Disabilities**, 415-282-7494, 2601 Mission St, Suite 606, www.supportforfamilies.org: Support groups for children, siblings, and parents—some in Spanish or Cantonese—as well as a parent mentor program, workshops, a drop-in center and resource library, a help line, short-term counseling, and a newsletter.
- **La Leche League,** www.lalecheleague.org: Provides a wealth of information on breastfeeding and also runs support groups at locations throughout the Bay Area.
- **Petit Appetit**, 415-601-4916, www.petitappetit.com; San Francisco–based resource for preparing all-natural food for babies and toddlers, offers private and group classes, cookbook, and food services.

EAST BAY
- **The Nurture Center**, 3399 Mt. Diablo Blvd, Lafayette, 925-283-1346, www.nurturecenter.com: Provides childbirth information, support groups for new parents.
- **Neighborhood Parents Network**, 877-648-KIDS, www.npnonline.org: Based in the East Bay, provides educational community forums, newsletters, school information, events and support for Bay Area parents.

SOUTH BAY/PENINSULA
- **Las Madres Neighborhood Playgrounds**, 877-LAS-MADRES, www.lasmadres.org: South Bay group that hosts regular mommy and baby park days in local parks, field trips, parties, educational speaker nights, classes, discounts, Mom's Night Out, Couple's Night Out, baby sitting co-ops, sit 'n play groups, and more.

- **The Parenting Corner,** 1922 The Alameda, Suite 217 San Jose, 408-247-2030, www.theparentingcorner.com: Offers a range of parenting classes and support services, and offers classes in Spanish.
- **Community Arts & History Support Family Institute**, 408-251-1776, www.cahsworld.org/cahs_family.html: Runs family support groups in San Jose, Milpitas, and Santa Clara.
- **Parents Helping Parents**, 3041 Olcott St, Santa Clara, CA, 95054, 408 727-5775, www.php.com: Family resource center serving parents of special-needs kids. Extensive network of education, referrals, support groups, community events, and on-line tools.
- **Special Parents Information Network (SPIN)**, www.spinsc.org: Though based in Santa Cruz, this group has a wealth of online information with links to support and information services throughout California for parents of children with special needs and disabilities.

ITHOUT EXAGGERATION, IT IS FAIR TO SAY THAT THE BAY AREA is a shopper's paradise. Whether you like to shop in familiar chain stores or enjoy finding unique boutiques, they're all here. If you don't want to spend a lot, used clothing, furniture, and appliances are available at secondhand stores, such as the Salvation Army or Goodwill, which run their own department stores. Numerous flea markets abound, and because of the mild climate, garage and yard sales occur year round. Discount shopping is also available from one end of the Bay Area to the other. If money is of no concern, you can be sure you'll have plenty of opportunities to hand it over to a delighted sales associate at an upscale emporium.

MALLS/SHOPPING CENTERS

No matter what you're looking for or how much or little you're willing to spend, you can probably find it at one of the following Bay Area shopping destinations. Check their web sites for mall specials, directions, and store directories.

SAN FRANCISCO
- **The Cannery/Del Monte Square**, 2801 Leavenworth St, 415-771-3112, www.thecannery.com
- **Crocker Galleria**, 50 Post St, 415-393-1505, www.shopatgalleria.com
- **Embarcadero Center**, One Embarcadero Center, 415-772-0500, www.embarcaderocenter.com
- **Ghirardelli Square**, 900 North Point, 415-775-5500, www.ghirardellisq.com
- **Japan Center**, Sutter and Buchanan sts, 922-6776
- **Metreon**, A Sony Entertainment Center, 101 4th St, 415-369-6000, www.metreon.com

- **San Francisco Shopping Centre**, 865 Market St, 415-495-5656
- **Stonestown Galleria**, 3251 20th Ave, 415-759-2623, www. stonestowngalleria.com

NORTH BAY

- **Larkspur Landing**, Larkspur, 415-277-6800
- **Northgate Mall**, San Rafael, 415-479-5955, www.themallatnorth gate.com
- **Strawberry Village**, Mill Valley, 415-381-3089, www.strawberry village.com
- **Town & Country**, Corte Madera, 415-924-2961
- **The Village**, Corte Madera, 415-924-8557, www.villageat cortemadera.com

EAST BAY

- **Bayfair Mall**, San Leandro, 510-357-6000, www.bayfair-mall.com
- **Hilltop Mall**, Richmond, 510-223-1933
- **Jack London Square**, 866-295-9853
- **NewPark Mall**, Newark, 510-794-5523, www.newparkmall.com
- **South Shore Center**, Alameda, 510-521-1515, www.southshore center.com
- **Sun Valley**, Concord, 925-825-2042, www.shopsunvalley.com
- **The Willows**, Concord, 925-825-4000, www.willowshopping center.com

PENINSULA

- **Hillsdale Mall**, San Mateo, 650-345-8222, www.hillsdale.com
- **Serramonte Center**, Daly City, 650-992-8686, www.serramonte center.com
- **Stanford Shopping Center**, Palo Alto, 650-617-8230, www.stanford shop.com
- **The Shops at Tanforan**, San Bruno, www.theshopsattanforan.com
- **Westlake Shopping Center**, Daly City, 650-756-2161

SOUTH BAY

- **Great Mall of the Bay Area**, Milpitas, 408-945-4022, www.great mallbayarea.com
- **Oakridge Mall**, San Jose, 408-578-2910
- **The PruneYard**, Campbell, 408-371-4700, www.thepruneyard.com
- **Santana Row**, San Jose, www.santanarow.com
- **Sunnyvale Town Center**, Sunnyvale, 408-245-6585
- **Town and Country Village**, Sunnyvale, 408-736-6654

- **Vallco Fashion Park**, Cupertino, 408-255-5660
- **Valley Fair Shopping Center**, San Jose, 408-248-4450

OUTLET MALLS

Whether these places actually offer more affordable merchandise than elsewhere is debatable but what is certain is their nationwide popularity and rapid growth. Check the web at www.outletsonline.com for more information. In the South Bay, the city of Gilroy is famous for its outlets—packed together along Highway 101. Bay Area residents frequently take special weekend trips just for shopping. Below are a few of the outlet malls located in the Bay Area:

- **Gilroy Premium Outlets**, 408-847-4155, Highway 101 at Leavesley exit
- **Marina Square**, 1259 Marina Blvd, San Leandro, www.outlets online.com/swmsca.htm
- **Vacaville Commons**, Vacaville, 707-447-0267, 2098 Harbison Dr

DEPARTMENT STORES

- **Gumps**: The upscale grand dame of San Francisco department stores, Gumps stocks furniture and other home accessories with special attention paid to objets d'art, impeccably displayed. The service is top-notch; 135 Post St, 800-882-8055, www.gumps.com
- **JC Penney**: This national department store chain sells just about everything you'd need for your home, including major appliances, televisions, stereos, VCRs, linens, bedding and furniture as well as clothing, shoes, jewelry, and cosmetics. Numerous Bay Area locations, but none in San Francisco, including Tanforan, San Bruno, 650-873-4100; Southland Mall, Hayward, 510-783-0300; Richmond Hilltop Mall, Richmond, 510-222-4411.
- **Macy's**: The Union Square store is reportedly the largest in the nation, outside of the flagship store in Manhattan. You could fully stock your closets and furnish your entire home here if you were so inclined, as Macy's carries clothing, shoes, linens, bedding, appliances, cookware, gourmet items, luggage, and more. Service, once notoriously bad, has improved of late. Bay Area locations include **San Francisco**: Union Square, Stockton & O'Farrell sts, 415-397-3333; **Peninsula**: 1 Serramonte Center, Daly City, 650-994-3333; **East Bay**: Bayfair Mall, San Leandro, 510-357-3333; **North Bay**: Northgate Mall, San Rafael, 415-499-5200.
- **Mervyn's**: Known for big and frequent sales, this medium-priced department store specializes in clothing, shoes, linens, bedding, and

home accessories. Numerous locations across the Bay Area: **San Francisco**: 2675 Geary Blvd, 415-921-0888; **Peninsula**: 63 Serramonte Center, Daly City, 650-756-9022; **East Bay**: South Shore Center, Alameda, 510-769-8800; Southland Mall, Hayward, 510-782-8000; **North Bay**: Northgate Mall, San Rafael, 415-499-9330

- **Neiman-Marcus**: The opulent Texan retailer carries expensive non-necessities, has nice restaurants, a fairly good gourmet department, and is known for the Christmas tree in the rotunda. Geary at Stockton, **San Francisco**, 415-362-3900; 400 Stanford Shopping Center, **Palo Alto**, 650-329-3300, www.neimanmarcus.com.

- **Nordstrom**: Employees at this Seattle-based retailer have a reputation for being helpful, courteous, and knowledgeable about the products they sell. Merchandise ranges from shoes and clothing for the entire family to jewelry and cosmetics, though no home furnishings. Perhaps most popular here are the women's shoe sales. Their online service also is top-notch, www.nordstrom.com. Bay Area locations include: **San Francisco**: SF Shopping Centre, 865 Market St, 415-243-8500; Stonestown Galleria, 285 Winston Dr, 415-753-1344; **Peninsula**: Hillsdale Mall, San Mateo, 650-570-5111; **North Bay:** The Village at Corte Madera, 1870 Redwood Hwy, Corte Madera, 415-927-1690; **East Bay**: 1200 Broadway Plaza, Walnut Creek, 925-930-7959.

- **Saks Fifth Avenue**: This upscale retailer features clothing, jewelry, cosmetics, objets d'art. Located in San Francisco at 384 Post St on Union Square, 415-986-4300.

- **Wilkes Bashford**: Strictly speaking, Wilkes Bashford isn't a department store since it sells only clothing and decorative items, but most department stores don't sell much else these days either. It is the only San Francisco–based department store remaining and there's only one. It's still run by Wilkes Bashford himself. What you'll find here is high-end, high-style gear in a low-key, service-oriented environment, without the cookie cutter feel of many chain stores; 375 Sutter St, 415-986-4380, www.wilkesbashford.com.

DISCOUNT DEPARTMENT STORES AND OUTLETS

Discount chains such as **Target**, **Kmart**, and **WalMart** all do business throughout the Bay Area. Check the Yellow Pages for the nearest location of your favorite. Below are a few of the discount outlet stores in the area.

- **California Big & Tall**, 625 Howard St, 415-495-4484, for men; the exclusive outlet for Rochester Big & Tall
- **Georgiou Outlet**, 925 Bryant St, 415-554-0150
- **Gunny Saxe Discount Outlet**, 35 Stanford, 415-495-3326

- **Loehmann's**, 222 Sutter St, 415-982-3215, is a local favorite for discount designer clothes and shoes for both men and women
- **Marjorie Baer Outlet Store**, 2660 Harrison St, 415-821-9971, contains samples and discontinued items of costume jewelry
- **Nordstrom Rack**, 555 9th St, San Francisco, 415-934-1211; Metro Shopping Center, 81 Colma Blvd, Colma, 650-755-1444; the discount rack for all the Nordstrom stores
- **North Face Outlet**, 1238 Fifth St, Berkeley, 510-526-3530

COMPUTERS/ELECTRONICS/APPLIANCES

The Bay Area offers plenty of options when it comes to buying anything computer related. This is, after all, the headquarters of the global digital revolution. Locations are in San Francisco unless otherwise noted. Another good place to look for computer information is Computer User, www.computeruser.com. In addition, dozens of individually owned and operated electronics and appliance stores as well as all the familiar national chains can be found throughout the Bay Area. The list below includes some well-known computer and electronics retailers, and you can check the Yellow Pages for additional options.

- **Apple Store**, for the latest in everything Mac, One Stockton St, San Francisco, 415 392 0202; 3251 20th Ave, Stonestown Shopping Center, San Francisco, 415-242-7890; 1301 Burlingame Ave, Burlingame, 650-340-1167; 1516 Redwood Hwy, Corte Madera, 415-927-5820; 5664 Bay St, Emeryville, 510-658-8700; 451 University Ave, Palo Alto, 650-617-9000; 925 Blossom Hill Rd, Oakridge Shopping Center, San Jose; 408-362-4930; 1129 South Main St, Walnut Creek, 925-210-2020; 2855 Stevens Creek Blvd, Santa Clara, Valley Fair Shopping Center, 408-551-2150, www.apple.com
- **We Fix Macs**, 1245 Laurelwood Rd, Santa Clara, 408-562-3900; 3159 El Camino Real, Palo Alto, 650-813-6161, 591 Howard St, San Francisco, 800-933-4962; www.allmac.com
- **Best Buy**, 1717 Harrison St, San Francisco, 415-626-9682; 180 Donahue St, Marin City, 415-332-6529; 3700 Mandela Pkwy, Emeryville, 510-420-0323; 1127 Industrial Rd, San Carlos, 650-622-0050; 3090 Stevens Creek Blvd, San Jose, 408-241-6040; for more Bay Area locations visit www.bestbuy.com
- **Circuit City**, 1200 Van Ness Ave, San Francisco, 415-441-1300; 1880 South Grant St, San Mateo, 650-578-1400; 4080 Stevens Creek Blvd, San Jose, 408-296-5522; for more Bay Area locations visit www.circuit city.com
- **CompUSA**, 750 Market St, San Francisco, 415-743-3200; 1250 El Camino Real, San Bruno, 650-244-9980; 3839 Emery St, Emeryville,

510-450-9500; 3561 El Camino Real, Santa Clara, 408-554-1733, www.compusa.com
- **Fry's**, 340 Portage Ave, Palo Alto, 650-496-6000; 600 East Hamilton Ave, Campbell, 408-364-3700; 1077 East Arques Ave, Sunnyvale, 408-617-1300; 550 East Brokaw Rd, San Jose, 408-487-1000, www.frys.com
- **Good Guys**, 1400 Van Ness Ave, 415-775-9323, San Francisco; 2675 Geary Blvd, San Francisco, 415-202-0220, San Francisco; Serramonte Shopping Center, Daly City, 650-301-8855; 1247 West El Camino Real, Sunnyvale, 650-962-0101, www.goodguys.com

BEDS, BEDDING, & BATH

Some area department stores sell bedding as well as beds. For their names, locations, and phone numbers see the previous entries under **Department Stores**. Here's a list of just some of the San Francisco stores that deal exclusively in these items.
- **Beds and Bedding**, 9th and Harrison sts, 415-621-0746
- **Bed Bath and Beyond**, 555 9th St, 415-252-0490; call 800-GO-BEYOND (800-462-3966) to find numerous other Bay Area locations
- **Dreams Inc.**, 921 Howard St, 415-543-1800
- **Discount Depot**, 520 Haight St, 415-552-9279; 2020 San Pablo, Berkeley, 510-549-1478
- **Duxiana**, 1803 Fillmore St, 415-673-7134
- **Earthsake**, 1772 4th St, Berkeley, 510-559-8440, www.earthsake.com
- **Mattress Discounters**, multiple locations, 800-289-2233, www.mattressdiscounters.com,
- **McRoskey Airflex Mattresses**, 1687 Market St, 415-861-4532
- **Oysterbeds**, 1400 Tennesse St, 415-643-0818, www.oysterbed.com
- **Scheuer Linens**, 340 Sutter St, 415-392-2813
- **Warm Things**, 3063 Fillmore St, 415-931-1660

CARPETS & RUGS

- **Carpet Connection**, Hudson Ave, 415-550-7125
- **Conklin Brothers**, 1100 Selby St, 415-282-1822
- **Cost Plus World Market**, 2552 Taylor St, 415-928-6200; Hillsdale Mall, San Mateo, 650-341-7474; 101 Clay St, Oakland, 510-834-4440, www.worldmarket.com
- **Claremont Rug Company**, 6087 Claremont Ave, Oakland, 510-654-0816, fine antique carpets
- **The Floor Store**, 5327 Jacuzzi St, Suite 2A, Richmond, 510-527-3203

- **Omid Carpets**, 590-10th St, 415-626-3466, a full range of Oriental carpets
- **Pier One Imports**, 3535 Geary Blvd, 415-387-6642; 2501 El Camino Real, Redwood City, 650-364-6608; 1255 West El Camino Real, Sunnyvale, 650-969-8307; 20610 Stevens Creek Blvd, Cupertino 408-253-4512; 1009 Blossom Hill Rd, San Jose, 408-978-9555, www. pier1.com

FURNITURE

There are too many furniture stores in the Bay Area to list them all, but here are a few well-known names to get you started in your search for perfect and affordable home furnishings.

- **Busvans for Bargains**, 244 Clement St, San Francisco, 415-752-5353; 900 Battery St, 415-981-1405
- **Cort Furniture Clearance Center**, 2925 Meade Ave, Santa Clara, 408-727-1470; 426 El Camino Real, San Bruno, 650-615-0406; San Jose, 1830 Hillsdale Blvd, 408-264-9600
- **Crate & Barrel**, 55 Stockton St, San Francisco, 415-982-5200; Stanford Shopping Center, Palo Alto, 650-321-7800, The Village at Corte Madera, Corte Madera, 415-924-5412; Hillsdale Shopping Center, San Mateo, 650-341-900; 301 Santana Row, San Jose, 408-247-0600; Crate & Barrel Outlet Store, 1785 4th St, Berkeley, 510-528-5500; for more Bay Area stores check out www.crateandbarrel.com
- **Evolution Home Furnishings**, 511 East Francisco Blvd, San Rafael, 415-482-1600
- **Flegel's**, 1654 2nd St, San Rafael, 415-454-0502; 870 Santa Cruz Ave, Menlo Park, 650-326-9661; www.flegels.com
- **Fumiki**, 272 Sutter St, San Francisco, 415-362-6677, www.fumiki.com
- **Hoot Judkins**, offers a wide selection of finished and unfinished furniture at reasonable prices; 1142 Sutter St, San Francisco, 415-673-5454; 1269 Veterans Blvd, Redwood City, 650-367-8181; 1400 El Camino Real, Millbrae, 650-952-5600; 5101 Mowry Ave, Fremont, 510-795-4890; www.hootjudkins.com
- **IKEA**, 4400 Shellmound St, Emeryville, 510-420-4532; 1700 East Bayshore Rd, East Palo Alto, 650-323-4532, www.ikea.com
- **Limn**, high-end cutting-edge design furniture and housewares; 290 Townsend, San Francisco, 415-543-5466, www.limn.com
- **Macy's**, Union Square, San Francisco, 415-397-3333
- **Max Furniture**, 1633 Fillmore St, San Francisco, 415-440-9002, residential commercial design furniture
- **Nest**, San Francisco: 2300 Fillmore St, 415-292-6199; 2340 Polk St, 415-292-6198; East meets West eclectic

- **Noriega Furniture**, 1455 Taraval St, San Francisco, 415-564-4110
- **San Francisco Furniture Mart**, 1355 Market St, 415-552-2311, is open to the public twice a year, once in May and once in November, and offers wholesale prices.
- **Scandinavian Designs**, 317-South B St, San Mateo, 650-340-0555; 2101 Shattuck Ave, Berkeley, 510-848-8250; 1212 4th St, San Rafael, 415-457-5500
- **Slater/Marinoff**, 1823 4th St, Berkeley, 510-548-2001
- **The Wooden Duck**, 2919 7th St, Berkeley, 510-848-3575
- **Z Gallerie**, 2071 Union St, San Francisco, 415-346-9000; 1731 4th St, Berkeley, 510-525-7591; 320 Corte Madera Town Center, 415-924-3088; 340 University Ave, Palo Alto, 650-324-0693; Santana Row, San Jose, 408-615-9863, www.zgallerie.com
- **Zonal**, distressed and "found" furniture, San Francisco: 568 Hayes St, 415-255-9307; 1942 Fillmore St, 415-359-9111; 2139 Polk St, 415-563-2220

HOUSEWARES

Most department stores carry dishes, glassware, and other items needed for the home, so if you have a favorite that may be the place to start. There are also numerous specialty outlets from which to choose, including the following:

- **Bed Bath and Beyond**, 555 9th St, 415-252-0490; call 800-GO-BEYOND to find other Bay Area locations
- **Crate & Barrel**, 55 Stockton St, San Francisco, 415-982-5200; Stanford Shopping Center, Palo Alto, 650-321-7800; the Village at Corte Madera, Corte Madera, 415-924-5412; Hillsdale Shopping Center, San Mateo, 650-341-900; 301 Santana Row, San Jose, 408-247-0600; Crate & Barrel Outlet Store, 1785 4th St, Berkeley, 510-528-5500; for more Bay Area stores check out www.crateandbarrel.com
- **Dansk**, 1760 Fourth St, Berkeley, 510-528-9226
- **IKEA**, 4400 Shellmound St, Emeryville, 510-420-4532; 1700 East Bayshore Rd, East Palo Alto, 650-323-4532; www.ikea.com
- **Pier One Imports**, Pier One Imports, 3535 Geary Blvd, 415-387-6642; 2501 El Camino Real, Redwood City, 650-364-6608; 1255 West El Camino Real, Sunnyvale, 650-969-8307; 20610 Stevens Creek Blvd, Cupertino, 408-253-4512; 1009 Blossom Hill Rd, San Jose, 408-978-9555; www.pier1.com
- **Pottery Barn**, 2390 Market St, 415-861-0800; 1 Embarcadero Center, 415-788-6810; 2100 Chestnut St, 415-441-1787; for other Bay Area locations call 800-922-9934

- **Sur La Table,** 77 Maiden Lane, 415-732-7900; Ferry Building, 415-262-9970; 1806 Fourth St, Berkeley, 510-849-2252; 23 University Ave, Los Gatos, 408-395-6946; cookware, kitchenware, linens, small appliances, and tableware:
- **Viking Home Chef,** 3527 California St, 415-668-3191; 329 Town Center, Corte Madera, 415-927-3191; 1600 Saratoga Ave, San Jose, 408-374-3191
- **Williams Sonoma,** San Francisco Center, 415-546-0171; 150 Post St, San Francisco, 415-362-6904; 2 Embarcadero Center, San Francisco, 415-421-2033; Stonestown Galleria, San Francisco, 415-681-5525; Hillsdale Mall, San Mateo, 650-345-8222; 180 El Camino Real, Palo Alto, 650-321-3486; The Village, Corte Madera, 415-924-2940; 1009 Blossom Hill Rd, San Jose, 408-978-9555

HARDWARE/PAINTS/WALLPAPER/GARDEN CENTERS

Nearly everything you might need to fix up your new place is readily available at a local hardware store, but if the local store doesn't have that special color of paint you want for the sun porch you can head for one of many cavernous home improvement centers (see below). Unless otherwise indicated, the following hardware stores and garden centers are in San Francisco.

- **Bauerware Cabinet Hardware,** 3886 17th St, 415-864-3886, www.bauerware.com; offers knobs, pulls, and handles the array and design of which you may never have seen. You can't not find something you like here.
- **Restoration Hardware,** 1733 Fourth St, Berkeley, 510-526-6424; Hillsdale Mall, San Mateo, 650-577-9807; 281 University Ave, Palo Alto, 650-328-4004
- **Victoriana SF Moulding,** 2070 Newcomb Ave, San Francisco, 415-648-0313; specializes in Victorian moldings, wallpapers, draperies, tiles, fabrics, carpets, and more

ACE HARDWARE STORES

- **Cole Hardware,** 956 Cole St, 415-753-2653
- **Discount Builders,** 1695 Mission St, 415-621-8511
- **Cliff's Variety,** 479 Castro St, 415-431-5365
- **Fredericksen's Hardware,** 3029 Fillmore St, 415-292-2950
- **Golden Gate Building,** 1333 Pacific Ave, 415-441-0945
- **Standard 5-10-25,** 3545 California St, 415-751-5767

TRUE VALUE HARDWARE STORES

- **Creative Paint**, 5435 Geary Blvd, 415-666-3380
- **Sunset Hardware**, 3126 Noriega St, 415-661-0607
- **True Value Hardware**, 2244 Irving St, 415-753-6862

GARDENING STORES

- **Broadway Terrace Nursery**, 4340 Clarewood Dr, Oakland, 510-658-3729
- **Native Here Nursery**, 101 Golf Course Dr, Berkeley, 510-549-0211
- **Plant'lt Earth**, 2215 Market St, 415-626-5082
- **Smith and Hawken**, 2040 Fillmore St, San Francisco, 415-776-3424; 35 Corte Madera Ave, Mill Valley, 415-381-1800; 1330 10th St, Berkeley, 510-527-1076; 26 Santa Cruz Ave, Los Gatos, 408-354-6500; 705 Stanford Shopping Center, Palo Alto, 650-321-0403
- **Sloat Garden Centers**, a full range of garden supplies, plants and trees, classes, and friendly and helpful advice; 3rd Ave between Geary and Clement, San Francisco, 415-752-1614; 2700 Sloat Blvd, San Francisco, 415-566-4415; 2000 Novato Blvd, Novato, 415-897-2169; 1580 Lincoln Ave, San Rafael, 415-453-3977; 828 Diablo Blvd, Walnut Creek, 925-743-0288
- **Woolworth Nursery**, 4606 Almaden Expy, San Jose, 408-266-4400; 725 San Antonio Rd, Palo Alto, 650-493-5136

HOME IMPROVEMENT CENTERS

The big do-it-yourself centers are located outside of San Francisco, but the ones listed below are all within a 15- to 30-minute drive of the city.
- **Orchard Supply Hardware (OSH)**, 2245 Gellert Blvd, South San Francisco, 650-878-3322; 900 El Camino Real, Millbrae, 415-873-5536; 1151 Anderson Dr, San Rafael, 415-453-7288; 1025 Ashby Ave, Berkeley, 510-540-6638
- **Home Depot**, 1125 Old County Rd, San Carlos, 650-592-9200; 1781 East Bayshore, East Palo Alto, 650-462-6800; 1933 Davis St, San Leandro, 510-636-9600; 11955 San Pablo Ave, El Cerrito, 510-235-0800
- **Yardbirds**, 13901 San Pablo Ave, San Pablo, 510-236-4630; 1801 4th St, San Rafael, 415-457-5880

SECONDHAND SHOPPING

The Advertiser is a weekly newspaper that lists items sold by individuals or at flea markets. The publication is free and can be found at most supermarkets and many newsstands. Call 415-863-3151 to sell or buy anything from cars to computers, from bedroom sets to budgies.

Your mother might call it secondhand but today that pair of 1970 elephant bottoms in the bottom of a box in the basement may be high fashion "vintage" to an aficionado. In San Francisco, dressing in stylish cast-offs has been all the rage for decades and there are scores of stores specializing in it. There are also plenty of shops that sell secondhand items that don't quite qualify as vintage. Vintage is consistently more expensive than secondhand and usually in excellent condition. Shopping for secondhand furnishings can be just as much fun as shopping for new. The chance of finding a lost heirloom adds to the excitement of saving a bit of cash. Here are a few places to begin your bargain-hunting adventure. Locations are San Francisco unless otherwise noted.

- **The Apartment**, 3469 18th St, 415-255-1100, vintage furniture
- **Attic Shop**, Cathedral School, 1036 Hyde St, 415-776-6630, secondhand
- **Berkeley Outlet**, 711 Heinz Ave, Berkeley, 510-549-2896
- **Busvan Bonded Dealers & Appraisers**, two locations: 900 Battery St, 415-981-1405; 244 Clement St, 415-752-5353
- **Community Thrift Store**, 623 Valencia St, 415-861-4910
- **Cottrell's Moving and Storage**, 150 Valencia St, 415-431-1000
- **Discovery Shop**, 1827 Union St, 415-929-8053, secondhand
- **Goodwill**, 1500 Mission St, 415-575-2100, has multiple other San Francisco and Bay Area locations, www.sfgoodwill.org
- **Harrington Brothers**, 599 Valencia St, 415-861-7300
- **Home Consignment Center**, 863 East Francisco Blvd, San Rafael, 415-456-2765, www.thehomeconsignmentcenter.com
- **Hospice by the Bay Thrift Shop**, 1173 Sutter St, 415-673-3030, www.hospicebythebay.citysearch.com
- **Mickey's Monkey**, 214 Pierce St, vintage furniture, 415-864-0693
- **Out of the Closet**, 2415 Mission St, $1 clothing, 415-920-9521
- **People's Bazaar**, 3258 Adeline, Berkeley, 510-655-8008
- **Repeat Performance**, 2223 Fillmore St, 415-563-3123, vintage
- **St. Vincent de Paul Society**, 6298 Mission St, Daly City, 650-992-9271, secondhand, has multiple other Bay Area locations
- **St. Vincent de Paul**, 1745 Folsom St, 415-626-1515; 1519 Haight St, 415-863-3615; 186 West Portal Ave, 415-664-7119, secondhand
- **Salvation Army**, 1185 Sutter St, 415-771-3818, secondhand

- **Salvation Army**, 1509 Valencia St, 415-643-8040, secondhand, has multiple Bay Area locations
- **Second Act**, 12882 S Saratoga Rd, Saratoga, 408-741-4995
- **Third Hand Store**, 1839 Divisadero St, 415-567-7332, secondhand
- **Thrift Center**, 1060 El Camino Real, San Carlos, secondhand, 650-593-1082
- **Thrift Town**, 2101 Mission St, 415-861-1132, secondhand, second floor features furniture and housewares, www.thrifttown.com
- **Town School Closet**, 3325 Sacramento St, 415-929-8019, vintage
- **Victorian House**, 2318 Fillmore St, 415-923-3237, vintage

FLEA MARKETS

- **Alemany Flea Market**, 100 Alemany Blvd, specializes in antiques, every Sunday
- **Berkeley Flea Market**, 1937 Ashby Ave, Berkeley, 510-644-0744, a nonprofit, community service flea market
- **Coliseum Swap Meet**, 66th St off Highway 880, Oakland, 510-534-0325
- **Midgley's Country Flea Market**, 2200 Gravenstein Highway South, Sebastapol, 707-823-7874
- **Mission Village Flea Market**, 2955 18th St, eclectic goods, including occasional music equipment, collectibles, you can even get help fixing your bike at the popular bike kitchen, plans are in the works to add a summertime farmer's market, 415-643-3469 or 415-648-7562; www.cellspace.org/market/
- **Norcal Swap Meet**, Laney College, Oakland, 510-769-7266
- **San Francisco Flea Market**, United Nations Plaza, Hyde and Market sts, 415-255-1923
- **San Jose Flea Market**, 1590 Berryessa Rd, San Jose, 408-453-1110 or 800-BIG FLEA; this is a huge flea market with everything old for sale, plus live music, fresh produce, dozens of food stands, two playgrounds and more
- **Treasure Island Flea Market**, Ave C at 4th St on Treasure Island, an upscale outdoor market held every Sunday

ANTIQUES

There are pages of antique dealers listed in the San Francisco Yellow Pages; check there first for stores in your neighborhood. The 400 block of Jackson Street, in San Francisco's Financial District, is known for its high concentration of antique stores. Most of the Jackson Street dealers are members of the Antique Dealers Association of California, and if they don't have what you're looking for they can steer you in the right direction. Market Street at Franklin has several lower priced antique shops. Sacramento Street in Presidio Heights has an array of fine antique shops. In Marin County San Anselmo has a small antique row along Sir Francis Drake Boulevard.

FOOD

The Bay Area is blessed with a wide selection of supermarket chains that range from inexpensive to downright exorbitant. The budget grocery stores offer bulk quantities of your regular fare while the more expensive stores emphasize fresh produce, organics, and imported goods. The big grocery chains fall in between those two extremes. For budget shopping head for **Foods Co.**, **Food 4-Less**, **Grocery Outlet**, **Smart and Final**, or **Pak-N-Save**. **Bell Markets**, **Albertson's**, **Safeway**, and **SaveMart** are the next rung up the ladder. **Trader Joe's** offers an array of high-quality foods, as well as beers and wines, for reasonable prices. **Andronico's** reigns supreme at the high end. **Whole Foods** is the big chain health food store, and **Mollie Stone's** is a more local natural foods chain.

SPECIALTY GROCERS

SAN FRANCISCO
- **Bombay Bazar**, 548 Valencia St, 415-621-1717, has a variety of Indian spices, food, and clothing, not to mention the fantastic Bombay Ice Creamery next-door—featuring flavors like rose, cardamom, and clove.
- **Chinese** food markets are sprinkled throughout Chinatown, Irving St in the Sunset, and Clement St in the Richmond District.
- **Cost Plus World Market**, 2552 Taylor St, 415-928-6200, www.worldmarket.com; a discount clearing house for nonperishable imports with a variety of wines, beers, teas, and chocolates as well as housewares.
- **Ferry Building Marketplace**, the Embarcadero at Market St, 415-693-0996, www.ferrybuildingmarketplace.com; features a number of specialty shops including the North Bay's Cowgirl Creamery Cheese Shop, Acme Bread Company, and the San Francisco Fish Company. The outdoor plaza also hosts one of the Bay Area's most popular farmers' markets (see details below).
- **Good Life Grocery**, 448 Cortland Ave, 415-648-3221; friendly Bernal Heights shop with a good selection of produce, fine cheeses and wines.
- **Mollie Stone's**, 2435 California St, 415-567-4902, www.molliestones.com; a large, upscale natural foods shop with a wide variety.
- **Rainbow Grocery and General Store**, 1745 Folsom St, 415-863-0620, www.rainbowgrocery.org; this popular eco-friendly worker

owned co-op has a vast selection of bulk products from grains, to pastas, to teas, organic produce, a huge vitamin and mineral selection, and an amazing olive bar. You'll have to go elsewhere for your meat though.
- **Whole Foods**, 1765 California St, 415-674-0500; 399 4th St, 415-618-0066, www.wholefoodsmarket.com; the natural food giant offers a wide array of bulk products, a large prepared foods area, a decent house brand, popular salad bar, and everything to meet your basic grocery needs.

NORTH BAY
- **Mill Valley Market**, 12 Corte Madera, Mill Valley, 415-388-3222
- **Mollie Stone's**, 100 Harbor Dr, Sausalito, 415-331-6900; Bon Air Shopping Center, Greenbrae, 415-461-1164; www.molliestones.com
- **Whole Foods**, 414 Miller Ave, Mill Valley, 415-381-1200; 340 3rd St, San Rafael, 415-451-6333; www.wholefoodsmarket.com

EAST BAY
- **Berkeley Bowl**, 2777 Shattuck, Berkeley, 510-841-6346; a beloved local favorite that draws shoppers from throughout the Bay Area, offers bulk foods, organic produce, seafood, and a wide variety of goods and great prices
- **Cheese Board Collective**, 1504 Shattuck Ave, 510-549-3183, http://cheeseboardcollective.coop; this popular Berkeley co-op has a rotating variety of freshly baked breads, a wide selection of cheeses and a tasty pizza place a few doors down at 1512 Shattuck Ave
- **Cost Plus World Market**, 101 Clay St, Oakland, 510-834-4440, www.worldmarket.com
- **G.B. Ratto and Co.**, 821 Washington St, Oakland, 510-832-6503; ethnic import sausages, great fun
- **Market Hall**, 5655 College, Oakland, 510-652-0390; specialty stores for wine, coffee, tea, pasta, produce, poultry, meat, and fish
- **Monterey Market**, 1550 Hopkins, Berkeley, 510-526-6042; incredible produce
- **Monterey Fish Market**, 1582 Hopkins St, Berkeley, 510-525-5600
- **Pacific East Mall**, 3288 Pierce St, Richmond, 510-527-3000
- **Whole Foods**, 3000 Telegraph Ave, Berkeley, 510-649-1333, www.wholefoodsmarket.com

PENINSULA/SOUTH BAY
- **Cosentino's** vegetable haven, South Bascom and Union aves, San Jose, 408-377-6661; vegetables, bulk items, ethnic condiments
- **Cost Plus World Market**, 785 Serramonte Blvd, Colma, 415-994-7090

- **Draegers**, 1010 University Ave, Menlo Park, 650-688-0677; imported cheeses, deli, produce and wine
- **Fiesta Latina**, 1424 Cary Ave, San Mateo, 650- 343-0193
- **Mollie Stone's**, 164 South California Ave, Palo Alto, 650-323-8361; 1477 Chapin Ave, 650-558-9992, Burlingame; 22 Bayhill Shopping Center, San Bruno, 650-873-8075, www.molliestones.com,
- **Oakville Grocery**, 715 Stanford Shopping Center, Palo Alto, 650-328-9000
- **Takahashi**, 221 South Claremont, San Mateo, 650-343-0394; Southeast Asian, Hawaiian, and more
- **Whole Foods**, 774 Emerson St, Palo Alto, 650-326-8676; 1250 Jefferson Ave, Redwood City, 650-367-1400; 1010 Park Place, San Mateo, 650-358-6900; www.wholefoodsmarket.com

WAREHOUSE SHOPPING

Costco, www.costco.com, a giant in the club-shopping business, features cavernous warehouse-type facilities stacked from floor to ceiling with restaurant-trade items, such as gallon jars of olives, mayonnaise, six-packs of everything from chopped tomatoes to pet food, tires, cleaning supplies, clothing, and pharmaceuticals. Basic membership costs $45 a year, and there are over 20 locations around the Bay Area.

FARMERS' MARKETS

San Francisco is surrounded by some of the most productive farmland in the world (the San Joaquin Valley, and the counties of Sonoma, Salinas, and Monterey), and many of the men and women who run these farms take at least one day a week to hawk their fruits and vegetables at **Farmers' Markets** all around the Bay Area. Organic produce is also available and most sellers will offer you a taste before you buy. Below is a list of some of the markets held in or close to San Francisco. You can also get organic, locally grown fresh and tasty fruits and veggies delivered weekly from Planet Organics, www.planetorganics.com, 800-956-5855. The basic fruit and veggie box subscription is $28 and includes a weekly delivery of a seasonal selection of fruits and veggies, and a newsletter featuring recipes and nutrition tips. A range of more customized options is also available.

SAN FRANCISCO CITY & COUNTY
- **100 Alemany Blvd**, Saturday, dawn to dusk, year round
- **Ferry Plaza on the Embarcadero**, Saturday, 9 a.m. to 2 p.m., year round; and Thursday nights, 4 p.m. to 8 p.m., May through October.

- **Fillmore Farmers' Market**, Saturday 9 a.m. to 1 p.m., November-April, O'Farrell and Fillmore sts at the Fillmore Center Plaza.
- **United Nations Plaza**, Market St (between 7th and 8th sts), Sunday and Wednesday 7 a.m. to 5 p.m., year round

MARIN COUNTY
- **Corte Madera**: Village Shopping Center, Wednesday, 1 p.m. to dusk, May-October
- **Novato**: Downtown (Sherman Ave between Grant and Delong Aves), Tuesday, 4 p.m. to 8 p.m., May-October
- **San Rafael**: Downtown (4th at B St), Thursday, 6 p.m. to 9 p.m., April-October; Marin Civic Center, Sunday and Thursday, 8 a.m. to 1 p.m., year round
- **Sausalito**: Dunphy Park, Napa and Bridgeway, Saturdays, 9:30 a.m. to 1:30 p.m., 415-456-3276, www.marincountyfarmersmarkets.org

SAN MATEO COUNTY
- **Daly City**: Serramonte Center, Thursday, 10 a.m. to 2 p.m., year round
- **Menlo Park**: Downtown Parking Plaza, Sunday, 10 a.m. to 2 p.m., May-November
- **Millbrae**: 200 Broadway, Saturday, 8 a.m. to 1 p.m., year round

ALAMEDA COUNTY
- **Berkeley**: Center St at MLK (Martin Luther King) Way, Saturday, 10 a.m. to 2 p.m., year round
- **El Cerrito**: El Cerrito Plaza, Tuesday, 9 a.m. to 1 p.m., year round
- **Oakland**: Jack London Square, Sunday, 10 a.m. to 2 p.m., year round

SANTA CLARA COUNTY
- **Palo Alto**: Hamilton and Gilman, Saturday, 8:00 a.m. to noon, May-November
- **San Jose** downtown: Jackson between Seventh and Eighth, Thursdays, 10 a.m. to 2 p.m., May-November
  To find a farmers' market in another locale call 800-949-FARM.

COMMUNITY GARDENS

Why shop for fruit and veggies when you can grow your own? San Francisco, Berkeley, and Oakland are home to a variety of community gardens ranging from dense urban forests tucked in larger city parks to tiny backyard fields at local churches, schools, and community centers. Most of the time, you'll be assigned a plot of your own to care for and sometimes there is a waiting list. But urban gardening is a great way to get outdoors, enjoy the fresh air, and meet your neighbors. For information about community gardens in San Francisco contact the **San Francisco Urban Gardeners League (SLUG)**, 2088 Oakdale Ave, 415-285-SLUG, www.grass-roots.org/usa/slug.shtml.

SAN FRANCISCO
- **25th and De Haro Garden**, 25th and De Haro sts
- **3rd St Community Garden**, 6698 3rd St
- **Adam Rogers Garden**, 1220 Oakdale Ave
- **Alice St Community Gardens**, Bonifacio and Lapu Lapu sts
- **Alioto Park Community Garden**, Capp and 20th sts
- **Argonne Community Garden**, between 15th and 16th aves and Fulton and Cabrillo sts
- **Arkansas Friendship Garden**, 22nd St between Arkansas and Connecticut sts
- **Arlington Community Garden**, Arlington St and Highland Ave
- **Bayshore Gardens and Roses**, Bayshore Blvd near 3rd St and LeConte
- **Bernal Heights Garden**, Bernal Heights Blvd between Gates and Banks sts
- **Brooks Park**, Ramsell and Shields sts
- **Candlestick Point Garden**, 1105 Carroll Ave
- **Central YMCA Rooftop Garden**, 220 Golden Gate Ave
- **Clipper Community Garden**, Clipper St near Grandview Ave
- **Connecticut St Garden**, 22nd and Connecticut sts
- **Corona Heights Garden**, Corona Heights Park, 16th and Flint sts
- **Crags Court Garden**, end of Crags St off of Berkeley Way
- **Daniel E. Koshland Community Learning Garden and Page St Community Garden**, Page and Buchanan sts
- **Dearborn Community Garden**, between 17th and 18th sts and Valencia and Guerrero sts
- **Fort Mason Garden**, north of Building 201, Fort Mason
- **Golden Gate Senior Center Garden**, 6101 Fulton St
- **Good Prospect Garden**, Prospect St and Cortland Ave
- **Hooker Alley Garden**, Mason St between Bush and Pine sts
- **Howard Langton (SOMA) Garden**, Langton Alley and Howard St
- **Howard St Garden**, Howard St near 12th St
- **Juri Commons Community Garden**, between Guerrero and San Jose sts and 25th and 26th sts
- **La Grande Community Garden**, end of Dublin St near Russia St
- **McLaren Park Garden**, Leland Ave and Hahn St
- **Michelangelo Community Garden**, Greenwich St between Jones and Leavenworth sts

- **Miller Memorial Garden**, Brewster and Rutledge
- **Mission Creek Gardens**, 300 Channel St
- **New Liberation Community Garden**, Divisadero and Eddy sts
- **Noe Beaver Garden**, Noe and Beaver sts
- **Noe Valley Library Garden**, 451 Jersey St
- **Ogden Terraces Community Garden**, Ogden St between Prentiss and Nevada sts
- **Park St Community Garden**, end of Park St, west of Mission St;
- **Potrero Del Sol**, Potrero Ave and Cesar Chavez St
- **Potrero Hill Community Garden**, San Bruno Ave and 20th St
- **Rolph Playground Garden**, Potrero Ave between 25th and Cesar Chavez sts
- **Rose/Page Garden**, Page St between Laguna and Octavia sts
- **Sunset Community Garden**, 37th Ave and Pacheco St
- **Telegraph Hill Neighborhood Center Garden**, 660 Lombard St
- **Visitacion Valley Garden**, Arleta St, between Alpha and Rutland sts
- **White Crane Springs Garden**, 7th Ave, near Lawton St
- **Wolfe Lane Community Garden**, Rutledge and Mullen

BEYOND SAN FRANCISCO

For information on Community Gardens in **Oakland**, contact the city's **Community Gardening Coordinator**, 250 Frank Ogawa Plaza, Suite 3330, Oakland, 94612, 510-238-2197.

- **Arroyo Viejo**, 79th Ave and Arthur St, Oakland
- **Bushrod**, 584 59th St, Oakland
- **Golden Gate**, 1068 62nd St, Oakland
- **Lakeside Horticultural Center Kitchen Garden**, 666 Bellevue Ave, Oakland
- **Marston Campbell**, between 16th and 18th sts and Market and West sts, Oakland
- **Temescal**, 876 47th St; Verdese Carter, 96th and Bancroft aves, Oakland

   Berkeley is very community garden friendly and many schools have educational gardens; to find out more contact **Berkeley Community Gardening Collaborative**, P.O. Box 2164, Berkeley, CA 94702, 510-883-9096, www.ecologycenter.org/bcgc.

- **BYA Community Garden**, Allston Way between Bonar and West sts, Berkeley
- **Karl Linn Community Garden**, Peralta Ave and Hopkins St, Berkeley
- **Northside Community Gardens**, Northside Ave and Hopkins St, Berkeley
- **Ohlone Community Garden**, Hearst and McGee aves, Berkeley

- **People's Park Gardens**, Bowditch St between Dwight Way and Haste St, Berkeley
- **Peralta Community Art Garden**, Peralta Ave near Hopkins St, Berkeley
- **South Berkeley Community Garden**, Martin Luther King Jr. Way and Russell St, Berkeley
- **UC College of Natural Resources Garden**, Walnut and Virginia sts, Berkeley
- **West Berkeley Senior Center**, Senior Gardening, 1900 6th St, Berkeley

In **San Jose**, the **Garden Center for the Guadalupe River Park & Gardens**, 715 Spring St, in Guadalupe Gardens, is a great resource for local gardeners, 408-298-7657. In other cities, contact the local park and recreation department for information on community gardening programs.

ETHNIC FOOD DISTRICTS

San Francisco reportedly has so many restaurants that everyone who lives here could sit down to dinner at the same time, and there would still be table space left over for visitors. It's a city that, simply put, loves to eat, and to eat well. Thanks to a wealth of diverse cultural influences, San Francisco boasts not only some of the finest ethnic eateries in the USA, but some of the best markets as well. Whether you want a hard-to-find hot chili pepper from Mexico, handmade Japanese soba noodles, or freshly baked Russian rye bread, you can find it here.

The Mission: The heart of San Francisco's vibrant Latin American community, 24th Street between Potrero Avenue and Valencia Street, and Valencia and Mission streets between 16th and Cesar Chavez, the Mission boasts a wide variety of traditional Mexican bakeries; mom 'n' pop groceries stocked with fresh produce, homemade tortillas, and imported specialties; and makeshift corner stands with everything from flowers, to mangoes, to oranges sold from the back of pick-up trucks. If you're looking for food on the go, you can frequently find the famous Tamale Lady selling her cheap and tasty specialties late into the night at local bars.

Chinatown: Chinese moon pies, steamed pork buns, roasted duck, rice candy, Asian pears, and starfruit are all available here in a dense collection of markets, bakeries and the ever-popular produce stands. The markets are always packed, during the day, and on Sundays, trucks with the latest imported fruits and veggies often don't even bother to unload, opting instead to sell their goods directly to the gathering crowds. Grant Street between Market Street and Broadway is the main thoroughfare, but you'll find shops all along Washington, Stockton, Kearny, and smaller surrounding streets as well. Goodies from China, Thailand, Vietnam, and all across Asia can be found in the Inner Richmond on Clement Street between 4th and 9th avenues, referred to by many as "new Chinatown." Shops and restaurants also spill over onto nearby Geary Boulevard and California Street.

North Beach: While most of this old world district is fancy sit-down restaurants today, you can still fin a few gems—bakeries with fresh foccacia, delis offering fine imported cheeses, olive oil, and sweets, markets that sell freshly made pastas to go, and of course cafés that will pack their premium coffee for you to take home. Broadway and Columbus are the main streets here, but Grant, Union, and Vallejo streets, especially near Washington Square Park, are also filled with shops.

Japantown: "town" is kind of a misnomer here—Japan mall might be more appropriate, as the Japanese markets are almost all clustered under one roof here at the Kintetsu Mall, better known as Japan Center, on Geary Boulevard and Fillmore Street. A handful of smaller shops are also clustered alongside the mall on Post Street. In Japantown, you can find a remarkable array of Japanese delicacies from udon noodles, to seaweed wraps for sushi, to the latest in anime art. And yes, there are karaoke bars here as well. If you feel like taking a break from shopping, the fantastic Kabuki Day Spa is quietly hidden away here at the foot of Japan Center, near the Kabuki multiplex cinema, which annually plays host to the Asian American Film Festival. Even though Japantown is small, you can't miss it—just look for the large pagoda in the central outdoor plaza.

The Richmond: While the Inner Richmond is known for its Asian markets along Clement Street, the Outer Richmond is all about Russia and Eastern Europe. Here, you'll find locals lining up every morning to nab loaves of exquisite, freshly baked breads, as well as markets that carry imports from Russia, Hungary, Romania, and the Czech Republic.

RESTAURANTS

Depending on your interest in food, dining out here can be a convenience, a diversion, a hobby, a sport, a religion, or a vocation. Offering every cuisine imaginable, the San Francisco Bay Area is one of the food capitals of the world, with more restaurants per person than any other area in the USA. In fact, many new arrivals to the Bay Area are part of the food industry, serving as wait staff, suppliers, growers, chefs, managers, investors, etc. If you are interested in finding out more about dining out in the Bay Area, check out the weekly reviews features and columns in the *San Francisco Weekly* and the *San Francisco Bay Guardian* newspapers. You can also check out the food lover's old trusty companion, *Zagat Survey, San Francisco Bay Area Restaurants*, www.zagat.com.

WINES

- **Beltramos**, 1540 El Camino Real, Menlo Park, 650-325-2806, wines and beers
- **Beverages and More**, for Bay Area locations call 888-772-3866
- **Calistoga Wine Stop**, 1458 Lincoln Ave, #2, Calistoga, 707-942-5556
- **Cost Plus World Market**, 2552 Taylor St, San Francisco, 415-928-6200; 785 Serramonte Blvd, Daly City, 415-994-7090; 101 Clay St, Oakland, 510-834-4440, www.worldmarket.com
- **The Jug Shop**, 1567 Pacific Ave, San Francisco, 415-885-2922, 800-404-9548, www.jugshop.com
- **K&L Wine Merchants**, 3005 El Camino Real, Redwood City, 800-247-5987; 638 4th St, San Francisco, 800-437-7421, 877-KLWines, www.klwines.com, wine-of-the-month clubs, free newsletter, huge selection
- **Marin Wine Cellar**, 2138 Fourth St, San Rafael, 415-459-3823
- **North Berkeley Wine Company**, 1505 Shattuck Ave, Berkeley, 510-848-8910
- **The Wine Stop**, 1300 Burlingame Ave, Burlingame, 650-342-0570; 101 West 25th Ave, San Mateo, 650-573-1071

And don't forget to visit the hundreds of wineries in Napa and Sonoma.

WITH ALL THE DIVERSE AND HIGHLY ACCLAIMED CULTURAL EVENTS in the Bay Area, you may have trouble deciding what to do first. San Francisco boasts a world-class symphony and chorus, opera, ballet, and a vibrant live theater scene, with everything from the experimental and off-beat to big, brash Broadway musicals. And the surrounding Bay Area presents rich and varied cultural offerings as well. It's a rare evening here when one of the current stars of the pop music scene is not appearing locally. South of Market, the official nightlife district, is the nightclub hub.

Art lovers indulge themselves at major museums in San Francisco's downtown area and in Golden Gate Park as well as in smaller galleries throughout the City. Oakland, Berkeley, and the South Bay have myriad museums and galleries as well. Science museums, aquariums, planetariums, and top-notch zoos also abound. The South Bay, not surprisingly, has a number of technology-oriented museums.

All of the Bay Area's newspapers print entertainment schedules on a regular basis, so you'll have no trouble finding out what's happening. The most comprehensive listing can be found in the *San Francisco Chronicle's* Sunday "Datebook." The *Chronicle* also publishes a daily "Datebook" section in the morning newspaper. San Francisco's *Bay Guardian* weekly and the *SF Weekly* also have extensive listings and movie reviews, and they're free. Look for them in street-side racks and cafés.

Tickets for most events and performances may be purchased at the venue box offices or by calling **Ticketmaster** at 415-421-2277 in San Francisco, 510-625-2277 in the East Bay; 408-998-2277 for South Bay and Peninsula; 707-528-2277 for the North Bay, or order online at www.ticketmaster.com. It's always a good idea to get your tickets as far in advance as possible since many shows, concerts, exhibits, and events sell out in advance. When calling ahead, have your credit card ready and be prepared to pay service fees (if your sense of thrift won't allow you to pay the often-steep service fees, buy your tickets in person at the box office). For discount, same-day tickets to San Francisco theater productions and full-price tickets to other selected local events check out the **TIX Bay Area** ticket booth on the east side of Union Square. This is where last-minute open seats are sold for half-price; although your choices are usually limited, you can score great bargains. Call TIX at 415-433-7827—cash only for half-price tickets, VISA and MasterCard accepted for full-price purchases. Other ticket agencies are listed in the Yellow Pages under "Tickets."

MUSIC—SYMPHONIC, OPERA, CHORAL

SAN FRANCISCO/NORTH BAY

- The **San Francisco Symphony** is one of the country's premier orchestras. The symphony and its **Chorus** have both won Grammy awards and toured much of the world, performing to packed houses and critical acclaim. World-renowned conductor Michael Tilson Thomas, known as MTT, runs the show and is famous for his innovative approach. Along with showcasing Beethoven and Mozart classics as well classics of American music, the symphony has paired with such unusual partners as SF heavy metal legend Metallica for a special sold-out show. When at home, the San Francisco Symphony and Chorus perform separately and in tandem at their glittering glass, brass, and concrete home, the $33 million Louise M. Davies Symphony Hall. Opened in 1980, the structure underwent an acoustic upgrade in 1992. The concert hall and box office are located in the Civic Center area, at 201 Van Ness Avenue. Call the ticket office at 415-864-6000 or purchase tickets and view the full concert calendar online at www.sfsymphony.org. Ticket prices start around $10, and go up from there. Each new concert season kicks off in early September with a swank black tie and ballgown gala, and runs through June.
- The **San Francisco Opera** performs at the War Memorial Opera House, right across Van Ness Avenue from City Hall, north of Davies Symphony Hall. This company attracts many of the opera world's biggest stars and is known for its often-lavish productions. Tickets can be on the expensive side, with decent seats starting around $85. However, if you don't mind being on your feet for three-plus hours, standing-room tickets, available for $10 each (cash only), go on sale at 10 a.m. on the day of the show at the Opera box office, 301 Van Ness Avenue. A number of these tickets are also held aside to be sold two hours before the performance. If a show isn't sold out, students, seniors, and military personnel can try for special cash-only rush tickets ($15 for students, and $30 for seniors and military personnel). Rush tickets go on sale at 11 a.m. the morning of the performance at the

Opera box office. Call the day before to check for ticket availability. The curtain comes up on the opera season with a gala event in September and continues into the summer. For more information or to order tickets, call 415-864-3330. The opera also presents free performances in Stern Grove, Golden Gate Park, and Yerba Buena Gardens during the summer. Visit www.sfopera.com for more details and schedules.

- The highly acclaimed vocal ensemble **Chanticleer** calls San Francisco home. This a cappella group of 12 men works year-round, traveling all over the world, performing live and making new recordings. The ensemble specializes in "early music," but is also adept at classical choral works, jazz, pop, and spirituals. Catch them when they're in town—you'll be amazed by what you hear. To find out more, contact Chanticleer at 415-252-8589, www.chanticleer.org.
- San Francisco's own **Kronos Quartet** specializes in modern, experimental music, and they too travel the globe, playing to sold-out audiences. Check newspaper entertainment guides for the few times Kronos is in the Bay Area to play for its adoring local followers. If you like modern chamber music, you're sure to become one of Kronos's many fans. For a schedule of upcoming performances, check out www.kronosquartet.org.
- If you'd like to hear some of the professional musicians of the future, the place to go locally is the **San Francisco Conservatory of Music**. The school is scheduled to be settled into its new digs at 50 Oak St, in the Civic Center, in the fall of 2006. Frequent concerts are staged here, featuring classical and contemporary solo and ensemble performers. For more information on upcoming events at the conservatory, call 415-759-3477 or visit www.sfcm.edu.
- At **San Francisco Community Music Center**, 544 Capp St, 415-647-6015, www.sfcmc.org, you can take a class or view inexpensive, sometimes free performances by students, instructors, and professionals of worldwide acclaim.
- At the striking Frank Lloyd Wright–designed Civic Center in San Rafael you can hear the **Marin Symphony**. Call 415-479-8100 or visit www.marinsymphony.org for more details.

The areas surrounding San Francisco and the North Bay host an abundance of classical musical offerings. Not all musical groups have permanent homes; instead, some play at a variety of locations, which means that people have an opportunity to hear live classical music pretty close to home no matter where they live.

EAST BAY
In Contra Costa County the **Dean Lesher Regional Center for the Arts** houses a number of performance companies such as the **Contra**

Costa Chamber Orchestra, the **Diablo Light Opera Company**, and the **Center REPertory Company**, 1601 Civic Dr, Walnut Creek, 925-943-7469, http://dlrca.org. Also here:
- **Berkeley Opera**, 2640 College Ave, Julia Morgan Center for the Arts, Berkeley, 510-841-1903, www.berkeleyopera.org
- **Berkeley Symphony Orchestra**, various locations, 510-841-2800, www.berkeleysymphony.org
- **Oakland East Bay Symphony**, 2025 Broadway, the Paramount Theatre, Oakland, 510-444-0801, www.oebs.org

PENINSULA
In the groves of academe at Stanford University you can hear the **Stanford Symphony Orchestra**, the **Symphonic Chorus**, and the **Chamber Chorale**. Visit http://events.stanford.edu for a full events listing, or contact 650-723-2300.
- **Palo Alto Chamber Orchestra**, various locations, Palo Alto, 650-856-3848, www.pacomusic.org
- **Palo Alto Philharmonic**, various locations, www.paphil.org
- **West Bay Opera**, Lucie Stern Theatre, Palo Alto, 650-424-9999, www.wbopera.org

SOUTH BAY
- **Cupertino Symphonic Band**, various locations, 408-262-0471, www.netview.com/csb
- **Opera San Jose**, the California Theatre, 345 South First St, San Jose, 408-437-4450, www.operasj.org
- **San Jose Wind Symphony**, various locations, 408-927-7597, www.sjws.org
- **Symphony Silicon Valley**, performances at the California Theatre, 345 South First St, 408-286-2600, www.symphonysiliconvalley.org

BALLET & DANCE

At any given time dance lovers in the Bay Area can enjoy watching Celtic step dancing, Native American dancing, Russian or Balkan dancers, and modern dance companies. Look in the newspaper or any of the local weeklies for listings.

SAN FRANCISCO/NORTH BAY
- **Dance Mission Theater**, run by Dance Brigade, hosts a variety of shows, from performances by the resident six-woman contemporary

company to Afro-Cuban festivals; it's also a popular spot to take classes in everything from hip hop to salsa, to modern dance, to Afro Brazilian, 3316 24th St (at Mission) 415-273-4633, www.dancemission.com.

- **Fat Chance Belly Dance**, a San Francisco institution, performs tribal style belly dancing at a variety of festivals and events, as well as offering drop-in dance classes, for women only, at the studio, 670 South Van Ness Ave, 415-431-4322, www.fcbd.com.
- **Marin Ballet**, various locations, 415-453-6705, www.marin ballet.org, performs the Nutcracker every Christmas at the Marin Veterans Memorial Auditorium, 3501 Civic Center Dr.
- Michael Smuin, formerly a choreographer with the San Francisco Ballet, started his own company, **Michael Smuin Ballet**. They perform modern and classical pieces often reworked by Smuin at various locations including Yerba Buena Center for the Arts, 701 Mission St, and the Mountain View Center for the Performing Arts, 500 Castro St. Call 415-495-2234 or visit www.smuinballet.org for information.
- **ODC Theater** (Oberlin Dance Collective, with its roots at Oberlin College) performs modern dance at ODC Theatre, 3153 17th St, 415-863-9834, www.odctheater.org, and elsewhere. They also put on the popular "Velveteen Rabbit" for children each Christmas at Yerba Buena Center for the Arts.
- Other modern dance troupes include **Deborah Slater Dance Theatre**, 415-267-7687, **Margaret Jenkins Dance Company**, 415-826-8399, and **Footloose Dance Company and Shotwell Studios**, 415-289-2000, www.ftloose.org. This is only a partial list. New companies form, combine, and move in all the time.
- The **San Francisco Ballet** is a small company with a big reputation. The ballet season follows the opera season, starting with the perennially popular "Nutcracker" in November and proceeding throughout the late winter and spring. Performances are at the War Memorial Opera House at Van Ness and Grove. For performance and ticket information call 415-865-2000, or visit www.sfballet.org.
- **Theatre Flamenco of San Francisco**, 415-826-1305, enlivens the Spanish dancing scene.

EAST BAY

- **Axis Dance Company**, a contemporary company, integrates dancers with disabilities who create and perform their own original works; various locations, 510-625-0110, www.axisdance.org.
- **Cal Performances** presents dancers of world renown who perform through UC Berkeley at the Greek Theater, Hertz Hall, or Zellerbach Auditorium, 510-642-9988.

- **Julia Morgan Center for the Arts,** 2640 College Ave, Berkeley, 510-845-8542, www.juliamorgan.org, offers a wide variety of arts programs. The Center also houses the **Berkeley Ballet Theater**, which boasts the inclusive motto, "where all can dance," features both adult and youth companies, and teaches ballet lessons, 510-843-4687, www.berkeleyballet.org.
- **Oakland Ballet** performs at the beautiful Paramount Theatre and other locations. They are known for their innovative approach and the use of ethnic elements in their work; annually they perform a renowned modern reworking of the *Nutcracker*, "The Hard Nut." Call 510-452-9288 or visit www.oaklandballet.org to find out what they're up to.

PENINSULA/SOUTH BAY

- **Ballet San Jose Silicon Valley**, 40 North First St, San Jose, 408-288-2800, www.balletsanjose.org, showcases classic and contemporary works from *Romeo and Juliet* to *The Little Mermaid*; the ballet school's educational outreach program is dedicated to serving young audiences.
- **Peninsula Ballet Theatre**, various locations, 650-340-9448, presents a variety of classical ballet performances at affordable prices, including an annual rendition of the *Nutcracker* popular with families, www.peninsulaballet.org.
- **San Jose Dance Theater**, 408-286-9905, www.sjdt.org, hosts classics and children's favorites including *Alice in Wonderland*, *Sleeping Beauty*, *Beauty and the Beast*, and of course the *Nutcracker*.

THEATER

The San Francisco theater scene is an active one offering works that range from experimental to mainstream. The theater district, located two blocks west of Union Square on Geary Street, is where you'll find the Curran and Geary theaters. The Curran stages musicals such as the immensely successful 5-year run of *Phantom of the Opera* and other visiting Broadway productions, as well as shows being prepared for the trip to New York's Great White Way. The Geary Theater plays host to what many would consider more serious productions, such as works by Shakespeare, Chekhov, and Sam Shepard. It is also is home to one of the country's most respected companies, the American Conservatory Theatre. The Golden Gate Theater, in the nearby Tenderloin district, stages big, splashy musicals. The surrounding streets are on the seedy side, which puts many people off when it comes to attending shows here. However, there is safety in numbers, so if possible, stick with the crowd when traveling through this area.

Once you leave the theater district, productions take on a less commercial, more experimental feel, and there are many to choose from. Of course, local high schools, colleges, and universities also mount shows, as do many local theater groups. Look for listings for all of the above in newspaper entertainment guides, or call the theaters. Here are just a few **San Francisco theaters**:

- **American Conservatory Theater (ACT)**, San Francisco's major professional theater company, based at the Geary Theater, 415 Geary St, 415-749-2228, www.act-sf.org
- **Brava**, 2781 24th St, 415-641-7657, focuses on social and political issues.
- **Club Fugazi**, 678 Beach Blanket Blvd (Green St) 415-421-4222, home of the immensely popular *Beach Blanket Babylon*.
- **Curran**, 445 Geary St, 415-551-2000, www.bestofbroadway-sf. com, Broadway shows
- **Eureka Theatre**, 215 Jackson St, 415-788-7469, music, plays, classes
- **Exit Theatres**, 156 Eddy St and 277 Taylor St, 415-673-3847, www.theexit.org
- **Fort Mason Box Office** (Cal Theater, Young Performers Theater, etc.), Fort Mason, 415-441-3687, new and old plays, comedy and drama
- **Golden Gate**, 42 Golden Gate Ave, 415-551-2000, www.bestof broadway-sf.com musicals
- **Intersection for the Arts**, 446 Valencia St, 415-626-3311, www.theintersection.org, plays, readings, musicals, music, and dance
- **Lorraine Hansberry**, 620 Sutter St, 415-474-8800, known for top-notch African-American drama
- **Magic Theatre**, Fort Mason, Building D, 415-441-8822, www.magic theatre.org, experimental
- **Marines Memorial**, 609 Sutter St, 415-771-6900, varied, www.marines memorialtheater.com
- **New Conservatory Theatre Center**, 25 Van Ness Ave, 415-861-8972, traditional, new, musical, gay and lesbian themes
- **Orpheum**, 1192 Market St, 415-551-2000, www.bestofbroadway-sf. com, opera, musicals, serious drama
- **Post Street Theatre**, 450 Post St, 2nd Floor, 415-771-6900, www. poststreettheatre.com, drama, new works, classics
- **Theatre Rhinoceros**, 2926 16th St, 415-861-5079, www.the rhino.org, gay and lesbian themes

NORTH BAY
- **Marin Community Playhouse**, 27 Kensington Rd, San Anselmo, 415-456-8555, films, lectures, dance, drama, music

- **Marin Shakespeare Company**, 415-499-4488, www.marin shakespeare.org, various locations
- **Marin Theatre Company**, 397 Miller Ave, Mill Valley, 415-388-5208, www.marintheatre.org, new plays and classes
- **Mountain Play Association**, 177 East Blithedale, Mill Valley, 415-383-1100, www.mountainplay.org, yearly outdoor summer musicals

EAST BAY
- **Actors Ensemble of Berkeley**, 1301 Shattuck Ave, 510-525-1620
- **Aurora Theatre Co.**, 2315 Durant Ave, Berkeley, 510-843-4822, old standards and new plays
- **Berkeley Repertory Theatre**, 2025 Addison, Berkeley, 510-845-4700, www.berkeleyrep.org, nationally known, new, and reworked plays
- **Black Repertory Group**, 3201 Adeline St, Berkeley, 510-652-2120
- **Contra Costa Civic Theatre**, 951 Pomona Ave, El Cerrito, 510-524-9132
- **Dean Lesher Regional Center for the Arts**, and **Center Repertory Company**, 1601 Civic Dr, Walnut Creek, 925-943-SHOW, www.dlrca.org
- **Diablo Light Opera**, Dean Lesher Regional Center for the Arts, 1601 Civic Center Dr, Walnut Creek, 925-939-6161, www.dloc.org
- **East Bay Center for the Performing Arts**, 339 11th St, Richmond, 510-234-5624, www.eastbaycenter.org
- **Lamplighter Music Theatre**, Dean Lesher Center for the Performing Arts, 925-943-7469
- **Malonga Calquelourd Center for the Arts** (formerly the **Alice Arts Center**), 1428 Alice St, Oakland, 510-451-6100, www.malonga center.org

PENINSULA
- **Broadway by the Bay**, San Mateo Performing Arts Center, 600 North Delaware St, San Mateo, 650-579-5568, www.pclo.org
- **Palo Alto Players**, 1305 Middlefield Rd, Palo Alto, 650-329-0891, www.paplayers.org, full season of shows at reasonable prices
- **TheatreWorks**, Mountain View Center for the Performing Arts, 500 Castro St, and Lucie Stern Theater, 1305 Middlefield Rd, Palo Alto, 650-463-1960, www.theatreworks.org

SOUTH BAY
- **American Musical Theater of San Jose**, Center for the Performing Arts, 255 Almaden Blvd, San Jose, 408-453-7108, or 888-455-SHOW, www.amtsj.org

- **City Lights Theater Company**, 529 South Second St, San Jose, 408-295-4200, www.cltc.org, eclectic new plays
- **Louis B. Mayer Theatre**, Santa Clara University, Santa Clara, 408-554-4989
- **San Jose Repertory Theatre**, 101 Paseo de San Antonio, 408-291-2255, www.sjrep.com, classics and originals
- **San Jose Stage Company**, 490 South First St, San Jose, 408-283-7142, www.sanjose-stage.com/off-Broadway shows
- **Santa Clara Players**, Santa Clara Community Center, Santa Clara, 408-248-7993, www.scplayers.org

MOVIES—ART, REVIVAL, INTERNATIONAL

Mainstream theaters, some of which still offer bargain matinees in the afternoon, show the latest Hollywood blockbusters located throughout the Bay Area. Below is a list of harder-to-find "art houses" that specialize in foreign and/or alternative films.

SAN FRANCISCO
- **Artists' Television Access**, 992 Valencia St, 415-824-3890
- **Bridge**, 3010 Geary Blvd, 415-267-4893
- **Balboa**, 3630 Balboa St, 415 221-8184, www.balboamovies.com
- **Castro**, 429 Castro St, 415- 621-6120, www.castrotheatresf.com
- **Clay**, Fillmore at Clay St, 415-267-4893
- **Embarcadero**, 1 Embarcadero Center, 415-267-4893
- **Four Star**, Clement St and 23rd Ave, 415-666-3488
- **Lumiere**, California at Polk St, 415-267-4893
- **Opera Plaza**, Van Ness at Golden Gate Ave, 415-267-4893
- **Red Vic**, 1727 Haight St, 415-668-3994
- **Roxie**, 3117 16th St, and The Little Roxie, 3125 16th St, 415-863-1087
- **Vogue**, Sacramento St and Presidio Blvd, 415-221-8183

SURROUNDING BAY AREA
- **ACT I and II**, Center and Shattuck sts, Berkeley, 510-843-3456
- **Stanford Theater**, 221 University Ave, Palo Alto, 650-324-3700
- **Camera 12 Cinemas**, 201 South Second St, San Jose, 408-998-3300, www.cameracinemas.com
- **Los Gatos Cinemas**, 41 North Santa Cruz Ave, Los Gatos, 408-395-0203, www.cameracinemas.com
- **Towne Theatre**, 1433 The Alameda, San Jose, 408-287-1433
- **Christopher B. Smith Rafael Film Center**, 1118 Fourth St, San Rafael, 415-454-1222, www.cafilm.org

- **New Pacific Film Archive Theater**, 2725 Bancroft Ave, Berkeley, 510-642-5249, www.bampfa.berkeley.edu

FILM FESTIVALS

The Bay Area hosts several annual film festivals. If you're a film buff, you'll want to mark your calendar.

- **Festival Cine Latino** (September), 415-553-8135, www.cineaccion.com
- **International Lesbian & Gay Film Festival** (June), 415-703-8650, www.frameline.org
- **Jewish Film Festival** (July), 415-621-0556, www.sfjff.org
- **Mill Valley Film Festival** (October), 415-383-5256, www.mvff.com
- **San Francisco International Asian American Film Festival** (March), 415-865-1588, www.naatanet.org
- **San Francisco International Film Festival** (April), 415-561-5000, www.sffs.org

CONTEMPORARY MUSIC

San Francisco draws star entertainers as well as up-and-comers from all over the world. The city also has its own incredibly vibrant local music scene. If you're into hip-hop, dance music, rowdy pick-up bars, and late night clubbing, check out SOMA. About a decade ago, this area became the target of "clean-up" efforts instituted by then-head of the Southern Police Station, Capt. Dennis Martel. Frequent vice squad raids by the SFPD and the Federal Bureau of Alcohol led to tighter restrictions on club operating hours and ultimately shut down many of the city's most popular clubs. To this day, it's extremely difficult to get an after-hours license in San Francisco, so you'll be hard pressed to find anything (legally) open after 2 a.m. The best-known exception is **Ten 15**—a massive multi-tier dance club with different DJs spinning in every room. Long lines form every Friday and Saturday when the club is open all night long, 1015 Folsom Street, 415-431-1200, www.1015.com.

Rock and roll hipsters spend their nights following beloved local bands and DJs who spin at a seemingly ever-rotating pool of tiny bars and intimate nightclubs scattered throughout the city. Currently, 6th Street—where rents are cheap, space is freely available, and neighbors don't complain—is home to a crop of new nighttime hot spots. In recent years, a number of new bands, small clubs, and art/music spaces have also sprung up in Oakland—enticing die-hard San Francisco music lovers across the bridge on Friday and Saturday nights.

Even when the mix of venues is steady, many of the smaller club nights, and even a few of the bigger ones like the long-running, ever-popular 1980s tribute night New Wave City rotate—using different spots on different nights. For the latest on local bands, shows, and venues, check out the alternative weeklies: the *San Francisco Bay Guardian*, *SF Weekly*, and the *East Bay Express*. There are also a host of free monthly magazines devoted entirely to local music—*West Coast Performer* and *Mesh*. You can pick these up at local music stores, and at many coffee shops. In the wired world, there are also a number of popular online music sites: www.foopee. com/punk/the-list, the internet version of **"The List"**—Steve Koepke's tried and true old-school photocopied punk and indie rock listing—gives the weekly lowdown on Bay Area shows, good for lovers of more underground/less mainstream music. You can also sign up for the **Squid List**, http://laughingsquid.com/squidlist, a daily e-mail list of noncommercial/ underground music, art, culture, and performance events. You can also check their online event calendar at the same web address. Many events are also posted on the bulletin boards of popular social sites, **Friendster**, www.friendster.com (the "one that started it all" and began here in the Bay Area) and **MySpace**, www.myspace.com. MySpace also has an area specifically devoted to music. **Yahoo** (www.yahoo.com) also hosts a variety of subscriber bulletin board and discussion groups, including the popular **SF Indie List**. You have to register to use these sites and online community services, but membership is free. **Noise Pop**, the all-about indie rock festival held every February, is the place to check out local emerging rock stars and hot out-of-town acts, www.noisepop.com.

If big arena rock is your cup of tea, no doubt the name Bill Graham will be familiar to you. Graham, the prolific Bay Area concert promoter, died in 1991 returning from a Huey Lewis and the News concert on a windy night when his helicopter hit a transmission tower in the North Bay. Today Graham is best remembered for his early years in the 1960s and 1970s promoting San Francisco psychedelic rockers the Grateful Dead and Jefferson Airplane, first at local art spaces and later at the Fillmore. These days, the company he founded, **Bill Graham Presents (BGP)**, presses on, bringing big-time rock and roll acts to the Fillmore, the Warfield, as well as the large, centrally located Civic Center, now officially renamed the Bill Graham Civic Auditorium.

In the East Bay, the **Oakland Coliseum** (currently officially named, but called by no one, McAfee Coliseum) is one of the Bay Area's premier outdoor concert sites for big-name pop stars; it also has an indoor stage. A number of other outdoor facilities are used for concerts, chief among them the **Shoreline Amphitheatre** in Mountain View and the **Chronicle Pavilion** in Concord. Both have covered seating up front close to the stage, and loads of uncovered lawn behind the seats. Bring a blanket, stretch out, and listen to the music. Though it's not outdoors, Madonna and Bette Midler both stopped by the **HP Pavilion** in San Jose on recent tours, skipping San Francisco—which lacks a space large enough to host them—entirely.

Jazz and blues are the hallmarks of North Beach, especially along upper Grant Avenue. While it's no longer the Beat Generation mecca—and you'll be hard pressed to find a smoky bar with young intellectuals hanging on the words of poets waxing prolific to a bongo backbeat—you will find a mix of late night jazz clubs, and down home country and blues dive bars. Spots like **Grant & Green Blues Club**, **The Saloon**, and the **Gathering Café** are longtime favorites. Late into the night, jazz lovers congregate for cappuccino nightcaps and lively chats at the neighborhood's late night coffee houses.

Wherever you go be forewarned, there is no smoking indoors in public places in San Francisco—or in any of California for that matter. Smoking is officially banned in restaurants, bars, and clubs throughout the state. Of course, a handful of places openly flaunt their disobedience. You'll know them by the ashtrays scattered on the tables, and of course, by the thick clouds of smoke billowing out the door.

For the latest on who's playing where and when, you can consult the weeklies listed above, the *San Francisco Chronicle's* weekend "Datebook," or the paper's web site, www.sfgate.com.

BAY AREA CONCERT FACILITIES

- **Chronicle Pavilion at Concord**, 2000 Kirker Pass Rd, Concord, 925-363-5701, www.chroniclepavilion.com
- **Cow Palace**, Geneva Ave and Santos St, Daly City, 415-404-4111, www.cowpalace.com
- **Fillmore**, 1805 Geary Blvd, San Francisco, 415-346-6000, www.thefillmore.com
- **Great American Music Hall**, 859 O'Farrell St, San Francisco, 415-885-0750, www.musichallsf.com
- **Greek Theater**, UC Berkeley (near football stadium), Berkeley, 510-642-9988
- **HP Pavilion**, 525 W. Santa Clara St, San Jose, 409-287-6655
- **Oakland Coliseum & Arena**, Hegenberger Rd and I-880, Oakland, 510-569-2121, www.coliseum.com
- **Shoreline Amphitheatre**, 1 Amphitheater Pkwy, Mountain View, 650-967-3000, www.shorelineamp.com
- **Warfield Theatre**, 982 Market St, San Francisco, 415-775-7722

NIGHTCLUBS

We offer you a list of places to get you started, though this list is by no means comprehensive. Call ahead: here today, gone tomorrow is often the case in this fast-paced scene.

SAN FRANCISCO

- **Bahia Cabana**, 1600 Market St, 415-861-4202; this beloved Brazilian salsa club burned down in its original corner location, on New Year's Day 2000, but soon after managed to find a new home nearby; nights here are packed again with samba, salsa and flamenco, and there is also an excellent restaurant that serves up tasty Brazilian fare.
- **Biscuits & Blues**, 401 Mason St, 415-292-2583, www.biscuitsand blues-sf.com; blues, hosts a weekly Mardi Gras party, Tuesday nights at 8:45 p.m. with the Fat Tuesday Band; a new full-service restaurant recently opened upstairs and serves up home-style southern Cajun cuisine including jambalaya and fried chicken—and there's a raw oyster bar.
- **Bottom of the Hill**, 1233 17th St, 415-621-4455, www.bottomofthe hill.com; the long-reigning king of the indie rock music scene, hosts up-and-coming local bands and touring favorites, the outdoor patio is the place to mix and mingle, and to escape the noise, as well as a haven for smokers; when the weather is nice, the Sunday BBQs are a great way to while away the day.
- **Café du Nord**, 2170 Market St, 415-861-5016, www.cafe dunord.com; the stairwell that leads you down to this swanky little dark club reveals du Nord's former days as a bootleggers' paradise during prohibition; here you can catch up-and-coming local rock bands and in-house jazz regulars with a pint of speakeasy ale in your hand; arrive early to grab a bite to eat and a cozy table.
- **Edinburgh Castle**, 950 Geary St, 415-885-4074, www.castle news.com; the stage here is tiny, but the friendly pub atmosphere, excellent beer, and support of emerging bands make it a great place to check out new local rock acts; the Castle also hosts a handful of intimate but popular dance nights, including the beloved Brit pop night, Lovely; and drinkers square off for a test of wits at the Castle Quiz trivia night every Tuesday at 8:30 p.m.
- **Fillmore**, 1805 Geary Blvd, 415-346-6000, www.thefillmore.com; this old-fashioned, ornate and stalwart hall was closed for several years after being ravaged by the 1989 Loma Prieta earthquake. But today, you can once again wander the walls lined with posters and photos from its glory days in the 1960s and '70s while you listen to today's rock n' roll greats; a new upstairs lounge hosts DJs and smaller acts that play

between sets on the main stage as well as a snack bar to soothe your late night munchies. Arrive extra early to snag one of the premier balcony tables and leave quickly afterward to get one of the free concert posters the venue is famous for.

- **Gathering Café**, 1326 Grant St, 415-433-4247; sipping coffee in this crowded café while listening to blues singers belt out the classics, and jazz trumpeters raise the roof, will take you back to the days when North Beach was a poetry and jazz mecca.
- **Hotel Utah**, 500 4th St, 415-546-6300, www.thehotelutah saloon.com; a dive in the best sense of the word, with bar-style rock and blues bands, Monday night open mike.
- **Noe Valley Ministry**, 1021 Sanchez St, 415-454-5238, www.noe valleymusicseries.com; hosts the Noe Valley Music Series in a 110-year-old Victorian church, with a mix of world, jazz, folk, and classical performances.
- **Pearl's**, 256 Columbus Ave, 415-291-8255, www.jazzatpearls.com; this famous jazz and blues 1930s style supper club with French and Spanish food in the heart of North Beach offers two live music shows every night Monday-Saturday, 8 p.m. dinner show, 10:30 p.m. cocktail show.
- **Plough & Stars**, 116 Clement St, 415-751-1122; voted "Best Irish Pub" by the *SF Weekly*, the club offers a variety of imported pints and live Irish music Tuesday through Sunday, free most nights with a cover charge on Friday and Saturday.
- **Slim's**, 333 11th St, 415-522-0333, www.slims-sf.com; opened in 1988 by legendary R&B artist Boz Scaggs, this mid-size club in the heart of SOMA hosts rock, hip-hop, and blues touring and local acts.
- **330 Ritch**, 330 Ritch St, 415-541-9574; DJ dance nights, world, hip hop, hosts long-running popular Brit pop dance night, Pop Scene, every Thursday night.

NORTH BAY
- **19 Broadway**, 19 Broadway, Fairfax, 415-459-1091, www.19broadway. com; open seven nights a week, with two shows nightly, rock to raga, Monday nights open jam sessions.
- **Sweetwater**, 153 Throckmorton Dr, Mill Valley, 415-388-2820; a Marin fixture, this place has national and international musical acts.

EAST BAY
- **Ashkenaz**, 1317 San Pablo Ave, Berkeley, 510-525-5054, www. ashkenaz.com; all ages, rock, hip-hop, funk, blues, world, country.
- **Freight & Salvage**, 1111 Addison St, Berkeley, 510-548-1761, www.freightandsalvage.org; coffee house with coffee, tea and

desserts, acoustic, rock, blues, world, country, youth 16 and under half price, $1 off for seniors.

- **Kimball's East**, Emeryville Public Market, Emeryville, 510-658-0606, www.kimballs.com; intimate supper club, jazz, r&b, classic soul, shows at 8 p.m. and 10 p.m. Friday and Saturday, and at 5 p.m. and 8 p.m. Sunday.
- **La Pena Cultural Center**, 3105 Shattuck, Berkeley, 510-849-2568; hip-hop, soul, world.
- **Starry Plough**, 3101 Shattuck Ave, Berkeley, 510-841-2082; small, friendly pub atmosphere with local rock, country and world music acts, shows are frequently $5.
- **Yoshi's**, 510 Embarcadero West, Oakland, 510-238-9200, www.yoshis.com; this club in the heart of Jack London Square is where the giants of jazz play when they come to town, tickets are pricey, but shows are top-notch and you can enjoy sushi and classic Japanese fare at the adjoining restaurant. Shows are Monday-Saturday at 8 p.m. and 10 p.m., Sunday at 2 p.m. and 8 p.m.

PENINSULA
- **Fanny and Alexander**, 412 Emerson St, Palo Alto, 650-326-7183; rock
- **Los Altos Bar and Grill**, 169 Main St, Los Altos, 650-948-4332; rock, jazz, etc.
- **Ploneer Salon**, 2925 Woodside Rd, Woodside, 650-851-8487; country, rock

SOUTH BAY
- **The Blank Club**, 44 South Almaden Ave, San Jose, 408-29-BLANK, www.theblankclub.com; rock
- **Boswell's**, Pruneyard Shopping Center, 1875 South Bascom, Campbell, 408-371-4404; rock
- **J.J.'s Blues**, 14 2nd St, San Jose, 408-286-3066; blues, rock, hip-hop

SWING

Swing is the in thing here and has been for the last several years. What was an underground youth movement has caught the imagination of old timers, former hippies, young people, and everyone in between. There are numerous swing bands, swing street fairs, and swing clubs, and now the old swank night spots like Bimbos and Top of the Mark hire young swing bands to keep their patrons hopping. Vintage clothing stores have run out of original 1940s swing attire so smart young designers are making their own replicas of everything from zoot suits to flattering floral print rayons for the gals. Almost every venue hosts pre-event dance classes for the beginner, so there's no excuse not to lindy. Check out the Lindy List, www.lindylist.com, for Bay Area–wide classes and happenings.

COMEDY

There's a lot to laugh about in life, and San Francisco provides ample opportunity to do so at a number of comedy clubs. Some headline the big names in modern comedy, including San Francisco natives Margaret Cho and Marga Gomez, and touring stand-ups Jamie Kennedy and Bill Maher. Others offer open-mike opportunities for up-and-coming jokesters. If your funny bone needs tickling, here are a few of the places you may want to visit for comic relief:

- **Cobb's**, 915 Columbus Ave, San Francisco, 415-928-4320, www.cobbs comedyclub.com
- **Comedy on the Square**, various locations, comedy, 415-522-8900, www.comedyonthesquare.com
- **Josie's**, 3583 16th St, San Francisco, 415-861-7933
- **Punch Line**, 444 Battery St, San Francisco, 415-397-7573, www.punchlinecomedyclub.com
- **Rooster T. Feathers**, 157 West El Camino Real, Sunnyvale, 408-736-0921, www.roostertfeathers.com
- **National Comedy Theater**, 52 South First St, third floor, San Jose, 408-985-5233, www.national-comedy.com

MUSEUMS

San Francisco is blessed with excellent art museums, most notably the M.H. de Young Memorial Museum (undergoing renovations) in Golden Gate Park, the new Asian Art Museum, the San Francisco Museum of Modern Art at Yerba Buena Gardens, and the California Palace of the Legion of Honor in Lincoln Park. Those are the big ones. Throughout the Bay Area are also many smaller art museums and galleries, as well as museums related to history, culture, and science, and interesting one-of-a-kind centers. Here's a sampling:

ART MUSEUMS

SAN FRANCISCO/NORTH BAY
- **African-American Museum**, Fort Mason, Building C, 415-441-0640
- **Asian Art Museum**, 200 Larkin St, 415-581-3500, www.asianart.org; featuring artwork, ceramics, architectural displays, jade and textiles from China, Korea, India, Tibet, Japan and Southeast Asia. This is the

largest museum of its type on the West Coast and is indicative of the Bay Area's large Asian population. On Thursdays, the museum is free after 5 p.m. and stays open until 9 p.m. Kids 11 and younger free.

- **California Palace of the Legion of Honor,** 415-863-3330; a beautiful building perched atop a hill in Lincoln Park, it was given to the city in 1924 by the Spreckels family as a monument to the state's war dead. The art collection features European art from the medieval to the 20th century including a cast of Rodin's *The Thinker*, which sits outside the main entrance. Free on Tuesday, under age 12 free.
- **Headlands Center for the Arts,** 944 Fort Barry, Sausalito, 415-331-2787, www.headlands.org
- **M.H. de Young Museum,** named for Michael de Young, a former publisher of the *San Francisco Chronicle*, this museum has been located in Golden Gate Park since construction of the park began in 1917. The dramatically transformed new museum (reopened in fall 2005) features a stunning observatory tower as well as American works from Colonial to Modern, and African, British, Egyptian, Greek, Roman, and Asian items. The museum is also the site of many lectures and gala events. Call 415-863-3330 for more information.
- **Mexican Museum,** Fort Mason, Building D, the oldest (at merely 30) and largest (at 10,000 objects) collection of Mexican and Chicano art in the country. For information on exhibits, programs, and guided mural tours, contact 415-202-9700 or go to www.mexicanmuseum.org.
- **Museo Italo Americano,** Fort Mason, Building C, 415-673-2200, free for children 11 and under.
- **Performing Arts Library and Museum,** 401 Van Ness Ave, fourth floor, 415-255-4800, www.sfpalm.org, free.
- **SF Craft and Folk Art Museum,** Fort Mason, Building A, 415-775-0990, youth 18 and under free; Free the first Wednesday of the month, when the museum stays open until 7 p.m., and free every Saturday from 10 a.m. to noon.
- **San Francisco Museum of Modern Art (SFMOMA)** at Yerba Buena Gardens is one of the most exciting buildings in the city. Swiss architect Mario Botta designed the building, and its massive cylindrical skylight is a sight to behold. Exhibits include works by Henri Matisse, Pablo Picasso, and Jackson Pollock, to name just three. SFMOMA was the West Coast's first museum dedicated solely to 20th century art. Located at 151 3rd St, 415-357-4000, www.sfmoma.org. On Thursdays the MOMA is open until 9 p.m. and is half price after 6 p.m. Children 12 and under free. Free on the first Tuesday of the month.
- **Yerba Buena Center for the Arts,** 701 Mission St, 415-978-2787, www.ybca.org; under age 12 free. Free the first Tuesday of the month.

EAST BAY

- **Judah L. Magnes Memorial Museum**, 291 Russell St, Berkeley, 510-549-6950, www.magnes.org; Jewish art and objects, under 12 free.
- **Oakland Museum**, 1000 Oak St, 510-238-2200, California art and history, Open late the first Friday of the month, under age 12 free.
- **University Art Museum**, 2626 Bancroft Way, Berkeley, 510-642-0808; free the first Thursday of the month.

PENINSULA/SOUTH BAY

- **Cantor Arts Center,** 328 Lomita Dr & Museum Way, Palo Alto, 650-723-4177, www.stanford.edu, features modern art, sculpture, photography, and international exhibits; the highlight here is the outdoor Rodin Sculpture Garden, with 20 bronze statues by Auguste Rodin, including "The Gates of Hell"; admission is free.
- **San Jose Museum of Quilts and Textiles**, 110 Paseo de San Antonio, 408-971-0323, www.sjquiltmuseum.org, features contemporary and traditional quilt making and textile design.
- **De Saisset Museum**, Santa Clara University, 408-554-4528
- **Palo Alto Cultural Center**, 1313 Newell St, 650-329-2366, features contemporary local artwork.
- **San Jose Museum of Art**, 110 South Market St, San Jose, 408-294-2787, www.sjmusart.org, features 20th century traveling exhibits.
- **San Jose Institute of Contemporary Art**, 451 South First St, San Jose, 408-283-8155, www.sjica.org
- **Triton Museum of Art**, 1505 Warburton Ave, Santa Clara, 408-247-3754, features modern art.

HISTORY AND CULTURAL MUSEUMS AND CENTERS

- **Arion Press**, 1802 Hays St, The Presidio, 415-561-2542, www.arion press.com; this living, breathing museum of printing and book arts with historic type foundry was designated an "irreplaceable cultural treasure" by the National Trust for Historic Preservation.
- **Cable Car Museum**, get a close look at the history and inner workings of the nation's only moving landmark, San Francisco's world famous cable cars. Located at Washington and Mason sts in San Francisco, 1201 Mason St, 415-474-1887, www.cablecarmuseum.org.
- **California History Center**, 21250 Stevens Creek Blvd, DeAnza College Campus, Cupertino, 408-864-8712
- **Cartoon Art Museum**, 655 Mission St, San Francisco, 415-227-8666, www.cartoonart.org
- **Chinese Culture Center**, Holiday Inn, Third Floor, 750 Kearny St, San Francisco, 415-986-1822, www.c-c-c.org

- **Chinese Historical Society of America**, San Francisco's Chinatown has long been one of the largest Chinese communities in the country, and this small museum is dedicated to the Chinese-American story. Located at 965 Clay St, San Francisco, 415-391-1188, www.chsa.org
- **Contemporary Jewish Museum**, this modest historical museum doubles as an art museum featuring works by Jewish artists. Located at 121 Steuart St, San Francisco, 415-591-8800, www.thecjm.org
- **Cupertino Historical Museum**, 10185 North Stelling Rd, Quinlan Community Center, Cupertino, 408-973-1495
- **Falkirk Cultural Center**, 1408 Mission Ave, San Rafael, 415-485-3328
- **Jack London Square and Village**, Embarcadero between Alice and Broadway in Oakland, here you'll find shops and restaurants as well as a museum of African Antiquities. The Jack London Museum is at 30 Jack London Square.
- **Marin County Historical Society and Museum**, 1125 B St, San Rafael, 415-454-8538
- **Maritime Museum**, Hyde St Pier, San Francisco, 415-561-7100
- **Mission San Rafael**, 1104 5th Ave, San Rafael, 415-456-3016
- **Museum of American Heritage**, 351 Homer Ave, Palo Alto, 650-321-1004, historical tableaux of day-to-day life
- **National Japanese American Historical Society**, 1684 Post St, San Francisco, 415-921-5007
- **Paramount Theatre**, 2025 Broadway, Oakland, tours available, call 510-893-2300, www.paramounttheatre.com
- **Peralta Adobe**, 154 West St. John St, San Jose, 408-993-8300, www.historysanjose.org
- **San Francisco Museum and Historical Society**, free exhibits at City Hall and Pier 45, 415-537-1105
- **San Jose History Park** at Kelley Park, 1650 Senter Rd, 408-287-2290, www.historysanjose.org,
- **Santa Clara de Asis Mission**, Franklin and Market, San Jose, 408-554-4023
- **Santa Clara Historical Museum**, 1509 Warburton Ave, Santa Clara, 408-248-2787
- **Saratoga Historical Museum**, 20450 Saratoga-Los Gatos Rd, 408-867-4311

SCIENCE MUSEUMS & ZOOS

The Bay Area is a world scientific research center, home to the Lawrence Livermore and Lawrence Berkeley laboratories, medical research facilities at UCSF, and Stanford University Medical Center. In Silicon Valley, and elsewhere in the Bay Area, the next generation of computer, communications, and medical technologies is being developed. That said, you don't have to be a tech guru or rocket scientist to enjoy the abundant science museums in the Bay Area. Below is a partial list:

SAN FRANCISCO

- **California Academy of Sciences** has temporarily relocated to 875 Howard St while it rebuilds its spectacular facility in Golden Gate Park; the new building is expected to open in 2008. Founded in 1853, the Academy of Sciences was and is the oldest scientific institution in the western United States. The facility includes the **Morrison Planetarium** and the **Steinhart Aquarium**. One of the aquarium's most popular attractions is the Fish Roundabout, which allows you to watch as all manner of water creatures, including shark, bat rays, and eel, glide around you in a 100,000-gallon tank. There are astounding displays of reptiles and amphibians, as well as a varied display of underwater plant life. Call 415-321-8000 or visit www.calacademy.org for information on the academy and the aquarium. Free the first Wednesday of the month.
- **Exploratorium**, located in the Palace of Fine Arts in the Marina district, is a true "hands on" scientific experience for everyone. There are nearly 700 exhibits, many of them interactive, and all highly educational. One of the most popular attractions is the Tactile Dome. Reservations are required for the opportunity to tumble around inside this darkened dome, where you rely on nothing but touch and sound. Located at 3601 Lyon St, 415-397-5673, www.exploratorium.edu.
- **San Francisco Zoo**; this 65-acre facility is perhaps best known for its koalas and Gorilla World. The koalas are a real treat to see as they cling, fast asleep, to their habitat's eucalyptus branches. The gorilla display is reportedly one of the world's largest. There's also a Children's Zoo, which allows kids to pet some of the animals, and an Insect Zoo. Located on Sloat Blvd at 47th Ave, 415-753-7080, www.sfzoo.org.
- **Underwater World**, opened in 1996 at the tourist magnet of Pier 39, takes visitors literally into the aquarium through a long, inches thick, viewing tunnel. All around you the aquarium's residents glide by in an environment that can make you feel as though it is people, rather than fish, that are on display, 415-623-5300.

NORTH BAY

- **Bay Area Discovery Museum**, Fort Baker, 557 McReynolds Rd, Sausalito, 415-339-3900, www.baykidsmuseum.org, hands-on exhibits for kids
- **San Francisco Bay Model**, 2100 Bridgeway, Sausalito, 415-332-3870, no charge

EAST BAY

- **Holt Planetarium—Lawrence Hall of Science**, Centennial Dr, Berkeley, 510-642-5132, www.lawrencehallofscience.org
- **Oakland Zoo**, Oakland Zoo, 9777 Golf Links Rd, 510-632-9525, www.oaklandzoo.org
- **UC Berkeley Botanical Gardens**, 200 Centennial Dr, 510-643-2755, http://botanicalgarden.berkeley.edu; offers plants and hiking trails

PENINSULA AND SOUTH BAY

- **Children's Discovery Museum of San Jose**, 180 Woz Way, 408-298-5437, www.cdm.org
- **Hiller Aviation Museum**, 601 Sky Way Rd, San Carlos Airport, San Carlos, 650-654-0200
- **Intel Museum**, 2200 Mission College Blvd, Santa Clara, 408-765-0503
- **Lick Observatory**, 19 miles east of San Jose on Highway 130 near Mount Hamilton, 408-274-5061, www.ucolick.org
- **Los Gatos Museum**, 4 Tait Ave, Los Gatos, 408-354-2646
- **Minolta Planetarium**, 21250 Stevens Creek Blvd, DeAnza College Campus, Cupertino, 408-864-8814, www.planetarium.deanza.edu
- **NASA Ames Research Center**, Moffett Field, Mountain View, 650-604-6274, www.nasa.gov/centers/ames/events/index.html
- **Stanford Linear Accelerator**, 2275 Sand Hill Rd, Menlo Park, 650-926-2204, www.slac.stanford.edu, offers tours six times per month
- **The Tech Museum of Innovation**, 201 South Market St, San Jose, 408-795-6100, www.thetech.org

CULTURE FOR KIDS

There is so much for kids to do culturally in the Bay Area that they'll grow up before they can try it all. Beside numerous technical, history, science, nature, ethnic, and art museums, there are dozens of dance, theater, poetry, and musical performances aimed at or composed of children. Now that schools are less inclined to offer an array of language classes, kids can learn another language at some of the local cultural institutes as well. During the holidays the **San Francisco Ballet** performs its version of *The Nutcracker* and the **ODC** performs a modern version of the *Velveteen Rabbit*. This smattering of listings for events and places that children might enjoy represents only a little of what the Bay Area has to offer.

SAN FRANCISCO

- **Exploratorium**, the **San Francisco Zoo**, and **Underwater World** are made for kids. See descriptions above under **Science Museums & Zoos**.

- **Randall Junior Museum**, 199 Museum Way, 415-554-9600, www. randallmuseum.org; a perennial favorite among children, this museum features an earthquake exhibit, live animals, art and science programs, films, lectures, concerts, and plays.
- **Yerba Buena Gardens**, 4th and Mission sts, www.yerbabuena gardens.com, offers gardens, paths, waterfalls and fountains full of birds. At one end, you'll find the high-tech museum **Zeum**, an ice-skating rink, a kid-sized bowling alley, a playground, and a merry-go-round; at the other, the **Sony Metreon**, 415-369-6000, www. metreon.com, is home to 15 movie screens, an IMAX theater, restaurants, hot dog stands, shops, arcades, and a Where the Wild Things Are interactive exhibit.
- **Zeum**, 221 4th St, 415-777-2800, www.zeum.com, part of the large arts complex at Yerba Buena Gardens, includes hands-on science and technology exhibits for children, an outdoor playground, and an old-fashioned merry-go-round.

SURROUNDING BAY AREA
- **Berkeley Youth Orchestra**, 2322 Shattuck Ave, Berkeley, 510-653-1616, www.berkeley-youth-orchestra.org
- **Billy Jones**, Wildcat Railroad, Oak Meadow Park, Los Gatos, 408-395-7433, www.bjwrr.org
- **Children's Discovery Museum of San Jose**, 180 Woz Way, 408-298-5437, www.cdm.org
- **Coyote Point Museum for Environmental Education**, 1651 Coyote Point Dr, San Mateo, 650-342-7755, www.coyotepointmuseum.org, nature museum and animal center, hands-on children's exhibits
- **Emma Prusch Farm Park**, 647 South King Rd, San Jose, 408-926-5555
- **Happy Hollow Park and Zoo**, 1300 Senter Rd, San Jose, 408-277-3000, www.happyhollowparkandzoo.org
- **Marin Dance Theatre**, 1 St. Vincent's Dr, San Rafael, 415-499-8891, www.mdt.org, children and adult classical ballet classes and performances
- **Oakland Youth Orchestra**, 1428 Alice St, Oakland, 510-832-7710, www.oyo.org
- **Palo Alto Junior Museum & Zoo**, 1451 Middlefield Rd, Palo Alto, 650-329-2111, www.city.palo-alto.ca.us/ross/museum
- **Winchester Mystery House**, 525 South Winchester Blvd, San Jose, 408-247-2000, www.winchestermysteryhouse.com
- **Young People's Symphony Orchestra**, Berkeley, 510-849-9776

LITERARY LIFE

New York may be home to the major publishing houses, but San Francisco has a literary legacy and pulsing life all its own. The city's illustrious roster of once-wrote-heres includes beloved humorist Mark Twain, detective noir master Dashiell Hammett, and legendary newspaper columnist Herb Caen. And across the bay, Oakland proudly claims classic literary legend Jack London, for whom its waterfront square is named, as one of its own.

In the 1950s and '60s, San Francisco was a favorite stomping ground of Beat poets Allen Ginsberg and Jack Kerouac, while in the 1970s Armistead Maupin began a local soap-opera-esque newspaper serial that shone a light on San Francisco life, and eventually became the famed novel *Tales of the City.*

But those who think San Francisco's glory days as a writers' haven are long gone should take a closer look. Beneath the surface, a young, feisty new community of novelists, essayists, poets, and publishers is rising— forging an active local literary community and commanding national attention. Independent bookstores; community spaces like Dave Eggers' **826 Valencia**, which offers free writing workshops for teens; and the Grotto, a writers' collective that offers a variety of seminars, are coming to the fore. And while the big city loves the limelight, the East Bay—Berkeley and Oakland in particular—is home to some of the best spoken word and hip-hop poetry groups around.

Below you'll find a list of some of the Bay Area's best-loved independent bookstores, many of which host regular readings; cafés and clubs that host storytelling and open mike nights; writers' groups; local literary publications; and annual events. Local libraries, which offer a variety of pro grams—not to mention endless books to choose from, all for free—are an excellent place to start.

BOOKSTORES

The Bay Area has a large number of good independent, specialized, and used bookstores, many of which host author readings and other literary programs. Check their bulletin boards or get on their mailing or e-mail lists to be notified of upcoming events. Below is a list of just some of these, though once you move here, you'll probably discover many more. The university towns of Palo Alto and Berkeley have many good new and used bookstores encircling their campuses. Here are some of the familiar standards as well as a few interesting local independents worth visiting. Unless otherwise noted, the following establishments are in San Francisco.

- **Adobe Book Shop**, 3166 16th St, 415-864-3936; the store employees recently arranged all of the books here in color order, a la the rainbow. But not to worry, the art exhibit was only temporary and things are now back to "normal." Adobe hosts popular reading nights and occasional music and art events.
- **Alexander Book Co.**, 50 2nd St, 415-495-2992, www.alexander book.com; this three-level store in the heart of the Financial District specializes in African American literature and children's books, also maintains a large poetry collection.
- **Black Oak Books,** www.blackoakbooks.com, hosts author events at the main store, 1491 Shattuck Ave, Berkeley, 510-486-0698; also two San Francisco locations, 630 Irving St, 415-564-0877; 540 Broadway 415-986-3872.
- **Book Passage**, 51 Tamal Vista Blvd, Corte Madera, 415-927-0960 or 800-999-7909, www.bookpassage.com, is known for its great support of local authors, frequent readings, and writing workshops. There is now also a second shop in San Francisco Ferry Plaza, 1 Ferry Plaza, #46, San Francisco, 415-835-1020.
- **Booksmith**, 1644 Haight St, 415-863-8688, www.booksmith.com, offers a wide collection of new and used books, as well as a substantial magazine section. Recent author events have showcased everyone from local Green Party activist Medea Benjamin to baseball superstar Jose Canseco.
- **Bound Together Book Collective**, 1369 Haight St, 415-431-8355, specializes on anarchist and progressive books.
- **Builders Booksource**, 900 North Point, Ghirardelli Square, 415-440-5773; 1817 Fourth St, Berkeley, 510-845-6874, www.buildersbook source.com; offers architectural, design, and construction books for the amateur and professional.
- **Citylights Bookstore**, 261 Columbus Ave, 415-362-8193, www.city lights.com, the legendary Beat Generation bookshop founded by San Francisco's first poet laureate, Lawrence Ferlinghetti, was the first paperback bookstore in the country. Its creaky wooden floors and endless shelves are probably the best place to browse late in the evening. The store has an excellent collection of fiction, a poetry room upstairs, and a nook dedicated to zines; the store showcases local authors, operates its own publishing house, and hosts frequent poetry and fiction events.
- **A Clean, Well Lighted Place for Books**, 601 Van Ness Ave, 415-441-6670, www.bookstore.com, runs a 10 a.m. Saturday book group every other week, with coffee and cookies, and hosts frequent author events—from the well-known to the up-and-coming.

- **Cody's Books, Inc.**, www.codysbooks.com, 2454 Telegraph Ave, Berkeley, 510-845-7852, a Berkeley institution, features a huge book selection and an extensive magazine and zine collection. A second Berkeley location is at 1730 Fourth St, 510-559-9500. Fall 2005 marked the grand opening of Cody's Books in San Francisco, at 2 Stockton St, 415-773-0444.
- **Dog Eared Books**, 900 Valencia St, 415-282-1901, offers a great collection of used fiction—from the classics to recent works.
- **Europe Book Co**, 925 Larkin St, 415-474-0626, carries books in French, German, and Spanish.
- **Get Lost Books**, 1825 Market St, 415-437-0529, www.getlostbooks. com, offers travel-related books, maps, and gear.
- **Green Apple Books and Music**, 506 Clement St, and annex at 520 Clement St, 415-387-2272, www.greenapplebooks.com, offers a huge selection of used books, a wide fiction selection including small presses, a large magazine collection, and used CDs, DVDs, and videos.
- **Kepler's Books**, 1010 El Camino Real, Menlo Park, 650-324-4321, www.keplers.com; boasts an expansive collection of fiction and nonfiction, special children's section, and frequent author events, highly knowledgeable staff; stays open late and is next door to an outdoor café.
- **La Casa Del Libro**, 973 Valencia St, 415-285-1399, provides books in Spanish.
- **Marcus Books**, 1712 Fillmore St, 415-346-4222, www.marcusbooks. com, specializes in African American, African, and Caribbean literature.
- **Moe's Books**, 2476 Telegraph Ave, Berkeley, 510-849-2087, www.moesbooks.com, an East Bay favorite, Moe's features an excellent, huge collection of used fiction and nonfiction.
- **Modern Times**, 888 Valencia St, 415-282-9246, www.moderntimes bookstore.com, hosts frequent author events and a large leftist politics section, occasionally has music events too.
- **Nolo Press Outlet Bookstore**, 950 Parker St, Berkeley, 510-704-2248, www.nolo.com, publishes a variety of easy-to-read legal guides.
- **Rand McNally Map and Travel Store**, 595 Market St, 415-777-3131, stocks travel-related books and other items.
- **San Francisco Mystery Book Store**, 4175 24th St, 415-282-7444, www.sfmysterybooks.com, offers mystery and detective books as well as out-of-print pulp fiction.
- **Stacey's**, 581 Market St, San Francisco, 415-421-4687 or 800-926-6511, www.staceys.com; this large downtown San Francisco store is known for its huge selection and large collection of textbooks, as well as its excellent events roster, featuring readings and signing by such big names as financial guru Suze Orman and film critic extraordinaire Roger Ebert.

- **Thomas Bros. Maps and Books**, 550 Jackson St, 415-981-7520, 800-969-3072, www.thomas.com, features the indispensable city map books, wall maps, and related items.
- **William Stout**, 804 Montgomery St, 415-391-6757, stoutbooks.com, specializes in books on architecture and design.

BOOKSTORE CHAINS

These days there are pretty much two main players that dominate the big league bookstore game all across the country, Borders and Barnes & Noble. A few discount-style bookshop chains remain in local shopping malls. The Bay Area is also home to a handful of West Coast chains.

- **Barnes & Noble**, 2550 Taylor St, San Francisco, 415-292-6762; 1940 South El Camino Real, San Mateo, 650-312-9066; 2352 Shattuck Ave, Berkeley, 510-644-0861; 2020 Redwood Hwy, Greenbrae, 415-924-1016; 3600 Stevens Creek Blvd, San Jose, 408-984-3495; www.bn.com
- **Books Inc.**, Stanford Shopping Center, Palo Alto, 650-321-0600; 3515 California St, San Francisco, 415-221-3666, www.booksinc.net, specializes in discounted books. They have a good cookbook section. They also have a spot at SFO if you need to pick up something to read on the airplane.
- **Borders Books Music Movies & Café**, 15 Ranch Dr, Milpitas, 408-934-1180; 400 Post St, San Francisco, 415-399-1633; 5903 Shellmound, Emeryville, 510-654-1633; 588 West Francisco Blvd, San Rafael, 415-454-1400, www.bordersstores.com; have their own coffee shops inside where you can read, flip through magazines, or study.
- **WaldenBooks**, Four Embarcadero Center, San Francisco, 415-397-8181, 2242 South Shore Center, Alameda, 510-523-4463, also primarily a shopping mall bookstore chain, offers inexpensive popular paperbacks and discounted gift books.

RESOURCES

In addition to libraries and bookstores, San Francisco has a collection of active literary groups, creative collectives, nonprofits, and publications that host regular events. A great source of information is the *Literary Supplement*, a special pull-out section published quarterly in the *San Francisco Bay Guardian*.

- **826 Valencia**, 826 Valencia St, 415-642-5905, www.826valencia.org; Dave Eggers' strange pirate booty shop in the front/writing center in the back offers free youth writing classes and occasional adult workshops and events, and is also home to *McSweeney's*, an excellent literary quarterly.

- The **Alternative Press Expo (APE)**, www.comic-con.org/ape, held every spring at the Concourse Exhibition Center in San Francisco, showcases independent authors, publishers, and comic artists from all over.
- **Berkeley Poetry Slam**, 510-841-2082, www.daniland.com/slam; this popular open mike night showcases up-and-coming poets and spoken word artists and regularly draws crowds from throughout the Bay Area. Held every Wednesday at the Starry Plough, 3101 Shattuck Ave, Berkeley. Sign-up to read at 7:30 p.m.; show starts at 8:30 p.m.
- **City Arts and Lectures**, 415-392-4400, www.cityarts.net, brings big-wig talents and off-beat cult favorites to town for packed lectures, usually at the Herbst Theater.
- **Friends of the San Francisco Public Library** offers a way to get involved with your local library and operates two book bays with excellent deals: Fort Mason Center, Building C, 415-771-1076; Main Library, 100 Larkin St, 415-557-4238; www.friendssfpl.org.
- Every year, **Litquake**, www.litquake.org, a week-long extravaganza of fiction and nonfiction, celebrates local literary life with readings by some of the Bay Area's best-known authors.
- **Porchlight**, 415-861-5016, www.porchlightsf.com, a storytelling series hosted by local authors Beth Lisick and Arline Klatte, presents stories on specific themes at 7 p.m. on every third Monday of the month at Café Du Nord, 2170 Market St. Recent themes have included *Why Don't You Kill Me: Tales of Complete Loserdom* and *On the Couch: The Therapy Show*.
- **Radar Reading**, 415-557-4400, www.sfpl.org, queer reading series hosted by literary diva Michelle Tea at the San Francisco Public Library, 100 Larkin St, monthly, evenings (times/dates vary).
- **Selected Shorts**, public radio broadcast of actors reading short stories by notable authors, Saturdays at 8:30 p.m. Saturdays, KQED 91.5 FM.
- **The Commonwealth Club**, 595 Market St, 415-597-6700, www.commonwealthclub.org, hosts a range of impressive guests from political heavyweights to cultural icons, to literary giants; membership and single-ticket options available.
- **The Grotto**, www.sfgrotto.org, writers' collective space whose members frequently offer workshops and seminars at various locations, including a multimedia series in conjunction with the SF Public Library.
- **Writers with Drinks**, 415-647-2888, www.writerswithdrinks.com, is a "spoken word variety show" hosted at 7:30 p.m. on the second Saturday of every month by *Other Magazine* at the Make Out Room, 3225 22nd St.

SPECIALTY LIBRARIES

The **Main Library** in San Francisco, 100 Larkin Street, puts on a variety of excellent programs throughout the year from author readings, to poetry workshops for teens, to noontime film screenings—and it's all free. Call them at 415-557-4400 or visit www.sfpl.org to find out about current events. Local branch libraries are also a great resource; check the neighborhoods sections for more details and contact information. Home to two top-tier universities, Stanford and the University of California at Berkeley, and a cutting-edge scientific research facility at UCSF, the Bay Area offers a wide array of specialty libraries and research centers. Below are just a few. All libraries are located in San Francisco unless otherwise noted.

- **African American Historical Society**, Fulton Street Center, 762 Fulton St, 415-292-6172
- **Alliance Francaise**, 1345 Bush, 415-775-7755, www.afsf.com, maintains a large library of French books, videos, CDs, and magazines, as well as works in French with accompanying English translations. Alliance also offers a variety of French language classes and programs. Library open to all, but borrowing privileges are reserved for members and students enrolled in classes.
- **Bureau of Jewish Education**, 1835 Ellis St, 415-567-3327
- **The Foundation Center and Library,** 312 Sutter St, in the World Affairs Council Building, Suite 606, 415-397-0902, http://fdn center.org/sanfrancisco; for nonprofits, artists, students, and scholars, this is the place to go for information about grants and special funding opportunities. Anyone can use the library—which is full of stacks and stacks of helpful resource materials—and the staff is extremely knowledgeable. The online database is available on a first-come first-served basis, and there are also frequent specialized workshops.
- **Holocaust Center of Northern California**, 601 14th Ave, 415-751-6040
- **Hoover Institution Library and Archives**, Hoover Tower at Stanford University in Palo Alto, 650-723-2058, www.hoover.org, offers a mind-boggling collection of first-hand historical accounts recording major political, social, and economic transformations, with more than 1.6 million volumes, 60 million archive documents, and 100,000 original political posters. The institute is free and open to the public, but borrowing privileges are reserved for Stanford students, faculty, and research affiliates. The reading tower is worth a trip in itself for the spectacular views of the Peninsula.
- **Japanese American National Library**, 1619 Sutter St, 415-567-5006

- **The Law Library** houses a wealth of legal documents and information on various aspects of federal and state law. Access is free to the public, but borrowing privileges are reserved for members of the state bar in good standing and practicing law in the City and County of San Francisco, judges of courts within the City and County of San Francisco; and municipal, state, and federal officers. If you meet these requirements, you may qualify for a library card. There are three locations:
- **Veterans War Memorial Building**, 401 Van Ness Ave, room 400, 415-554-6821, www.sfgov.org/site/sfll_index.asp (main location)
- **Monadnock Building**, 685 Market St, Suite 420, 415-882-9310 (special emphasis on business law)
- **Courthouse Reference Room**, Courthouse, 400 McAllister St, Room 512, 415-551-3647 (quick answers to last-minute court preparations)
- **Performing Arts Library and Museum**, 401 Van Ness Ave, fourth floor, 415-255-4800, www.sfpalm.org, houses books, artwork, photographs, newspaper clippings, audio recordings, sheet music, video tapes, design plates, and artifacts that chronicle the history of dance, music, theater, and theater design in the San Francisco Bay Area. The museum is home to the archives of many local performing arts organizations, including the San Francisco Ballet, Opera, and Symphony, the Stern Grove Festival, the Ethnic Dance Festival, Pickle Family Circus, and The Lamplighters. Check the web site for special programs, presentations, and events.

HIGHER EDUCATION

California, the Bay Area in particular, is world renowned for its quality institutions of higher learning. Whether you are looking to enroll in a Bachelor's, Master's, continuing education, or night degree program, or perhaps you are interested in attending a lecture series or evening theatrical performance, the list of possibilities is endless.

SAN FRANCISCO
- **Golden Gate University,** 536 Mission St, 415-442-7000, www.ggu.edu, is a private, nonprofit, and accredited program, located in the downtown area. It offers a wide variety of graduate and undergraduate programs in business, law, and public administration.
- **San Francisco State University,** 1600 Holloway Ave, 415-338-1111, www.sfsu.edu; part of the California State University system, SFSU offers a wide range of undergraduate and graduate degrees. Serving more than 30,000 students a year, SFSU is one of the largest schools in the CSU system.

- **University of San Francisco**, Parker and Fulton sts, 415-422-5555, www.usfca.edu; founded in 1855 by Jesuit fathers, USF was San Francisco's first institution of higher learning. It is fully accredited and beautifully situated on a 50-acre hilltop. USF offers undergraduate and graduate degrees in nursing, business, education, law, and many other disciplines.

NORTH BAY

- **Dominican University of California**, 1520 Grand Ave, San Rafael, 415-457-4440, www.dominican.edu; affiliated with the Catholic Church, Dominican is known for its counseling psychology, education, and music programs; offers Bachelor's and Master's degrees.
- **Sonoma State University**, 1801 East Cotati Ave, Rohnert Park, 707-664-2880, www.sonoma.edu, was founded in 1960 and is one of the youngest universities in the California State University system. Located 50 miles north of San Francisco, the 220-acre campus east of Rohnert Park reminds many of a park. Degrees and certificates offered in a wide variety of disciplines.

EAST BAY

- **California State University, East Bay**, formerly California State University, Hayward, has two main campuses. One is situated on a hilltop overlooking the city of **Hayward** to the west, and the other is in the **Concord** foothills of Mt. Diablo. CSUEB also has a new professional development center in downtown Oakland. The main campus in Hayward is undergoing a massive $70 million makeover, including a new business and technology center, student union, and student housing. Located at 25800 Carlos Bee Blvd, Hayward, 510-885-3000, and 4700 Ygnacio Valley Rd, Concord, 925-602-4700; www.csu hayward.edu.
- **John F. Kennedy University**, 12 Altarinda Rd, Orinda, 925-254-0200, www.jfku.edu, founded in 1964, it offers courses geared toward the adult student looking for a BA and/or MA degree, in fields such as counseling, library or museum arts, management, law, and liberal arts.
- **Mills College**, 5000 MacArthur Blvd, Oakland, 510-430-2255, www.mills.edu, founded in 1852, is the oldest women's college in the western United States. Mills has a long history of excellence in the fields of liberal arts and science. The college offers women undergraduate and graduate degrees, and admits men to some graduate programs.
- **Saint Mary's College**, 1928 St. Mary's Rd, Moraga, 925-631-4000, www.stmarys-ca.edu, founded in 1863 by the Christian Brothers, is located in the hilly, wooded, secluded community of Moraga. Classes

are small and instruction excellent. Offers undergraduate and graduate degrees.

- **University of California, Berkeley**, 510-642-6000, www.berkeley.edu, is considered by many to be the finest school in the UC system. Founded in 1868 and located on a 1,500-acre wooded urban campus, UC Berkeley has top-notch facilities, faculty, and course offerings in hundreds of disciplines, undergraduate and graduate. Entrance competition is stiff, to say the least.

PENINSULA/SOUTH BAY

- **San Jose State University,** One Washington Square, San Jose, 408-924-2000, www.sjsu.edu, is located in the heart of Silicon Valley in downtown San Jose. SJSU offers some unique opportunities including the use of the nation's only undergraduate nuclear science lab, its own deep-sea research ship, and centers for the study of Beethoven and John Steinbeck. Graduate programs also offered.
- **Santa Clara University** is considered by many to be one of the finest universities in the country. Santa Clara was founded in 1851 by the Jesuits and is recognized as California's oldest institution of higher learning. Today it is known for its law, business, and engineering schools. Located at 500 El Camino Real, Santa Clara, 408-554-4000, www.scu.edu.
- **Stanford University,** 650-723-2300, www.stanford.edu, is certainly one of the nation's premier universities. Stanford is located in comfortable Palo Alto, at the northern end of Silicon Valley. Established in 1885 by former California Governor and Senator Leland Stanford and his wife Jane, Stanford is known for its excellence in the arts and sciences, and its highly regarded faculty and facilities, including its medical center.

SURROUNDING AREAS

- **University of California, Davis,** Mrack Hall, Davis, 916-752-1011, www.ucdavis.edu, is located about 70 miles northeast of San Francisco and 15 miles west of Sacramento. UCD is a top-notch research university offering undergraduate and graduate degrees in a wide range of fields. A beautiful college town, the city of Davis is known for being one of the most bicycle-friendly communities in the nation.

THE BAY AREA IS ONE OF THE BEST URBAN PLAYGROUNDS IN THE world. With its ocean beaches, wide-open greenspaces, nearby mountain ranges, and all the activities that accompany such environs, it may be difficult to decide what to do with your free time. Surfing (with a wet suit) at Ocean Beach is one option, as well as kayaking, windsurfing, or rowing—though probably not in the ocean. Biking, hiking, and running in Golden Gate Park, the Presidio, or Mount Tamalpais are popular choices. Bird watching is fabulous at the Palo Alto Baylands; and these are only a few of the opportunities available. However, if all you really want to do on your day off is kick back and be a spectator, you are in luck. The Bay Area has plenty of professional and college teams to cheer on.

PROFESSIONAL

Bay Area sports fans are blessed (although some might say cursed) with professional teams in all of the major leagues: baseball, basketball, football, hockey, and soccer. For the latest, consult the sports section of the *San Francisco Chronicle, Oakland Tribune, Marin Independent Journal*, or the *San Jose Mercury News*, or visit your team's web site.

BASEBALL

One of the Bay Area's most intense sports rivalries exists between the National League **San Francisco Giants** and the American League **Oakland Athletics** (the A's), and passions run high on both sides. Among the most popular matches are the inter-league games where the Giants and the A's face off against each other. The last time the A's and Giants met in the World Series was in 1989, a series disrupted by the

October 17th Loma Prieta earthquake that rattled then-Candlestick Park. (The game was canceled, and the A's went on to win the series four games to three.)

- **San Francisco Giants** (National League), SBC Park, 24 Willie Mays Plaza, San Francisco, CA 94107, 800-5-GIANTS, www.sfgiants.com; the big news for the Giants is their gorgeous new stadium, a 40,800-seat ballpark in China Basin that was completed in March 2000. For those wanting to attend a game, there are a number of ways to purchase tickets: online at http://sanfrancisco.giants.mlb.com; at the stadium's Double Play Ticket Window; from www.tickets.com, 800-352-0212; or from any Giants Dugout Store—check the Giants' web site for more details. Individual ticket prices for the 2005 season ranged from $12 for bleacher seats all the way up to $72. Season tickets are difficult, if not impossible, to obtain. For those on a more last-minute schedule, 500 day-of-the-game tickets are available at the stadium two hours before each scheduled home game.
- **Oakland Athletics** (American League), Oakland Coliseum (McAfee), I-880 and Hegenberger Rd, Oakland, 510-638-0500, http://oakland.athletics.mlp.com; fans were in an uproar when the team traded some of its stars players recently, but things seem to be settling down a bit. A's fans have a reputation for throwing a good party, and the bleachers—where you can catch the game live for a mere $9—can get rowdy at times, especially during heated night games. If this sounds like a fun night out, you can track down tickets several ways: purchase online at the A's web site (web address above) or call A's ticket services, 510-568-5600; purchase through www.tickets.com, 800-352-0212; or go to the Oakland Coliseum ticket window. Ticket prices for the 2005 season ranged from $9 for bleacher seats to $36 for a Plaza Club seat.

BASKETBALL

The NBA's **Golden State Warriors** play their home games in Oakland's Arena, just off I-880 in Southern Oakland, from November through June. Tickets can be purchased at the Warrior Ticket Office, 510-986-2222, or at the Oakland Arena on the day of the game. For more information check the Warriors' web site, www.nba.com/warriors.

FOOTBALL

Similar to the baseball rivalry between the A's and the Giants, competition between the **Oakland Raiders** and the **San Francisco 49ers** is fierce. These teams, two of the most successful franchises in the National Football

League, rarely play each other because they are in different conferences, but when they do, the air is thick with anticipation and the cheers are passionate and loud.

- The **Raiders** play at the Oakland Coliseum, I-880 and Hegenberger Rd, Oakland, 510-638-0500, www.raiders.com. For tickets, call 888-44-RAIDERS or purchase them at www.ticketmaster.com, 415-421-8497.
- The **San Francisco 49ers**, www.sf49ers.com, play at Monster Park (formerly known as Candlestick Park), which is notoriously cold and windy. For tickets call the 49ers' ticket office, 415-656-4900, or contact them via e-mail at 49ersTicketOffice@niners.nfl.net. You can also purchase tickets through Ticketmaster on the web at www.ticketmaster. com or by calling 415-421-8497.

HOCKEY

The **San Jose Sharks** of the National Hockey League are the ice hockey team for the Bay Area. Pre-season starts in September; the season runs until April. They play in the HP Pavilion (aka San Jose Arena), affectionately known as the "Shark Tank." As a result of a bargaining dispute, the entire NHL cancelled its 2004-2005 season, much to the dismay of Sharks fans. However, things appear to be back on track for the 2005-2006 season. Tickets for the Sharks are available at the arena ticket office, 408-999-5757, or through Ticketmaster, 415-421-8497, www.ticketmaster.com. Consult the Sharks' web site, www.sj-sharks.com, for more information.

HORSE RACING

Pack your mint juleps and don your Kentucky Derby hat—horse racing is not far from San Francisco. You have two choices: Just across the bay you can attend **Golden Gate Fields**, located at 1100 Eastshore Highway, in the City of Albany. Entrance fees range from $3 to $15, depending on the location of your viewing stand. Fall season runs from November to January, and spring season from April to June. For more information call 510-559-7300 or visit www.goldengatefields.com. On the Peninsula, you can bet on the horses at **Bay Meadows**, 2600 South Delaware St, San Mateo, 650-574-7223, www.baymeadows.com. Take CalTrain from the Peninsula, South Bay, or San Francisco right to the tracks.

SOCCER

The year 1996 brought professional soccer to the Bay Area for the first time in years, in the form of Major League Soccer's San Jose Clash. At the inaugural match against DC United, the Clash won, 1-0. Today, the renamed

San Jose Earthquakes, www.sjearthquakes.com, play at Spartan Stadium on 7th Street, just south of downtown San Jose. The season runs from April through September. For ticket information call the San Jose Earthquakes' ticket sales office at 408-985-4625. You can also purchase tickets through Ticketmaster on the web at www.ticketmaster.com or by calling 415-421-8497.

In 2001 the Bay Area welcomed the newly formed professional women's soccer team, the **Cyber Rays**, to compete in the Women's United Soccer Association (WUSA) league. Unfortunately, the financial bottom fell out of WUSA in 2003 and operations were suspended. But in 2004, a group of former League officers joined with the Players' Association in an effort to revive WUSA. For the latest information on the future of the WUSA and the Cyber Rays, visit http://wusa.com.

COLLEGE SPORTS

If you'd like to watch the sports stars of tomorrow, check out one of the Bay Area college or university teams. Probably the most closely followed collegiate sports contest in the Bay Area is football's annual Big Game that pits the **University of California Golden Bears** against the **Stanford Cardinal**. It's usually a spirited event, and a consistent sellout, so get your tickets early.

Another popular attraction is the Stanford women's basketball team. Under Coach Tara VanDerveer, the Stanford women have been one of the best teams in the country, and Cardinal fans are hoping that trend continues. **Stanford University** plays basketball at Maples Pavilion and football at Stanford Stadium, both located on the university campus in Palo Alto. For information call 800-STANFORD or check www.gostanford.com. The **University of California at Berkeley** plays basketball in the Harmon Arena and football at Memorial Stadium, both on the Berkeley campus. For more information call 800-462-3277, or check www.berkeley.edu.

The following schools also stage sporting events:

- **Cal State East Bay**, 510-885-3000, www.csuhayward.edu
- **San Francisco State University**, 415-338-2218, http://athletics.sfsu.edu
- **St. Mary's College**, 925-631-4392, www.stmarys-ca.edu/athletics
- **Santa Clara University**, 408-554-4063, http://santaclarabroncos.collegesports.com
- **San Jose State University**, 877-757-8849, www.sjsuspartans.com

PARTICIPANT SPORTS & ACTIVITIES

The Bay Area is a haven for sports enthusiasts. Popular activities include walking, running, biking, hiking, camping, sailing, tennis, baseball, football, soccer, swimming, lifting weights, and aerobics. Crissy Field in the Golden Gate National Recreation Area is home to some of the world's best windsurfing, and Mount Tamalpais and the Marin Headlands have excellent hiking and biking trails. Area **Parks and Recreation Departments** can assist those interested in specific programs:

- **California Department of Parks and Recreation**, P.O. Box 942896, Sacramento, 94296, 916-653-6995, 800-777-0369, www.cal-parks.ca.gov
- **East Bay Regional Park District**, 2950 Peralta Oaks Court, P.O. Box 5381, Oakland, 94605, 510-562-PARK, www.ebparks.org
- **Marin County Parks**, 3501 Civic Center Dr, Room #415, San Rafael, 415-499-6387
- **Mid-Peninsula Regional Open Space District**, 330 Distel Circle, Los Altos, 94022, 650-691-1200, www.openspace.org, www.co.marin.ca.us/depts/PK/Main/pos/parks.cfm
- **Napa Valley Parks**, 1195 Third St, Room 310, Napa, 707-253-4580, www.co.napa.ca.us/LIVING
- **San Francisco Recreation and Park Department**, 501 Stanyan St, San Francisco, 94117, 415-831-2700, www.parks.sfgov.org
- **San Mateo County Park and Recreation Department**, 455 County Center, 4th Floor, Redwood City, 650-363-4020, www.eparks.net
- **Santa Clara County Parks and Recreation**, 298 Garden Hill Dr, Los Gatos, CA 95032, 408-355-2200, www.parkhere.org
- **Solano County Parks**, 707-784-7514, www.co.solano.ca.us
- **Sonoma County Regional Parks**, 2300 County Center Dr, 120A, Santa Rosa, 707-565-2041, www.sonoma-county.org/parks

Parks and recreation departments for specific cities are listed below:
- **Alameda Recreation and Parks**, 1327 Oak St, 510-747-7529, TTY: 510-522-7538, www.ci.alameda.ca.us/arpd
- **Berkeley Parks Recreation and Waterfront Department**, 2180 Milvia St, Third Floor, 510-981-6700, TTY: 510-981-6903
- **Cupertino Parks and Recreation Department** (and Quinlan Community Center), 10185 North Stelling Rd, 408-777-3120
- **Daly City Parks and Recreation Department**, 111 Lake Merced Blvd, 650-991-8001
- **Emeryville Recreation Department**, 4300 San Pablo Ave, 510-596-3782

- **Foster City Parks**, 650 Shell Blvd, Foster City, 650-286-3392
- **Fremont Recreation Services**, 3300 Capitol Ave, Building B, 510-494-4600
- **Hayward Area Recreation and Park District**, 1099 E St, 510-881-6700, www.hard.dst.ca.us/top
- **Menlo Park Community Services Department**, 701 Laurel St, 650-330-2200
- **Mill Valley Parks and Recreation Commission**, 26 Corte Madera Ave, 415-383-1370
- **Milpitas Recreation Service Department**, 457 East Calaveras Blvd, 408-586-3210
- **Mountain View**, Community Services Department, Recreation Division, 201 South Rengstorff Ave, 650-903-6331
- **Newark Leisure Services Administration**, 34009 Alvarado-Niles Rd, 510-675-5353
- **Newark Recreation Services**, Community Center, 35501 Cedar Blvd, 510-742-4437
- **Novato Community Services**, 75 Rowland Way, #200, 415-899-8200, www.ci.novato.ca.us/parks/index.cfm
- **Oakland Parks and Recreation**, 250 Frank Ogawa Plaza, Suite 3330, 510-238-PARK, TTY: 510-615-5883
- **Pacifica Parks**, Beaches and Recreation Department, 650-738-7381
- **Palo Alto Parks and Golf Division**, 3201 East Bayshore Rd, 650-463-4900
- **Piedmont Recreation Department**, 358 Hillside Ave, 510-420-3070
- **Redwood City Recreation**, 1120 Roosevelt Ave, Redwood City, 650-780-7317
- **Richmond Recreation & Parks Department**, 3230 Macdonald Ave, 510-620-6793
- **San Bruno Recreation Services Department**, 567 El Camino Real, 650-616-7180
- **San Jose Park, Recreation and Neighborhood Services**, 4 North Second St, Suite 600, 408-277-4661
- **San Rafael Parks and Recreation Commission**, 618 B St, 415-485-3333, www.cityofsanrafael.org/parkandrecreation
- **San Ramon Parks and Recreation and Community Center**, 925-973-3200 or visit www.ci.san-ramon.ca.us/parks/parks.htm
- **Santa Rosa Parks and Recreation Commission**, 618 B St, 415-485-3333, www.cityofsanrafael.org/parkandrecreation
- **Sausalito Parks and Recreation Department**, 420 Litho St, 415-289-4152

- **Sunnyvale Parks and Recreation Department,** 550 East Remington Dr, 408-730-7350
- **Greater Vallejo Recreation District**, 395 Amador St, 707-648-4600, www.gvrd.org

BASEBALL/SOFTBALL

Play ball! There are a number of softball and baseball leagues around the Bay Area. The **Northern California Amateur Softball Association** sponsors slow and fast pitch adult and junior leagues. For more information, visit their web site at www.norcalasa.org. For **Little League** contact www.littleleague.org, and for **Pony Baseball/Softball** contact www.pony.org.

City parks and recreation departments are another good place to look for baseball and softball games. (See above and also see **Neighborhood** listings.)

BASKETBALL

San Francisco has a **professional/amateur basketball league**, one for men and one for women. Teams play at Kezar Pavilion on Stanyan and Waller streets. Check www.sanfranciscoproam.com for information about dates and times. For something a little less competitive, check with your local parks and recreation department (see above) or try your community gymnasium or health club, which may have its own league. Among other neighborhood basketball programs are the **Eureka Valley's** league, 415-554-9528, and the **SOMA** league, 415-554-9528. The Sunset has a men's over-35 league, 415-753-7098. For information on **women's basketball teams,** check out www.bayareawomensbasketball.com. **Dream League,** www.dreamleague.org, runs programs for at-risk teens. **San Francisco Gay Men's Basketball**, www.gaybasketball.com/sf/ runs the **Castro Basketball League** at the Upper Noe Recreation Center and open court games at the 6th Street Gym. The YMCA, 415-885-0460, www.ymcasf.org, offers organized youth programs and pick-up games for all ages. **Dolores Park**, at 19th Street and Dolores, also almost always has a pick-up game going.

BICYCLING

Numerous biking trails and bike lanes throughout the Bay Area offer a wide variety of terrain and views. One of the most exciting developments in recent years is the installation of a biking/walking trail ringing the entire bay. While only portions of the Bay Trail have been built to date, supporters insist it will eventually be completed, and will be a definite boon to cyclists.

According to California law, bike riders younger than 18 must wear a bike helmet. Violators are subject to fines.

If pro-bicycle activism interests you, consider joining the local Critical Mass campaign. Since 1992, this bicyclists' movement (they adamantly call themselves a "movement" and not a "group") has taken to the streets on the last Friday of every month. Literally hundreds (sometimes thousands) gather at Justin Herman Plaza and then bicycle, en masse, through the city streets. Their goal is to make their presence known, in the hope that drivers will be more courteous and city leaders will be inspired to make the streets safer for cyclists. This monthly "movement" usually has a police escort to protect them from irate drivers who resent being held up by the group.

Some of the best biking in **San Francisco** is in Golden Gate Park, along the Embarcadero and the Golden Gate Promenade beneath the south end of the Golden Gate Bridge. The stretch runs from the Marina all the way to Fort Point. For more information about trails in San Francisco, bicycle groups, and resources, call the **San Francisco Bicycle Coalition**, 995 Market Street, Suite 1150, 94103, 415-431-BIKE, www.sfbike.org.

The South Bay and the Peninsula have more than 440 miles of biking trails. On the **Peninsula**, the Long Ridge Open Space Preserve provides lovely views, great oaks, grassy knolls, and some of the best single track riding in the area. The trail parallels Skyline Blvd between Page Mill Road and Highway 9. Another great ride is along Montebello Road just off Stevens Canyon Road in **Cupertino**. Here, you'll find creeks, steep hills, and the Ridge Winery. Upper Stevens Creek County Park is another spectacular ride with steep canyons amidst hardwood forests. For more information about biking in the mid-Peninsula, contact the **Silicon Valley Bicycle Coalition** at 408-806-8582, www.svbcbikes.org. In San Mateo County, check out the **Peninsula Bike and Pedestrian Coalition**, www.PenBiPed.org. Another good resource for maps and hooking up with other bikers is through the **Trail Center**, www.trailcenter.org.

Taking your bike across to the biking trails in the **East Bay** and **Marin County** is a fairly easy task as the BART system accommodates bicycles in the last train car, during non-commute hours. Some bus systems also accommodate bikes, as do the many ferryboats that crisscross the bay. Marin Headlands and Mount Tamalpais are fantastic areas to ride. For more information call the **Bicycle Trails Council of Marin**, www.btcmarin.org. In the East Bay check with **The Bicycle Trail Council for the East Bay**, 510-466-5123, www.btceb.org. For some exceptional trails try Tilden Park (see under **Hiking**), Redwood Regional Park, Wildcat Canyon, and Briones Park.

There are many bicycle shops in the Bay Area; consult your Yellow Pages for local listings.

BOWLING

Some might argue that it's not quite a sport, but few would argue that it's a lot of fun. Since the much-bemoaned closure of the famous Japantown Bowl, the city has been left with just two bowling spots. But, you can find more opportunities in the rest of the Bay Area:

- **The Rooftop at Yerba Buena Center Gardens Ice Skating and Bowling Center**, 750 Folsom St, San Francisco, Skating Center, 415-777-3727
- **Presidio National Park Bowl**, Building #93 (between the Presidio's Moraga and Montgomery sts), San Francisco, 415-561-2695
- **Albany Bowl**, 540 San Pablo Ave, Albany, 510-526-8818, www.albanybowl.com
- **AMF Bowling Center**, 300 Park St, Alameda, 510-523-6767
- **Bel Mateo Bowl**, 4332 Olympic Ave, San Mateo, 650-341-2616
- **Fourth Street Bowl**, 1441 North Fourth St, San Jose, 408-453-5555
- **Mel's AMF**, 2580 El Camino Real, Redwood City, 650-369-5584
- **Moonlight Lanes**, 2780 El Camino Real, Santa Clara, 408-296-7200
- **Palo Alto Bowl**, 4329 El Camino Real, Palo Alto, 650 948-1031
- **Serra Bowl**, 3301 Junipero Serra Blvd, Daly City, 650-992-3444
- **Sea Bowl**, 4625 Coast Highway, Pacifica, 650-738-8190

CHESS

Throughout the day you can see groups eagerly gathering around a small line of checkered tables on **Market Street** near the corner of 5th Street. If you're looking for a good pick-up match, this is the place; all levels are welcome. Tables are usually set up by 2 p.m. and taken down at dusk. It generally costs 50 cents to join a game, and often players agree to bet $1 per match. Another outdoor spot with more atmosphere hasn't quite caught on yet. But if you don't mind bringing your own pieces, and your own opponent, you can play at one of the stone tables with built-in game boards at **Yerba Buena Gardens**. The tables are located on the southwest side of the gardens, near the pedestrian bridge to the Zeum, and there's no place better to be on a sunny afternoon.

In the North Bay, the **Depot in Mill Valley** has permanent chess tables set up throughout the square. Donated by famed local music promoter Bill Graham, these tables are busy with pick-up games of both casual and speed chess from afternoon until evening; occasionally a pro even stops by.

A good first stop for chess-loving newcomers is **The Northern California Chess Association**, P.O. Box 136, Berkeley, CA 94701, www.calchess.org. Cal Chess maintains lists of active local clubs, events, and tournaments. Below are a few club contacts to get you started. For more information also try the **US Chess Federation**, www.uschess.org.

- **East Bay Chess Club**, 1940 Virginia St, Berkeley, 510-845-1041, www.eastbaychess.com; open daily for drop-in games, organizes lectures, exhibitions, and tournaments
- **Fremont Chess Club**, meets Fridays at 7 p.m. at the Centerville Library, 3801 Nicolet Ave, 510-656-8505, www.fremontchessclub.org
- **Kolty Chess Club**, meets Thursday evenings at the Campbell Community Center, 408-902-8590, Campbell, www.angelfire.com/ca2/kolty
- **The Mechanics' Institute Chess Club**, 57 Post St, San Francisco, 415-421-2258, www.chessclub.org; daily drop-in games, Tuesday night marathons, programs for children
- **San Mateo-Burlingame Chess Club**, meets Thursdays at 7 p.m. at the Burlingame Lions Club, 990 Burlingame Ave, Burlingame, new players welcome, 650-591-8857, www.BurlingameChessClub.com

If you're interested in chess lessons try one of the following or look under "Chess Instruction" in the Yellow Pages:

- **Academic Chess**, 4524 Anza St, San Francisco, 415-668-8841, www.academicchess.com; classroom and after-school programs
- **The Berkeley Chess School**, P.O. Box 136, Berkeley, 510-843-0150, www.berkeleychessschool.org; teaches chess in Bay Area schools, runs summer chess camps, and offers Friday night chess games
- **Know Chess**, 4019 Rector Common, Fremont, 510-794-9850, www.knowchess.com; programs throughout Bay Area schools for children

FENCING

Those interested in the fine art of the foil may want to contact the **Northern California Division of the United States Fencing Association**, www.norcalfence.org, which keeps a list of local fencing teachers, as well as information on competitions. **The Bay Cup**, www.thebaycup.org, sponsors Bay Area fencing competitions for youth and adults at various skill levels, and maintains a list of active clubs in the area and information on fencing summer camps. Bay Cup membership is $40. Another good source of information is www.fencing.net, a national web site that offers information on technique, tournaments, and equipment, and also hosts discussion forums. Below are a few local clubs and instruction centers; many colleges and universities have competitive fencing teams, and a few park and recreation departments also offer classes. Contact your local park and recreation department to find out about offerings in your neighborhood.

SAN FRANCISCO
- **Golden Gate Fencing Center**, 2417 Harrison St, 415-626-7910, www.gofencing.com
- **Halberstadt Fencers' Club**, 621 South Van Ness Ave, 415-863-3838, www.halberstadtfc.com
- **Massialas Foundation at Halberstadt**, www.fencingUSA.com
- **San Francisco City College**, 50 Phelan Ave, San Francisco, 415-239-3000

PENINSULA AND SOUTH BAY
- **Accademia di Scherma Classica**, 14 Bancroft Rd, Burlingame, 650-401-3838, www.scherma.org
- **California Fencing Academy**, 5289F Prospect Rd, San Jose, 408-865-1950, www.calfencingacademy.com
- **Cardinal Fencing** (Stanford Fencing Club), 375 Santa Teresa St, Stanford, 650-725-0733, www.cardinalfencingclub.com
- **Coastside Fencing Club**, Sea Crest Parks and Recreation, 901 Arnold Way, Half Moon Bay, 650-219-5335, www.geocities.com/anthony joslin@sbcglobal.net
- **Elite Musketeers Fencers Club**, 160-B Constitution Dr, Menlo Park, 650-353-0717, www.emfc.net
- **The Fencing Center**, 110 Stockton Ave, San Jose, 408-298-8230, www.fencing.com
- **First Place Fencing Club**, 853J Industrial Rd, San Carlos, 650-954-3196, www.firstplacefencing.com

EAST BAY
- **East Bay Fencers' Gym**, 3265 Market St, YMCA, Oakland, 510-654-9622, www.eastbayfencers.com
- **Fremont Fencers**, 3355 Country Dr, Fremont, and Centerville Community Center, Fremont, 510-791-4324, www.fremontfencers.com
- **Las Positas Fencing Center**, Forresters Hall, 171 South J St, Livermore, 925-373-5862, www.laspositasfencingcenter.com
- **Pacific Fencing Club**, 2329 Santa Clara Ave, Alameda, 510-814-1800, www.pacificfencingclub.com
- **Sport Fencing Center**, 5221 Central Ave #9, Richmond, 510-528-5110, www.sportfencingcenter.com
- **Sword Play Fencing Academy**, 1061 Shary Circle, Suite A-1, Concord, 925-687-9883, www.swordplayfencing.net

NORTH BAY
- **La Spada Nimica**, 309 Todd Way, Mill Valley, 415-388-8939, http://home.pacbell.net/parsec-e
- **Marin Fencing Academy**, P.O. Box 518, San Anselmo, CA 94979, 415-458-4271, www.marinfencing.com
- **Sonoma Fencing Academy**, 239 Water St, Petaluma, 707-763-8290, www.sonomafencing.com

FISHING

You'll find a large number of fishing spots across the Bay Area (the following only details a smattering of the fishing opportunities). Check with your local outfitter for more ideas. In San Francisco, people fish for bass, perch, shark, and even crab right off the pier near Crissy Field in the Presidio. The piers near Fisherman's Wharf are also popular fishing spots.

Lake Merced is stocked with trout and catfish, and the Lake Merced Boating and Fishing Company, 415-753-1101, sells lures and can provide more information about fishing here. Lake Anza, north of Berkeley, in Tilden Park is open for fishing throughout the year. Oakland's Lake Temescal, located next to the junction of highways 24 and 13, is stocked periodically with rainbow trout. Other fish in Lake Temescal include large-mouth bass, red-eared sunfish, bluegill, and catfish. The pier in Pacifica is also a popular spot, and is a great place to watch the sunset.

For those more interested in fishing on the open ocean, check www.sfsportfishing.com, where the San Francisco Bay Area commercial fishing fleets have pooled charter information onto one page. This web site lists the fleet of boats leaving from Fisherman's Wharf, Emeryville Marina, Berkeley Marina, Half Moon Bay, Point San Pablo, Sausalito, and San Rafael. The California Department of Fish and Game, 1416 Ninth Street, Sacramento, requires you to obtain a permit/license to fish. You can contact them at 916-227-2245, www.dfg.ca.gov. Or visit your local bait and tackle store.

However, if you're planning to take your catch of the day home for dinner, you should be aware that because of higher mercury levels, PCBs, and other chemicals found in the San Francisco Bay, public health officials advise adults to eat a maximum of two servings per month of fish caught in Bay waters. Striped bass over 35 inches long—as well as croakers, surf-perches, bullheads, gobies, and shellfish from the Richmond Harbor Channel should not be eaten at all. Pregnant women, nursing mothers, and children should not eat more than one serving of SF Bay fish per month. They should avoid entirely striped bass over 27 inches and shark. These advisory guidelines do not apply to salmon, anchovies, herring, and smelt from the Bay; other fish caught in the delta or ocean; or commercial fish. For more information check out www.dfg.ca.gov.

ULTIMATE FRISBEE AND DISC GOLF

Contact the local **Ultimate Players Association**, 800-UPA-4384, www.upa.org, for more information.

For disc golfers, San Francisco has a new popular 9-hole course in **Golden Gate Park**, at Marx Meadow between 25th and 30th avenues on the north side of the park off of Fulton Street, here on a trial basis, and efforts are now underway to make it permanent. For more information check out the **San Francisco Disc Golf Club**, www.sfdiscgolf.org, which also lists courses throughout the Bay Area.

GOLFING

The Bay Area is home to a fantastic array of golf courses. San Francisco offers a Resident Golf Card, good for booking advance tee times and local course discounts. The card costs $40 and is valid for one year. Contact Parks and Recreation for more information, 415-831-2700.

SAN FRANCISCO
- **Gleneagles**, 2100 Sunnydale Ave, 415-587-2425, 9-hole course in McLaren Park.
- **Golden Gate Park Golf Course**, 47th Ave and Fulton St, Golden Gate Park, 415-751-8987; 9-hole course, a good spot for beginning golfers.
- **Harding Park**, 1 Harding Rd, 415-664-4690, www.harding-park.com; undoubtedly the most popular public course in San Francisco, and host to a variety of competitions; situated near the beach at Lake Merced, 18-hole tournament course and 9-hole practice course.
- **Lincoln Park Golf Course**, 34th Ave and Clement St, 415-750-GOLF, www.playlincoln.com; a local favorite, this 18-hole course offers sweeping scenic views of the Golden Gate Bridge; make a day of it, walk the nearby Lands End trail after your game, and stop to take in the latest exhibit at the Palace of the Legion of Honor Museum.
- **Mission Bay Golf Center**, 1200 6th St, 415-431-7888; practice your swing at this local driving range and putting green.
- **Presidio Golf Club**, 300 Finley Rd (in the Presidio), 415-561-4661, www.presidiogolf.com; not just for high-ranking military officers anymore, this 18-hole course set in the lush Presidio National Park is now open to the public.

NORTH BAY
- **Indian Valley Golf Club**, 3035 Novato Blvd, Novato, 415-897-1118, www.ivgc.com, 18 holes, instruction, bar and grill.
- **Mare Island Golf Course**, 1800 Club Dr, Vallejo, 707-562-GOLF, www.mareislandgolfclub.com, recently expanded into a full 18-hole facility.
- **McInnis Park Golf Center**, 350 Smith Range Rd, San Rafael, 415-492-1800, www.mcinnisparkgolfcenter.com, 9 holes, golf academy, driving range, miniature golf course, batting cages, restaurant.
- **Mill Valley Golf Course**, 280 Buena Vista Ave, Mill Valley, 415-388-9982, 9 holes.
- **Napa Municipal Golf Course at Kennedy Park**, 2295 Streblow Dr, Napa, 707-255-4333, www.playnapa.com, 18 holes.
- **Peacock Gap Golf & Country Club**, 333 Biscayne Dr, San Rafael, 415-453-4940, www.peacockgapgolf.com, 18 holes, two putting greens, driving range, instruction, restaurant and bar.
- **San Geronimo Golf Course**, 5800 Sir Francis Drake Blvd, San Geronimo, 415-488-4030, 18 holes.
- **Stone Tree**, 9 StoneTree Lane, Novato, 415-209-6090, www.stonetreegolf.com, new 18-hole championship course.

EAST BAY
- **Chuck Corica Golf Course**, 1 Clubhouse Memorial Rd, Alameda, 510-747-7800, two 18-hole courses, par 3 executive course, putting greens, restaurant, lighted driving range.
- **Lake Chabot Golf Course**, 11450 Golf Links Rd, Oakland, 510-351-5812, 27 holes, panoramic views.
- **Metropolitan Golf Links**, 10051 Doolittle Dr, Oakland, 510-569-5555; practice your swing at this local driving range.
- **Montclair Golf Course**, 2477 Monterey Blvd, 510-482-0422, 9-hole course.
- **Tilden Park Golf Course**, Grizzly Peak Blvd and Shasta Rd, Berkeley, 510-848-7373, 18 holes.

PENINSULA/SOUTH BAY
- **Blackberry Farm**, 22100 Stevens Creek Blvd, Cupertino, 408-253-9200, www.blackberryfarm.org, 9-hole course.
- **Cinnabar Hills**, 23600 McKean Rd, San Jose, 408-323-5200, www.cinnabarhills.com, 27 holes.
- **Coyote Creek** 1 Coyote Creek Golf Dr, San Jose, 408-463-1400, www.coyotecreekgolf.com, two 18-hole courses.

- **Crystal Springs**, 6650 Golf Course Dr, Burlingame, 650-342-0603, www.playcrystalsprings.com, 18-hole championship course, tournaments, restaurant and bar.
- **Cypress Golf Course**, 2001 Hillside Blvd, Colma, 415-992-5155, www.cypressgc.com, 9 holes, driving range, instruction.
- **Deep Cliff Golf Course**, 10700 Clubhouse Lane, Cupertino, 408-253-5357, 18-hole course.
- **Half Moon Bay Golf Links**, 2 Miramontes Point Rd, Half Moon Bay, 650-726-4438, www.halfmoonbaygolf.com, two 18-hole championship courses, ocean views, lessons, restaurant.
- **Mariner's Point**, end of Mariner's Island Blvd, Foster City, 650-573-7888, www.marinerspoint.com, 9 holes, bayside course.
- **Palo Alto Municipal Golf Course**, 1875 Embarcadero, Palo Alto, 650-856-0881 www.city.palo-alto.ca.us/golf, recently renovated 18 hole championship course, lighted driving range, restaurant and bar, putting green area.
- **Poplar Creek**, 1700 Coyote Point Dr, San Mateo, 650-522-4653, www.poplarcreekgolf.com, 18 holes, restaurant, junior golfer program.
- **San Jose Municipal Golf Course**, 1560 Oakland Rd, San Jose, 408-441-4653, 18 holes.
- **Santa Clara Golf and Tennis Club**, 5155 Stars & Stripes Dr, Santa Clara, 408-980-9515, 18 holes, restaurant, Santa Clara residents get preferential rates and tee time sign-ups at this municipal course.
- **Sharp Park Golf Course**, foot of Sharp Park Rd off Interstate 280, Pacifica, 650-355-8546 or 650-359-3380, 18 holes.
- **Shoreline Golf Links**, 2600 North Shoreline Blvd, Mountain View, 650-969-2041, 18 holes.

HANG GLIDING/PARAGLIDING

Originated by French mountain climbers eager to descend the mountain before sundown, paragliding is a popular sport in the Bay Area. Venture down to Fort Funston to watch the paragliders and hang gliders soar through the air. Suspended in a harness, hang gliders are attached to large kite-like gliders that help them sail through the air. Increasingly popular is the art of tandem gliding, where two people ride the same glider together. If you've never been before, check out a program or club that can offer you lessons in the basics—launching, turning, and landing. For more information check out the **US Hang Gliding Association's** web site, www.ushga.org and www.all-about-hang-gliding.com. Local clubs include **The Fellow Feathers Fort Funston**, www.flyfunston.org; the **Marin County Hang Gliding Association**, www.mchga.org; and the **Bay Area Paragliding Association**, www.sfbapa.org. There are a number of options for lessons, including the **San Francisco Hang Gliding Center**, 510-528-2300, www.sfhanggliding.com, which offers gliding lessons at Mt. Tamalpais in Marin.

HIKING

If taking off for a hike away from the urban bustle is something that strikes your fancy, you'll have many opportunities to indulge without straying too far from home. San Francisco offers plenty of hikes, including the famous **Golden Gate Bridge walk** (the Bridge is about a mile and a half long). Contact the folks at the Golden Gate Bridge Plaza, San Francisco, 415-921-5858, for more details. Longer hikes can be found at **Presidio National Park** in San Francisco. Along the water, Crissy Field is a popular place for walking and running. A wide paved pathway along the waterfront makes this area accessible to wheelchairs and baby strollers as well. **Marin Headlands**, just beyond the northern end of the Golden Gate Bridge, is nice. An enjoyable option for a long afternoon is to take the ferry to Angel Island to hike the island. **Mount Tamalpais** in Marin County and **Tilden Park** in the Oakland/Berkeley hills are great places to explore. Drive a little further north (about 90 minutes) to the popular **Point Reyes National Seashore** for exceptional hiking and views. See also **Trails** in the **Running** section, later in this chapter.

If you want to escape for more than a day, consider **Yosemite National Park**, located about a four-hour's drive to the east, in the Sierra Nevada. Yosemite is a popular vacation destination for Bay Area residents, many of whom visit in the fall or early spring to avoid the summer tourist season. Despite what you may have heard about the crowds in the park, though, the only consistently crowded part is Yosemite Valley; if you set out on foot for the high country, you can leave the motor homes behind. For more park information contact **Yosemite National Park**, Wilderness Permits, P.O. Box 545, Yosemite, CA 95389, 800-436-7275. **Lake Tahoe** and the **Sierras**, which offer prime hiking and camping, are also about four hours away. Consult with the **Forest Service** for the best hikes: US Forest Service Information, Room 521, 630 Sansome Street, San Francisco, CA 94111.

HORSEBACK RIDING

Public trails and riding areas abound on the coast in and around Half Moon Bay, as well as in the wooded hills of Woodside, Portola Valley, and in Marin

County. If you have your own horse and are looking for a place to board in San Francisco, Golden Gate Park is home to **Golden Gate Park Stables**, 415-668-7360. The East Bay regional parks (see details below) offer a variety of boarding and trail options, and on the peninsula **Huddart Park** in Woodside is a popular riding spot. And whether you're an expert or beginner, you can saddle up at one of the popular stables in Half Moon Bay that offer guided rides along the water's edge. In the North Bay, the **National Golden Gate Recreation Area** offers a range of spectacular horse-friendly coastal trails, and **Miwok Stables** in Tennessee Valley, 415-383-8048, runs guided rides in the park.

In the East Bay, you can rent a horse for a trail ride at **Las Trampas Stables, Little Hills Regional Recreation Area, Las Trampas Regional Wilderness**, in Danville, 925-838-7546, and kids can ride ponies at **Tilden Regional Park**, Berkeley, 510-527-0421. There are also stables in a handful of East Bay regional parks including the **Chabot Stables and Skyline Equestrian Center**, in Anthony Chabot Regional Park, Skyline Boulevard and Keller Avenue, 510-336-0850. For more information on these programs call 510-562 PARK.

For further information on places to take guided rides, rent horses for the day, or take lessons, see "Horse Rentals" and "Horse Stables" in your local Yellow Pages.

KAYAKING

Sea kayaking is another way to enjoy the Bay. It's best to kayak early in the morning when the water is more likely to be calm. The semi-secluded, relatively calm waters of Tomales Bay, in Marin County, are protected from the pounding waves of the Pacific and the winds of nearby Inverness, making this one of the most popular spots in the Bay Area for this sport. Contact **Tomales Bay State Park**, 415-669-1140.

- **Blue Waters Kayaking**, Point Reyes National Seashore, Inverness, 415-669-2600
- **California Adventures**, 2301 Bancroft Way, Berkeley, 510-642-4000
- **California Canoe & Kayak**, 409 Water St, Oakland, 510-893-7833
- **Environmental Traveling Companions**, Fort Mason Center, Building C, 415-474-7662
- **Sea Trek Ocean Kayaking Center**, Schoonmaker Point Marina, Sausalito, 415-488-1000, all year

RUNNING

Running clubs are a great way to get in shape, enjoy the outdoors, and make new friends in a new city. Many Bay Area clubs welcome walkers as well as those training for marathons, and several sponsor their own events and races. Most have some sort of annual membership fee, in the $20–$30 range, that helps support the club.

- **Diablo Road Runners**, www.diablorunners.com; Contra Costa County club with regular Wednesday evening and Saturday morning runs at a variety of spots from tracks to trails, open to many ages and ability levels, sponsors of the annual Brickyard 4- and 8-mile race.
- **Golden Gate Running Club**, www.goldengaterunningclub.org; Sunday runs in the park at 10 a.m., followed by brunch, open to all ability levels, track workout Wednesday night at Kezar Stadium, meeting at the southeast corner of the track at 7 p.m.
- **Hoy's Excelsior Running Club**, www.tkecapital.com/hoys-excelsior. htm; regular Tuesday and Thursday 6 p.m. track runs at Kezar Stadium, Sunday morning long Golden Gate Park and Bay Area trail runs, competitive teams.
- **Lake Merritt Joggers and Striders**, 510-644-4224, www.lmjs.org; club hosts runs at Lake Merritt in Oakland every fourth Sunday at 9 a.m: 5K, 10K, 15K, and a 5K walk. On the morning of San Francisco's Bay-to-Breakers, the club sponsors an alternative race in the Berkeley Hills—the Tilden Tough Ten, the first race in the renowned Triple Crown Trail Championship.
- **Palo Alto Run Club**, www.parunclub.com; 5- to 7.5-mile runs on the first Sunday of the month, at 8:30 a.m., followed by a pot-luck tailgate brunch; Wednesday runs 6:15 p.m. leave from the Lucie Stern Community Center, 1305 Middlefield Rd, in Palo Alto.
- **Pamakid Runners Club**, 415-333-4780, www.pamakids.org; weekly fun runs, racing teams practice at Kezar Stadium on Thursdays at 6:30 p.m.
- **San Francisco Dolphin South End Runners**, 415-978-0837, www.dserunners.com; open to all levels and encourages women runners, older runners, beginners, and kids. Walkers welcome. The DSE holds runs throughout San Francisco almost every Sunday at 9 a.m. and sponsors special challenge events throughout the year.
- **San Francisco FrontRunners**, 415-978-2429, www.sffront runners.com; club for the LGBT community and friends, regular Tuesday evening run along the Embarcadero and dinner, and Saturday morning brunch and run in Golden Gate Park, open to walkers.
- **San Francisco Road Runners Club**, 415-273-5731, www.sfrrc.org; Saturday 7:45 a.m. runs at Marina Green divided into pace groups, training programs for beginners and marathon and half-marathon runners, Tuesday tack runs at Kezar Stadium at 7 p.m., Wednesday night runs at Marin Green, distance runs throughout San Francisco and Marin County.

- **Stevens Creek Striders**, www.stevenscreekstriders.org; runs every Saturday at 8:30 a.m. in Stevens Creek County Park, followed by breakfast. From April through late October a group also runs at Rancho San Antonio County Park & Open Space Preserve in Cupertino on Tuesdays and Thursdays at 6 p.m.
- **Tamalpa Runners' Association**, 415-721-3791, www.tamalpa runners.org; holds regular runs on Mt. Tamalpais; racing teams for road, cross country, and distance trips; coaching and youth activities; Saturday 9 a.m. 7- to 10-mile fun run on Mt. Tam, Tuesday morning training sessions, Wednesday night 7-mile runs at Blackie's Pasture in Tiburon.

RACES

- **Bay to Breakers**, 415-359-2800, www.baytobreakers.com; San Francisco's moveable Mardi Gras includes as many (or more) costumed revelers as serious racers, from the Embarcadero up the Hayes Street Hill through Golden Gate Park, 12K, May
- **Bridge to Bridge**, 415-995-6868, www.bridgetobridge.com; 12K (shorter 7K route) run from the Bay Bridge to the Golden Gate, October
- **Escape from Alcatraz**, 831-373-0678, www.tricalifornia.com; Triathlon—1.5-mile swim from Alcatraz Island in the San Francisco Bay, 18-mile bike ride out the Great Highway, through the Golden Gate Park, concluding with an 8-mile run through the Golden Gate National Recreation Area, finishing at the Marina Green, July
- **San Francisco Marathon**, 415-284-9653, www.runsfm.com; also shorter half-marathon and 5K run/walk option, July

TRAILS

With its fantastic weather and stunning landscape, the Bay Area has a host of amazing trails, including those listed below:
SAN FRANCISCO
- **The Coastal Trail**: Runs from the Golden Gate Bridge just over 9 miles south through China Beach, Land's End, and the Cliff House, Lake Merced, and Fort Funston.
- **The Embarcadero**: This long concrete, palm-lined promenade stretches along the Bay from the Ferry Building to Fisherman's Wharf for about 2 miles.
- **Golden Gate Park**: The city's main park has a number of trails of varying length, both paved and dirt. A 7.4-mile perimeter loop goes around the entire park; a 2-mile loop circles around Stow Lake and goes up Strawberry Hill.

- **Golden Gate Promenade**: This 3.5-mile multi-use path at Crissy Field is extremely popular with joggers, walkers, bicyclists, and dog walkers; the paved path starts a little past the Yacht Harbor and ends near the Fort Point Coast Guard Station. This run offers fantastic views of the Bay and the Golden Gate Bridge. If you're feeling really ambitious, you can even run across the bridge—but be warned, it's usually quite windy!
- **Lake Merced**: Check out the 4.5-mile paved and dirt loop alongside the water at Lake Merced Boulevard and Skyline.
- **Ocean Beach**: You can run on the sand or along the esplanade. The run alongside the beach is pretty flat and you can make it a few blocks or a few miles—depending on your endurance; head up toward the Cliff House for great views and a steeper workout.

For more information on San Francisco trails, contact **The Golden Gate National Recreation Area**, 415-561-4700, www.nps.gov/goga, or the **San Francisco Recreation and Park Department**, 415-831-2700, www.parks.sfgov.org

PENINSULA AND SOUTH BAY

- **Edgewood Park**: This park has a handful of dirt hillside trails trekking up and downhill amid the dense forested areas and the open grasslands. In the spring, the fields here are blanketed with colorful wildflowers. The trails are also excellent for hikers; see bulletin boards in the park for information on free guided nature walks. Main park entrance is at Edgewood Rd off of I-280 in Redwood City.
- **Huddart Park**: Set in the high hills amid lush redwoods, the park offers a number of trails of varying length and difficulty; park entrance is at the top of Kings Mountain Rd in Woodside.
- **Rancho San Antonio Open Space Preserve**: A popular site with runners and hikers, the reserve offers more than 20 miles of scenic, hilly trails; Cristo Rey Dr off of Foothill Expressway in Mountain View.
- **San Bruno Mountain**: Twelve miles of trails snaking up and downhill. Summit Trail heads 1,314 feet to the top and boasts the best views; wildflowers and butterflies abound in the spring. Main park entrance is at Guadalupe Canyon Pkwy in Brisbane, $3 fee for cars.
- **Sawyer Camp Trail**: This 12-mile waterside loop is the most popular trail on the peninsula. The path is paved with some dirt areas, and mostly flat. You'll meet lots of fellow runners here, as well as bicyclists, walkers, parents pushing strollers, and rollerbladers. The scenic trail winds around the blue waters of Crystal Springs Reservoir, and mile markers are posted along the way to help you keep track. The main entrance is at Skyline Blvd and Highway 92 in San Mateo.

- **Stanford University**: Lots of paved trails weave through the Palo Alto palm tree–lined campus; routes are popular with bikers and walkers too. For a map check www.stanford.edu.
- **Sweeney Ridge**: Steep and rolling coastal hills with ridges overlooking the peninsula and the Pacific Ocean. There are three trails with about 10 miles of space; the Sweeney Ridge Trail is the easiest. Take Sneath Lane west to Sweeney Ridge or you can access the main trail from Skyline College, just off of parking area 2, San Bruno.

For more information on Peninsula trails, contact the **San Mateo County Park and Recreation Department**, 650-363-4020, www.eparks.net; for more on South Bay trails, contact Santa Clara County Park and Recreation, 408-355-2200, www.parkhere.org.

EAST BAY

- **Coyote Hills Regional Park**: Offering vistas of the Bay, marshlands, hills, and multiple trails, the Alameda Creek Trail is a popular, long, paved, flat 12-mile trail along the south side of the creek from the mouth of Niles Canyon west to the Bay; there's an additional 3.5-mile loop trail making the run west from Niles Canyon along the trail, through Coyote Hills, and back again a full marathon length. There are markers along the way at quarter-mile intervals; 8000 Patterson Ranch Rd, Fremont.
- **Nimitz Way**: One of the most popular multi-use pathways in the East Bay, this paved 8-mile trail starting at Inspiration Point has terrific views; Wildcat Canyon Road, Tilden Park, Berkeley.

For more information on East Bay trails, contact the **East Bay Regional Park District**, 510-562-PARK, www.ebparks.org.

NORTH BAY

- **The Dipsea Trail**: This 7.1-mile trail from Mill Valley to Stinson Beach is probably the best known trail in the North Bay. Twisting dirt trails wander amid shady trees, bringing you through Mt. Tamalpais State Park, Muir Woods National Monument, and the Golden Gate Recreational Area. There are a few steep steps to climb at one point along the way—676 to be exact!
- **The Marin Headlands**: There are a number of trails here, including several near Point Bonita Lighthouse and Hawk Hill with spectacular views of San Francisco and the Golden Gate Bridge.
- **Tennessee Valley**: Follow the main trail from to the beach and back, about 4 miles total. Take the Highway 1 exit off of 101, and follow the signs.

- **Wolf Ridge Loop**: This 5.5-mile path starts at Rodeo Beach and climbs almost 900 feet upward before dropping back down to sea level again. Rodeo Beach has strong currents and undertows; swimming here is not recommended.

For more information on Marin County trails, contact the **Golden Gate National Recreation Area**, 415-561-4700, www.nps.gov/goga, or Marin County Parks, 415-499-6387.

ROCK CLIMBING

To keep your finger muscles in shape, the Bay Area has a number of climbing gyms including:
- **Berkeley Ironworks**, 800 Potter St, Berkeley, 510-981-9900
- **Mission Cliffs**, 2295 Harrison St, San Francisco, 415-550-0515, www.touchstoneclimbing.com
- **Planet Granite Rock Climbing Gym**, 2901 Mead Ave, Santa Clara, 408-727-2777
- **Twisters Gym**, 2639 Terminal Blvd, Mountain View, 650-967-5581
- **Vertex Climbing Center**, 3358a Coffey Lane, Santa Rosa, 707-573-1608, www.climbvertex.com

A number of local parks in Berkeley also have excellent outdoor climbing areas:
- **Contra Costa Rock Park**, 869-A Contra Costa Ave
- **Cragmont Rock Park**, 960 Regal Rd
- **Glendale La Loma Park**, 1339 La Loma Ave
- **Great Stoneface Park**, 1930 Thousand Oaks Blvd
- **Grotto Rock Park**, 879 Santa Barbara Rd
- **Indian Rock Park**, 1950 Indian Rock Ave
- **Mortar Rock Park**, 901 Indian Rock Ave
- **Remillard Park**, 80 Poppy Lane

For more information contact the **Berkeley Parks, Recreation and Waterfront Department**, 2180 Milvia St, Third Floor, 510-981-6700.

SAILING

According to aficionados, the sailing and windsurfing in San Francisco Bay is top-notch. The annual opening day on the Bay brings out hundreds of sailors and spectators each May. Although sailing is possible here year round, this event serves as the ceremonial, if not official, kickoff of the summer sailing season. Throughout the year the Bay is the place for various sailing regattas, from the casual Friday night beer can race to the competitive world championship.

Many of the local yacht clubs have summer sailing programs for children and classes for adults wanting to learn how to sail. For information on sailing schools, check out the nonprofits and clubs below or look in the Yellow Pages under "Sailing Instruction."

SAN FRANCISCO

- **Cal Sailing Club**, nonprofit membership sailing club that offers lessons at the Berkeley Marina, membership is $60 for 3 months or $200 per year, all activities are free to members—lessons, cruises, and use of the club's sailboats and sailboards; visit www.cal-sailing.org to become a member or find out more.
- **Lake Merced, Learn-to-Sail** program for at-risk youth on Lake Merced, offered by America True with the San Francisco Parks and Recreation Department and San Francisco State University; contact America True, Pier 40, San Francisco, 415-974-1018, www.america true.org.
- **The Lake Merritt Boating Center** offers beginning, intermediate, and advanced sailing classes, youth programs and summer camp at Lake Merritt. Advanced classes also take to the waters of the San Francisco Bay from the Oakland Estuary. Windsurfing, kayaking, canoeing, and rowing programs are also available at the lake, 568 Bellevue Ave, Oakland, 510-238-2196, www.oaklandnet.com.
- **Robert W. Crown Memorial Beach**; during summer weekends you can rent sailboards and take lessons at this shoreline gem, located at 8th St and Otis Dr in Alameda; contact the East Bay Regional Park District for more information, 510-562-PARK.
- **Sailing Education Adventures**; this nonprofit offers adult beginning and advanced classes, and youth summer sailing camps; boats are located at the Clipper Yacht Harbor in Sausalito, Building E, Room 235, Fort Mason Center, San Francisco, 415-775-8779, www.sailsea.org
- **Shoreline Aquatic Center**, 3160 North Shoreline Blvd, Shoreline Park, Mountain View, offers sailing, windsurfing, and kayaking lessons and youth summer sailing camps on a 50-acre man-made salt lake 650-965-7474, www.shorelinelake.com

SCUBA AND FREE DIVING

Northern California's waters are not warm, so be sure you have a thick wetsuit when you scuba dive in Monterey Bay. With the rich kelp forests, you'll probably be underwater with the sea otters. If you have strong lungs, try free diving (diving without a tank) for abalone off the northern coast of California by Mendocino. Make sure to get a fishing license if you are catching abalone or any fish. Also familiarize yourself with the rules regarding size and limits. Contact the **Department of Fish and Game** at 916-227-2245, www.dfg.ca.gov, for more information.

- **Any Water Sports**, 1130 Saratoga, San Jose, 408-244-4433, www.anywater.com
- **Cal School of Diving**, 1750 6th St, Berkeley, 510-524-3248, www.caldive.net
- **Diver Dan's**, 2245 El Camino Real, Santa Clara, 408-984-5819
- **Mistix State Park Reservation System**, Point Lobos, Bluefish Cove, Whalers Cove, and Monastery Beach (the latter is for experienced divers only), 800-444-7275, www.reserveamerica.com
- **Monterey Bay Dive Center**, 225 Cannery Row, Monterey, 831-656-0454, www.montereyscubadiving.com
- **Monterey Bay Harbormaster**, 408-646-3950

SKATING—ROLLER / IN-LINE / ICE

Every Friday night in-line skaters, sometimes more than 500 at a time, meet at San Francisco's Ferry Building to tour the city on wheels.

Roller-skating, in-line skating, and skateboarding (see below) are all popular activities in San Francisco, especially on weekends in Golden Gate Park. If you don't own your own skates, head for Fulton Street along the northern end of the park in the morning and look for the brightly colored rent-a-skate vans parked there. Alternatively, there are plenty of skate shops that will be more than happy to outfit you in the latest gear.

If you'd rather skate at an ice rink, you're in luck. After years without a regular indoor ice skating rink, San Francisco now offers an NHL-sized (200' by 85') hockey rink at the Yerba Buena Gardens downtown.

SAN FRANCISCO
- **DLX SF Skateboards**, 1831 Market St, 415-626-5588
- **FTC Skate Shop**, 1632 Haight St, 415-626-0663, www.ftcsf.com
- **Golden Gate Park Skate & Bike**, 3038 Fulton St, 415-668-1117
- **Skates on Haight**, 1818 Haight St, 415-752-8375
- **Yerba Buena Center Gardens Ice Skating and Bowling Center**, 750 Folsom St, 415-777-3727

NORTH BAY
- **Adrenaline Zone Sports**, 124 Calistoga Rd, Santa Rosa, 707-538-7538
- **Brotherhood Board Shop**, 1216 Mendocino Ave, Santa Rosa, 707-546-0660

- **Luckies Skate & Snow**, 1214 Grant Ave, Novato, 415-209-9887
- **Redwood Empire Ice Arena**, 1667 West Steele Lane, Santa Rosa, 707-546-7147, www.snoopyshomeice.com

EAST BAY
- **Berkeley Iceland Ice Skating**, 2727 Milvia St, Berkeley, 510-647-1600
- **Golden Skate**, 2701 Hooper Dr, San Ramon, 925-820-2525, www.thegoldenskate.com, roller skating rink
- **Oakland Ice Center**, 519 18th St, Oakland, 510-268-9000

PENINSULA/SOUTH BAY
- **Belmont Iceland**, 815 Country Rd, Belmont, 650-592-0532
- **Environment Skateboards**, 159 South B St, San Mateo, 650-344-3825
- **Ice Centre of San Jose**, 1500 South Tenth, San Jose, 408-279-6000
- **Ice Chalet**, 2202 San Mateo Fashion Island, San Mateo 650-574-1616
- **Ice Oasis**, 3140 Bay Rd, Redwood City, 650-364-8090
- **Redwood Roller Rink**, 1303 Main St, Redwood City, 650-369-5558
- **The Winter Lodge**, 3009 Middlefield Rd, Palo Alto, 650-493-4566, www.winterlodge.com

SKATEBOARDING

When the X Games came to San Francisco in 1999, kids of all ages and adults packed the bayside bleachers for a chance to see legends like Tony Hawk take on seemingly impossible vertical feats. These days, that daredevil waterside legacy lives on in the summertime at Pier 7, which, while not a sanctioned spot, is a popular gathering place for skaters. Years after shouting the mantra "skateboarding is not a crime," and tangling with frustrated office building owners over oh-so-sleek and inviting staircases, planters, and benches, skateboarding is finally getting its due, and its own public space. Skateparks are popping up all over the peninsula, offering kids and adults alike a place to flip kick and ollie freely—and legally. Below are a just a few local favorite spots; check with your local park and recreation department to find the spot closest to you, try visiting www.caliskatz.com or www.sk8parklist.com, or check out *Thrasher*, www.thrashermagazine.com or *Transworld* magazine, www.skateboarding.com.

Most parks operated by parks require safety gear—helmets, knee and elbow pads; many allow roller blades and a handful also allow BMX bikes, but call ahead to find out. San Francisco has only one official skate park, but the greater Bay Area has stepped up to offer skaters quite a bit more.

SAN FRANCISCO

- **Crocker Amazon Skate Park**, Crocker Amazon Playground, Geneva Ave and Moscow St, 415-831-2700; bowl, ramps, rails, and ledges.

EAST BAY

- **Antioch Skatepark**, 4701 Lone Tree Way, at Prewett Family Park, Antioch, 925-779-7070, www.ci.antioch.ca.us; rails, volcano, pyramid with box, vert wall, stairs.
- **Berkeley Skatepark**, Harrison and Fifth sts, Berkeley, 510-981-6700; 18,000 square feet, double bowl, ramps, recently reopened after chemical clean-up.
- **Cityview Skatepark**, 1177 West Redline Ave, Alameda Point, Alameda, 510-747-7529; recently revamped with design input from local skateboarders, this 15,000-square-foot park has a bowl, banks, a pyramid, ledges, and excellent views. There's a big controversy going on here over bikes, which are not officially allowed, but BMXers have been fighting to get access rights.
- **501 Skateboarding**, 2500 Telegraph Ave, Berkeley, 510-843-1863.
- **Kennelly Skatepark**, Moraga Ave off of Pleasant Valley Rd, Piedmont, 510-420-3070; bowl, concrete features.
- **Livermore Skatepark**, east end of Pacific Ave, in Sunken Gardens Park, Livermore, 925-373-5700, www.larpd.dst.ca.us/skatepark.html; 11,000 square feet, bowls, fun box, pyramid, rails.
- **Pleasanton Skateboard Track**, Sports and Recreation Park, Parkside Dr and Hopyard Rd, Pleasanton, 925-931-5340, www.ci. pleasanton.ca.us; 10,000-square-feet Skatetrack is located at the front of a 105-acre Sports Park.

SOUTH BAY AND PENINSULA

- **Campbell Skatepark**, 1 West Campbell Ave, Campbell, 408-866-2105, www.ci.campbell.ca.us; pyramid, quarter pipe, fun box, rails, half pipe.
- **Derby Skatepark**, 508 Woodland Way, Santa Cruz, 831-420-5270, www.santacruzparksandrec.com; Derby is a classic, one of the first public skateparks in this area with a long concrete snakerun and bowls.
- **The Fun Spot**, Beach St at Washington Ave, Santa Cruz, 831-420-5270, www.santacruzparksandrec.com; 14,000-square-feet asphalt with wooden ramps.
- **Greer Skateboard Park**, 1098 Amarillo Ave, in Greer Park, Palo Alto, 650-329-2390; popular three-bowl complex.
- **Millbrae YMCA Skatepark**, 541 Millbrae Ave, YMCA, Millbrae, 650-697-6852; $5 entrance fee, at the Peninsula Family YMCA.

- **Mountain View Skatepark**, 201 South Rengstorff Ave at Crisanto Ave, northwest corner of Rengstorff Park, Mountain View, 650-903-6331; Sundays the park is reserved exclusively for skaters age 12 and under from 9:30 to 11:30 a.m.; ramp, quarter pipe, mini half pipe, fun box, rails.
- **Phil Shao Memorial Skatepark**, St. Francis St off of Jefferson St, in Red Morton Park, Redwood City, 650-780-7250; new, 13,000 square feet, bowl, concrete features.
- **Sunnyvale Skatepark**, 540 Fair Oaks Ave, in Fair Oaks Park, Sunnyvale, 408-730-7350; 18,500 square feet, big bowl, vertical and street course elements, local favorite.

NORTH BAY
- **Mill Valley Skatepark**, Sycamore Ave, east end of the middle school parking lot, Mill Valley, 415-383-1370.
- **Novato Skatepark**, 1200 Hamilton Pkwy, at Sport Court Island, Novato, 415-893-1100; new 15,000-square-foot park, bowls, walls, curbs, stairs, rails, and ramps.
- **Santa Rosa**, 1725 Fulton Rd, at Youth Community Park, Santa Rosa, 707-543-3292; pool-style features, concrete half acre, three bowls connected by runs, fun box, curb.

SKIING

Sierra Nevada ski resorts are about a four-hour drive east of the Bay Area, along Interstate 80 and Highway 50. If you don't own skiing equipment, several local businesses will rent everything you need to hit the slopes or cross-country ski trails in style, including the national chain, **Recreational Equipment Incorporated (REI)**, 1338 San Pablo Avenue, Berkeley, 510-527-4140. Other places to check: **Boardsports** (snowboarding), 415-929-7873, www.boardsports.com, or **Lombardi Sports**, 415-771-0600, both in San Francisco. For additional outfitters, try the Yellow Pages under "Ski Equipment-Retail."

SKYDIVING

Call one of the listings below for information about lessons, equipment, and getting connected with an instructor for this exhilarating sport:
- **Adrenaline Air Skydiving of Santa Rosa**, 707-573-8116, www.skydivesantarosa.com
- **Skydive Monterey Bay**, 888-229-5867, www.skydivemontereybay.com
- **Skydive San Francisco**, 415-584-6332, www.skydivesf.com

SOCCER

Soccer is a popular sport in the Bay Area. If you are interested in organized games, contact your local parks and recreation department (see above). The **Palo Alto Adult Soccer League (PAASL)**, for men and women ages 25 and over, has an informative web site about local and international soccer, www.paasl.org. PAASL games generally take place at Jane Lathrop Stanford Middle School (next to Mitchell Park) in Palo Alto. Also included on the PAASL web site is a list of pick-up games in the Bay Area. Many such pick-up games are now so crowded that participation may be limited to the first 20 players to arrive. Bring both a white and a colored t-shirt. For youth, the **American Youth Soccer Organization (AYSO)** is the main organization with teams throughout the Bay Area, offering boys and girls a chance to play outdoors, 800-872-2976, www.soccer.org.

SWIMMING POOLS

For those few days when it actually gets hot enough to swim outdoors in San Francisco, you might want to check out a public pool; visit www.parks.sfgov.org for more information. Hours vary, so the best bet is to call ahead. Below is a list of public pools in San Francisco, unless otherwise noted:

- **Alameda Swim Center**, 2256 Alameda Ave, Alameda, 510-522-8107
- **Angelo Rossi**, Arguello Blvd and Anza St, 415-666-7014
- **Balboa Park**, Ocean and San Jose aves, 415-337-4701
- **Coffman Swimming Pool**, Visitacion and Hahn, 415-337-4702
- **Garfield Pool**, 26th and Harrison sts, 415-695-5001
- **Hamilton Recreation Center**, Geary Blvd and Steiner St, 415-292-2001
- **King Swimming Pool**, Keith and Carroll sts, 415-822-2807
- **Sava Swimming Pool**, 19th Ave and Wawona St, 415-753-7000

Some private clubs have pools, including the **Golden Gateway Tennis and Swim Club (GGTSC)**, 370 Drumm St, 415-616-8800, the **Bay Club** at 1 Lombard St, 415-433-2550, and the **Presidio YMCA** at the Presidio, 415-447-9680.

Outdoors, **Lake Anza**, north of Berkeley, in Tilden Park has a sandy beach that is sheltered from the wind. Lifeguards are posted here during the swim season, April 15 to October 15. Picnic grounds are located nearby. There is an entrance fee to the swim area, which has changing rooms and a refreshment stand. The lake is open for fishing throughout the year.

Originally constructed as a storage lake for drinking water, **Lake Temescal**, next to the junction of highways 24 and 13 in Oakland, was opened to the public in 1936. Temescal is a popular urban oasis, with many coming for swimming, fishing, sunbathing, and picnicking. The swim area is open spring through fall. Lifeguards are on duty during posted periods. A snack stand is nearby, and many facilities are accessible to the disabled. There are picnic areas at both ends of the lake (several of them can be reserved for groups), and eight acres of lawn. For more information about Temescal, call 510-562-PARK.

People actually swim in San Francisco Bay, and some more than once. Many such intrepid souls belong to **The Dolphin Club**, 502 Jefferson St, 415-441-9329 or the **South End Rowing Club**, 500 Jefferson St, 415-776-7372. After a cold dip, you can enjoy the clubs' sauna and shower facilities.

TENNIS AND RACQUET SPORTS

San Francisco alone boasts 140 public tennis courts, most of which operate on a first-come, first-served basis. At the east end of **Golden Gate Park** are 21 courts that may be reserved by calling 415-753-7100. There are also quite a few private clubs in and around San Francisco, including the **Golden Gateway Tennis and Swim Club**, 370 Drumm, 415-616-8800; **The Bay Club**, 1 Lombard St, 415-433-2550; **San Francisco Tennis Club**, 645 5th St, 415-777-9000; and the **California Tennis Club**, 1770 Scott St, 415-346-3611. In addition, the **Presidio YMCA** has access to the numerous courts spread throughout the Presidio. Call 415-447-9622 for details. For more information about public tennis and lessons in San Francisco, call 415-751-5639. For courts outside San Francisco check with your local parks and recreation department (see above).

VIDEO ARCADES

Does Ms. Pac-Man make your heart sing? Are you a sucker for Dance Dance Revolution? Whichever it is, you can get your game on at Bay Area arcades, mini golf lands, and family fun centers. If you're feeling hungry too, pizzerias—most notably the massive kids' party land **Chuck E. Cheese**—are usually a good bet to get your gaming fix.

SAN FRANCISCO
- **Bonkers**, 483 Pine St, San Francisco, 415-986-2637
- **Metreon**, a Sony Entertainment Center, 101 4th St, San Francisco, 415-369-6000, www.metreon.com
- **Pier 39**, San Francisco, 415-981-7437, www.pier39.com

NORTH BAY
- **Pinky's Pizza Parlor**, 345 3rd St, San Rafael, 415-453-3582
- **Starbase Arcade**, 1545 4th St, San Rafael, 415-459-7655, www.starbasearcade.com

SOUTH BAY AND PENINSULA
- **Capitol Flea Market**, 3630 Hillcap Ave, San Jose, 408-225-5800
- **Great Mall**, 447 Great Mall Dr, Milpitas, 408-945-4022, www.great mallbayarea.com
- **Malibu Castle**, 320 Blomquist St, Redwood City, 650-367-1906, www.malibugrandprix.com/redwood/
- **Milpitas Golfland**, 1199 Jacklin Rd, 408-263-6855, milpitas. golfland.com
- **Nickel City**, 1711 Branham Lane, San Jose, 408-448-3323
- **Santa Cruz Boardwalk**, 400 Beach St, Santa Cruz, 831-423-5590, www.beachboardwalk.com.
- **Town and Country Billiards**, Mission and San Pedro, Daly City, 650-992-7900

EAST BAY
- **The Bearcade**, UC Berkeley campus, Student Union, lower level, Telegraph Ave and Bancroft Way, Berkeley, 510-642-6000
- **Escapade Family Entertainment Center**, in the Public Market, Emeryville, 510-653-3323

VOLLEYBALL

Whether you are a pro looking to join an indoor tournament team, or a parent looking to sign your kids up for some outdoor summer fun, the Bay Area offers a variety of options for volleyball lovers. Many local park and recreation departments offer lessons, leagues, and special summer camps. If you're new in town, and looking to join a league, a good place to start is the **Northern California Volleyball Association (NCVA)**, 72 Dorman Ave, San Francisco, 415-550-7582, www.ncva.com. Another good resource is www.volleyball.org/bay_area.
- **City Beach Volleyball**, 4020 Technology Place, Fremont, 510-651-2500, and 2911 Mead Ave, Santa Clara, 408-654-9330, www.city beach.com/sports/, sponsors tournaments and runs two game facilities that offer indoor and outdoor volleyball classes.
- **Industrial Volleyball League, Inc.**, 947 Emerald Hill Rd, Redwood City, 650-365-2666, www.ivlinc.com., organizes indoor volleyball competition on the Peninsula and in the South Bay, and runs an open play night for individuals and teams on Fridays from 7 p.m. to 10 p.m. in the large gym at Wilcox High School, 3250 Monroe St, Santa Clara; the fee is $6.
- **Stanford University** runs a popular volleyball clinic for adults in the summer; the cost is $100 per session; for more information or to sign

up visit http://gostanford.collegesports.com/marketplace/events/ volleyball-adult-form.html or call 800-stanford.

WINDSURFING

San Francisco Bay hosts some of the world's best windsurfing. The inexperienced should take instruction before heading out on the Bay, as understanding the ocean's tides and currents is key to staying safe. Check www.iwindsurf.com for updates on wind speed and direction on the Bay. (True windsurfing addicts can even get a pager called "call of the wind," that beeps in with updates on the Bay's wind and tide conditions.) Favorite local spots to ride the wind include **Crissy Field/Golden Gate Bridge**, 415-561-4700, and **Candlestick Point Recreation Area**, 415-671-0145, in San Francisco; **Crown Beach** in Alameda, 510-562-7275; and **Brannan Island State Park** in the Sacramento Delta, 916-777-6671, home of Windy Cove.

Area windsurfing clubs and outfitters include:

SAN FRANCISCO
- **CityFront Sailboards**, 2936 Lyon St, 415-929-7873
- **San Francisco Board Sailing Association**, www.sfba.org
- **WOW: Women on Water**, 415-385-1224, www.uswindsurfing. org/WOW/WOWhome.htm; women's windsurfing club offers lessons at Crown Beach in Alameda

EAST BAY
- **Berkeley Board Sports**, 1601 University Ave, Berkeley, 510-527-7873
- **California Adventures**, Berkeley Marina, 510-642-4000
- **California Sailing Club**, Berkeley Marina, www.cal-sailing.org (see **Sailing** for more information)

SOUTH BAY
- **ASD-Advanced Surf Designs**, 302 Lang Rd, Burlingame, 650-348-8485
- **Helm Ski and Windsurf**, 333 North Amphlett Blvd, San Mateo, 650-344-2711
- **Shoreline Aquatic Center**, 3160 North Shoreline Blvd, Mountain View, 650-965-7474

THE SACRAMENTO DELTA
- **Delta Windsurf Co.**, 3729 West Sherman Island Rd, Rio Vista, 916-777-2299
- **Windcraft Windsurfing**, 17124 East Sherman Island Levy Rd, Rio Vista, 916-777-7067, www.windcraft.com

YOGA

Yoga is popular in the Bay Area, and many health clubs offer yoga classes. In addition, several studios are devoted solely to the fine art of bending, stretching, and breathing. Here are a few:

SAN FRANCISCO
- **Funky Door Yoga**, 186 Second St, 415-957-1088 (Bikram); for other San Francisco locations check out www.funkydooryoga.com
- **Integral Yoga**, 770 Dolores, 415-821-1117
- **Iyengar Yoga Institute of San Francisco**, 2404 27th Ave, 415-753-0909, http://iyisf.org
- **Mindful Body**, 2876 California St, 415-931-2639, www.themind fulbody.com
- **Yoga Society of San Francisco**, 2872 Folsom St, 415-285-5537
- **Yoga Tree**, multiple locations, 425-701-YOGA, www.yogatreesf.com

NORTH BAY
- **Bikram Yoga San Rafael**, 1295 2nd St, San Rafael, 415-453-9642
- **Yoga Center of Marin**, 142 Redwood Ave, Corte Madera, 415-927-1850

EAST BAY
- **4th Street Yoga**, 1809C 4th St, Berkeley, 510-845-9642, www.4th streetyoga.com
- **Funky Door Yoga**, 2567 Shattuck Ave, Berkeley, 510-204-9642 (Bikram), www.funkydooryoga.com
- **Piedmont Yoga Studio**, 3966 Piedmont Ave, Piedmont, 510-652-3336, www.piedmontyoga.com

PENINSULA/SOUTH BAY
- **Willow Glen Yoga**, 1188 Lincoln Ave, San Jose, 408-289-9642
- **Yoga Source**, 525 Alma St, Palo Alto, 650-328-9642
- **Yoga Wellness Studio**, 105 East 3rd Ave, San Mateo, 650-401-6423

HEALTH CLUBS, GYMS, YMCAS

The Bay Area has no shortage of health clubs, so whether you're seeking the latest, most up-to-date exercise machine with a pulse-pumping sound-track or the quietest, most peaceful yoga center, you can find it here.

SAN FRANCISCO
- **Bay Club**, 555 California St, 415-362-7800; 150 Greenwich St, 415-433-2200, www.sfbayclub.com

- **Club One**, 1 Sansome St, 415-399-1010; 450 Golden Gate Ave, 415-876-1010; 1755 O'Farrell St, 415-749-1010; 535 Mason St, 415-337-1010
- **Crunch**, 1000 Van Ness Ave, 415-931-1100
- **Curves**, 425 Battery St, 415-391-7418; 638 Stanyan St, 415-221-6932; 2529 Van Ness Ave, 415-771-0445, women only; for other San Francisco locations visit www.curves.com
- **Gold's Gym**, 2301 Market St, 415-626-4488
- **Golden Gateway Tennis and Swim Club**, 370 Drumm, 415-616-8800, www.ggtsc.com
- **Gorilla Sports**, 2324 Chestnut St, 415-292-8470; 2330 Polk St, 415-292-5444
- **Pinnacle**: 345 Spear St, 415-495-1939; 1 Post St, 415-781-6400
- **24 Hour Fitness**, numerous locations, 800-204-2400
- **Valencia Street Muscle and Fitness Center**, 333 Valencia St, 415-626-8360, www.valenciastreetmuscle.com
- **YMCA**: 169 Steuart St (Embarcadero), 415-957-9622; Presidio, 415-447-9622; Stonestown, 333 Eucalyptus Dr, 415-242-7100; Chinatown (men only), 855 Sacramento St, 415-576-9622; Central, 220 Golden Gate Ave, 415-885-0460
- **YWCA**, 1830 Sutter St, 415-775-6502

NORTH BAY
- **Gold's Gym**, 10 Fifer Ave, Corte Madera, 415-924-4653
- **Mill Valley Personal Fitness**, 34 Sunnyside Ave, Mill Valley, 415-381-4279
- **Nautilus of Marin**, 1001 4th St, San Rafael, 415-485-1001
- **24 Hour Fitness**, 1001 Larkspur Landing Circle, Larkspur, 415-925-0333

EAST BAY
- **Curves**, 2855 Telegraph Ave, Berkeley, 510-540-9256; 1969-A Mountain Blvd, Oakland, 510-338-0302; women only; for other East Bay locations visit www.eastbaycurves.com
- **In Forma**, 23 Orinda Way, #A, Orinda, 925-254-6877
- **World Dance Center**, 1831 Solano Ave, Berkeley, 510-528-1958
- **YMCA**, 2350 Broadway Oakland, 510-451-9622, www.ymca eastbay.org

PENINSULA/SOUTH BAY
- **Curves**, 839 Emerson St, Palo Alto, 650-566-1515; 1799 El Camino Real, Millbrae, 650-589-9790; women only; for more locations visit www.curves.com

- **Optimum Results**, 2624 Fayette Dr, Mountain View, 650-941-9148
- **Prime Physique Fitness Specialists**, 3635 Union Ave, San Jose, 408-558-1800
- **Right Stuff Health Club-Women**, 1145 South De Anza Blvd, San Jose, 408-973-1088
- **YMCA**, 4151 Middlefield Rd, #211, Palo Alto, 650-856-3955

SPORT AND SOCIAL CLUBS

Sport and Social Clubs offer organized athletic activities specifically geared towards singles. One part athletic outing, one part date night, they offer an alternative way for singles to meet through shared activities. Ski clubs and hiking groups hosting short getaways are the most popular here. And often good old-fashioned coed leagues offered through your local parks department serve the same purpose. Whether your love is diving, rock climbing, or bowling, the best way to find a club is to look in the yellow pages or on-line under the specific sport. Below are a few to get you started:

- **Bay Area Ski Connection**, www.jaws.com/baski/home.html; a clearinghouse of information on local clubs, here you'll find links to various Bay Area singles ski and snowboard clubs, information on group travel, and the singles racing league.
- **Golden Gate Sport & Social Club**, 415-921-1161, www.ggsport andsocialclub.com; based in San Francisco, offers adult recreational sports leagues including softball, soccer, basketball, and night bike riding, coed activities, parties and social nights, membership is free.
- **Single Sailors Association of Alameda**, http://sail-ssa.org; for beginning and experienced sailors alike, the groups organizes lunch and dinner sails to Tiburon, Sausalito, and San Francisco as well as multi-day cruises to the Delta, Drakes Bay, Monterey, and other spots. Membership is $85 ($55 renewal). Meetings are the second Thursday of every month, 6:30 p.m. social hour, 7:30 p.m. at Ballena Bay Yacht Club, 1150 Ballena Blvd, Alameda.
- **The Diving Singles Club**, www.garlic.com/~triblet/singles/ index.html; Silicon Valley singles club based around a shared love of scuba diving. The group organizes several diving trips every month to Monterey for beginner to advanced divers, and also hosts get-togethers occasionally for dinner, hiking, and wine tasting. Membership is free, meetings are held the third Sunday of the month at Round Table Pizza, 101 Town and Country Village, in Sunnyvale, 6:30 social hour, 7:00 p.m. meeting.

PARKS

Everyone knows about San Francisco's Golden Gate Park, and many have heard about the Presidio and Marin Headlands, but most newcomers are probably unaware of the profusion of little gem-like parks scattered throughout the Bay Area. These little havens, some of them perched atop hillsides, are perfect for romping with the kids, taking in the views, and breathing in the misty morning air. In fact, in San Francisco alone there are 230 parks and recreation facilities; among them, you'll find 6 scenic golf courses and 52 playgrounds—not bad for a city of 48 square miles. And then there are the beaches...

If you're interested in National Parks beyond the Presidio, discussed below, refer to **National Parks** in the **Quick Getaways** chapter.

SAN FRANCISCO

GOLDEN GATE PARK

The idea to create a large park in San Francisco first surfaced in the mid-1860s as city leaders strategized about how to wrest control of a large, sandy area occupied by squatters. Today this area spreads out about three miles from its eastern border of Stanyan Street to the Pacific Ocean, is about a half mile wide, and separates the Richmond district to the north and the Sunset to the south.

Visit Golden Gate Park and you will find that the rolling sand dunes of the 1800s have been transformed into rolling fields of green and wooded groves. The method for turning the land into the greenspace it is today was reportedly hit upon by accident. It seems William Hammond Hall, the park's designer and its first Superintendent (1871–1876), noticed a horse's barley nosebag fall to the sand and then sometime later the barley that spilled sprouted. Hall took note of this and decided to sow barley, grass, and other plants throughout the sandy areas needing transformation, and the rest is history. Hall is also credited with keeping traffic moving slowly through the park by insisting on the design of park roads that twisted and turned.

Hall appointed John McLaren as Assistant Superintendent, and by 1890, McLaren, a native of Edinburgh, Scotland, became Superintendent. He went on to make a name for himself by continuing the transformation process. Word has it that with the advice of horticulturists from around the world as to what kinds of plants and trees might thrive in this region, he alone planted more than one million trees in the park. Following his death in 1943, "Uncle John," as he was lovingly known, was honored by City leaders who named the park's headquarters (his former home) after him, the McLaren Lodge.

Today Golden Gate Park is the City's 1,017-acre playground, seven days a week. It's huge—New York's Central Park comes in at a mere 840 acres. No matter what the weather, you'll find walkers, joggers, roller skaters, and bike riders out using the trails. The meadows and groves are popular picnic sites. (The grills require reservations on weekends; see below.) The park also boasts numerous lakes and streams, baseball diamonds, soccer fields, tennis courts, playgrounds, an antique carousel, two art museums, a science museum and an aquarium, a Japanese tea garden, and much more. You can get your groove on with free swing dancing lessons every Sunday at Lindy in the Park from 11 a.m. to 1:30 p.m, weather permitting, beginner's lesson at 12:30 p.m. This activity, normally in the bandshell, has temporarily relocated to John F. Kennedy Drive near 10th Avenue during the massive construction and closure of the main concourse. For more information visit www.lindyinthepark.com. Despite all the activity, Golden Gate Park also offers quiet places for those seeking a bit of solitude.

For further information or reservations visit www.parks.sfgov.org or call:

- **Beach Chalet Visitor Center**, 415-751-2766
- **Boating** (Stow Lake), 415-752-0347
- **Fly casting** (Angler's Lodge), 415- 386-2630
- **Golf** (9-hole course), 415-751-8987
- **Guided walks**, 415-263-0991
- **Horses** (stables), 415-668-7360
- **Japanese Tea Garden**, 415-752-1171
- **Lawn bowling**, 415-487-8787
- **M. H. de Young Art Museum**, 415-863-3330
- **Park Senior Center**, 415-666-7015
- **Permits & Reservations**, 415-831-5500

•**Sharon Arts Studio**, 415-753-7004
•**Strybing Arboretum**, 415-661-1316
•**Tennis** (21 courts), 415-753-7100

PRESIDIO NATIONAL PARK

Located at the northern tip of the San Francisco peninsula, the 1,480-acre Presidio is one of the City's biggest treasures. Only recently part of the National Park system, it was originally settled by the Spanish in 1776, and functioned as a military post. In 1847, under US rule, its military functions continued, serving as a training base for Union troops in the Civil War and, in the aftermath of the 1906 earthquake that destroyed much of San Francisco, as a refuge for displaced residents. During World War II, the Presidio functioned as command center for the Sixth Army Command. It wasn't until October 1, 1994, when the National Park Service assumed control, that the US Sixth Army packed up and moved out. It is now part of the Golden Gate National Recreation Area and boasts some of the City's prime real estate, with more than one hundred miles of roads and wooded trails, ocean vistas, and a world-class golf course. Bikers and hikers enjoy the trails that meander through the eucalyptus groves; windsurfers and kite surfers head for Crissy Field. Fishermen look for crab, bass, perch, shark, or whatever else will bite at the pier near Fort Point.

Unique in the National Park System, the Presidio is run by the Presidio Trust, an independent federal agency, in combination with the National Park Service. The US Congress has mandated that the Presidio be completely self-sufficient by the year 2013, and to that end, the Presidio Trust has had to be creative about how to accomplish self-sufficiency. Finding big business tenants seems to be the way the Trust has decided to go. The extended San Francisco arm of Lucas Films, a new multimedia mega-complex, the Letterman Digital Arts Center, opened in the Presidio in 2005. Another project may be a theater built by Robert Redford's Sundance Institute. Area organizations/businesses have offices here, including non-profits and some dot-coms, and the Presidio is also a residential area with houses and apartments—available primarily to those who work here. Regardless of the politics surrounding how best to manage the area, the Presidio is a San Francisco treasure, offering art, history, and cultural centers, a shorebird lagoon, and recreation space. For more information on what the park has to offer, call the **Visitor's Center** at 415-561-4323. Military history buffs may want to visit the **Presidio Army Museum**, at Funston Avenue and Lincoln Boulevard, 415-561-4331. Golfers interested in teeing off at the **Golf Course** call 415-561-4663. Keglers can try out the park's 12-lane **Bowling Alley** in Building #93 (between Moraga and

Montgomery Streets); call 415-561-2695 for more information. Visit the Presidio's web site at www.nps.gov/prsf, and check the **Sports and Recreation** chapter for more details about these and other sports.

ADDITIONAL SAN FRANCISCO PARKS

- **Sigmund Stern Memorial Grove**, 19th Ave and Sloat Blvd, 415-252-6252
- **Harding Park**, popular public golf course, Harding Dr off Skyline Dr, 415-664-4690
- **McLaren Park**, University and Woolsey sts
- **Dolores Park**, Dolores and 19th sts
- **Balboa Park**, Ocean Ave and San Jose St
- **Glen Canyon Park**, Bosworth St and O'Shaughnessy
- **Crocker Amazon**, Moscow and Italy sts

Most San Francisco neighborhoods have parks with playgrounds, tennis courts, various flora and fauna, views, and secluded sunbathing groves. **Washington Square Park** in North Beach, **Alamo Square** at Fulton and Scott streets, **Lafayette Park** and **Alta Plaza** in Pacific Heights, and **Buena Vista Park** in the Haight are just a few. For more information about parks and recreational opportunities in your area, call the **San Francisco Parks & Recreation Department**, 415-831-2700, or visit their web site at www.parks.sfgov.org.

BEYOND SAN FRANCISCO—BAY AREA PARKS

The park system throughout the rest of the Bay Area is vast and varied. Included here are city, county, and national parks. There are too many parks to list completely but the following will give you an idea of what to expect.

For information about additional parks in the western United States, call the **National Park Services' Pacific West Information line** at 415-561-4700.

NORTH BAY

Part of the Golden Gate National Recreation Area, **Marin Headlands** is located on the Marin side of the Golden Gate Bridge, and offers spectacular views of the city, the bridge, and the ocean. Hiking, camping, and mountain biking are available, and it's only moments away from the city. Near Rodeo Beach you'll find the Marine Mammal Center, 415-289-SEAL, which provides shelter and medical assistance to elephant seals and sea lions. For more information about the Marin Headlands, contact the

Visitors' Center in Sausalito at Bunker Road, 415-331-1540, or visit the Golden Gate National Recreation Area's web site at www.nps.gov/goga or call 415-561-4700.

Located in the center of San Francisco Bay is **Angel Island State Park**. People come here mostly by ferry, though a few arrive via sailboats. Ferries leave from Tiburon, San Francisco (at Pier 41, Fisherman's Wharf), and Vallejo. Once on the island, you can hike, bike, picnic, camp, enjoy a softball game, or even climb the 750-foot Mount Livermore. For more information about Angel Island, call 415-435-2131 or visit www.angelisland.org. For the San Francisco and Vallejo ferries, call the Blue and Gold Fleet at 415-773-1188. For information about the Tiburon Ferry, call 415-435-2131.

Mount Tamalpais (elevation 2,586 feet), in Mount Tamalpais State Park, features 50 miles of hiking and biking trails. On clear days, the views of San Francisco Bay and the city are stunning, especially by Trojan Point and Pantoll. You can even see the Farallon Islands, some 25 miles out to sea. In the spring the outdoor Mountain Theater presents plays. For information about Mount Tamalpais, call 415-388-2070. On your way to Mount Tamalpais, you'll pass **Muir Woods**, an eerily beautiful grove of ancient redwoods. Visit in the winter when there are fewer tourists, lots of greenery, and creeks that are running full blast. For more information call 415-388-2595 or visit the Golden Gate National Park Recreation web site at www.nps.gov/goga.

Samuel P. Taylor State Park, 15 miles west of San Rafael on Sir Francis Drake Boulevard, offers over 2700 acres of hilly forested countryside, complete with hiking trails, fire roads, and a paved bike trail. The groves of redwoods and Papermill Creek make the area a popular camping spot. For more information, call 415-488-9897. To reserve a campsite (61 sites), contact Reserve America at 800-444-7275, www.reserve america.com

Located between the towns of Bolinas and Tomales, **Point Reyes National Seashore** includes 80 miles of coastline and 70,000 acres of pristine wilderness. Amidst its rugged bluffs, wooded canyons, dense forests, and open meadows, you'll find spectacular hiking, biking, camping, bird watching, and whale watching. Mountain lions live here, so if visiting with children, be sure to keep them nearby at all times. In 1995, a fire destroyed some 13,000 acres of the park, and though you can still see the effects of the fire, most of the area has recovered. For information about camping at Point Reyes, contact the Visitors' Center at 415-663-1092. Make sure to reserve camping sites ahead of time.

To learn more about city parks in Marin County, contact the **Marin County Department of Parks and Recreation** at 415-499-6387, www.co.marin.ca.us/depts/PK/Main/pos/parks.cfm.

EAST BAY

The East Bay has some spectacular parks, especially up in the Berkeley and Oakland hills. Call the **East Bay Regional Park District** at 510-562-7275 for information or visit their web site at www.ebparks.org.

In Berkeley, the Aquatic Park, at Seventh and Heinz streets, 510-843-2273 is alive with the sounds of sculling teams and migrating birds. You can join a kite-flying contest at Berkeley Marina off University Avenue in Berkeley, 510-644-6376. Many would argue that the crown jewel here is **Tilden Park**. Located in North Berkeley, it has hiking trails and Anza Lake for swimming (see **Sports and Recreation** for swimming details), a merry-go-round, miniature trains, golf course, a steam train, and a petting zoo. For more information, call 510-562-7275.

Tucked away in Oakland are a number of lovely green havens. **Lake Temescal Recreation Area**, 510-562-7275, has a reservoir for swimming and trout or bass fishing. Only a few miles from downtown Oakland, **Redwood Regional Park**, 510-562-7275, offers stately redwoods, horseback riding, a swimming pool, and picnic areas. At **Anthony Chabot Regional Park** you can row along the 315-acre lake—no swimming allowed though. To reserve one of the 75 campsites (the cost is $18) call 510-562-2267. Another Oakland Park is the 425-acre **Joaquin Miller Park**, 510-562-7275, off Highway 13 on Joaquin Miller Road, where you'll find plenty of hiking trails. If you drive up Skyline Boulevard check out the new **Chabot Observatory and Science Center**, 510-530-3480, with its high-powered telescopes, planetarium, and Dome IMAX theater.

In Richmond, **Wildcat Canyon** offers hiking trails that are less crowded than many other Bay Area trails.

In Alameda you can walk lazily along **Crown Memorial Beach**, Shoreline Drive, 510-562-7275, or if you are energetic, try windsurfing or kitesurfing. The **Crab Cove Visitor Center**, which offers marine education as well as tide pooling, is another favorite recreation spot. Call 510-521-6887 for more details.

In Contra Costa County check out the 19,000-acre **Mount Diablo State Park**, 925-837-2525, for hiking, camping, mountain biking, and incredible city views.

Located between Martinez and Lafayette is the hilly **Briones Regional Park**, 510-562-7275. Its 5,000 acres offer 45 miles of trails through meadows and wooded areas among lakes and waterfalls.

PENINSULA

In San Mateo County, along Highway 1 from Pacifica to Santa Cruz, you'll find stunning coastline, big waves, and lovely beachcombing. Beware of sharks; they have been known to chomp on surfboards.

Located about 55 miles south of San Francisco is the **Año Nuevo State Reserve**, which hosts the world's largest breeding colony of northern elephant seals. Every year, the elephant seals mate and give birth to their 75-pound pups along the sand dunes. This is truly a remarkable area and if you are lucky, you may witness a female giving birth. Breeding season is from December to late March. For more information, call 650-879-0227.

On the San Francisco Bay, the **Coyote Point County Recreational Area**, Coyote Point Drive, 650-573-2592, has a well-visited Nature Museum along with swimming, boating, windsurfing, and some kiteboarding. Windsurfing is also popular by **Candlestick Park State Recreation Area**, a few miles south of Coyote Point and near the San Francisco Airport. **Crystal Springs Reservoir**, located 13 miles south of San Francisco on Interstate 280, is another refuge as well as a source of water for San Francisco and the surrounding areas. Trails here are used for hiking, biking, and horseback riding. The reservoir itself holds 22.6 billion gallons of Hetch Hetchy water for delivery to San Francisco and northern peninsula towns.

At **Huddart County Park** in Woodside, 650-851-1210, you'll find groves of second growth redwoods. The park also features a playground designed specifically for the physically challenged. Additional San Mateo County Parks are **Memorial Park** where you can fish for trout, plunge into a swimming hole, hike, bike, ride, or visit a nature museum; the 7,500-acre **Pescadero Creek County Park** with ridgetop ocean views and hiking and biking; and the **Sam MacDonald County Park** with 42 miles of hiking trails. Call 650-879-0212 for camping information at the above parks.

For more information on **San Mateo's County Parks** call the **Parks and Recreation Department** at 650-363-4020.

There are also many preserves and open spaces such as **Pulgas Ridge Open Space Preserve** in San Carlos and the **Thornewood Open Space Preserve** in Woodside. Call the **Mid-Peninsula Regional Open Space District Office** at 650-691-1200 to learn more.

SOUTH BAY

There are 28 parks in Santa Clara County; contact the **Santa Clara Department of Parks and Recreation** at 408-355-2200 or visit www.parkhere.org. Below is just a sampling.

The 3,600-acre **Sanborn Skyline County Park**, nestled in the Santa Cruz Mountains between the city of Saratoga and Skyline Boulevard, is a steep and wooded area. It offers camping, an outdoor theater, and a youth hostel; call 408-867-9959 for more information. **Stevens Creek County Park**, in Cupertino, 408-867-3654, is great for riding or bicycling around its reservoir. Within the City of San Jose is **Alum Rock**, 408-259-5477, which has trickling mineral springs, as well as hiking, biking, and horse-back riding trails.

Bird lovers from all over the country flock to **Palo Alto's Baylands Preserve**. Here, among the 2,000 acres of bird-beckoning salt marsh, you'll find more than 100 species of birds, including white egrets, California clappers, and thousands of tiny shorebirds. In the fall and winter the tiny black rail makes its appearance. For more details call 650-329-2506 or check www.ci.palo-alto.ca.us. Remember to bring your binoculars.

With more than 87,000 acres, **Henry Coe State Park** is the largest state park in northern California. People come to hike, mountain bike, back-pack, camp, fish, and ride horses. Located in Morgan Hill (south of San Jose), the park has blue oaks, ponderosa pines, wild pigs, deer, birds, and much more. There is a $5 per vehicle parking fee. For more information, call the visitor center at 408-779-2728 or visit their web site at www.coepark.org.

BEACHES

If you think all of California's beaches are like the ones seen on "Baywatch," erase that image from your mind. Those are southern California beaches. Northern California beaches are much different than the miles-long ocean-front playgrounds seen on TV. Weather here is frequently foggy and cold, and the undertow can be extremely dangerous. Although Bay Area beaches do host hardy surfers and sunbathers, you won't be out of place if you consider the beaches here more akin to the North Sea—places to walk with a stick and a dog and warm clothing.

With the shore often socked-in by morning fog, temperatures rarely top the 70s, even by mid-afternoon. Nevertheless, **San Francisco** boasts a number of popular beaches. In addition to the beaches listed below, dog walkers love the beach at **Fort Funston**, south of **Ocean Beach**, and nud-ists throw caution to the wind at **Land's End** (located on the northern edge of Lincoln Park). **China Beach**, a few steps away from popular **Baker Beach**, is a small, secluded stretch of sand adjacent to the upscale Sea Cliff neighborhood. Daring swimmers willing to endure the cold Bay water take the plunge at the beach in **Aquatic Park** near Fisherman's Wharf.

In **Marin County**, **Stinson Beach** is perhaps the Bay Area's most popular beach (see listing below for more details). As a matter of fact, it is so popular that on summer weekends you should beware of the thousands of vehicles, and inevitable traffic jams, on Highway 1 along the coast north of San Francisco as city dwellers rev up their engines in search of peace and quiet. Keep in mind that the car trip there includes a winding road, which can make even the sturdiest stomach queasy. For clothing-optional beaches in Marin try **Muir Beach**, just before Stinson. Just past Stinson is the town of Bolinas, which has a small beach, popular for surfing.

There are much quieter beaches along the **San Mateo County** coastline, so if you'd like to avoid the crowds, head south from San Francisco down Highway 1, through **Pacifica** and **Half Moon Bay** and keep your eyes peeled for a beach that fits the bill. Remember, though, that the water is cold, and the underwater currents are strong. For more details on the state beaches listed below and others throughout the Bay Area check out www.parks.ca.gov.

To find out more about area parks and to make camping reservations, call 800-444-7275 or log onto the **National Recreation Reservation Service** at www.reserveusa.com. The **National Park Service** is located in Fort Mason, Building 201, San Francisco, 415-561-4700, www.nps.gov.

SAN FRANCISCO AND NORTH BAY BEACHES

- **Baker Beach**: Smaller than Ocean Beach, but also more picturesque, Baker Beach is nestled at the bottom of the deeply wooded Point Lobos, just beneath the Golden Gate Bridge—offering great views of the bridge and the Marin Headlands; North Baker is a popular nude beach. On a nice day, sunbathing is the main activity here.

- **Ocean Beach**: San Francisco's main beach is a long, flat sandy shoreline stretching out along the city's western edge, just a few steps from the foot of Golden Gate Park. Packed with sun worshipers on those rarest of days when the weather is warm, Ocean Beach is popular year-round with surfers, hang-gliders, paragliders, kite fliers, city strollers, joggers, and dog walkers (officially on-leash). The weather here is typically foggy and brisk, with high wind gusts that kick sand into your food and your face; waters here are icy and the waves are rough so swimming is hazardous; on summer evenings, the beach lights up with campfire gatherings. Highway 1, easily accessible from the MUNI LRV: N Judah.

- **Point Reyes**, 415-464-5100, www.nps.gov/pore/visit.htm, is one of the Bay Area's greatest gems with 100 square miles of beaches, forests, marshes, and trails snaking along the northern coastline—a great place to camp and spend the weekend hiking, kayaking, biking, bird watching, picnicking, or just relaxing. The rough Pacific currents make swimming in the ocean dangerous, but many intrepid water-lovers take the cold plunge at Bass Lake, dubbed by the park service as the best unofficial place to take a dip. The hike to Bass Lake via the Coastal Trail can be challenging in spots.
- **Red Rock Beach**, www.redrockbeach.com: This popular "clothing optional" beach is about half a mile south of Stinson Beach, at Milepost 11 on Highway 1. There's a turnout for parking, but no signs. It's about a 15-minute hike down a steep trail to the water. There are no facilities at Red Rock Beach, and poison oak is reportedly rampant here so wear shoes on the trail and use caution.
- **Stinson**, www.stinsonbeachonline.com: This well-loved long sandy beach and adjoining 51-acre park are packed with wall-to-wall families in the summertime; swimming is permitted here and there are lifeguards on duty from May through October; there are also lots of picnic tables and a snack bar open during peak season. If you want to avoid the crowds, try visiting on a weekday. Restrooms and showers. Highway 1 to the Stinson Beach exit.
- **Tomales Bay State Park**, 415-669-1140: Right next to Point Reyes, this 2,000-acre park is home to four protected, gentle and surf-free beaches, making it a prime spot for swimming, boating, and kayaking; four miles north of Inverness on Pierce Point Road.

For more information on San Francisco and Marin County beaches, contact the **Golden Gate National Recreation Area**, San Francisco, 415-561-4700, www.nps.gov/goga.

PENINSULA, SOUTH BAY, AND EAST BAY BEACHES

- **Half Moon State Beach**, a half-mile west of Highway 1 on Kelly Avenue, is actually three beaches under one title: Dunes, Francis, and Venice combine to make up four miles of broad, sandy beaches along Highway 1. For those interested in an overnight experience, Francis Beach has a campground for tents and RVs. Reservations are recommended. **Francis Beach**, end of Kelly Avenue in Half Moon Bay; **Venice Beach**, end of Venice Boulevard off Highway 1; **Dunes Beach**, end of Young Avenue off Highway 1. Contact Half Moon Bay Beaches, 650-726-8819, for more information. Campsite reservations must be made through Reserve America by calling 800-444-PARK (7275) or through their website at www.reserveamerica.com.

- **San Gregorio State Beach**: A perennial favorite with families and school field trips, San Gregorio's clay cliffs and caves, hiking trails, and picnic facilities make it a perfect children's adventure land. There is also an estuary here, home to many birds. The beach is located 10.5 miles south of Half Moon Bay on Highway 1. Call 650-879-2170 for more information.
- **Año Nuevo State Reserve**: Fifty-five miles south of San Francisco a rocky point juts out into the ocean—home to the largest mainland breeding colony in the world for the northern elephant seal. During the breeding season, December through March, access to the reserve is available by guided walks only. This 4,000-acre reserve is truly something special, well worth a day trip. For more information call 650-879-0227.
- **Montara State Beach**: The tide pools and fishing are great here. Point Montara also has one of the best youth hostels in the country—offering visitors the chance to spend the night at the lighthouse 20 miles south of San Francisco, on Highway 1. There are two beach access points from the bluff area, one across from Second Street and the second about a half-mile north on the ocean side of Highway 1. The paths down to the beach are steep, and dogs are allowed on leash. For information on staying overnight contact American Youth Hostels, 650-728-7177.
- **Pacifica**, 650-738-7381, www.ci.pacifica.ca.us: Pacifica has a handful of spectacular beaches; Linda Mar (also known as Pacifica State Beach) runs along a wide curving mouth, and is popular with families. Kids love what locals call the world's most beautiful Taco Bell, while the wave-pounded shores here and at nearby Rockaway are favorites with surfers. All of Pacifica's beaches are accessible from Highway 1 in Pacifica.
- **Pescadero State Beach**, 650-879-2170: The sandy shores, rocky cliffs, and picnic tables make this a popular family spot in the summer; get here early to check out the tide pools. Across the highway Pescadero Marsh Natural Preserve is an excellent spot for bird watching. The beach is located about 15 miles south of Half Moon Bay on Highway 1.
- **Robert W. Crown Memorial State Beach**: The City of Alameda's 2.5-mile sandy playground is a popular spot for family picnics, BBQs, and windsurfing; swimming is permitted year-round. The beach is also home to the Elsie Roemer Bird Sanctuary and Crab Cove marine reserve. Rental sailboards and lessons are available on summer weekends. Contact the East Bay Regional Park District, 510-562-7275, or www.ebparks.org for more information.

LIVING ON THE WEST COAST IS TRULY A BLESSING FOR MANY, THOUGH
it is not without risk. While bad weather events are not as much of an
issue as they can be in the frigid upper Midwest, the hurricane-prone
coastal South, or the tornado-torn heartland, the concern here is with
earthquakes and now, being a sizable population zone, terrorist strikes.
While only chance dictates who will be in the wrong place at the wrong
time during a quake or terrorist attack, there are precautions you can take to
aid your survival, including establishing a family emergency plan and creating a stock of emergency supplies (see the end of the chapter). The following sources of general information and assistance may also be helpful:

- **American Red Cross Bay Area Chapter** offers disaster preparedness information, this number also operates as a 24-hour disaster hotline, 415-427-8000, www.bayarea-redcross.org
- **California Office of Emergency Services**, 510-286-0895,
  www.oes.ca.gov
- **Federal Emergency Management Agency (FEMA)**, 800-480-
  2520 or 510-627-7100, www.fema.gov

EARTHQUAKES

One of the biggest fears about living in California is earthquakes. While
most natives aren't too frightened by the swaying or bumps of small temblors, no one relishes the thought of the proverbial "big one." San
Francisco has been victimized by major earthquakes twice in nearly 100
years: 1906 and 1989. In 1906 the 8.3 magnitude quake toppled buildings
and sparked fires that destroyed much of the city, and killed 700 people.
The 1989, 7.1 magnitude Loma Prieta temblor killed 67, brought down a
section of a major East Bay freeway, dislodged part of the Oakland–San
Francisco Bay Bridge, sparked fires in the Marina district, and brought the

World Series to an abrupt, albeit temporary, halt. And without a doubt, the San Francisco Bay area will be hit with more earthquakes. In fact, earthquake experts say there is a 62% chance that the Bay Area will be hit by the "Big One," an ominous shaker of 6.7 or greater, by 2032. While no one can control the whims of Mother Nature, if you choose to settle down in earthquake country, there are many preventative steps you can take to help keep you, your loved ones, and your home safe.

HOME PREPARATION AND INSURANCE

Simple steps you can take prior to an earthquake that will make your home a bit safer include fastening computers, televisions, and other big pieces of equipment to desks and counters so that they won't fall off during the quake. Large furniture items, such as bookcases, should be bolted to the wall. Small items, such as fragile collectibles, should be taped or glued to their shelves or stuck with clay. Strap the water heater and other large appliances to the wall. The folks in the earthquake supply stores will be more than happy to sell you what you need to do this or go to a hardware/home supply store and get the equivalent. Chances are it will be less expensive at the latter. For information about retrofitting your home call the **California Earthquake Authority**, 916-325-3800. They'll tell you what needs to be done to your home to make it safer and will give you information on contractors and financing. Additional information on seismic safety can be found at http://quake.abag.ca.gov. *Peace of Mind in Earthquake Country* by Peter Yanev might be useful.

Bolted wood frame buildings (such as Victorians) are considered quite safe, and steel-reinforced concrete buildings (such as downtown skyscrapers) are reasonably safe. The most dangerous building to be in during a quake is non-reinforced masonry. For this reason, brick buildings can no longer be constructed in San Francisco, but a handful of older ones remain. Many such buildings have warning plaques in their entryways. Dozens of San Francisco buildings are still being retrofitted following the 1989 earthquake. You might want to find out whether the building you live or work in has been retrofitted or bolted.

If you're buying a home in California the seller is required by law to tell you if the property is in the vicinity of an earthquake fault line. Before buying you may want to engage the services of a civil engineer to give your prospective home the once-over, just to make sure it's as safe as it can be. Rental property owners are not required to disclose information about nearby faults to prospective tenants.

Property owners are strongly advised to buy a homeowner's insurance policy that covers quake damage. The California Insurance Commissioner requires that companies that sell homeowners and renters policies in California must also offer earthquake insurance. The most common type of earthquake insurance is normally added as an endorsement on a standard homeowner's insurance policy. Typically, there is a deductible of 5 to 10%, and sometimes 15%, of the value of the home. An important coverage is temporary living expense, which pays for motel and meals if you have to move out of your home. There is usually no deductible on this coverage. The yearly cost of residential earthquake insurance is normally about $1.50 to $3 per $1,000 of coverage on the structure. To find out more about earthquake insurance, ask your insurance agent or call the **California State Department of Insurance** at 800-927-4357.

WHAT TO DO DURING AN EARTHQUAKE

- If you're inside when the earth shifts, remember the three potentially life-saving words that all California school children know by heart—duck, cover and hold. Get under a strong table or desk. Cover your head and face to protect them from broken glass and falling debris. Hold onto the table or desk and be prepared to move with it. Stay there until the shaking stops. Do not run outside. Stay away from windows and avoid elevators and stairwells. Keep an eye out for falling objects.
- If you're driving when the earthquake strikes, pull over to the shoulder of the road. Stay away from bridges, overpasses, power lines, and large buildings. Remain in your car and wait for the shaking to stop.
- If you're outside, go into an open area away from trees, power lines and buildings.
- If you're in a crowded public area stay calm, do not jam the exit, and avoid elevators and stairwells. Instead look for a safe place to duck and cover until passage is safe and clear.

AFTER THE SHOCK

- One of the first things you should do following a quake is check to see if your natural gas line is leaking. If you detect a leak, and only if you detect a leak, turn the shutoff valve. Quake-prepared residents leave the appropriate tool for shutting off the gas valve right next to it at all times. Remember, don't turn the gas off if you don't think it's leaking. The gas company will no doubt be very busy fixing numerous emergency problems following the earthquake so it may be days before someone can get to those who shut things off unnecessarily. If your water supply is working fill the tub and sinks with water. Although the pipes are running now they may not later and you can use this water for washing. Outside check for downed utility lines, and turn on the radio for instructions and news reports.

- Stay calm, help others, make sure all household members and pets are all safe and accounted for. Turn the radio on for emergency announcements, and follow emergency workers' instructions. To leave roads clear for emergency vehicles, avoid driving. Check gas, water, electrical, and sewer lines, and turn off anything that appears to be leaking or broken at the source. Report any problems immediately to your utility company.
- Check your home for damages—paying attention to the roof, foundation, and chimneys, as well as cracked walls, etc.
- Check for downed power lines; steer clear and warn others to stay away.
- Be prepared for aftershocks.
- If you must leave your home, leave a note telling others where you are.
- If you have to leave your residence and haven't found your pets or they have run off or hidden, remember to leave food and water. Leave the toilet seat up, fill the bathtub, open cans of food and tear open entire bags of dry food. They might be hanging around for several days before you are allowed to return.

BASIC EARTHQUAKE FACTS: BAY AREA FAULTS

The mother of all Bay Area faults, and the source of much geological anxiety, is the San Andreas. Named in 1895 by geologist A.C. Lawson for the San Andreas Lake, a pond roughly 20 miles south of San Francisco, this master fault spans almost the entire length of California. A fault system made of up of various segments, the San Andreas is more than 800 miles long, and at its greatest depth, dips 10 miles beneath the surface. Here, two of the continent's great tectonic plates, the Pacific and the North American, meet, creating what geologists call a strike slip fault—for the way the plates crash, then dip, one beneath the other. Earthquakes in the San Francisco Bay Area result from the pressure buildup and strain across the region as these plates push against one another. From the San Andreas, a web of smaller faults splinter off, weaving in and out from inland areas all along the coast. These smaller Bay Area faults include the Rodgers Creek, Concord–Green Valley, Greenville, Hayward, San Gregorio, and Calaveras faults.

For more interesting facts about the science of earthquakes, as well as up-to-the-minute information on quakes happening all over the world, visit the US Geological Survey's informative web site at www.usgs.gov.

Other **earthquake information sources**:
- **American Red Cross Bay Area Chapter**, 415-427-8000, www. bayarea-redcross.org, offers disaster preparedness information; this number also operates as a 24-hour disaster hotline

- **California Earthquake Authority**, 916-325-3800, www.earth quakeauthority.com, for seismic safety and earthquake insurance information
- **California Office of Emergency Services**, 510-286-0895, www. oes.ca.gov
- **California Seismic Safety Commission**, 1900 K St, Sacramento, CA 95814, 916-263-5506, www.seismic.ca.gov, publishes "The Homeowner's Guide to Earthquake Safety" as well as other materials on quake preparedness
- **Federal Emergency Management Agency (FEMA)**, 800-480-2520 or 510-627-7100, www.fema.gov
- **Northern California Earthquake Data Center at UC Berkeley Seismology Laboratory**, http://quake.geo.berkeley.edu
- **US Geological Survey**, 345 Middlefield Rd, Menlo Park, CA 94025, 888-275-8747, 650-853-8300 www.usgs.gov; this office helps to determine the size of the quakes and offers a treasure trove of information on all things seismic

DISASTER KITS AND SAFETY PLANS

Aside from luck, the secret to surviving a local disaster is found in the time-proven Boy Scout adage "be prepared." There are dozens of good books on the market about how to get ready for a seismic onslaught or terrorist strike, and plenty of free information available from local, state and federal agencies. They all tell you that you need to be ready to be on your own for three to seven days, because it may take that long for emergency crews to restore power, water, and telephone service to affected areas. You should also have at least a basic disaster kit prepared. Remember to store your supplies away from areas likely to be damaged in a big earthquake. The kit should include the following:

- Water (at least one gallon per person, per day)
- Food for each family member and your pets (canned goods such as stews, beans, soups, evaporated milk, cereals, granola bars and nuts, dried fruit, cookies)
- Non-electric can opener
- Flashlights and extra batteries
- Portable radio and extra batteries
- Blankets/sleeping bags/pillows
- Camping stove or your barbecue with plenty of appropriate fuel
- Swiss Army knife or similar tool
- Cooking and eating utensils, paper plates and cups
- Proper sized tent

- Water purification tablets
- Small bottle of chlorine bleach
- Toiletries, including toilet paper, feminine hygiene products, and contact lens supplies, diapers
- Waterproof matches
- Plastic garbage bags and ties
- Toys, games, cards, crosswords, paper and pencils, books
- Red lipstick to scrawl a message on the front of the building door (or ruins) if you must leave
- Sturdy shoes
- Rain gear
- Sunglasses and sunscreen
- Dust masks
- Cold weather clothing, gloves, scarves, hats
- Fire extinguisher
- Whistle
- Pet carrier and photos of your pets to identify them if they take off
- A basic tool kit with hammer, pliers, wrenches, etc., for minor repairs
- Cash (bank ATMs may not work after a big temblor and merchants may not be accepting credit cards!)
- First aid kit, including the following:
  - plastic adhesive strips
  - ACE bandages
  - gauze pads and tape
  - scissors
  - tweezers
  - safety pins
  - chemical ice packs
  - cotton balls or swabs
  - aspirin or the equivalent
  - antibiotic ointments
  - hydrogen peroxide
  - rubbing alcohol
  - insect repellent
  - thermometer
  - over-the-counter medications for diarrhea and upset stomach
  - First Aid Manual
  - Prescription medications that are not past their expiration dates

Once you've gathered everything together put it all in a container, such as a big plastic garbage can with a lid, and stash it in a place that's not likely to be buried in a quake. If you're living in a house, the backyard may be best. If you're living in an apartment building you'll have to be creative when it comes to protecting your kit.

Several Bay Area stores sell earthquake/disaster preparedness equipment and information. They also sell earthquake kits as well as individual components. These can be pricey, but when you consider that your life, following a major quake, may depend on how well prepared you are, it is probably worth the expense. Here are just a few of the stores specializing in quake supplies:

- **Earthquake Supply Center**, 3095 Kerner Blvd, San Rafael, 415-459-5500, www.earthquakesupplycenter.com
- **Earth Shakes**, 466 Cumberland Rd, Burlingame, 650-548-9065
- **REI—Recreational Equipment Inc.**, 1338 San Pablo Ave, Berkeley, 510-527-4140; 1119 Industrial Rd, San Carlos, 650-508-2330; www.rei.com

As you put your disaster kit together you should also come up with a **family emergency plan**, in case disaster strikes when you're not all in the same place. You can do the same thing with your apartment building neighbors. Emergency preparedness experts say you should:

- Agree on someone out of the area you can all call to check in, for example, Aunt Mildred in Omaha. She'll want to know how you are as well, so let her be the clearinghouse for family information. Make sure each family member knows the number. The only chink in this armor is that telephone lines and satellite service may not be working for a few days—keep trying; eventually they will be restored.
- Should your home suffer severe damage, create a planned meeting place, such as the local high school football field or a department store parking lot, someplace that is not likely to come tumbling down during an initial quake or any aftershocks.

S AN FRANCISCO'S DIVERSITY IS MOST EVIDENT IN THE MULTITUDE
of churches, temples, ashrams, mosques, and other houses of worship to be found throughout the Bay Area. Below is a list describing
just a few of the many religious organizations here. For more information
about worship in the Bay Area, talk to leaders or fellow congregants at your
current place of worship. You'd be surprised at how many people across
the USA have ties to the San Francisco area. To find a place of worship close
to your new home, check the Yellow Pages under "Churches" or
"Synagogues" or go online to www.qwestdex.com and do a key word
search. You can also check out http://directory.sanfrancisco.com/san-fran-
cisco/churches.zq.html

CHURCHES

BAPTIST

- **Ebenezer Baptist Church**, 275 Divisadero St, San Francisco, 415-431-0200
- **First Chinese Baptist Church of San Francisco**, 1-15 Waverly Place, San Francisco, 415-362-4139; 3010 Noriega St, San Francisco, 415-753-3950, www.fcbc-sf.org; serving San Francisco since its inception in 1880, the Waverly location is newly renovated and seismically retrofitted. The congregation is multi-generational, bilingual, and bicultural.
- **Third Baptist Church, Inc.**, 1399 McAllister St, San Francisco, 415-346-4426, www.thirdbaptist.org, headed by pastor Amos Brown, former member of the San Francisco Board of Supervisors, youth activities, broadcasts regular radio program.

EASTERN ORTHODOX

- **Greek Orthodox Cathedral of the Annunciation**, 245 Valencia St, 415-864-8000, www.annunciation.org, hosts fantastic, packed events with Greek music, food, and dancing, and its whitewashed façade evokes the beauty of the Greek islands.
- **Greek Orthodox Cathedral of the Ascension**, 4700 Lincoln Ave, Oakland, 510-531-3400, www.ascensioncathedral.org; this Cathedral is known for its lovely stained glass. Overlooking the Bay Area from atop the Oakland hills, the church offers youth and senior programs and a choir.
- **Greek Orthodox Diocese of San Francisco**, 372 Santa Clara Ave, San Francisco, 415-753-3075, www.sf.goarch.org
- **Holy Virgin Cathedral**, 6210 Geary Blvd, 415-221-3255, located in the Outer Richmond, in the heart of San Francisco's vibrant Russian community, towers majestically above the fog. This dazzling Russian Orthodox cathedral—with its five ornate golden domes and stunning frescoes—is a true San Francisco landmark. The church offers services in Russian and is also home to a Russian high school. It's definitely worth seeing, regardless of your faith. Also be sure to check out the wonderful Russian bakeries nearby.
- **Russian Orthodox Church of Our Lady of Kazan**, 5725 California St, 415-752-2502, is located in the Richmond District. The Church's glistening, onion-domed Cathedral with mosaics, icons, and frankincense is an exquisite place to visit, even if you aren't a member. The singing is spectacular. Several Russian bakeries and restaurants nearby offer mouthwatering breakfasts and lunches after services.

EPISCOPAL

- **Grace Cathedral**, and the **Episcopal Diocese of California**, 1055 Taylor St, San Francisco, 415-749-6300, www.gracecathedral.org; perched atop Nob Hill, this is a lovely cathedral, complete with stained glass windows, murals, and lofty ceilings. Episcopalians come from all over the city to worship here. In particular, midnight mass on Christmas Eve, the Easter service that includes an egg roll at nearby Huntington Park, and the Evensong on Sundays are attended by members and non-members alike. The church also hosts concerts and indoor/outdoor art exhibits, and offers an associated boys' school, a café, and a shop of religious items including music and Christmas cards. Just walking inside or strolling through the outdoor labyrinth offers a peaceful and meditative experience. There are a number of other Episcopal churches throughout the city and the Bay Area; check the Yellow Pages under "Churches."

JEHOVAH'S WITNESSES

Jehovah's Witnesses in San Francisco can contact the **Excelsior Congregation**, 11 Bright St, 415-586-9194, or to find your local Kingdom Hall, visit www.watchtower.org.

LATTER DAY SAINTS/MORMON

Whether you are a member of the Church of Jesus Christ of Latter Day Saints or not, the **Mormon Temple**, 4770 Lincoln Avenue off of Highway 13 in Oakland, is well worth a visit. Built in the 1960s and nested high in the Oakland hills overlooking the Bay, the five spires of this impressive temple dominate the skyline and can be seen from miles away. The church boasts a large, active membership from throughout the Bay Area, including a large Asian-American community. The temple itself is reserved for religious services, but the exquisitely kept grounds and visitors' center are open to the public. For more information call 510-531-3200. For more information on finding a ward near you visit www.lds.org.

LUTHERAN

- **St. Mark's Lutheran Church**, 1111 O'Farrell St, San Francisco, 415-928-7770, www.stmarks-sf.org, is known for its music programs and social outreach activities; childcare provided all Sunday morning.
- **St. Matthews Lutheran Church**, 3281 16th St, San Francisco, 415-863-6371, offers services in German as well as English.
- **West Portal Lutheran Church**, 200 Sloat Blvd, San Francisco, 415-661-0242, www.westportallutheran.org, multicultural community.
- **Zion Lutheran Church and School**, 495 9th Ave, San Francisco, 415-221-7500, www.zionsf.org, traditional and contemporary services.

METHODIST

- **Glide Memorial Methodist Church**, 330 Ellis St, San Francisco, 415-771-6300, www.glide.org; the charismatic Reverend Cecil Williams, a prominent San Francisco figure, and his poet wife have instituted 52 programs at Glide including food giveaways, recovery meetings, classes, and housing programs. But what draws parishioners, the down and out, tourists, the movers and shakers of San Francisco society, and many others, at least once, is the lively music and singing at the services.

PRESBYTERIAN

- **Calvary Presbyterian Church**, 2515 Fillmore St, San Francisco, 415-346-3832, located at the top of the hill in Pacific Heights, offers concerts, a preschool, and singles and elder groups.
- **Menlo Park Presbyterian Church**, 950 Santa Cruz Ave, Menlo Park, 650-328-2340, www.mppc.org, is a popular church with loads of groups for singles and single parents, group activities, and outreach programs. Contact www.mppc.org.
- **Noe Valley Ministry**, 1021 Sanchez St, San Francisco, 415-282-2317, www.noevalleyminstry.org, holds popular concerts, including jazz, folk, classical, and religious music. For a detailed listing of musical programs visit www.noevalleymusicseries.org. The church also offers community classes that range from belly dancing to ecology.
- **The Old First Presbyterian Church**, 1751 Sacramento St, San Francisco, 415-776-5552, www.oldfirst.org, claims to be the oldest Presbyterian church in the city. The church also frequently hosts popular chamber music concerts. For more information visit www.oldfirst concerts.org.

QUAKER

Known worldwide for promoting peace and justice, as well as fellowship and spirituality, the Quakers, also known as the Religious Society of Friends, have an active meeting house in San Francisco, at 65 Ninth Street, a library that includes multimedia offerings on Quaker history and peace studies as well as children's books, and a school, http://sffriendsschool.org. The San Francisco Friends hold a silent peace vigil in front of the Federal building at Golden Gate and Larkin streets every Thursday at noon that is open to all. The San Francisco meeting house holds regular worship services every Sunday at 11 a.m; newcomers are encouraged to attend the Orientation to Meeting held beforehand at 10:40 a.m. To find out more, contact **San Francisco Friends Meeting**, 415-431-7440 or www.sfquakers.org. Outside of San Francisco, to find the meeting house nearest you visit www.quakerfinder.org.

ROMAN CATHOLIC

There are 48 different Catholic parishes in San Francisco. For a comprehensive list, contact the San Francisco Archdiocese at 415-565-3600, or check their web site, www.sfarchdiocese.org. The office of the Archdiocese of San Jose, 900 Lafayette Street, Suite 301, 408-983-0100, www.dsj.org, can tell you about churches in the South Bay. Numerous churches in the Bay Area offer services in Italian, Chinese, Tagolog, French, Spanish, Latin, Vietnamese, Korean, and more. Check the web sites listed previously to find one that may be of interest to you.

- **The Cathedral of St. Mary of the Assumption,** 1111 Gough St, San Francisco, 415-567-2020, www.stmarycathedralsf.org, is the main church of the diocese in San Francisco. Referred to as St. Mary's Cathedral, it is a bright and airy modern structure, completed in 1971 after the original cathedral burnt down.
- **Mission Dolores**, 3321 16th St, San Francisco, 415-621-8203, the oldest building in the city, is rich in history and tucked away on the edge of Dolores Park. Sunday services are at 8 a.m. and 10 a.m. for English speakers, there is a noon mass in Spanish.
- **St. Dominic's** at 2390 Bush St in San Francisco, 415-567-7824, www.stdomincs.org, has a school for children, K-8, a special shrine to St. Jude, and holds weekday and evening masses, morning prayer sessions, and services in Spanish at 1:30 p.m. every Sunday.
- **St. Ignatius**, Fulton and Parker sts, San Francisco, 415-422-2188, you can see the gorgeous, towering spires of this Jesuit parish, located on the University of San Francisco campus, from many of the city's hilltops—watching the sun set over this magnificent work of architecture is simply stunning.
- **St. Vincent de Paul Church** at 2320 Green St, San Francisco, 415-922-1010, www.svdp-sfparish.org, has one of the largest and most active young adult groups, meets every second and fourth Monday of the month (not every other Monday), from 7:30 p.m. to 9 p.m.

SEVENTH-DAY ADVENTISTS

Known for their worship music programs, Seventh-day Adventist churches are located throughout the city—including churches specifically dedicated to Chinese, Japanese, Latin-American, Russian, and gay and lesbian communities. For newcomers, a good place to start is the **San Francisco Central Seventh-day Adventist Church**, 2889 California Street, 415-921-9016, www.sfcentral.org. The church offers a variety of services, including Saturday services, and Sabbath school for children. To find a church or school near you visit www.adventistdirectory.org or http://cc.adventist.org.

UNITARIAN UNIVERSALIST

Known for their progressive views, social activism, and embrace of people from varied religious backgrounds, Unitarian Universalist churches are active throughout the Bay Area. For a list of local churches go to www.uua.org.

- **First Unitarian Universalist Church and Center**, 1187 Franklin St, San Francisco, 415-776-4580, www.uusf.org, welcomes people of all faiths, operates the King's Gallery art space, and offers a variety of programs including a Social Justice Committee, UUs for Peace, the Faithful Fools Street Ministry—addressing poverty through art and activism, a Wednesday night bridge club, and a choir.

JEWISH CONGREGATIONS

The **Jewish Community Center** at 3200 California Street, San Francisco, 415-346-6040, www.jccsf.org, offers Jewish education classes and workshops, social and singles events, programs for interfaith couples and families, preschools, after-school programs, a teen center, summer and day camps, youth sports classes and leagues, dance, music, ceramics and art classes, and older adult programs. In Palo Alto, the **Albert L. Schultz Jewish Community Center**, 650-493-9400, www.paloaltojcc.com, also offers classes and community events.

For a wealth of information log onto the **Jewish Community Federation's** web site, www.sfjcf.org, where you can find out about volunteer opportunities, trips to Israel for young people, and a great deal more. Resource, www.sfjcf.org/resource, is an excellent guide to Jewish life in the Bay Area and maintains a thorough list of local congregations, organizations, and social events.

The **Jewish Community Information & Referral**, 415-777-4545, www.jewishfed.org/resource should also be able to assist you.

For more on Jewish congregations and organizations in the Bay area, go to www.jewishsf.com, where you can bring up information about cooking, personal ads, classifieds, entertainment, a calendar of events, etc.

There are at least twenty different Jewish congregations in the City. Below are just a few.

CONSERVATIVE

- **Beth Shalom**, 1301 Clement St, San Francisco, 415-221-8736, is a traditional conservative congregation with more than 600 household members.

CONSERVATIVE REFORM

A conservative reform synagogue mixes conservative and reform traditions, and tends to have more English and less Hebrew in the service than a conservative synagogue.

- **Beth Israel**, 625 Brotherhood Way, San Francisco, 415-586-8833; offers a reform service on Fridays at 8 p.m., and a conservative service on Saturdays at 10 a.m. Parking is not a problem.

ORTHODOX

A good place for Orthodox newcomers to begin is www.jewish.org, a Silicon Valley–based web resource clearinghouse for the Orthodox community.
Chabad of Noe Valley, 94 29th St, San Francisco, 415-821-7046, www.chabadnoevalley.org, offers Shabbat and holiday services, Torah study, and a variety of other programs.

PROGRESSIVE REFORM

- **Sha'ar Zahav**, 290 Dolores St, San Francisco, 415-861-6932, www. ShaarZahav.org, is a progressive reform synagogue for people of all sexual identities.

RECONSTRUCTIONIST

- **Keddem Congregation**, 650-947-9913, www.keddem.org, a community-led congregation based in Palo Alto

REFORM

- **Temple Emmanu-El**, 2 Lake St, San Francisco, 415-751-2535, www.emmanu-el.org, celebrated its 150th anniversary in 2000; a beautiful temple, it's one of the centers of reform Jewish life in San Francisco.
- **Temple Sherith Israel**, 2266 California St, San Francisco, 415-346-1720

ISLAMIC WORSHIP

There are dozens of mosques, Islamic community centers, libraries, schools, and political and social groups in the Bay Area. For starters, in San Francisco contact the **Islamic Society of San Francisco** at 415-863-7997; in the South Bay, contact the **Muslim Community Association of the San Francisco Bay Area**, 408-970-0647. You can reach the **South Bay Islamic Association** at www.sbia.net, which offers details about Bay Area mosque locations, schools, elder groups, restaurant listings, charities, and more.

FAR EASTERN SPIRITUAL CENTERS

HINDU

To find out more about the practice of Hinduism and its related yogic meditations, visit the **Sivanda Ashram Yoga Center**, 1200 Arguello Boulevard, 415-681-2731. There are a number of yoga centers sprinkled throughout the city. Voted one of the best places to practice yoga by the *San Francisco Bay Guardian* is the **Mindful Body**, 2876 California St, 415-931-2639.

* **Hindu Temple and Cultural Center**, 3676 Delaware Dr, Fremont, 510-659-0655.
* **The Vedanta Society of Northern California** at 2323 Vallejo St, 415-922-2323, www.sfvedanta.org, while not a religious organization, offers lectures, scripture classes, a bookshop, and library.

BUDDHISM

The **San Francisco Buddhist Center**, at 37 Bartlett Street, 415-282-2018, www.sfbuddhistcenter.org, is a good resource for newcomers wanting to contact other Buddhist centers in the Bay Area.

Bay Area Zen Buddhist centers offer peaceful and sheltered environments for ceremonies, meals, meditations, chanting, and more, to members and non-members alike. The old brick **Zen Center** at 300 Page Street, in San Francisco, 415-863-3136, and Marin County's **Green Gulch Farm Zen Center** in Sausalito, 415-383-3134, are just two of the many centers in the Bay Area. (Vegetables grown at Green Gulch are used at Green's Restaurant in Fort Mason.) For more information and links to local centers, visit www.sfzc.com.

GAY AND LESBIAN

* **A Common Bond**, the support network for current and former gay, lesbian, bisexual, and transgender Jehovah's Witnesses, began in San Francisco and has expanded nationally. The group meets in the various homes of its members. For more information check out www.gayxjw.org.
* **Congregation Sha'ar Zahav**, 290 Dolores St, San Francisco, 415-861-6932, www.shaarzahav.org, is a reform synagogue for people of all sexual identities.
* **Dignity San Francisco**, San Francisco, 415-681-2491, www.dignity sanfrancisco.org, is for Catholic gay, lesbian, bisexual, and transgender people and their friends. Services are held at the Seventh Avenue Presbyterian Church, 3129 7th Ave.

- **Metropolitan Community Church**, 150 Eureka St, San Francisco, 415-863-4434, www.mccsf.org, offers social activities, recovery groups, counseling. The parishioners also serve meals to and provide showers for the homeless, and tutor children at the Harvey Milk Civil Rights Academy.
- **Most Holy Redeemer Church** (Catholic), 100 Diamond St, San Francisco, 415-863-6259, www.mhr.org, offers services, reconciliation and confession, and AIDS support groups.
- **Saint Francis Lutheran**, 152 Church St, San Francisco, 415-621-2635, www.st-francis-lutheran.org; this entire church is excommunicated from the mainstream Lutheran Church. They offer over 30 self-help groups, senior meetings, and bingo.

RELIGIOUS STUDIES

- **The Graduate Theological Union**, 1798 Scenic Ave, Berkeley, 510-849-8272, www.gtu.edu, nicknamed Holy Hill, is on the north side of the University of California at Berkeley. It includes the Pacific School of Religion, the Bade Museum (of religious items), the Flora Lamson Hewlitt Library, at 2400 Ridge Rd, 510-649-2500, as well as six schools of theology and six religious centers. Combined, these schools and centers offer seminars on every imaginable subject about any known religion. For more about lectures, presentations, and public prayer services, call 510-649-2400.

THE MISSIONS

For California history buffs, Roman Catholics, or anyone who wants to get a sense of old California, a tour of some of Northern California's missions is a must. Spanish missionaries settled California during the 1700s and several mission sites are still in existence today. Some are active, consecrated churches, others exist only as crumbling remnants.

- **Mission Dolores**, 3321 16th St, 415-621-8203, www.mission dolores.org, in the heart of San Francisco, is the area's most well known and still operating mission.
- Little of **Santa Clara's** original mission remains, but a replica has been placed on the University of Santa Clara campus.
- **Mission San Jose**, 43300 Mission Blvd, in Fremont has been reconstructed and re-consecrated.
- **Mission San Rafael**, 1104 5th Ave, 415-456-3016, once a sanitarium for the California natives who were sickened by exposure to European diseases, is today a consecrated church.

If you want to head out of town to see the historic sites, check out **Mission Soledad**, 36641 Fort Romie Road, **Sonoma Mission**, 114 East Spain Street, 707-938-1519, or **Carmel Mission**, 3080 Rio Road in Carmel. To find out more, visit www.californiamissons.com.

GIVING BACK TO THE COMMUNITY IS A REWARDING EXPERIENCE. Whether you are skilled at building houses, caring for the elderly, tutoring underprivileged children, or canvassing neighborhoods (having bilingual skills in any of these areas can be particularly useful), you can find a volunteer project that suits your talents and beliefs. Helping out in your new community is also a great way to meet people and can make the transition to an unfamiliar place less stressful.

HOW YOU CAN HELP

THE HUNGRY AND THE HOMELESS

Scores of volunteers concern themselves with shelter for the city's homeless. Jobs include monitoring and organizing the shelters; providing legal help; ministering to psychiatric, medical, and social needs; raising money; manning phones; and caring for children in the shelters. Many people solicit, organize, cook, and serve food to the destitute at sites throughout the city. Still others deliver meals to the homeless and the homebound.

CHILDREN

If involvement with children is especially appealing, you can tutor in and out of schools, be a big brother or sister, teach music and sports in shelters or at local community centers, run activities in the parks, entertain children in hospitals, and accompany kids on weekend outings. Schools, libraries, community associations, hospitals, and other facilities providing activities and guidance for children are all worth exploring.

HOSPITALS

The need for volunteers in both city-run and private hospitals is manifold: From interpreters to laboratory personnel to admitting and nursing aides, many volunteers are required. Assistants in crisis medical areas—emergency rooms, intensive care units, and the like—are wanted if you have the skills, as are volunteers to work with victims of sexual abuse. If you just want to be helpful, you might assist in food delivery or work in the gift shop.

THE DISABLED AND THE ELDERLY

You can read to the blind, help teach the deaf, work to prevent birth defects, and help the retarded and developmentally disabled, among others. You can also make regular visits to the homebound elderly, bring hot meals to their homes, and teach everything from nutrition to arts and crafts in senior centers and nursing homes.

EXTREME CARE SITUATIONS

Helping with suicide prevention, Alzheimer's and AIDS patients, rape victims, and abused children is a special category demanding a high level of commitment—not to mention emotional reserves and, in many cases, special skills.

THE CULTURE SCENE

Area museums are constantly in need of volunteers to lead tours or lend a hand in any number of ways. Libraries, theater groups, and ballet companies have plenty of tasks that need to be done. Fundraising efforts also require many volunteers to stuff envelopes and/or make phone calls. The Public Broadcasting Service (PBS) is a good example. Its large volunteer staff raises money for its stations through extensive on-air fundraising campaigns that include collecting pledges.

THE COMMUNITY

Work in your neighborhood. You can help out at the local school, community garden, neighborhood block association, nursing home, settlement house, or animal shelter.

VOLUNTEER REFERRAL SERVICES

The agencies listed below can put you in touch with the many service organizations in the Bay Area in need of your assistance.

- **Center for Volunteer and Nonprofit Leadership of Marin**, 415-479-5710, www.centerforleadershipmarin.org
- **Contra Costa Volunteer Center** (also serving Alameda County), 925-472-5760 or 800-123-CARE, www.helpnow.org
- **Hayward Area Volunteer Services**, 510-888-0102
- **Volunteer Center of San Francisco** (also serving San Mateo County), 415-982-8999, www.thevolunteercenter.net

If you already know which type of volunteer work suits you, try one of the agencies below.

AREA CAUSES

ALCOHOL AND DRUG ABUSE RECOVERY

- **Alcoholics Anonymous**, 415-674-1821, www.aasf.org
- **Glide Memorial Church**, 415-771-6300, www.glide.org
- **Haight-Ashbury Free Clinic**, 415-487-5638, www.hafci.org
- **Narcotics Anonymous**, 415-621-8600, www.sfna.org

ANIMALS

- **Marine Mammal Center**, 415-979-4357, www.tmmc.org
- **Peninsula Humane Society**, 650-340-7022, www.peninsulahumanesociety.org
- **Pets Unlimited**, 415-563-6700, www.petsunlimited.org
- **Randall Museum**, 415-554-9600, www.randallmuseum.org
- **San Francisco Society for the Prevention of Cruelty to Animals**, 415-554-3000, www.sfspca.org
- **San Francisco Zoo**, 415-753-7080, TTY 415-753-8141, www.sfzoo.org

ARTS AND CULTURE

- **Asian Art Museum**, 415-581-3500, www.asianart.org
- **Cartoon Art Museum**, 415-227-8666, www.cartoonart.org
- **De Young Museum and Legion of Honor**, 415-863-3330, www.thinker.org

- **Photo Alliance**, 415-781-8111, www.photoalliance.org
- **San Francisco Museum of Modern Art**, 415-357-4000, TTY 415-357-4154, www.sfmoma.org
- **Yerba Buena Center for the Arts**, 415-978-2787, www.ybca.org

CRIME

- **San Francisco District Attorney Victim Services Unit**, 415-553-9044, www.victimservicessf.org

DISABLED ASSISTANCE

- **Council of the Blind**, 800-221-6359
- **Crisis Line**, 800-426-4263
- **Hearing Society**, 415-693-5870
- **The Janet Pomeroy Center** (recreation center for the handicapped), 415-665-4100, www.janetpomeroy.org
- **Rose Resnick Lighthouse for the Blind**, 415-431-1481, www.light house-sf.org
- **United Cerebral Palsy of the Golden Gate**, 510-832-7430, www.ucp.org

DISASTER

- **American Red Cross Bay Area Chapter**, 415-427-8052, www.bayarea-redcross.org
- **United Way of the Bay Area**, 800-CARE-123, www.theunited way.org

ENVIRONMENT

- **California Conservation Corps**, 800-952-5627, www.ccc.ca.gov
- **Nature Conservancy**, 415-777-0487, http://nature.org
- **Sierra Club**, 415-977-5500, www.sierraclub.org

GAY AND LESBIAN

- **Gay Youth Talk Line**, 415-863-3636
- **LYRIC (Lavender Youth Recreation and Information Center)**, 415-703-8510, www.lyric.org
- **Metropolitan Community Church**, 415-863-4434, www. mccsf.org

- **New Leaf**, 415-626-7000, www.newleafservices.org
- **The Center**, 415-865-5585, www.sfcenter.org

HEALTH

- **American Cancer Society**, 415-394-7100, www.cancer.org
- **American Heart Association**, 415-433-2273, www.american heart.org
- **Blood Centers of the Pacific**, 415-567-6400, www.blood centers.org
- **Haight-Ashbury Free Clinic**, 415-487-5638, www.hafci.org
- **Mental Health Association**, 415-421-2926, www.mha-sf.org

HISTORY

- **California Historical Society**, 415-357-1848, www.california historicalsociety.org
- **San Francisco Maritime National Historic Park**, 415-561-7000, TTY 415-556-1843, www.nps.gov/safr

HIV/AIDS

- **AIDS Emergency Fund**, 415-558-6999, www.aidsemergency fund.org
- **AIDS/HIV/HEP C Nightline**, 415-984-1902, TTY 415-781-2228
- **California AIDS Hotline**, 415-863-2437 or 800-367-AIDS, www.sfaf.org
- **Shanti**, 415-674-4700, www.shanti.org
- **Project Inform**, 415-558-8669 or 800-822-7422, www.project inform.org
- **Project Open Hand**, 415-447-2404, www.openhand.org

HUNGER AND HOMELESSNESS

- **Community Awareness & Treatment Services, Inc. (CATS)**, 415-241-1199, www.catsinc.org
- **Glide Memorial Church**, 415-771-6300, www.glide.org
- **Home Away From Homelessness**, 415-561-5533, www.home away.org
- **Meals on Wheels**, 415-920-1111, www.mowsf.org
- **Project Open Hand**, 415-447-2404, www.openhand.org
- **SF Food Bank**, 415-282-1907, www.sffoodbank.org

- **Salvation Army**, 415-553-3500, www.tsagoldenstate.org
- **St. Anthony's Dining Hall**, 415-592-2748, www.stanthonysf.org
- **St. Vincent de Paul**, 415-977-1270, http://vincent.org

LEGAL

- **ACLU**, 415-621-2493, www.aclunc.org
- **Asian Law Caucus**, 415-896-1701, www.asianlawcaucus.org
- **Bay Area Legal Aid**, 415-982-1300, www.baylegal.org
- **The Legal Aid Society of San Francisco and Employment Law Center**, 415-864-8848, TTY 415-593-0091, www.las-elc.org
- **Legal Services for Children**, 415-863-3762, www.lsc-sf.org

LITERACY

- **Project Read**, 415-557-4388, http:sfpl.lib.ca.us

SENIOR SERVICES

- **Institute on Aging**, 415-750-4180
- **Legal Assistance to the Elderly**, 415-538-3333
- **Meals on Wheels**, 415-920-1111, www.mowsf.org
- **Mission Hospice of San Mateo County**, 650-554-1000, www.missionhospice.org

WOMEN'S SERVICES

- **Planned Parenthood Golden Gate**, 415-441-7858, www.ppgg.org
- **WOMAN Inc. (Women Organized to Make Abuse Nonexistent)**, 415-864-4722, www.womaninc.org
- **Women Against Rape**, 415-861-2024
- **The Women's Building**, 415-431-1180, www.womensbuilding.org

YOUTH

- **Big Brothers/Big Sisters of San Francisco and the Peninsula**, 415-503-4050, www.sf-bbbs.org
- **Boys & Girls Clubs of San Francisco**, 415-445-5482, www.bgcsf.org
- **Break the Cycle**, 415-341-1765, www.breakthecycle.org

- **Child Care Coordinating Council of San Mateo County**, 650-655-6770, www.thecouncil.net
- **Girlventures**, 415-864-0780, www.girlventures.org
- **Larkin Street Youth Services**, 415-673-0911, www.larkinstreet youth.org
- **Polly Klaas Foundation**, 800-587-4357, www.pollyklaas.org
- **San Francisco Child Abuse Prevention Center**, 415-668-0494, www.sfcapc.org
- **San Francisco School Volunteers**, 415-749-3700, www.sfsv.org
- **YMCA of San Francisco**, 415-777-9622, www.ymcasf.org

BY CAR

CALIFORNIA IS WIDELY KNOWN FOR ITS "CAR CULTURE." HOWEVER, if you are planning to live and work in San Francisco, having a car—with the endless hassles of parking, the merciless traffic, and the staggering price of gas—can often seem more like a hindrance than a help. Living car-free in San Francisco is common, thanks to an excellent public transportation system that makes getting around town easy and inexpensive. However, living car-free outside San Francisco is quite a different story. Despite the best efforts of alternative transportation advocates, a long history of poor regional planning, abysmal connections, and sparse suburban options have left those who live and/or work outside the city little choice but to get into their cars and go. Thus Bay Area freeways clog every weekday morning, afternoon, and evening, often to the point of gridlock. According to *Commute Profile 2004* published by RIDES for Bay Area (www.rides.org or www.511.org), more than 3.3 million people in the Bay Area commute to work, and of these vast majority—64%—drive alone in their cars.

However, the situation is getting better. The number of solo drivers has been slowly decreasing, as the stress- and money-saving option of carpooling becomes more popular. And with the recent opening of its much anticipated airport extension—which includes several new stops along the peninsula including SFO—BART has also become a way of life for many of those who work along its corridor. Plans are in the works to extend BART further still, to provide better links between Santa Clara and Alameda County. And with plans inching forward throughout the region to create so-called transit corridors—improving links between BART, CalTrain, light rail, ferries, buses, and shuttles as well as expanding bike and pedestrian pathways—residents may soon have more reliable, easy-to-use, eco-friendly commute options.

For details on Bay Area transit options including fares, routes, and schedules as well as traffic updates, ridesharing, bicycling, and trip planning options, check out 511, a new phone and web information service provided by the Metropolitan Transportation Commission (MTC). Simply dial 511 from anywhere in the nine Bay Area counties, 24 hours a day, 7 days a week, or visit www.511.org.

TRAFFIC

When the dot-com boom bubble burst, it took not only many jobs with it, but many cars too. With a sharp decline in the hordes of commuters heading south into the heart of the Silicon Valley, congestion on local highways declined in 2003 for the third year in a row, according to a study by the Metropolitan Transportation Commission. But that doesn't mean it's all smooth sailing. Particular routes remain stubborn problems—most notoriously the dreaded Bay Bridge commute, which brings throngs of East Bay residents to work in San Francisco and back, backing up not only Interstate 80 but the connecting highways as well as several city blocks starting in the late afternoon. In fact, the MTC named the Bay Bridge morning commute the area's most congested strip of highway. Replacing the South Bay as the new heart of the Bay Area's traffic woes, the East Bay now boasts three of the Bay Area's worst commutes along Interstate 580 in eastern Alameda County. If taking BART or some other form of mass transit is not feasible, the travel information line, 511 (no area code needed), will give you up-to-the-minute highway condition reports for the entire Bay Area. Or tune into KALW-FM at 91.7, KGO-AM at 810, and KCBS-AM at 740, during morning and afternoon commute hours. Real-time traffic incidents are available at http://cad.chp.ca.gov.

CARPOOLING

Rides for Bay Area Commuters Inc. is a free carpool and vanpool matching service. To be matched with a fellow commuter who is on a similar work schedule and lives and works close to you, call the service at 511 or check www.511.org. In the Bay Area you'll find carpool lanes, also called diamond lanes, on the major freeways. The number of passengers required to qualify as a carpool and the hours during which the lane may be used exclusively by buses, vanpools, and carpools varies. Call the above number for more details, or check your route for posted information. During commute hours, 5 a.m. to 10 a.m., and 3 p.m. to 7 p.m., the Bay bridges offer free tolls for those driving with three or more people in a vehicle. Commute hours for the Golden Gate Bridge are 5 a.m. to 9 a.m. and 4 p.m. to 6 p.m. There are also 150 Park & Ride lots throughout the area where you can leave your car to join a van or carpool. Contact Rides to join a van or carpool. There's no need to drive down that lonesome highway all alone!

CAR SHARING

If you prefer to live car-free but might need your own set of wheels every once in awhile for errands, moving, etc., car sharing programs let you reserve cars by the hour. In San Francisco and the East Bay, **City CarShare** maintains a fleet of Volkswagen Bugs that can be picked up and dropped off at a variety of locations. There is a $30 application fee that includes driver orientation. Membership is $10 per month, plus a $300 deposit. Vehicles are $4/hour and 44 cents per mile at peak times and include gas and insurance. For more information call 415-995-8588 or visit www.city carshare.org

CAR RENTALS

All the big rental outfits are represented in the Bay Area, most with numerous locations. Here are a few numbers to get you started:
* **Alamo**, 800-327-9633, www.alamo.com
* **Avis**, 800-831-2847, www.avis.com
* **Budget**, 800-527-0700, www.budget.com
* **Dollar**, 800-800-4000, www.dollar.com
* **Enterprise**, 800-325-8007, www.enterprise.com
* **Hertz**, 800-654-3131, www.hertz.com
* **National**, 800-227-7368, www.nationalcar.com
* **Thrifty**, 800-847-4389, www.thrifty.com

TAXIS

The Bay Area is served by a number of cab companies, but they are not always easy to find and it almost always seems that once you sight a cab it's already full. Particularly on a rainy day, holidays (especially Halloween and New Year's), and during rush hour, it is best to call ahead. If you are already out and about and need a cab, you might have better luck hailing one in front of a hotel, a department store, or a hospital.

SAN FRANCISCO
* **De Soto Cab**, 415-970-1300
* **Luxor Cab**, 415-282-4141
* **Veteran's Cab**, 415-552-1300
* **SuperShuttle**, 415-558-8500

NORTH BAY
- **Marin Cab**, 415-455-4555
- **North Bay Cooperative Taxi**, 415-332-2200
- **Yellow Cab of Marin County**, 415-453-6030

EAST BAY
- **Berkeley Yellow**, 510-528-9999
- **Contra Costa Cab**, 925-235-3000
- **Veteran's Cab**, 510-533-1900
- **Yellow Cab**, 510-317-2200

PENINSULA
- **A-One Airport Transportation**, 650-571-0606
- **Burlingame Rainbow Cab**, 650-344-6718
- **Hillsborough Yellow Cab**, 650-340-0330
- **Peninsula Cab Co.**, 650-344-2627
- **Yellow Cab,** 650-321-1234

SOUTH BAY
- **American Cab**, 408-727-2277
- **Santa Clara Cab**, 408-773-1900
- **San Jose Taxicab**, 408-437-8700
- **United Cab**, 408-971-1111
- **Yellow Cab**, 408-293-1234

BY BIKE

Many Bay Area residents commute to work by bicycle. To find out everything you need to know about using your bike as transportation in the Bay Area call 511 (no area code needed) and ask for the "**RIDES Bicycle Resource Guide**" or check www.511.org. At this site you can find out about bike racks at your place of work, track down a bike buddy, learn about bicycle routes and lanes, and find a bicycle club. If you choose this manner of commuting, make sure to purchase a bike light for the winter months, and wear a helmet! Bicycles are allowed on BART with the following restrictions: Bikes are allowed on at the Embarcadero Station during morning commute hours (7:05 a.m. to 8:50 a.m.) only for trips to the East Bay. For the evening commute (4:25 p.m. to 6:45 p.m.), bicycles coming from the East Bay must exit at the Embarcadero Station. During morning and evening commute hours bikes are not allowed in the 12th and 19th Street Oakland Stations. During non-commute times, bicyclists are allowed in any car except for the first car. There is no extra cost for bringing your bike. Most ferries and buses (not all) also accommodate bikes. But be fore-warned, most city bus racks can only hold one bicycle at a time!

For the latest about proposed bike routes, bicycle commuting initia-tives, safety information, and bike laws go to **California's Department of Transportation** web site, http://www.dot.ca.gov/hq/tpp/offices/bike/bicycle_prgm.htm. Another resource is the **San Francisco Bicycle Coalition** at 415-431-BIKE, www.sfbike.org. To learn more about recre-ational bicycling in the Bay Area, consult the **Sports and Recreation** chapter.

A note of interest: on the last Friday of every month, **Critical Mass**, a large group of bike riders, gathers at the Ferry building in downtown San Francisco to ride together throughout the city. Their intent is to be noticed, particularly by city leaders and drivers, in the hope that more attention will be paid to biking as an alternative form of transportation. Take a look at their web site for more information, www.critical-mass.org.

PUBLIC TRANSPORTATION

BAY AREA RAPID TRANSIT (BART)

The king of local transportation systems is Bay Area Rapid Transit, a high-speed, above- and below-ground train system that whisks travelers between San Francisco, the East Bay, and San Mateo County, through one of the world's longest underwater tunnels. BART transports about 350,000 people daily, and has a reputation for being clean, quiet, and on time.

Currently BART runs five lines on more than 100 miles of track between 43 stations. Recently, the much-awaited extension to the San Francisco International Airport opened, bringing with it three additional stations en route – South San Francisco, San Bruno, and Millbrae. Trains currently run weekdays from 4 a.m. to midnight, Saturdays, 6 a.m. to midnight, and Sundays, 8 a.m. to midnight. Fares are based on distance traveled, and range from $1.25 to $7.45, one way. Discount tickets (75% off) for senior citizens, children 5–12 years old, persons with disabilities who have proper identification, and students on a chaperoned field trip are sold at participat-ing banks, retailers, social service agencies, and other community-based organizations. These tickets are not sold at any of the BART stations.

BART stations are also connection points for local bus services, making it fairly easy to get just about anywhere in the Bay Area on public transit. You can pick up free transfers from BART stations in San Francisco and Daly City for discounts on connections with MUNI. All BART stations are wheel-chair accessible. Bicycles are allowed on BART; see **By Bike** above for details. For schedule and fare information drop by the Customer Service window at the Lake Merritt BART station in Oakland, or at the Embarcadero or Montgomery stations in San Francisco during normal business hours, or call 510-465-2278 or 415-989-2278 or 650-992-2278; TTY: 510-839-2278. BART also has an informative web site, www.bart.gov.

SAN FRANCISCO MUNICIPAL RAIL (MUNI)

San Francisco's bus system or MUNI employs a variety of vehicles including diesel and electric buses, electric trolleys (some of them vintage), MUNI Metro light-rail vehicles, and the world-renowned cable cars. In total, MUNI operates 80 lines, 17 of them express, as well as special service to Monster Park (formerly called Candlestick Park) for 49ers games and other events. In general, service is available 24 hours, although not on all lines. The current adult fare is $1.50 one way. Cable car rides cost $5. Exact change is required on all MUNI vehicles, except for the cable cars. Transfers are available on all MUNI lines, as are discounts for seniors, youths and the disabled. A monthly pass costs $10.00 for seniors, youths, and disabled people, and $45.00 for everyone else. You can also buy a weekly pass for $15.00. The monthly pass is also valid on specific BART, CalTrain, and SamTrans routes within the city (routes 24B and 34 and only within San Francisco), as well as cable cars. If you are taking BART and then MUNI, you can get a 25-cent discount on your bus ride. Just stop off before you exit the BART gates near the addfare machine to pick up a transfer discount coupon.

You can also always request a transfer to ride on another MUNI bus for free from the MUNI bus driver. Bus transfers are valid for 90 minutes and can be used for any direction. The popular light rail service has been gradually expanding over the years, and a new 3rd Street extension—linking southeast San Francisco with downtown—is slated to open in 2006.

For more information on MUNI service call 415-673-MUNI; TTY: 415-923-6366 or visit their web site at www.sfmuni.com. Call 415-923-6070 for information about services for passengers with disabilities.

ALAMEDA–CONTRA COSTA TRANSIT (AC)

AC Transit, 510-891-4700, TTY 800-448-9790, www.actransit.org, is the bus system connecting the East Bay to San Francisco, and serves Alameda and Contra Costa counties. Widely used are the commute-hour Transbay Express Routes from San Francisco to cities in the East Bay such as Oakland, Berkeley, Alameda, Emeryville, Richmond, and more. AC Transit also connects with all East Bay BART stations. Ticket prices vary depending on distance traveled; they range from $1.50 to $3 down to $.75 for seniors, the disabled, and those under 12. You can purchase transfers for $.25. Transfers from BART are $1.25.

SAN MATEO COUNTY TRANSIT (SAMTRANS)

SamTrans, 800-660-4287, TTY 650-508-6448, www.samtrans.com, provides Peninsula residents with local bus service and offers routes to downtown San Francisco. It also offers direct service from SFO to downtown San Francisco. The cost varies depending on distance traveled.

GOLDEN GATE TRANSIT (GGT)

Golden Gate Transit, 415-923-2000; TTY 415-257-4554, www.goldengate transit.org, provides **local bus service** for Marin County communities, as well as **commuter bus and ferry service** between Marin and Sonoma counties and downtown San Francisco. The ferries depart for San Francisco from the Larkspur Ferry Terminal and a Sausalito dock located just off Bridgeway, the city's main street. There is plenty of free parking at the Larkspur facility and metered parking close to the Sausalito launch point. There is no more civilized or more relaxing way to commute than on the ferry, and more and more people are choosing to take the boat these days. Another added bonus about the scenic ferry is that numerous romances have blossomed on these morning and evening cruises. Drinks and snacks are served. The trip across the bay takes about 30 minutes. The cost varies depending upon distance traveled.

ADDITIONAL BUS SERVICES

- **Contra Costa County Connection** provides local bus service in Contra Costa County, call 925-676-7500, TTY: 800-735-2929.
- **Santa Clara County Transit** or **Valley Transit Authority** offers bus and light rail service to the South Bay, call 800-894-9908; TTY: 408-321-2330.

FERRIES

ALAMEDA, OAKLAND, AND VALLEJO FERRIES

Providing an aquatic link to downtown San Francisco for East Bay residents, the **Alameda/Oakland Ferry**, 510-522-3300, www.eastbay ferry.com, is similar to the Golden Gate ferry service outlined above. Those who use the boat regularly often develop friendships that continue on land, and you can be sure plenty of professional networking takes place on board. The boats leave seven days a week from Oakland's Jack London Square, at the foot of Broadway, and from Alameda's Main Street terminal.

They dock at San Francisco's Ferry Building and at Fisherman's Wharf. Food and beverage service is available. One-way fares range from $1.25 to $5.50, and ticket books are also available.

Baylink, 707-64-FERRY or 877-64-FERRY, www.baylinkferry.com, operates daily commuter ferry service from San Francisco to Vallejo. One-way fares are $4.75 to $9.50, and various passes are also available.

The **Harbor Bay Ferry**, 510-769-5500, www.harborbayferry.com, operates from the San Francisco Ferry Building to Bay Farm Island (part of the City of Alameda) in the East Bay. Travel time is approximately 30 minutes. One-way fares are $5.50 for adults, with various passes available.

The **Golden Gate Ferry Service**, 415-455-2000, www.goldengate ferry.org, is the premier north county water link, with daily service connecting San Francisco with Larkspur and Sausalito. One-way fares range from $3.20 to $6.45.

Long-range regional transportation planning talks frequently have expanded ferry service on the table, but whether this will become a reality remains to be seen.

ADDITIONAL FERRY SERVICE

- **Angel Island–Tiburon Ferry**, 415-435-2131
- **Blue and Gold Fleet**, 415-773-1188

COMMUTER TRAINS

CALTRAIN

For Peninsula and South Bay residents, the commuter rail option is CalTrain, 800-660-4287, TTY: 415-508-6448, www.caltrain.com. This service runs between Gilroy in the South Bay and San Francisco's Fourth Street Station. Once you get to San Francisco you'll need to take a bus, cab, or walk to the Financial District. There is talk of extending CalTrain's tracks to the Transbay Terminal at First and Mission streets. Fares on CalTrain are based on distance traveled, range from $2.00 to $5.25, and can be purchased at any CalTrain station. From San Jose, trains run Monday–Friday, 4:44 a.m. to 10:30 p.m., and from San Francisco, 5 a.m. to 11:59 p.m. Bikes are allowed in the northernmost car, which is the designated bicycle car. Some trains also have an added, second bicycle car.

AMTRAK

Amtrak trains don't board in San Francisco; instead you take the Amtrak bus at the Ferry Building, Pier 39 (near Fisherman's Wharf), or at Powell and Market, which will then drive you over the Bay Bridge to the Amtrak station in Emeryville. Or you can take BART, disembark at the Richmond station, and catch an Amtrak train one block away at 16th and MacDonald. Oakland has a new train station just two blocks off Jack London Square at Embarcadero and Alice Street. Amtrak provides connecting bus service to San Francisco, or you can head off on your own and catch the ferry. In San Jose, Amtrak is located at 65 Cahill just south of the Alameda. Here you can connect up with local commuter trains and buses.

For more information call the central line at 800-USA-RAIL or check www.reservations.amtrak.com. When visiting online, look for "rail sale" entries, where you'll find discounts of up to 60% on long-distance coach train tickets. Regional Amtrak information can be found at Amtrak California, www.amtrakcalifornia.com, which lists local specials and promotions.

ALTAMONT COMMUTER EXPRESS (ACE)

Altamont Commuter Express is a new commuter train service for those traveling between Stockton and San Jose, with additional stops in Lathrop/Manteca, Tracy, Livermore, Pleasanton, Fremont, and Santa Clara. Currently, there are two morning and two afternoon trains. Fares depend on the distance traveled and range from $3 to $10 one-way. Monthly passes are available and range in price from $65 to $259. For more information, contact 800-411-RAIL or visit the ACE website at www.acerail.com.

GREYHOUND

Greyhound has numerous stations throughout the Bay Area. For more information, call 800-231-2222, or visit their web site at www.greyhound.com.

AIRPORTS & AIRLINES

SAN FRANCISCO INTERNATIONAL AIRPORT (SFO)

Located 15 miles south of downtown San Francisco, SFO sits just off Highway 101 near the Peninsula cities of Millbrae and San Bruno. The granddaddy of Bay Area airports, it seems to be under continuous construction. Presently a new international terminal is being built, and airport officials warn of increased traffic congestion and long-term and short-term parking shortages due to this construction.

There is no shortage of transportation options between the airport and San Francisco. One of the best is BART, which runs directly to SFO, where it connects with a new air tram that will shuttle you straight to your terminal. Be sure to check the schedule ahead of time though, as service is less frequent outside rush hours and on weekends. A taxi or a limo will set you back about $40. One of the many shuttle vans, such as SuperShuttle, 415-558-8500, www.supershuttle.com will cost about $15 (additional passengers in your party are $8 each) but you may have to sit through a number of stops before you get to your destination (they claim no more than three stops per trip). If you've got time to kill and you need to conserve cash, catch a SamTrans bus at one of several stops right outside the terminals for a ride directly into downtown San Francisco. (For more on SamTrans see above.)

For more information on SFO call 650-761-0800, or visit their web site at www.sfoairport.org. Airlines serving SFO include:

- **Air Canada**, 888-247-2262, www.aircanada.ca/home.html
- **Air China**, 800-986-1985, www.airchina.com.cn/en/index.jsp
- **Air France**, 800-237-2747, www.airfrance.com/us
- **AirTran**, 800-247-8726, www.airtran.com
- **Alaska**, 800-426-0333, www.alaskaair.com
- **America West**, 800-235-9292, www.americawest.com
- **American**, 800-433-7300, www.aa.com
- **ATA**, 800-435-9282, www.ata.com
- **British Airways**, 800-247-9297, www.british-airways.com
- **Continental**, 800-523-3273, www.flycontinental.com
- **Delta**, 800-221-1212, www.delta-air.com
- **Hawaiian Airlines**, 800-367-5320, www.hawaiianair.com
- **Japan**, 800-525-3663, www.japanair.com
- **Lufthansa**, 800-645-3880, www.lufthansa.com
- **Mexicana**, 800-531-7921, www.mexicana.com
- **Northwest-KLM**, 800-225-2525, www.nwa.com
- **Qantas**, 800-227-4585, www.qantas.com
- **USAir**, 800-428-4322, www.usairways.com
- **United**, 800-241-6522, www.unitedairlines.com
- **Virgin Atlantic**, 800-862-8621, www.virgin-atlantic.com

OAKLAND INTERNATIONAL AIRPORT

This East Bay airport is easier to use than San Francisco International for one simple reason: It is much smaller than its trans-bay Goliath. While SFO is serviced by many major US and international carriers, Oakland Airport focuses on commuter and low-cost airlines, the most popular being Southwest and the United Shuttle. Oakland Airport is fairly easy to get in and out of by car, and is also served on a regular basis by a shuttle from BART's Coliseum station. Parking is usually available at Oakland Airport,

TRANSPORTATION

433

even during peak holiday travel periods. The airport is located at the west end of Hegenberger Road, a clearly marked exit from Highway I-880.

- **Alaska**, 800-426-0333, www.alaskaair.com
- **Aloha**, 800-367-5250, www.alohaairlines.com
- **America West**, 800-235-9292, www.americawest.com
- **American**, 800-433-7300, www.aa.com
- **Continental**, 800-523-3273, www.flycontinental.com
- **Delta**, 800-221-1212, www.delta-air.com
- **Jet Blue**, 800-538-2583, www.jetblue.com
- **Mexicana**, 800-531-7921, www.mexicana.com
- **Southwest Airlines**, 800-435-9792, www.swavacations.com
- **United Shuttle**, 800-748-8853, www.united.com

For general information on Oakland Airport call 510-577-4000. For the latest on airport parking call 510-633-2571.

SAN JOSE INTERNATIONAL AIRPORT

Located just north of downtown, San Jose International Airport, like Oakland Airport, is relatively easy to navigate and to find parking at. Large and small air carriers fly to San Jose International. For general information call 408-277-4SKY or look at their web site at www.sjc.org.

Some of the airlines serving San Jose include:

- **Alaska**, 800-252-7522, www.alaskaair.com
- **American**, 800-433-7300, www.aa.com
- **Continental**, 800-523-3273, www.flycontinental.com
- **Delta**, 800-221-1212, www.delta-air.com
- **Mexicana**, 800-531-7921, www.mexicana.com
- **Northwest-KLM**, 800-225-2525, www.nwa.com
- **Southwest**, 800-435-9792, www.swavacations.com
- **United**, 800-241-6522, www.unitedairlines.com

ONLINE RESOURCES—AIR TRAVEL

A number of travel-related web sites all tout great deals including Travelocity.com, Intellitrip.com, Expedia.com, Orbitz.com, Lowestfare.com, and Cheaptickets.com—take your pick. If cost far outweighs convenience, check Priceline, www.priceline.com, where you may be able to pin down a cheap fare at an inconvenient hour (often in the middle of the night). Some airlines post last-minute seats at a reduced rate, usually online. Northwest, www.nwa.com, posts last-minute cybersavers on Wednesdays at 12:01 a.m. Check with other airlines' web sites for similar deals.

To register a complaint against an airline, contact the Department of Transportation: 202-366-2220, Aviation Consumer Protection Division, C-75 Room 4107, 400 7th Street SW, Washington, DC 20590.

Information about flight delays can be checked online at www.fly.faa.gov.

U NTIL YOU FIND YOUR FIRST BAY AREA HOME OR APARTMENT, YOU'LL need an interim place to hang your hat. Besides hundreds of hotels, motels, and bed and breakfasts aimed at San Francisco's considerable tourist trade, there are old-fashioned, homey residential clubs in better neighborhoods that may be more economical. Also, although most of the hotels in the city are downtown or at Fisherman's Wharf, there are neighborhood hotels where you can get a sense of what it might be like to live in a particular area of San Francisco. If you are an adventurous and/or budget-minded newcomer, you may want to consider one of the single-room occupancy hotels, called SROs, that dot much of downtown. Keep in mind that these establishments typically offer just a small room with little more than a bed, dresser, chair, and a desk. They are popular because they are cheap and because they rent by the day, week, or month. Unfortunately, these low-rent buildings are often located in the seedier parts of town, 6th and Mission streets south of Market, and the Tenderloin, which is just north of Market.

Reservations for bigger, more mainstream and chain hotels can be had by calling a hotel directly or through a reservation service such as **Central Reservation Service**, 800-548-3311, **Hotel Reservations Network**, 800-964-6835, **Quikbook**, 800-789-9887, or **San Francisco Reservations**, 800-333-8996. Or go online at the following web sites for similar information: www.quikbook.com, www.hotels.com, www.hotel discount.com, www.hotelres.com. Always ask about the cancellation policy when booking through discount sites, as charges may apply. Some companies ask for full payment upon making the reservation.

Low rates quoted below are for one person per night, and for the most part, high rates quoted are for two persons per night. Of course, prices are subject to change depending on the season. If you are a real bargain hunter, try negotiating a lower price.

Unless otherwise noted, all listed establishments are in San Francisco.

RESIDENCE CLUBS

Residence clubs offer secure housing, maid service, some meals, community rooms for television, videos, reading, games, message service, and the opportunity to meet dozens of people in the same situation as yourself. They are not the cheapest form of housing, but the pampering you receive while you search for something permanent may be worth the added expense. Prices typically range from $175 to $300 per week and up.

- **The Gaylord Apartment Hotel**, 620 Jones St, 415-673-8445, a pretty, California Mission–style hotel
- **Harcourt Residence Club**, 1105 Sutter St, 415-673-7721
- **Kenmore Residence Club**, 1570 Sutter St, 415-776-5815
- **Mary Elizabeth Inn**, 1040 Bush St, 415-673-6768, www.meinn.org, women only, minimum two-week stay
- **Monroe Residence Club**, 1870 Sacramento St, 415-474-6200
- **San Francisco Residence Club**, 851 California St, 415-421-2220

INEXPENSIVE HOTELS

San Francisco has a range of basic, inexpensive motels and hotels located downtown and along outer Lombard Street in the Marina. Prices range from as little as $50 to $150 per night. The greater Bay Area has a variety of options too, many of them located just off of major highways.

- **Capri Motel**, 2015 Greenwich St, 415-346-4667
- **Comfort Inn**, 2775 Van Ness Ave, 928-5000, and 1370 Monument Blvd, Concord, 925-827-8998
- **Days Inn**, 2650 El Camino Real, Redwood City, 650-369-9200, suites with kitchenettes available; to find other Bay Area locations call 800-453-7070, www.daysinn.com
- **Hotel Sheehan**, 620 Sutter St, 800-848-1529, www.sheehan hotel.com, downtown; indoor swimming pool
- **The Phoenix Hotel**, 601 Eddy St, 415-776-1380, www.jdvhospitality. com, a San Francisco legend, this arty hotel is built around an enclosed courtyard pool, with popular adjoining bar; a frequently used pit stop for touring rock bands; good for young, energetic, music-loving set
- **Royal Pacific Motor Inn**, 661 Broadway, 415-781-6661
- **San Remo**, 2227 Mason St, 800-352-REMO, a charming old hotel (it has chain toilets) with odd-shaped rooms, a Victorian ambiance, a wine bar, and lots of European guests; located in North Beach

- **Seal Rock Inn**, 545 Point Lobos, 415-752-8000, located in the fog belt of the Richmond district, a good place to stay if you want to get a taste of the Richmond or Sunset districts

MEDIUM-PRICED HOTELS

The next step up, mid-range hotels run a bit more; room rates vary from about $100 to $250 per night.
- **Berkeley City Club**, 2315 Durant Ave, 510-848-7800
- **Berkeley Travelodge**, 1820 University, 510-843-4262
- **Canterbury Hotel**, 750 Sutter St, 415-474-6464, downtown
- **Chancellor Hotel**, 433 Powell St, 415-362-2004, downtown
- **Claremont Resort and Spa**, Ashby and Domingo, Berkeley, 510-843-3000, www.claremontresort.com, a rambling Victorian spa
- **Courtyard by Marriott**, 2500 Larkspur Landing Circle, Larkspur Landing, 800-321-2211
- **Holiday Inn Express Hotel and Suites**, 93 West El Camino Real, Mountain View, 650-967-6957, www.hitowncenter.com, geared for business travelers, offers a variety of extended stay options
- **Hotel Boheme**, 444 Columbus Ave in North Beach, 415-433-9111; an ode to the beatniks
- **Hotel California**, 2431 Ash St, Palo Alto, 650-322-7666
- **Hotel Rex**, 562 Sutter St, 415-433-4434, www.thehotelrex.com, cozy boutique hotel in the heart of the theater district with tasty restaurant downstairs
- **King George Hotel**, 334 Mason St, 415-781-5050, www.king george.com, downtown, an interesting, skinny, green building with a popular tea room
- **Madison Street Inn**, 1390 Madison St, Santa Clara, 408-249-5541
- **The Maxwell**, 386 Geary St, 415-986-2000, $149-$225; downtown
- **Oakland Marriott**, 1001 Broadway, 510-451-4000, downtown with great views of Lake Merritt and the Bay
- **San Ramon Marriott**, 2600 Bishop Dr, San Ramon, 925-867-9200
- **York Hotel**, 940 Sutter St, 415-885-6800, downtown, houses the Plushroom, a cabaret venue

LUXURY HOTELS

The finest the Bay Area has to offer; if you can afford to splurge, you'll be well taken care of here:
- **The Archbishop's Mansion**, 1000 Fulton St, 415-563-7872; located in the Western Addition/Alamo Square, the decor of each room is based on a different opera

- **The Clift**, 495 Geary St, 415-775-4700, located downtown, considered to be one of the best in the city; houses the elegant Redwood Room, an ever-popular piano bar
- **Cupertino Inn**, 10889 North De Anza Blvd, Cupertino, 408-996-7700
- **El Drisco**, 2901 Pacific Ave, 800-634-7277; in Pacific Heights, an old gem with great views
- **The Fairmont**, 950 Mason St, 415-772-5000, at the top of Nob Hill, one of the city's opulent, old-world hotels
- **The Fairmont**, 170 South Market St, San Jose, 408-998-1900, in the heart of downtown
- **Garden Court Hotel**, 520 Cowper St, Palo Alto, 650-322-9000
- **The Grand Hotel**, 865 W. El Camino Real, Sunnyvale, 800-786-0827, www.svgrandhotel.com
- **The Grand Hyatt**, 345 Stockton St, 415-398-1234, downtown
- **Hotel Sausalito**, 16 El Portal, 888-442-0700, Sausalito
- **The Mark Hopkins**, 1 Nob Hill Circle, 415-392-3434, www.markhopkins.net, old-fashioned luxury atop Nob Hill, what a view!
- **The Palace**, 2 New Montgomery St, 415-512-1111, downtown, with a Palm Court reminiscent of days gone by
- **Ritz-Carlton**, 600 Stockton St, 415-296-7465, in Nob Hill, luxurious
- **Stanford Park Hotel**, 100 El Camino Real, Menlo Park, 650-322-1234
- **Westin St. Francis**, 335 Powell St, 415-397-7000, luxurious grand hotel in the heart of Union Square

EXTENDED-STAY ESTABLISHMENTS

Short-term apartment rentals are usually not cheap. Generally, these residences cater to corporations, not individuals. However, many will rent directly to individuals who are moving to a new city. And if you are getting assistance from your employer as part of a job relocation, this can be a great way to start out. In general, short-term rentals are less costly than extended hotel stays and give you a comfortable, homey place to rest your head when you arrive, while leaving you time to house hunt in person once getting settled in the Bay Area. Most offer month-to-month or week-to-week fully furnished accommodations—typically in studios or one-bedroom apartments with kitchens—and the majority require a 30-day minimum stay. Higher end spots can also come loaded with hotel-style amenities including laundry service, restaurants, and fitness centers.

- **BridgeStreet Worldwide**, 800-278-7338, www.bridgestreet.com, has several corporate housing sites in San Francisco, including Avalon at Mission Bay, as well as apartments in the East Bay, Peninsula, and

South Bay; weekly, monthly and year-long rentals available. Fully furnished units, fitness facilities, parking, families welcome.

- **California Suites/Suite America** (short-term rentals nationwide), 800-367-9501
- **ExecuStay**, 800-500-5110, or 888-340-2565, www.execustay.com, a nationwide Marriott Hotel–affiliated service that offers fully furnished apartments, kitchens, and in-unit washers and dryers; some apartments can also accommodate pets and children.
- **Fox Plaza**, 1390 Market St, 415-626-6902; a prime example of high-rise temporary apartments, you'll find studios, one- and two-bedroom units, each with a panoramic view of San Francisco. The building has 24-hour security, a fitness center, underground parking, and restaurants in the building. Cats are the only pets allowed, provided you pony up a $500 deposit.
- **Key Housing Connections**, 800-989-0410, www.keyhousing.net, offers furnished accommodation Bay Area wide for a minimum of 30 days, up to three months, depending on availability.
- **Oakwood Corporate Apartments**, 800-888-0808, www.oakwood.com; this company owns the buildings they lease to renters all over the South Bay and Peninsula. Fully furnished apartments are customized to suit your needs. The minimum stay is 31 days. Prices vary depending on location. A few of their spots include Oakwood/San Jose South, 700 South Saratoga in San Jose, and Oakwood/Mountain View location, 555 West Middlefield Rd in Mountain View.
- **Trinity Plaza**, 1169 Market St, 415-861-3333; studios and one-bedrooms charged by the month. Trinity Properties offer numerous short-term rentals around San Francisco but none such a bargain as at Trinity Plaza. Call 415-433-3333 or 474-0330 for information about others.

BED & BREAKFASTS

There are hundreds of B&Bs in the Bay Area, ranging in price from as low as $65 per night for a simple room in a private home to as much as $200 per night for an opulent unit in an historic Victorian or a self-contained carriage house or private cottage. **Bed and Breakfast International** has been providing information and reservations about local B&Bs since 1978 and boasts connections to more than 300 B&Bs and similar lodgings. Check out Bed and Breakfast International on the web at www.ibbp.com.

HOSTELS/YMCAS

In addition to the facilities listed below, you can find out more information on local youth hostels at www.hostelweb.com or www.hiayh.org.

SAN FRANCISCO/NORTH BAY

- **Adelaide Hostel**, 5 Isadora Duncan Lane, 415-441-2261, www.adelaide hostel.com, basic, funky, private rooms and dorm style options, full of budget-minded Europeans; located in downtown San Francisco
- **AYH Hostel Union Square**, 312 Mason St, 415-788-5604
- **AYH Hostel Fort Mason**, Fort Mason, Bldg, #240, 415-771-7277
- **Globetrotters Inn**, 494 Broadway, 415-346-5786
- **HI Marin Headlands**, 941 Fort Berry, Sausalito, 415-331-2777, dorms and private rooms—must have at least two people in your party to stay in a private room
- **YMCA**, Administrative Office, 44 Montgomery St, 415-391-9622
- **YMCA Hotel**, 220 Golden Gate Ave, 415-885-0460
- **YMCA Hotel**, 855 Sacramento St, 415-576-9622

SOUTH BAY

- **Hidden Villa Hostel**, 26870 Moody Rd, Los Altos Hills, 650-949-8648
- **Sanborn Park Hostel**, 15808 Sanborn Rd, Saratoga, 408-741-0166

ACCESSIBLE LODGING FOR THE DISABLED

Hyatt Hotels, 800-233-1234, ITT Sheraton, 800-325-3535, and **Microtel Inn and Suites**, 888-771-7171, offer rooms specializing in the needs of the disabled.

A S WONDERFUL AND DIVERSE AS THE BAY AREA IS, EVERYONE LIKES to get away from city living now and again. Whether it's skiing, water sports, scenery, gambling, historical tours, wining and dining, or just rest and relaxation, there are dozens of nearby destinations to suit most anyone. Interesting possibilities abound outside the immediate Bay Area; in fact, you can go skiing on Saturday and sailing on Sunday, and be back to work by Monday. Following are just a few of the many quick getaways Northern California has to offer.

NORTH OF SAN FRANCISCO

If you don't want to drive far and you want to keep an eye on San Francisco, **Angel Island** may be the ticket. Located in the middle of San Francisco Bay, Angel Island is a short jaunt, either by ferry or sailboat, and a good place to picnic, barbecue, join a softball game, bike, kayak, hike the scenic trails, and camp. Call 415-435-1915 or visit www.angelisland.org for more information. For the San Francisco and Vallejo ferries, contact the Blue and Gold Fleet at 415-773-1188; the Tiburon Ferry information is at 415-435-2131.

In Marin County a stay in a cedar lodge with meals included is available at **Green Gulch Farm Zen Center**, 1601 Shoreline Highway, Sausalito, 415-383-3134. Here you can witness a Japanese tea ceremony, join in classes and meditation, and even learn about organic gardening. Most of the fruits and vegetables grown at Green Gulch end up as a vegetarian meal at Greens Restaurant in Fort Mason. If this kind of getaway appeals to you, get a copy of *Sanctuaries, the Complete United States: A Guide to Lodging in Monasteries, Abbeys, and Retreats* by Jack and Marcia Kelly.

On a hot summer day, you may want to drive windy Highway 1, past the Green Gulch Farm Zen Center, and venture to **Stinson Beach** for sunbathing, body surfing, swimming, or just exploring the shore. Be aware that you may not be the only one with this plan; traffic can be horrible. Another great beach getaway is **Point Reyes National Seashore**, which includes 30 miles of coastline and 70,000 acres of pristine wilderness. Amidst its rugged bluffs, wooded canyons, dense forests, and open meadows, you'll find spectacular hiking, biking, camping, bird watching, and whale watching. For information about camping at Point Reyes contact the Visitors' Center at 415-464-5100. Make sure to reserve camping sites ahead of time. If you don't want to camp and instead pine for an upscale romantic lodge, Manka's Inverness Lodge, 415-669-1034, is lovely. While you are in the area try some oysters at Hog Island Oyster Company, 415-663-9218.

One of the most popular Bay Area getaways is a journey to **Napa** and **Sonoma counties** for fine wines and steaming mud. If you're a gourmand these areas offer dozens of world-renowned **vineyards** and **wineries**, most with tours, tastings, and some with fine restaurants. Connoisseurs recommend Auberge du Soleil, 180 Rutherford Hill Road, Rutherford, www.aubergedusoleil.com; Tra Vigne, 1050 Charter Lane, Saint Helena, www.travignerestaurant.com; and The French Laundry, 6640 Washington Street, Yountville, www.frenchlaundry.com. You can even take a wine train to eat, drink, and view the gentle landscape all the way from St. Helena to Napa, without having to designate a driver. For information about the train call 800-427-4124.

In addition to wineries, Napa and Sonoma counties host numerous **spa-type resorts**. Facilities range from the funky to the glamorous. Most of the spas are in the town of Calistoga. Below is a list of some of the spas, many which have indoor and outdoor pools, mineral baths, steam rooms, dirty but oh so cleansing mud baths, salt scrubs, massage, and more. This list is far from comprehensive:

- **Calistoga Indian Springs Resort**, 1712 Lincoln Ave, Calistoga, 707-942-4913, www.indianspringscalistoga.com
- **Calistoga Spa Hot Springs**, 1006 Washington St, Calistoga, 707-942-6269, www.calistogaspa.com.
- **Dr. Wilkinson's Hot Springs**, 1507 Lincoln Ave, Calistoga, 707-942-4102, www.drwilkinsons.com
- **Lavender Hill Spa**, 1015 Foothill Blvd, Calistoga, 707-942-4495, www.lavenderhillspa.com
- **Sonoma Mission Inn**, 18140 Sonoma Hwy, Boyes Hot Springs, 707-938-9000, www.sonomamissioninn.com
- **White Sulphur Springs**, 3100 White Sulphur Springs Rd, St. Helena, 707-963-8588, www.whitesulphursprings.com

If all this isn't enough, you can ride a hot air balloon, take a tram up a mountainside, sail through the air on a glider, hike, bike, horseback ride, picnic, or shop at posh designer outlets. For further information about the entire region, go to www.co.napa.ca.us or www.sonoma.com.

Another North Bay getaway is a visit to the old logging region of **Russian River**. In the 1920s and '30s, the area was a working class summer resort. During and after the Depression it suffered from neglect and overuse, and was quite deteriorated by the 1970s when entrepreneurs, many from the gay community, arrived and began restoring the old buildings. Today Russian River is again a resort destination with lodging, fine restaurants, wineries, camping, hiking, horseback riding, and more. The natural environs of the Russian River, with its sandy beaches, redwood groves, and placid river, make it a pleasant place to spend a day or even a weekend. Canoeing down the river is a popular way to explore the area. Begin in Forestville and the local canoe company will meet you and your canoe 10 miles down river in Guerneville. After canoeing, take a trip down the Russian River Wine Road (www.wineroad.com) to sample fine wine. For more information about the many things to do here, contact the Russian River Visitors Bureau at 800-253-8800 or visit www.rrvw.org.

Moving toward the coastline around **Mendocino**, located about three and half hours north of San Francisco, is simply breathtaking. The town of Mendocino reminds some of fishing villages on the East Coast. Here you can watch for whales, wade in the tide pools, hike in Mendocino Headlands State Park, 707-937-5397, or camp among redwoods at Van Damme State Park, 707-937-4016. At the **Jug Handle State Reserve** you can view tectonic uplifts and pygmy forests. If riding horses along the beach appeals to you, take a trail ride at Ricochet Ridge Ranch, 707-964-7669. Many opt to explore the area by train, allowing the engineer of the Skunk Train to do the driving through 40 miles of redwoods and gulches, 866-45-SKUNK, or 800-866-1690, www.skunktrain.com.

The community of **Sea Ranch**, located 100 miles north of San Francisco on Highway 1, offers house rentals with ocean views and nearby trails. Abalone diving, kayaking, horseback riding, and swimming are only some of the activities, not to mention the golf course. For more details go to www.searanchvillage.com or call 707-785-2468.

Fort Bragg, about four hours north of San Francisco on Highway 1, was built to protect the peace-loving Pomo Indians from less peaceful settlers, though the actual fort hasn't been here since the 1860s. These days Fort Bragg is a lumber town, and during the annual Paul Bunyan Days you can watch lumberjacks test their skill in a number of competitions. Contact the Mendocino Coast Fort Bragg Chamber of Commerce at 707-961-6300 or visit www.mendocinocoast.com for more information.

PENINSULA/SOUTH BAY

The coastline from San Francisco all the way south to Santa Cruz offers a scenic getaway with bluffs, beaches, and great surfing spots. In Half Moon Bay, you can pick pumpkins at any of the numerous pumpkin patches along the highway. Sixty miles south of San Francisco brings you to

Año Nuevo State Reserve, home to large numbers of northern elephant seals. The reserve offers memorable tours during breeding season from December to March. Call 650-879-0227 for more information.

Monterey/Carmel is also known as John Steinbeck country, as he based many of his novels here, including *Cannery Row, Of Mice and Men,* and *The Grapes of Wrath*. Now the canneries are closed, and resorts and tourist sites stand in their stead. Another attraction is the Monterey Bay Aquarium, where you can come eye to eye with strange-shaped sunfish or marvel at the elegant jellyfish. For more information call 800-756-3737, www.monterey.com.

These days, Carmel is tourist oriented—full of restaurants, art galleries, gift shops, inns, and hotels—and is an easy place for children and elderly folks to get around. The scenery is spectacular, with sea lions and coves, rocky beaches, wind-whipped cypress trees, and well-maintained indigenous gardens. Nor can we forget the famous Pebble Beach Golf Course, where Tiger Woods etched his name into the golfing record books, winning the 100th US Men's Open by 15 shots. The Carmel Mission on Rio Road and Lasuen Drive, 831-624-3600, dates from 1797. The missionaries assigned here must have counted their blessings to be in such a scenic place and gentle climate. In the early 1900s, Carmel-by-the-Sea became a mecca for artists and writers. Robert Louis Stevenson, Ansel Adams, Sinclair Lewis, Edward Weston, Upton Sinclair, and Mary Austin settled at one time in Carmel. Poet Robinson Jeffers' home has been made into a museum; contact Tor House at 831-624-1813 for details. The Henry Miller Library, with memorabilia from that famous author, is located nearby in Big Sur. Call 831-667-2574, or check www.henrymiller.org for more details. Residents and tourists alike gather to watch the sunset at Nepenthe Restaurant along the cliffs of Big Sur.

Those looking for a more spiritual outing may want to drive to **Big Sur** to the famous Esalen Institute/Hot Springs, 831-667-3000. The institute, designed to foster personal and social transformation, offers seminars, lodging, dining, hot springs, a pool, massages, and awesome views of the California coastline.

On the northern part of Monterey Bay sits **Santa Cruz**, a striking contrast to the more conservative town of Carmel. The bohemian-hippie enclave of Santa Cruz is as lovely as any beach town, with wind-swept trees, rolling hills, and ocean vistas, though most outsiders come here for the Santa Cruz Beach Boardwalk, 400 Beach Street, 831-423-5590, www.beach boardwalk.com. Here you can ride the wooden roller coaster or the merry-go-round and experience an old-style amusement park. The University of California at Santa Cruz, with its laid-back student body, adds to the beachy feel of this friendly town—despite its many resident panhandlers. Visit the Santa Cruz Municipal Wharf for the Santa Cruz Surfing Museum on West

Cliff Drive, 831-420-6289. Come in the summer and sit on the beach to listen to Summertime Summer Nights Concerts, or attend an opera at the Capitola Theatre, 120 Monterey Avenue, Capitola, 831-462-3131. If thrift shopping is your thing, junk-stores on Capitola Avenue are quite popular; they even offer a guide and map for your convenience. Call 800-833-3494 to order one. For a perfect place to watch the sunset or build a fire on the beach after dusk, try New Brighton, Seacliff, Rio del Mar, or Manresa State Beaches. There are fire rings for barbecues and roasting marshmallows. For more information, contact 800-833-3494 or checkwww.ci.santa-cruz.ca.us.

Amateur and professional geologists alike flock to the epicenter of the 1989 Loma Prieta quake at what's known as the **Earthquake Trail** in **Nicene Marks State Park**. Located 80 miles south of San Francisco, just a few miles outside of Santa Cruz, the area is lovely, sheltered by pines and oaks with gentle streams running through. There are 10,000 acres of forest here, so plenty of non-geology folk visit as well. Call 831-763-7064 for more information. Call the Aptos Chamber of Commerce at 831-688-1467 for further sightseeing and hotel ideas.

SIERRAS AND GOLD COUNTRY

Twenty-five miles north of Auburn in the **Sierra Nevada foothills** is **Gold Country**. View what the '49ers experienced when they flocked here from around the world in search of their fortunes. In this old mining territory you can pan for gold, swim, or sun on a rock while being sprayed by the cooling foam of the Yuba River. Bird watching is popular, or if you're a homesick Northeasterner, come in the autumn to take in the brilliantly colored maple and aspen leaves. In summer and fall you can fish for trout or bass. Hiking is possible at Buttermilk Bend, Independence Trail, or if you're up to it, try the steep Humbug Trail. Call 800-655-6569, or check out www.nevadacitychamber.com for information, or go to www.nevada cityinns.com to find a place to stay. Some of the best whitewater rafting and kayaking can be had along the American, Stanislaus, Tuolumne and Merced rivers, all weaving through the Sierra foothills.

In winter, many head north on I-80 to ski in the Sierras. There are dozens of choices in **Lake Tahoe** for downhill or cross-country skiers. You can also ice-skate, snowboard, or sled. Lake Tahoe is loads of fun in the summer too. That's when folks go water-skiing in the icy waters of Lake Tahoe. You can also kayak, river raft, or even try inner tubing the chilly Truckee River. Camping, rock climbing, and hiking in the Sierras are first rate. If you want to reserve a roof over you head, contact Lake Tahoe Central Reservations at 800-824-6348 or at www.mytahoevacation.com.

Nearby, **Reno**, which proudly sports the moniker "The Biggest Little City in the World," in big flashing lights, offers a mini Las Vegas–style quick getaway. Roulette wheels, card tables, cocktails, and slot machines are the name of the game here. Along with 24-hour casino entertainment, you'll find hearty buffets, big name country and pop music performers, late night lounge acts, and a host of golf courses including PGA Tour host Montreux Golf and Country Club. For more information contact 775-337-3030 or www.reno-sparkschamber.org. For hotel and resort reservations check out www.reno.com.

NATIONAL PARKS

To learn about the camping and tour reservation system for the National Park system, contact www.reservations.nps.gov or call 800-365-2267. The National Park Service Office for the Bay Area is located at Fort Mason, Building 201, 415-561-4700.

YOSEMITE NATIONAL PARK

Beloved by Californians and out-of-state tourists alike, Yosemite is a popular destination for many, though most Bay Area visitors come in the fall, after the summer crowds have gone. President Theodore Roosevelt called Yosemite "the most beautiful place on earth," and it seems photographer Ansel Adams and naturalist John Muir were equally awestruck, having spent years here documenting the incredible natural beauty, including Half Dome, El Capitan, and Nevada Falls. Yosemite has gotten much more popular and crowded since Muir and Adams made their way around the valley. The valley floor is often packed with tourists, and many try to avoid it, preferring to head to the backcountry hiking trails. Intrepid folks hike 17 steep miles to the top of Half Dome, while rock climbers finesse their way up El Capitan. There's a hut system for luxury backcountry camping, but the permits for these are issued by lottery and therefore can be difficult to obtain. Wilderness permits are required for any overnight travel into the park's back-country; call 209-372-0740 for more details about hut and wilderness permits. For more details about Yosemite, contact Yosemite National Park, P.O. Box 577, Yosemite, CA 95389, 209-372-0200 or check www.nps.gov/yose or www.yosemitepark.com.

NATIONAL FOREST SERVICE

If you are planning a camping trip, call the National Forest Service's toll-free reservation line at 877-444-6777, TDD, 877-833-6777. You can reserve up to 240 days in advance. You can also make your reservation online at www.reserveusa.com.

ALMOST EVERY DAY OF THE YEAR THERE IS SOMETHING SPECIAL TO do or see in this culturally rich region. Many local events take place on an annual basis so you can look forward to them year after year. Here are just a few of the celebrations and events you may want to experience for yourself. Specific dates are not provided as they may change depending on the particular year. Locations are provided when possible, although they too sometimes change from year to year. If none is given, then assume San Francisco and call for details.

JANUARY

- **Chinese New Year Celebrations** begin toward the end of the month and go into February in Chinatown, San Francisco, 415-391-9680
- **Martin Luther King, Jr., Birthday Celebration**: San Francisco Annual Freedom March from CalTrain station to Civic Center, SF Martin Luther King Civic Committee, 415-643-5121, www.sfmlk.org; for information about events happening throughout the Bay Area, contact the Northern California Martin Luther King, Jr., Birthday Observance Committee, 510-268-3777, www.norcalmlk.org
- **Peninsula Orchid Society Show & Sale**, Fair Oaks Community Center, 2600 Middlefield Rd, Redwood City, Redwood City, 650-780-7500 http://penorchidsoc.org
- **San Francisco Sports and Boat Show**, Cow Palace, Daly City, 415-404-4111, www.fredhall.com
- **San Jose International Auto Show**, McEnery Convention Center, San Jose, 408-277-3900, www.motortrendautoshows.com/sanjose
- **Tall Ships Exposition**, Jack London Square, Oakland, 800-200-5239, www.jacklondonsquare.com

- **Tet Festival**, Vietnamese New Year (sometimes in February), in San Francisco at the Civic Center and Tenderloin District, 415-391-8050; huge celebration in the South Bay, Santa Clara County Fairgrounds, San Jose, 408-494-3247
- **Whale Watching** (through March), Point Reyes National Seashore, 415-669-1534, www.pointreyes.net

FEBRUARY

- **American Indian Art Show**, Marin Center, San Rafael, 415-499-6400, www.americanindianartshow.com.
- **Black History Month Celebrations**, Oakland Museum of California, Oakland, 510-238-2200, www.museumca.org; Oakland Public Libraries, Oakland, 510-637-0200 or www.oaklandlibrary.org; Westlake Park, Daly City, 650-991-8001; MLK Jr. Community Center, San Mateo, 650-522-7470
- **Chinese Community Street Fair**, Chinatown, 415-982-3000, www.sanfranciscochinatown.com
- **Chinese New Year Golden Dragon Parade**, Chinatown, 415-391-9680, www.chineseparade.com
- **Golden Gate Kennel Club Dog Show**, Cow Palace, Daly City, 415-404-4111
- **Pacific Orchid Exposition**, Fort Mason, 415-345-7575, www.orchid sanfrancisco.org
- **Russian Festival**, Sutter and Divisadero sts, 415-921-7631, www. russiancentersf.com
- **Tribal Folk and Textile Art Show**, Fort Mason, 415-455-2886, www.caskeylees.com
- **Valentine's Day Walk**, benefits American Heart Association, Lake Merritt, Oakland, 510-904-4000

MARCH

- **Farm Day**, celebration of National Agriculture Day, Marin County Exhibition Hall, San Rafael, 415-499-4204, www.growninmarin.org
- **International Women's Day Celebration**, call San Francisco location, 415-431-1180
- **Russian River Wine Barrel Tasting**, local wineries strut their stuff; call for locations in Sonoma County, 800-723-6336
- **Saint Patrick's Day Celebration**, Happy Hollow Park & Zoo, San Jose, 408-277-3000, www.happyhollowparkandzoo.org
- **Saint Patrick's Day Parade**, Market St, San Francisco, 415-675-9885

- **San Francisco International Asian American Film Festival**, 415-865-1588, www.nataanet.org
- **Sonoma County Home and Garden Show**, Sonoma County Fairgrounds, Santa Rosa, 800-655-0655, www.sonomacountyfair.com
- **White Elephant Sale**, benefits Oakland Museum of California, call for location, Oakland, 510-536-6800, www.museumca.org/events/elephant.html

APRIL

- **Berkeley Bay Festival**, Berkeley Marina, canceled for 2006 due to lack of funding, but the city hopes to revive the long-standing tradition, 510-981-6720
- **Cal Day**, open house at UC Berkeley for the community, 510-642-5215, www.berkeley.edu/calday/
- **Cherry Blossom Festival**, Japantown, 415-563-2313, www.nccbf.org
- **Earth Day Events**, Civic Center Park, Berkeley, 510-548-2220, multiple events and locations in Oakland, 510-238-7611; College of Marin, Marin, 415-456-3469 x 2, www.marinearthday.org
- **Grand National Rodeo**, for the cowpoke inside us all, Cow Palace, Daly City, 415-404-4111, www.grandnationalrodeo.com
- **New Living Expo**, a must for New Age aficionados, Concourse in San Francisco, 415-382-8300, www.newlivingexpo.com
- **Opening Day on the Bay**, kicks off the local yachting season on the San Francisco Bay, 415-331-0702, www.picya.org
- **San Francisco International Film Festival**, 415-561-5000, www.sffs.org
- **Spring Flower Festival**, Marin Art & Garden Center, Ross, 415-454-5597
- **Youth Arts Festival**, Berkeley Arts Center, Berkeley, 510-644-6893
- **Zoo & Aquarium Month**, Happy Hollow Park & Zoo, San Jose, 408-277-3000, www.happyhollowparkandzoo.org

MAY

- **Arboretum Plant Sale**, San Francisco County Fair Building, 415-661-3090
- **Bay to Breakers**, a seven-mile, cross-city, run/walk, with incredible sights and costumes, in San Francisco, 415-359-2800, www.baytobreakers.com
- **Carnaval**, Latin street party in San Francisco, 24th and Mission sts, 415-821-1155

- **Charmarita Pentecost Festival**, Portuguese extravaganza, IDES Hall, Half Moon Bay, 650-726-2729; IDES Hall, Pescadero, 650-726-5701
- **Cherry Festival**, Marin Center, San Rafael, 415-456-3276
- **Cinco de Mayo Parade**, in San Francisco, 24th and Mission sts, 415-821-1155
- **Cinco de Mayo Celebration**, Stanford University, Palo Alto, 650-723-2089; downtown San Jose, 408-277-4000
- **Civil War Memorial & Re-Creation**, San Jose Historical Museum, San Jose, 408-287-2290
- **Grecian Festival**, Zorba would feel welcome, Nativity of Christ Church, Novato, 415-883-1998, www.nativityofchrist.org
- **Greek Festival**, Greek Orthodox Cathedral, Oakland, 510-531-3400
- **Hometown Days**, local arts & crafts, Burton Park, San Carlos, 650-594-2700
- **Jack o' the Green Spring Faire**, Old English celebration, Bodega Bay, 707-875-3704
- **Marin a la Carte**, gourmet treats, Marin Center, San Rafael, 415-472-3500
- **Maritime Day**, a nautical observance, Jack London Square and Waterfront, Oakland, 866-295-9853, www.jacklondonsquare.com
- **Nikkei Matsuri Japanese Festival**, Japantown, San Jose, 408-277-3900
- **Polish Spring Festival**, Golden Gate Park, San Francisco, 415-396-3023, http://capolonia.com
- **Sequoia Auto Show**, Sequoia High School, Redwood City, 650-368-8212
- **Stanford Pow-Wow**, massive gathering of Native Americans, Stanford University, Palo Alto, 650-725-6944
- **Tiburon Wine Festival**, Point Tiburon Plaza, Tiburon, 415-435-5633
- **Youth Arts Festival**, Yerba Buena Arts Center and Zeum, 415-750-8630, www.sfyouthartsfestival.org

JUNE

- **Alameda County Fair**, Alameda County Fairgrounds, Pleasanton, 925-426-7600
- **Art & Wine Festival**, call for location, Sunnyvale, 408-736-4971
- **Black & White Ball**, open to the public, this glamour symphony fundraiser is held every other year in San Francisco, call for locations, 415-864-6000.
- **Cherry Festival**, call for location, San Leandro, 510-577-3462

- **Good Guys Rod and Custom Classic Car Show**, Alameda County Fairgrounds, Pleasanton, 925-838-9876, www.good-guys.com
- **Haight Ashbury Street Fair**, fun and frolic at the free love flash point, Haight and Ashbury sts, San Francisco, 415-863-3489, www.haightstreetfair.org
- **International Lesbian & Gay Film Festival**, call for locations, 415-703-8650, www.frameline.org
- **Juneteenth Celebration**, marking Lincoln's Emancipation Proclamation: San Francisco parade and celebration, Fillmore St, 415-931-2729, www.sfjuneteenth.org; Berkeley, 510-655-8008; Plaza de Cesar Chavez, San Jose, 408-292-3157, www.sjaacsa.org/juneteenth.htm
- **Lesbian Gay Bisexual Transgender Celebration & Parade**, numerous San Francisco locations, 415-864-3733
- **Midsummer Mozart Festival**, call for locations, 415-392-4400
- **Mill Valley Wine & Gourmet Food-Tasting**, Lytton Square, Mill Valley, 415-388-9700
- **North Beach Festival**, an Italian blowout, North Beach 415-989-2220, www.sfnorthbeach.org/festival
- **Novato Art, Wine & Music Festival**, Old Town, Novato 415-897-1164, www.novato.org
- **Puerto Rican Cultural Festival "Dia de San Juan,"** Santa Clara County Fairgrounds, San Jose, 888-200-1488, www.wrprcouncil.org
- **San Anselmo Art & Wine Festival**, San Anselmo Ave, San Anselmo, 415-454-2510
- **San Francisco Jazz Festival** summer sessions, call for locations, June–October, 415-776-1999, www.sfjazz.org
- **San Jose Gay Pride Festival** & **Silicon Valley Pride Parade**, Discovery Meadow, San Jose, 408-278-5563, www.sjgaypride.com
- **Shakespeare on the Beach**, call for location, Stinson Beach, 415-868-1115, www.shakespeareatstinson.org
- **Silicon Valley Concours d'Elegance**, fine wine and vintage cars, Guadalupe River Park, San Jose, 408-277-3900
- **Sonoma-Marin Fair**, Petaluma Fairgrounds, Petaluma, 707-763-0931
- **Stern Grove Midsummer Music Festival**, in San Francisco, Stern Grove, June–August, 415-252-6252, www.sterngrove.org
- **Summer Concert Series**, through August, call for locations, Milpitas, 408-586-3000
- **Trips for Kids Bike Swap**, huge bicycle event, San Rafael High School, San Rafael, 415-458-2986
- **Twilight Concerts in the Park**, Tuesday nights through July, various parks, call for locations, Palo Alto, 650-463-4940

- **Union Street Festival**, Cow Hollow event with music, art, and gourmet food, Union and Fillmore sts, San Francisco, 800-310-6563, www.unionstreetfestival.com

JULY

- **Berkeley Kite Festival** and **West Coast Kite Flying Championships**, Cesar Chavez Park, Berkeley, 510-235-5483, www.highlinekites.com
- **Books by the Bay**, a celebration of independent book sellers, Yerba Buena Gardens, 5th and Mission sts, San Francisco, www.booksbythebay.com
- **Chinese Summer Festival**, Kelly Park, San Jose, 408-842-1625, www.chcp.org
- **Festa Italia**, plenty of pasta and pesto, San Mateo, 650-349-9879, www.festafoundation.org
- **Fillmore Jazz Festival**, Fillmore and California sts, 800-731-0003, www.fillmorestreetjazzfest.com
- **Fourth of July Celebrations**, call for details: San Francisco, fireworks at Pier 39, 415-705-5500, www.pier39.com; Alameda, 510 747-7400; Berkeley, 510-981-CITY; Redwood City, 650-780-7000, www.parade.org; San Jose, 408-277-4000; Oakland, 866-295-9853, www.jacklondonsquare.com
- **Gilroy Garlic Festival**, a pungent party, Christmas Hill Park, Gilroy, 408-842-1625, www.gilroygarlicfestival.com
- **Jewish Film Festival**, through August, UC Theatre, Berkeley, 415-621-0556, www.sfjj.org
- **Los Altos Art & Wine Festival**, downtown Los Altos, 650-917-9799, www.los-altos.downtown.org
- **Marin County Fair**, Marin County Fairgrounds, San Rafael, 415-499-6800, www.marinfair.org
- **Marin Shakespeare Festival**, Dominican College, San Rafael, 415-499-4485, July–September, www.marinshakespeare.org
- **Mill Valley Chili Cook-off**, Blithedale Plaza, Mill Valley, 415-381-1070
- **Obon Festival**, Buddhist Church, San Jose, 408-293-9292
- **San Francisco Jazz Festival** summer sessions, call for locations, June–October, 415-776-1999, www.sfjazz.org
- **San Jose American Festival**, Guadalupe River Park, San Jose, 408-294-2100 x 444, www.americanfestival.com
- **San Jose International Mariachi Festival**, Guadalupe River Park, San Jose, 408-928-5563, www.mhcviva.org
- **Scottish Highland Games**, Dunsmuir House, Oakland, 510-615-5555, www.dunsmuir.org

- **Shakespeare in the Park**, through October call for locations, 415-422-2222, www.shakes.org
- **Stern Grove Midsummer Music Festival**, in San Francisco, Stern Grove, June–August, 415-252-6252, www.sterngrove.org
- **Summer Festival & Chili Cook-off**, Mitchell Park, Palo Alto, 650-463-4921, www.cityofpaloalto.org
- **Tahiti Fete**, island music and delicacies sure to please, San Jose State University Event Center, San Jose, 408-924-6350, www.tahitifete.com

AUGUST

- **California Small Brewers Festival**, microbrew beer bash, Franklin and Evelyn sts, Mountain View, 888-875-BREW, www.smallbrewersfest.com
- **Nihonmachi Street Fair**, a celebration of Japanese culture, Japantown, 415-771-9861, www.nihonmachistreetfair.org
- **Palo Alto Festival of the Arts**, University Ave, Palo Alto, 650-324-3121, www.paloaltochamber.com
- **Park Street Art & Wine Faire**, Park St, Alameda, 510-523-1392
- **San Francisco Aloha Festival**, Pacific Islander cultural celebration, San Francisco Presidio Main Parade Grounds, 415-281-0221, www.pica-org.org/AlohaFest
- **San Francisco Jazz Festival**, summer series continues, call for locations, June–October, 415-776-1999, www.sfjazz.org
- **San Jose Jazz Festival**, Plaza de Cesar Chavez, San Jose, 408-288-7557, www.sanjosejazz.org
- **San Mateo County Fair**, San Mateo County Expo Center, San Mateo, 650-574-3247, www.sanmateocountyfair.com
- **Santa Clara County Fair**, Santa Clara County Fairgrounds, San Jose, 408-494-3100, www.thefair.org
- **Stern Grove Midsummer Music Festival**, in San Francisco, Stern Grove, June–August, 415-252-6252, www.sterngrove.org
- **West Marin Music Festival**, call for locations, 415-663-9650, www.sonicstew.com/WMMF.html

SEPTEMBER

- **A la Carte a la Park**, gourmet food in the park, Sharon Meadows, Golden Gate Park, 415-458-1988
- **American Indian Trade Fest**, Marin Museum of the American Indian (Miwok Museum), Novato, 415-897-4064
- **Art in the Park**, Memorial Park, Cupertino, 408-777-3120
- **A Taste of Chocolate**, a chocoholic's dream come true, Ghirardelli Square, 415-775-5500

- **Black Filmworks**, honoring African-American films and filmmakers, call for locations, Oakland, September–October, 510-465-0804
- **Black Diamond Blues Festival**, Diamond and 5th sts, Pittsburg, 510-836-2227, www.bayareabluessociety.net
- **Cupertino Golden Jubilee**, Memorial Park, Cupertino, 408-252-7054, www.cupertino-chamber.org
- **Fall Arts Festival**, Old Mill Park, Mill Valley, 415-383-5256, www.mvfaf.org
- **Folsom Street Fair**, Folsom between 7th and 12th sts, 415-861-3247, www.folsomstreetfair.com
- **Harvest Faire**, Marin Center, San Rafael, 415-456-3276
- **How Berkeley Can You Be? Festival**, 510-644-2204, www.how berkeleycanyoube.com
- **Mountain View Art & Wine Festival**, Castro St, Mountain View, 408-968-8378, www.mountainviewchamber.org
- **Opera in the Park**, free arias, Sharon Meadows, Golden Gate Park, 415-861-4008, http://sfopera.com
- **Pacific Coast Fog Fest**, clearly a good time in the fog, Palmetto & Salada Aves, Pacifica, 650-359-1460, www.pacificcoastfogfest.com
- **Renaissance Pleasure Faire**, journey back to Elizabethan England, call for locations, September–October, 800-523-2473, 408-849-3247, www.norcalrenfaire.org
- **Sandcastle Classic**, architects vs. amateurs in sandcastle building, Aquatic Park, 415-861-1899, www.leap4kids.org/scc/about.html
- **San Francisco Blues Festival**, Great Meadow, Fort Mason, 415-979-5588, www.sfblues.com
- **San Francisco Fringe Festival**, a celebration of the offbeat, call for locations, 415-931-1094, www.sffringe.org
- **San Francisco Jazz Festival** summer sessions, call for locations, June–October, 415-776-1999, www.sfjazz.org
- **Sausalito Art Festival**, Bay Model Visitors Center and Marinship Park, Sausalito, 415-331-3757, www.sausalitoartfestival.org
- **Santa Clara Art & Wine Festival**, Central Park, Santa Clara, 408-615-3155, www.santaclaraartandwinefestival.com
- **Sir Francis Drake Kennel Club Dog Show**, Marin Center, San Rafael, 415-472-3500
- **Solano Stroll**, massive street fair, Solano Ave, Albany and Berkeley, 510-527-5358, www.solanoavenueassn.org/strol.htm
- **Tiburon Chili Festival**, Main St, Tiburon, 415-435-5633, http://sanrafaelchamber.com

OCTOBER

- **Castro Street Fair**, Castro St, 415-467-3354, www.castrostreet fair.org
- **Days of the Dead Community Festival**, Oakland Museum of California, Oakland, 510-238-3818, www.museumca.org
- **Fleet Week**, celebrating San Francisco's long relationship with the US Navy, call for locations, 415-705-5500
- **Great Halloween & Pumpkin Festival**, Polk St, 415-346-4446
- **Half Moon Bay Pumpkin Festival**, Main St, Half Moon Bay, 650-726-9652, www.miramarevents.com/pumpkinfest
- **Halloween Celebration**, Jack London Square, Oakland, www.oaklandcvb.com
- **Halloween Night**, The Castro, www.halloweensf.com
- **Halloween at the Winchester Mystery House**, a sprawling, 160-year-old Victorian mansion, San Jose, 408-247-2101, www.winchester mysteryhouse.com,
- **Italian Heritage Day**, honoring, among others, Christopher Columbus, North Beach, 415-434-1492
- **Mid Autumn Festival**, Milpitas Community Auditorium, Milpitas, 408-586-3210
- **Mill Valley Film Festival**, call for locations, Mill Valley, 415-383-5256
- **Milpitas Main Street USA Parade**, a flag-waving good time, Main St, Milpitas, 408-942-2470
- **Moon Viewing Festival**, Lake Merritt, Oakland, during the full moon, 510-482-5896
- **Novato Harvest Festival**, Farmers Market, Novato, 415-456-3276
- **Open Studios**, a citywide, month-long tour of artists' studios, www.mesart.com/openstudios_SanFrancisco.jsp, 415-641-4867
- **Pacific Fine Arts Festival**, Santa Cruz Ave, Menlo Park, www.pacific finearts.com
- **Potrero Hill Festival**, a neighborhood favorite, call for location, 415-826-8080
- **Pumpkin Festival**, Marin Center, San Rafael, 415-507-2000
- **Reggae in the Park**, Sharon Meadow, Golden Gate Park, 415-383-9378
- **San Francisco International Accordion Festival**, can you stand it? Fisherman's Wharf, 415-775-6000
- **San Francisco Jazz Festival**, twelve days of jazz around the city, call for locations, June–October, 415-776-1999, www.sfjazz.org
- **Sunny Hills Grape Festival**, Larkspur Landing, Larkspur, 415-256-1580

NOVEMBER

- **American Indian Film Festival**, Palace of Fine Arts, 415-554-0525, www.aifisf.com
- **Arts & Crafts Faire**, Strawberry Recreation Center, Mill Valley, 415-383-6494,
- **Celebration of Craftswomen**, Fort Mason, 415-383-3470, www.miramarevents.com/craftswomen
- **Christmas Tree Lighting**: Ghirardelli Square, 415-775-5500
- **Dias de los Muertos (Day of the Dead)**, Mexican celebration of spirits, parade, altars in the park, great costumes and food, 24th and Bryant sts to Garfield Park, the Mission District, 415-821-1155
- **Festival of Lights Parade**, downtown, Los Altos, 650-917-9799, www.losaltos-downtown.org
- **Great Dickens Christmas Faire**, travel back in time to 19th Century London, Cow Palace, Daly City (runs through early December), 415-392-4400, www.dickensfair.com
- **Harvest Festival**, Concourse Exhibition Center in San Francisco, 707-778-6300, www.harvestfestival.com; McEnery Convention Center, San Jose, 707-778-6300, www.harvestfestival.com
- **Holiday Faire**, Santa Clara County Fairgrounds, San Jose, 408-494-3247
- **Holiday Harmony**, multicultural holiday celebration, Pier 39, 415-705-5500, www.pier39.com.
- **Jack London Square Tree Lighting**, Jack London Square, Oakland, 866-295-9853, www.jacklondonsquare.com
- **Marin County Holiday Antique & Collector's Fair**, Marin Center, San Rafael, 415- 472-3500
- **Native American Culture Day**, Oakland Public Library, Oakland, 510-482-7844
- **San Francisco International Auto Show**, Moscone Center, 415-331-4406, www.sfautoshow.com
- **Spirit of the Holidays Gift Faire**, Sonoma County Fairgrounds, Santa Rosa (runs through early December), 707-861-2035, www.sonoma giftfair.com
- **Thanksgiving Farmers Market**, Marin Center, San Rafael, 415-456-3276, http://marincountyfarmersmarkets.org
- **Union Square Tree Lighting**, Christmas window displays, Union Square, San Francisco, 415-781-7880
- **Union Street Festival of Lights**, Union St between Franklin and Steiner sts, San Francisco, 800-310-6563

- **Veterans Day Parade**: Market St, 415-441-5051; downtown San Jose, 408-277-4000
- **Victorian Christmas**, Open House, Angel Island, 435–3522, www.angelisland.org
- **Winter Wonderland & Parade of Lights**, downtown San Rafael, 415-453-8388

DECEMBER

- **Christmas in the Park**, Plaza de Cesar Chavez, San Jose, 408-995-NOEL, www.christmasinthepark.com
- **Christmas Revels**, Scottish Rite Temple, Oakland, 510-452-9334, www.calrevels.org
- **Christmas at Sea**, holiday fair with a nautical bent, Hyde St Pier, 415-561-6662
- **Hanukkah Family Celebration**, Marin Jewish Community Center, San Rafael, 415-479-2000
- **Kwanzaa Celebration**, MLK Jr. Community Center, San Mateo, 650-522-7470
- **Kwanzaa Gift Show**, Oakland Marriott Convention Center, Oakland, 510-534-1594, www.kwanzaagiftshow.com/
- **Lighted Yacht Parade**, Jack London Square & Waterfront, Oakland, 866-295-9853, www.jacklondonsquare.com
- **Lighted Yacht Parade**, Sausalito, 415-331-7262
- **Messiah Sing**, Point Reyes Station, 415-663-1075
- **San Jose Holiday Parade**, downtown, San Jose, 408-277-3303, www.holidayparade.com
- **Sing-a-long Messiah**, Santa Rosa High School Auditorium, Santa Rosa, 707-537-6809, www.sing-along-messiah.org
- **Sing-it-yourself Messiah**, Davies Symphony Hall, 415-864-6000, www.sfsymphony.org
- **Trains for Tots**, South Bay, Peninsula, and San Francisco stops with Santa along the CalTrain corridor, 800-660-4287, www.caltrain.com
- **Victorian Christmas**, San Jose Historical Museum, San Jose, 408-287-2290
- **Winterfest**, Oakland Museum of California, Oakland, 510-238-3818

A BAY AREA READING LIST

THERE ARE HUNDREDS, IF NOT THOUSANDS, OF BOOKS ABOUT SAN Francisco and the Bay Area. Below is a small selection of guides, works of fiction, and historical books that will help you get acquainted with your new home.

ART

- *Art in the San Francisco Bay Area: 1945-1980: An Illustrated History* by Thomas Albright
- *Artful Players: Artistic Life in Early San Francisco* by Brigitta Hjalmarson
- *Bay Area Wild: A Celebration of the Natural Heritage of the San Francisco Bay Area* by Galen Rowell; captures the natural beauty of the Bay Area with the author's photographs and insightful text

FICTION AND LITERATURE

- *The Best of Adair Lara* by Adair Lara
- *China Boy* by Gus Lee
- *City Lights Pocket Poets Anthology*, Editor Lawrence Ferlinghetti
- *Everyone Into the Pool: True Tales* by Beth Lisick
- *Eyes of a Child* by Richard North Patterson
- *A Heartbreaking Work of Staggering Genius* by Dave Eggers
- *The Joy Luck Club* by Amy Tan
- *Letters from the Earth* by Mark Twain
- *The Maltese Falcon* by Dashiell Hammett
- *San Francisco Stories: Great Writers on the City* edited by John Miller
- *The Subterraneans* by Jack Kerouac
- *San Francisco Poems* by Lawrence Ferlinghetti
- *Tales of the City* by Armistead Maupin
- *Jack London Stories of Adventure* by Jack London
- *Valencia* by Michelle Tea
- *West from Home: Letters of Laura Ingalls Wilder, San Francisco, 1915* by Laura Ingalls Wilder
- *The Woman Warrior* by Maxine Hong Kingston

LOCAL LIT JOURNALS
- *McSweeney's*
- *Instant City: A Literary Exploration of San Francisco*

FOOD

- *Bread and Chocolate: My Food Life in San Francisco* by Fran Gage
- *The Cheese Board: Collective Works: Bread, Pastry, Cheese, Pizza* by Alice Waters and the Cheese Board Collective
- *Chez Panisse Cooking: New Tastes and Techniques* by Paul Bertolli with Alice Waters
- *The Chowhound's Guide to the San Francisco Bay Area*
- *Eat this San Francisco* by Dan Leone
- *The Eclectic Gourmet Guide to San Francisco* by Richard Sterling
- *Patricia Unterman's San Francisco Food Lover's Guide* by Patricia Unterman
- *San Francisco in a Teacup* by Ulrica Hume; where to find tea, accoutrements, and afternoon teas
- *The San Francisco Chronicle Cookbook Volume II* by Michael Bauer
- *San Francisco a la Carte* by the Junior League of San Francisco
- *Zagat Survey, San Francisco Bay Area Restaurants*

HISTORY

- *Baghdad by the Bay* by Herb Caen
- *The Barbary Coast* by Herbert Asbury
- *Historic San Francisco* by Rand Richards
- *The Mayor of Castro Street: The Life and Times of Harvey Milk* by Randy Shilts
- *Reclaiming San Francisco History, Politics, Culture; a City Lights Anthology* edited by James Brook, Chris Carlsson, and Nancy J. Peters
- *San Francisco: A Cultural and Literary History* by Mick Sinclair
- *San Francisco Then & Now* by William Yenne
- *Tales of San Francisco* by Samuel Dickson
- *The World of Herb Caen* by Herb Caen
- *The Wild Parrots of Telegraph Hill* by Mark Bittner

KIDS

- *Best Hikes with Children: San Francisco's North Bay* by Bill McMillon with Kevin McMillon
- *The Cable Car and the Dragon* by Herb Caen

- ***The City by the Bay: A Magical Journey Around San Francisco*** by Tricia Brown
- ***Fun Places to go with Children in Northern California*** by Elizabeth Pomada
- ***Humphrey, the Lost Whale: A True Story*** by Wendy Tokuda and Richard Hall
- ***San Francisco*** by Deborah Kent
- ***San Francisco: A Mini-History*** by Phyllis Zauner

LIVING HERE

- ***Connecting in San Francisco*** by Diane de Castro; once you've found your job and your home, this'll help you find friends
- ***How to Get a Job in the San Francisco Bay Area*** by Robert Sanborn and Will Flowers

OUTDOORS

- ***Adventuring in the San Francisco Bay Area*** by Peggy Wayburn; information about camping, hiking, fishing, area wildlife and weather
- ***Backcountry Adventures: Northern California*** by Peter Massey and Jeanne Wilson
- ***Bay Area Backroads*** by Doug McConnell
- ***Cruising Guide to San Francisco Bay*** by Carolyn Mehaffy and Bob Mehaffy
- ***Bay Area Bike Rides*** by Ray Hosler
- ***East Bay Trails: Outdoor Adventures in Alameda and Contra Costa Counties*** by David Weintraub
- ***Foghorn Outdoors: 101 Great Hikes of the San Francisco Bay Area*** by Ann Marie Brown
- ***Foghorn Outdoors Bay Area Biking: 60 Of the Best Road and Trail Rides*** by Ann Marie Brown
- ***Golden Gate Trailblazer: Where to Hike, Walk and Bike in San Francisco and Marin*** by Jerry Sprout and Janine Sprout
- ***Inside/Out Northern California: Best Places Guide to the Outdoors*** by Dennis J. Oliver
- ***The New San Francisco at Your Feet: Best Walks in a Walkers' City*** by Margot Patterson Doss; offers a selection of walking tours rated for their difficulty
- ***Roaming the Backroads of Northern California*** by Peter Browning
- ***Sailing the Bay*** by Kimball Livingston; about sailing on San Francisco Bay

- *San Francisco Running Guide: the 45 Best Routes in the Bay Area* by Bob Cooper
- *Short Bike Rides in and around San Francisco* by Henry Kingman

BAY AREA GUIDES

These off-beat and theme-oriented guides to San Francisco will get you out and exploring, but away from the hordes of tourists.
- *The Dog Lover's Companion to the Bay Area* by Maria Goodavage; the name says it all—amongst the concrete walls of the City, there are places for your dog
- *Get Lost! The Cool Guide to San Francisco* by Claudia Lehan; a hip guide to the Bay Area
- *Romantic Days and Nights in San Francisco: Intimate Escapes in the City by the Bay* by Donna Peck; with this book, you can truly leave your heart in San Francisco
- *San Francisco As You Like It: 20 Tailor-Made Tours for Culture Vultures, Shopaholics, Non-Bohemians, Fitness Freaks, Savvy Natives, and Everyone Else* by Bonnie Wach; there's an old hippie tour, a tour for gourmet lovers, kids tours, and others
- *San Francisco Secrets* by John Snyder; full of little-known information about the city for lovers of trivia and history
- *Underground Guide to San Francisco* by Jennifer Joseph; if you need a new tattoo or an unusual museum to show a visiting friend, here's the guide for you
- *San Francisco Bizarro* by Jack Boulware; proving the old adage that truth is definitely sometimes stranger than fiction
- *Ghost Hunter's Guide to the Bay Area* by Jeff Dwyer; full of local legends and lore
- *Footsteps in the Fog, Alfred Hitchcock's San Francisco* by Jeff Kraft; the master of cinematic suspense shot a number of his famous films in and around San Francisco
- *San Francisco Noir* by Nathaniel Rich; a look at the city's rich past as a the stunning backdrop for a host of Hollywood whodunits
- *Jazz on the Barbary Coast* by Tom Stoddard

SHOPPING

- *Bargain Hunting in the Bay Area* by Sally Socolich
- *Mr. Cheap's San Francisco* by Mark Waldstein

ONCE YOU ORDER PHONE SERVICE, WITHIN TWO WEEKS SBC will deliver the White and Yellow Pages to your door. To get them faster, call SBC at 800-248-2800 and have them deliver the books to you by UPS—this will take three to five days—or you can purchase a phone book at any Safeway grocery store. To obtain a phone book from outside your county you will have to order by mail and pay the additional cost. The prices vary considerably from county to county, although counties other than your own but within your area code generally are free. You can access SBC's online Yellow Pages at www.smartpages.com. Although not as extensive as the print Yellow Pages, the list below should be of some assistance:

AMBULANCE, All areas, 911

ANIMALS

- Animal bites, 911
- Animal Control, 415-554-6364
- Homeless Cat Network, 650-286-9013, www.homelesscatnetwork.org
- Humane Society of Contra Costa County, 925-279-2247, www.cc humane.org
- Humane Society of East Bay, 510-845-7735, www.behumane.org
- Humane Society of Marin County, 415-883-4621, www.marin-humane.org
- Humane Society of Peninsula, 650-340-8200, www.peninsulahumane society.org
- Humane Society Silicon Valley, 408-727-3383, www.hssv.org

- Humane Society of Sonoma County, 707-542-0882, www.sonoma humane.org
- Pets Unlimited, 415-563-6700, www.petsunlimited.org
- San Francisco Lots Pet Services, 415-567-8738
- Second Chance Rescue, 415-721-1721, www.secondchance rescue.com
- Silicon Valley Friends of Ferals, www.svff.org
- SPCA (Society for the Prevention of Cruelty to Animals), 415-554-3000, www.sfspca.org
- Tri-Valley SPCA Maddie's Adoption Center, 925-479-9670, www.east bayspca.org

AUTOMOBILES

- American Automobile Association (AAA), 800-AAA-HELP, 800-922-8228, www.aaa.com
- BBB Auto Line, 800-955-5100
- California Department of Motor Vehicles, 800-777-0133, www.dmv.ca.gov

SAN FRANCISCO
- Abandoned Automobiles, 415-781-5861
- City Tow, 415-621-8605
- DMV, 800-921-1117 (automated 24-hour number), 800-777-0133 to speak with an agent

PARKING AND TRAFFIC
SAN FRANCISCO
- Web Site, www.ci.sf.ca.us/dpt
- Information, 415-554-7275
- Citation Division, 415-255-3900; Pay Traffic/Parking Citations with Credit Card, 415-255-3999, 800-531-7357
- Parking Permits, 415-554-5000
- Towed Vehicles, 415-553-1235

NORTH BAY
- DMV, Corte Madera, 800-921-1117 (automated 24-hour number), 800-777-0133 to speak with an agent
- Marin County Traffic Authority—Parking, 800-281-7275

EAST BAY
- DMV, El Cerrito, 800-921-1117 (automated 24-hour number), 800-777-0133 to speak with an agent

- DMV, Hayward, 800-921-1117 (automated 24-hour number), 800-777-0133 to speak with an agent
- DMV, Oakland, 800-921-1117 (automated 24-hour number), 800-777-0133 to speak with an agent
- Oakland Parking Bureau, 510-238-3099
- Traffic Division of the Superior Court, 510-268-7673

PENINSULA/SOUTH BAY
- DMV, San Mateo, 800-921-1117 (automated 24-hour number), 800-777-0133 to speak with an agent
- DMV, Daly City, 800-921-1117 (automated 24-hour number), 800-777-0133 to speak with an agent
- DMV, Redwood City, 800-921-1117 (automated 24-hour number), 800-777-0133 to speak with an agent
- DMV, San Jose, 800-921-1117 (automated 24-hour number), 800-777-0133 to speak with an agent
- DMV, Santa Clara, 800-921-1117 (automated 24-hour number), 800-777-0133 to speak with an agent
- San Mateo, Parking Permits, Residential & City Parking Facilities, 650-522-7326

BIRTH/DEATH CERTIFICATES

- Alameda County, 510 272-6362 , www.acphd.org
- Marin County, 415-499-6094
- San Francisco County Health Department, 415 554-2700, www.dph.sf.ca.us
- San Mateo County, 650-363-4712, www.smhealth.org
- Santa Clara County, 408-299-2481, www.co.santa-clara.ca.us

CITY/COUNTY GOVERNMENT

SAN FRANCISCO
- Assessor-Recorder's Office, 415-554-5516, www.ci.sf.ca.us/assessor
- Board of Supervisors, 415-554-5184, www.ci.sf.ca.us./bdsupvrs
- California Governor, 916-445-2841, 415-703-2218, www.governor.ca.gov
- California Public Utilities Commission, Public Advisor's Office in San Francisco, 866-849-8390, www.cpuc.ca.gov
- California Registrar of Voters, 800-345-8683
- City Attorney, 415-554-4700
- City Hall, 415-554-4000

- County Clerk, 415-554-4950
- District Attorney, 415-553-1752
- Health Department, 415-554-2500, www.dph.sf.ca.us
- Marriage Licenses, 415-554-4950
- Mayor's Office, 415-554-6141
- Parks and Recreation, 415-831-2700, www.parks.sfgov.org
- Recycling Program,
- Rent Stabilization Board, 415-252-4600, www.sfgov.org/rentboard
- Residential Parking Permits, 415-554-5000
- San Francisco Public Utilities Commission, 415-554-3155, http://sf water.org
- San Francisco Unified School District, 415-241-6000, http:// portal.sfusd.edu/template/index.cfm

NORTH BAY—ONLINE
- Corte Madera, www.ci.corte-madera.ca.us
- Fairfax, www.town-of-fairfax.org
- Marin County, www.co.marin.ca.us, www.marin.org
- Mill Valley, www.cityofmillvalley.org
- Napa County, www.co.napa.ca.us
- Novato, www.ci.novato.ca.us
- San Rafael, www.cityofsanrafael.org
- Sausalito, www.ci.sausalito.ca.us
- Santa Rosa, www.ci.santa-rosa.ca.us
- Sonoma County, www.sonoma-county.org
- Tiburon, www.tiburon.org

EAST BAY—ONLINE
- Alameda City, www.ci.alameda.ca.us
- Alameda County, www.co.alameda.ca.us
- Albany, www.albanyca.org
- Antioch, www.ci.antioch.ca.us
- Berkeley, www.ci.berkeley.ca.us
- Concord, www.ci.concord.ca.us
- Contra Costa County, www.co.contra-costa.ca.us
- Danville: www.ci.danville.ca.us
- Fremont, www.ci.fremont.ca.us
- El Cerrito, www.el-cerrito.ca.us
- Emeryville, www.ci.emeryville.ca.us
- Hayward, www.ci.hayward.ca.us
- Livermore, www.ci.livermore.ca.us
- Martinez, www.cityofmartinez.org
- Newark, www.ci.newark.ca.us

- Oakland, www.ci.oakland.ca.us, www.oaklandnet.com
- Piedmont, www.ci.piedmont.ca.us
- Pinole, www.ci.pinole.ca.us
- Pittsburg, www.ci.pittsburg.ca.us
- Pleasanton, www.ci.pleasanton.ca.us
- Richmond, www.ci.richmond.ca.us
- San Leandro, www.ci.san-leandro.ca.us
- San Ramon www.ci.san-ramon.ca.us
- Union City, www.ci.union-city.ca.us
- Walnut Creek, www.ci.walnut-creek.ca.us

PENINSULA/SOUTH BAY—ONLINE
- Atherton, www.ci.atherton.ca.us
- Belmont, www.ci.belmont.ca.us
- Brisbane, www.ci.brisbane.ca.us
- Burlingame, www.burlingame.org
- Campbell, www.ci.campbell.ca.us
- Cupertino, www.cupertino.org
- Daly City, www.ci.daly-city.ca.us
- Foster City, www.fostercity.org
- Half Moon Bay, www.half-moon-bay.ca.us
- Hillsborough, www.hillsborough.net
- Los Altos, www.ci.los-altos.ca.us
- Los Gatos, www.los-gatos.ca.us
- Menlo Park, www.ci.menlo-park.ca.us
- Millbrae, www.ci.millbrae.ca.us
- Milpitas, www.ci.milpitas.ca.gov
- Mountain View, www.ci.mtnview.ca.us
- Pacifica, www.ci.pacifica.ca.us
- Palo Alto, www.city.palo-alto.ca.us
- Redwood City, www.ci.redwood-city.ca.us
- San Bruno, www.sanbruno.ca.gov
- San Carlos, www.cityofsancarlos.org
- San Jose, www.sjliving.com, www.sanjose.org, www.ci.santa-clara-ca.us
- San Mateo City, www.ci.sanmateo.ca.us
- San Mateo County, www.co.sanmateo.ca.us
- Santa Clara City, www.ci.santa-clara.ca.us
- Santa Clara County, www.co.santa-clara.ca.us
- Saratoga, www.saratoga.ca.us
- South San Francisco, www.ci.ssf.ca.us
- Sunnyvale, www.ci.sunnyvale.ca.us
- Woodside, www.woodsidetown.org

COMMUNITY EVENTS AND RESOURCES ONLINE

- *Bay City Guide*, www.baycityguide.com or www.sanfrancisco online.com
- City of San Francisco, www.ci.sf.ca.us or www.sfgov.org
- KTVU Channel 2, www.bayinsider.com
- *San Francisco Bay Guardian*, www.sfbg.com
- *San Francisco Chronicle*, www.sfgate.com
- San Francisco Citysearch, http://sanfrancisco.citysearch.com
- *San Francisco Magazine*, www.sanfran.com
- *San Jose Mercury News*, www.mercurynews.com
- *SF Weekly*, www.sfweekly.com
- The Boulevards Guide to San Francisco, www.sanfrancisco.com

CONSUMER AGENCIES

- Alameda County Bar Association, 510-893-7160
- Better Business Bureau, 415-243-9999, www.bbb.goldengate.org
- California State Directory Information Service, 916-657-9900
- California Attorney General, 800-952-5225, http://caag.state.ca.us
- California Department of Consumer Affairs, 800-952-5210, 510-785-7554, www.dca.ca.gov
- California Public Utilities Commission, 415-703-1282
- Department of Consumer Complaints, 800-952-5210
- Federal Communications Commission, 888-225-5322, www.fcc.gov
- Federal Consumer Information Center, 800-688-9889, TTY, 800-326-2996 www.consumer.gov
- Federal Citizen Information Center (and Consumer Action Handbook), 888-878-3256, www.pueblo.gsa.gov, www.consumeraction.gov
- Federal Trade Commission, 877-FTC-HELP, www.ftc.gov
- Financial Consumer Information, www.mymoney.gov
- San Francisco Bar Association Lawyer Referral Service, 415-989-1616
- San Francisco District Attorney, 415-553-1752
- San Francisco Public Utilities Commission, 415-554-3155, www.ci.sf.ca.us/puc
- San Mateo County Bar Association, 650-369-4149
- Santa Clara County Bar Association, 408-287-2557
- State Bar of California, 415-538-2000, www.calbar.ca.gov
- Telecommunications and Research Action Center, www.trac.org
- The Utility Reform Network (TURN), 415-929-8876, 800-355-8876, www.turn.org

CRISIS LINES

- Gay Youth Talk Line, 415-863-3636
- Suicide Prevention, 415-781-0500
- Suicide Prevention, Marin, 415-499-1100
- Westside Crisis Services, 415-353-5055

ALCOHOL AND DRUG DEPENDENCY
- Alcoholics Anonymous, 415-674-1821, www.aasf.org
- Behavioral Health Services Community Access, 800-750-2727
- Cocaine Anonymous, 415-821-6155
- Contra Costa County AA, 925-939-5371
- Drug Crisis, 415-362-3400, TDD 415-781-2224
- East Bay AA, 510-839-8900
- Marin County Alcoholics Anonymous, 415-499-0400
- Napa County AA, 707-255-4900
- Narcotics Anonymous, 415-621-8600, www.sfna.org,
- San Mateo County Alcoholics Anonymous, 650-577-1310
- Santa Clara County AA, 408-374-8511
- Smoker's Hotline, 800-662-8887

CHILD ABUSE/PROTECTION
- Alameda County Child Protective Services, 510-259-1800
- Child Abuse Council of Santa Clara County, 408-293-5450
- Marin Child Abuse Prevention Council, 415-507-9016
- Marin Child Protective Services, 415-499-7153
- Domestic Violence Hotline, 415-553-9225; for emergencies dial 911
- San Francisco Child Abuse Prevention Center, 415-668-0494
- San Francisco Child Abuse Response Unit, 415-558-5500, for emergencies dial 911

RAPE/DOMESTIC VIOLENCE
- Bay Area Women Against Rape (Crisis Line), 510-845-7273
- Casa de Las Madres, 877-503-1850, www.lacasa.org/ (offers shelter and advocacy to battered women and children)
- Domestic Violence Hotline, 415-553-9225
- Marin Rape Crisis Center, 800-670-7273
- National Domestic Violence Hotline, 800-799-SAFE
- San Francisco General Hospital 24-hour Rape Treatment Center, 415-206-8256
- Women Against Rape, 415-647-7273, www.sfwar.org
- YWCA Rape Crisis Center (Crisis Hot-Lines), 408-287-3000 , 650-617-7273

ENTERTAINMENT

- San Francisco Events, 415-391-2001
- www.sgbg.com
- www.sfgate.com
- www.sfstation.com
- www.sftoday.com
- www.sfweekly.com
- Tix Bay Area (discount tickets), 415-433-7827
- Ticketmaster at 415-512-7770, www.ticketmaster.com
- www.sfgate.com
- 777-FILM

EARTHQUAKE INFORMATION

- American Red Cross, Bay Area Chapter, 415-427-8000, www.bayarea-red cross.org
- Bay Area Quake Information, http://quake.abag.ca.gov.
- California Earthquake Authority, 916-325-3800, www.earthquake authority.com
- California Seismic Safety Commission, 916-263-5506, www.seismic. ca.gov
- Federal Emergency Management Agency (FEMA), 800-480-2520, www.fema.gov
- US Geological Survey, 888-275-8747, 650-853-8300, www.usgs.gov

ELECTED OFFICIALS

SAN FRANCISCO CITY AND COUNTY
- Mayor's Office: 415-554-6141, TTY: 415-252-3107
- Board of Supervisors: 415-554-5184, TTY: 415-554-5227
- City Hall: 415-554-4000
- County Clerk, 415-554-4950
- District Attorney, 415-553-1752
- Assessor-Recorder, 415-554-5516

STATE OF CALIFORNIA
- Governor's Office, 916-445-2841, www.govmail.ca.gov
- State Assembly, 916-319-2856, www.assembly.ca.gov
- State Senate, 916-319-2856, www.sen.ca.gov

UNITED STATES
- US Senate, 202-224-1388, www.senate.gov
- US House of Representatives, 202-224-3121, www.house.gov
- White House, 202-456-1111, TTY: 202-456-6213, www.white house.gov

EMERGENCY NUMBERS

- 24-Hour SF Rape Treatment Center, 415-437-3000
- FEMA Disaster Assistance Information, 800-525-0321, www.fema.gov
- Fire, Police, Medical Emergency, 911
- Office of Emergency Services, 415-558-2700
- Poison Control Hotline, 800-876-4766
- San Francisco Fire Department, non-emergency, 415-558-3268
- San Francisco General Hospital, 415-206-8000, 24-hour Emergency Services, 415-206-8111
- San Francisco Police Department non-emergency, 415-553-0123
- San Jose Police Department non-emergency, 408-277-8900

HEALTH AND MEDICAL CARE

- American Board of Medical Specialties—Board Certification Verification, 866-275-2267
- Berkeley Drop-in Center, 510-653-3808
- Berkeley Free Clinic, 800-6-CLINIC, www.berkeleyfreeclinic.org
- Cancer Care, 800-813-4673
- Dental referral, 800-DENTIST
- Lead Poisoning Prevention Program, www.aclppp.org
- Marin County Department of Health and Human Services, 415-499-7118
- Medical Board of California, 800-633-2322
- Medi-Cal information, 415-904-9600
- Poison Control, 800-876-4766
- Public Health Department, San Jose, 408-299-6120
- San Francisco General Hospital, 415-206-8000
- San Francisco Department of Public Health, 415-554-2500, www.dph.sf.ca.us
- Sexually Transmitted Disease, 415-487-5500
- Suicide Prevention, 415-781-0500

HIV-TESTING
- AIDS/HIV and Hep C Nightline, 415-984-1902
- HIV/AIDS and Hep C Testing Hotline, Marin, 415-499-7515

- AIDS Testing Hotline, San Jose, 408-885-7000
- California AIDS Hotline, 800-367-2437
- UCSF HIV/AIDS Testing and Referral Hotline, 415-502-8378

HOUSING

- Bay Area Legal Aid, 2 West Santa Clara St, 8th floor, San Jose, 408-283-3700; call for a pre-screening.
- Berkeley Rent Stabilization Program, 510-644-6128, www.ci.berkeley.ca.us/rent
- California State Fair Employment and Housing Department, San Francisco, 800-884-1684, www.dfeh.ca.gov
- California Tenants Association, www.catenants.com
- Contractors State License Board, 800-321-2752
- Franchise Tax Board, 800-852-5711, www.ftb.ca.gov
- East Palo Alto Rent Stabilization Program, 650-853-3109
- Eviction Defense Center, 510-452-4541
- Housing Rights, Inc., 2718 Telegraph #100, Berkeley, 510-548-8776, 800-261-2298, www.housingrights.org
- Legal Aid Society Housing Counseling Program, 408-283-1540
- Project Sentinel, specializes in landlord/tenant disputes in Sunnyvale, 408-720-9888
- St. Peter's Housing Committee, 415-487-9203
- San Francisco Rent Board, 415-252-4600
- San Francisco Tenants Union, 415-282-6622, www.sftu.org
- San Jose Rental Rights and Referrals, 408-277-5431

LEGAL MEDIATION OR REFERRAL

- AIDS Legal Referral Panel, 415-701-1100 or 510-451-5353 www.alrp.org
- Alameda County Bar Association, 510-893-7160
- American Civil Liberties Union of Northern California, 415-621-2488, www.aclunc.org
- California Courts, www.courtinfo.ca.gov
- California Community Dispute Service, 415-865-2520
- East Bay Community Mediation, 510-763-2117
- Legal Aid Society of Santa Clara County, 408-998-5200
- Legal Aid of the North Bay Area, 800-498-7666
- San Francisco Bar Association Lawyer Referral Service, 415-989-1616
- San Mateo County Bar Association, 650-369-4149

- Santa Clara County Bar Association, 408-287-2557
- State Bar of California, 415-538-2000

SMALL CLAIMS COURTS
See **Consumer Protection** section in the **Helpful Services** chapter.

PUBLIC LIBRARIES

- Berkeley Central Branch, 510-981-6100, www.berkeleypublic library.org
- Marin County Library, 415-499-6056, www.countylibrary.marin.org
- New Main, San Francisco, 415-557-4400, www.sfpl.org
- Oakland Public Library, Main Branch, 510-238 3134, www.oakland library.org
- Peninsula Library System, 650-780-7018, www.plsinfo.org
- San Jose Public Library, 408-808-2000, www.sjlibrary.org
- Santa Clara County Library System, 408-293-2326, 800-286-1991, www. santaclaracountylib.org

MARRIAGE LICENSES

- Alameda County, 510-272-6363
- Contra Costa County, 925-646-2956
- Marin County, 415-499-3003
- San Francisco City and County, 415-554-4950
- San Mateo County, 650-363-4712
- Santa Clara County, 408-299-7310

PARKS AND RECREATION DEPARTMENTS

- East Bay Regional Park District, 510-562-7275, www.ebparks.org
- Golden Gate National Recreation Area, 415-561-4700, www.nps. gov/goga
- Golden Gate Park, 415-831-2700
- Marin County Department of Parks and Recreation, 415-499-6387, www.marincountyparks.org
- San Francisco Recreation and Parks Department, 415-831-2700, www.parks.sfgov.org
- San Mateo County Parks and Recreation Department, 650-363-4020, www.co.sanmateo.ca.us
- Santa Clara Department of Parks and Recreation, 408-355-2200, www.parkhere.org

POLICE

- BART Police: 877-679-7000
- California Highway Patrol, Emergency, 911, Non-emergency, 707-551-4100, TTY: 707-648-5363
- Domestic Violence Response Unit, 415-553-9225
- Emergency, 911
- Road conditions, 800-427-7623
- San Francisco Police Chief, 415-553-1551
- San Francisco Police, Non-emergency, 415-553-0123; TTY:415-626-4357
- San Jose Police, Non-emergency, 408-277-8900

POST OFFICE, 800-275-8777, www.usps.com

SANITATION—GARBAGE & RECYCLING

CALIFORNIA
- California Department of Conservation, 800-732-9253.
- Earth 911, 800-CLEAN-UP, www.earth911.org

SAN FRANCISCO
- Golden Gate Disposal & Recycling Company, 415-626-4000, www.goldengatedisposal.com
- Norcal Waste Systems: Sunset Scavenger, 415-330-1300, www.sunset scavenger.com
- Recycling Hotline, 415-554-7329, www.sfenvironment.com
- Recycle Central (Norcal), 415-330-1400
- San Francisco League of Urban Gardeners (SLUG), 415-285-7585

NORTH BAY
- Marin Recycling Center, 415-453-1404
- Marin Sanitary Services, 415-456-2601, www.marinsanitary.com

EAST BAY
- Allied Waste/BFI, 510-657-3500
- East Bay ROT-line, 510-444-SOIL
- Pleasanthill Bayshore Disposal, serves most of Contra Costa County, 925-685-4711, www.pleasanthillbayshoredisposal.com
- StopWaste.org (Alameda County Waste Management Authority), 510-430-8509, www.stopwaste.org
- Tri-Cities Waste Management, East Bay, 510-624-5900

PENINSULA/SOUTH BAY

- BFI: BFI Daly City (serving Daly City, Colma, Broadmoor), 650-756-1130, www.bfidalycity.com
- BFI San Mateo County, 650-592-2411, http://bfisanmateocounty.com
- Norcal Waste Systems of San Jose 408-576-0057
- Recycle Palo Alto Program, 650-496-5910
- RecycleWorks, San Mateo County, 888-442-2666, www.recycle-works.org
- Santa Clara County Recycling Hotline, 408-924-5453 or 800-533-8414, www.recyclestuff.org
- Santa Clara County, BFI, 408-432-1234
- South San Francisco Scavenger (northern San Mateo County), 650-589-4020, www.ssfscavenger.com

SENIORS

- AARP California, 888-OUR-AARP, www.aarp.org
- Elder Care Locator, 800-677-1116
- Legal Assistance for Seniors and HiCap, Oakland, 510-832-3040
- Institute on Aging, 415-750-4180
- Legal Assistance to the Elderly, 415-538-3333
- Marin Adult Protection Services, 415-499-7118
- Meals on Wheels, 415-920-1111, www.mowsf.org
- Mission Hospice of San Mateo County, 650-554-1000, www.mission hospice.org
- Richmond Resource Center, 415-752-2815
- United Way of the Bay Area, 415-773-0111

SHIPPING SERVICES

- DHL Worldwide Express, 800-225-5345, www.dhl.co.id
- FedEx, 800-238-5355, www.fedex.com
- United Parcel Service (UPS), 800-742-5877, www.ups.com
- US Postal Service Express Mail, 800-222-1811, www.usps.com

SPORTS

- www.sfgate.com
- Golden State Warriors, 510-986-2222, www.nba.com/warriors
- Oakland A's, 510-638-0500, http://oakland.athletics.mlp.com
- Oakland Raiders, 888-44-RAIDERS, www.raiders.com
- San Francisco 49ers, 415-656-4900, www.sf49ers.com
- San Francisco Giants, 800-5-GIANTS, www.sfgiants.com

- San Jose Earthquakes, 408-985-4625, www.sjearthquakes.com
- San Jose Sharks, 408-287-7070, www.sj-sharks.com
- Women's United Soccer Association, http://wusa.com

STREET MAINTENANCE

- Report an overflowing litter receptacle, 415-28-CLEAN
- Report Illegal Dumping, 415-28-CLEAN
- San Francisco Department of Public Works, 415-554-6920, TTY: 415-554-6900
- Sign Posting Guidelines, www.amlegal.com
- Street Cleaning, 415-554-6920
- Street Construction Coordination Center, 415-554-SCCC
- Street Use Permits, 415-554-5810
- Tree planting, San Francisco, Friends of the Urban Forest (FUF) 415-561-6890
- Tree Removal and Pruning, 415-28-CLEAN

TAXES

- Internal Revenue Service, 800-829-1040, www.irs.ustreas.gov
- San Francisco Tax Collector, 415-554-4400
- State Franchise Tax Board, 800-338-0505, www.ftb.ca.gov
- State of California Department of Finance, www.dof.ca.gov

TELEPHONE

- AT&T, 800-222-0300, www.att.com
- GTC Telecom, 800-486-4030, www.gtctelecom.com
- MCI, 800-444-3333, www.mci.com
- Qwest, 800-860-2255, www.qwest.com
- Sprint, 800-877-4646, www.sprint.com
- SBC, 800-310-2355, TTY: 800-772-3140, www.sbc.com
- Utility.com, www.utility.com
- Verizon, 800-483-4000, www.verizon.com
- Working Assets, 800-788-0898, www.workingforchange.com, this company donates a portion of monthly fees to nonprofits

TICKETS

- Ticketmaster, 415-512-7770, www.ticketmaster.com
- TIX Bay Area, 415-433-7827
- Tickets.Com, 800-352-0212, www.tickets.com

TIME, 415-POP-CORN

TRAVEL AND TOURISM

- International Association for Medical Assistance to Travelers, 716-754 4883, www.iamat.org
- National Park Service, www.nps.gov
- National Passport Information Center, 877-4USA-PPT (877-487-2778), TTY: 888-874-7793, www.travel.state.gov
- San Francisco Convention and Visitors Bureau, 415-391-2000, www. sfvistor.org
- US Department of State, Bureau of Consular Affairs, http:// travel.state.gov/

TRANSPORTATION

- Bay Area Public Transportation, go to www.511.org or dial 511 (no area code needed when dialed from anywhere in the Bay Area)
- Carpool and Vanpool Services, www.rides.org , 800-755-7665 or 511, www.511.org
- Real Time Traffic Updates, http://cad.chp.ca.gov

TRAINS AND BUSES
- AC Transit, 510-891-4700; TTY: 800-448-9790, www.actransit.org
- Altamont Commuter Express, 800-411-RAIL, www.acerail.com
- Amtrak, 800-USA-RAIL, www.reservations.amtrak.com, www.amtrak california.com
- BART (Bay Area Rapid Transit), 510-465-2278, 415-989-2278, 650-992-2278; TTY: 510-839-2278, www.bart.gov.
- CalTrain, www.caltrain.com; 800-660-4287; TDD/TTY, 415-508-6448
- Contra Costa County Connection, 925-676-7500; TDD/TTY, 800-735-2929
- Golden Gate Transit, 415-923-2000, TTY: 415-257-4554, www.golden gatetransit.org.
- Green Tortoise Bus, 415-956-7500
- Greyhound, 800-231-2222, www.greyhound.com
- MUNI (San Francisco Municipal Rail) 415-673-MUNI, TTY: 415-923-6366, www.sfmuni.com
- SamTrans, 800-660-4287; TTY: 650-508-6448, www.samtrans.com.
- Santa Clara County Transit (Valley Transit Authority) offers bus and light rail service to the South Bay, call 800-894-9908; TTY: 408-321-2330
- Sonoma County Transit, www.sctransit.com
- SuperShuttle, 415-558-8500

AIRPORTS

- Oakland International Airport, 510-577-4000; parking, 510-633-2571
- San Francisco International Airport, 650-761-0800, www.sfoairport. org, parking, 650-877-0227
- San Jose International Airport, 408-277-4759, www.sjc.org; parking, 408-293-6788

FERRIES

- Alameda Oakland Ferry, 510-522-3300, www.eastbayferry.com.
- Angel Island–Tiburon Ferry, 415-435-2131
- Baylink (Vallejo-SF) 707-64-FERRY or 877-64-FERRY, www.baylink ferry.com.
- Blue and Gold Fleet, 415-773-1188
- Golden Gate Ferry Service, (Marin-San Francisco) 415-455-2000 or www.goldengateferry.org
- Harbor Bay Isle Ferry (Alameda-SF), 510-769-5500, www.harborbay ferry.com

TAXIS, see **Transportation** chapter

UTILITIES

- City of Palo Alto Utilities (CPAU), 650-329-2161
- PG & E (Pacific Gas and Electric), 800-743-5000; TTY, 800-652-4712, www.pge.com
- Santa Clara Green Power. 408-244-SAVE
- Silicon Valley Power, 408-615-2300, www.siliconvalleypower.com

See **Water** in the **Getting Settled** chapter for water district numbers and web sites.

UTILITY EMERGENCIES
- Pacific Gas & Electric, 800-743-5002

WEATHER, Regional Weather Reports, www.wrh.noaa.gov/mtr/

ZIP CODE REQUEST, 800-275-8877, www.usps.com

INDEX

SABRINA CRAWFORD lives to write and writes to earn a living. She is a former staff reporter for the *San Francisco Examiner*, writes erratically for the *San Francisco Bay Guardian* about music and film, and publishes the feminist zine *Cherrybomb*. When not jet-setting, she lives in San Francisco with her cat, plays drums in a rock and roll band, and is working on her first novel. Sabrina has a fancy Ivy League degree but owes much of her smarts to the excellent education she received in Bay Area public schools thanks to fabulous teachers—and to her dad, who for better or worse, always has something to say.

We would appreciate your comments regarding this third edition of the *Newcomer's Handbook° for Moving to and Living in the San Francisco Bay Area.* If you've found any mistakes or omissions or if you would just like to express your opinion about the guide, please let us know. We will consider any suggestions for possible inclusion in our next edition, and if we use your comments, we'll send you a *free* copy of our next edition. Please send this response form to:

Reader Response Department
First Books
6750 SW Franklin, Suite A
Portland, OR 97223-2542
USA

Comments:

_____

_____

_____

_____

_____

_____

Name: _____

Address _____

_____

_____

Telephone ( )_____

E-mail

6750 SW Franklin, Suite A
Portland, OR 97223-2542
USA
503-968-6777
www.firstbooks.com

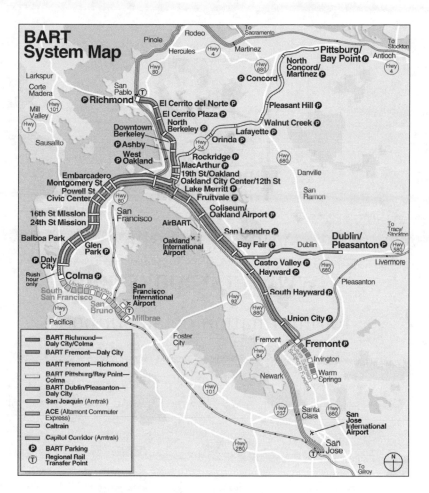

BAY AREA RAPID TRANSIT SYSTEM MAP

FIRST BOOKS®

Visit our web site at
www.firstbooks.com
for information on all our books.